CHAUCER'S PILGRIMS

CHAUCER'S PILGRIMS

An Historical Guide to the Pilgrims in *The Canterbury Tales*

Edited by
LAURA C. LAMBDIN
and
ROBERT T. LAMBDIN

GREENWOOD PRESS
Westport, Connecticut • London

Library of Congress Cataloging-in-Publication Data

Chaucer's pilgrims : an historical guide to the pilgrims in The
    Canterbury tales / edited by Laura C. Lambdin and Robert T. Lambdin.
        p.   cm.
    Includes bibliographical references and index.
    ISBN 0–313–29334–1 (alk. paper)
        1. Chaucer, Geoffrey, d. 1400. Canterbury tales.   2. Occupations
in literature.   3. Chaucer, Geoffrey, d. 1400—Characters—Pilgrims.
4. Christian pilgrims and pilgrimages in literature.   5. Literature
and history—England.   6. Occupations—England—History.
7. Professions—England—History.   I. Lambdin, Laura C.
II. Lambdin, Robert T.
PR1875.O26C48   1996
821'.1—dc20   95–34160

British Library Cataloguing in Publication Data is available.

Library of Congress Catalog Card Number: 95–34160
ISBN: 0–313–29334–1

First published in 1996

Greenwood Press, 88 Post Road West, Westport, CT 06881
An imprint of Greenwood Publishing Group, Inc.

Printed in the United States of America

The paper used in this book complies with the
Permanent Paper Standard issued by the National
Information Standards Organization (Z39.48–1984).

10 9 8 7 6 5 4 3 2 1

Copyright Acknowledgments

The editors and the publisher are grateful to the following for granting permission to quote from
their material:

Larry D. Benson (Editor), *The Riverside Chaucer*, Third Edition. Copyright © 1987 by Houghton
Mifflin Company. Reprinted with permission.

Excerpts from *The Complete Poetry and Prose of Geoffrey Chaucer*. Second Edition by John H.
Fisher, copyright © 1989 by Holt, Rinehart and Winston, Inc., reprinted by permission of the
publisher.

To Our Dear Elizabeth Ann

Contents

Preface

The premise behind this reference text goes beyond its obvious value as another scholarly tool or resource in the study of Geoffrey Chaucer's *Canterbury Tales*. In our studies, we have found critical volumes that discuss every possible angle concerning the pilgrims of this timeless text; these secondary sources run the gamut from feminist studies to exegetic examinations. However, very rarely do we find works that define the sorts of "sondry folk" who are woven into this collection of tales, and there is no work that details the pilgrims' various vocations in any depth. In essence, it is difficult to find explanations of the role of a medieval cook, or to pinpoint the differences between a friar and a monk. It is this critical fissure that this work repairs.

For some six hundred years, the notion of presenting a text that describes the pilgrims' various vocations has been neglected; now this gap is filled. Each of the scholars contributing to this volume has selected a pilgrim and provided an in-depth entry describing that pilgrim's specific function in fourteenth-century England. Medievalists from twenty-five or so universities all over the United States—from California to Washington to Florida to New York—have contributed information that will be useful to all teachers and students of Chaucer, from high school to graduate school. It is our belief that these descriptions of the pilgrims' vocations add to the intricate readings of other scholars and highlight some of the problems found in the text of the *Canterbury Tales* (for example, the textual problem of the "Shipman's Tale"). Furthermore, cultural attitudes toward the pilgrims are more greatly defined and clarified where possible. Each contributor has meticulously researched and gleaned many sources and synthesized the often scant material to present a unified entry concerning each pilgrim, those enlisted from the start of the journey at the Tabard, as well as the Canon and his Yeoman who appear in the later stages of the work.

The bulk of each portion is an examination of the historical position of the various vocations foreworded in the "General Prologue" of the *Canterbury Tales*. Some, for example the Pardoner or the Knight, are characters defined by jobs that no longer exist in our world. Others, like the poor Parson, were involved in professions that are still common but have changed tremendously (i.e., clergy today usually do not have to beg for each meal). Most of each work is devoted to making clear the parameter of that pilgrim's profession in Chaucer's time, as well as making some mention of its origins and current, if any, mutations.

The secondary area in each chapter is the link between each pilgrim's profession and the content or direction of his or her tale where it is applicable. In most of the tales it seems likely that Chaucer cleverly united the narrative content and the world view shaped by the character's position. For example, the "Friar's Tale" probably attacks summoners because there was some monetary competition between various branches of the Church; the Canon and his Yeoman may expose the fallacy of alchemy because Chaucer himself was duped by a wayward alchemist. In the instances where these links occur, the contributors have provided keen analysis of the impression this technique delivers.

Third, where possible, another link has been made: the profession and tale are discussed in terms of the pilgrim's character as defined in the "General Prologue." How does the pilgrim look or act like someone who would tell a particular story or even a particular type of story, display those distinct mannerisms, or work in that specific vocation? For example, it seems clear that the Pardoner's tale and vocation are well matched with his physical appearance and characteristics. Also the work examines in what ways, if any, the pilgrim's character goes a bit beyond what one might normally expect from a member of such a group, like the Prioress's secular love symbol which is an interesting and controversial addition to her character. We also learn of the laws and conflicts concerning class stature simply because of the way some of the pilgrims are dressed, in direct clash with the sumptuary laws, especially in the studies concerning the five guildsmen and the Miller.

The fascinating last two areas (tale and character) involve critical analysis, but the bulk of each chapter concerns historical background and a more general view of the actual vocation. However, although the essays involve more historical research than literary criticism, they are followed by a bibliography containing recent critical works relative to each pilgrim.

Before we begin our examination of the pilgrims, we might benefit from an overview concerning the roles of pilgrimages in society. In late fourteenth-century England, a pilgrimage to the Shrine of St. Thomas à Becket, martyred archbishop of Canterbury Cathedral, involved traveling down the old Pilgrims' Way leading from Hampshire to Kent over the Sussex Downs, via Winchester. Geoffrey Chaucer's route, as recorded in the *Canterbury Tales,* led from the Tabard Inn in the Southwark district of London to Canterbury, which is sighted but never reached in the text. Inasmuch as the *Canterbury Tales* were composed in part around 1387, Chaucer may well have made such a pilgrimage in April of that very year to gain healing for his wife, Philippa, the sister of John of Gaunt's third wife and a lady-in-waiting to Edward III's Queen. Philippa died several months later, and some reconstructions of Chaucer's life place him in Calais, rather than up the road in Canterbury, that year.

Such pilgrimages to achieve spiritual assistance by visiting holy places are part of many religious traditions. Ancient Egypt witnessed pilgrimages to the pyramids at Giza and to the Temples of Amun at Karnak; in India, pilgrims walked to Varnasi or Benares on the sacred Ganges River; Chinese pilgrims journeyed to Mount Tai; the Israelites went up to Jerusalem on the occasion of each Passover. Classical Greeks traveled to Eleusis, the Mystery Shrine, and to the Shrine of Apollo at Delphi; in the ninth century Christians sought out Jerusalem, Bethlehem, and Nazareth after the impetus of the discovery of the True Cross (now disputed) by St. Helena, the mother of the Emperor Constantine. Santiago de Compostela in Spain became one of the great shrines of the Middle Ages after the reputed miracle that located the tomb of the apostle James the Greater. The Pilgrimage to Mecca remains one of the special obligations of Islam.

The Crusades were launched to protect the Holy Land route and destination; since 1300 the popes have set aside holy years (jubilees) for special pilgrimages to Rome, the sight of the martyrdom of St. Peter and St. Paul. Indeed, one of the explanations for the origin of the *Chanson de Roland* connects it with the songs sung to entertain Compostella pilgrims.

This leads us to the pilgrims of the *Canterbury Tales*. Chaucer includes himself as one of the thirty pilgrims, each to tell four tales (two going, two returning) but actually only twenty-three get to tell a single tale and the incompleteness of the plan is obvious (just as some strange gender uncertainty is evidenced when the Second Nun refers to herself as an "unworthy son of Eve" and the Shipman several times classifies himself among the women). Therefore, it seems likely that Chaucer never considered the text to be complete. Although it has been determined that the bulk of the *Canterbury Tales* was composed in the late 1380s and early 1390s, the entire composition was never realized. Perhaps Chaucer tired of the project or simply ran out of tales to tell. The point is moot, however, for by his death in 1400 he did leave us with the partial script of a drama that has lasted some six hundred years.

Although it is disputed whether or not Chaucer knew Boccaccio's *Decameron,* it remains the most obvious similarity in terms of the *Canterbury Tales'* style. However, there were other possible paradigms: the *One Thousand and One Arabian Nights,* Ovid's *Metamorphosis, Disciplina Clericalis* of Peter Alphonsus, the romance of *The Seven Sages,* Gower's *Confessio Amantis,* Chaucer's own *Legend of Good Women,* and, in 1374, the *Novelle* of Giovanni Sercambi with its pilgrimage setting. In addition, the fourteenth century abounded with allegorical writing—both sacred and secular—presenting personified types: Courtesy, Gentleness, Envy, Slander, Hypocrisy (perhaps stemming from the anonymous cycle drama *Everyman*). Writers using these character types include Theophrastus in late Hellenistic Greek, and much later, La Bruyère in French and Bacon in English.

Some of the leading figures of the *Canterbury Tales* may be traced with a degree of certainty to well-known contemporaries, as Harry Bailly to Henricus Bailly, host of the Tabard, and Thomas Pinchbek, sergeant-at-law. Most of the pilgrims seem to have been invented by Chaucer and reflect his artistry in using physiognomy as a guide to character traits, a habit typical in medieval writing. It seems clear, too, that Chaucer wished to reflect the constant tension between laity and clergy, and between gentry and peasant, although no characters of royalty or the upper nobility are included (the Knight is the character of highest social rank). Oddly, we can still appreciate these conflicts today, given the quickly changing political landscape and the influence of various religions. We can understand the precarious social standing of millers and reeves and the nature of their conflict in the *Canterbury Tales*. Twentieth-century dress codes for various jobs are similar to the clothing that links these pilgrims and their vocations in the fourteenth century.

Significantly, Chaucer himself was a man who was involved in many different fields: accomplished courtier, experienced soldier, wily ambassador, spy, poet, story teller, and gentleman of the world. In 1357 Chaucer was a page in the household of Prince Lionel (later Duke of Clarence); 1359–1360 found him in the army of Edward III, captured in France, and ransomed. From 1372 to 1373 and again in 1378 Chaucer was on diplomatic tours of Italy. His long royal service, from 1374 to 1391, finally paid off handsomely when he was appointed comptroller of the customs on fur and hides for the Port of London, and was also made a prestigious clerk of the King's Works. Furthermore, during his lifetime, he was a poet of some renown. His works were evidently popular and well accepted; they are perhaps timeless because they offer sly, insightful comments illuminating an age long since past. In the *Canterbury Tales* Chaucer presents a perspective of medieval England unparalleled in literary history. His pilgrims range from common to clerical, rich to poor, each one presenting a unique world view. Part of Chaucer's artistry is shown in the way he carefully linked the characters with a tale and a vocation perfectly suited for that personality type. Examining the trades of this mysterious time yields much for both the casual reader and the serious scholar. In an effort to make the work more relevent, the contributors have included the most current scholarship in their references. In the few instances where recent research is lacking, the most current scholarship was examined and used. All quotes from the *Canterbury Tales* are from *The Riverside Chaucer*, Third Edition, edited by Larry D. Benson. So it is now time for us to join the pilgrims and leave the Tabard. And just as in the *Canterbury Tales*, our study will begin with the Knight.

—*Laura C. and Robert T. Lambdin,*
with Elton E. Smith

CHAUCER'S PILGRIMS

Chapter 1

A Knyght Ther Was

MICHAEL A. CALABRESE

INTRODUCTION

Chaucer's Knight, the first pilgrim described, the first to tell a tale, and the overall most gentle and respected of the Canterbury pilgrims, is an English fourteenth-century version of a very long and complex military profession that we refer to as knighthood. He has fought in a host of fourteenth-century wars against various "pagan" peoples in Eastern Europe and the Middle East at the tail end of the Crusades, a series of European Christian attempts to re-conquer the Holy Land and/or devastate the heathen peoples, mainly the Muslims, but including at different times and to different degrees, pagans, Jews, and schismatics. This knight then is a warrior on horseback, coming to pilgrimage fresh from battle, for Chaucer tells us that he is in military dress and his clothes are still soiled—a chilling detail designed to link this man of arms to war. And we must know first and foremost that knights, although they appear in many roles in medieval literature, legend, and history, were created for and made their living through war. The knight is a medieval soldier.

The Knight's dress, his character, and his war record all provide insight into what "knighthood" meant to Chaucer and his readers. What kind of a profession was it? What are its origins? Where does its religious element come from? Does this knight represent the crown and glory of medieval chivalry, a code of social and religious virtue recalling the legendary glory of the Round Table? Or does he display the old, decayed, lost hopes of a Christian world that never saw its dreams of conquering the Holy Land and converting heathens realized? Does he also represent a European military culture that never comprehended the paradox of its rather un-Christian hatred for non-Christian peoples? Did Chaucer admire the Knight? Do the other pilgrims? Can we admire him in spite of the clear record of what may seem to a twentieth-century audience no more than racist brutality? The Knight is often called one of the "ideal" pilgrims along with the Parson and sometimes the Clerk because unlike the other portraits, Chaucer offers no attack or satire against them. But in what ways could the Knight have been a fourteenth-century ideal?

For many years the Knight was not controversial, and most readers agreed that both Chaucer and the pilgrims admired him and that we should too. But some readers have challenged the ideal view and cast a dark eye on the Knight and his fourteenth-century crusading spirit. The Knight, in turn, has his own "men at arms," critics who defend him, or at least contextualize his actions in the world in which he lived. We don't have to conclude here whether the Knight is the object of attack or high praise, but we will explore the world of the Knight so that readers can turn to the text and draw their own conclusions about one of the most fascinating figures and most historically complex professions in the *Canterbury Tales.*

THE PROFESSION IN CHAUCER'S TIME

Throughout the Middle Ages in the many countries of Europe, being a knight could mean many things. In his important book on Chaucer's Knight, Terry Jones comments that when he set out to understand knighthood in Chaucer's day he sadly found that "there is no clear cut and dried answer" as to what a knight was because "throughout the Middle Ages the meaning of the word 'knight' had been elastic" (Jones 4; see also 4–13 and Barber 3–24). Before we retrace the specific history that established the English figure in the *Canterbury Tales,* let me run through some of the identities that a "knight" could have had in medieval Europe. Some knights were wealthy; some were poor. Some paid extra taxes to be knights; others were exempt. Some were parts of royal orders and had high aristocratic status; some worked up through the ranks to attain the knightly rank; though in other times, the low born were forbidden to become knights. Some men avoided knighthood but were compelled by kings to pay taxes and arm themselves. Some were part of fervent religious orders, created and sanctified by the Church. Some lived in the Holy Land and established kingdoms, accommodating in "hospices" visiting pilgrims and European knights who came to help them in their cause of converting or conquering the heathen. Some who called themselves knights were actually mercenaries, and some were thugs who lived by extorting peasants. Some, in the later Middle Ages were not warriors but "dispensers of justice and keepers of the peace" (Barber 14), members of Parliament, or representatives of local government, like Chaucer's Franklin. Indeed, Chaucer himself was a kind of knight, for in 1386 he was made "knight of the shire" a member of the House of Commons (Benson, *The Riverside Chaucer* xxiii; Jones 9–10).

This complex jumble of religious, political, and military identity made up what we call medieval "knighthood." In fourteenth-century England specifically, as Jones notes, "in fact the words 'knight' and 'knighthood' were terms widely used to designate [simply] the upper class of layman" (10). But the complexity and the generality of the term should not make us despair, because Chaucer creates his Knight in such historical detail that we can easily explore the specific kind of knight he might have been and the military, political, and ideological world he may have lived in.

Readers should know primarily that this Knight, and indeed what most people mean when they refer to "knights" in the Middle Ages, was a "man of arms" who rode on horseback and fought wars. Arthurian legend, furthermore, makes us associate knights with England, but "real knights originated in France and were unknown in England until the Norman conquest" (Gies 3). At this time, when William the Conqueror invaded England, "the native writers unhesitatingly applied the Old English word 'cniht' to his military followers . . . whom William rewarded with grants of the land they had helped him conquer" (Jones 5). This explains the use of the English word, but, looking back further than William the Conqueror, let us consider how knighthood starts and how Chaucer's particular image of knighthood betrays the evolution of the early European warrior. Let us trace some features of that evolution because knowing something of the prehistory of knights will allow us to see how the values and the overall identity of the fourteenth-century Crusading, honorable Christian knight, who is bound to duty and to war, came to be.

His manners, courtliness, and chivalry, along with nobility, authority, and honor, are all late medieval manifestations, indeed ways of ordering and controlling the armed horse-riding Germanic warrior, who initially had no definitive class, Christian, or "courtly" identity. And, quite importantly, not until the Church orders and sanctifies powerful violent military men into Christian warriors bound for Crusades do we perceive that odd mix of military and religious identity that we see in Chaucer's Knight. Our English fourteenth-century figure, then, is the product of a series of transformations, which had occurred in the eleventh and twelfth centuries as knights became knights of God and attained class identity just below that of the nobility. So as Chaucer created this figure, he was creating a man who displayed the social, military, and religious evolution of medieval knighthood, and as we read his portrait, we read that history.

Knighthood has a long, roughly eight-hundred-year history, beginning with the Carolingian cavalry and even extending through the establishment of gunpowder and of great national armies in Europe, when knights "were still prominent, though increasingly obsolescent" (Gies 2). Scholars debate the origins of medieval knighthood but like to make clear that medieval knights are *not* descended from the Roman "knightly" class but rather from Frankish, that is, Germanic warriors who, in the eighth century "became horsemen, abandoning their old method of fighting on foot" (Barber 10). The hardware of these early knights changes as technologies evolved, such as the revolutionary step of using stirrups (adopted from Arabs but traceable to fifth-century Korea), the throwing of lances, the use of swords, and the advent of "shock combat," in which knights clash head to head in a violent charge. Technology changes constantly, as armor has to improve to combat greater and greater onslaughts, and puts a constant economic strain on generations of knights and would-be knights who will struggle to stay armed and up to date.

Throughout most of Europe, these early knights were men of modest standing; they did not constitute a class or order, and they had no clear religious mission. They certainly dispel the mythic image we have of the Knights of the Round Table, who seek the Holy Grail and maintain a kind of just, courtly order, while exploring personal Christian virtue in a mystic, mythic landscape—a situation that one critic has called a "bizarre time warp in which knights in gleaming plate armor galloped anachronistically through the primitive countryside of post-Roman Britain" (Gies 3).

The establishment of the forces that will later be called "knights" was driven not by divine or Arthurian authority but simply by fear and political necessity in Europe. From the eighth century on, during and after the Frankish rule and the reign of Charlemagne, in a Europe fearing attacks by Saracen, Dane, and Hun, royal vassals needed to recruit men for warrior service. In these violent times, the establishment of bands of loyal armed men, which we may call "proto-knights," flourished (Gies 4). Since these early forms of medieval knighthood emerged in the ninth and tenth centuries, in what Gies calls "turmoil-filled" centuries (3), the early knight, three hundred years before Chaucer's, was "a crude and violent figure virtually uncurbed by a society that had lost control over its military class" (Gies 4). He was, as Gies says, "ignorant and unlettered, rough in speech and manners," and "he earned his living largely by violence" (17).

Both the violence and the kind of loyalty infusing the military bond of warrior to gift-giving lord are familiar to students of the Old English Epic *Beowulf,* where prechivalric, prefeudal warriors swear oaths and fight their lords' battles against rival tribes and monsters alike. In this old Germanic structure, a lord, such as Hygelac or Hrothgar, provides arms, land, and support to powerful fighting men who pledge their loyalty to that lord in battle.

Such a practice helps form the basis of the later medieval feudalism, which flourished throughout Europe in full maturity in the thirteenth century. In this socioeconomic system, knights were given a gift of land, the most valuable medieval commodity, by virtue of their military commitment to a more powerful, wealthier lord. As Gies summarizes, "In this dominant economic (and political) order of the Middle Ages, a lord granted land to a vassal in return for military and other less important services. Lord and vassal swore an oath, of protection and support on the part of the lord, of loyalty on the part of the vassal. At the height of the feudalism, the knight was the cornerstone of the institution" (3). The vassals would retain knights to loyally defend the lord in battle and accompany him when the nation called for war. Barber describes feudalism as the "perfect pyramid," which, in its "purest form" has "each vassal owing service to one lord only, his lord in turn doing homage to a higher lord or to the king'' (Barber 13).

We realize that the term *vassal,* though now ''tinged with derogation,'' as Morris Bishop says, refers to men who were actually part of the nobility, just above the knights they would employ for their lord. The lord-vassal oath is worth noting; as Bishop recounts for us:

The bond between the lord and vassal was affirmed or reaffirmed by the ceremony of homage. The vassal knelt, placed his clasped hands within those of his master, declared, ''Lord, I become your man,'' and took an oath of fealty. The lord raised him to his feet and bestowed on him a ceremonial kiss. (96)

So too the knights' ceremonial initiation, or ''dubbing,'' was ritualistic and sacred:

The candidate took a symbolic bath, donned clean white clothes and a red robe, and stood or knelt for ten hours in nightlong silence before the altar, on which his weapons and armor lay. At dawn mass was said in front of an audience of knights and ladies. His sponsors presented him to his feudal lord and gave him his arms, with a prayer and a blessing said over each piece of equipment. . . . An elder knight struck the candidate's neck or cheek a hard blow with the flat of the hand of the side of his sword. This was the only blow a knight must always endure and never return. (Bishop 64)

This perfect, idealized, ritualized pyramid system goes through various evolutions and permutations in the Middle Ages. The confused status of the loyalty oath when fiefs were inherited or divided, plus allegiance by vassals to more than one lord—which makes one's loyalty in battle confused—help to break the smooth system down (see Barber 13–14), constantly changing the ways men could ensure forces and a king would raise an army. In general, we see a movement away from the feudal levy, the perfect pyramid system described above, to the system of ''indenture,'' by which a man swears loyalty to a lord or king in return for pay or sponsorship of some kind (see Jones 7–9; McKisack 235–236). Beyond a mere mercenary system, which never had a noble or honored reputation, this method preserved some of the old personal feudal loyalty. Chaucer's own son, for example, was indentured to Chaucer's patron, John of Gaunt (Jones 9).

So when Chaucer tells us that his Knight fought in his ''lord's war,'' (line 47), we know that behind these acts lies a long history of personal oaths, loyalty, and commitment, such as had in the finest times been the noble personal bond of honor and loyalty. Students may remember the loyalty of Wiglaf, who helps a struggling Beowulf kill the powerful dragon. The Knight's virtues, as we see them in this fourteenth-century text, recall that distant Germanic past, that time of honor.

Along with feudal and pseudofeudal bonds and pledges, other influential forces worked throughout the Middle Ages on the concept of "knighthood." In the eleventh century knights begin to take on class identity not just as fighting men but as men of means who could afford the expensive paraphernalia needed for battle. As Barber points out, "the new class was a compound of men whose families were well established without being noble, and of newcomers whose wealth had been won by adventure or ambition" (12). The rise of European knights, including great control of land, gave rise to what Barber calls the "heyday" of knighthood in which they are in an "almost unchallenged position": "Only the clergy held comparable power as a class . . . but they lacked the knights' individual power as landowners" (17).

Although the situation varies from country to country in Europe, in general, as time goes on knighthood became ever more expensive. In England, furthermore, knights had to pay "scutage" or a shield tax and other dues. The old mail (chain-link armor) war replaced by plates, and as Barber states, "all this was expensive, and not easy to obtain" (19). These forces made knighthood more specialized and exclusive—not all could afford to commit to the costly life. So by the thirteenth century we hear of the "poor knight," struggling to maintain the expensive trappings of warfare, and we hear of many squires who simply opt not to attempt to raise themselves to the knightly rank.

But Chaucer's man has avoided at least devastating poverty and has always found plenty of employment. So let's turn specifically to the fourteenth century and to such men, who were the products of all these forces and influences that shaped medieval military and knightly identity. What did a fourteenth-century knight like Chaucer's do when not telling tales and attending holy pilgrimage? Even though the portrait does not explain what Christian wars our Knight fought in Western Europe, most English knights fought in English wars against the Irish, Welsh, Scots, or the French, the last in the series of struggles generally known as the Hundred Years' War (1337–1453). In England, since the old feudal levy was gone, English kings of the thirteenth and fourteenth centuries, starting with Edward I "offer[ed] pay systematically to all ranks of the army except the very highest" (McKisack 234). Various lords were indentured to the king, making a contract pledging to supply fighting men in times of battle. In the actual service, "the commanding officers were the leading members of the aristocracy together with those captains of lower rank who had won renown through deeds of prowess" (McKisack 237) "All were knights," continues the historian, "but a graduated scale of payments reveals a hierarchy within the order of knighthood" (237). So within the army, men of different classes, aristocratic and not, were nonetheless *knights,* a military term referring here to those in armor on great war horses. Chaucer's Knight, if he were in such an army would not have been part of the nobility but a professional man at arms. He was not the kind of knight who would sit with the king and plan strategy. He would not have belonged, say, to one of the noble knightly orders established in the fourteenth century by Edward III, such as the nostalgic Order of the Round Table or the Order of the Garter (see McKisack 251–252), which is familiar to readers of the fourteenth-century Arthurian poem, *Sir Gawain and the Green Knight.*

But in any rank in the army, all knights, of course, need weapons and accouterment, including what one critic calls a "pit team," akin to that of a modern auto racer, which would attend to the technical needs of the man and his arms (Peirce 152). The costs were always high, and Peirce observes that the initial stage of production of a twelfth-century battle sword alone could take as long as fifteen hours, making the arms an overall expensive undertaking. McKisack tells us that in the fourteenth century armor "was in process of transition from mail to plate" and was, as always, "elaborate and costly" (238). Good war horses could cost over £100, for although men fought on foot, they needed horses for travel and for "the pursuit of a broken enemy" (239). One couldn't be a knight without a horse.

With the costs so high, aside from the desire for battle and the commitment one has made for economic reasons, why would a man want to pursue knighthood? One reason in fourteenth-century England was profit, for many warriors made their fortunes during the Hundred Years' War. Chaucer himself, as a diplomat, found employment in the king's service during the war, which created jobs, so to speak, in ways that the modern military industry still does in the late twentieth century.

But profit came not only through the creation of wartime roles, but through simple plunder too. McKisack tells us: "The spoils of war were on a scale which made it possible for the commons in the Good Parliament of 1376 to suggest that, if the king had better councilors and servants, he need levy no subsidies because the war should pay for itself" (247). Peace could actually be "disheartening" to the "poor knights, squires, and archers of England whose comforts and stations in society depended upon war" (248). A "policy of peace, retrenchment, and reform was," says McKisack, not likely to appeal to the knightly classes (250). As Michael Bennett reports, "throughout the middle ages, military service remained the most celebrated avenue of social advancement" (162). And despite the obvious disjunction between Christian charity and war, in the fourteenth century, as in most historical periods, "society was organized for war" and "the profession of arms was supremely honorable" (McKisack 250). All these appeals and benefits made knighthood a respected profession and help explain the prominence Chaucer gives to this Knight and the lavish words of respect for his military prowess and for his personal virtue. The Knight, Chaucer tells us, was "ever honored for his worthiness" and was a "verray, parfit gentil knyght" [I (A) 72] ["true, perfect, noble knight"]. These words may sound lofty, but they bespeak fourteenth-century culture's judgment of its chivalric, military heroes—or at least the best of those possible judgments.

Chaucer's Knight is at once a great military man and also kindly, noble, and Christian, for his religious identity cannot be separated from his social and military positions. This odd paradox is worth looking at because modern readers may wonder at how Christianity and violence could be so harmonized. The

Knight's battles include the Crusade siege of Alexandria in 1365. Few English knights were there, but some were, including Chaucer's. The Crusading soldiers' violence against the Moslems had won them hatred and powerful retaliatory retribution. In this battle according to Bradford, they "showed that they learned nothing from the blood thirsty errors of their forefathers, and that they were still possessed by . . . maniac savagery. . . . Making no distinction between Coptic Christians, Jews or Moslems, they put the whole city to the sword, looting, ransacking, raping and murdering" (Bradford 72). Jones reports that most historians' accounts make the entire deadly expedition sound like the My Lai massacre of villagers by American soldiers during the Vietnam War (Jones 42). Surely *our* knight couldn't have done any of this, for he is, as Chaucer says, as meek as a maid (line 69). To understand why he massacred and looted in the name of religion, or why he could have, we first have to understand the Church's project of re-imagining violence and channeling knightly prowess against the common enemies of Christendom.

In the tenth and eleventh centuries, the Church confronted the problem of Christian violence and civil chaos brought on by powerful bands of early knights. It proclaimed the Peace of God and the Truce of God, signifying that no one should plunder churches or church lands and that Christians should not harm one another. Gies calls the Church's motivation a mix of idealism and pragmatic fear for their lands and property. But whatever the reason, cultivating the virtue of the armed men of Europe, by making the knights "soldiers of Christ," paved the way to the preaching of the Crusades (see Gies 30).

Pope Urban II, in one of the most important moments in the history not only of knighthood but of Western history itself, further developed the idea of a Christian knighthood by calling the European men to arms against a common enemy. The Crusades gave a holy identity and direction to the overflowing and dangerous violence that men of arms wreaked upon each other:

Listen and learn! You, girt about with the badge of knighthood, are arrogant with great pride; you rage against each other and cut each other in pieces. This is not the (true) soldiery of Christ which rends asunder the sheep-fold of the Redeemer. The Holy Church has reserved a soldiery for herself to help her people, but you debase her wickedly to her hurt. Let us confess the truth, whose heralds you ought to be; truly you are not holding to the way which leads to life. You the oppressors of children, plunderers of widows; you, guilty of homicide, of sacrilege, robbers of another's rights; you who await the pay of thieves for the shedding of Christian blood—as vultures swell fetid corpses, so do you sense battle from afar and run to them eagerly. Verily this is the worst way, for it is utterly removed from God! If forth you wish to be mindful of your souls, either lay down the girdle of such knighthood, or advance boldly, as knights of Christ, and rush as quickly as you can to the defense of the Eastern Church. . . .We say this, brethren, that you may restrain your murdering hands from the destruction of your brothers, and in behalf of your relatives in the faith oppose yourselves to the gentiles. Under Jesus Christ, our Leader, may you struggle for your Jerusalem, in Christian battle live, most invincible line, even more successfully than did the sons of Jacob of old—struggle that you may assail and drive out the Turks, more execrable than the Jebusites, who are in this land, and you may deem it a beautiful thing to die for Christ in that city in which he died for us. (Peters 8–9)

The year was 1095, and although Chaucer's crusading Knight answers this call in battles some 250 years later, he answers it nonetheless. Pope Urban hopes, as we can see in his vivid attack on inter-Christian violence, for a virtuous knighthood, and he makes no mention of extending to non-Christian peoples God's mercy or the fruits of Christian charity. He never tries to purge violence out of the knight, just to direct its cannon blasts at human evil, in the form of the Turks who encroached on Eastern Church lands. Urban recognized that war and violence could not be stopped but perhaps Christian on Christian violence could.

Of course, he was wrong, for despite the Crusades, what one historian calls the "seven great gales out of the west and north that thundered over [the] eastern land" (Bradford 13), Christian wars did not end. Chaucer's portrait cleverly highlights this fact, for the Knight's portrait makes no mention of the Hundred Years' War between England and France, but only of battles against "muslims, schismatics and pagans" (see L. Benson 801). Is the poet trying to ignore the fact that Christian knights did indeed fight one another because that history, which Chaucer himself took loyal part in, is embarrassing from a Christian perspective? Why does he only refer to Crusades, and how do this Knight's crusading actions relate to history? His very moral status is at stake, and all Chaucer tells us is that "no man had ridden further in both Christian and in heathen lands" (11. 48–49).

Taking on the Knight's crusading record, Terry Jones wrote a very detailed book connecting the Knight to the fourteenth-century mercenaries, "men who made their bread and butter out of fighting," bands who "debased the very concept of knighthood" (24). The knight's poverty, that is, his lack of ostentatious dress, hints that he is of this group. Jones takes the standard appreciation of the Knight and turns it on his head. Critics have often pointed to Chaucer's comment that the Knight is a worthy man who loves "chivalrie" and "trouthe and honour, freedom and curteisie" as evidence of his goodness. But according to Jones: "The apparently unequivocal praise of these opening lines . . . contrasts sharply with the picture of the knight that would have unfolded to the contemporary reader throughout the rest of the description" (31). The rest of the description, according to Jones, depicts a man who could have been part of a "huge band of blood thirsty marauders roam[ing] Europe, killing, raping, burning and pillaging without let or hindrance" (31). The Knight-slaying critic concludes:

By the end of Chaucer's description of the Knight no contemporary reader would have been left in any doubt as to what sort of fellow this was. They would not have seen a militant Christian idealist but a shabby mercenary without morals or scruples—the typical product of an age which saw war turned into a business. (141)

In part defending the knight, Maurice Keen shows that the Crusading spirit was still alive and, contrary to common scholarly belief, formed a vital part of the late fourteenth-century political and religious world, so that the Knight's crusade activities, far from making him a bloodthirsty mercenary, connect him to a proven record of aristocratic knightly aspiration, as many famous and noble knights fought in the campaigns Chaucer attributes to him. Keen shows that Crusading enthusiasm remained "alive in the time of Chaucer," "that knights did still respond to its promptings . . . and that it was still widely respected as the highest expression of chivalric dedication" (60). According to Keen, then, the Knight is one of those figures whose "lives indicate patterns of virtuous living that are not outmoded, but which too few in Chaucer's opinion, made a sufficiently serious effort to follow" (47).

One of the most prominent students of the Knight, Jill Mann, comments on the oddity of Chaucer's emphasis on the Knight as Crusader, saying this only refers to half a medieval knight's duty; the other, unmentioned, half made him official "defender of churches, widows and orphans" (Mann 114). Mann links the Knight up to the kind of chivalric/monastic knight envisioned by St. Bernard, a holy warrior who does not plunder and so remains poor and humble. But Mann is still uncomfortable with the focus of the portrait and concludes on a dubious note:

If we examine the Knight's portrait closely, we see that the immediate ends of his professional activities are undefined. Is their aim conversion of the heathen? or their extermination, to make way for the permanent occupation of the Holy Land by Christians? The Knight's role, as it is described in his portrait, is merely to fight, win and move on. One might say that his campaigns have a religious *character,* but not a religious *aim*. . . . The relevance of his profession to the lives of the [other pilgrims] is not made clear. (115)

From these critical historical discussions we learn that we cannot separate the Knight from his profession, and we cannot evaluate or even comprehend him without knowing something about these controversial dimensions of medieval knighthood. And unlike the case for pilgrims like the Pardoner and Summoner, the moral universe of the Knight is hard to read, wrapped up as it is with the historical, political universe of Christian European history.

It seems that Christian peoples of the fourteenth century, although they preserved a Crusading spirit, also expressed dismay over the war and the slaughter of the "Saracen." Jones describes the "growing realization that heathens were human beings the same as Christians." He also quotes from a pamphlet of 1395 that criticizes the Crusaders: "And knights, who run into 'hethnesse' to get themselves a name for slaying men, are greatly blamed by the King of Peace; for by humility and tolerance our faith was multiplied, and Jesus Christ hates fighters and man slayers and threatens them: Qui gladio percutit, gladio peribit. [Who strikes with the sword, shall die by the sword]" (Jones 36). And yet we can view the wars our Knight had *no* known part in in equally debased terms. As Morris Bishop says in discussing the Battle of Crécy of 1346, one of the major battles of the Hundred Years' War:

War became a business, a rather dirty business. It was conducted by contract armies, recruited anywhere without concern for nationality. The knights themselves fought no longer from feudal obligation and loyalty but for advantage. Their dream was to capture and hold some noble for an enormous ransom. (Bishop 385)

The fourteenth century both praised and condemned the wars the Knight took part in, and they celebrated and profited by the ones he—as far as Chaucer tells us—did not take part in. Yet, from a larger perspective, later these were potentially embarrassing Christian wars, seemingly inexcusable acts of violence between Christians. Furthermore, Chaucer offers nothing but praise for what the Knight has done, and his omission of references to the French wars might be his way of criticizing that tragically Christian war (see L. Benson 801). A portrait that seems on the surface such a clear-cut piece of praise finally leads us in circles trying to grasp the politics and the history behind the stately images.

Chaucer never settles these questions for us. Does the Knight's behavior and interactions with the other pilgrims shed any light on the subject? He reconciles the Host and the Pardoner, making them kiss after they have exchanged vicious insults. And although he interrupts the interminable "Monk's Tale," he does so in terms more polite than those of the outspoken Host. Whether such social authority befits a man of his class and that class's history, or whether a peace-making, humble knight bespeaks a horrible irony—an irony underlined by the stories of brutality behind his many Crusading battles—we cannot say for sure. Whether anachronism, idealization of the past, or even as embodiment of Christian military terror and failure, the Knight emerges as the focal point of histories that Chaucer wanted his readers and future generations to confront. We need not be afraid, in the twentieth century, to admit the paradoxes, ironies, and excesses that constitute that history. As long as we are ready to recognize the possibility that Chaucer may, through the Knight, be celebrating battles and ideals he saw as glorious, however inglorious they may now seem to us, we can understand the character as being "worthy." Perhaps Chaucer did not intend, if he were looking so far ahead, for us so easily to understand and judge his Knight. Perhaps he wanted to preserve a figure, who through action, character, appearance and experience, would ever force future generations to confront English Christian identity and military ideology. If so, then Chaucer succeeded.

THE KNIGHT AND HIS TALE

The Knight tells a tale about the wars and political adventures of Duke Theseus of ancient Athens, a long "romance" about his conquest of the Amazons and the love triangle that ensues between two knights he captures in battle and the sister of his Amazon wife. In the most general way, it makes sense that a man of arms would tell a war story and would create classical versions of knights and ladies and lords, replete with detailed combat and martial tournament scenes. Clearly, as narrator the Knight likes the "locker room" details of battle, the arming scenes, and the hosts of great men brought together for the battle over Emily. The story is in many ways suited to him.

We should be careful about pressing these connections too far, however, because the "Knight's Tale" was an independent story of Chaucer's, based on Boccaccio's *Teseida,* long before Chaucer wrote the *Canterbury Tales* or gave this tale to the Knight. So the tale does not necessarily reflect his character. The Knight makes no biographical references, no self-reflective statements, he offers no specialist's insights or comments on the actions of the characters—however knightly they may be—and he simply does not involve himself personally in the tale, aside from the rather conventional, common Chaucerian apology that he's not much of a story teller: "I've got a large field to dig, and the oxen in my plow are weak" (886–887).

We should, however, feel free to explore the possible connections between the themes of the portrait and tale. David Aers argues that the tale "involves a most illuminating scrutiny of the versions of order, styles of thought and life embodied in Theseus, rulers like him and their culture" (174–175). In this type of context, is the tale in any way a comment on war or violence in the manner that the portrait's emphasis on Crusading might be? Battle and violence sometimes bring success, such as the conquest over the Amazons and over the tyrant Creon. But sometimes violence brings disaster, as in the endless battles and tragically useless tournament war between the two uncompromising knights in love with Emily. Is the tale saying that violence is outdated, anachronistic like the crusty old Knight himself? Jones sees the tale as appropriate because a vicious mercenary like the Knight is a suitable teller of a tale that "extol[s] the power and glory of a tyrant" and is a "hymn to worldly success and the right of might" (219). But in response to reductive, oversimplifying readings like Jones's, other critics have simply said, as C. David Benson puts it, that the relationship between the Knight and the tale is "general and nominal" (65). Chaucer clearly does not develop the tale-teller relationship here as he does with such characters as the Miller, Wife of Bath, Friar and Summoner, Pardoner and Parson, where the tale forms part of the identity of the pilgrim and the drama of the entire plot.

REFERENCES

Aers, David. "Imagination, Order and Ideology: The Knight's Tale." Chapter 7 of *Chaucer, Langland and the Creative Imagination.* London, Boston, and Henley: Routledge and Keegan Paul, 1980.

Barber, Richard. *The Knight and Chivalry.* New York: Charles Scribner's Sons, 1970.

Bennett, Michael J. *Community, Class and Careerism.* Cambridge: Cambridge University Press, 1983.

Benson, C. David. *Chaucer's Drama of Style.* Chapel Hill: University of North Carolina Press, 1986.

Benson, Larry D., ed. *The Riverside Chaucer.* Boston: Houghton Mifflin, 1987.

Bishop, Morris. *The Horizon Book of the Middle Ages.* New York: American Heritage Publishing Co., 1968.

Bradford, Ernle. *The Shield and the Sword: The Knights of St. John, Jerusalem, Rhodes, and Malta.* New York: E. P. Dutton, 1973.

Gies, Frances. *The Knight in History.* New York: Harper and Row, 1984.

Howard, Donald R. *The Idea of the Canterbury Tales.* Berkeley: University of California Press, 1976.

Jones, Terry. *Chaucer's Knight: The Portrait of a Medieval Mercenary.* New York: Methuen, 1985.

Keen, Maurice. "Chaucer's Knight, the English Aristocracy and the Crusade." In *English Court Culture in the Later Middle Ages.* V. J. Scattergood and J. W. Sherborne, eds. New York: St. Martin's, 1983.

———.*Chivalry.* New Haven, Conn. and London: Yale University Press, 1984.

McAlpine, Monica E. *Chaucer's Knight's Tale: An Annotated Bibliography: 1900 to 1985.* Toronto: University of Toronto Press, 1991.

McKisack, May. *The Fourteenth Century: 1307–1399.* Oxford: Clarendon Press, 1959.

Mann, Jill. *Chaucer and the Medieval Estates Satire: The Literature of Social Classes and the "General Prologue" to the "Canterbury Tales."* Cambridge: Cambridge University Press, 1973.

Nolan, Barbara. *Chaucer and the Tradition of the Roman Antique.* Cambridge: Cambridge University Press, 1992.

Peirce, Ian. "The Knight, His Arms and Armor in the Eleventh and Twelfth Centuries." In *The Ideals and Practice of Medieval Knighthood.* Christopher Harper-Bill and Ruth Harvey, eds. Suffolk and New Hampshire: Boydell Press, 1986.

Peters, Edward, ed. *The First Crusade. The Chronicle of Fulcher of Chartres and Other Source Material.* Philadelphia: University of Pennsylvania Press, 1971.

Runciman, Steven. *A History of the Crusades. Volume I: The First Crusade and the Foundation of the Kingdom of Jerusalem.* Cambridge: Cambridge University Press, 1951.

Tomasch, Sylvia. "Mappae mundi and the Knight's Tale: The Geography of Power, the Technology of Control." In *Literature and Technology.* Mark L. Greenberg and Lance Schachterle, eds. Cranbury, N.J.: Associated UP, 1992.

Wetherbee, Winthrop. *Geoffrey Chaucer: The Canterbury Tales.* Landmarks of World Literature. Cambridge: Cambridge University Press, 1989.

Chapter 2

A Yong Squier

PEGGY HUEY

THE PROFESSION IN CHAUCER'S TIME

In the Middle Ages, England was divided for political purposes into manors, which were awarded to knights for services rendered to the king or other nobles. These manors were sufficient to maintain the family and their retainers; the manor remained in the family's hands, then, as long as the knight rendered the service (primarily military support) due the lord. Since the rules of chivalry demanded that a man's father or grandfather had been a knight in order for him to be knighted, his sons could inherit the manor by following in their father's footsteps. As Bradford Broughton explains in his discussion of the word "knighthood" in his *Dictionary of Medieval Knighthood and Chivalry,* "chivalry was designed essentially to ameliorate the horrors and brutality of war, to provide a means whereby men were encouraged to view their enemies as fellow humans whose misfortunes in war were to be considered with pity rather than with revenge" (291). Using this definition of the term, we can perceive chivalry as a precursor to the Geneva Convention of 1864, which governs the treatment of prisoners of war as well as the sick and wounded today. The nature of chivalry, however, with all of its complexity both on the battlefield and in the court, required a training period before the rank and responsibility of knighthood (and its various ramifications) could be assumed. During this training, which was traditionally available to the younger sons of peers and their eldest sons as well as the eldest sons of knights and their eldest sons, the young man was referred to as a squire.

Throughout the chivalric world prevalent in Western Europe of the twelfth century, the term *squire* had evolved as people realized there was a rank in society beneath that of knight. Depending on what the individual was actually doing for the knight, several Latin words were available at this time to label this subordinate rank: *armiger, serviens, scutiger/scutifer,* and *valletus.* In preconquest Normandy, *armiger* (Latin for "armour bearer") was the last step before being knighted; by the time of England's Edward I (1272–1307), it generally was reserved for the "body-squires" or "Squire of the Body," which included the "master-cook and chamberlain" of the household (Crouch 167), who rendered personal service to kings and great noblemen as well as their ladies (Broughton 23–24, 298). A related term, *serviens,* evolved into the military term *sergeant* as an infantry and light cavalry rank (via OFr. *serjant*), but its role late in the twelfth century was to refer to other less important servants in attendance on the knight (Broughton 415; Crouch 164). *Scutiger/scutifer* (from OFr. *escuier,* "shield-bearer" [Crouch 164], or "shield-maker" [Bennett 2]) evolved into our term *esquire* or *squire,* primarily for the person attending the knight's horses. The final option available was *valletus,* "little vassal" (from OFr. *vadlet/vaslet*), which evolved into "valet" and "varlet" (Crouch 164), but it also referred to a "yeoman" during Edward I's reign (Broughton 465). Through history, the words melded and separated, jumbling the clear differentiations inherent in the original labels. For example, in Edward I's account books, the same people appear bearing different titles under various accounts "in the Pay Rolls and the Wardrobe Book . . . [and] the Marshal's Register of feudal retinues" (Bennett 2), adding to the confusion. This makes it extremely difficult to trace the role of the "squire" logically through time.

Nevertheless, when Geoffrey Chaucer wrote the *Canterbury Tales* in the fourteenth century, the "shield-bearer" aspect of the squire was firmly established in people's minds. This image led to the creation of the Squire who participates in the pilgrimage depicted in the *Canterbury Tales.* However, discussing Chaucer's Squire as a person is difficult without talking about the Knight. The problem here is twofold. First, the Squire is the Knight's son; because of that relationship, we expect certain similarities between them in background, personality, interests, and so on. Second, his role both as the knight's son and a squire is that of a knight-in-training, learning the skills necessary to be a leader of men during combat; in this role, the squire is comparable to today's military academy or Regular Officer Training Corps (ROTC) cadets. This correlation is especially clear if we consider fighter pilots as modern-day knights, strapping on the "armor" of their jet aircraft to engage in hand-to-hand combat with the enemy (only fighting with missiles instead of lance and sword).

Part of the difficulty in separating discussion of the squire from that of the knight stems from Chaucer's use of his characters—the order in which each one appears in the Prologue follows a definite plan (see H. F. Brooks for complete details on this idea). As the first pair appearing in the Prologue, the Knight and his son "are strongly contrasted, on a basis of affinities. . . . They are both idealized representatives of the same military class, the son a likely candidate for the order of knighthood in which the father is so eminent" (Brooks 14).

The idealized relationship between the two characters allows Chaucer's Squire (along with Aurelius in the "Franklin's Tale") to fit the first definition Larry Benson uses in his "Glossary" to the Riverside edition of Chaucer, that of a "knight bachelor, the first degree of knighthood" (1293), which just adds to the confusion discussed earlier regarding the role of a squire. To clarify Benson's understanding of the word, we can turn to *The Oxford English Dictionary (OED)*, which describes a knight bachelor as someone who is "not a member of any special order" of knighthood (like a Knight of the Bath or a Knight of the Garter). This definition places the character beyond the bounds of the meaning of the word *squire* according to the *OED:* "one ranking next to a knight under the feudal system of military service and tenure"; or the related word *esquire,* "a young man of gentle birth, who as an aspirant to knighthood, attended upon a knight, carried his shield, and rendered him other services." The latter description presents the image most of us conjure up when we picture squires in conjunction with the concept of chivalry.

In fact, this image is justifiable when we consider how squires were depicted in the manuscripts of the period. They were generally unarmed themselves, though one of their main jobs was to bear the knight's armor, spear, and shield for him. To help us picture the squire more clearly, we can turn to Edward L. Cutts for his description of a typical squire's activities in *Scenes and Characters of the Middle Ages:*

we see the squire starting into activity to catch his master's steed, from which he has been unhorsed by an antagonist of greater strength or skill, or good fortune. We see him also in the lists at a tournament, handing his master a new spear when he has splintered his own on an opponent's shield; or helping him to his feet when he has been overthrown, horse and man, under the hoofs of prancing horses. (352)

In addition to his role as assistant to the knight, the squire was learning by observation how to conduct himself in courtly environments. At this time, the squire's appearance was extremely important both to him and the knights. Squires are usually seen wearing a *hacqueton,* a quilted armor "made of buckram [a coarse cotton fabric stiffened with glue], and stuffed with cotton" formed into a sleeved tunic, according to Cutts (345). In the Romance of King Meliadus (part of the King Arthur cycle), folio 66 v shows a squire "who has a round cap with a long feather. . . . In several other instances the squire rides bareheaded, but has his hood hanging behind on his shoulders ready for a cold day or a shower of rain" (Cutts 352). Chaucer's Squire appears similarly in a short gown "with sleves longe and wyde" (I.93). Portrait miniatures of the pilgrims from the Ellesmere MS (now in the Huntington Library) were completed early in the fifteenth century, within twenty years of the poet's death. Therefore, they would be relatively accurate portrayals of the pilgrims. The Squire's mount "rises in a posture called courbetting (or curvetting) . . . [which] suggests the social aspiration and possibly the travels of the rider" (Hussey 29). As Chaucer describes him, the Squire's portrait reveals "the poet's admiration for the Squire.

. . . With his long sleeves blowing out behind him from his padded *gipoun* or doublet, the Squire has managed to keep on the tall hat under which his crimped hair can be seen. His hose are of a length to put him to extreme disadvantage if he were forced to walk'' (Hussey 48).

In contrast to this apparently typical portrait of a squire, *The Book of the Knight of La Tour-Landry* tells the tale of a squire who appeared before a company of French noble persons wearing ''a coat-hardy'' (or ''cote-hardie'') (''a close-fitting garment with sleeves, formerly worn by both sexes'' according to the *OED*), which was apparently common among the Germans. Two brothers who would not hesitate to correct in public someone they considered as a peer ''asked him where was his fiddle or his rebec (*ribible*), or such an instrument as belongeth unto a ministrel'' (quoted in Rickert 140). Chastised, the squire immediately changed to a more suitable gown since he was making every effort to fit in with this elite company.

The last line of the Squire's introductory portrait in the ''General Prologue,'' ''And carf biforn his fader at the table'' [''and carved before his father at the table''], indicates one of the more important tasks of the squire—attending the nobles at the dinner table, assisted by ''older professional servitors of villein stock'' who would pass to the squires the dishes, which were then ''presented on bended knee by noble hands to noble guests'' under the guiding hand of a seneschal (Davis 123).

As part of his definition of ''knighthood,'' Broughton describes what he considers as three lesser levels of squires (in comparison with the Squire of the Body) whose duties centered around the table: the Squire of Table, corresponding to our Squire's portrait; the Squire of Wines; and the Squire of Pantry (299), which would seem to contradict the honor associated with the task. Ernest Kuhl and Henry Webb believe ''he who carved probably held the position of greatest esteem'' based on their reading of several medieval texts on the subject that were collected in *Early English Meals and Manners* (283). The importance of this role is logical when we consider that the squire would be in close contact with the nobles his lord was entertaining; as such, his training would be subject to evaluation by his lord's guests. A significant portion of this stage of the squire's education involved his learning to behave with propriety in distinguished company, including standing at perfect ease, not staring blankly, keeping his fingernails clean, and putting ''a little from every plate into the basket of collected leavings for the poor'' (Davis 123–124).

The initial triad of the Knight and the Squire in the ''Prologue'' adds the Yeoman, with whom the Squire is also set in contrast. This time, however, the contrast is in terms of social class, thereby creating a real-life picture of fathers, sons, and servants. This contrast also ties the Squire to the second definition of a Squire: that of a ''servant to a knight'' (Benson 1293), which is used twice in the ''Knight's Tale'' (I.1410, I.2502). This definition fits the alternate picture we might have when we think of a Squire: Sancho Panza serving Don Quixote, the Dwarf serving the Red Cross Knight, R2D2 serving Luke Skywalker. This role today is filled by the batman of the British army—the army officer's soldier-servant. (If we extend our analogy of the fighter-pilot as knight, the closest relative in the American military might be the crew chief, who cares for the pilot's "armor," or more generally the entire ground support crew.)

In *Scenes and Characters of the Middle Ages,* Cutts offers an ironic description of this servant-class of squire and his activities: "The squires are unarmed, and mature men of rather heavy type, different from the gay and gallant youths whom we are apt to picture to ourselves as the squires of the days of chivalry attendant on noble knights adventurous. . . . We see the squires looking on very phlegmatically while their masters are in the height of a single combat; perhaps a knight adventurous was not a hero to his squire" (Cutts 352).

To help us understand the relationship of the servant-class of squire and his lord, we can consider an entry in John of Gaunt's Register, which records "A Squire's Indentures of Service" between himself and Symkyn Molyneux in 1374:

The said Symkyn is retained and will remain with our said lord for peace and for war for the term of his life, as follows: that is to say, the said Symkyn shall be bound to serve our said lord as well in time of peace as of war in whatsoever parts it shall please our said lord, well and fitly arrayed. And he shall be boarded as well in time of peace as of war. And he shall take for his fees by the year, as well in time of peace as of war, ten marks sterling from the issues of the Duchy of Lancaster by the hands of the receiver there who now is or shall be in time to come, at the terms of Easter and Michaelmas by even portions yearly for the whole of his life. And, moreover, our lord has granted to him by the year in time of war five marks sterling by the hands of the treasurer of war for the time being. And his year of war shall begin the day when he shall move from his inn [his private dwelling house] towards our said lord by letters which shall be sent to him thereof, and thenceforward he shall take wages coming and returning by reasonable daily [payments]; and he shall have fitting freightage for him, his men, horses, and other harness within reason, and in respect of his war horses taken and lost in the service of our said lord, and also in respect to prisoners and other profits of war taken or gained by him or any of his men, the said our lord will do to him as to other squires of his rank. (Quoted in Rickert 139)

The squire described thus is one who has either no desire to assume the golden spur that designates the knight or is not of a suitably aristocratic background.

For now, let us focus on the knight-in-training aspects of the role of a squire. Just as a person enters into training to become a medical doctor or a priest, boys from aristocratic families (as noted earlier) entered into training to become knights. This training frequently began as early as the age of seven or eight, when the boy would be sent to

the court of his father's lord or of some distinguished relative. While there he would be expected not only to develop skill in all martial exercises but also to become familiar with the ways of life in and about the halls of the great. Though never treated as a menial, he would have to make himself useful in a variety of tasks, from running errands for ladies to assisting knights with their horses and harness. (Stephenson 45)

This aspect of his training is quite possibly what has lead to the confusion of Benson's seemingly contradictory definitions of a squire: a first-degree knight versus a servant. In addition, the squire's training at this stage included horsemanship, hawking, and hunting as well as "religion and courtesy in words and deeds and actions" (Broughton 298). By the fourteenth century, this training was also extended to sons of merchant families in order to increase the supply of soldiers for the king, although these boys tended to start at a later age. Chaucer himself, the son of a vintner, utilized this avenue to an eventual position at court by entering into service (at the age of fourteen) in the Ulster household in 1357.

During this early period of training, the boy was referred to as a *valet* or *damoiseau* in French, a page in English. He held that title until he reached the age of fourteen, when he was promoted to the rank of squire; he held that rank until he was at least twenty-one (apparently, the earliest age at which he could be knighted unless he would one day be king—Henry III was nine when he was knighted; Edward I was fifteen). In a formal, religious ceremony, he was girded with his own sword, making him a squire. To continue his training, he attached himself to one particular knight, whom he accompanied on all journeys and assisted as needed. During a joust or "in the event of battle, the squire carried the knight's reserve of arms, led his extra horse if he had one, laced on his defensive armor, rescued him when dismounted or wounded, and took charge of any prisoners he might capture. Through such activity the squire learned the brutal business of war at first hand" (Stephenson 46). Meanwhile, he practiced his skills against other squires attached to his knight or other knights. When he had finally proven himself through his participation in actual battle, he would be rewarded with knighthood.

We know from Chaucer's description of the Squire in the "General Prologue" that "he hadde been somtyme in chyvachie / In Flaundres, in Artoys, and Pycardie" (I.85–86) ["he had been once / In Flanders, in Artois, and Picardy"]. This implies that the Squire has already received all the training necessary to become a knight and has apparently proven himself in battle; we assume he is just waiting for the proper occasion so that he can be formally knighted. We also know, from Chaucer's biography, that he too had seen service in France; however, he was captured and had to be ransomed as a *valettus* (worth about £16) by the king (Howard 4). Therefore, he had not acquitted himself honorably in battle. Perhaps the same was true of the Squire, especially since the Crusade he had participated in was not very successful and had been launched purely for political reasons.

With the increased cost of full-plate armor (necessitated by the arrival of artillery warfare replacing hand-to-hand combat) along with all the accouterments required or expected of the knight, many men began avoiding the knighting ceremony until forced by the distraint process to participate. The distraint process required anyone holding a "knight's fee" or having an estate worth at least £20 a year to accept knighthood. Knights, who had tired of riding off to battle at the beck and call of the monarch, preferred instead to send a "knight's fee" (comparable to a tax on their holdings) to cover their obligation, which enabled the king to hire mercenaries to fight directly for him instead of under the knight. As the number of knights avoiding service increased, the role of knight with its civil as well as military aspects changed, and with that the role of the squire as a knight-in-training. To fill the void, squires began to assume some of the civil responsibilities associated with a knight, including representing the shire. In fact, by the end of Edward III's reign in 1377, standard policy dictated "that sergeants or esquires were to be *known* as knights of the shire in parliament," a policy that became law in 1445 (Powicke 175 and note). This shift in perspective evolved into the men who in more modern times are referred to as "country squires" (like Squire Allworthy in Henry Fielding's *Tom Jones*), the principal landowner in a village or district.

The shift in perspective also saw squires continuing their learning at the Inns of Court instead of on the tournament field, improving their verbal jousting, getting legal training before entering the royal household. This was the training Chaucer received that led to his spending several years as envoy for the court of Edward III before getting his position at the customhouse.

Chaucer's place in the society of the 1370s adds to the ambiguity regarding the definition of a squire. In 1374 Chaucer, who was living in "apartments granted him by the Mayor and Aldermen of the City," was ranked as a squire beneath "the Mayor of London [who] ranked as an Earl, [and] the aldermen as barons or tenants-in-chief of the Crown" (Robertson 265). In this role, Chaucer himself fits the *OED*'s third definition of a Squire: "an officer charged with personal attendance upon a sovereign, nobleman, or other high dignitary." According to Derek Brewer, part of his pay for this position included a ration of "two Paris (i.e., tallow) candles and a supply of firewood" in winter (83). D. W. Robertson helps us understand Chaucer's role as a squire by explaining that "as a royal servant he would outrank the Squire in the General Prologue, not to mention Aurelius in the Franklin's Tale." Therefore, "it is a mistake, as well as a grievous oversimplification, to consider Chaucer as a member of the 'middle class' " (293), which we might try to do since he came from the merchant class and was never knighted.

THE LINK BETWEEN THE PROFESSION AND TALE

The Squire is one of the few pilgrims whose portrait in the "General Prologue" is actually a physical description, so we can picture this young man who is accompanying his father on the pilgrimage:

> A lovyere and a lusty bacheler,
> With lokkes crulle as they were leyd in presse.

Of twenty yeer of age he was, I gesse.
Of his stature he was of evene lengthe,
And wonderly delyvere, and of greet strengthe.
And he hadde been somtyme in chyvachie
In Flaundres, in Artoys, and Pycardie,
And born hym weell, as of so litel space,
In hope to stonden in his lady grace.
Embrouded was he, as it were a meede
Al ful of fresshe floures, whyte and reede.
Syngynge he was, or floytynge, al the day;
He was as fressh as is the month of May.
Short was his gowne, with sleves longe and wyde.
Wel koude he sitte on hors and faire ryde.
He koude songes make and wel endite,
Juste and eek daunce, and weel purtreye and write.
So hoote he lovede that by nyghtertale
He sleep namoore than dooth a nyghtyngale.
Curteis he was, lowely, and servysable,
And carf biforn his fader at the table.

                                        (I.80–100)

[A lover and a lively bachelor,
With locks curled as they were laid in a press.
Of twenty years of age he was, I guess.
Of his stature he was of moderate height,
And marvelously agile, and of great strength.
And he had been sometime on a cavalry expedition
In Flanders, Artois, and Picardie,
And conducted himself well, as of so little time,
In hope to stand in his lady's grace.
Embroidered was he, as was a meadow
All full of fresh flowers, white and red.
Singing he was, or piping, all the day;
He was as fresh as is the month of May.
Short was his gown, with sleeves long and wide.
Well could he sit on his horse and fairly ride.
He could songs make and well compose,
Joust and also dance, and well draw and write.
So passionately he loved that at nighttime
He slept no more than does a nightingale.
Courteous he was, humble, and willing to serve,
And carved before his father at the table.]

Like the Physician and the Shipman, the Squire makes "only token appearances, or none, outside the General Prologue" except for the tale he tells (C. Benson 9). Therefore, we have to rely on this portrait for our introduction to the character, especially since, as R. M. Lumiansky points out, each tale that is told is suited to the teller; to understand the Squire's unfinished story about Cambuskan, Cambalo, and Canace, we need to understand the Squire. To make our task more difficult, C. David Benson explains, the portraits in the "General Prologue" vary greatly, some indicating only casual knowledge of the pilgrim (as with the Yeoman) while others reveal personal secrets (for example, the Wife of Bath and the Friar). We know the Squire must have been an educated person, because he had some musical ability (he was singing or playing the flute all day). Derek Brewer also sees him as fitting "the normal courtly ideal," because he dressed well, was a good soldier and jouster, could write, draw, compose poetry and write the music to it (178).

The "Prologue" also offers other clues to our interpretation of the pilgrims. Some of the pilgrims are arranged in obvious groups (like the Knight, Squire, and Yeoman), whereas others (like the Doctor) appear as individuals. The group consisting of the Knight, Squire, and Yeoman make up the "military class" of the pilgrims; as such, they are set in contrast with the regular clergy, the middle-class merchants, and the churls and rascals. In terms of this contrast between groups, the pilgrims represent "ideal types" (Brooks 13). Robertson observes that "in general, Chaucer's 'ideal' portraits demonstrate interest in intangibles, so that the Knight, for example, loves chivalry, truth, honor, generosity, and courtesy; the Clerk is preoccupied with moral virtue" (278). The Squire, it is generally agreed, represents youth, love, and springtime, offering a youthful point of view to the pilgrimage.

That Chaucer's portrait of the Squire is an ideal can be confirmed by the marked similarities between the description of the Squire and the description of Aurelius (also identified as "a squier" [V.926]) in the "Franklin's Tale":

> Upon this daunce, amonges othere men,
> Daunced a squier biforn Dorigen,
> That fressher was and jolyer of array,
> As to my doom, than is the month of May.

> (V.925–928)

> [Upon this dance, among other men,
> Danced a young knight before Dorigen,
> That younger was, and jollier of condition,
> In my opinion, than is the month of May.]

This was a May that

> . . . hadde peynted with his softe shoures
> This garden ful of leves and of floures;
> And craft of mannes hand so curiously
> Arrayed hadde this gardyn, trewely,
> That nevere was ther gardyn of swich prys

But if it were the verray paradys.

(V.907–912)

[. . . had painted with his soft showers
This garden full of leaves and flowers;
And craft of man's hand so skilfully
Prepared had this garden, truly,
That never was there a garden of such price
But if it was the true paradise.]

Chaucer has placed both of the squires "in the popular context of the activities of the month of May. In his young manhood (a Squire was always under twenty-one) he is a perfect symbol of that time of the human year" (Hussey 48).

When joined with the Knight and the Franklin, the Squire also presents the qualities of the ideal aristocrat who has been educated in "religion and morality, war and athletics, and literary and cultural pursuits" (Orme 43). Stanley Kahrl convincingly argues "that because Chaucer has so carefully associated the Squire with his father, both in the "General Prologue" and through verbal echoes within his tale, we are permitted, indeed forced to conclude that if the "Knight's Tale" is a celebration of classical order in the chivalric world, the "Squire's Tale" presents the growing impulse toward exoticism and disorder at work in the courts of late medieval Europe" (195).

The father and the son also contrast image-wise, representing two different stages of life. Brooks observes that "the youth, fashion, grace, exuberance, and promise of the Squire contrast with the Knight's maturity and experience, his long record of achievement, his concentration on essentials, like good horses and prompt thanksgiving, at the expense if necessary of his appearance" (14). Carrying the contrast to its logical conclusion, we realize the Squire has the "proper attributes to go with his being a young lover: a fine figure, a dashing military career . . . ; and all the courtly accomplishments described in the *Roman de la rose* as being appropriate for winning one's lady" (Cooper 36). As such, he becomes a recognizable model, quite familiar to Chaucer's audience. When his turn comes to perform, he relates a tale appropriate for what we earlier learned of his character; this gay, lighthearted young man tells, or begins to tell, "the romantic story of far-off Tartary, in which are evident certain attitudes that the Squire has acquired from his father, the Knight. There are no dramatic complications—no antagonisms pursued or axes ground—as contexts for the performances in this category" (Lumiansky 8). Because he is a romantic, the story he tells is a romance. This is the crux of the connection between his profession and his tale.

Considering the subject matter he chose, we can determine that the Squire's purpose "was in fact to outdo the more traditional Arthurian romances" whose style his father had followed (Kahrl 199). It is interesting that in his tale, he "refers to the great knights of Arthurian days as dead and gone, perhaps figments to begin with" (Howard 434); yet this is the elite company he is seeking to join. Marie Neville sees him as trying to double or triple the effects achieved by the Knight in his tale. Robert Haller says Chaucer is actually satirizing "the pseudo-genre of romance" by having the Squire show off his knowledge of rhetoric as he embellishes the rhetorical devices available to him (286). He is basically using the old romances, the primary textbooks to teach both the manners and the manner of a knight, as models for himself and his tale. As he tells his story,

his concentration on the rhetorical surface and on feeling prevents him from seeing the extent to which the meaning of what he says is a judgment on his way of life. . . . The Squire is as disordered philosophically as he is poetically. . . . What better way to show the Squire's rhetorical failure than to have him tell a tale which, it would seem, could go on forever, but which is also complete, if not finished, at any point. (Haller 293)

Kahrl reminds us that "it is the Squire, not Chaucer," whose project is to combine several tales into one story "without possessing the ability to maintain a coherent narrative thread" (196). Obviously, the Squire is more concerned with esoterics than coherence.

Equally obvious is the fact that the Squire is proud of his acquaintance with the colors of rhetoric, considering the extensive use he makes of all the figures of rhetoric like *inventio, occupatio,* and *descriptio.* His style focuses on the processes of telling the story rather than on its advancement, which is the main reason why he does not conclude the story. His rhetorical elaboration is at a premium, and it frequently calls attention to itself in the process. His subject matter may be novel, in keeping with the age's fascination with "matters Oriental," but it is leading nowhere, with conventional details that are "handled without grace or a feeling for their fitness in a particular context" (Kahrl 207). This places his tale in direct contrast with the "Knight's Tale," and the careful, considered, even artistic use the Knight makes of the same figures.

The Squire's lack of skill in this area is emphasized by the Franklin's being so impressed "by the superficial and empty rhetorical extravagances of the Squire, which seem to him to demonstrate 'gentilesse,' . . . the superficial and empty splendor of his 'array,' both literal and verbal" (Robertson 279). In this manner, the Squire has provided the Franklin "with an opening for a tale in which he can expound his own ideas of gentilesse" in the next tale in the sequence (Haller 293). The Franklin ends his tale (lines 1543–1544) with an acknowledgment that a squire can be as good as a knight: "Thus kan a squier don a gentil dede, / As well as kan a knyght, withouten drede." ["Thus can a squire do a noble deed, / As well as can a knight, without dread."] Even though the Franklin's tale reveals that his concept of "gentilesse," like his admiration for the Squire's rhetoric, is not quite all it should be, he does provide "a narrative as satisfyingly whole as the Squire's was inconclusive. His tale is a rhetorical rather than a narrative completion of the Squire's" (Lee 190). This makes it clear that Chaucer is purposely poking fun at the Squire's skills, even if the tale, according to A. W. Pollard, may be "one of Chaucer's rare attempts at a more or less original plot" (viii). Brian Lee also observes that "the Aristotelian formula for a work of art, that it should have a beginning, a middle and an end, applies to the 'Franklin's Tale' because it is fundamentally a literary work; whereas the 'Squire's Tale' is conceived in the oral mode, which being coterminous with experience stops only when the speaker falls silent, for reasons not necessarily prompted by the tale he is telling" (191). The Squire speaks only as long as his rhetoric can support him; when he loses that support, the Franklin gracefully interrupts him—to everyone's relief.

REFERENCES

Barber, Richard. *The Knight and Chivalry.* 1970. New York: Harper, 1982.

Bennett, Matthew. "The Status of the Squire: The Northern Evidence." *The Ideals and Practice of Medieval Knighthood: Papers from the first and second Strawberry Hill Conferences.* Woodbridge, Suffolk: Boydell Press, 1986.

Benson, C. David. *Chaucer's Drama of Style: Poetic Variety and Contrast in the Canterbury Tales.* Chapel Hill: University of North Carolina Press, 1986.

Benson, Larry D., ed. *The Riverside Chaucer.* Boston: Houghton Mifflin, 1987.

Brewer, Derek. *Chaucer in His Time.* London: Thomas Nelson, 1963.

Brooks, Harold F. *Chaucer's Pilgrims: The Artistic Order of the Portraits in the Prologue.* New York: Barnes and Noble, 1962.

Broughton, Bradford B. *Dictionary of Medieval Knighthood and Chivalry: Concepts and Terms.* New York: Greenwood Press, 1986.

Chaucer, Geoffrey. *The Canterbury Tales. The Riverside Chaucer.* Ed. Larry D. Benson. Boston: Houghton Mifflin, 1987. pp. 3–328.

Cooper, Helen. *Oxford Guides to Chaucer: The Canterbury Tales.* Oxford: Oxford University Press, 1989.

Crouch, David. *The Image of Aristocracy in Britain, 1000–1300.* London: Routledge, 1992.

Cutts, Rev. Edward L. *Scenes and Characters of the Middle Ages.* 7th ed. London: Simpkin Marshall, 1930.

Davis, William Stearns. *Life on a Mediaeval Barony: A Picture of a Typical Feudal Community in the Thirteenth Century.* New York: Harper, 1923.

Denholm-Young, N. *The Country Gentry in the Fourteenth Century: With Special Reference to the Heraldic Rolls of Arms.* Oxford: Clarendon Press, 1969.

Furnivall, Frederick J., ed. *Early English Meals and Manners.* London: EETS, 1894.

Haller, Robert S. "Chaucer's *Squire's Tale* and the Uses of Rhetoric." *Modern Philology* 62 (1965): 285–295.

Howard, Donald R. *Chaucer: His Life, His Works, His World.* New York: E. P. Dutton-NAL Penguin, 1987.

Hussey, Maurice. *Chaucer's World: A Pictorial Companion.* Cambridge: Cambridge University Press, 1967.

John of Gaunt, Duke of Lancaster. *John of Gaunt's Register.* Ed. Sidney Armitage-Smith. 2 vols. London: Publications of the Royal Historical Society, 1911. Camden Third Ser., XX–XXI. Included in Rickert.

Kahrl, Stanley J. "Chaucer's *Squire's Tale* and the Decline of Chivalry." *Chaucer Review* 7 (1973): 194–209.

Kuhl, Ernest P., and Henry J. Webb. "Chaucer's Squire." *ELH* 6 (1939): 282–284.

La Tour-Landry, Geoffrey de. *Book of the Knight of La Tour-Landry*. 1371. Ed. Thomas Wright. London, 1868. EETS, Orig. Ser., XXXIII: 158–159. Included in Rickert.

Lee, Brian S. "The Question of Closure in Fragment V of *The Canterbury Tales*." *Yearbook of English Studies* 22 (1992): 190–200.

Life-Records of Chaucer. Part II. Ed. F. J. Furnivall. London: Chaucer Society, 1900. Second Ser. XIV: 67–70. Included in Rickert. (From Harl. MS 642, fol. 55).

Lumiansky, R. M. *Of Sundry Folk: The Dramatic Principle in the Canterbury Tales*. Austin: University of Texas Press, 1955.

Neville, Marie. "The Function of the *Squire's Tale* in the Canterbury Scheme." *Journal of English and Germanic Philology* 50 (1951): 167–179.

Orme, Nicholas. "Chaucer and Education." *Chaucer Review* 16, 1 (1981): 38–59.

Oxford English Dictionary. 2nd ed. 1989.

Pollard, A. W. *Chaucer's Canterbury Tales: The Squire's Tale*. London: Macmillan, 1921.

Powicke, Michael. *Military Obligation in Medieval England: A Study in Liberty and Duty*. Oxford: Clarendon Press, 1962.

Rickert, Edith, comp. *Chaucer's World*. Eds. Clair C. Olson and Martin M. Crow. New York: Columbia University Press, 1962.

Robertson, D. W., Jr. *Essays in Medieval Culture*. Princeton, N.J.: Princeton University Press, 1980.

Stephenson, Carl. *Mediaeval Feudalism*. 1942. Ithaca, N.Y.: Great Seal-Cornell University Press, 1956.

Chapter 3

A Yeman Had He

JOHN W. CONLEE

> A Yeman hadde he and servantz namo
> At that tyme, for hym liste ride so,
> And he was clad in cote and hood of grene.
> . . . .
> A forster was he, soothly, as I gesse.

(I.101–117)

> [A yeoman had he and no other servants
> At that time, for preferred to ride so,
> And he was clad in a coat and a hood of green
> . . . .
> A forester he was, truly, as I guess.]

The third person to undergo the narrator's wide-eyed scrutiny in the "General Prologue" to the *Canterbury Tales* is the Yeoman. Like the Squire who precedes him, he is a member of the Knight's small entourage; but in contrast to the Squire and his father the Knight, who are members of the nobility, the Yeoman is a commoner. In fact, were it not for his association with the Knight and the Squire and for the narrator's apparent desire to present the Knight and his retinue as a discrete social entity, the Yeoman's more humble status probably would have earned him a place among the final group of pilgrims rather than the first. Indeed, by any objective measure the Yeoman must be viewed as a relatively minor member of the assembled pilgrims. His portrait takes up just seventeen verses, making it one of the shortest in the collection—only the Merchant, Cook, and Plowman are given fewer lines—and the Yeoman is one of only two pilgrims described at any length in the "General Prologue" to whom Chaucer assigned no tale, a distinction he shares with the Plowman. Nor has the figure of the Yeoman attracted much attention from scholars; the body of commentary on this man is among the slimmest for any of the characters described in the "General Prologue." Yet few of Chaucer's pilgrims have failed to generate controversy, and the Yeoman, in his own small way, proves no exception. Indeed, a basic issue for each of the pilgrims is the extent to which his or her portrait contains satire; in the case of the Yeoman, as in nearly every other case, scholarly opinions on this issue differ.

For most of the Canterbury pilgrims, the labels attached to them in the "General Prologue" reflect their profession or occupation or social position in fairly obvious ways. Figures such as the Knight, the Monk, the Physician, the Miller, or the Summoner occupied specific niches in late medieval society. In the case of the Yeoman, however, a particular occupation or social position is not so readily indicated simply because of the label assigned him, for in the fourteenth and fifteenth centuries the word "yeoman" had a wide range of meanings and possible applications. And thus when someone is referred to as "a yeoman," it is necessary to consider very carefully the context in which this occurs. Quite often the full implications of the term can be ascertained only by carefully noting who this person serves and the kinds of responsibilities he has been given. There can be a world of difference between one kind of yeoman and another, as there probably is between the Yeoman of the "General Prologue" and the character introduced late in the *Canterbury Tales* known as the Canon's Yeoman.

In the case of the Yeoman described in the "General Prologue," it is safe to say that he is actually a yeoman in several senses of the term. He is a yeoman first of all because he serves as an attendant in a noble household—one of the standard meanings of "yeman"—a fact suggesting that he enjoyed a fairly high social standing. He is also a yeoman in a more specialized military sense of the word, one often used to refer to the fighting men who in the later Middle Ages wielded England's long bowman so effectively. And he is also a yeoman in the sense of being an expert in hunting and woodcraft, skills undoubtedly required by his peacetime occupation as his noble lord's forester.

Before examining the various facets of the Yeoman's life as suggested by the specific details contained in his portrait, it is essential to consider this man in relation to the Knight and the Squire, the aristocratic personages whom he serves and with whom he travels. The Yeoman's portrait begins with the statement—"A Yeman hadde he and servants namo / At that tyme, for hym liste ryde so . . . (101–102) ["A yeoman had he and servants no more / At that time for he preferred to ride so . . ."]. This statement explicitly links the Yeoman to the Knight's party, but it has also created two questions in the minds of Chaucer scholars. First of all, do the pronouns "he" and "hym" refer to the Squire or to the Knight? That is, which of these two men does the Yeoman actually serve? And second, why would a pair of noblemen travel with only a single attendant in their retinue? Do they travel this way by choice, or perhaps by necessity?

The question of whether the Yeoman is "the Knight's Yeoman" or "the Squire's Yeoman" is one on which Chaucer editors and commentators have expended a surprising amount of energy. It has been a matter of contention since William Thynne's 1532 edition of the *Canterbury Tales* in which the Yeoman was called "The Squyers Yoman." In the eighteenth century Thomas Tyrwitt questioned the Yeoman's assignment to the Squire, but W. W. Skeat, the great nineteenth-century Chaucer editor, favored it, while at the same time sensibly pointing out that "both the squire and the squire's man were necessarily servants to the knight, who, in this way, really had *two* servants" (V.11). Most twentieth-century scholars, including the editors of the *Riverside Chaucer* (803), believe that the word "he" in the first line of the Yeoman's portrait refers to the Knight, not the Squire. Among the dissenters to this view is Earle Birney, who suggests that the Yeoman's attire and accouterments make him "peculiarly adapted to the service of the Squire, and the Squire only" (10). One of the best pieces of evidence to justify assigning the Yeoman to the Knight rather than the Squire, I believe, occurs in the second line of the portrait in the phrase, "At that tyme . . . hym liste ryde so" (102). These words indicate that someone has decided how many servants should be brought along. Surely it is the Knight, not the Squire, who would make that decision and who would select the members of his own entourage.

In any event, the fact that the Knight and the Squire are accompanied by only one servant raises the more significant question—does the Knight travel with this very abbreviated cortege because he chooses to or because it is all he can muster? There is evidence, certainly, that the Knight is maintaining only the minimum number of attendants required to uphold the honor of his rank. The Caxton translation of Raymond Lull's *Book of the Ordre of Chyvalry,* for example, states that "it behoveth [a knight] that there be gyven to hym a squyer & a servaunt that may take hede to his horse" (19). Anything less, presumably, would be an affront to his honor. A pertinent illustration of this occurs in the late medieval poem *A Gest of Robyn Hode,* in an episode in which Robyn encounters a knight whose financial condition has forced him to ride without any attendants:

> "It were greate shame," sayde Robyn,
>   "A knight alone to ryde,
> Withoute squyre, yoman, or page,
>   To walke by his syde."
>
> (317–320)

Robyn then lends this indigent knight Lytell Johnn to serve him in a "yeman's stede" (323). Because Chaucer's Knight rides with a minimal retinue, some readers have interpreted this to indicate that he is a very low-ranking member of the nobility or that he is a knight who is now down-on-his-luck financially. Other readers, however, have not seen this as reflecting the knight's indigence but rather his desire to shun ostentation and as "further testimony to his 'meekness' or humility" (Robertson 579). A different tack in the matter of how the

Yeoman reflects on the Knight has been taken by William McColly, who argues that because the Knight's retainer holds the position of forester—which would imply that the Knight possessed a sizable estate—then the Knight was probably a figure of some prominence within the higher nobility (14–27).

What these discussions seem to ignore, however, is the simple fact that these three men are probably meant to be representative, representative first of all of particular social types, but representative also of the three main groups of fighting men who were recognized in England during the fourteenth and fifteenth centuries as forming an elite military unit. With respect to the first point, throughout the "General Prologue" Chaucer presents us with individual examples of figures drawn from a wide variety of professions and occupations. And aside from the Prioresse's often-questioned *preestes thre* (164), there is no duplication among the pilgrims. Thus the inclusion of one knight, one squire, and one yeoman is consistent with this larger pattern; giving the Knight several servants, however, would have violated it. Less obvious, however, is the fact that these three figures represent the basic English fighting unit—a unit sometimes referred to as a "lance"—which consisted of a knight, a squire, and a yeoman. This was the fighting unit that was instrumental in achieving England's great military victories during the earlier stages of the Hundred Years' War; and it was also, as Terry Jones has pointed out, a fighting unit that typified English mercenary groups, such as the White Company, later on in the fourteenth century (212). Working in tandem, knights, squires, and yeomen—a term commonly applied to English archers who used the long bow—provided the solid core of England's military power throughout the Hundred Years' War and well beyond.

The military importance of these three groups, as well as their interconnection and interdependence, is frequently attested in Middle English literature. The author of the fourteenth-century poem *Wynnere and Wastoure,* for example, identifies the three constituent groups in Wastoure's army as being "sadde men of armes" [knights], "Bolde sqwyeres of blode" [squires], "and bowmen many" [yeomen] (193–194). Thomas Malory, when setting the stage for King Arthur's final battle in the *Morte D'Arthur,* tells us that Arthur was awakened from his vision of Gawain by "knyghtes, squyars and yomen" (*Works* 711). And in *A Gest of Robyn Hode,* Robyn instructs Lytell Johnn not to harm any "gode yeman / That walketh by grene-wode shaw, / Ne no knyght ne no squyer / That wol be a gode felawe" (53–56) ["good yeoman / That walks by the green woods, / Nor any knight nor any squire / That will be a good fellow]. And as a final example of the close-knit relationship of knight, squire, and yeoman, consider these verses from the fifteenth-century political poem, "The descryuyng of mannes membres":

> The shuldre and the bakebon,
>   I likne to lordis of the lond;
> The armes, to knygtes, to fende fro fon;

The squyers, I likne to the hondes;
The fyngres, to yemen that byfore gon
With bent bowes and brygt brondes.

(33–38)

[The shoulder and the backbone,
  I liken to the lord of the land;
The arms, to knights, to fend from foes;
  The squires, I liken to the hounds;
The fingers, to yeomen that before went
  With bent bows and bright torches.]

There is considerable evidence, then, to indicate that during Chaucer's time knights, squires, and yeomen formed a distinctive military unit within the larger social estate of "those who fight."

Although it seems quite clear that Chaucer's Yeoman was a yeoman in the military sense of the word—and it should be noted that Chaucer uses the word *yeman* with its military meaning in the "Knight's Tale" also (I.2509 and I.2728)—it is important to consider the additional aspects of this man's yeomanry. As was noted earlier, the word "yeoman" (which was usually spelled *yeman* or *yoman*) had a wide range of possible applications during the later Middle Ages. Chaucer's writings reflect this fact, and he uses the term in a variety of contexts with a variety of meanings. According to the *Oxford English Dictionary,* one of the most common meanings of "yeoman" was simply "servant or attendant," and the word could be used with this meaning in reference to servants of fairly low social standing, or, conversely, to servants of considerable standing such as attendants in a noble household. The Yeoman who attends upon the Knight and the Squire in the "General Prologue," because he is also identified as a forester and because he seems to be this nobleman's hand-picked retainer, probably enjoyed a fairly high status. On the other hand, the Canon's Yeoman, a character that Chaucer introduces much later in the *Canterbury Tales* as servant to the Canon obsessed by the allure of alchemy, was probably a servant of quite humble status, judging from the menial tasks that the Canon has him perform.

By the fifteenth century, and probably somewhat before that, the word "yeoman" was used to denote a free-born person below the rank of gentleman who possessed a small freeholding of land. This is probably what Malory has in mind when he says that "all men of worshyp may discover [i.e., differentiate] a jantyman frome a yoman and a yoman frome a vylayne" (*Works* 232), a statement establishing the yeoman's social status as being intermediary to those of a gentleman and a villein. In all likelihood, this is also the social status the term reflects when we are told in the "Miller's Tale" that Alisoun was suitable "For any lord to leggen in his bedde, / Or yet for any good yeman to wedde" (I.3269–3270) [For any lord to lay in his bed, / Or yet for any good yeoman to wed]. Such is also the case in the "Reeve's Tale," when we learn that Symkyn selected his wife in order "To saven his estaat of yomanrye" (I.3949) ["to save his estate of yeomanry]—that is, to help preserve or even enhance his social position as a yeoman. This meaning of the word—a freeborn person with a small holding of land—may or may not be applicable to the Yeoman of the "General Prologue." Some commentators have suggested that the Yeoman "may have been an independent farmer holding land from the Knight (by 'yeo-man-service')" (Schmidt 129). However, there is no explicit support for this supposition in the language of the Yeoman's portrait.

It also became common for the word "yeoman" to be used in a very general way to describe outdoorsmen or hunters, possibly because they, like England's celebrated military yeomen, were viewed as being skillful archers. In many of the Robin Hood poems and ballads, for example, Robin's men are regularly called yeomen, more likely because of their expertise with the bow and arrow than because they enjoyed a particular social standing or were small landholders. In Chaucer's "Friar's Tale," the huntsman encountered by the summoner is also called a *yeman:*

> . . . he saugh bifore hym ryde
> A gay yeman, under a forest syde.
> A bowe he bar, and arwes brighte and kene;
> He hadde upon a courtepy of grene. . . .

(III.1379–1382)

> [. . . he saw before him ride
> A gay yeoman, under a forest side.
> A bow he bore, and arrows bright and keen;
> He had on a coat of green. . . .]

Like the Yeoman in the "General Prologue," this man who suddenly appears before the Summoner "under a forest syde" is garbed in the traditional green of the hunter, and he carries a bow and an impressive set of arrows. Perhaps it wouldn't be stretching the point too far to note that the yeoman in the "Friar's Tale," who is actually a fiend from hell, is searching out certain kinds of law-breakers (in his case, unrepentant sinners), just as Chaucer's Yeoman, in performing his duties as the Knight's forester, would have kept a sharp eye out for violators of forest laws.

In any case, "A forester was he, soothly, as I gesse" (117), the narrator says of the Yeoman in the final line of his portrait. And assuming that the narrator is correct about this, then the Yeoman, when he was not accompanying his lord on military campaigns, was engaged in overseeing a hunting preserve on his lord's own estate or in a royal preserve where the Knight has been granted hunting rights by the king. As a forester the Yeoman would have had a great many duties, among which, typically, was the responsibility for husbanding a forest's valuable resources, especially its timber and game animals. It is quite likely that he would have supervised the work of gamekeepers and falconers and others who served under him. But perhaps more than any other thing, a medieval forester was charged with enforcing the forest laws of "vert and venison"—special laws that restricted access to the use of wood and animals.

Chief among a forester's enemies were poachers, men who dared to violate the established laws of the forest and who did so at great personal risk. Such a man is the solitary hunter whose activities are depicted in the opening section of the Middle English poem *The Parlement of the Thre Ages.* The first one hundred lines of this poem provide a great deal of specific information about medieval hunting techniques, including the way in which this lawbreaking hunter attempts to thwart the forester. After a lengthy description of the hunter's stalking, killing, and dressing of a large *hert,* we learn that he "heuede alle into ane hole and hidde it with ferne, / With hethe and with horemosse hilde it about, / That no fostere of the fee [i.e., the forester] scholde fynde it theraftir . . ." (92–95) ["heaved all into a hole and hid it with fern, / With heath and with moss held it about, / That no forester should find it thereafter . . ."]. Chaucer also offers a comment on the forester's role as law enforcer when the Physician observes in his tale that "A theef of venysoun, that hath forlaft / His likerousnesse and al his old craft, / Kan kepe a forest best of any man" (VI.83–85) ["a thief of venison, that has abandoned / His greedy appetite and all of his old craft, / Can keep a forest better than any man"]—a variation on the adage that it takes a thief to catch a thief. Indeed, Chaucer's familiarity with many different aspects of medieval hunting is reflected throughout his poetry, as O. F. Emerson has amply demonstrated. Much of this knowledge undoubtedly stems from the fact that Chaucer, when he was a young man serving in the household of the countess of Ulster, would have participated in many noble hunting parties, perhaps similar to those he describes in the *Book of the Duchess,* the "Knight's Tale," and the *Legend of Dido* in the *Legend of Good Women.* Chaucer's professional duties during the late 1380s actually included his overseeing of hunting lodges in some of the royal forests. It isn't likely, however, that his appointment to the position of deputy forester at North Petherton in Somerset, in the early 1390s, involved him directly in the performance of a forester's duties.

Chaucer's Yeoman, on the other hand, in his capacity as forester to his lord the Knight, would have been deeply involved in performing the everyday duties of a forester, a fact surely reflected in the narrator's statement that "Of wodecraft wel koude he al the usage" (110) ["Of woodcraft well could he all the usage"]. The term *wodecraft* probably encompasses the Yeoman's knowledge of the rules and conventions that governed medieval hunting practices, as well as his skill in applying them. As treatises such as William Twiti's *The Art of Hunting* and Edward, duke of York's *The Master of the Game* clearly reveal, hunting in the Middle Ages was a complex business, a fact also reflected in poems such as *Sir Gawain and the Green Knight, Sir Tristrem,* and the *Parlement of the Thre Ages.* In regard to the elaborate conventions that surrounded this favorite aristocratic pastime in the Middle Ages, the authors of medieval

romances often credited Sir Tristr~   eing the one who elevated hunting
and hawking to its highest level o   ation. As Malory writes:

> And every day sir Trystram wolde go i   tynge, for he was called that tyme the
> chyeff chacer of the worlde and the nol   · of an horne of all maner of mesures.
> For . . . of sir Trystram cam all the goc   f venery and of huntyng, and all the
> syses and mesures of all blowyng wyth   id of hym we had fyrst all the termys
> of hawkynge, and whyche were bestis c   l bestis of venery, and whyche were
> vermyns; and all the blastis that longed   r of game. . . . (*Works* 416)

> [And every day sir Tristram would go ri   ing, for he was called that time the
> chief chaser of the world and the nobles   a horn of all manner of measures.
> For . . . of sir Tristram came all good ter   y and of hunting, and all the sizes
> and measures of all blowing with a horn; and of him we had first all the terms of
> hawking, and which were beasts of chase and beasts of venery, and which were vermin;
> and all the blasts that longed to all manner of game. . . .]

Like Sir Tristrem, Chaucer's Yeoman would have been very familiar with the
appropriate *mesures* and *blastis* to sound on his hunting horn; and it is certainly
possible that he may have served on occasion as master of the hunt, in the
fashion of the *mayster-hunte* in Chaucer's *Book of the Duchess,* who "With a
gret horn blew thre mot / At the uncouplynge of hys houndes" (376–377)
["With a great horn blew three must / At the uncoupling of his hounds"].

The Yeoman's hunting horn, and the baldric from which it hangs—"An horn
he bar, the bawdryk was of grene" (116) ["a horn he bore, the baldric was of
green"]—are the last details in his description, whereas his "cote and hood of
grene" (103) had been the very first. Thus all the other specific details in the
portrait are bracketed by the references to the Yeoman's hunting attire, emphasizing the fact that this man is above all else a hunter. In addition to wearing
the green apparel traditionally associated with hunters, the Yeoman possesses
"a myghty bowe" (108), a "sheef of pecok arwes, bryght and kene" (104),
and "a gay bracer" (111), i.e., an archer's arm guard, implements that appear
to be scrupulously maintained. Indeed, the Yeoman's arrows have been fletched
so well that they "drouped noght with fetheres lowe" (107), probably meaning
that they didn't fall short in flight; and the yeoman carries them in their sheaf
under his belt "ful thriftily" (105). His dagger, too, is "Harneished wel and
sharp as point of spere" (113). All in all this Yeoman, with his "broun visage"
and "not heed" (closely cropped hair), appears to be an efficient, meticulous,
and seasoned outdoorsman, a conclusion that accords with the narrator's statement that "Wel koud he dresse his takel yemanly" (106).

Two of the items that would appear to belong to the inventory of the Yeoman's hunting tackle, his "myghty bowe" and his "gay daggere," may also
reflect on the Yeoman in his capacity as a fighting man. The other items in the
Yeoman's portrait that clearly pertain to his role in the military are the "swerd"
that hangs by his side and his "bokeler" (a small round shield), both of which

are mentioned in line 112. It is not surprising that the Yeoman carries these weapons during a peacetime excursion, for a nobleman's attendant would customarily be armed with sword and shield when in attendance upon his lord, as the Yeoman is here. The presence of the Yeoman's mighty bow, however, may be a little more difficult to explain. Judging from the adjective "myghty," the bow the Yeoman is carrying would appear to be a long bow, a weapon originally introduced into England's military arsenal by Welsh archers. And while practicing with the long bow on England's village greens had become a common recreational activity of English youths during the fourteenth century, using the long bow for hunting would not have been common, nor would it have been practical, for the weapon was ill-suited to that purpose. And thus the Yeoman's mighty bow more properly belongs with his military tackle than with his hunting tackle. The fact that the Yeoman carries a bow and a sheaf of arrows, a sword, a dagger, and a shield has led to the perception of some scholars that this man is "armed to the teeth" (Jones 212).

The Yeoman's weaponry contributes to an overall appearance that has raised the eyebrows of some readers, who suspect that Chaucer is treating this man somewhat satirically or ironically. It has been suggested in this regard that Chaucer establishes a contrast between the Knight and the Yeoman that is similar to but more muted than the contrast between the Knight and the Squire; and that this contrast serves to emphasize the Knight's humility while implying that the Yeoman is overly concerned with making an impression on his fellow pilgrims. It is certainly true that the Yeoman's clothing is not battle-stained like the Knight's, and it is also true that his weapons may be somewhat showy. His "bracer" (111) is said to be "gay" (probably meaning brightly colored), while the Knight's horse is said not to be "gay" (74), and his dagger is "Harneised wel" (114), perhaps implying that it was expensively mounted. Furthermore, the Yeoman wears "A Cristopher on his brest of silver sheene" (115), at a time when the possession of silver ornaments such as this St. Christopher's medal was unusual among the lower classes.

The Yeoman, one can't help believing, *is* making an effort to dress for the occasion. In that respect perhaps he is more akin to the colorfully attired Squire, who appears to be highly self-conscious about his appearance, than to the more soberly dressed Knight, who may be truly unconcerned about his appearance. And yet the suggestion that Yeoman's attire "can be taken to sound a quietly humorous echo to the study of the Squire" (Birney 13), while it cannot be entirely discounted, seems nonetheless unconvincing. Whereas it would be acceptable, perhaps even admirable, for a person of the Knight's status to err in the direction of modesty in his outward appearance—the Sergeant of the Lawe may be striving consciously to achieve a similar effect (328–330)—for a man of much lower status to be dressed only in his ordinary, workaday clothing might seem disrespectful of the occasion. Indeed, it seems quite natural that a yeoman-forester would want to put on his Sunday best for a pilgrimage to one of England's most holy places.

Chaucer's Yeoman is one of just two pilgrims who receive the narrator's full descriptive treatment in the "General Prologue" but who are not given a chance to tell their tales. It is clear that Chaucer intended for the Yeoman to have a tale, since in the final dramatic link that precedes the "Parson's Tale" the Host declares, "Now lakketh us no tales mo than oon" (X.16), indicating that every pilgrim except for the Parson has told a tale. One can do no more than speculate about the kind of tale the Yeoman would have told, although it is certainly possible that Chaucer had in mind adapting the "Tale of Gamelyn," a non-Chaucerian version of which was inserted into some of the Chaucer manuscripts. This tale of forest adventures, which later provided the plot for Shakespeare's *As You Like It,* might have been an appropriate tale for Chaucer's Yeoman-forester to relate to his fellow pilgrims. But whatever Chaucer's plan for the Yeoman may have been, it was never completed. And so we are left to regret, along with Muriel Bowden (88) and many other readers of the *Canterbury Tales,* that we encounter "this sound and likable fellow" only in the seventeen lines comprising his portrait in the "General Prologue."

REFERENCES

Birney, Earle. "The Squire's Yeoman." *Review of English Literature* 1 (1960): 9–18.

Bowden, Muriel. *A Commentary on the General Prologue to the Canterbury Tales.* New York: Macmillan, 1949.

"The Descryuyng of Mannes Membres." Ed. J. Kail. *Twenty-Six Political Poems.* Early English Text Society 124, p. 65. London, 1904.

Edward of Norwich, Second Duke of York. *The Master of the Game.* Eds. William A. and Florence N. Baillie-Graham. London, 1904.

Emerson, Oliver Farrar. "Chaucer and Medieval Hunting." *Romanic Review* 13 (1922): 115–150.

"A Gest of Robyn Hode." Eds. Helen Child Sargent and G. L. Kittredge. *English and Scottish Popular Ballads.* Boston: Houghton Mifflin, 1965. Pp. 256–278.

Jones, Terry. *Chaucer's Knight.* New York: Methuen, 1985.

Krappe, Edith S. "A Note on Chaucer's Yeoman." *Modern Language Notes* 43 (1928): 176–177.

Lull, Raymond. *The Book of the Ordre of Chyvalry.* Trans. Wm. Caxton. Ed. Alfred T.P. Byles. London: Oxford University Press, 1926.

Malarkey, Stoddard. "Chaucer's Yeoman Again." *College English* 24 (1963): 289–295.

Malory, Sir Thomas. *Works.* Ed. Eugene Vinaver. Oxford: Oxford University Press, 1977.

Mann, Jill. *Chaucer and Medieval Estates Satire.* Cambridge: Cambridge University Press, 1973.

McColly, William. "Chaucer's Yeoman and the Rank of His Knight." *Chaucer Review* 20 (1985): 14–27.

McKisack, May. *The Fourteenth Century, 1307–1399.* The Oxford History of England. Vol. 5. Oxford: Clarendon-Oxford University Press, 1959.

Parlement of the Thre Ages. Ed. M. Y. Offord. Early English Text Society 246. London, 1959.

Robertson, D. W., Jr. "Some Disputed Chaucerian Terminology." *Speculum* 52 (1977): 571–581.

Schmidt, A.V.C. *The General Prologue to the Canterbury Tales and Canon's yeoman's Prologue and Tale.* New York: Holmes and Meier, 1974.

Sir Gawain and the Green Knight. Eds. J.R.R. Tolkien and E. V. Gordon. 2nd ed. Rev. Norman Davis. Oxford: Clarendon-Oxford University Press, 1967.

Sir Tristrem. Ed. G. P. McNeill. Scottish Text Society 8. Edinburgh, 1886.

Skeat, Walter W., ed. *The Complete Works of Geoffrey Chaucer.* 7 Vols. Oxford: Clarendon-Oxford University Press, 1894–1897.

Test, George A. "Archer's Feathers in Chaucer and Ascham." *American Notes & Queries* 2 (1964): 67–68.

Twiti, William. *The Art of Hunting.* Ed. B. Danielsson. Stockholm: Almqvist & Wiskell International, 1977.

Wynnere and Wastoure. Ed. Stephanie Trigg. Early English Text Society 297. London, 1990.

Chapter 4

Ther Was Also A Nonne, A Prioresse

MAUREEN HOURIGAN

Ther was also a Nonne, a Prioresse,
That of hir smylyng was ful symple and coy;
Hire gretteste ooth was by Seinte Loy;
And she was cleped madame Eglentyne.
Ful weel she soong the service dyvyne,
Entuned in her nose ful semely,
And Frenssh she spak ful faire and fetisly,
After the scole of Stratford atte Bowe,
For Frenssh of Parys was to hire unknowe.

(117–125)

[There was also a Nun, a Prioress,
That of her smiling was very uneffected and quiet;
Her greatest oath was by Saint Loy;
And she was named madam Eglentine.
Very well she sang the liturgy,
Intoned in her nose in a seemly manner,
And French she spoke very well and elegantly,
In the manner of the school of Stratford atte Bowe,
For French of Paris was to her unknown.]

INTRODUCTION

The Prioress, as Florence H. Ridley points out in her explanatory notes to the *Riverside Chaucer,* "has attracted more critical commentary and controversy than almost any other character in the General Prologue" (803). And her tale, which might seem "on first or even tenth reading to require little interpretive assistance" (Friedman 118), has continued to receive just such assistance from the critics. From the early 1900s to the 1950s, most critical articles discussed analogues and sources of the "Prioress's Tale." From the 1950s on, the seemingly blatant anti-Semitism displayed in the 238-line poem (the shortest of the completed *Canterbury Tales*) has led to a spirited debate among critics and a proliferation of critical articles that focus on the Prioress's personality. Of special interest are the limits and nature of the Prioress's religious vocation and the relationship of her courtly manners to the theme of her tale.

Some critics, reluctant to attribute the tale's anti-Semitism to Chaucer himself, find the poem a satire on a prioress whose "own lack of Christian virtue makes her an unworthy judge of whom she hates" (Rex 121–122). Other critics argue that Chaucer's treatment of the Jews is similar to their treatment in the analogues (Friedman 118) and that "the attitudes for which Madame Eglentine is condemned by twentieth-century critics were shared by most of her countrymen" and probably were "shared by Chaucer himself" (Ridley 35). Finally, Albert B. Friedman asserts that the anti-Semitism in the tale is "incidental" and the "whole critical enterprise directed toward explaining away Chaucer's bigotry is misguided and unnecessary" (127, 119). Whatever their interpretations, critics generally turn to an analysis of the social, intellectual, and cultural milieu of the late fourteenth century in order to support their conclusions. In doing so, critics generally focus on one aspect of the Prioress's personality—her courtly manners, for example—or on one aspect of her tale—its Marian allusions, perhaps—thereby losing sight of what Hardy Long Frank contends Chaucer has presented: "a full-fledged characterization of a thoroughly competent, shrewd professional woman of the late fourteenth century" (229).

THE PROFESSION OF PRIORESS

The inferior "Stratford" French that the Prioress speaks points to the Benedictine priory of St. Leonard's at Stratford at Bowe or its neighbor the Benedictine abbey at Barking in Essex as the likely home of the fictive Madame Eglentine. By the time the Prioress appeared in Chaucer's "General Prologue," her profession had been in existence for more than eight centuries. Importantly, the history of that profession provides a context for those critics who judge the nature of her religious vocation.

The first monastic rule for nuns in the West was written by Caesarius, bishop of Arles, in A.D. 512. His rule demanded strict cloister or separation from the world; all but the abbess were strictly forbidden from leaving the cloistered walls of the convent until the day they died. Even the abbess's comings and goings were strictly regulated, as Caesarius's *Regula sanctorum viginum* demonstrates: "The Abbess is absolutely not to dine outside the congregation unless compelled to do so by lack [of food], or by illness, or by business." Her dining elsewhere was a practical rather than a social matter, for if there was not enough food for all the sisters, the abbess, responsible as she was for the business affairs of the community, would benefit her sisters by her absence at the table.

In A.D. 529, some seventeen years after Caesarius wrote the *Regula,* St. Benedict of Nursia founded the Benedictine monastic order at Monte Cassino, Italy. So many men and women were attracted to Benedict's widely respected sanctity that before long he had to establish additional monasteries and nunneries to accommodate them. When he could no longer personally train all those who sought religious instruction, he appointed abbots and abbesses to take charge of the spiritual training of the men and women who entered (Ebaugh 13). The early years of Benedict's religious life had been spent as a member of a community of hermits who were not bound by a rule; each was free to order his life as he saw fit. He organized his own monastic communities, however, according to an exact, stabilized rule that was binding upon all members in the community (Hilpsich 14).

The Rule of St. Benedict mirrored the structure of the feudal society that emerged in Europe following the collapse of the Roman Empire. The abbot or abbess, elected by the whole community, served as a feudal lord; the rest of the community served as serfs. While the abbot or abbess was aided in the government of the monastery or nunnery by the prior or prioress and the cellarer or cellaress (who dealt with the outside tradesmen and was responsible for adequate provisions of food and drink), full responsibility for the protection, care, and spiritual guidance of all the members of the community fell solely on the abbot or abbess. (Smaller communities were called priories; in these, the prior or prioress assumed the responsibilities of the abbot or abbess.) Although Benedict bound the abbots and abbesses to the Rule, he gave them ''far reaching powers to modify certain things according to conditions of time and place'' (Hilpsich 14). By the late fourteenth century, when Madame Eglentine appeared as one of Chaucer's pilgrims, things had been modified indeed.

The main work of monastic communities was prayer, including silent prayer of the heart and daily recitation of the Divine Office or the Little Office of the Virgin Mary, an abridged version commonly used in nunneries. There was also time for reading of both classical and religious works and the manual labor that permitted the monastic communities to remain economically self-sufficient. So popular was Benedictine monastic life that within a century Benedictine communities had spread across Europe. The Benedictine abbey at Barking in Essex, one of the two nunneries that Chaucerian scholars associate with the Prioress, was founded during Anglo-Saxon times and was one of the oldest and wealthiest in England.

From its inception, monastic life was open to women of upper class families who believed that ''having a member in an order of consecrated virgins would bring blessings to both the family and the cities'' (Ebaugh 13). Passages from *Ancrenne Wisse,* an early-thirteenth-century work addressed to ''dear sisters'' of an anonymous ordered community of nuns, make explicit the social status of many communities. Instructing the nuns on the sacrament of Penance, the anonymous author makes it clear that the self-denial that one must put up with in religious life and the endurance of slights from one's social inferiors is a particular sign of submission to God's will: ''Shame I call it to be always accounted of no social rank, and to beg like a wretch, if need is, for one's livelihood, and to be another's pensioner, as you are, dear sisters, and you endure often the arrogance of such a one sometimes as might have been your slave" (Dobson 3). Although many upper class women freely chose monastic life, families sometimes chose the veil for their daughters. Thus nunneries came to house not only aristocratic women with religious vocations but also daughters of feudal lords who were unwilling or unable to go to the trouble and expense of finding them husbands, unfaithful wives who were put away by their husbands, and women who had lost their families in plagues. The head of a monastic community was an important and powerful person. As Eileen Power notes in *Medieval Nunneries,* from the very beginning of monasticism, the mother superior was usually a woman of some social station. "If a great lady retired to a nunnery, she was very like to end as its head" (69). Scholars generally point out that the abbey at Barking claimed three queens and two princesses among its abbesses.

By the tenth and eleventh centuries, nunneries and monasteries had accumulated considerable communal wealth and power. Eileen Power explains their social and political circumstance: "Socially in all cases, and politically when their houses were large and rich, abbots and abbesses, priors and prioresses, ranked among the great folk of the countryside. They enjoyed the same prestige as did lords of neighboring manors and some extra deference on account of their religion. It was natural that the Prioress should be 'holden digne of reverence' " (69).

However, an accumulation of power and wealth combined with the lack of a religious vocation on the part of some nuns led to a decline in Benedict's ascetic ideal, and many orders grew lax in following the prescribed Rule. Prioresses and abbesses broke the cloister by venturing forth on the pretense of doing business related to the monastery. While most sensible persons would consider attendance at a funeral or a religious ceremony or religious procession as legitimate reasons for breaking the rule of cloister, other relaxations of the rule soon followed. Some prioresses attended weddings, others danced, many wore fancy clothes and jewelry, and some lodged themselves in separate quarters with servants to care for them. Many went on pilgrimages, the one excuse for breaking the rule of cloister that was strongly discouraged by the bishops: A council had forbidden the practice in 791 and again in 1195; in 1318, an archbishop of York ordered nuns who had vowed to break cloister to journey on a pilgrimage "to say as many psalters as it would have taken to perform the pilgrimage so rashly vowed" (Power, *People* 95). (One has only to consider the kinds of pilgrims that Madame Eglentine encounters on her way to Canterbury to understand why bishops discouraged such journeys.) All in all, prioresses and nuns alike neglected the study and skilled common work that had attracted so many people to monasteries to begin with. By the middle of the twelfth century, such laxities led to several major reform movements and the questioning of the viability of a cloistered lifestyle in a world where the Church was embarking on Crusades to evangelize new lands.

But the most important reaction against the relaxation of the rules came from Boniface VIII who issued his famous *Periculoso* bull at the end of the thirteenth century. He began by declaring his desire "to provide for the perilous and detestable state of certain nuns, who, having slackened the reins of decency and having shamelessly cast aside the modesty of their order and sex, sometimes gad about outside their monasteries in the dwellings of secular persons." He ended with a proclamation that imposed cloister on all religious orders, a restriction that was to remain in force until the twentieth century:

We the present constitution, which shall be irrefragably valid, decree with healthful intent that all and sundry nuns, present and future, to whatever order they belong and in whatever part of the world, shall henceforth remain perpetually enclosed within their monasteries; so that no nun tacitly or expressly professed in religion shall henceforth have or be able to have the power of going out of those monasteries for whatsoever reason or cause, unless perchance any be found manifestly suffering from a disease so great and of such a nature that she cannot, without grave danger or scandal, live together with others. (Power, *Nunneries* 344)

That Councils and bishops were forced to issue similar mandates during the fifteenth, sixteenth, and seventeenth centuries is a measure of *Periculoso*'s failure. The Council of Trent (1543–1563), for example, stipulated that all nuns must be cloistered or suffer excommunication from the Church. Nor did the Church's attitude toward cloister change much in the subsequent four centuries. From 1600 to 1950, the Church issued pronouncement after pronouncement that required nuns to wear religious habits and veils, to travel outside the convent in pairs, and to recite the Divine Office daily in their communities. For fifteen hundred years, from the time St. Benedict founded his first abbey until the Second Vatican Council (1962–1965), the cloistered life had remained essentially unchanged. For fifteen hundred years, celibate orders of nuns, whose primary work had changed from prayer to the care of the ill and infirm, to the staffing of schools and hospitals, had lived together under a superior. After the Second Vatican Council, religious orders retained commitment to a celibate life but abandoned the cloistered lifestyle.

Today, some thirty years after Vatican II, it is not unusual to find five or six nuns living together in a single community, but seldom is there a superior among them. Oftentimes, nuns are permitted to live alone, reporting to no local superior. All in all, life in the convent after Vatican II hardly resembles life before it. With the loss of cloister has come the loss of mystery and respect from the laity; nuns who had once lived their lives separated from the world now find their lives totally immersed in it. Ultimately, Helen Ebaugh predicts that this elimination of cloister, combined with the increasing opportunities for women to pursue professional careers once reserved for men, "makes it highly likely that religious orders as we have known them for fifteen hundred years in the

Catholic Church will not survive their current crisis'' (29). In sum, the Prioress's profession will exist no more.

DUTIES OF THE PRIORESS

Sweeping social changes had occurred from the inception of the Benedictine Order in the sixth century to the election of Chaucer's fictive prioress in the late fourteenth century. With the establishment of medieval towns, society had become more urbanized, and the beginnings of world trade had led to a greater contact with the Eastern world. Paul A. Olson describes the skills a successful fourteenth-century prioress needed in order to negotiate this new world:

She had to have the administrative skill of a baron and the spiritual authority of a parson. She had the authority to see the liturgical services properly said, to oversee all management of the convent property, to supervise the education of convent novices, children, and youths, to supervise convent arts, crafts, and eleemonsynary work, and to provide for the disciplining of sisters violating humility, continence, voluntary poverty, or worship-and-work disciplines. (134)

In addition to providing for the spiritual needs of the house, the prioress was responsible for all of its business matters: she had to furnish both the house and its inhabitants, hire and fire the staff, and examine the financial accounts to be certain that the farms turned a profit, that the churches that belonged to the priory paid their tithes, and that the merchants who purchased the convent goods paid a good price. Moreover, despite *Periculoso*'s injunction against travel, the business of a fourteenth-century convent might easily require its abbess or prioress to travel to London for legal matters, estate matters, or even church matters (Frank 232).

Important, too, were her duties as a hostess. Historical records show that neighboring lords and ladies often dined with the prioress and that on occasion visitors traveling from one estate to another spent the night. Sometimes country gentlemen who would be away for a year at war or on a pilgrimage would board their wives there. While the bishops disapproved of the arrangement, they were unable to effectively prohibit the practice, as the nuns needed the money that their boarders brought in. In addition to money for their lodging and meals, boarders also brought their worldly trappings—fashionable clothes and small dogs—with them, tempting those gently born prioresses who shared the spirit, manners, and tastes of their race. Of Madame Eglentine, Power concludes that ''only the mention of her chanting of divine service [in the ''General Prologue''] differentiates her from any other well-born lady'' (*Nunneries* 9). Her table manners, like those of ladies of the court, are dainty (''She leet no morsel from hir lippes falle''); her dogs, like theirs, small and well-fed; her clothes, like theirs, fashionable; her gold brooch, like theirs, ''ful sheene.'' Of Madame Eglentine's resemblance to real fourteenth-century prioresses, she declares, ''We may wade through hundreds of visitation reports [bishops' registers] and injunctions and everywhere the grey eyes of [Chaucer's] prioress will twinkle at us out of their pages, and in the end we must always go to Chaucer for her picture, to sum up everything that historical records have taught us" (*People* 96).

THE PRIORESS AND HER CRITICS

Was the Prioress religious? Ambiguities in Chaucer's portrait of Madame Eglentine in the "General Prologue" account for quite different answers to that question from critics. As Joseph Dane points out, "this opposition between nun and romance heroine" can be "explained, defended, or even subjected to psychoanalysis" (Dane 219). "Everyone wonders to what extent she understands the implications of her courtly conduct," maintains Edward I. Condren in a recent essay on the Prioress (193), and he divides critical interpretations of the nature of the Prioress's personality and her tale into two camps—the "hard," which questions the nature of her religious vocation, and the "soft, which views her favorably. At the far end of the continuum are critics who see the Prioress as a childish, cruel, hateful bigot, unworthy of her profession and office, and see her tale as proof of her bigotry and imperfect understanding of Christian charity. E. T. Donaldson regards her as a "romance hero masquerading as a nun" and contends that her tale's "harsh, un-Christian attitude to the Jews and preoccupation with vengeance . . . ill accords with a tone of tender piety" (quoted in Friedman 121). Even those critics of the "hard" school who are charmed by Madame Eglentine's delicate manners and impeccable cleanliness are more likely "to admire the woman inside the nun than the nun inside the woman." Their delight in the woman, however, often seems to entice them to judge her "wanting in pious character" (Condren 193).

"Soft" critics like Hardy Long Frank contend that the Prioress is "a woman of many facets whose weaknesses are simultaneously her strengths, whose courtliness, be it native or acquired, is part and parcel of her professional adroitness." Moreover, Frank continues, "it is not simply her appearance or her social standing that arouses their respect but the consummate piety and professionalism manifest in her *Tale*" (232). More critics are found in the "hard" camps than in the "soft." Perhaps members of the "hard" school hold the Prioress to twentieth-century standards of what a nun should be, thereby blinding themselves to the reality of her real role in the fourteenth-century priory, as both Condren and Frank suggest.

Critics are as much taken with the satirical elements in Chaucer's portrait of the Prioress as they are its ambiguities. While some argue that her care for her little dogs demonstrates the gentleness of her nature, others point out that her concern for small animals draws into question the nature of her religious perspective. If even ladies of the court were admonished for lavishing affection and comforts on their small dogs, should not the Prioress be more blameworthy for doing the same? After all, she keeps them in defiance of the pope's order that forbade nuns to have pets (Bowden 98–99). Her clothing also raises collective critical eyebrows. The Prioress's veil is supposed to be pinned so tightly against her own eyebrows that none of her forehead shows, yet clearly hers is visible, for Chaucer as narrator mentions its breadth. The most famous ambiguity in the entire portrait is the gold brooch that hangs from her rosary. Its motto, "A crowned A, / and after *Amor vincit omnia,"* has inspired many critics to try to resolve the double meaning of *amor.* Does Madame Eglentine mean divinely inspired love conquers all, or does she mean sensual love conquers all? John Livingston Lowes offers perhaps the most frequently quoted response to these incompatible meanings: "Now is it earthly love which conquers all, now heavenly; the phrase plays back and forth between the two. *Which of the two loves does 'amor' mean to the Prioress?* I do not know; but I think she thought she meant love celestial" (quoted in Bowden 97). Albert Friedman argues that "she seems to have been as blithely oblivious of her irregularities as she was of the delicious ambiguity of the motto on her brooch" (120). Ironically, she points out the monk's failings when she speaks of the abbot who buried the little martyr in her tale: the abbot "was an hooly man / As monkes been—or elles oghte be" (VII.641–42) ["was a holy man / As monks are—or else ought to be"]. Friedman sees this as a "pointed reflection" on her fellow pilgrim, "whose impatience with the crabbed life of the cloister and whose unmonkish outer accouterments and diversions she is obliquely chastizing" (120).

While critics may disagree about the Prioress's personality, they are in general agreement that her tale is particularly well-suited to her, albeit for very different reasons. The tone of "prayerful seriousness" in the tale, claims Friedman, "suits to perfection the religious lady cast as the speaker," and the "Prologue" to her tale "is something of a *tour de force* since the significant phrases and the very cadences echo the Office recited daily by nuns" (118, 124). Marie Hamilton finds Chaucer's selection of a Mary legend particularly fitting for a nun who is a frustrated mother, while J. M. Manly finds it an excellent complement to the induction of Philippa Chaucer (Frank 233). Frank holds that its Mary legend is "perfectly suitable to both a pious nun and her worldly hearers"; moreover, "its economy and its effectiveness" are exactly what one would expect from one so well-experienced at telling stories at table (232). Condren contends that, despite the incongruities inherent in a gentle woman telling a bloody tale of ritual murder, "despite the crossed purposes of both her secular and religious impulses, each paradoxically reaches fruition in her 'Tale' " (212).

The critical controversies surrounding Chaucer's depiction of the Prioress and his authorial purpose in the "Prioress's Tale" seem destined to remain a matter of generous speculation. Was she religious? Chaucer says little on the subject. With the exception of her singing of the divine service and her address to the Virgin Mary at the beginning of her tale, he says only that she was "so charitable" and "so piteous." "So," in Eileen Power's words, "we take our leave of her, characteristically on the road to Canterbury" (*People* 97).

REFERENCES

Bowden, Muriel. *A Commentary on the General Prologue of the Canterbury Tales.* 2nd ed. New York: Macmillan, 1967.

Condren, Edward I. "The Prioress: A Legend of Spirit, a Life of Flesh." *Chaucer Review* 23 (1989): 192–218.

Dane, Joseph A. "The Prioress and Her *Romanzen.*" *Chaucer Review* 24 (1990): 219–222.

Dobson, E. J. *The Origins of* Ancrene Wisse. Oxford: Clarendon Press, 1976.

Ebaugh, Helen Rose Fuchs. *Women in the Vanishing Cloister: Organizational Decline in Catholic Religious Orders in the United States.* New Brunswick, N.J.: Rutgers University Press, 1993.

Ferris, Sumner. "Venus and the Virgin: The Proem to Book III of Chaucer's *Troilys and Criseyde* as a Model for the Prologue to the 'Prioress' Tale." *Chaucer Review* 27 (1993): 252–259.

Frank, Hardy Long. "Seeing the Prioress Whole." *Chaucer Review* 25 (1991): 229–237.

Friedman, Albert B. "*The Prioress's Tale* and Chaucer's Anti-Semitism." *Chaucer Review* 9 (1974): 118–129.

Hilpsich, Stephanus, OSB. *Benedictinism Through Changing Centuries.* Collegeville, Minn.: St. John's Abbey Press, 1958.

Olson, Paul A. *The Canterbury Tales and the Good Society.* Princeton, N.J.: Princeton University Press, 1986.

Power, Eileen. *Medieval English Nunneries c. 1275 to 1535.* New York: Biblo and Tannen, 1964.

———. *Medieval People.* Garden City, N.Y.: Doubleday, 1924.

Rex, Richard. "Chaucer and the Jews." *Modern Language Quarterly* 45 (1984): 107–122.

Ridley, Florence H. *The Prioress and the Critics.* Berkeley: University of California Press, 1965.

Chapter 5

Another Nonne With Hire Hadde She

REBECCA STEPHENS

INTRODUCTION

In contrast to her more fully described companion, the Prioress, Chaucer's Se-
conde Nonne calls for greater imagination on the reader's part to create her
physical and spiritual portrait. Described in the "General Prologue" simply as
"another nonne" and chapeleyne (chaplain) to the Prioress (Fisher 12), this
pilgrim must instead be understood through her hagiographic tale and the large
body of knowledge that exists regarding religious life in the Middle Ages.

Because all of Chaucer's religious figures suffer some degree of irony at their
creator's hands, it is tempting to read the second nun as a caricature of the
profession. The Prioress is drawn in this manner: worldly in her excessive zeal
at the dinner table, wastefully indulgent of her pets, and improper in revealing
her forehead in public. This depiction, as well as that of the Nun's Priest and
other religious officials, points an accusing finger at the corruption and materialism which had weakened the Church during Chaucer's lifetime. The writings
of the reformer Wyclif and our later knowledge of the Reformation uphold this
view of the condition of the Church and those who supposedly had devoted
their lives to its service.

Yet the Second Nun's tale of the martyr St. Cecilia, prefaced by an exhortation against the sin of idleness and an invocation to the Virgin Mary, offers
not one shadow of a double voice or other distancing narrative device. For this
reason, and because Chaucer offers no descriptive details to the contrary, it is
possible and likely that the Second Nun belonged to the large group of cloistered
women who had chosen their vocation and embraced its life of sacrifice. H. S.
Bennett writes that, in spite of the growing corruption in the Church, Chaucer's
England was predominantly a Catholic country and that religious beliefs infused

the lives of its people, almost without thought or doubt (12). The irony and satire that Chaucer directed to his learned audience would have fallen on deaf ears among large numbers of the devout.

MONASTIC LIFE IN THE MIDDLE AGES

A monastic life was available to both men and women in the Middle Ages, but originally only to those of gentle or noble birth. In fact, convents (also called monasteries) were often founded by the nobility for female relatives who would not or could not marry in accordance with the expectations of their social standing. Williams and Echols suggest that some women ''vigorously objected to enclosure,'' while others found the lifestyle an acceptable, often preferable, alternative to marriage (122). In later years, the daughters of wealthy townsmen could be found among the sisterhood as well. Yet throughout the Middle Ages the orders remained small, averaging twenty or so members. Eileen Power estimates that the total number of nuns in England at the middle of the fourteenth century was 3,500. She writes that this number declined steadily thereafter, reaching 1,900 in the year 1534 (89).

The abundance of factual material that exists about medieval nunneries suggests that their generally standard philosophical foundations met with a wide range of interpretations in practice. The strict code established by St. Benedict of Nursia in the sixth century provided the rules governing everyday life in the monastery:

The three main tasks under his *Benedictine rule* were the divine service, manual labor, and study. Nuns or monks observed strict silence, except for certain rest periods, and owned no personal property—everything was communal. In most houses, each day was divided by seven offices [services]. (Williams and Echols 120)

Eileen Power describes these seven offices which each nun said daily:

She rose at 2 a.m., went down to choir for Matins, followed by Lauds, returned to bed at dawn and slept for three hours. She got up for the day at 6 a.m. and said Prime. Tierce, Sext, None, Vespers and Compline followed at intervals through the day; the last at 7 p.m. in winter and 8 p.m. in summer, after which she was supposed to go straight to bed. (92)

When not praying or resting, the nun engaged in certain labors. In the more prosperous nunneries, these tasks might include embroidery, or copying or illustrating manuscripts. In the poorer communities, nuns did housekeeping chores for themselves and for neighboring clerics (Williams and Echols 121). Some were familiar with even heavier labor: ditch digging, gardening, and haymaking (Power 93).

In principle, the nun's first responsibility was to save her own soul ''by avoiding the temptations of the turbulent outside world'' (Williams and Echols 120). Second to this purpose, she served God through prayer and sometimes through charitable acts. Finding the means for this charity could be difficult among the poorer cloisters; in fact, nuns were known to fast in order to feed the poor.

Such poverty stands in contrast to the nunneries of the highborn, which often required a dowry from novitiates. A secure economic base, together with the social status and political influence that came from family connections to the nobility, led to a strikingly different lifestyle in these convents, particularly in the nature of their contact with the outside world and their quotidian application of the Benedictine rule. The well-connected nunneries often housed schools for the young women of the community, in spite of the disapproval of the Church. In addition, female relatives and friends of the nuns typically viewed convents as boarding houses or inns, open to their use while traveling, or as permanent homes for widows. Vows of poverty faced difficult battles against the worldly materialism that outside guests brought into the nunneries. Chaucer's prioress, with her discriminating yet vociferous appetite and her attempt at courtly manners, betrays some degree of contact with the world outside her cloistered walls.

Powers notes a general decline in the intellectual and moral standards of English nunneries beginning in the fourteenth century. Records from this time show monks writing to nuns in French, as fluency in Latin waned. Carelessness in reciting prayers and in singing the services has been documented, and a general frivolity prompted discipline from Church authorities:

The bishops were especially shocked to find nuns retaining the vanities of their sex. The three D's (dances, dresses, dogs) drew special condemnation. The Church reprobated dancing at the best of times and especially in nunneries. Yet in spite of this account rolls of expenses of medieval nunneries contain payments for wassails at New Year and Twelfth Night, Mayday games, bonfire nights, harpers and players at Christmas and so on. (Power 98)

The Papal Bull *Periculoso*, issued by Pope Boniface in 1300, was one of a number of attempts to secure nuns physically and spiritually within the convents. The Bull ordered nuns never to leave their walls or to have contact with secular persons without special permission. A combination of active and passive resistance made the Bull and subsequent orders impossible to enforce. Sisters at a nunnery in the diocese of Lincoln, Power writes, were so upset with the bishop who presented the bull that they ''pursued him to the gate when he was riding away and threw the Bull at his head'' (99).

The Second Nun, however, represents the opposite extreme of this general decline in spirituality and devotion. Her tale celebrates the martyrdom of St. Cecilia, one of several such inspirational figures for the more serious medieval nuns. This nun would likely have been familiar with a number of similar stories, romanticized portraits of physical deprivation, spiritual ecstasy, and power dynamics.

The Example of Saints' Lives

One type of inspirational story developed from the model of the queen-saint, which dates back to the Merovingian and Anglo-Saxon periods. An early example is St. Clotilda, queen of the Franks, who converted her husband Clovis to Christianity. St. Clotilda's great-granddaughter, the Anglo-Saxon queen Bertha, converted her husband, King Aethelbert of Kent, to Christianity as well. Jane Tibbetts Schulenberg finds in this pattern of the queen saint a powerful combination of private and public influence: "Through their royal offices, pious queens appointed bishops and abbotts: they worked to formulate alliances between the crown and bishroprics or monasteries; they influenced and affected religious policy and organization" (106). Schulenberg notes a connection between noblewomen and the cloisters; at least half of the Anglo-Saxon women who achieved sainthood were nuns, and the majority of these were economically and politically powerful founding abbesses (108).

The story of St. Cecilia follows the paradigm of this queen-saint story, elaborating on the intimacy of the private relations which the queen-saint infuses with her spiritual ecstasy. Another example with which the Second Nun might have been familiar is the story of Margaret, daughter of the exiled Prince Edward of England and Agatha of Hungary. Margaret, born circa 1045, married King Malcolm III of Scotland. She lived the life of a secular nun, teaching and providing charity, and eventually ordering the reform of the Scottish church. Her husband supported her efforts, both spiritually and economically.

Williams and Echols cite a variation of this story, typified by St. Elizabeth of Portugal. In this narrative framework, the queen-saint marries a man who doubts her piety and remains unsupportive of her work until he himself is converted and his worldly life reformed by a new faith. Married to Diniz, king of Portugal in 1283, Elizabeth devoted her life to charity. She founded an agricultural school for the wives of farmers and even gave away land to some of her graduates. Her husband the king disapproved of this work. He was also unfaithful. Elizabeth responded with more intensity of faith and effort, as well as regular fasting. Once, when he accused her of giving money away, he opened her hand and found, instead of silver, a rose, a sign of sanctity. This sign inspired Diniz to appreciate his wife's holiness (119).

Complicating the echoes of the queen-saint paradigm which underlie the Second Nun's Life of St. Cecilia is a suggestion of mysticism, and possibly hereticism, to which some medieval nuns subscribed. In the tale an angel appears to protect Cecilia from physical intimacy with her husband, Valerian. The two see invisible crowns that can only be smelled by Valerian's brother Tiburce. And Cecilia survives her physical torture, including severe neck wounds, for three days so that she may continue her preaching. These preternatural elements, together with the involvement of the reputedly heretical Urban, push the story beyond the realm of orthodox Catholic doctrine, suggesting the mystical state that Delaney describes as follows:

A connection always exists between any soul which is in the state of grace and God. However, what differentiates the mystical from the non-mystical soul is the fact that the former is actually *conscious* of that connection, whereas the latter only knows it by faith or inference. The means of communication between God and the soul may be compared to a wireless. (27)

Williams and Echols write that heretical sects existed on the Continent in the Middle Ages but did not take hold in England. Similarly, mysticism, defined in simple terms as a state of perpetual communion with God, was documented in Germany, Sweden, and the Low Countries. However, the English may have sensed a suggestion of mysticism, or may even have suspected heretical beliefs, among the recluse nuns who lived in cells attached to parish churchyards. These silent women—one of whom occupied a cell in the Tower of London—would pray and offer consultations and advice to the public. The intensity of their devotion could be witnessed by parishioners. Knowledge of these phenomena would have supplied Chaucer with additional means of exposing excesses of the religious life, however sincere or pious the intention.

The Second Nonne as Story Teller

Chaucer's nun, of course, finds her voice when summoned to tell a tale. The structure of her tale, particularly its three-part preface, offers a number of clues that place her faith and vocation somewhere in the moderate middle range of religious passion; she is neither worldly woman nor reclusive mystic.

Immediately preceding the tale is an interpretation or etymology of the name Cecilia. With this recitation of five possible interpretations of the name, she dispels any doubt of her application to the study required by the Benedictine rule. She alludes to "the philosophers" when drawing an analogy between the swiftness of heaven and that of Cecilia's good works, and she commends the saint's sapience as well. From this discourse it becomes apparent that this nun was not part of the intellectual decline noted by Powers.

Prior to the etymology is an invocation to Mary, a typically intimate and private exchange with a saint which is still practiced among Roman Catholics today. Commonly accepted as source of the invocation is St. Bernard's prayer in Canto xxxiii of Dante's *Paradiso* (Gerould 664). Shared with the Canterbury pilgrims and centuries of readers, this invocation confirms the piety of its speaker. Calling herself a "flemed wrecche, in this desert of galle" (Fisher 311), she recalls the words of the devoted Gertrude the Great, who considered earthly life a "place of exile" (Williams and Echols 122).

The invocation also raises the issue of the female gender. Seen in the Middle Ages as a "defect" to be overcome in the quest for perfection in God's eyes, the female body prompted a number of responses. Here the nun celebrates Mary's triumph over the sin of the female body, a triumph achieved when she bore the son of the Creator. Similarly, some nuns spoke of a union with Christ as if it were a sexual union; some nuns, known as "bridal mystics," considered themselves spiritual wives of Christ (Williams and Echols 124). Other nuns responded to the "female defect" with extreme fasting, a denial of the earthly body altogether. Chaucer's Second Nun expresses such a disdain for her body in the invocation:

> And of thy light my soule in prison lighte,
> That troubled is by the contagioun
> Of my body, and also by the wighte
> Of erthely lust and fals affeccioun;
>
> [VIII (G) 71–74]

> [And of thy light my soul in prison light,
> That troubled is by the contagion
> Of my body, and also by the weight
> Of earthly lust and false affection;]

Temporary fasting, in the Middle Ages and now, is carried out with the intention of retaining food and resources for those in need. Among some medieval nuns, however, this practice carried the further connotation of purity through denial of physical hunger or bodily function.

The prologue of the tale, a treatise on the sin of idleness, provides an outer frame of piety against which to read the invocation, the etymology and the tale itself. Gerould writes that no source has been discovered for this material (664). One possibility, and one with which the Second Nun may have been familiar, is a document known as the *Ancren Riwle* or the *Regula Inclusarum*. This thirteenth-century document, of which four copies are extant, was translated from "a curious Anglo-Saxon language" into modern English in 1853 (*The Nun's Rule* xi). It describes the rules by which recluse nuns were to live and comport themselves. A combination of rules, biblical references, homilies, and anecdotes, the work discusses such topics as "Different Kinds of Evil Speech," "Felicity of the True Anchoresses," and "Parlour Windows to be Avoided." The rules also exhort clearly against idleness:

Be never idle; for the fiend immediately offers his work to her who is not diligent in God's work; and he beginneth directly to talk to her. For while he seeth her busy, he thinketh thus: It would avail nothing if I were now to accost her, nor would she take time to listen to my teaching. From idleness ariseth much temptation of the flesh, "All the wickedness of Sodom came out of idleness, and of a full belly." Iron that lieth still soon gathereth rust; and water that is not stirred soon stinketh. (319)

The Second Nun's "Prologue" resounds with similar sentiments, particularly the capacity of honest labor to deter the vigilant eye of evil:

For he that with his thousand cordes slye
Continuelly us waiteth to biclappe,
Whan he may man in ydelnesse espeye,
He kan so lightly cacche hym in his trappe—
Til that a man be hent right by the lappe
Hy nys nat war the feend hath hym in honde.
Wel oghte us werche and ydelnesse withstonde.

(8–14)

[For he that with his thousand cords cunning
Continually wait to trap us suddenly,
When he may a man in idleness spy,
He can so lightly catch him in his trap—
Til that a man be taken right by the hem
He is not aware that the fiend has him in hand.
Well should we work and idleness withstand.]

When the Second Nun is contextualized in her time, and numerous possibilities concerning her faith and lifestyle are explored, the tale itself takes on a life that sourcebooks and other textual backgrounds may fail to appreciate. In contrast to the other pilgrims affiliated with the Church, the Second Nun escapes the irony that undercuts the centrality of her faith and devotion. Although she is far from silent—one blatant breach of the code that would have governed her cloistered life—her voice is reserved for the word of God as she would have received, believed, and celebrated it.

REFERENCES

Bennett, H. S. *Chaucer and the Fifteenth Century.* New York: Oxford University Press, 1947, 1954.

Fisher, John H., ed. *The Complete Poetry and Prose of Geoffrey Chaucer.* New York: Holt, Rinehart and Winston, 1989.

Gerould, G. H. "The Second Nun's Prologue and Tale." In *Sources and Analogues of Chaucer's Canterbury Tales.* W. F. Bryan and Germaine Dempster, eds. London: Routledge and Kegan Paul Ltd., 1958.

Gilchrist, Roberta. " 'Blessed Art Thou Among Women': The Archaeology of Female Piety." In *Woman Is a Worthy Wight: Women in English Society c. 1200–1500.* P. J. P. Goldberg, ed. Wolfeboro Falls, N.H.: Alan Sutton Publishing, 1992.

Labarge, Margaret Wade. *A Small Sound of the Trumpet: Women in Medieval Life.* Boston: Beacon Press, 1986.

The Nun's Rule Being the Ancren Riwle Modernised by James Morton with Introduction by Abbot Gasquet. New York: Cooper Square Publishers, 1966.

Power, Eileen. *Medieval Women.* M. M. Postan, ed. Cambridge: Cambridge University Press, 1975, 1986.

Schulenberg, Jane Tibbetts. "Female Sanctity: Public and Private Roles, ca. 500–1100."

In *Women and Power in the Middle Ages.* Mary Erler and Maryanne Kowaleski, eds. Athens: University of Georgia Press, 1988.

Williams, Marty Newman, and Anne Echols. *Between Pit and Pedestal: Women in the Middle Ages.* Princeton, N.J.: Markus Wiener Publishers, 1994.

Chapter 6

And Preestes Thre

CATHERINE COX

In the "General Prologue" of the *Canterbury Tales,* the description of the Prioress concludes with an indication that she is traveling in the company of other religious figures: "Another Nonne with hire hadde she, / That was hir chapeleyne, and preestes thre" (I.163–164) ["Another nun with her had she, / Who was her chaplain, and priests three"]. These other pilgrims are the so-called Second Nun, who serves the Prioress in a secretarial capacity, and the Nun's Priest, who accompanies the nuns for purposes that remain ambiguous in the context of the "General Prologue." (The number "thre" in line 164 may have been erroneously added by a scribe, for only one priest accompanies the Prioress [Pearsall 135].) Both the Second Nun and the Nun's Priest participate not only in the Canterbury pilgrimage, but in the tale-telling competition as well, thus distinguishing themselves as the only tale-telling pilgrims lacking an individual Prologue portrait. Even so, the Nun's Priest provides the *Canterbury Tales* collection with one of its best-known and best-loved narratives, that of the mighty rooster Chauntecleer and his outwitting of Russell the fox.

Despite virtual anonymity in the "General Prologue," however, the Nun's Priest represents a ubiquitous and well-defined vocation in Chaucer's day. In the late fourteenth century, ministers (Latin, "servants") were authorized to perform specific religious services according to title and rank; the title "priest" was used to correspond to those ministers of the medieval Roman Catholic Church situated in the established religious hierarchy just below the rank of bishop. The full hierarchy of ecclesiastical "orders" (Latin *ordin-,* "degrees" or "steps") included the pope, bishop of Rome, at the top; then the bishops, each of whom was the head of a specific territory or *diocese;* then the priests, who mediated between the people and God; the deacons, who were charged in the service of the poor; and the subdeacons, who sang the designated portions of scripture at the Eucharist. From the thirteenth century onward these positions were collectively known as the "major orders," as they are today with the exception of the office of subdeacon, abolished by the Roman Catholic Church in 1972. Below the major orders were the "minors," including the acolytes, or, as they are known today, altar boys, who served as attendants at the altar during public worship; exorcists, believed to exorcise evil spirits; lectors, readers of scripture; and ostiaries, or doorkeepers. Of the four medieval minor orders, only the acolytes and lectors are still officially used and recognized by the Roman Catholic Church today.

Priests were members of the "secular" clergy (Latin *saecularis,* "worldly"), actively integrated into the society that they served, and, indeed, occupying a place in the ecclesiastical hierarchy wholly to serve the laity, that is, the non-ordained members of the Church who constituted the majority of people in most church congregations. Priests served the worshipers of a specifically designated territory known as their *parish;* a parish was a portion of the larger ecclesiastical district known as the *diocese,* which was supervised and administered by a bishop. By the late fourteenth century in England, there were eighteen dioceses comprising approximately 9,500 parishes, of which memberships varied from as few as fifty to as many as three hundred parishioners (Ackerman 38–39). Each parish was administered by a priest residing within the parish, who was frequently assisted by other lesser clergy, though only the priest was the holder of a *benefice* which designated his ecclesiastical office in terms of the specific duties it entailed as well as the specific revenues stipulated to be provided in return. The priest of the parish, or "parson," as he was known by his medieval Latin title, was a familiar figure to his parishioners, as were the parishioners to the parish priest; the parish was an important social, as well as religious, unit. For a secular community the parish priest was the most important religious figure, and, despite the significant cultural and social influence of the Church during the Middle Ages, priests were in many cases the only clergy known personally to most of the laity.

The title "priest" is a contracted form of the label "presbyter" (Greek, "elder") used by members of the early Church hierarchy to identify Church elders. The label was used initially to denote members of the boards of elders that oversaw local churches in Palestine during the early Christian centuries (Osborne 119–127). Its original usage in the Christian sense is found in Acts 14.22, wherein it is noted that St. Paul determined that the Church should make appointments according to an organizational strategy designed to maintain order and consistency and to promote the faith: "Et cum constituissent illis per singulas ecclesias presbyteros, et orassent cum ieiunationibus, commendaverunt eos Domino, in quem crediderunt" ["And when they had ordained to them priests in every church, and had prayed with fasting, they commended them to the Lord, in whom they believed"]. By the second century A.D., such boards of elders comprised members of two different and distinct titles: the "presbyters," who constituted the local boards or councils, and the "bishops" (Greek, "overseer''), who governed these local groups and from whom the presbyters derived their authority and responsibilities. A third distinct group, just below the rank of presbyter, also emerged at this time: the ''deacons,'' who were responsible for the collecting and administering of alms. From the second century on, priests were responsible largely for ministering to the people, much as they are within today's Catholic Church organization.

In the fourteenth century priests were distinguished not only by their place in the ecclesiastical hierarchy but in contrast to other types of environments in which clergy fulfilled their religious duties as well. Outside of the ecclesiastical hierarchy of the major and minor orders were the independent communities of monks and nuns, and the mendicant (begging) orders of friars. Such groups included the Franciscan, Dominican, and Carmelite friars; and the Camaldolese, Carthusian, and Cistercian orders of Benedictine monastic communities, founded according to the Rule of St. Benedict in the sixth through eighth centuries (Cantor 165–175; Southern 217–240). In addition, communities of nuns, called *convents,* paralleled the monastic orders in Rule and chronology. Within the monastic orders a hierarchy distinct from that of the major and minor orders was established: an *abbot* would oversee the monks of a community and had complete responsibility for and authority over them. As the superior cleric of the monastery, or abbey, the abbot was regarded as the father of the house. Elected for life by the monks of his house, the abbot assumed the full duties of the office without further negotiation or other involvement by the monks, which ensured that the monks could devote themselves fully to their work and prayer without the distractions of administrative decision making. In communities of nuns (feminine form of Latin *nonnus,* monk), the superior held the title of *abbess* and assumed similar authority. In this relatively large abbey, the second-in-command was given the title of *prior* (monastery) or *prioress* (convent); smaller houses would be presided over by a prior or prioress. In what were known as *conventual houses,* the prior or prioress assumed self-governing authority or, in *obedientiary houses,* were dependencies of abbeys and overseen by its respective abbot or abbess.

In contrast to the secular clergy, members of the monastic orders were called ''regular'' clergy (Latin *regula,* ''rule''), most of whom resided in a cloistered environment in which they fulfilled their vows of poverty, chastity, and obedience to their abbot. Mendicant orders, though less highly structured and governed than the monastic orders, also functioned outside of the ecclesiastical hierarchy of the major and minor orders. The regular clergy were bound by the Rule under which their orders operated, and their occupational activities and privileges were exempted from episcopal (Greek *episcopos,* ''bishop'') jurisdiction.

Although some of the duties and interests of the regular and secular clergy overlapped, each group denoted a specific spiritual way of life, with its own obligations, responsibilities, and privileges. Certainly, there was no shortage of professional rivalry between members of the regular and secular orders, especially during the rise of the mendicants—particularly the Dominicans and Franciscans in the thirteenth century—who were in competition for financial and political support from the laity. Although not the normal practice, a man could belong to both the regular and secular orders. Pope Gregory the Great (ca. 540–604), for example, was a monk when elected pope and continued to fulfill his monastic vows even while serving as bishop of Rome. Owing to the monastic reforms of the late eleventh century, many monks chose to be ordained as priests as well. But because the regular clergy had chosen to separate themselves in their communities, away from the distractions of the secular world, they were generally forbidden to provide clerical services to lay congregations (unless the monastery itself provided and supported a church for such a congregation), since this was the main duty of the secular clergy. Of greater potential consequence to the secular clergy were the mendicant orders, for friars could compete with a priest in providing services to the laity for financial gain, and yet, unlike the priest, were not answerable to the priest's bishop. Such tensions between the regular and secular clergy are illustrated in the *Canterbury Tales,* for example, in the animosity shown between the Friar and Summoner and further developed in their respective tales.

Men in the late fourteenth century who desired to enter the priesthood did so by way of securing the approval of a bishop and undergoing the ritual of Holy Orders, the ceremony by which they were ordained. A candidate for priesthood was required by the Church to meet specific qualifications in addition to the candidate's stated desire to join the ordained clergy. These qualifications, established by the early thirteenth century, included both personal and moral specifications: the candidate had to be of legitimate birth, unmarried, and age twenty-five or over; in addition, he was expected to have been educated sufficiently to take up his official duties, to exhibit strong and decent moral character, and to have secured a *titulus,* that is, either a position of employment with the Church or some other respectable and reliable means of financial support, be it through private wealth or employment in professions deemed suitably respectable, such as teaching (De Boulay 23–25; Lynch 294). As holder of a benefice, a priest did receive a portion of his parish's tithes, but in most of the poorer rural parishes these sums could not be relied on to provide adequate support for the priest. (Priests and candidates for the priesthood were expected to shun potentially lucrative but morally questionable employment—as a tavern-keeper or financial administrator, for instance.) Having undergone the process of examination, approval, and the ceremony of ordination, a priest was expected to maintain throughout his career the same high standards of character and behavior that were initially required of him as a candidate.

Candidates would be examined in their command of Latin and, ideally, would have further education relevant to their vocation as well. A standard education would include the basic four-year grammar school curriculum of Latin, including the study of such basics as the *Ars Minor* of Donatus, brief portions of the Bible such as the Psalms, and some classical works, including Ovid and Virgil (Ackerman 43–44). Grammar-school education was available in most urban areas and was provided, usually for a fee, by priests through cathedral and collegiate churches, or by monasteries, or, in some cases, merchant guilds or municipalities. Well-educated priests were deemed highly desirable and in great demand; parishes often sought candidates for their parish-priest positions who had continued their education beyond the grammar-school basics, that is, who had received some university training as well. Because the grammar-school curriculum did not include the study of theology, canon law, or church rituals, further education was necessary if a priest was to have formal training in the specific disciplines informing his office. The curricula at most universities centered on the classical Roman curriculum of the seven liberal arts, divided into the disciplines of words and numbers: the *trivium* of grammar, rhetoric, and dialectic, and the *quadrivium* of arithmetic, geometry, astronomy, and music. Typically, the bachelor's four-year education comprised *trivium* studies, while further study in the disciplines of the *quadrivium* led to a master's degree in about three years' time beyond the bachelor's. Beyond the undergraduate level, a candidate would have the opportunity for substantial study in theology and related areas. Although the set of seven core disciplines had been the norm at such cathedral schools as Chartres, Benevento, and Canterbury from the ninth through twelfth centuries, the universities, which evolved during the thirteenth century, placed greater emphasis on dialectic (based on Aristotelian logic), which resulted in the evolution of university education into a more philosophical, "scholastic" undertaking, particularly at the University of Paris under the influence of St. Thomas Aquinas in the mid-thirteenth century (Dillon 74–75, 92–93; Knowles 80–84). At Oxford, which emerged as an important center of learning late in the thirteenth century, theology, philosophy, and mathematics were areas of equal emphasis and repute. A student—or "clerk" as both university students and men in the Holy Orders were known, like Chaucer's "Clerk of Oxenford"—completing a master's level university training would be well informed and capable of critical and insightful thinking, speaking, and writing (Pantin 105–122). Candidates without university training were expected to acquaint themselves with these areas through some form of self-education: reading the important texts, listening to sermons, and conversing with others having relevant clerical interests. Although such a practical education was in most cases less comprehensive than that provided by a university, most fourteenth-century priests in England were in fact not formally educated or trained.

In addition, a successful candidate, once ordained into the priesthood, was expected to remain celibate. Celibacy for priests meant that they could not marry, though in the popular perception of the laity celibacy pertained to abstinence from all sexual activity, not just that occurring within marriage. The movement toward celibacy for the clergy, known also as the "monasticization of the priesthood," was fueled in part by the laity's desire for priests of strong moral character (Brundage 150–152, 401–405). Celibacy, it was believed, was a sign of a priest's commitment to the clerical calling; not only were his attention and devotion undistracted by the responsibilities attending wedlock, but also, and more important in the general opinion of the laity, his willingness to accept celibacy demonstrated his willingness to sacrifice for his vocation, to deny himself ordinary human pleasures in order to maintain the highest level of moral character. This condition was a relatively recent development for the clergy of the fourteenth century; the Second Lateran Council of 1139 set forth the guidelines for clerical celibacy, including the stipulation that married priests should be removed from office and marriage henceforth forbidden as a condition of ordination (though a married couple could separate and remain continent as a prerequisite to entering the regular, but not secular, orders). The celibate priest represented to his parishioners a man wholly committed to his spiritual vocation.

In practice, however, the reality frequently diverged, often markedly, from the ideal. Candidates for the priesthood often failed to meet even the most basic entry requirements, such as those pertaining to legitimacy and age; a papal dispensation could be easily arranged to circumvent these constraints. Similarly, other more significant shortcomings were often willfully ignored. Candidates were sometimes attracted to a career in the major orders not because they felt any deep sense of spiritual calling, but because the priesthood offered an attractive degree of economic stability, social privilege, and, in some cases, political power. In addition, some candidates chose the priesthood by default; there simply were no other opportunities available to them at the time the option became available. The Church employed vast numbers of clerics from all walks of life; a man from any social class could find a place in the Church hierarchy, and priests were much in demand to staff parishes throughout England, despite the relatively meager income that many sparsely populated rural parishes could offer. Although some of these opportunistic priests provided an acceptable level of professional service and commitment to their parishes, many were mediocre at best and sometimes woefully inadequate, indifferent, or corrupt.

Moreover, the inconsistencies in the priests' training and education created problems at both the high and low end of the spectrum. Poorly educated priests often found themselves insufficiently prepared for their office. Historical evidence suggests that many priests were ignorant and ill-trained in the thirteenth and fourteenth centuries, sometimes lacking even a knowledge of Latin sufficient for reading the Vulgate Bible or liturgical handbooks. The modest level of competency in Latin provided by most grammar schools enabled candidates to pass examination by the bishop—which often included only brief translation exercises, perhaps a declension or two—but did not suffice for the actual demands of the office on a day-to-day basis. Perhaps not surprisingly, many of the priests who were unable to read the Bible and other pertinent texts of Church doctrine were not fully aware of other requirements and responsibilities of their vocation as well, and the popular perception—held by both the clergy and the laity— was that a poorly educated priest was probably lax in his moral conduct as well as inadequate in his professional duties (De Boulay 74–83). Yet at the same time, priests with extensive university training were found to be potentially ill-suited for their office, owing to the reality that most priests with unusually strong educational backgrounds were ambitious enough to desire a position of greater import in the Church hierarchy. In the fourteenth century, for instance, an estimated two-thirds of bishops were university graduates, while only a very small percentage of parish priests were similarly trained (Ackerman 42; Pantin 29). Exceptionally well-educated parish priests were frequently dissatisfied with, and even contemptuous of, their lowly positions and sought promotion elsewhere.

The celibacy requirement, too, was an ideal that was often compromised in practice. While marriage was strictly and overtly forbidden, sexual activity by some priests nevertheless took place. Indeed, some priests even lived in a state of concubinage, while maintaining an image of continence and piety. Some saw the celibacy requirement as a way of enjoying the benefits of sexual relationships without having to fulfill any of the social or economic obligations of marriage. The extensive number of written rules and regulations regarding the sexual behavior of clergymen throughout the Middle Ages points to the widespread existence of such behaviors and the relatively futile measures that the Church took to try to contain them (Brundage 536–539). Sexual and financial abuses of clerical offices were so rampant in the fourteenth century that by Chaucer's day the priesthood was one of the more criticized vocations, the subject of negative popular sentiment second perhaps only to the antifraternal backlash in its ferocity and indignation. Examples of such criticisms, known today as the literary genre of "estates satire," include John Gower's *Vox clamantis,* in which Gower speaks of "the waywardness of those among the secular clergy who have usurped the office of priesthood for themselves" (Miller 218; see also Owst 231–232), and William Langland's *Piers Plowman,* which lambastes not only the friars—"alle the foure ordres, / Preched the peple for profit of hemselven" (B.Prol.58–59) ["all the four orders, / Preached to the people for the profit of themselves"]—but also the "parisch prest" who wishes to "syngen . . . for symonye, for silver is swete" (B.Prol.86). Indeed, the other priest of the *Canterbury Tales,* "a povre Persoun of a toun" (I.478), is described in the "General Prologue" as living a life of celibacy and honesty, "clennesse" (I.506). The rather idealized portrait of Chaucer's Parson is the complete opposite of the popular satiric portraits and serves as a reminder of just what ideals the office of priesthood was supposed to represent. This is not to say, of course, that priests in general had moral failings; the majority of priests took their vocation seriously and performed their duties well, or at least adequately. The scoundrels in their ranks, however, did much to denigrate by association the entire vocation.

The specific responsibilities of priests during Chaucer's day were many and varied, but a priest's most important function was to perform the set of all prescribed public services of the Church, known collectively as the *liturgy.* In particular, he would conduct the ceremonies known as *sacraments.* A sacrament was, and still is, a complex concept, dealing with matters of spiritual grace and its signification to the laity. A sacrament, in effect, makes visible and known a sacred thing by way of material elements and form. Sacraments are considered valid by the Church when the right matter (e.g., water for Baptism, bread and wine for the Eucharist), the right form (i.e., the consecratory words), and the right intention (i.e., the purpose of doing the Church's work) are combined (Baldwin 6–13; Lynch 273–274; Moorman 122–126). The specific rites and rituals that constitute a sacrament has varied throughout Church history, but in Chaucer's time a group known collectively as "The Seven Sacraments," initially catalogued in Lombard's *Sentences* (c. 1155–1158), was recognized almost universally as the most significant and essential of the Church rites. The Seven included Baptism, a symbolic washing-away of the stain of original sin and the first sacrament received by any Christian; Confirmation, a ceremony marginal to most of the laity that indicated a person's initiation into Christianity and confirmed a person's status as baptized; the Eucharist, a ceremony also known as the Mass, which included prayers, readings from scripture, and, most important, communion, the central act of Christian worship in which the Body and Blood of Christ were conveyed by way of bread and wine; Penance, the ritual associated with the confession and absolution of sin; Extreme Unction, the annointing of the sick or, as it is usually reserved for those approaching death, the "last rites" for the dying; Holy Orders, whereby men were ordained into the major orders of clergy, administered through the ritual "laying on of hands" by a bishop; and Matrimony, the blessing of a conjugal union. Only bishops were permitted by the Church to perform the sacraments of Confirmation and Holy Orders, which had little impact on the lives of most parishioners; the others had greater relevance for most people in the diocese. Baptism was considered to be of such crucial importance to salvation that, in those instances where a clergyman was unavailable to perform the sacrament, anyone could substitute for the priest in a legitimate emergency. The remaining sacraments, however, required a priest's services.

The most popular of the sacraments, in terms of parish demand and lay interest, was the Eucharist or Mass (from Latin *missal,* "to send forth"), which was performed by the parish priest according to guidelines set forth by the Fourth Lateran Council of 1215 (Beckwith 36–37; Lynch 280–285). One of the Council's chief stipulations was that, at a minimum, every Christian over the "age of reason" (age twelve in most cases) should receive the Eucharist at Easter in his or her own parish church. In addition, parishioners were required to undergo confession and penance prior to the receipt of the Easter Eucharist. Thus the two sacraments became closely associated and constituted services that could be provided to parishioners only by their own parish priests.

Because only priests could administer the sacraments of Penance and the Eucharist, their services were essential to the parishioners to whom they were assigned. Most parish priests were assigned to minister to the laity residing in urban centers and agrarian village communities, but some priests served other parishioners as well, including convents. This is the specific professional status of Chaucer's "Nonnes Preest." Even established religious communities needed the service of an ordained priest to say the daily Mass and to administer the sacraments of Penance, Eucharist, and, if need be, Extreme Unction. But while monastic communities and mendicant houses never lacked clergy qualified in this regard, communities of nuns could not rely on their regular membership for sacramental services. Women were not permitted to hold major orders and were thus forbidden to administer the sacraments, even on behalf of the convent, based largely on the theological arguments of the patristics St. Augustine and St. Jerome, developed extensively by St. Thomas Aquinas. Why women were denied Holy Orders has long been the subject of much study and debate, and it remains a controversial issue to this day (e.g., McLaughlin; Osborne 86–88; Shahar 22–37). Whatever the specific conventional and ideological foundations informing the proscription against female clergy, it is clear that communities of nuns in the fourteenth century, like the Benedictine nunnery of St. Leonard's with which Chaucer's Prioress has long been associated (Manly 204–206), did not enjoy the same autonomy and self-sufficiency as did their monastic counterparts.

Nunneries were therefore of necessity compelled to establish a formal relationship with at least one priest. Depending on the size and needs of the convent, the priest could be either a resident of the convent, serving a parish wholly comprising a sizable community of nuns, or he could be the local parish priest in whose territory a smaller convent was located (Pearsall 135–136; Sherbo). The larger convents often had several residential priests. Although no "General Prologue" portrait of Chaucer's Nun's Priest is provided (other than the brief and contested line attached to the Prioress's portrait), the exchange between the Host and the Nun's Priest prior to the "Nun's Priest's Tale" (and continued as the "Epilogue") does shed some light on the Nun's Priest both as a representative of his profession and as an individual in late fourteenth-century society. It is ambiguous whether Chaucer's Nun's Priest is a parish priest providing services to Madame Eglentine's convent, or her priest-in-residence. That he is a resident of the convent, however, seems more likely in the context of the *Canterbury Tales*. Although the Prioress holds the superior position in her convent, the rituals of the nunnery would be contingent on the services supplied by the Nun's Priest. Despite his crucial service to the convent, however, the Priest is in the service of the Prioress, her subordinate in social status, and hence it is he who is identified as her traveling companion; she is not the Priest's Nun, but rather he is the Nun's Priest.

That a priest would accompany nuns on a pilgrimage as well as provide clerical services for their convent is appropriate for a priest's vocation in the fourteenth century. For in addition to providing his services as a confessor, a priest accompanying nuns on a pilgrimage would serve as a kind of bodyguard, a deterrent against those who might attempt to rob, rape, or otherwise abuse the nuns. Outside the relative security of the convent walls, the two nuns would be vulnerable and unprotected. On the Canterbury pilgrimage, moreover, the two nuns and the Wife of Bath are the only three women present in a company of perhaps thirty-three pilgrims. The disproportionate numbers alone hint at the risks to which the women might be exposed, especially if one considers the more vulgar and impulsive members of the group such as the Miller or Summoner. Late fourteenth-century nuns were discouraged, or even forbidden, to travel unless absolutely necessary, and in fact nuns were specifically forbidden to go on pilgrimages, if the York decrees of 1195 and 1318 were still to be observed (Shahar 48). Still, nuns did in fact venture outside their convents, and if Madame Eglentine chooses to disobey the bishop's injunction against frivolous travel, she nonetheless adheres to the stipulation that nuns not travel alone (Power, *People* 82–83). Indeed, the burly and virile Nun's Priest—in the Host's words, "See, whiche braunes hath this gentil preest, / So gret a nekke, and swich a large breest! / He loketh as a sperhauk with his yen" (VII.3455–3457) ["See, such brawn has this gentle priest, / So great a neck, and such a large breast! / He looks as a sparrow hawk with his yen"]—would make a formidable enough bodyguard for the nuns, especially given that most, though not all, of their fellow *Canterbury Tales* pilgrims seem decent and restrained enough.

Of course, the presence of a male cleric either residing in a community of women or accompanying them on a worldly adventure such as a pilgrimage frequently gave rise to gossip and rumor regarding improprieties, some of which are corroborated by historical evidence. In addition to the generic abuses criticized in the literature of estates satire (Mann 55–67, 128–137), abuses by priests specifically residing within convent communities were targeted for additional criticism and ridicule as well. (Again, however, although the abuses became fodder for gossip and mirth, these were the exceptions rather than the norm. Inappropriate relationships between and among members of religious communities were a recognized problem in Chaucer's day, but many communities had few problems of this sort.) Some of the more notorious cases, documented in Bishops' Registers, include those at the houses of Ilchester in 1323 and Moxby in 1325, both of which involved resident priests seducing nuns within the convent (Power, *Nunneries* 443–447). Chaucer's Nun's Priest, however, seems largely unimpugned (Lumiansky 110–111). He is made the target of the Host's joking innuendo—

> But by my trouthe, if thou were seculer,
> Thou woldest ben a trede-foul aright.
> For if thou have corage as thou hast myght,
> Thee were nede of hennes, as I wene,
> Ya, moo than seven tymes seventene.

(VII.3450–3454)

> [But by my truth, if you were secular,
> You would be a rooster excellent.
> For if you have heart as you might have,
> You would need hens, as I know,
> Ya, more than seven times seventeen.]

—but the text supplies no corroboration or additional emphasis.

The "Nun's Priest's Tale" itself, one of the *Canterbury Tales'* most striking and delightful tales, suits the vocation of its teller in terms of subject matter, genre, and narrative performance. The tale is an example of the beast-fable genre; in an entertaining and instructive fashion, animal characters are used to demonstrate moral positions that apply to humans. In addition to the fable's moral quality, it contains elements of tragedy, comedy, and romance as well, often in the form of parody. The many themes and intertexts of the "Nun's Priest's Tale" clearly correspond as well to the extensive intellectual background and theological training that might be attained by a fourteenth-century priest of extensive learning. Using the characters of rooster and fox, quite familiar to fourteenth-century audiences by way of numerous antecedents (Aesop's fable of the fox and crow, Marie de France's fable, the French *Roman de Renart,* John Bromyard's *Summa praedicantium,* among others [Hulbert 645–663]), the Nun's Priest achieves the balance of "sentence" and "solaas" that the Host has so persistently sought throughout the tale-telling competition. Readers have noted as well the humorous parallel that the tale suggests: just as Chauntecleer is surrounded by a harem—"This gentil cok hadde in his governaunce / Sevene hennes for to doon al his plesaunce, / Whiche were his sustres and his paramours" (VII.4055–4057) ["This gentle cock had in his governance / Seven hens for him to do all his pleasure, / Which were his sisters and his concubines"]— so, too, the Nun's Priest is surrounded by the community of nuns whom he serves (Broes 158–159), albeit in a spiritual, rather than conjugal, manner.

So little is otherwise revealed about the Nun's Priest himself in the *Canterbury Tales* that it is difficult to establish any definitive connections between the individual narrator and the specific tale that he tells. In fact, many readers find that the tale reveals far more about Chaucer's personality and interests than about the pilgrim who tells the story. As one critic observes, "the Nun's Priest seem[s] a closer alias for Chaucer than the pilgrim-persona he assigns himself" (Cooper 350). As a nun's priest, however, he chooses a tale that is both appropriate and elucidating with regard to his vocation. Though not specifically a sermon per se, the tale contains many elements associated with preaching (Donovan 498–508): moral *exempla,* authoritative citations, a closing prayer, and an invitation for the audience to contemplate the significance of the story's many elements (Spearing 169–175). As the Nun's Priest instructs,

> But ye that holden this tale a folye,
> As of a fox, or of a cok and hen,
> Taketh the moralite, goode men.
> For Seint Paul seith that al that writen is,
> To oure doctrine it is ywrite, ywis;
> Taketh the fruyt, and lat the chaf be stille.

(VII.4628–4633)

> [But you that hold this tale a folly,
> As of a fox, or of a cock and hen,

Take the morality, good men.
For Saint Paul said that all that is written,
To our doctrine it is written, certainly;
Take the fruit, and let the chaff be still.]

The Nun's Priest's closing comments set up his tale in marked contrast to that of his fellow priest, the Parson. Although the "Parson's Tale" insists on a straightforward, perhaps even heavy-handed, didacticism, the Nun's Priest successfully engages his audience's attention—both the fictional fourteenth-century audience of the imaginary world of the *Canterbury Tales* and those of us reading the tale today—by providing a tale that truly delights *and* instructs.

REFERENCES

Ackerman, Robert. *Backgrounds to Medieval English Literature.* New York: Random House, 1966.

Baldwin, Marshall W. *The Mediaeval Church.* Ithaca, N.Y.: Cornell University Press, 1953.

Beckwith, Sarah. *Christ's Body: Identity, Culture, and Society in Late Medieval Writings.* London: Routledge, 1993.

"Biblia sacra iuxta Vulgatam Clementinam." Eds. Alberto Colunga and Laurentio Turrado. 4th ed. Madrid: Biblioteca de Autores Cristianos, 1965.

Broes, Arthur T. "Chaucer's Disgruntled Cleric: The *Nun's Priest's Tale.*" *PMLA* 78 (1963): 156–162.

Brundage, James A. *Law, Sex, and Christian Society in Medieval Europe.* Chicago: University of Chicago Press, 1987.

Cantor, Norman F. *Medieval History: The Life and Death of a Civilization.* 2nd ed. London: Collier-Macmillan, 1969.

Chaucer, Geoffrey. *The Canterbury Tales. The Riverside Chaucer.* 3rd ed. Gen ed. Larry D. Benson. Boston: Houghton-Mifflin, 1987.

Cooper, Helen. *The Canterbury Tales.* Oxford Guides to Chaucer. Oxford: Oxford University Press, 1989.

De Boulay, F. R. H. *The England of Piers Plowman.* Cambridge: D. S. Brewer, 1991.

Dillon, Janette. *Geoffrey Chaucer.* Writers in Their Time. New York: St. Martin's Press, 1993.

Donovan, Mortimer J. "The *Moralite* of the Nun's Priest's Sermon." *JEGP* 52 (1953): 498–508.

Gower, John. *Vox clamantis.* Trans. Eric W. Stockton. Rpt. *Chaucer: Sources and Backgrounds.* Ed. Robert P. Miller. Oxford: Oxford University Press, 1977. Pp. 215–228.

Holy Bible, Douay-Rheims Version. Rockford, Ill.: Tan, 1971.

Hulbert, J. R. *The Nun's Priest's Tale. Sources and Analogues of Chaucer's Canterbury Tales.* Eds. W. F. Bryan and Germaine Dempster. 1941. Rpt. New York: Humanities Press, 1958. Pp. 645–663.

Knowles, David. *The Evolution of Medieval Thought.* New York: Random House, 1964.

Langland, William. *The Vision of Piers Plowman: A Complete Edition of the B-Text.* Ed. A. V. C. Schmidt. London: Dent, 1978.

Lumiansky, Robert M. *Of Sundry Folk: The Dramatic Principle in the Canterbury Tales.* Austin: University of Texas Press, 1955.

Lynch, Joseph H. *The Medieval Church: A Brief History.* London: Longman, 1992.

McLaughlin, Eleanor Commo. "Equality of Souls, Inequality of Sexes: Woman in Medieval Theology." *Religion and Sexism.* Ed. Rosemay Radford Ruether. New York: Simon and Schuster, 1974. Pp. 213–266.

Manly, John M. *Some New Light on Chaucer.* New York: Holt, 1926.

Mann, Jill. *Chaucer and Medieval Estates Satire.* Cambridge: Cambridge University Press, 1973.

Miller, Robert P., ed. *Chaucer: Sources and Backgrounds.* Oxford: Oxford University Press, 1977.

Moorman, John R. H. *A History of the Church in England.* 3rd ed. London: Adam and Charles Black, 1973.

Osborne, Kenan B., O.F.M. *Priesthood: A History of the Ordained Ministry in the Roman Catholic Church.* New York: Paulist Press, 1988.

Owst, G. R. *Literature and Pulpit in Medieval England.* New York: Barnes and Noble, 1966.

Pantin, W. A. *The English Church in the Fourteenth Century.* Medieval Academy Reprints for Teaching. 1955. Toronto: University of Toronto Press, 1980.

Pearsall, Derek, ed. *A Variorum Edition of the Works of Geoffrey Chaucer, vol 2, part 9: The Nun's Priest's Tale.* Norman: University of Oklahoma Press, 1984.

Power, Eileen. *Medieval English Nunneries c. 1275–1535.* Cambridge: Cambridge University Press, 1922.

———. *Medieval People.* 8th ed. London: Methuen, 1946.

Shahar, Shulamith. *The Fourth Estate: A History of Women in the Middle Ages.* Trans. Chaya Galai. London: Routledge, 1983.

Sherbo, Arthur. "Chaucer's Nun's Priest Again." *PMLA* 64 (1949): 236–246.

Southern, R. W. *Western Society and the Church in the Middle Ages.* New York: Penguin, 1970.

Spearing, A. C. "The *Canterbury Tales* IV: Exemplum and Fable." *The Cambridge Chaucer Companion.* Eds. Piero Boitani and Jill Mann. 1986. Cambridge: Cambridge University Press, 1993. Pp. 159–177.

ADDITIONAL BIBLIOGRAPHY

Allen, Mark, and John H. Fisher. "The Nun's Priest and His Tale." *The Essential Chaucer: An Annotated Bibliography of Major Modern Studies.* Boston: G. K. Hall, 1987. Pp. 159–163.

Gallick, Susan. "A Look at Chaucer and His Preachers." *Speculum* 50 (1972): 456–476.

Hussey, Maurice. Introduction. *The Nun's Priest's Prologue and Tale.* By Geoffrey Chaucer. Cambridge: Cambridge University Press, 1965. Pp. 1–42.

Lenaghan, R. T. "The Nun's Priest's Fable." *PMLA* 78 (1963): 300–307.

Manning, Stephen. "The Nun's Priest's Morality and the Medieval Attitude Toward Fables." *JEGP* 59 (1960): 403–416.

Oerlemans, Onno. "The Seriousness of the *Nun's Priest's Tale*." *Chaucer Review* 26 (1992): 317–328.

Pizzorno, Patrizia Grimaldi. "Chauntecleer's Bad Latin." *Exemplaria* 4 (1992): 387–409.

Watkins, Charles A. "Chaucer's *Sweete Preest*." *ELH* 36 (1969): 455–469.

Chapter 7

A Monk Ther Was, A Fair for the Maistrie

JOHN P. HERMANN

INTRODUCTION

Although monasticism was central to the life of the spirit in the Middle Ages, it is peripheral, sometimes thrillingly so, for most modern Christians. If we wish to make sense of Chaucer's monks, then, it is helpful to learn the history of a vocation that strikes some as irrelevant to contemporary life and others as a solution to its enigmas. To begin with, the modern notion of religious vocation as a "divine calling" does not apply to medieval monasticism, which was usually determined by societal and familial, rather than individual, choice. While it is true that monks in the modern world still behave much as they did in medieval times, since the ancient focus on work and prayer still governs their daily lives, the worldly context for this vocation has undergone striking changes.

Monks have traditionally lived their lives apart, separated from normal secular activities and concerns, in order to facilitate the contemplation of God. Unlike friars, who perform some special work in the world like preaching or teaching, monks focus their efforts exclusively on their relationship with God. While some early monks lived lives of spectacular solitude, most were, as they still are, members of a community following a set of regulations, or rule, designed to enable them to maintain their vows. Seclusion from the world has long been considered essential to the asceticism, or self-denial, associated with the pursuit of the life of the spirit, not only in the West but in India, Japan, and China as well. Asceticism involves the struggle against worldly desires, even when these desires are not, strictly speaking, sinful. For example, there is nothing inherently sinful about the desire for property, sexuality, or freedom, but the monk relinquishes such desires in order to focus with single-minded devotion on the contemplation of God. The monk's asceticism, then, stems from his love of God.

In order to love God with such intense and exclusive focus, the monk believes he must surrender his will to God's, relinquishing his desires for many of the world's goods. Such focus on the love of God requires, as it did during the Middle Ages, the exclusion of other loves—for his mate, his children, his neighbors, or even himself.

Monks living in solitude, known as eremites, were the originators of monasticism. While eremitic monasticism was frequently practiced in the Middle Ages, the mainstream of monasticism was cenobitic. Cenobites live out their solitude within a community. This paradoxical phenomenon of an essential loneliness felt even when one is not literally alone is commonplace in the modern world, ordinarily taking on a negative cast: one feels lonely in urban crowds, say, or at large gatherings. But for cenobites, this solitude is a positive opportunity to concentrate on the love of God and salvation of the soul, still, as they were in the Middle Ages, the monk's primary duties. Monks perform works of service to others only in order to further their own spiritual development, not to serve the world's needs. This may sound cold, but it is not necessarily so. For example, the premise of monastic concern for the sick and dying does not reside in the belief that people's lives need to be extended whenever possible, but in the hope that such care can give the monk, as well as the sick and dying, an opportunity to experience the love of Christ. Such social charity is always related to the essential loneliness of the soul's pilgrimage toward union with God and to the foreshadowings of that union that can be found in loving one's neighbor.

The roots of this solitude extend deep into the soil of monastic history. The modern word "monk" descends from the Anglo-Saxon *munuc,* which itself is simply the English form of Greek *monachos,* ultimately deriving from Greek *monos,* "lonely" or "single." Whether this word is glossed as "solitary" or "one," the notion of an intense solitude, along with a burning desire to be spiritually united with one's fellow monks in the contemplation of God, is central. But this paradoxical union presented early medieval monasticism with the concrete problem of the spiritual irregularities of wandering monks, ever on pilgrimage but not necessarily toward union with God. And it presented later medieval monasticism with the problem of the obedientiaries. While wandering monks traded on the hospitality of their hosts, disturbing the peace of the community, obedientiaries threatened to become little more than administrative functionaries who honored the call of the spirit more in the breach than in the observance.

Some of the great early monks such as St. Martin of Tours, Cassiodorus, Cassian, and Caesarius of Arles wrote rules to negotiate the delicate balance between solitude and community, but the *Rule* of St. Benedict (ca. 535–540) would become the norm. This first occurred in Italy itself, where the *Rule* satisfied the need for a fixed code of laws to supplement dependence on the personality of the individual abbot. Benedict's rewriting of preceding monastic customs allowed his monks food, wine, and sleep in sufficient quality and quantity, as a least common denominator of asceticism which all could reach. However, it should be noted that he allowed only one meal a day, with very little wine, followed by regularly interrupted sleep. He also recommended complete separation from the world outside the monastic walls, even forbidding the telling of tales of worldly life by obedientiaries, whose duties took them out into the world. Social intercourse with outsiders, when they were occasionally allowed to enter the monastery, was strictly limited. Curiosity was considered a monastic vice, not a virtue.

Central to the *Benedictine Rule*'s vision of monasticism were the vows of stability, conversion of life, and obedience. Benedict specifically emphasized the vow of stability of place, the explicit renunciation of the desire to travel. This geographical focus was intended to help lead the monk to an intense conversion of the spirit from secular concerns to union with God. Monastic democracy was not at all valued, since the control of the abbot was totalitarian and, in his role as an earthly representation of the heavenly father, paternalistic. Although poverty and chastity were not mandated explicitly in the *Benedictine Rule,* or in the system of monastic vows that developed from it, they are so clearly implicit throughout that they go without saying. Ideally, a monk absolutely renounced private property, the pursuit and enjoyment of which is essential to the smooth running of the modern consumer society. He also renounced the desire for a spouse and children, as we have seen, and avoided sexual experience in all forms. Accompanying these vows and practices were regulations forbidding leisure activities and meat-eating, and requiring extensive periods of manual labor.

Benedict's *Rule* for Monte Cassino began to exert widespread influence almost immediately. After Monte Cassino was burned by the Lombards in 577, Monk and Pope Gregory the Great introduced the *Benedictine Rule* into the monastery of St. Andrew in Rome. When Gregory sent Augustine to convert the Angles and Saxons in 597, he also introduced the rule into England: Canterbury was one of the earliest Benedictine monasteries outside Rome itself. Wilfrid of York and Benedict Biscop spread the *Benedictine Rule* in England, and the Anglo-Saxon monk St. Boniface, who converted much of the European continent, founded monasteries and spread the *Rule* as he went. To be a monk eventually came to mean following a rule based on that of St. Benedict.

Monks chiefly devoted themselves to prayer, not only in private, but also in the communal *Opus Dei,* or Divine Office. Early in the morning, sometime around 3 A.M.—although in the winter, as much as an hour earlier—monks were awakened so that the office of Matins could be sung. Lauds, sung at sunrise, was followed by the shorter daily offices of Prime, Terce, and Nones, named after the first, third, and ninth hours of the day, respectively. Monks rested after Nones, then sang the evening office of Vespers—after which the only meal was taken—followed by Compline at dusk. According to the *Rule,* the entire Psalter was to be recited each week, chiefly at Matins, along with lessons from the Bible or Church Fathers and responsories (meditative verses) based on these lessons. Not all monks observed this order as stated in the *Ben-*

edictine Rule, however, and substantial transformations occurred in different periods, places, and communities.

Confession of sins took place in chapter—that is, in public. Mass took place on Sundays only. When not praying, monks were working, reading, eating, or sleeping in carefully prescribed fashion. Conversation was strictly controlled, and there was no prescription for recreational activities. Indeed, idleness was seen as the devil's workshop, a dangerous interruption in the unceasing monastic combat against the devil.

Monastic labor generally meant agriculture, crafts, or housekeeping. Early monasticism required prodigious feats of forest-clearing in order to sustain life in the remote places where monks dwelled, accomplishments that served the spiritual needs of monks and secular needs of their benefactors at the same time. Architectural labors were also continual, in the form of the construction of new buildings or repair of the old ones. The various arts and crafts were utilized for the spiritual development of the community.

The production of manuscripts, which formed the indispensable monastic contribution to the survival of classical culture, was linked to the educational mission of the monastery. The monastic *scola,* or school, originally had a military as well as an educational tenor, since knowledge was meant to be deployed in the struggle against evil which, it was presumed, could only be helped by the nuanced reading of the Word. The objective of this study had more in common with some modern field like military science than it did with the arts and sciences as currently conceived at the close of the twentieth century. However, the warfare was internal, a struggle against pride, covetousness, lust, anger, gluttony, envy, sadness, and sloth. These capital sins might be deadly, depending on the degree of a monk's consent to their depradations. In other words, they could, if unresisted, cause a permanent breach in the ability of the soul to unite with the divine will.

The chief monastic orders were the Benedictines and their offshoots, the Cluniacs and Cistercians; other orders were spawned as well, such as the Carthusians, Premonstratensians, and Augustinian canons regular. In the early tenth century, the abbot of Cluny assumed a position of great authority over a vast number of dependent houses. Such monastic feudalism would eventually develop into a monastic empire in Western Europe. The Cistercians, who preserved a stronger sense of the relative autonomy of the individual monastery, were founded at the end of the eleventh century, with Cîteaux constituting the house of prime authority. When the English Cistercians originated in the early twelfth century, they renounced wealth, refusing to accept manors, monopoly rights, and patronage and avoiding elaborate processions and litanies as well. But eventually they were given lands that were no longer in desert places, and they began to rear flocks of sheep, like the other religious orders in England.

The contemplative ideal was modified by monastic foundations that performed specific works, such as the legendary Templars, Hospitallers, and Teutonic Knights, which were military orders, and the several orders of canons regular.

In England, the two chief branches of monasticism were the Benedictines and the Augustinian canons regular. The *Rule of St. Augustine,* which exerted a deep and widespread influence after its discovery at the end of the eleventh century, was far less strict than the *Benedictine Rule.* An interpolated version of one of Augustine's letters, with additional regulations covering monastic observances, the *Augustinian Rule* allowed priests to develop their own monastic communities. It differed from the *Benedictine Rule* chiefly in a shorter office, a less restricted diet, and a reduction in manual labor. As the Augustinian canons regular were spreading, Benedictine monks began to be ordained in increasing numbers as well, in a process of rapidly increasing clericalization that had begun, although to a far lesser degree, within a century of Benedict's death. From the twelfth century onward most monks were also priests, a development unforeseen by the *Benedictine Rule.* The *Augustinian Rule* spawned other orders of canons such as the Victorines, Premonstratensians, and Gilbertines. This last order, originating with a Lincolnshire parish priest named Gilbert, never appealed to the social elite. This fact in itself made the order exceptional, since most monasteries attracted the wealthy and powerful, albeit with sizable numbers of lay brothers clearly marked by their inferior social status.

The Fourth Lateran Council (1215), which attempted to regulate the defective aspects of a monastic system that often fell short of the ideals of the *Benedictine* and *Augustinian Rules,* had its greatest influence in England, where a national order of Benedictines and Cluniacs was formed; only the Cistercians failed to join. As a result of this national organization, great wealth accrued to many monasteries. Their buildings grew to enormous size and were fitted out with great splendor. Reformist orders like the Cistercians, which had originally protested against the dangerous tendencies toward monastic worldliness, "had by the end of the twelfth century acquired . . . an unenviable reputation for avarice and group acquisitiveness" (Lawrence 161). Lawrence goes on to say that

Much has been written about the relaxed discipline in the monasteries of this period. There are widespread indications of a drift away from strict observance of the Rule. It was not a question of scandalous vice—though cases were not unknown—so much as a general dilution of community life in favour of the individual. The most conspicuous breaches in the coenobitic principle were over privacy and individual ownership. In many houses the common dormitory was replaced by individual chambers; monks received a cash allowance from the common fund with which they could buy clothes, books, and luxuries; and the constraints imposed by the rules of enclosure were greatly relaxed. (Lawrence 222)

Monastic wealth required administrative supervision of the lands and businesses that produced revenues. Such managers were called obedientiaries because their various managerial assignments were known as obediences. The typical English monastery had about a dozen of them: prior, sacrist, precentor, novice-master, cellarer, hosteller, infirmarian, as well as the various outriders, whose duties required them to spend long stretches of time away from the monastery. Potential for serious abuses arose with the further delegation of managerial supervision of lands, tithes, and offerings to subordinate obedientiaries. Ever larger numbers of monks were involved in such duties as managing estates and other monastic holdings (including entire villages and towns), interviewing bailiffs, examining accounts, and meeting with tenants. Outriders sold and bought products of the holdings, including timber, peat, fish, and salt, which were often legally sanctioned monastic monopolies; they collected tolls on cargo traveling past the monastery by road or on the river; they supervised winemaking, horse-raising, mining, and agricultural ventures. Leases had to be redrawn so that monasteries could acquire land for farming and sheepraising, and lawsuits set in motion to acquire title to land, business activities requiring careful legal supervision. Sheep farming by the Cistercians and Augustinian canons took place on a grand scale.

Inevitably, monasteries began to emphasize administrative rather than contemplative attitudes and skills in order to meet these specialized managerial demands. Originally based on renunciation of the world in order to cultivate the soul's pilgrimage to God, monasteries frequently departed from the genuine spiritual sources of their influence by focusing on the fruits of this world. Obedientiaries required not only extended periods of travel, but also a compensatory limiting of time devoted to the *Opus Dei*. For some monks, this was not much of a sacrifice, since their interests and concerns had become administrative rather than spiritual. Monasteries grew to be heavily involved in banking, functioning like modern savings and loan associations. Monastic labor was increasingly performed by paid servants, and, as we have seen, monks themselves began to receive a regular dole; their diets began to include the better cuts of meat and finer grades of wine. Critics emerged to castigate monastic wealth, gluttony, and sloth, and to urge a return to the simple but strict patterns set by the *Benedictine* and *Augustinian Rules.*

The state of the monasteries in the fourteenth century was deeply affected by the Hundred Years' War and the Black Death, which contributed to a pervasive social disintegration. The Black Death, which swept England in Chaucer's early childhood, not only directly infected monasteries with bubonic and pneumonic plague, but also decreased the number of potential new recruits at the same time that it increased the rights and remuneration of wage laborers on monastic holdings. In the later fourteenth century, John Wycliffe would criticize the monks as possessioners whose love of wealth had caused them to wander so far from the principles of Christianity and of their orders, that only confiscation of their holdings could restore the ideals set forth in the *Benedictine Rule.* Wycliffe's ideas contributed to the critiques of monasticism found in the works of writers like Chaucer and his contemporary Langland. But where Langland made use of bitter sarcasm, Chaucer tended to employ an urbane irony.

CHAUCER'S MONK

Now how might this historical background help make sense of Chaucer's monks? I use the plural since, in addition to the "General Prologue" portrait of the Monk and the "Monk's Tale" itself, the "Shipman's Tale" contains an incisive monastic portrait. Careful reading can tell us a good deal about Chaucer's attitude toward fourteenth-century monasteries, just as our historical knowledge can inform such a reading.

We are first told that Chaucer's monk was "fair for the maistrie (165)," glossed in the *Riverside Chaucer* as "extremely fine or handsome." This seems an odd initial description of a cleric. But when next we are told that he was "an outridere, that lovede venerie" (166), it begins to look as if the "General Prologue" portrait might be somewhat critical. The criticism does not simply reside in his being an "outridere," since that was a legitimate monastic office, though one that drew contemporary criticism, as we have seen. Nor does it reside in his love of hunting, an activity frequently forbidden monks, as we discover a few lines later on ("He yaf nat of that text a pulled hen, / That seith that hunters ben nat hooly men" [177–178]) ["He gave not of that text a pulled hen, / That said hunters were not holy men"]. These are minor criticisms in comparison to the narrator's suggestion that the monk held the sacred spiritual traditions of monasticism in low esteem, and instead devoted himself to the world:

> The reule of Seint Maure or of Seint Beneit—
> By cause that it was old and somdel streit
> This ilke Monk leet olde thynges pace,
> And heeld after the newe world the space.
>
> (173–176)

> [The rule of Saint Maurus or of Saint Benedict—
> Because it was old and somewhat strict
> This same Monk let old things pass,
> And held after the new world the space.]

In other words, this monk actively strove to forget the *Rule* of St. Benedict, which had been introduced into France by his follower St. Maurus, because "it was old and too strict." Of course, these are curious reasons for his behavior, since the Gospels themselves were even older than the *Rule* and monastic strictness was precisely the reason monks left the world and followed the rule in the first place: such restriction allowed them to focus on the life of the spirit to the exclusion of worldly concerns. Such cleaving to the Gospels and *Rule* is especially distasteful to the monk of the "General Prologue," who disliked such hallowed traditions and wished instead to follow the ways of "the newe world" (176). He did not observe the many admonitions against monks hunting, or the commonplace injunction of Jerome, Antony, and Caesarius of Arles that ''a monk out of his cloister dies spiritually, like a fish out of water.'' Chaucer's monk specifically invokes this ancient maxim, only to assert that it was ''nat worth an oystre'' (181). Clearly, it interfered with his consuming interest in monastic administration. The many food images establish his deep interest in consuming food, as they do in the portrait of the Prioress, who was ''nat undergrowe'' (156). Moreover, the pilgrim narrator Geoffrey agrees (ironically?) with his exceptionally lax opinions: why should the monk study, or labor, as the *Augustinian Rule* stipulated?

With admirable economy, Chaucer establishes the monk's abandonment of two fundamental characteristics of monastic life, *stabilitas loci* and vegetarianism (or at least an ascetic diet). He further departs from the monastic ideal in his recreational hunting, and his vow of poverty is questionable: he had ''ful many a deyntee hors'' (168) and his bridle resounded as clearly as the chapel bell of the subordinate monastery of which this monk was the ''kepere'' (172), that is, either the prior or the cellarer. In place of the monastic vows, this monk's modern desire is expressed in the question ''How shal the world be served?'' (187). His desire is centered on hunting, where he makes valuable business and government contacts, and he spares no expense to support this recreation, even to the extent of owning greyhounds (expressly forbidden to monks) especially bred for speed. There is no evidence that he focuses on the love of learning and the desire for God, characteristics of the monasteries at their best.

His clothing was lined with expensive squirrel fur, or ''grys'' (194) which, once again, was strictly forbidden to monks; he wore an expensive golden pin (196); he was ''ful fat'' (200); and he wore costly leather boots that were especially ''souple'' (203) or pliant, as only the best leathers are. He had a very well-conditioned horse (203), and he loved to eat a fat swan better than any other roast (206). In other words, the various details of the portrait indicate that he honors the *Rule* more in the breach than in the observance. If we compare him to another priest on the pilgrimage, say, the Parson, we find none of the Parson's spirit of self-sacrifice, charity, rectitude, and spiritual discipline. He has more in common with the Prioress, who is more worldly than one would wish for a cleric charged with the education and spiritual formation of younger nuns. Some critics even find possible double entendres on ''venerie'' (166) and ''prikyng'' (191), signs of a lechery that would put the Monk quite comfortably into the company of the Friar: friars were members of mendicant orders descended from the original monastic foundations, but Chaucer's Friar is a pious fraud.

Perhaps it is wisest to say that we should locate Chaucer's Monk somewhere between the shallow and comical snobbery of the Prioress and the greed and lechery of the Friar, an evaluation that does not place him in particularly admirable ecclesiastical company. The Monk's evident departure from the historical foundations of monasticism might well lead us to reconsider his initial description as ''fair for the maistrie.'' We know that he is not ''handsome,'' with his bulging eyes and massive girth; the phrase would seem better taken as indicating that he is "extremely fine" as a representative monk. His fineness, then, resides in his representativeness, not his moral excellence, just as a piece of contemporary sportswriting, which is seldom fine, might nonetheless be a fine example of the genre precisely because of its exemplary literary wretchedness.

The "Monk's Tale" itself is a series of tragedies lugubriously recounting the fall of famous figures. But no Christian or even philosophical message of any merit emerges from these accounts, no revaluation of the claims of the world in terms of eternal values. Indeed, the Monk seems to think that losing the gifts of fortune is the worst thing that could possibly happen and that the remedy for such loss is sorrow and lamentation. The pompousness and unremitting gloom of his performance reveal a spiritual life characterized by intellectual shallowness and funereal hypocrisy. Most critics of the "Monk's Tale" have noted the theoretical shabbiness of his notion of tragedy and have related it to his spectacularly uncontemplative lifestyle as an "outridere" more attached to the world than the spirit. The Monk mourns the loss of worldly pleasures, when he should have been learning the discipline of transcending them.

We can test this view of the monk against the other notable monk in the *Canterbury Tales,* Daun John in the "Shipman's Tale." Like the "General Prologue" Monk, Daun John is an outrider who knows a good deal about hunting: socializing with wealthy merchants during the hunt was clearly advantageous to such monastic "officers." But Daun John deploys his hunting lore in a context noteworthy for its eroticism and cruelty. Our pleasure at his gruesome comparison of husbands to hares just about to be torn to pieces by hounds (102–105) is followed by the monk's reference to the wife's sexual relations with her husband as "labour" (108). He moves from satirizing husbands as hunted animals to risqué comments about lovemaking, which eventually lead to his devious approach to sexual intercourse with the merchant's devious wife. The monk "torends" the body of Christ by his wantonness. The merchant in the tale and his wife are one flesh torn apart by Daun John, who does not sow the seed of the Word, but of his phallus. Daun John takes over the merchant's role when he copulates with his wife, first dispensing funds to members of the merchant's household to purchase their good will and, more importantly, their silence. His financial acuity is significant. Monasteries, as we have seen, were heavily involved in banking in the fourteenth century, as well as in buying property, for which they exacted rent-charges. Daun John is accustomed to dealing in loans and buying property as an officer of his monastery.

He is also a seasoned liar who violates his religious vows in a stunning manner. He alleges false kinship with the monk, claiming the merchant "for cosynage" (36) since they were born in the same village. But the monk goes further, allowing the merchant he gulls to think they are knit with an "eterne alliaunce" (40), each assuring the other of "bretherhede" (42). As the monk pledges brotherhood to the merchant he cozens, he violates the "eterne alliaunce" of his monastic vows of brotherhood. Of course, the eternal alliance in which Daun John and the merchant are actually joined is of a sort rather different, and rather more sinister, than either might have been expected to imagine. The monk then makes a vow of secrecy to the wife that operates like a seal of confession upon the seduction:

> "... but telleth me youre grief.
> Paraventure I may, in youre meschief,
> Conseille or helpe; and therfore telleth me
> Al youre anoy, for it shal been secree.
> For on my porthors here I make an ooth
> That nevere in my lyf, for lief ne looth,
> Ne shal I of no conseil yow biwreye."
>
> [VII.9127–9133]

> ["... but tell me your grief.
> That I may, in your mischief,
> Counsel or help; and therefore tell me
> All your trouble, for it shall be secret.
> For on my breviary here I make an oath
> That never in my life, like it or not,
> Nor shall I of no counsel you betray."]

This oath sworn upon the breviary that is itself a sign of his monastic vows is echoed in comically empty fashion by the wife: " 'The same agayn to yow,' quod she, 'I seye./ By God and by this porthors I yow swere ...' " (134–135). The breviary is no sign of her commitment to any values more exalted than simple expediency; the monk offers it as a stage prop that can be used to validate a promise that entails breaking her marriage vows. The monk, after a kiss to seal their promises, admits that he is not related to her merchant husband, swearing this on his "professioun" (155). This oath belies his earlier vow to the merchant, a vow that itself paralleled his monastic vows of stability, conversion of life, and obedience, along with poverty and chastity. As if the monk's reduction of oaths to empty signs were not enough, he swears this vow to the merchant's wife upon his previous "professioun" of monastic vows. Daun John lends her the money she wants, which he has borrowed from the merchant, gains his sexual profit from the loan, and then leaves her to repay the money to the husband she has cuckolded. The humor of his role involves his systematic degradation of the monastic commitment. Although there is no way of knowing whether the "General Prologue" Monk is better or worse than Daun John in the "Shipman's Tale," we can be certain that neither one lives up to his monastic commitment wholeheartedly and that Chaucer's poetry invites us to laugh at such departures from sacred ideals. His humor is ethical and oftentimes merciless to the quarry he skewers for our entertainment and edification.

REFERENCES

Beichner, Paul E. "Daun Piers, Monk and Business Administrator." *Speculum* 34 (1959): 611–619. Rpt. in Richard Schoeck and Jerome Taylor, eds. *Chaucer Criticism.* Vol. 1. Notre Dame, Ind.: University of Notre Dame Press, 1960. Pp. 52–62.

Butler, Lionel, and Chris Given-Wilson. *Medieval Monasteries of Great Britain.* London: Michael Joseph, 1979.

The Catholic Encyclopedia. Eds. Charles G. Herbermann et al. New York: Encyclopedia Press, 1913.

Duckett, Eleanor Shipley. *The Gateway to the Middle Ages: Monasticism.* Ann Arbor: University of Michigan Press, 1961.

Hermann, John P. "Dismemberment, Dissemination, Discourse: Sign and Symbol in the *Shipman's Tale.*" *Chaucer Review* 19 (1985): 302–337.

———, and John J. Burke, Jr., eds. *Signs and Symbols in Chaucer's Poetry.* Tuscaloosa: University of Alabama Press, 1981.

Knowles, David. *The Monastic Order in England: A History of Its Development from the Times of St. Dunstan to the Fourth Lateran Council, 943–1216.* Cambridge: Cambridge University Press, 1949.

———. *The Religious Orders in England.* Cambridge: Cambridge University Press, 1950.

Lawrence, C. H. *Medieval Monasticism: Forms of Religious Life in Western Europe in the Middle Ages.* London: Longman, 1984.

Leclercq, Jean. *The Love of Learning and the Desire for God: A Study of Monastic Culture.* 2nd ed. Trans. Catharine Misrahi. New York: Fordham University Press, 1974.

Milis, Ludo J. R. *Angelic Monks and Earthly Men: Monasticism and Its Meaning to Medieval Society.* Woodbridge, England: Boydell, 1992.

Ramanzani, Jahan. "Chaucer's Monk: The Poetics of Abbreviation, Agression, and Tragedy." *Chaucer Review* 27 (1993): 260–276.

Chapter 8

A Frere Ther Was, A Wantowne and a Meryee

INTRODUCTION

A friar belongs to one of the religious groups known as the fraternal or mendicant orders, so called from the practice of supporting themselves by begging, or mendicancy. Created in the early thirteenth century, these orders quickly achieved both great popularity and controversy. All but four were regulated out of existence by the end of the same century, and all four still exist today. These orders are the Franciscans (Gray Friars), officially known as the Order of Friars Minor; the Dominicans (Black Friars), or the Order of Friars Preachers; the Carmelites (White Friars), or the Order of Our Lady of Mount Carmel; and the Augustinians (Austin Friars), or the Order of the Hermits of St. Augustine. Before the friars, clergy had three principal choices in their vocations: monasticism, the secular clergy, or the Canons Regular. The new orders had some characteristics of all the established groups but in a combination that made them distinctly different.

In name, at least, friars have a certain affinity with monks. The word "friar" comes from the Latin *frater, brother.* Monks too are called *brother,* but the word does not describe their order, and a friar's vocation differs from that of a monk in important ways. Like a monk, a friar lives under a set of regulations that guide his daily behavior; hence both are members of "regular" orders. A monk, however, retreats from the world to a life of contemplation and prayer. His monastery is usually located in a remote area. By contrast, a friar has a mission in the world, modeled on that of the Apostles, to teach the Christian faith and to save souls. Most medieval friaries, the places where friars lived, were therefore located in towns and cities. Both monk and friar live communally with other members of their order, but a monk is bound by a vow of stability to a particular monastery. The friar belongs to an international order, and his residence in a convent more closely resembles the posting of a Foreign Service officer to an embassy. While attached to a particular house, he obeys certain geographical limits, but he can frequently move from house to house as the need arises.

Because a friar ministers to the spiritual needs of the laity, he also performs many of the same functions as the secular clergy. Medieval friars maintained their own churches where they preached, celebrated Mass, and buried patrons. Groups of friars also made regular tours of the surrounding areas, preaching in public places, giving confession, and collecting alms. In all these functions they competed directly with parish priests. Money given to the friars was money diverted from the traditional tithes, which naturally aroused great resentment among the secular clergy.

Occupying something of a middle ground between the monastics and the seculars, the mendicant orders most closely resemble the orders of Canons Regular. Indeed, St. Dominic himself was originally a canon, and the first rule for his order was derived from the Praemonstratensian Canons. A Franciscan resembles a Canon Regular less than the other orders, but there are certain generic resemblances for all. Like the friar, the canon lives in a quasi-monastic fashion, under a communal rule but not completely withdrawn from the world. Many of their duties are also similar. Both friars and canons are typically involved with education, for example. A different focus to their tasks, however, leads to somewhat different priorities. Canons traditionally devote themselves to the celebration of the Mass. Their work outside the cloister is incidental to their calling. For friars, as has been mentioned above, apostolic teaching is the primary goal. Toward this end they subordinate much else, including liturgical services, which were often shortened to allow more time for preaching.

The most important distinction between friars and the other orders, and the one that caused the most controversy throughout the Middle Ages, was their vow of poverty, given its strictest and most idealistic expression by St. Francis. A monk makes an individual vow of poverty, relinquishing all personal property when entering the order. A monastery, however, may own possessions as a corporation, usually in the name of its patron saint. Many held large tracts of productive farmland, collected rent from tenants, and even supplied knights for feudal service. A member of the secular clergy takes no vow of poverty at all and may own property just as the laity does. The friars, on the other hand, made vows to both individual and corporate poverty. As Francis envisioned it, this poverty was to be absolute. The order owned nothing itself, collected no income from rents, and did not accept wages for labor. Instead it relied on donors to provide lodging, clothing, and food.

Although the other orders never adopted a vow quite so strict, critics took Franciscan poverty as the standard by which all the mendicants should be judged. As the orders expanded, practical administrative problems arose that forced compromises. Even within Francis's lifetime, a majority of Franciscans believed they needed to find ways around the idealistic letter of his rule. These accommodations caused fierce controversy both within the Franciscan order and in the polemics between the mendicants and other ecclesiastics. They also made the orders vulnerable to charges of hypocrisy, charges most deftly and bitingly made in the portrait of Friar John in "The Summoner's Tale."

EARLY HISTORY OF THE ORDERS

The two oldest and largest mendicant orders, the Franciscans and the Dominicans, began in the separate efforts of their founders Francis and Dominic to address the religious problems of the early thirteenth century. In the previous century, the Roman church had proven unable to satisfy the spiritual demands of a burgeoning urban populace. The secular clergy were widely perceived as both worldly and uneducated, lacking credibility as true spiritual leaders. Bishops, who were obligated to preach only four times a year, often seem to have neglected even this rather light burden.

In this environment, numerous religiously motivated groups sprang up outside the Church's direct control. Some were separate sects with serious doctrinal differences from Rome. The Cathars became so popular in Southern France and Northern Italy that they set up an independent church hierarchy, almost supplanting the Catholic Church altogether in those regions. Others, like the Waldensians, began as expressions of lay piety with few, if any, unorthodox beliefs. Many of the lay movements espoused a life of apostolic poverty, taking literally Christ's instructions to the rich man, "if you wish to be perfect, go, sell your possessions, and give to the poor" (Matt., 19:21). The Church was unsympathetic to both kinds of movements, particularly when the laity showed the desire to engage in tasks such as preaching, which were considered clerical prerogatives.

By the beginning of the thirteenth century, however, the church's attitude was changing. While still fiercely hostile to heretics, it became more flexible about the movements it would permit, particularly if these groups clearly accepted papal authority. In the first decade of the thirteenth century, Pope Innocent III sanctioned a number of groups practicing poverty, some of which, like the Humilitati, had been condemned decades earlier. Among these groups was one originally calling themselves the *Pauperes minores,* or "Lesser Poor," led by the son of an Assisi cloth merchant, Francis. When Innocent III approved Francis's rule in 1209 or 1210, the future saint had eleven followers. By his death in 1226 his order, now named the *Ordo fratrum minorum* (Order of Lesser Friars), numbered in the thousands and had spread throughout Latin Christendom. In the following centuries, numerous Franciscans traveled throughout the world on missions of conversion, their work in the New World being the most famous. For a time in the fourteenth century, they even maintained a mission in China.

Francis and his followers intended to live as Jesus had instructed his disciples in the New Testament (see Matt., 10). Without money, staff, or change of clothes, they were to wander through the world preaching the Gospel. Francis particularly hated money and ordered his followers to avoid it at all costs. The great popularity of the Franciscans, however, made this rigor difficult to maintain as admiring benefactors donated large gifts of land, goods, and money to the Friars Minor. In order to avoid direct ownership, a distinction was created between use and ownership of property. In theory, at least, the property was owned by another, either the original donor or the papacy itself, but was reserved for the use of the friars.

Out of the problems created by such property sprang a long and complex battle within the Franciscans. Roughly speaking, two internal camps developed over these issues: the Spirituals, who insisted on maintaining the original rigor of Francis's rule, and the Conventuals, who accepted the compromises imposed on the order by the papacy. The Spirituals remained a minority faction throughout the fourteenth century. Many adopted such radical ideas about poverty that they were suppressed as heretics. In the fifteenth century groups of Franciscans, called Observants, were once again expressing the desire for a strict observance of the rule. By the sixteenth century, the Observants had become the dominant faction and unable to resolve their differences with the Conventuals, they were split into separate orders.

The Dominicans, as their official name *The Order of Friars Preachers* indicates, were principally created to preach the word of God. They grew from Dominic's experiences in Southern France preaching against the Cathars. Neither the local clergy nor specially appointed delegates had made any effective progress, and so Dominic's response was to organize a group designed to produce the most effective preachers possible. He carefully instituted an organized system to educate his friars. Every priory was required to have at least one doctor of Theology to guide the friars' studies, and the Preachers quickly became a major presence at the universities. To free his preachers from as many distractions as possible, Dominic also prohibited manual labor. Most necessary tasks for maintaining the priory fell to lay brothers, leaving the friars more time for their studies.

Although the Dominicans also adopted mendicancy, its purpose and hence its character differed from the Franciscan rule. Dominic felt that preachers who set an example of humility and poverty would be more persuasive to their listeners than richly attired prelates. Poverty thus served the ultimate goal of preaching, rather than being an end itself.

The emphasis on preaching rather than poverty made a vast difference in the order's internal history. While the Preachers were certainly not obeying their own rule of poverty very strictly by the fourteenth century, mendicancy never became the divisive theoretical problem it did for the Franciscans. Dominicans were not forbidden to touch money, as were their Franciscan colleagues, nor was a distinction between use and ownership necessary. The Preachers owned the lands on which their priories were built but were prohibited from owning any additional lands from which they might collect rents.

The origins of the other two mendicant orders are more obscure. Both the Carmelites and the Augustinians existed by the twelfth century, originally as loosely organized groups of hermits, and so are technically older than the Franciscans or the Dominicans. Reflecting the great esteem in which the ideal of poverty was held at the time, they adopted a mendicant way of life in the mid-thirteenth century. Both orders modeled their revised rules on the Dominican constitutions and began to move from their isolated hermitages into urban areas. Although well established by the end of the thirteenth century, neither order ever achieved quite the presence of the Dominicans or the Franciscans, perhaps in part because they retained something of their original eremetical spirit.

Mendicancy proved extremely popular, both to the men who rushed to join the orders and to the lay populace who supported them. The thirteenth century held the idea of a holy poverty in great respect, and the friars were also effective preachers, much better trained than most parish priests. The Dominicans reached England in 1221 and the Franciscans in 1224, each with a handful of brothers. On the eve of the Black Death in 1348, the four orders had, according to one estimate, as many as 190 houses and 5,300 friars in England and Wales alone. In addition to the friars themselves, orders of nuns and lay congregations also associated themselves with the mendicants. The women led a cloistered existence, essentially indistinguishable from nuns of the older monastic orders. The lay congregations comprised people who wished to lead a pious and penitent life without leaving society for a religious order. They also provided much of the manual labor for the friars.

Even the four orders and their affiliates could not contain the initial enthusiasm for the mendicants. Throughout the thirteenth century, a variety of other mendicant groups such as the Crutched Friars and the Friars of the Sack were formed as well. Reacting to this proliferation, the Second Council of Lyons in 1274 stopped recruitment to all mendicant groups except the Franciscans and Dominicans, and forbade the formation of any new orders without explicit papal approval. The Augustinians and Carmelites received permission in 1298 to admit new members and so survived, but all other groups were forced either to disavow mendicancy, join one of the established orders, or quietly wither away. The larger mendicant orders were not averse to the ban. The people of any one area could only give so much in alms, and too many mendicants reduced the inflow of charity to the individual houses.

MENDICANT PRIVILEGES

In general, the papacy strongly supported the mendicants. Early on it gave the orders special privileges that allowed them wide latitude in their ministry, making them responsible only to their own order and the pope himself. They were largely independent of the system of parish and diocese within which the secular clergy worked. Friars were free to preach, to confess, and to bury parishioners without any consent from the parish priest or the bishop. Nor could the bishop easily regulate the friars' behavior within his diocese. Chaucer refers to this independence from episcopal control when Friar Huberd, at the beginning of his tale, boasts of his immunity from the Summoner, a representative of the church court: "For we been out of his correccioun. / They han of us no jurisdiccioun" (III.1329–1330) ["For we are exempt from his authority. / They have of us no jurisdiction"].

In competition with the parish priests and exempt from episcopal control, the friars incurred the rancor of those who were losing both money and status to these new orders. Many clergy further perceived the mendicants as a rebuke to their worldly way of life. Nor were the friars always discreet in the use of their privileges. The secular clergy complained that friars held services at the same time as the parish churches and cathedrals, and even allowed the laity to attend services while an area was under interdict. A series of papal bulls followed, alternately favoring the seculars and the mendicants. Finally, in 1300 Boniface VIII promulgated the bull *Super cathedram,* permanently incorporated into canon law in 1317, which tried to impose a compromise between seculars and mendicants. These regulations did not end all controversy (attacks against the mendicants' privileges continued throughout the fourteenth century), but a method had been established allowing friars and secular clergy to coexist which was still in effect in Chaucer's time. Bishops finally gained a measure of control, not over the orders themselves, but over the activities of friars within their dioceses.

All four orders considered preaching essential to their ministry. Under the terms of the *Super cathedram,* Mendicants were given free rights to preach within their own churches. Franciscans and Dominicans could also preach in public places within the territory assigned to their houses, as long as they did not do so at the same time as the bishop was preaching. Augustinians and Carmelites needed a license from the bishop to give a public sermon. To preach in the parish church, as Friar John does in "The Summoner's Tale," required the permission of the local priest or special approval by the bishop.

To act as a confessor, a friar had to present himself in person before the local bishop and receive a license. The confessional powers granted by such a license were equivalent to those of a parish priest. A friar could not absolve parishioners from so-called reserved sins, those that required absolution from the bishop himself, without a special license, called penitential commissions. Friar Huberd claims he can confess exactly these reserved sins, but we have only his word that he has been given a penitential commission: "For he hadde power of confession, / As seyde hymself, moore than a curat" (I.219–220) ["For he had power of confession, / more than a curate"]. From complaints in the episcopal records, it appears that some friars, including perhaps Huberd, overstepped the limits of their licenses and confessed reserved sins without permission.

Since bishops had no jurisdiction over the internal workings of the mendicant orders, the confessional license was the principal means by which they could control the activities of the friars in their dioceses. Many bishops set quotas, only issuing new licenses as substitutes for superannuated ones. The language used in these licenses has led some scholars to suggest that English bishops often tried to gain greater control over the mendicants by licensing both preaching and confession, which would overstep the authority given to them by the *Super cathedram.* These licenses, however, could easily have resulted from the slightly different rights of each order. Since the right to preach in public places applied only to Franciscans and Dominicans, Augustinians and Carmelites still needed a license to preach as well as to confess. Thus it might have proved more convenient for bishops to draft a standard license that would cover all four orders. In his study of the English episcopal registers, Arnold Williams cites only one instance of a license solely to preach, and that was issued, appropriately, to a Carmelite (Williams, "Relations" 42). Furthermore, while bishops often complain of friars confessing without proper license, there are no complaints of unlicensed preaching which would be permitted by the *Super cathedram.*

The last major issue that the *Super cathedram* settled was the right of the friars to bury parishioners. Although such funerals were not as common as either preaching or confession, they represented a major source of income, since the deceased generally bequeathed handsome sums of money to the institution that buried them. Some of the secular clergy's most bitter complaints were over the losses of funerary bequests which they suffered after the coming of the friars. Under the new rules, mendicants retained the right to bury parishioners who so desired in their churches, but the local parish was entitled to one-fourth of the fees and legacies given to the friars.

ORGANIZATION OF THE ORDERS

The government of the mendicant orders was organized geographically, in a systematic hierarchy. A whole order, headed by the master general, was divided into provinces, which generally correspond to a country, like England or France. Often the provinces were subdivided into areas which the Franciscans called custodies and the Dominicans vicariates. Within each province, the individual friaries, which might be called convents, priories, or monasteries, were the basic organizational unit. By the mid-thirteenth century, the orders were acting to assign each house its own territory which did not overlap with any other of the same order.

Depending on its size and location, each mendicant house divided its territory into districts, or limits. These districts could apparently contain dozens of parishes, but few records survive to indicate the actual details of the boundaries. The friars who went out on regular tours within these territories begging, preaching, and confessing were known as "limiters," a title Chaucer applies to both Huberd and John. Friars generally traveled their limits in twos, although Dominican friars were usually paired with a lay brother instead of another friar. There is evidence, at least for fifteenth-century France and Germany, that the practice had arisen of giving individual limits to friars for a fixed tax. In some cases the limits were even auctioned off to the highest bidder. This arrangement led to a more stable income for the friary, but anything the friar collected beyond the agreed tax was his to keep, a practice hardly in keeping with the ideals of apostolic poverty. The remark made of Friar Huberd in the ''General Prologue'' that ''His purchas was wel bettre than his rente'' (I.256) has often been understood to indicate that Huberd pays just such a tax for the privilege of his limit, although some have doubted that the practice actually existed in Chaucer's England and interpreted ''rent'' as a spiritual obligation owed to God rather than a literal fee paid to the order.

The friary was the central place around which most friars' lives were organized. At a minimum, a friary provided a dormitory for the brothers to sleep, and in most cases a church. Most of the friars lived in a common room, but private cells were often provided for senior friars such as the prior, known by the Franciscans as the guardian. Supported by generous donations, the friars' churches were often built on a lavish scale. The Franciscan church in London, for instance, had marble floors and pillars, and many stained glass windows. Friar John's convent seems to have similar ambitions for their church, as John tells Thomas ''we owen fourty pound for stones'' (III.2106).

Not every friar was a limiter. Apart from those responsible for the management of the house and novices still in training, some were assigned to celebrate the divine offices; others, particularly in university towns, held teaching positions. Even the limiters spent a fair proportion of their time at their friary. The Dominicans, for example, required every friar to reside in his priory for a minimum of six months a year, and it was customary for limiters to return frequently to the friary during their tours. Between his visits to Thomas's house, Friar John tells us, he has been at his convent. When traveling through the larger territories, where it was difficult or impossible for the friars to return to the friary each night, the original practice was to beg shelter for each night. A more stable arrangement sometimes adopted was to establish satellite institutions known as preaching houses as temporary residences for the limiters. Friar John and his confrere plan to stay at an inn, a practice generally considered to be unseemly by Church authorities, although the practical necessity was acknowledged when there were no other options.

EDUCATION AND CONTROVERSY

Despite some initial reluctance by Francis, all the mendicant orders recognized the importance of education. To be effective preachers and confessors, friars needed an intimate knowledge of theology and canon law. Early on, therefore, the mendicants established a thorough system to train their members, both in the local houses and at the newly forming universities, where they quickly became a major presence. Not only did several renowned theologians such as Alexander of Hales become friars, but also the products of the mendicant schools soon achieved an eminence that made them the rivals of the secular masters. The most famous thinkers of the time, Thomas Aquinas, Albertus Magnus, Roger Bacon, Duns Scotus, and Bonaventure, were all friars. Even the ordinary friars working among the laity were required to be well educated. Friar John, for instance, has a Master of Theology degree, probably from Oxford. In keeping with the nature of their ministry, friars were active in developing a new systematic training in the arts of preaching, writing both theoretical rhetorical handbooks and practical collections of sermon material for the daily use of working preachers. The mendicants' prestige and their numbers at the universities soon threatened the seculars' supply of students but even more their political control over the university.

Friction was not universal. At Oxford, the friars enjoyed the early support of Robert Grosseteste, bishop of Lincoln and the university's first chancellor. Mendicants and seculars coexisted relatively peacefully in England until the mid-fourteenth century. At the University of Paris, however, extremely violent quarrels erupted between the mendicants and secular masters which led to a stream of antifraternal literature from which Chaucer was later to draw for his own attacks on the friars.

In 1252 the masters of theology in Paris attempted to limit the growing power of the mendicants by restricting each religious order to no more than one chair of theology each. The Dominicans, who already held two chairs, refused to comply, and in the acrimony that followed the secular masters declared the mendicants excommunicate and expelled them from the university.

Early in the ensuing legal battle, Pope Innocent IV favored the seculars. In 1254 he upheld the university statutes and in the bull *Etsi animarum* drastically restricted the privileges of the mendicant orders. Shortly after *Etsi animarum*, however, Innocent IV died, and the new pope, Alexander IV, was wholly committed to the mendicant cause. He quickly reversed his predecessor's rulings, restoring the friars' earlier privileges and ordering the reinstatement of the mendicants to the university. When the seculars proved obdurate, Alexander ordered the ringleaders excommunicated and deprived them of their benefices.

The battle in Paris is most significant for the polemic literature it produced. Writing for the mendicants were Aquinas and Bonaventure, two of the century's ablest minds. The leader of the secular masters in the Faculty of Theology was William of St. Amour, whose most famous tract was *De periculis novissimorum temporum* (*On the Perils of the Last Times*). Although the reputations of Bonaventure and Aquinas far outstrip that of William of St. Amour today, the *De periculis* achieved a much wider circulation than the mendicant works and was more effective as a work of propaganda. Despite being condemned as heretical, the many surviving manuscript copies attest to its popularity. Moreover, William's work was the ultimate source for a variety of vernacular satires, including Faus Semblant in Jean de Meun's *Roman de la Rose* and Chaucer's own friars.

The *De periculis* is an apocalyptic work that gathers together a variety of biblical passages to show that the friars are false apostles who signify the end of the world. William's argument has two major theses. First, he asserts that there is no justification for the mendicants' existence as an organization within the church. William argues that the secular clergy is the true inheritor of the apostolic function and that other groups are pseudo-apostles. Second, he claims that the friars are hypocrites whose seeming piety hides their desire for worldly gain. William links the mendicants to Jesus's denunciation of the Pharisees (Matt. 23). The *De periculis* concludes with forty-one signs by which true and false apostles can be distinguished. False apostles are those who, among other things, preach for material gain and support themselves by begging. They seek out the rich rather than the poor, and they speak in honeyed, deceptive words.

In England, early complaints against the friars were sporadic. Except for the occasional carping of monks like Matthew Paris, the mendicants faced only occasional opposition until the 1350s, when Archbishop Richard FitzRalph began an extended polemic against the privileges of the friars. He pled his case before the pope himself, and this argument, the *Defensio curatorum,* was widely disseminated both in Latin and in an English translation by John Trevisa. FitzRalph's argument echoes some of the complaints made a century before by William of St. Amour, but they lack his predecessor's apocalyptic outlook. FitzRalph was more concerned with the first of William's arguments, the role of the mendicant orders within the church hierarchy, and claimed that the mendicants unnecessarily duplicated the functions of the secular clergy. The *Defensio curatorum* attacks the theoretical justification for mendicancy and raises many practical objections to the ministry of the friars, but FitzRalph does not directly accuse the friars of hypocrisy. At most, he suggests that the mendicant way of life tempts the friars to sin and abuse of their privileges.

FitzRalph died in 1360. His suit against the friars, still undecided, was quietly allowed to fall into obscurity. His writings, however, began a new spate of antifraternal attacks in England, both in Latin and the vernacular. Chaucer, Wycliffe, Langland, and Gower, drawing both on FitzRalph's work and on the antifraternal writings of the previous century, all targeted the friars as examples of corrupt, hypocritical churchmen.

Chaucer closely models his portraits of Friar Huberd and Friar John on the conventions established by the antifraternal literary tradition. Thus, it can sometimes be difficult to tell what reflects historical reality and what is literary convention. At the beginning of her tale, for example, the Wife of Bath complains about the omnipresence of friars: ''In every bussh or under every tree / Ther is noon oother incubus but he'' (III.879–880) [''In every bush or under every tree / There is not another incubus but he'']. Even granting the license of hyperbole, however, this complaint reflects a literary topos created more than a century before Chaucer wrote much more than it does the real population of friars. While the rapid expansion of friars in the first half of the thirteenth century must have made them seem common indeed, by the end of the fourteenth century conditions were quite different. First, the actual number of mendicants dropped significantly during the fourteenth century, particularly after the Black Death in 1348. Since friaries were generally located in towns and cities, often in already unhealthy areas, plague hit the mendicants particularly hard, killing perhaps as much as 60 percent of their membership. Afterward, they returned to their previous numbers slowly. They found it more difficult to recruit new friars, and the minimum age for novices was lowered. Furthermore, however many friars were living in their houses, the number of mendicants actually ministering to the laity was carefully controlled both by the local bishops and by the orders themselves. In short, while itinerant friars would have been a visible presence, they hardly could have been "As thikke as motes in the sonne-beem" (III.868).

On the other hand, just because something is literary convention does not necessarily imply that it has no historical basis in fact. Many of John and Huberd's vices can be found echoed in complaints made by Franciscans against other members of their own order, and many details in "The Summoner's Tale" do reflect the real life of fourteenth-century friars. The most difficult questions to answer are how widespread were real abuses among the mendicants and how representative of general public feeling were the antifraternal attacks. Episcopal registers and other legal records give a perhaps unrepresentative sample of mendicant transgressions, since friars who carried out their ministries with devotion went largely unnoted by these documents. Of the major antifraternal writers, Wycliffe and Langland were, respectively, a secular university master and a member of the parochial clergy, two groups traditionally opposed to the friars. Both Chaucer and Gower belonged to the same small coterie of London public servants, and that their views were widely shared cannot be established. The very wealth that made the mendicants a target for attack testifies to their great popularity among a large cross-section of society. The friars received regular alms from the king and other important nobles, but did not depend solely on such important patrons. Where records survive, as at Oxford, many wills record the bequests of all ranks of society to the mendicants. Friars were also popular as private confessors. Even Chaucer's own patron, John of Gaunt, had a mendicant as a confessor. The friars' opponents attributed the mendicants' success to the foolish credulity of the laity, but a more sympathetic view suggests that friars filled a real spiritual need in the lives of those who supported them, in many instances more effectively than the secular clergy.

CHAUCER'S PILGRIM AND HIS TALE

Chaucer does not specify to which order either the pilgrim Huberd or his parodic double John belongs. Much of the satire in both the "General Prologue" and the "Summoner's Tale" depends on the implicit contrast between the Franciscan ideals of poverty and the friars' actual behavior. The presence in the "Summoner's Tale" of a third companion, a layman, to carry the alms and John's reference to his friary as a convent also hint that he is Franciscan. Other references to Elijah, however, imply that John may be a Carmelite, the order with which the prophet was exclusively associated. Taken as a whole, Chaucer's friars should probably be seen as representatives for all the orders, not particular individuals.

The quarrels of the Friar Huberd and the Summoner comprise Chaucer's version of the controversies between mendicants and seculars. The Summoner, as a minor official in the episcopal court, stands for the secular clergy, but Chaucer's choice of representatives is unique. Most of the polemic literature about mendicancy takes a partisan position, attacking one side and defending the other. Pairing Huberd with another extortionist, however, effectively sharpens the nature of the debate, satirizing both sides. Chaucer omits entirely any lofty consideration of religious poverty or how the Church can best minister to the laity, and instead reduces the debate to a grasping competition for money.

If attacking the Summoner is a logical choice for a greedy friar, Huberd's tale also reflects his training as a preacher. Almost all the analogs to the "Friar's Tale" are found in the literature written for practicing preachers: collections of sermons and sermon exempla. The tale itself is recounted as a sermon against extortion and greed, complete with a concluding moral and exhortation to his audience. The principal failings of the Summoner in the "Friar's Tale" are his hardened cynicism and his inability to distinguish between the literal word and the intent behind it. This latter lapse is a particularly appropriate accusation from a preacher, whose profession centered on interpretation, or "glosyng" of the text. The tale's main irony, of course, is that such charges are equally appropriate to Huberd himself, as the Summoner will point out in his own tale.

Chaucer's attack on the friars is so bitingly effective that it has been taken to reflect the real decline of the mendicant orders in the fourteenth century. Even historians from the fraternal orders themselves have sometimes accepted Huberd as an accurate reflection of Everyfriar. Decline, however, depends on one's perspective. Compared to the practice of St. Francis, the mendicant orders were undoubtedly not following the strict life of poverty by the late fourteenth century. It is important to remember, however, that the other orders, and even many Franciscans, never completely accepted all of Francis's assertions about poverty. Moreover, the wealth the friars acquired was the direct result of their success among the laity, many of whom clearly felt that the mendicants provided better spiritual ministry than the secular clergy. In short, we cannot generalize from the personalities of Huberd and John to the characters of real medieval mendicants. Chaucer's friars are powerfully vivid characters, but they remain literary figures, not real people.

REFERENCES

Brooke, Rosalind B. *Early Franciscan Government: Elias to Bonaventure.* Cambridge: Cambridge University Press, 1959.

————. *The Coming of the Friars*. Historical Problems: Studies and Documents 24. London and New York: George Allen and Unwin, 1975.

Douie, D. L. *The Conflict Between the Seculars and the Mendicants at the University of Paris in the Thirteenth Century*. Aquinas Paper 23. Blackfriars, 1954.

Erickson Carolly. "The Fourteenth-Century Franciscans and Their Critics, I: The Order's Growth and Character." *Franciscan Studies* 35 (1975): 107–135.

————. "The Fourteenth-Century Franciscans and Their Critics, II: Poverty, Jurisdiction, and Internal Change." *Franciscan Studies* 36 (1976): 108–147.

Fleming, John V. "The Antifraternalism of the *Summoner's Tale*." *Journal of English and Germanic Philology* 65 (1966): 688–700.

Hinnebusch, William A. *The History of the Dominican Order*. 2 vols. Staten Island, N.Y.: Alba, 1966.

Jeffrey, David Lyle. "The Friar's Rent." *Journal of English and Germanic Philology* 70 (1971): 600–608.

Kedar, Benjamin Z. "Canon Law and Local Practice: The Case of Mendicant Preaching in Late Medieval England." *Bulletin of Medieval Canon Law,* New Series, 2 (1972): 17–32.

Knowles, David. *The Religious Orders in England*. 3 vols. Cambridge: Cambridge University Press, 1948–1956.

————, and Hadcock, R. Neville. *Medieval Religious Houses in England and Wales*. London: Longman, 1971.

Kolve, V. A. " 'Man in the Middle': Art and Religion in Chaucer's *Friar's Tale*." *Studies in the Age of Chaucer* 12 (1990): 5–46.

Lenaghan, R. T. "The Irony of the *Friar's Tale*." *Chaucer Review* 7 (1972–1973): 281–294.

Little, Andrew G. *The Grey Friars in Oxford*. Oxford, 1892.

Miller, Robert P. *Chaucer Sources and Backgrounds*. New York: Oxford University Press, 1977.

Moorman, John. *A History of the Franciscan Order: From Its Origins to the Year 1517*. Oxford: Clarendon Press, 1968.

Pantin, W. A. *The English Church in the Fourteenth Century*. Notre Dame, Ind.: University of Notre Dame Press, 1962.

Szittya, Penn R. *The Antifraternal Tradition in Medieval Literature*. Princeton, N.J.: Princeton University Press, 1986.

Tugwell, Simon, ed. *Early Dominicans: Selected Writings*. New York: Paulist Press, 1982.

Williams, Arnold. "Chaucer and the Friars." *Speculum* 28 (1953): 499–513.

————. "Relations Between the Mendicant Friars and the Regular Clergy in England in the Later Fourteenth Century." *Annuale Medievale* 1 (1960): 22–95.

————. "The 'Limitour' of Chaucer's Time and his 'Limitacioun.' " *Studies in Philology* 57 (1960): 463–478.

Chapter 9

A Marchant Was Ther With a Forked Berd

NANCY M. REALE

By including a merchant among the pilgrims in the *Canterbury Tales,* Chaucer brought to bear across the entire interpretive range of his poem an aspect of his personal experience of London that had deep resonances for an England in the process of developing its own mercantile character and accommodating itself to the burgeoning of fourteenth-century continental mercantilism. Chaucer underscored the contemporary conditions in which through social station and occupation he was personally enmeshed by including in various tales characters who are merchants or who behave in ways that mimic business transactions. The careful punctuation of the *Canterbury Tales* with figures representative of the merchant class should alert modern readers to the social, political, and moral tensions that permeated fourteenth-century London society resulting from emerging market conditions in the context of feudal relations. Chaucer knew and lived out these tensions from at least three vantage points as vintner's son, employee of the Crown, and professional poet with continental literary connections. The presentation of merchants in the *Canterbury Tales* constitutes part of a fictional record of what must have been Chaucer's acute awareness of the interstitial position fourteenth-century merchants inhabited. He fuses the social instability for which merchants are figures in the poem and his poetic interest in the instability of language in the formulation of mercantile discourses that serve as alternatives to more traditional systems of meaning represented by other narrative voices.

One of the most interesting aspects of Chaucer's representation of merchants is the complex web of allusion and association he weaves among the various merchants he depicts in the whole of the *Canterbury Tales.* We are initially offered a portrait of the merchant pilgrim, who tells a tale about the marriage of the Lombard knight January. As Winthrop Wetherbee has noted, January is "also a projection of the Merchant, who announces himself as having made a similarly bad choice" of a wife (*Chaucer* 70). The attributes January displays reflect the narrator-pilgrim both insofar as January, like the tale itself, is presented by Chaucer as a construction of that speaker's mind and also insofar as the Lombard knight is intended consciously by the Merchant to represent his personal experience. Other direct references to merchants can be found in the "Shipman's Tale," in which a merchant, portrayed rather unflatteringly, is a central figure; the "Parson's Tale," in which deceit among merchants is mentioned; and the "Man of Law's Tale." One could also claim along with Peggy Knapp that Chaucer intends that the Wife of Bath be understood as an entrepreneur whose negotiations involve not just her body but also the property she inherits from her husbands (117, 122–124); she too may be viewed as a merchant then, even if not expressly named as such in the stereotypical shorthand of the "General Prologue" in which the pilgrim Merchant is portrayed.

Chaucer's representation of and references to merchants are in part a conscious continuation of the practices of his literary predecessors, especially Boccaccio. The *Decameron* is especially interesting in this regard, and it is a reflection of Chaucer's debt to his continental predecessors that Boccaccio's collection of novellas contains a tale (7, 9) that is directly related to the story told by Chaucer's merchant. What we also see in the Chaucerian treatment of merchants, however, is a preoccupation with the role of what we might loosely call the middle class in the fabric of fourteenth-century English society. As Jill Mann has argued, much of the complexity of the "General Prologue" of the *Canterbury Tales* rests on the interplay between the idealized presentation of (the occupations of) some pilgrims and the corrupted versions of others (13). Mann demonstrates that in his catalog of a variety of occupations that we might consider "middle class," or, to use the Middle English term, part of the third "estate," "Chaucer is ironically substituting for the traditional moral view of social structure a vision of a world where morality becomes as specialised to the individual as his work-life" (xi; for the view that there were actually more than three distinguishable estates, see Strohm 10–11). What this irony involves and what occasions it can best be seen when one considers side-by-side the representations of merchants in Chaucer's poem and the personal experience he must have had of mercantile life.

Among the pilgrims described by the narrator of the *Canterbury Tales,* the Merchant is the tenth character to be described, and he is referred to in a brief but revealing manner:

> A marchant was ther with a forked berd,
> In mottelee, and hye on horse he sat;
> Upon his heed a Flaundryssh bever hat,
> His bootes clasped faire and fetisly.
> His resons he spak ful solempnely,
> Sownynge alwey th'encrees of his wynnyng.

He wolde the see were kept for any thyng
Bitwixe Middelburgh and Orewelle.
Wel koude he in eschaunge sheeldes selle.
This worthy man ful wel his wit bisette:
Ther wiste no wight that he was in dette,
So estatly was he of his governaunce
With his bargaynes and with his chevyssaunce.
For sothe he was a worthy man with alle,
But, sooth to seyn, I noot how men hym calle.

[I (A) 270–284]

[A merchant there was with a forked beard,
In motley, and high on his horse he sat;
Upon his head a Flemish beaver hat,
His boots clasped fairly and neatly.
His opinions he spoke very solemnly,
Making known always the increase of his profit.
He wished the sea was kept at all costs
Between Middleburgh and Orwell.
Well could he in exchange shields sell.
This worthy man very well used his wits:
There no man knew that he was in debt,
So dignified was he of his management
With his buying and selling and with his borrowing.
For truthfully he was a worthy man indeed,
But, truth be known, I do not know his name.]

The forked beard and motley of the Merchant immediately call attention to his potentially duplicitous nature by suggesting a lack of integrity, but they may also be a fairly accurate reflection of the kind of livery associated with particular London merchant groups (Robinson 657, n. 270, 271). In a society in which sumptuary legislation was looked to as a means of preserving class distinctions, dress was extremely important, so Chaucer's decision to refer to the Merchant first by means of his appearance is a way of providing a critical first impression of his character. The beard and multicolored clothing suggest a social delineation by class and specific occupation, but they simultaneously signify a lack of integrity and the Merchant's ability to appear differently from different vantage points—a talent, as we shall see, that Chaucer repeatedly associates with the merchants he represents. This in part reflects a negative view of the characterological traits of the quintessential merchant, but, in a less critical way, it might also be indicative of the fourteenth-century reality that the merchant tended to be seen as "a man of mixed enterprise, who primarily represented wholesale trade but combined it with one or more of a number of other interests" (Thrupp 6).

This merchant-pilgrim sits proudly on his horse, well outfitted in boots and Flemish beaver hat, both of which articles of clothing suggest connections with the importing and exporting of goods in which a merchant would naturally be engaged. The very appearance of the Merchant, then, intimately ties his occupation to his character, about which we are given additional information in the following two lines. We are told that the Merchant's principal concern is for profit, and here Chaucer's use of the word "solempnely" efficiently implies a negative comparison between the Merchant's use of language in the service of profit ('th'encrees of his wynnyng") and the use of language for religious purposes (on the Merchant's "assumed solemnity," see Strohm 89). Furthermore, we learn that the Merchant is interested in the sea not for either natural or political reasons but for his ability to traverse it safely for trading purposes. Thus, both man's ability to use speech (a talent with which Chaucer is obviously intimately concerned) and the world itself are shown in one stroke to be—for the merchant—valuable primarily (if not exclusively) in the interest of profit. With this brief but damning observation (especially given Chaucer's uses of language and relatively wide experience of the European world), Chaucer's pilgrim encapsulates and reflects a disdain and distrust for mercantilism that was very much alive in the fourteenth century. (On the tensions between the inherited social order and what Strohm calls "a depiction of social relations as horizontally arrayed, communal, secular, and bound in finite time" [x], see his preface and first chapter.)

Chaucer's specific mention of Orwell and Middelburg (a port on an island on the Dutch coast) possibly links the Merchant with the wool trade, one of the most important facets of foreign trade in which English and continental merchants were engaged (see Robinson 657–658, n. 276–277). Pearsall notes that during Chaucer's lifetime, London commerce prospered, "especially trade with the rapidly growing commercial centres in Flanders and Italy, and England was beginning to make its mark as an exporter of finished cloth, having been for centuries merely an exporter of raw wool" (23). At various times in its history, England's principal export was raw wool, and trade with the Low Countries largely involved cloth, with Ghent, Bruges, and Ypres as important clothmaking centers (Lloyd 61–62). The so-called Merchants of the Staple exported wool and skins, and the Merchant Adventurers dealt in various items, cloth among them (see *Riverside Chaucer* 809, n. 277; Thrupp 53). The reference to the Flemish-style hat is thus an appropriate and efficient way of calling up an entire world of which the Merchant is a part. By associating his pilgrim-merchant with the world of foreign exchange, Chaucer is to some extent advertising the status of his character within the upper portion of the mercantile middle class while providing an explanation for the professional wide-ranging travel of the Merchant, which in part accounts for the setting of his tale about the "worthy knyght" who "was dwellynge in Lumbardye" ("Merchant's Tale," 1–2).

The next bit of information that the pilgrim-narrator provides about the "worthy" Merchant (the adjective, which appears often in the *Canterbury Tales,* is significant since it raises the question of how worth can be or should be measured) is that he applies his wit successfully to making money by exchanging currency and by concealing the fact that he is in debt. This view of the dissembling, often foolish, and even unsuccessful, merchant is a literary commonplace in fourteenth-century literature. One need only look to the *Decameron* to find merchants like Bernabo and Ambrogiuolo (2,9), Arriguccio Berlinghieri (7,8), and many others whose wit and/or ethical practices are called into question. The appearance of questionable merchant characters similarly pervades the fabliau literature Chaucer would have known, so this unforgiving portrait of the Merchant is hardly unusual from the standpoint of literary context.

Despite the fact that twice in merely five lines the pilgrim-narrator asserts that the merchant is a "worthy man," the implication is made rather clearly that, in addition to being dishonest about representing himself, this merchant engages in the disreputable—and unlawful—practice of usury as he "in eschaunge sheeldes selle[s]." "Sheeldes" is a (plural) translation of the Old French *escu*, a coin, and by extension a reference to money-lending (see the note in *Riverside* 809; Robinson 658, n. 278). The two words "estatly" and "governaunce," which seem to point not only to positive but indeed to noble qualities, are undercut by the pair of nouns "bargaynes" and "chevyssaunce." According to the *Oxford English Dictionary,* "bargaynes" sometimes had a negative connotation in Chaucer's time, suggesting a transaction with unpleasant consequences or a struggle for mastery; "chevyssaunce," which referred to borrowing and lending for profit, was often used to denote usury (see *Middle English Dictionary* and Robinson 658, n. 282). The duplicitous nature of the Merchant initially suggested by the opening lines of the description is thus made explicit: while the Merchant comports himself as if he were a gentleman, he is in fact a fraud and a criminal whose profit is made unlawfully at the expense of others. This is an especially interesting charge given the socioeconomic climate of Chaucer's London, which was "full of rich merchants who were eager to imitate the manners and customs of their aristocratic superiors" (Pearsall 21).

Chaucer deliberately sets against this reference to the Merchant's dishonesty the narrator's double references to truth ("For sothe" and "sooth to seyn") in the next two lines and the final, perhaps disingenuous, but certainly damning, remark: "I noot how men hym calle." When all is said, this merchant remains unknown and unknowable; our narrator can perceive the gulf between the Merchant's self-presentation and his actions, but he cannot tell us who the Merchant really is. While it is true that many of the pilgrims to Canterbury remain unnamed precisely so that they can be seen as representative types, the fact that this particular description ends with an assertion of the limitations of the narrator's knowledge in the face of the dishonesty of the Merchant lends a decidedly negative—perhaps even hostile—note to the presentation of this figure.

Why might Chaucer elect to cast his Merchant in such a light? What was his experience of merchants in England and on the continent? What was the fabric of the world in which Chaucer moved that would give rise to such an attitude about merchants? We know that Chaucer had considerable first-hand experience with merchants from his youth. His father was a rather wealthy vintner who apparently held extensive properties, and Chaucer probably lived as a boy quite near to the Italian merchant population of London, which was evidently the early source for knowledge of the Italian language that would figure so importantly in his poetic career (Pearsall 18). The status of his family enabled Chaucer to work in the service of royalty. As royal esquire, Chaucer served Edward III and Richard II, and he eventually became controller of the Wool Custom, the Wool Subsidy, and the Petty Custom. This was a job of considerable responsibility which required that Chaucer "oversee the export taxes and a heavier subsidy in the port of London on wool, sheepskins, and leather. These efforts placed him in the company of collectors, rich merchants whose records were checked against Chaucer's independent accounts to assure that the revenue was properly received" (Richmond 21; for Chaucer's public life, see Howard; Pearsall; Richmond 15–35; and Strohm). Moreover, Chaucer traveled to France, Italy, and Flanders, all of which had extensive trade relations with London. In fact, there is evidence that Chaucer's trip to Italy in 1372 involved negotiations with the Bardi, a Florentine banking family, and that Chaucer was accompanied on this venture by two Italian merchants who were in the service of Edward (Howard 180–181; Pearsall 102–109). Later, in his 1378 mission to Lombardy, he negotiated with the lord of Milan, Bernabò Visconti, on behalf of the English war effort against France (Pearsall 106–107; Richmond 21). Chaucer later had other political appointments which included his being named clerk of the King's Works for Richard II, an office that carried with it oversight of considerable funds used for public projects (Richmond 23). This sort of intimate involvement with the business transactions of both merchants and aristocrats (and the intersection of these two worlds) clearly provided Chaucer with a wealth of experience on which to draw as he rendered his various portraits of merchants in the *Canterbury Tales*.

It was more than personal experience alone that Chaucer was speaking from as he fashioned these portraits, however. Chaucer began the poem in the late 1380s while he was living near London in Kent, and he continued to work on it until his death on October 25, 1400. (For a good summary of the chronology of the *Canterbury Tales,* see Pearsall 226–231). During that time, which was marked by considerable social unrest that was directly related to economic matters, Chaucer had various official relationships with the Crown, so he would have had both personal and professional experience of the economic discontent that was in the air. In June of 1381, Wat Tyler was a leading force in an invasion of London by artisans and peasants from Kent and Essex that has become known as the Peasants' Revolt. This insurrection was one of a number of similar rebellions of members of the third estate who were asking for economic reform to ease the burdens that had been imposed on them by war with France, the Black Death, and other epidemics in the middle of the century, and the recently levied poll tax (one shilling for each person over the age of sixteen, regardless of economic status). The unrest of the period resulted in no dramatic political or economic reforms on behalf of the rebels, but there were some tangible changes: "the poll tax was abandoned; rent increases were restrained and villeinage further relaxed; great lords began to maintain about them armed bodies of liveried retainers; amelioration kept the repressive society stable'' (Pearsall 145). In short, the old feudal system of England was bending under the weight of the financial pressures experienced by the commoners. (For more on this subject, see Pearsall 143–151; and Susan Crane, "The Writing Lesson of 1381," in Hanawalt 204–221.)

The London Chaucer knew was by far the largest city in England with a population of approximately 40,000 or 50,000 people (Pearsall 18; Richmond 28). It was a city that attracted merchants from all over Europe; London Bridge was the home of about 150 shops (Richmond 28), but most merchants conducted business and stored their goods in their large homes, which were the urban equivalents of manor houses (Richmond 30; Thrupp 130–131). Merchants apparently tended to associate with their own kind, marrying and transferring property among themselves as a means of consolidating wealth (Thrupp 28). Marriage settlements involved both liquid capital and land which ''in the hands of merchants . . . did constant service as security for business loans'' (Thrupp 122). The holding of land was also important to merchants as a way of blurring the distinction between their class and the landed aristocracy, and a successful merchant might have as much as half of his fortune in the form of land (Thrupp 127). Chaucer would have had intimate knowledge of ''the increased social mobility of the later fourteenth century, which had London merchants rising to the rank of knighthood or even higher, and members of the nobility cultivating their rich friends in the city and joining their guilds and confraternities'' (Pearsall 245; see also Strohm, chapters 1 and 2).

Like the rest of England, London had seen hard times, but it is important for understanding Chaucer's depictions of merchants to recall that there were still sufficient vestiges of the old feudal hierarchical structures that outright revolution was not in the air. Rather, dissatisfaction and distrust were more comfortably addressed toward the third estate which could be demonized as having pretenses to aristocracy as its wealth increased, thereby posing a threat to the established social hierarchy and inherited systems of governance. It was often charged that merchants abused their financial control to acquire land and that they mismanaged the land they did acquire, monopolizing hunting rights and felling timber improperly (Thrupp 129). Moreover, merchants in particular were associated with the currencies with which they often necessarily dealt, and money itself could be seen to represent a movement away from the inherited social structures that signified from a conservative perspective God's divine plan for man's proper social organization. Thrupp reminds us that ''the central psychological prop of the economic and political inequalities that developed was in the individual's inescapable respect for authority'' and that ''the bourgeois context did nothing to free the individual from this kind of pressure but seems rather to have intensified it'' (16).

The merchant class in Chaucer's London was actually comprised of a diverse population that is difficult to categorize broadly. The most critical distinction among merchants was between the enfranchised and the unenfranchised. "Only the former, who had sworn loyalty to the city government and undertaken to bear their share of taxation and public duty, could style themselves citizens or freemen and claim the various privileges that were guaranteed to the community by royal charter" (Thrupp 2–3). Some merchants were native Londoners, some were Englishmen from other parts of the kingdom who were known as "foreigners" (this group also included the London-born who were unenfranchised), and some were nonnatives, or "aliens." That each of these groups was subject to different trade regulations, which changed often and were enforced with varying degrees of consistency, was a source of tension locally, nationally, and internationally. The waters were further muddied by the fact that English merchants were often called upon to serve in diplomatic service for the Crown, as in fact was Chaucer himself (Howard; Pearsall; Strohm; Thrupp 553–557). Personal and public interests thus intersected in ways that affected both local politics and international relations.

In addition, merchants were directly engaged in representing their cities or regions in Parliament. In London, in particular, "to be a merchant . . . was to be known . . . as belonging to a group with a distinctive economic position, referring to the conduct of wholesale trade, and with a distinctive political position, that of controlling municipal government" (Thrupp ix). Indeed, Thrupp goes so far as to characterize the government of London for the period between 1250 and 1500 as having been controlled by "a merchant elite, with the acquiescence and assistance of the rank and file of the wholesale merchants" (84).

Merchants organized themselves according to the types of trade in which they engaged, forming groups called "misteries," "companies," or "fellowships," which in turn had their own kinds of internal regulation. Within these groups, there were further divisions into "liverymen," who were entitled to wear the clothing or livery that represented the association to which they belonged, and those not allowed to wear the company colors. The liverymen controlled the company by means of meetings from which the yeomanry, the unliveried merchants, were excluded (Thrupp 29). Typically, a wealthy and influential merchant would be admitted to the livery when he was about thirty years old, after first learning his trade by working for others and then setting up his own independent business (Thrupp 13).

The alien merchants did not participate in these companies, but they formed their own associations. Merchants from individual cities were often granted charters by the Crown, which in itself occasioned organization into groups on the basis of place of origin. It was considered difficult to control the behavior of alien merchants. As a result, such groups were often required to "accept collective responsibility for the debts or trespasses of individuals" who were part of the organization (Lloyd 127). Present in Chaucer's London were a number of important alien merchant confederations, principal among them Italian banking companies and the German Hanseatic league (see Lloyd, chaps. 4–7 on the organization of aliens from different places in Europe). There were also a number of private Italian merchants who "represented only themselves or small partnerships," some of whom even acquired citizenship (Lloyd 173–174).

The Italians are especially important for the *Canterbury Tales* both because of Chaucer's personal experiences referred to above and because in a more general sense the influence of the Italians was being felt culturally. Barbara Hanawalt's comment that "trade, diplomacy, and travel were making Englishmen aware of an Italian grandeur that did not stem from noble blood . . . but was evident in men of business with cultivated tastes" is perhaps a bit too simple a construction, but it does point rightly to the effects of an Italian presence in London in particular (*Chaucer's England* xiv). Nigel Saul notes that during the thirteenth and fourteenth centuries some Italians were pointing toward classical sources to support the idea that virtue was more important than lineage in determining noble status ("Chaucer and Gentility" in Hanawalt 50–51); Chaucer would have been aware of this both from his relations with merchants who had settled in England with whom he had contact throughout his life and from his exposure to Italian writers like Dante and Boccaccio.

It is no accident, then, that the "Merchant's Tale," like the "Clerk's Tale" before it, is set in Lombardy. One can see in the relation of the two tales at least three kinds of association: hearing the "Clerk's Tale" might simply have caused the Merchant to think of the story he knew about the Lombardy of his experience; the behavior of Walter and Griselda might also have reminded him, by constrast rather than comparison, of his own Italian tale of marriage; finally, the Merchant might have consciously balanced the Clerk's account of aristocratic values and behaviors against his own account of the business-like deportment of January, who is nominally a knight. Each of these three relationships to the Clerk's Tale can act as a springboard for one of the many readings that can be done of the "Merchant's Tale," but that is a project beyond the scope of this chapter. For the present purposes, it must suffice to demonstrate that the tale the Merchant tells very much describes a world of commercial transaction, even in a situation in which such exchange is apparently inappropriate, and that this description to some extent implies—if not defines—the Merchant's engagement with such a world. As we read about January's decision to take a wife and his subsequent treatment of May, we realize that the story

is about buying and controlling, about what can and cannot be bought and controlled. One might posit either a Merchant who fully understands the import of his tale or—in a familiar move for this fiction—one who *inadvertently* indicts the entrepreneurial temper, but in either case, he is an appropriate teller. (Knapp 113)

As the Merchant appears to be approving of January's aspirations and even his behavior toward May, he is nonetheless painting a picture of married life that David Aers calls an "appalling human reality," at least from the point of view of the fictional May and historical wives bound by law to their husbands' dominion (67). Aers considers the "Merchant's Tale" to be "one of the most disturbing visions of traditional Christian marriage as an institutionalisation of human and sexual degradation'' that accepts the premise that women ''exist as objects in the acquisitive male field of vision, commodities to be purchased and consumed'' (71–72). This idea is crucial, since it yokes together a traditional religious way of understanding the subjugation of women (and the related denigration of their sexuality) and a market-based social formulation that accomplishes the same end. The latter is a purely secular rationale that seems at odds with the religious perspective until one examines the similar effects of the two systems on the texture and quality of marital relations.

When considering this issue, we must recall not only the personality of the Merchant who is speaking the tale, but also the complex map of social relations that is suggested by the interaction of the various pilgrims and the tales they tell. Again Aers is helpful when he points out that the very emphasis on the pilgrims' occupations in the ''General Prologue'' and the interplay between these and the ''moral vocabulary and judgements'' offered ''dramatises the way a market society dissolves . . . traditional ideology and its ethical discourses while it shapes human relationships around the exchange of commodities'' (19, 20; see also Strohm, chapters 1 and 2 on this subject). The tale of January and May must call up for the reader of the *Canterbury Tales* not only the Merchant's relation to his own tale but also other marriages, other husbands and wives, discussed on various fictive levels in the poem, the Wife of Bath and the characters in the ''Clerk's Tale,'' the ''Shipman's Tale,'' and the ''Miller's Tale'' figuring as exemplary among them. Any effort to come to terms with what Chaucer might be saying about the union of matrimony requires that we hold before us the polyvalence and disparateness of each of the voices we hear on this subject and the complicated harmonies they produce.

The Merchant is, of course, a man who is deeply embittered by his own marital experience:

> A, goode sire Hoost, I have ywedded bee
> Thise monthes two, and moore nat, pardee;
> And yet, I trowe, he that al his lyve
> Wyflees hath been, though that men wolde him ryve
> Unto the herte, ne koude in no manere
> Tellen so muchel sorwe as I now heere
> Koude tellen of my wyves cursednesse!
>
> [IV (E) 1233–1239]

> [Ah, good sir host, I have married been
> These two months, and more not, by God;
> And yet, I trust, he that all his life
> Wifeless has been, though that men would him stab
> In the heart, nor could in no way
> Tell so much sorrow as I now here
> Could tell of my wife's cursedness!]

The Merchant goes on to claim that he is unable "for soory herte" (1244) to refer more specifically to his own marital troubles, but it soon becomes clear that his tale is in effect his personal indictment of feminine promiscuity and disobedience in marriage.

While he implicitly identifies with the cuckolding of his character January whom he presents as a victim of his spouse's deceit, that very identification turns back on the Merchant as his own narrative progressively reveals January to be not only a misogynist but a violent man. Furthermore, the discourse of commerce that permeates the tale creates another level of association between the Merchant and January's deplorable behavior that reflects negatively on the speaker. The Merchant's apparently unwitting intrusion of commercial linguistic patterns becomes the verbal equivalent of the attitudes about women as property displayed by the knight, who believes he can purchase marital contentment.

January is well aware that his "greet prosperitee" will enable him to buy the bride he desires despite his advanced years (1245–1266). The Merchant concurs with January's determination that it is wise to find a young wife to provide heirs: "Thanne is a wyf the fruyt of his tresor. / Thanne sholde he take a yong wyf and a feir, / On which he myghte engendren hym an heir" (1270–1272) ["Then is a wife the fruit of his treasure. / Then should he take a young wife and a fair, / On which he might beget him an heir"]. This attitude can be understood as characteristic of both the nobility (the "second estate") to which the knight belongs and the fourteenth-century merchant class in the business of consolidating wealth, so here is yet another kind of indirect identification between the Merchant and his character. Moreover, the description of a wife as the fruit of her husband's treasure is essential for both the unfolding of the Merchant's story in itself and the relation between the tale and its teller since the phrase conjoins the fertility of the wife with the estimation of her worth as part of her husband's holdings while it anticipates the appearance of the pear tree which will be the locus of May's adultery (and the references to food that pervade the tale).

The Merchant follows the words quoted above with a lengthy and impassioned discourse on the benefits and drawbacks of taking a wife. His commercial language continually reveals his devaluation of women as property even as he professes to speak of the inestimable worth of wives: "A wyf is Goddes yifte verraily; / Alle othere manere yiftes hardily, / As londes, rentes, pasture, or commune, / Or moebles—alle been yiftes of Fortune / That passen as a shadwe upon a wal" (1311–1315) ["A wife is God's gift verily; / All other kinds of gifts certainly, / As lands, rents, pastures, or common lands, / Or personal property—all are gifts of Fortune / That pass as does a shadow on a wall"]. When he finally returns to his account of January's search for a wife, the Merchant provides the list of requirements for a wife which January recites to his friends. So the narrative, even while shifting voice, remains within a world of male assessment of prospective female property. Chaucer forcefully underscores this fact by sustaining here, as elsewhere in the tale, references to eating, to the woman as food and the husband as consumer, he who both eats and spends wastefully (see the *Oxford English Dictionary* on the etymological history from Latin through French of the word "consume"). Most often cited by critics is January's reflection that "bet than old boef is the tendre veel," but lines 1415–1468 are full of figurative language involving food that betrays January's desire to consume his wife.

The eating imagery becomes directly tied to January's concern about heirs when he remarks that "were me levere houndes had me eten / Than that myn heritage sholde falle / In straunge hand" (1438–1440) ["would rather that my hounds would eat me / Than that my heritage should fall / Into strange hands"]. It is January's assumption that the world of marital arrangements, like the world of commerce and the natural world, is a world in which one must eat or be eaten: it is the role of the powerful male to provide for his appetites and to protect his possessions. To the extent that a wife can be useful in accomplishing these ends, January believes that the union in which husband and wife "yelde hir dette whan that it is due" can be both pleasurable and advantageous (1452; the "debt" here refers to the legal obligations both spouses had to participate in sexual intercourse). We shall see that he maintains that belief at the end of the tale, even though the Merchant has provided ample evidence that January is mistaken.

The introduction of Justinus and Placebo allows for yet two more male views of wives and the marriage contract (this noun is certainly more appropriate in this context than "sacrament"), and the emphasis remains explicitly on the male point of view as January begins to consider his female neighbors for their suitability: "Many fair shap and many a fair visage / Ther passeth thurgh his herte nyght by nyght, / As whoso tooke a mirour, polisshed bryght, / And sette it in a commune marketplace" (1580–1583) ["Many fair forms and many fair visions / There passed through his heart night by night, / And who should take a mirror, polished bright, / And set it in the common marketplace"]. January is doing his mental shopping, and he eventually settles on a woman who displays all the qualities he seeks—"fresshe beautee," "age tendre," "wise governaunce," and "gentillesse"—despite the fact that she is of low social status, of "smal degree" (1601–1625).

This last quality should give us pause, since the Merchant's mention of May's inferior social status calls up questions about how individuals can or should be characterized and judged, a concern that appears repeatedly in the *Canterbury Tales*. Strohm has remarked that "just as Chaucer's life was intersected by contrary social experiences and competing systems of social explanation, so does his poetry provide an intersection for different, ideologically charged ideas about social relations" (xi). What the Merchant says, what January says, and how January ultimately behaves in relation to his wife reflect very different views, but the critical point of intersection is that all three consider May to be "of smal degree."

Consequently, May, like Griselda before her, is a property without a voice, and she comes to her marriage bed "as stille as stoon," apparently unable to free herself from the marriage bonds—the debt—into which January's lust and her own desirability have placed her (1818). May's only recourse is predictable; the progress of her affair with Damian is the record of her effort to satisfy her own desires through adultery as a response to January's domination, to express herself through the only language to which she has access.

As May and Damian move closer to consummation of their desire (here we should recall the food imagery referred to above), we see January's attempts to control his wife (to hoard his treasure) grow. His extreme jealousy is testament to his unconscious awareness of his own impotence and ineffectuality and perhaps even to his knowledge that treasures must inevitably be spent, no matter how closely "wyket" and "clyket" are guarded (2044–2045). At the same time, his blindness reflects his moral bankruptcy and his inability to see the woman he professes to value so highly. With his wife's act of adultery, January's enclosed garden of delight becomes the scene of his humiliation (May even stands on his back to begin her climb into the pear tree toward her lover, figuratively reversing the relative social status of husband and wife) and the site of a reinterpretation of a marriage debt defined and controlled not by male assumptions but by female assertions.

The Merchant concludes the tale with his own assertion of January's continuing delight in his wife, and we are very much aware that, despite what we know has transpired in the garden, it is a male voice that appears to have the final authority to ascribe meaning to what has occurred. January is content, but the Merchant knows better, and his own use of irony requires that his story be understood as an indictment of adulterous wives. Clearly, however, Chaucer expects us to read beyond the Merchant's motivation and to see both the inhumanity of January's treatment of May and the Merchant's implicit approval of it. In a sense, May *has* spoken, despite her status as a lower class woman, in a voice that perhaps can even be said to overwhelm the two male perspectives that structurally encompass hers. As we see before us at least three apparently mutually exclusive possible ways of understanding the Merchant's narrative, we must be made uneasy by the dissonances among them, and it is precisely to recognize what these dissonances mean that we must return to Chaucer's relations to merchants in fourteenth-century England.

The knight January and the Merchant are allied with respect to their attitudes toward women and property, and it is this alliance that makes the telling of the tale possible. Beyond that bond, however, are differences between the characters' assumptions that resonate throughout the Merchant's discourse. January attempts to establish for himself a private, ordered world in which things are as they appear—an effort that eventually renders him blind. The Merchant, on the other hand, is aware from the start that January's efforts are in vain, that wives cannot be controlled no matter how closely their actions are curtailed. His is a world of newly married experience set off against January's refusal to acknowledge experience, and in this sense merchant and knight are men of their social classes, the merchant recognizing (however reluctantly) the reality of what Strohm calls "horizontal" social interaction (x) and the knight clinging to established assumptions despite his deep reservations. Set against both of these points of view are the implied religious view of marriage as a sacred bond, the views represented by Placebo and Justinus and the various classical figures introduced, and May's experience of marriage. Chaucer has indeed created in his text a place, as Strohm puts it, "crowded with many voices representing many centers of social authority" (xiii).

While the "Merchant's Tale" is obviously (perhaps primarily) important because of the issues it raises about the relations between spouses, it is given to the Merchant to tell precisely because his experience with trade and his familiarity with the language of commerce call attention to the fact that for fourteenth-century England the air was full of different conceptions of social order that traversed traditionally understood categories in uncomfortable ways that could not be neatly compartmentalized. If feudal hierarchies and sexual boundaries and religious discourse and classical social systems were to various degrees becoming brittle, fragmented, or even supplanted in Chaucer's world, one can readily imagine that for Chaucer it would be precisely the voice of the Merchant—with his professional experience of the world—that could highlight that disintegration by negotiating the spaces between and thereby implicitly challenging these inherited systems.

In his own ambiguous and possibly often awkward social position (see Strohm 10–11, 142), Chaucer must have experienced firsthand the collision of different ways of imagining social relations. He probably saw in mercantile interactions a powerful demonstration of the possibility that new market-based social relations could transect, puncture, or even replace feudal and religious social assumptions in ways previously unimaginable. For Chaucer the public citizen and employee of the Crown, the social role of merchants may have put into high relief the potential for enormous social flux which Chaucer the poet would seek to engage imaginatively through the polyvalent interplay of merchants' voices within the *Canterbury Tales*. Taken together, the mercantile discourses that emerge in the poem serve to complicate, impinge upon, and threaten to revise the voices with which they compete.

REFERENCES

Aers, David. *Chaucer.* Atlantic Highlands, N.J.: Humanities Press International, 1986.
Boccaccio, Giovanni. *Decameron.* Trans. G. H. McWilliam. London and Harmondsworth: Penguin, 1972.
Boitani, Piero, and Jill Mann, eds. *The Cambridge Chaucer Companion.* Cambridge: Cambridge University Press, 1986.
Brewer, Derek. *Chaucer and his World.* London: Methuen, 1978.
Chaucer, Geoffrey. *The Riverside Chaucer.* Ed. Larry D. Benson. 3rd ed. Boston: Houghton Mifflin, 1987.

————. *The Works of Geoffrey Chaucer.* Ed. F. N. Robinson. 2nd ed. Boston: Houghton Mifflin, 1957.

————. *The Merchant's Prologue and Tale from The Canterbury Tales.* Ed. Maurice Hussey. Cambridge: Cambridge University Press, 1966.

Coleman, Janet. "English Culture in the Fourteenth Century." *Chaucer and the Italian Trecento.* Ed. Piero Boitani. Cambridge: Cambridge University Press, 1983.

Hanawalt, Barbara A., ed. *Chaucer's England: Literature in Historical Context.* Medieval Studies at Minnesota 4. Minneapolis: University of Minnesota Press, 1992.

Howard, Donald R. *Chaucer: His Life, His Works, His World.* New York: E. P. Dutton, 1987.

Knapp, Peggy. *Chaucer and the Social Contest.* New York and London: Routledge, 1990.

Lloyd, T. H. *Alien Merchants in England in the High Middle Ages.* Sussex and New York: Harvester and St. Martin's, 1982.

Mann, Jill. *Chaucer and Medieval Estates Satire.* Cambridge: Cambridge University Press, 1973.

Pearsall, Derek. *The Life of Geoffrey Chaucer: A Critical Biography.* Oxford, UK and Cambridge, USA: Blackwell, 1992.

Quiller-Couch, Sir Arthur T. *The Age of Chaucer.* London: Dent, 1926.

Richmond, Velma Bourgeois. *Geoffrey Chaucer.* New York: Continuum, 1992.

Shoaf, R. A. *Dante, Chaucer, and the Currency of the Word.* Norman, Okla.: Pilgrim Books, 1983.

Strohm, Paul. *Social Chaucer.* London and Cambridge, Mass.: Harvard University Press, 1989.

Thrupp, Sylvia. *The Merchant Class of Medieval London (1300–1500).* Ann Arbor: University of Michigan Press, 1948.

Wetherbee, Winthrop. *Chaucer: The Canterbury Tales.* Cambridge: Cambridge University Press, 1989.

Chapter 10

A Clerk Ther Was of Oxenford Also

BERT DILLON

As with a number of the portrayals of the pilgrims in the "General Prologue," that of the Clerk presents an ostensibly straightforward and idealized portrait of an admirable and fairly familiar member of medieval society. Moreover, the Prologue and Epilogue of the "Clerk's Tale" seem to confirm this view. Furthermore, the contrasts with the other clerks in the *Canterbury Tales* serve to confirm the exemplary demeanor of the pilgrim. In the very broadest sense, Chaucer's Clerk is explicitly or tacitly admired for four qualities: his meekness, his poverty, his intellectual eagerness, and his moral rectitude. From his association with Oxford at the beginning of his description in the "General Prologue" to the "merry words of the Host" after the Envoy to his Tale, the Clerk emerges as a representation of the medieval scholar, although, ironically, that term is used only about the Friar and in the description of Nicholas in the "Miller's Tale" and Aleyn and John in the "Reeve's Tale."

It is very clear that in the development and representation of the pilgrim Chaucer has inventively exploited the quality of reticence, a quality that Chaucer the pilgrim also exhibits. That means that it is necessary for the reader to infer a number of things about the Clerk. In fact, a whole succession of readers have felt forced to do so. Consequently, the Clerk and his tale have occasioned a fairly extensive bibliography (see Ruggiers for the most recent and fullest treatment). For example, there have been ongoing debates about frustrating questions raised by the details that are left vague, such as the clerk's age, his stage in his academic career, his ecclesiastical status, why he tells such a gender-biased tale, and why his Envoy is so cynical.

From the outset, the Clerk is a study in ambiguities. To begin with, this most unworldly of men is wedged between two very crass materialists, the Merchant and the Man of Law. This may mean that Chaucer is trying to empower a man who uses his mind as opposed to men who use wealth and the law to further their position in society. Furthermore, his placement is not far removed from three very materialistic religious counterparts, the Prioress, the Monk, and the Friar. He is about equidistant between two other "ideal" pilgrims, the Knight and the Parson. This placement means that we are forced to glance in several directions when we read about him.

The first two things we are told about the Clerk are that he is at Oxford and that he has studied logic for a long time, presumably well beyond the study of those texts that would have been taken as part of the *trivium* (grammar, logic, rhetoric) in his initial years in the university. This relates to one of the questions indicated above: just where does he fit in the scheme of things at Oxford? Typically, he would have entered Oxford when he was about fourteen, and he would have normally taken seven years to complete his Master of Arts, although he could have been lecturing as a Bachelor of Arts by the time he was nineteen (Courtenay; Rashdall). The epiphonema (a kind of witty summary) that closes his portrait, "And gladly wolde he lerne and gladly tech" [I (A) 308], means that he could easily have been teaching as a B.A. for two or three years before he proceeded to his M.A., or he could have been a regent (one to five years) master. In his fifth year, if he was progressing satisfactorily, he was allowed to lecture on one of the texts in the arts course and licensed to determine, that is to lecture on one of the official books in logic. This lecturing usually made the student a bachelor of arts (Courtenay). Generally, at the end of his seventh year, a student who had "determined" could be put forward for "inception" as a new M.A. For the M.A. the candidate had to be at least twenty years old, be shown to be of good moral character, and "learned," by which was meant he had met all of the academic requirements for the degree. The candidate's qualification was determined by a group of regent masters. The successful candidate was then presented by his master to the chancellor for license to teach (*licentia docendi*), and within one year the licentiate was "incepted" as a new master. His inception was publicly acknowledged in two acts: he gave a disputation, and he was invested with the book and cap of the master. He also gave a brief inaugural lecture (the *principium*), determined (gave the final solution) two answers, and was required to offer forty days of public disputations and lecture as a regent master for two years (Courtenay). As Courtenay points out, the medieval student would have left the university for another career at an age when a modern student who was interested in an academic career would just be beginning. The implication is, however, that he had persisted in his study of logic rather than moving on to the higher study of theology. Actually, this would not have been unusual in fourteenth-century Oxford because during that period, Oxford was noted throughout Europe for the study of logic and for the masters who did the teaching and the writing. Indeed, the youth of the masters may explain why Oxford's greatest contributions to the intellectual life of Western Europe in the fourteenth century were in logic, linguistics, mathematics, and physics (Courtenay; Rashdall). This commitment to logic would also explain

Chaucer's statement, which presumably is a paraphrase of something he had managed to worm out of the Clerk, that he would rather have twenty books of Aristotle than the material comforts that seem to have been far more important to most students:

> For hym was levere have at his beddes heed
> Twenty bookes, clad in blak or reed,
> Of Aristotle and his philosophie
> Than robes riche, or fithele, or gay sautrie.

[I (A) 293–296]

> [For he would rather have at the head of his bed
> Twenty books, bound in either black or red,
> Of Aristotle and his philosophy
> Than rich robes, or a fiddle, or an elegant psaltry.]

Incidentally, this rather fantastic wish invites the comparison of the Clerk and that most famous clerk in the "Miller's Tale," "hende Nicholas," whose handsomely furnished *private* room is quite sumptuously described right down to the "sautrie."

> A chambre hadde he in that hostelrye
> Allone, withouten any compaignye,
> Ful fetisly ydight with herbes swoote;
> And he hymself as sweete as is the roote
> Of lycorys or any cetewale.
> His Almageste, and bookes grete and smale,
> His astrelabie, longynge for his art,
> His augrym stones layen faire apart,
> On shelves couched at his beddes heed;
> His presse ycovered with a faldyng reed;
> And al above ther lay a gay sautrie,
> On which he made a-nyghtes melodie
> So swetely that all the chambre rong;
> And *Angelus ad virginem* he song;
> And after that he song the Kynges Noote.

[I (A) 3203–3217]

> [A chamber had he in that inn
> Alone, without any company,
> Very elegantly adorned with sweet smelling herbs
> And he himself as sweet as is the root
> Of licorice or any zedoary.
> His Almageste, and books large and small,
> His astrolabe, necessary for his art,
> His counter stones lay far apart,
> On shelves at the head of his bed;
> His linen press covered with a coarse red woolen cloth;

And all above there lay a great psaltry,
On which he made at night melody
So sweetly that all the chamber rang;
And "The angel to the virgin" he sang;
And after that he sang the King's Tune.]

The Clerk's fervent need serves to reinforce the truth that at Oxford Aristotle and the study of the seven liberal arts and philosophy were inextricably linked just as logic and Aristotle were linked for the Clerk. The twenty books could easily have been copies the Clerk had made from an exemplar or that he paid to have done at a stationer. (These pieces were called *peciae* and very much resemble the course packets students now purchase at Kinko's.) As Bennett has discovered, a fourteenth-century father was required to provide £4 for his son's books and £5 for his clothes, and, as an added note, it was possible to buy a copy of Aristotle's *Physics* for £1.6s.8d. It is also interesting to note that at the end of the fourteenth century, there were approximately 300 MSS in Meron College and 180 in Balliol (Courtenay). Consequently, the Clerk's aspiration would have been out of the ordinary but not entirely ridiculous. If he intended to become a master, he certainly would have acquired some basic texts (Courtenay and Bennett). One final point about philosophy and poverty: Chaucer plays on the fact that alchemy was "philosophical" in that the "philosopher's stone" could transmute baser metals into gold, but our Clerk had very little gold. In other words, either all of his study had been in vain, or he paid no attention to such vain pursuits (unlike the Canon).

Chaucer's observation about the Clerk's study of logic quite illogically prompts him to observe the physical poverty of the Clerk, an ever-present condition of the majority of students at Oxford at the time because, of the approximately 1,500 students (Courtenay; Rashdall), a substantial number were from the rural middle class (Rashdall). Physically, we see a raggedly dressed, presumably young man on a lean nag. The implication is that the Clerk is poorly dressed (he has on a short coat, not a long gown) and that he is probably riding a College horse or a rented one: in either case, such an unappealing mount would be in keeping with the image of a poor scholar. Presumably the Clerk lived in a hall, which meant that he had to share a room even though he had his own bed and that he had to suffer student hardships: little food, paper windows, expensive candles, no heat, and so forth (Rashdall).

We are told that the Clerk, because of his commitment to learning (the fourteenth-century version of the "perpetual student"), had not been awarded a church (benefice), nor had he gotten a job (a worldly "office") that would employ someone who could read and write. The fact that he has no ecclesiastical living has led to the argument that because he chose to remain at university, he had not taken the minor orders needed to qualify for a benefice. In either case, it is clear that the Clerk, unlike most of the young men passing through Oxford, was interested in taking degrees and in teaching—both of which were the exception rather than the rule.

Like many poor scholars, he was reduced to begging (and certain students were, in fact, licensed to beg) or becoming a servitor to a college or a particular master to a well-to-do student (Rashdall). But any money he got he spent on books or fees. Chaucer also reports that the Clerk sought to repay some of his debts by saying prayers for those who would give him money for school. This could be taken to mean that he was, in fact, in minor orders because that would be the only way his prayers would be "effective." In any case, the Clerk relied on some form of patronage—a not unusual condition in the fourteenth century. As Courtenay points out, students were often patronized by friends of the family, persons in the student's hometown or region, or a particular college or school.

We know that, unlike the Monk, studying (i.e., pouring over books) was of paramount importance to him; and unlike the Friar, he was brief and decorous in his speech. However, like his ideal counterpart the Parson, the Clerk was morally upright and just as the Parson practiced what he preached, so the Clerk taught what he learned and vice versa.

Whatever his status at Oxford, the Clerk would have participated fully in the daily life of the university. In the morning (beginning as early as 5:00 A.M. in the summer and as late as 9:00 A.M. in the winter), he would attend the "ordinary" lectures of regent masters. These lectures were bipartite: in one, a division of the text was explained line by line; in the other, the lecturer picked out and solved a question that might arise from the interpretation of the text (Courtenay). In the afternoon, he would attend (or perhaps perform himself since they could be given by bachelors) "extraordinary" lectures that were "cursory": these lectures were literal or paraphrastic expositions of a particular text that had been treated in one of the "ordinary" lectures. He would also be expected to attend a weekly disputation by his master and a weekly "repetition" (i.e., a weekly review session) which, were he a B.A., he could conduct himself.

Since the Clerk seems to participate and enjoy the rigorous life of a conscientious student, his afternoons and evenings were taken up with study and reading. This is quite the opposite of what Rashdall/Emden tell us of the "unideal" student who was guilty of poaching, hawking, drinking, gambling, dancing, wenching, quarreling, practical joking, violence, and "bibulosity." The statutes and prohibitions indicate that most students were more inclined to pleasures of the flesh than to pleasures of the mind.

Before we turn to the "Clerk's Tale," mention should be made that the Clerk is one of the three pilgrims Harry Bailly singles out by name when it is time to draw lots (the other two are the Knight and the Prioress). With this singular mark of respect, the Host reiterates his modest and studious nature: "And ye, sire Clerk, lat be youre shamefastnesse, / Ne studieth nought . . ." [I (A) 840–841] ["And you, sir Clerk, leave off your modesty, / Nor study not . . ."].

In the "Clerk's Prologue" we learn more about this enigmatic pilgrim. Initially, Harry Bailly relates some of what we already know from the "General

Prologue": that the Clerk is shy and silent and, like the typical scholar, lost in abstruse thought:

"Sire Clerk of Oxenford," oure Hoste sayde,
"Ye ryde as coy and stille as dooth a mayde,
Were newe spoused, sittynge at the bord;
This day ne herde I of youre tonge a word.
I trowe ye studie about some sophyme;
But Salomon seith 'every thyng hath tyme.' "

[IV (E) 1–6]

["Sir Clerk of Oxford," our Host said,
"You ride as demurely and still as does a maiden
Who was newly wed, sitting at the dinner table;
This day I have not heard from your tongue a word.
I trust that you study sophism;
But Solomon said 'every thing has time.' "]

Here again we hear the echo of the Clerk with the Prioress ("coy") and the Knight ("mayde"). Since, of course, Harry Bailly is not privy to the information we have from the "General Prologue," it is not surprising that he accuses the Clerk of stereotypical faults of academics: intellectual wool-gathering, "I trowe ye studie aboute som sophyme" and high-flown language, "Youre termes, youre colours, and youre figures, / Keepe hem in stoor til so be ye endite / Heigh style, as whan that men to kynges write" [IV (E) 16–18] ["Your terms, your figures of speech, and your rhetorical devices, / Keep them in stock until occasion brings / Elaborate style, as when men write to kings."]. The reference to a sophism could perhaps refer to the fact that before advancing to bachelor, a student had to spend one year, usually the fourth, in "sophistica" disputation, during which time he was designated *sophista*. These public and often rambunctious debates were on difficult or enigmatic problems in grammar or logic (which included "insolubles") or problems in science (Courtenay). It is amusing to hear and not without irony that the Clerk submits by agreeing to the Host's demands "As fer as *resoun* axeth" (25). But the Clerk does involve the high style, both in referring to Petrarch and Lynyan, a laureate poet and a legal philosopher, and in beginning his tale with Petrarch's "heigh stile." Incidentally, the references to having been in Italy and having heard the tale from Petrarch and having heard of Lynyan, have all been used to suggest that the Clerk is indeed older and perhaps an M.A. (Ussery), particularly because Petrarch died in 1374. It should also be noted that in the fourteenth century there were quite a number of English scholars in Italian universities, particularly Padua and Bologna (Courtenay).

As to the Clerk's tale, it is certainly appropriate to the teller, even though its relentless "hero," Walter, is repellent to a great many modern readers. It should be remembered that the tale comes from a scholarly, clerical source: it is Petrarch's Latin translation of Boccaccio's last story in the *Decameron* (X.10), a translation he made because of the moral earnestness and importance he took to be the real worth of the story. As far as Petrarch is concerned, Griselda is a heroine because she represents obedience and faith. Those are the qualities that the Clerk would be expected to admire and present. In his reprise, the Clerk praises the virtue of patience and calls attention to the fact that the song he is going to sing from Chaucer is an antifeminist jibe aimed at the Wife of Bath, whose fifth husband, "joly Jankyn," was a clerk, and wives in general. The double ballade is used to return the Clerk to his enigmatic description in the "General Prologue." The Clerk's performance in the "Epilogue" does in fact seem to contradict his shyness and may be more indicative of the combative behavior we would expect of an Oxford schoolman.

Thus, the composite portrait we have of the Clerk is that of a shy, witty, and acerbic young man who is representative of academic life of the fourteenth century. He is certainly admirable, but not without foibles; he may be ideal, but he certainly is not perfect.

REFERENCES

Bennett, J.A.W. *Chaucer at Oxford and Cambridge.* Oxford: Clarendon Press, 1974.

Boyd, Beverly. *Chaucer and the Medieval Book.* San Marino: Huntington Library, 1973.

Cato, J.J. *The Early Oxford Schools.* Vol. I of *The History of the University of Oxford,* ed. T.H. Aston. Oxford: Oxford University Press, 1989.

Courtenay, William. *Schools and Scholars in Fourteenth-Century England.* Princeton, N.J.: Princeton University Press, 1987.

Englehardt, George T. "The Ecclesiastical Pilgrims of the *Canterbury Tales:* A Study in Ethology." *Medieval Studies* 37 (1975): 287–315, esp. 287–291.

Frese, Dolores Warwick. *An Ars Legendi for Chaucer's Canterbury Tales.* Gainesville: University of Florida Press, 1991.

Ginsberg, Warren. "And Speketh Pleyn: The Clerk's Tale and Its Teller." *Criticism* 20 (1978): 307–323.

Green, A. Wigfall. "Chaucer's Clerks and the Medieval Scholarly Tradition as Represented by Richard de Bury's *Philobiblon.*" *ELH* 18 (1951): 1–6.

Hansen, Elaine Tuttle. *Chaucer and the Fictions of Gender.* Berkeley: University of California Press, 1992.

Haskins, Charles Homer. *The Rise of Universities.* New York: Holt and Co., 1923. Rpt. Ithaca, N.Y. and London: Cornell University Press, 1990.

Knapp, Peggy. *Chaucer and the Social Contest.* New York: Routledge, 1990.

LeGoff, Jacques. *Intellectuals in the Middle Ages.* Oxford: Blackwell, 1993.

McKisack, May. *The Fourteenth Century.* Oxford: Oxford University Press, 1959.

Mann, Jill. *Chaucer and the Medieval Estates Satire: The Literature of Social Classes and the "General Prologue" to the "Canterbury Tales."* Cambridge: Cambridge University Press, 1973.

Morse, J. Mitchell. "The Philosophy of the Clerk of Oxenford." *MLQ* 19 (1958): 3–20.

Murray, Alexander. *Reason and Society in the Middle Ages.* Oxford: Clarendon Press, 1978.

Pantin, W.A. *The English Church in the Fourteenth Century.* Cambridge: Cambridge University Press, 1955.

Piltz, Anders. *The World of Medieval Learning.* Trans. David Jones. Oxford: Blackwell, 1981.

Rashdall, Hastings. *The Universities of Europe in the Middle Ages.* New Edition by F.M. Powlicke and A.B. Emden. 3 vols. Oxford: Oxford University Press, 1895; 1936, Rpt. 1969.

Ruggiers, Paul. *The Art of the Canterbury Tales.* Madison: University of Wisconsin Press, 1965.

————, and Daniel J. Ransom, gen. eds. Vol. II of the *Variorum Edition of the Works of Geoffrey Chaucer.* Part One A. Malcolm Andrew, Charles Moorman, and Daniel J. Ransom. Part One B. Explanatory Notes. Malcolm Andrew. Norman: University of Oklahoma Press, 1993.

Salter, H.E. *Medieval Oxford.* Oxford: Clarendon Press, 1936. Rpt. 1976.

Ussery, Huling. "How Old Is Chaucer's Clerk?" *TSE* 15 (1967): 1–18.

————. "Fourteenth Century English Logicians: Possible Models for Chaucer's Clerk." *TSE* 18 (1970): 1–15.

Chapter 11

A Sergeant of the Lawe, War and Wyse

JOSEPH HORNSBY

Chaucer's "General Prologue" portrait of the Man of Law provides us with a thumbnail sketch of a common lawyer. Common lawyers practiced in the courts where the king's law, the common law, was observed, as opposed to those courts where the church's law, the canon law, held sway. This particular lawyer has attained the position of sergeant and hence ranked among an elite group of men in the legal profession. Though lists vary, during Richard II's reign only twenty-two or twenty-three new sergeants were called to take up the order (Baker, *The Order of Serjeants at Law* 158–159; Eberle 28; *Year Books of Richard II, 1378–79* xxxiii–xxxiv). Next to justice of one of the king's courts at Westminster, the rank of king's sergeant-at-law was the highest in the legal profession in Chaucer's day. By the fifteenth century, sergeants-at-law had a virtual monopoly on the practice of law in one of the king's courts, the court of common pleas. Attaining the rank of sergeant placed one next in line for an appointment to the bench of one of the king's courts. It also gave the holder of that rank entree to an array of legal business unavailable to lawyers entitled to practice only in inferior courts. Consequently, appointment to the position of king's sergeant-at-law practically granted a license to begin amassing a significant personal fortune (Postan 157). The emergence of a professionally and socially superior group of lawyers is one of the first signs of the stratification of the legal profession into categories designating both experience and expertise and was a relatively new phenomenon in the fourteenth century. It coincides with other events that mark the formation of a legal profession with a distinct sense of professional identity and forms of self-governance. To appreciate the novelty of the Man of Law for his time, a look at the evolution of the English legal profession is in order before taking up the details of his portrait. Here too I should note that while Chaucer calls this pilgrim a "A Sergeant of the Lawe" (309) in the "General Prologue," because the profession had not quite defined itself by the fourteenth century, I follow the Host and use the broader appellation, Man of Law (*Introduction to the Man of Law's Tale* 33).

THE PROFESSION

Paul Brand's *The Origins of the English Legal Profession* argues that, prior to the middle of the twelfth century, the legal profession did not exist in England (1–13). In the two hundred intervening years, a profession centered around the king's courts did begin to organize itself. But as Nigel Ramsay points out, the performance of no single activity or types of activity defined membership in such a profession; "[r]ather, there were several types of activity whose practitioners were seen as lawyers" (Baker, "The English Legal Profession" 75–76; Ramsay 62). One way to identify members of the profession was by the offices to which they were appointed. For instance, king's sergeants were appointed for life, while attorneys were appointed on an ad hoc basis. Another way was by title. Legal records refer to the following types of lawyers: sergeant at law, apprentice at law, man learned in the law (Ramsay 63).

By the fifteenth century, the common law courts divided the profession into students (apprentices), senior apprentices, and sergeants. The senior apprentices and sergeants actually practiced law in the courts. Even later in the fifteenth century, the profession would settle into a clear-cut hierarchy of sergeant, barrister, and solicitor, with the attorneys essentially mutating into the solicitors and the senior apprentices into the barristers (Brand 159). But fourteenth-century titles for types of lawyers are somewhat slippery. Another way to distinguish members of the profession from one another was according to the court in which they practiced. This was the route taken by Caxton in his *Game and Playe of the Chesse,* printed in the late fifteenth century, when the profession's mutations had become somewhat more distinct:

I suppose that in all Christendom are not so many pleaders, attorneys and men of the law as be in England only, for if they were numbered all that belong to the courts of the Chancery, King's Bench, Common Pleas, Exchequer, Receipt and Hell, and the bag-bearers of the same, it should amount to a great multitude. And how all these live, and of whom, if it should be uttered and told it should not be believed. (Baker, "The English Legal Profession" 75)

Caxton's complaint about the proliferation of lawyers and courts is myopic. It only mentions the courts of Westminster and the place in Westminster Hall where records were kept—the "Receipt and Hell" (Baker, "The English Legal Profession" 75, n. 1). Local courts, church courts and the practitioners therein are not mentioned. Moreover, lawyers active in one court might be active in another, and active in courts of London and other locales (Ramsay 63). Finally, because no professional regulatory body or centralized program of legal education existed in Chaucer's period (though one was taking shape in London as I mention below), anyone claiming legal expertise or holding himself out as expert in the law might be considered a lawyer (Ramsay 65).

Out of this morass of so-called lawyers infesting the courts of the fourteenth and fifteenth centuries, the king's sergeant stands most clearly defined in terms of where he practiced and how he practiced law (Baker, *An Introduction to English Legal History* 180). In general, however, the majority of medieval English lawyers fell into two groups according to their function in court. They either stood before the court as attorney or pleader for their client (Lyon 139). The term *attorney* comes from the Latin verb *attornare,* meaning to appoint (Brand 46). Simply put, an attorney was someone appointed to take a litigant's place in court and to authorize the various procedural steps in the lawsuit (Baker, "The English Legal Profession" 84). The words and actions of the attorney in court were binding to the litigant. A pleader did much more than that. The pleader, known as a *countour* or *narrator,* actually counted or pled the litigant's case before the judges and then countered arguments made in court against his version of the case (Baker, *An Introduction to English Legal History* 179). In essence, they told their client's story, hence the name *countour* or *narrator* (Brand 94). The pleader, or counter, had to master a complicated series of responses and counter responses to the various steps involved in pleading the lawsuit. One misstatement in the pleadings could so seriously weaken a client's case that a judge would have no other choice than to dismiss it.

In the early thirteenth century, *countours* in the king's courts began to be referred to as sergeants, a term derived from the Latin *serviens* and the French *serjant,* or "servant." "[T]he term may have come to be applied to the serjeant because of the perceived analogy between the way in which he was liable to disavowal by his client for what he had said in court and the way in which a lord whose servants had performed a particular action without his express prior approval were subject to a similar right of avowal or disavowal after the deed" (Brand 94–95). Eventually, the term *sergeant* replaced the term *counter* because "counting had started to be a less important part of the counter's employment than pleading and advocacy in general" (Brand 95; see also Baker, *The Order of Serjeants at Law* 27, n. 3).

Out of the ranks of counters of the king's courts sprang the elite order of sergeants of law in the fourteenth century, a group composed of expert pleaders in the king's courts. Records, however, indicate that these counters were not regularly referred to as sergeants of the law or sergeants-at-law until the 1370s (Baker *The Order of Serjeants at Law* 21–22). By singling out a select group of lawyers deemed superior to all lawyers and granting them special rank and privilege in the king's courts, those courts were taking crucial steps toward defining the perimeters of the legal profession. This process was manifest as well in the interest the king's courts began to take in supervising the training and delineating the academic credentials necessary in order to become a common lawyer. Both interests were realized when the inns of court became virtual colleges of law in the late fourteenth century. When this occurred, other avenues for entrance into the profession began to close. The instability of the profession in the fourteenth century, however, is implied by the triptych established in the "General Prologue" through the juxtapostion of the Man of Law's portrait with those of the Clerk and the Franklin. On the one hand, the Clerk's university training would give him appropriate credentials to do legal work; on the other, the Franklin is a *countour* ("General Prologue" 359).

Originally, lawyers came out of the universities. There they would have received training in philosophy as well as in canon law, the law of the Roman Catholic Church, and in civil law, with Roman law stemming from the tradition of Justinian. The student of canon law studied Gratian's *Decretum* and Gregory IX's *Decretals,* the two primary compilations of papal edicts, along with the glosses of and the commentary on those edicts. The course in civil law consisted of lectures on Justinian's *Code* and the *Digest* (Brand 145). Essentially, civil law was studied as an addendum to canon law. Students trained in both disciplines were qualified to practice as advocates in the church courts of England. At times a student weary from following Chaucer's Clerk's philosophy to "gladly . . . lerne and gladly teche" ("General Prologue" 308) and the threadbare lifestyle attendant to the scholar's life might want to reap more tangible profits from his labors. One of the men mentioned by Chaucer at the end of *Troilus and Criseyde,* Ralph Strode, found his way into the practice of law after a career as an Oxford logician. In 1373 he abandoned the university, moved to London, and commenced the practice of law as common sergeant and pleader for the city of London (Delasanta 205–210). In the trajectory of his professional life, then, Strode embodied aspects of both the Clerk and the Man of Law.

As the courts began to develop an educational regimen to monitor and screen those who were competent to plead in the common law courts, another route developed for becoming a lawyer. Aspiring pleaders could apprentice to the law courts at Westminster and take up lodging with other apprentices in the inns of court. The court of common pleas had a place reserved for them, the crib, where they could learn by example (Brand 111). The earliest description of the educational regimen undertaken by these apprentices is that of Sir John Fortescue in his *De laudibus legum anglie,* a treatise on the English legal system. Even though that account stems from the mid-fifteenth century, it hints at the education of fourteenth-century apprentices. According to Fortescue:

laws are taught and learned in a certain public academy, more convenient and suitable for their apprehension than any University. For this academy is situated near the king's courts, where these laws are pleaded and disputed from day to day, and judgements are rendered in accordance with them by judges, who are grave men, mature, expert and trained in these laws. So those laws are read and taught in these courts as if in public schools, to which students of the law flock every day in term-time. (Fortescue 117)

Records indicate that at least by 1388, though some historians argue for as early as 1340, a program of legal instruction like the one Fortescue describes had begun in the inns of court, his "public academy," to supplement what the apprentices had learned about pleading and the law in the courts (Baker, *Readings and Moots at the Inns of Court in the Fifteenth Century,* vol. II, xv–xxxiii). Those inns—the Inner Temple, the Middle Temple, Gray's Inn, and Lincoln's Inn—comprised what later lawyers termed the third university of England (Baker, "Learning Exercises in the Medieval Inns of Court and Chancery" 7). Fortescue's description of the education provided in the inns is vague. But he implies that they had become more than a school of law, a kind of "finishing school" for the upwardly mobile young bourgeois:

In these greater inns, indeed, and also in the lesser, there is, besides a school of law, a kind of academy of all the manners that the nobles learn. There they learn to sing and to exercise themselves in every kind of harmonics. They are also taught there to practise dancing and all games proper for nobles, as those brought up in the king's household are accustomed to practise. In the vacations most of them apply themselves to the study of legal science, and at festivals to the reading, after the divine services, of Holy Scripture and of the chronicles. (Fortescue 119)

In other words, apart from the hands-on experience the apprentices received in the law courts when they were in session, by the middle of the fourteenth century, when the courts were in recess, apprentices were also engaged in the "study of legal science" at the inns. The essence of this study was the participation in legal exercises designed to reinforce what they learned about pleading and law from the crib. These exercises consisted of taking part in moots and readings. During moots, apprentices were given a legal crux and asked to argue what law solved it. Readings were performed by expert lawyers who lectured on statutes like the Magna Carta by explicating them phrase by phrase (Brand 112). If readings were part of the educational curriculum of the inns in the fourteenth century, then Chaucer's observation about his Man of Law that "every statut koude he pleyn by rote" ("General Prologue" 327) may not be as hyperbolic as it appears. Instead it may describe the fact that experienced lawyers were called on to explicate statutes line by line for the educational benefit of apprentices.

To augment the readings and moots, apprentices could turn to central treatises on the common law. Two important *summa* of the common law were *Glanvill,* a twelfth-century treatise, and Bracton's thirteenth-century *De legibus et consuetudinibus Angliae.* Apprentices also seem to have been responsible for the compilation of yearbooks, the records of pleadings, and pronouncements from the bench in the court of common pleas (Brand 111).

Apprentices were not always confined to the crib of the court of common pleas or limited to exercising their blossoming legal expertise in moots (Simpson 250). At some stage in their career, students in the inns of court became actual pleaders. One theory accounting for the rise of the inns of courts posits that at first the inns were merely residence halls for provincial attorneys who needed a place to stay while conducting business with the central courts (Dawson 30–32; Ives 17–19). These attorneys were called apprentices, and they were permitted to plead in all of the courts of Westminster but the court of common pleas, where only sergeants could plead (Ives 17–18). As the fourteenth century progressed, the inns took on the task of educating aspiring lawyers, and "apprentice" came to denote both student and practitioner.

If the Man of Law's legal career were to be charted, then, he would have begun as an apprentice-at-law learning the art of pleading and argumentation from the crib. Were he a member of one of the inns of court, he might also have participated in the earliest versions of the learning exercises. He probably also began pleading in other Westminster courts, establishing the reputation that would eventually earn him promotion to sergeant. His companion on the pilgrimage seems to have taken another career track, but one that also involves the law. Among his many titles is that of *countour*. Unlike the Man of Law, a sergeant, whose professional status at law was fairly well defined, the Franklin, it seems, was a member of that larger, amorphous group of men who worked the provincial courts, holding themselves out to be experts in the law—apparently to great profit.

In his 1598 edition, Thomas Speght included a biography that reported that Chaucer had been a member of one of the inns of court, the Inner Temple (Hornsby 8). If so, he would have had first-hand knowledge of the training that went into the making of his Man of Law. Unfortunately, Speght's evidence is flimsy, and no fourteenth-century documentation exists to support this legend. Nevertheless, the tantalizing possibility remains that Chaucer's portrait of the Man of Law benefits from a more intimate perspective on that profession than do the portraits of the other pilgrims.

After serving an apprenticeship in the law under the supervision of the justices of the common law courts and the lawyers who practiced therein, if one had sufficiently distinguished himself, he might become one of an elite group of lawyers nominated by the king or his council to assume the coif and robes of sergeant-at-law. The nomination would come in the form of a writ from the king ordering the nominee to prepare himself to assume the title and status of sergeant. Baker translates one of the earliest writs calling an apprentice to take the degree of sergeant. Found in the fifteenth-century formulary of Thomas Hoccleve, it reflects both the esteem and the expanded professional horizons conferred by the elevation. It also indicates the immediate financial distress that would occur if the apprentice declined the call (Baker, *The Order of Serjeants at Law* 28).

The king etc. to our good friend A. de B., apprentice of the law, greetings! Forasmuch as we have ordered by the advice of our council that you amongst others should give gold and at (such a time) next coming should before our justices of the Common Bench take the estate of serjeant, in order to plead before our said justices in the said Bench and in all our other courts whatsoever for all who wish to plead therein: We firmly charge you to prepare yourself and make ready to give the gold and take the estate of serjeant, as above, at the aforesaid time. And this in no wise omit, upon the faith and allegiance that you owe to us and upon pain of 100s. which we shall cause to be levied to our use from your lands and goods if you should do contrary to this our command. (Baker 28)

The writ clearly notes the change in estate from apprentice to sergeant bestowed by the king, as well as the right to plead before the common bench and all other courts. It also alludes to one of the first rituals established to mark the passing into sergeantry: the giving of gold rings to the host of worthies present at the investiture ceremony. This sometimes meant that the new sergeant had to distribute hundreds of rings (Baker 94–96). That ritual, combined with the robes he would receive at the investiture and the grand week-long feast he and the other new sergeants were to provide the lords and lawyers who cared to partake, meant that the honor bestowed on the new sergeants was a costly one. When Fortescue became a sergeant in the fifteenth century, his creation ceremony cost him around 266 pounds, with 50 pounds going for rings, 50 pounds for liveries, and the rest marking his contribution to the feast (Baker 99; see also Fortescue 121–127). It is no small wonder that occasionally someone tapped to take on the rank of sergeant would desperately seek to avoid the honor. Such an enormous expenditure at the outset, however, particularly the giving of gold, prefigured the great return on his investment that the sergeant hoped to receive over the course of his career (Baker 95).

Before placing Chaucer's Man of Law definitively in this elite fraternity, we must remember that the term *sergeant* was somewhat unsettled in the fourteenth century and still could apply to a pleader in another court as well as to the more prestigious king's sergeant (Brand 109, 114). Arguably, then, the Man of Law could be a common sergeant like Ralph Stode who practiced in the city courts of London, or a sergeant of the king who practiced in the king's courts. Chaucer's life records indicate that he was acquainted with both, and both kinds of sergeants could serve as justices in assize as did Chaucer's lawyer. In recognizing this ambiguity, Jill Mann notes that Chaucer's lawyer's credentials are somewhat exaggerated. Thus he has attributes associated with both lawyers and judges, enabling broad comment on the legal profession (86–87).

But the aggregate details of the Man of Law's portrait seem to confirm his status as king's sergeant-at-law. The place where he entertains clients, the "Parvys," and his parti-colored robes imply the status of king's sergeant. We are told in the "General Prologue" that he "often hadde been at the Parvys" (310) and that "He rood but hoomly in a medlee cote, / Girt with a ceint of silk, with barres smale" (328–329) ["He rode but simply in a parti-colored coat, / Encircled with a belt of silk, with small stripes"]. Most commentators take "Parvys" to refer to the portico in front of St. Paul's Cathedral (*The Riverside Chaucer* 811, n. 310). Baker notes that according to tradition each new sergeant was assigned a pillar in St. Paul's Cathedral where he could consult

with clients. He then suggests that the "Parvys" was probab.   nnaded
north aisle" of the Cathedral (Baker 101–102). Wherever thὲ   ·ation
of the "Parvys" in the Cathedral, it is generally agreed that th\   ·s to
the place where each sergeant conducted business. Like his   he
"Parvys," his robes singled him out and symbolized the status ⌐
Medieval versions of the "power suit" worn to court by today's law.
colored robes were worn by sergeants-at-law in the fourteenth century
of their profession (Baker, *The Order of Serjeants at Law* 74). Genera
cloaks were made of two different cloths with the right side being of onὲ ⌐pe
and hue and the left side being of a contrasting type and hue. According to
Baker, blue and green were generally the colors marking a sergeant's cloak. But
the sergeant pictured in the Ellesmere manuscript of the *Canterbury Tales* wears
a red coat with contrasting blue rays (Baker 74). The motley attire of Chaucer's
Man of Law signifies far more than its "hoomly" appearance might suggest: it
is an advertisement for his exalted place in his profession.

The Man of Law's mastery of the finer points of land law and draftsmanship
also implicitly links him to the order of sergeants. Sergeants often traded on
their expertise in land law to increase their own landholdings (Ives 285–307).
Conveniently, the Man of Law is an expert conveyancer of land: "So greet a
purchasour was nowher noon: / Al was fee symple to hym in effect; / His
purchasyng myghte nat been infect" ("General Prologue" 318–320) ["So great
a land buyer was nowhere none: / All were unrestricted possession to him in
effect; / His buying might not be invalidated"]. Not surprisingly, the English
legal profession was born out of the land law as formulas for pleading in cases
became increasingly more complex (Brand 36–42). This was especially true of
disputes concerning possession of real property. Different types of actions to
regain property required different forms of writs to instigate the lawsuit, while
at trial subtle pleading formalities had to be observed to keep the lawsuit in
play. Laymen inexperienced in the art of pleading found it impossible to negotiate the maze of pleadings and counterpleadings. To fill the gap of experience
formed by the law's burgeoning complexity, there arose a professional group of
pleaders who made it their business to master the forms of actions and pleadings
and then speak for the untrained litigant in court—for a fee. Brand points out
that one of the complications in lawsuits to recover land wrongly taken from a
lawyer's client was that the plea had to precisely match the facts alleged in the
writ instigating the lawsuit. This meant that when he made his plea, the party
claiming a "right" to property had to recount all of the ancestors through which
his right to the party descended (Brand 38–39). By necessity, then, it was crucial
that a pleader plead not only the correct line of descent, but also that the property
was held in fee simple. Hypothetically, he might have to trace the claim all the
way back to the time of William the Conqueror. Chaucer's Man of Law's expertise in property law, his ability to deliver an impeccable title of possession
to land, and his extensive knowledge of case law reaching all the way to the

time of "kyng William" ("General Prologue" 324) reflects the historical origins of his profession.

Novae Narrationes, a thirteenth-century formulary containing forms for pleadings responding to different writs, has a wealth of examples attesting to the complexities involved in correctly counting or responding to a count. One lengthy example of a pleading on a writ of right, arguing that a client had been wrongly dispossessed of a tract of land, demonstrates the complexities involved in counting when the line of descent for title to land had to be traced back through many generations:

Walter de Freland, by his attorney who is here, lays before you this: that Richard Bremel who is there by attorney, wrongfully deforces him of the manor of Folham [here follows a detailed account of the appurtances to that manor]. And wrongfully because it is his right and his heritage, and of it a certain ancestor of his, Adam by name, was seised in his demesne as of fee and of right, in time of peace, in the reign of king Richard, cousin of the present king Edward [here follows a detailed list of the homage and rents taken in the granting of land]. From Adam the right of the tenements aforesaid, excepting the exceptions, descended and ought to descend to Abraham as to his son and heir. From Abraham the right descended and ought to descend to Alice as to daughter and heir. From Alice because she died without heir of her body, the right resorted and ought to resort to Isaac as to uncle and heir brother of Abraham [who was] the father of Alice. From Isaac because etc. the right descended and ought to descend to Jacob as to brother and heir. From Jacob because he left the world and took religious habit in the order of friars minor at London, in which order he was professed by which demise and profession without heir of his body, the right descended and ought to descend to Katherine, Joan, and Rose as to three sisters and one heir. (*Novae Narrationes* 144–145)

So far the pleading has followed a detailed but simple and linear pattern of descent. Now, however, the path of descent that must be traced in the count becomes more convoluted. Although the three sisters take as one heir, for purposes of descent, each has a one-third share in the property. When one sister dies without an heir, then her share effectively reverts to the other sisters, giving them an equal share of the property. When one of those two sisters enters a convent with an heir, her share descends to that heir. Keeping track of who had what share when could be extremely challenging. Moreover, one mistake in tracing the chain of descent fouls the count's initial assertion of the litigant's right to the property.

From Katherine, because she died without heir of her body, the right of her share descended to Joan and Rose as to sisters and heir. From Joan, because she left the world and became a nun at St. Ellen of London and was there professed, by which demise and profession the right of her share descended etc. to W. as to son and heir. From W. the right of his share descended etc. to Mabel as to daughter and heir. From Mabel because etc. [the right] of her share etc. resorted etc. to Rose as to cousin and heir, sister of Joan, [who was] mother of W. [who was] father of Mabel. From Rose because etc. [the right] of the whole [resorted] to Joram as to cousin and heir, brother of W. [who was] father of A. [who was] father of Adam [who was] father of Rose. From Joram [the right] descended to Richard as to son and heir. From Richard [the right] descended etc. to Gregory as to son and heir. From Gregory the right descended etc. to Walter as to son and heir who now demands. And that such is the right of Walter, he has suit and good proof. (*Novae Narrationes* 145)

In following the pattern of descent, the counter has had to count forward and backward over the generations. Once Joan's heirs run out with Mabel's death, then the whole share and right reverts back to Rose. But because she dies without issue, the right reverts to the closest living relative, who happens to be her great uncle—or cousin as the plea designates him—Joram the brother of W., Rose's great grandfather. Once settled in Joram the line of descent flows linearly to Walter, the current claimant. Keeping in mind that this entire performance was oral, before opposing counsel eager to leap on any misstep, and ready with a counter plea offering another account of the line of descent and right to possession, one must bow to the discipline of the memory required to flawlessly plead a case. Remember also that the example above is only the first step in pleading the case. In light of the vast amount of data a pleader had to marshall in counting a case, the claim that the Man of Law knew all of the "termes" ("General Prologue" 323) or yearbooks from King William's day to his is not as exaggerated as it might seem (Eberle 28; Wentersdorf).

Expertise in land law and the techniques of acquiring unencumbered possession of land also helped most sergeants acquire estates in land for themselves and thus begin to recoup the costs of their investiture ceremonies. Henry and Geoffrey Scrope, pleaders in the court of common pleas in the early thirteenth century, were able to add significantly to their family estates by loaning money to neighbors, securing those loans with the neighbor's property, and then seizing that property when the loan was forfeited. Geoffrey seems to have manipulated legal procedure to quash an inquiry into one such seizure (Vale 99). The fifteenth-century sergeant Thomas Kebell also acquired a sizable personal estate through his mastery of the intricacies involved in securing clear title to land (Ives 285–307). Expertise in property law, no doubt, helped William Paston increase his family estates during the course of his career as lawyer too (Barber 13).

Of course, it was not just through his ability to negotiate his way through the labyrinth of feudal encumbrances and potential claimants to land that a sergeant earned his "fees and robes" ("General Prologue" 318). Baker points out that being named sergeant virtually lifted one into the ranks of the nobility (*The Order of the Serjeants at Law* 49). Indeed, the social presence conferred by the title "sergeant" is captured in the opening lines of the Man of Law's portrait: he was a "Sergeant of the Lawe, war and wys," "ful riche of excellence," "Discreet," "and of greet reverence" ("General Prologue" 309, 311–312). This was the cachet that a sergeant traded on and that his clients depended on.

King's sergeants could take on other clients, but their first allegiance was to the king and to prior clients. A sergeant's clientele could be diverse. He might serve as one among several lawyers retained by a magnate or seigneurial household. In addition, ecclesiastical authorities and monastic orders regularly retained sergeants to handle matters of secular law. Towns and other corporate bodies also required legal representation. Finally, his clientele might range through the mercantile class to members of his own profession (Ives 131). The financial arrangements between sergeant and client would vary. Sergeants often were retained for life by a client. In this situation, the sergeant was generally paid an annual pension in exchange for representing that client in court or providing legal advice when the need arose (Brand 100–105). But they also could be compensated by grants of life estates in land or robes. Dyer estimates that the annual income of a sergeant was around 300 pounds (47). The retainer fee generally fell between 20 and 40 shillings per annum (Brand 100–101). Along with pleading and representing a litigant in court, their legal activities were diverse. Sergeants supervised conveyances of property that did not involve litigation, drafted legal documents like wills, obligations, indentures, contracts, and deeds for clients, settled estates, and served as arbitrators in disputes. Some sergeants went so far, as we have seen with the Scropes, as to lend money to secure property; or to put it in a darker light, some sergeants were usurers (Ives 115–146).

By virtue of being the king's sergeants, they also were expected to go about the business of preserving the king's law. In this respect, sergeants routinely performed significant service in a wide array of judicial capacities. The editors of *Chaucer Life-Records* traced the judicial careers of the six sergeants who served with Chaucer as justice of the peace in Kent from 1385 to 1389: Robert Belknap, Walter Clopton, David Hanmer, William Rickhill, Robert Tresilian and William Brenchley. The list of judicial commissions these men presided over during their careers is extensive: it included not only justice of peace, but also "justice of assize, justice of jail delivery, justice of oyer and terminer, justice *ad inquirendum,* justice to supress rebels, justice in eyre, justice of array &c" (*Chaucer Life-Records* 361). Each of these men also became justice in either the king's bench or the court of common pleas.

J. M. Manly speculated that Chaucer makes a pun on the name of another sergeant, Thomas Pynchbek, in his description of the Man of Law's consummate skill at drafting unimpugnable legal documents: "Ther koude no wight pynche at his writyng" ("General Prologue" 326; Manly 150–157) ["There could no man find a flaw in his writing"]. Pynchbek might have been the inspiration for Chaucer's portrait of a common lawyer. Chaucer may have even had a score to settle with Pynchbek; as justice of the court of the exchequer, he issued a writ to arrest Chaucer for debt (*Life-Records* 386). To cement the connection he made between Pynchbek and Chaucer's Man of Law, Manly reported that Pynchbek purchased a great deal of land while sergeant (153). Conceivably, the account of the Man of Law's uncommon ability to deliver clean title for every piece of property he handled was directed at Pynchbek to insinuate that he manipulated land law for his own enrichment ("General Prologue" 318–320). Chaucer's experience with sergeants, however, was sufficiently broad so that no one lawyer need be singled out as the model for his lawyer.

The other judicial functions performed by sergeants, apart from their exclusive role as pleaders in the court of common pleas, indicate that they played an important part in maintaining English law throughout the realm. Their active service on behalf of the king's justice also argues that they did much more than simply use their privileged position to enrich themselves. As the list quoted from *Chaucer's Life-Records* attests, sergeants were busy pleading in or presiding over a wide array of courts. At Westminster, they could be found in any of the king's courts: the court hearing civil matters, the court of common pleas, or the court adjudicating criminal matters, the king's bench. But, as Caxton's list indicates, lawyers might represent litigants at other Westminster courts. The chancery was the chancellor's court, a court of equity instituted to hear matters that could not be brought before the king's courts for want of the necessary writ. The exchequer of pleas was a court of limited jurisdiction that handled matters involving officers of the exchequer and other exchequer personnel responsible for rendering accounts to the exchequer. Debtors to the king could also use that court to recover money owed them so that they in turn could pay their debt to the Crown (Baker, *An Introduction to English Legal History* 57). Litigants might also petition the king to have their case heard directly by the king and his council. Courts grew out of the offices of the various councilors to the king who were called on to settle disputes from time to time. The chancellor, the admiral, and the marshall each had his own court (Baker 113). Outside Westminster, various commissions and inquests were held to hear local civil and criminal matters. Extensions of the king's jurisdiction, these tribunals could be assembled on a regular or ad hoc basis. The most significant of these commissions were the assizes which brought the king's justice to the provinces. The assizes met twice yearly when Westminster courts were recessed. They were broken into six circuits; each circuit was presided over by two justices appointed from the ranks of sergeants of law and king's justices (Baker 25). The terms of the king's commission to the justices determined the scope of their power, but generally assize justices had authority to deliver the gaols ("to try or release prisoners in the gaol specified" in the commission) and to "oyer and terminer" ("to enquire into, hear and determine the offences specified") (Baker 20). To ease the congested dockets of the assizes, local commissions of the peace, like the one Chaucer served on in Kent, were also appointed. These commissions were presided over by "justices" of the peace, local knights, and lawyers, who were empowered to hear matters that otherwise might be brought before the assizes (Baker 29). That king's sergeants were sufficiently skilled in the law both to practice in the king's courts at Westminster and to preside over local commissions is also a testament to their versatility and expertise. Given the number of courts where one might find a sergeant as pleader or justice, it is no wonder that the Man of Law appears to be so busy: "Nowher so bisy a man

as he ther nas, / And yet he semed bisier than he was'' (''General Prologue''
321–322) [''Nowhere so busy a man as he there was not, / And yet he seemed
busier than he was''].

THE TALE

While the ''Man of Law's Tale'' is not explicitly about law, underlying the
tale are assumptions about the interrelation of divine and human law. Those
assumptions may be at the heart of the claim made for the Man of Law in the
''General Prologue'' that ''In termes hadde he caas and doomes alle / That from
the tyme of kynge William were falle'' (''General Prologue'' 323–324). Some
controversy revolves around the plausibility of that claim. The debate centers
around the meaning of the word ''terms'' and whether or not the Man of Law
could possibly have known all of the legal precedents from his day back to the
time of William the Conqueror (Eberle 28). Earlier, I suggested one reason why
this statement might not be a gross exaggeration of his knowledge. But whether
these lines are read as hyperbole or irony, they also disclose something about
memory and the common law that exposes the ideology of common lawyers.
The lines do not characterize just the breadth of the Man of Law's legal knowledge, but also ideas about the origin and authority of the common law. It is
telling that the law the Man of Law knows extends beyond the point of time
legally defined as the limit of legal memory. Statutes of 1275 and 1293 had
fixed 1189, the date of Richard I's coronation, as that limit of legal memory.
Practically speaking, that meant that a litigant did not have to present evidence
from earlier than 1189 to prove his claim (Clanchy 123). Extending beyond that
limit to King William's reign, the Man of Law's memory of law reflects an
assumption that at least by the fifteenth century was a commonplace: that the
common law was as old as time itself.

The historian J.G.A. Pocock has argued that by the sixteenth century common
lawyers accepted as fact the notion that the common law extended as far back
as history, that it was the only law England had known. Not only was it immemorial, but it was peculiarly English (Pocock 30–31). This idea seems to be
part of the mythology developed about the common law and its keepers as soon
as a defined legal profession came into being. This myth emerges in an aside
during an exchange between justice Danby and lawyer John Catesby recorded
in a fifteenth-century yearbook. The question Catesby was arguing before the
justices of the court of common pleas was whether or not that court had jurisdiction over someone affiliated with the court of the king's bench who claimed
that by custom he could be tried only by the king's bench. In discussing Catesby's arguments about the privilege, Danby noted, ''the privilege is beyond
the time of memory, and as old as the common law.'' In response Catesby
observed, ''common law has existed since the creation of the world'' (*Year
Books of Edward IV* 38). This fiction about the antiquity of the common law
proposes an originary myth that proved quite valuable to the legal profession in

England: it made lawyers privy to a mysterious, unwritten truth, one whose survival was owed to a dutiful legal profession that shepherded that truth along the generations. In locating the underpinnings of the common law in an ideology constituted from notions about memory, Peter Goodrich observes that "where legal memory is genuinely a question of time out of mind or of time immemorial, it is language which is exemplary of the unwritten inscription of things and thereby stands for or symbolises the origin of things" (Goodrich 42). "Such a practice of memory refused even to contemplate the possibility of a theory of memory not because it lacked a past but because its memories were not the memories of man, of the lifeworld or of a lived history and language, but rather they were those of a sacred presence or of an eternal and mythic continuity of the spirit, the breath and voice of divine reason and natural law" (Goodrich 50). The common law then was inextricably bound with the sacred. Passing down the law over time, preserving the common law, was preservation not of something secular but something divine. "Memory in the hands of the legal tradition is not an historical method but rather a technique of faith: through the recollection of previous instances of legal presence, through establishment of precedent, the law continuously rediscovers itself; it is made present to itself as *logos* or the word incarnate. Memory within such a rigorously internal history of a discipline is simply the witness of presence, the testimony of authority, the repetition of externally given truths" (Goodrich 50). The common lawyer's role was a sacred duty then, making the common lawyers a priesthood that preserved the sacred spirit of the common law.

The "Man of Law's Tale" takes place before England was Christianized. By situating his tale beyond the limit of legal memory, in time immemorial, the Man of Law can subtly insinuate the connection between the common law and divine law, and by extension assert the divine office of those who are entrusted with keeping the memory of that law alive, the common lawyers. Implicitly, those who are the elite of the profession, the judges and sergeants, through their expertise in the common law are privy as well to the mysteries of God's law. That assumption is registered in the tale in two ways: First, in the tale's relentless promotion of the absoluteness of divine law; and second, in the various references to legal procedure, references which demonstrate that God's law and the common law are one.

When he asks the Man of Law to tell his tale, Harry Bailly acknowledges that lawyers are in a unique position to sustain the social order because of their exclusive access to the foundations of that order, the mysteries of law (see Patterson 280–281). The lawyer's response to the Host's request that he keep his promise and tell a tale subtly exposes his own assumptions about the law. He replies, "Bihest is dette" ("Prologue to the Man of Law's Tale" 41)—"A promise ought to be kept." The Host's law, to tell a tale when called on, like the common law, is absolute and must be strictly followed. His tale concerns itself with the virtues of obediently submitting to the law of the Father and of the father. The tale is about the travails of Custance, who time and again submits to the will of either God or her own father, despite the apparent dangers she is subjected to because of her abject obedience. Initially, her father marries her to a heathen in hopes of converting him. The marriage accomplishes this, but her jealous mother-in-law has all the Christians at the wedding murdered and sets Custance adrift in a rudderless boat.

Traveling under God's protection, she winds up in Northumberland. Here the Man of Law infuses his tale with elements from early common law. In doing so, he neatly links English law and God's law. During her stay in Northumberland, Custance rebukes the amorous advances of a knight. To spite her, the knight murders Custance's friend and protector, Hermengyld, and frames Custance for the murder by placing the murder weapon, a knife, in her bed. The procedural details of her trial are based on those for an appeal of felony—the procedure for bringing someone to trial for the commission of a felony. The Man of Law alludes to three elements of the appeal: the appeal or accusation, the oath attesting to the truth of that appeal, and trial by battle (Hornsby 145). When Custance is brought before the king, the knight appeals and accuses her of the murder. "This false knyght, that hath this tresoun wroght, / Berth hire on hond that she hath doon thys thyng" ("Man of Law's Tale" 619–620) ["This false knight, that has this treason wrought, / Accuses her falsely that she has done this thing"]. Next, the Man of Law alludes to trial by battle when he acknowledges that Christ is Custance's only hope. Battle was the mode of proof for determining the guilt or innocence of the appellee. "Allas! Custance, thou hast no champioun, / Ne fighte kanstow noght, so weylaway! / But he that starf for our redempcioun, / And boond Sathan (and yet lith ther he lay), / So be thy stronge champion this day!" (631–635) ["Alas! Custance, you have no champion, / Nor fight can you not, so alas! / But he that died for our redemption, / And bound Satan (and lying there he lies still), / So be your strong champion today!"]. The trial never makes it to that ultimate step, because when the knight swears to the proof of his accusation, the step in the proceedings immediately prior to battle, his falseness is exposed in a graphic demonstration of the efficacy of modes of proof based on oaths.

> A Britoun book, written with Evaungiles,
> Was fet, and on this book he swoor anoon
> She gilty was, and in the meene whiles
> An hand hym smoot upon the nekke-boon,
> That doun he fil atones as a stoon,
> And bothe his eyen broste out of his face
> In sighte of every body in that place.
>
> (666–672)

> [A British book, written with the Gospels,
> Was fetched, and on this book he swore at once
> She guilty was, and in the meanwhile
> A hand him smote on the neck-bone,

That down he fell at once as a stone,
And both his eyes burst out of his face
In sight of everybody in that place.]

The king, Alla, impressed by this dramatic display of God's justice and Custance's innocence converts to Christianity and marries her (Hornsby 146–147).

When Alla is away seeing to the affairs of his realm, Custance delivers their child. But the king's mother, Donegild, intercepts the birth announcement to her son and, in hopes that the king will reject both wife and son, substitutes for it the message that the child is deformed because the mother was an elf. When the king accepts the birth, his mother forges a letter in his name to the constable instructing him to send both mother and child out to sea. The language of the letter echoes that of common law writs, essentially letters of instruction from the king to local authorities commanding them to restore justice.

> "The king comandeth his constable anon,
> Up peyne of hangyng, and on heigh juyse,
> That he ne sholde suffren in no wyse
> Custance in-with his reawme for t'abyde
> Thre dayes and o quarter of a tyde;
>
> But in the same ship as he hire fond,
> Hire, and hir yonge sone, and al hir geere,
> He sholde putte, and croude hire fro the lond,
> And charge hire that she never eft coome theere."

                                                      (794–802)

> ["The king commanded his constable immediately,
> On pain of hanging, and on high judicial sentence,
> That she should suffer in no way
> Custance within his realm for to abide
> Three days and a quarter of a tide;
>
> But in the same ship as he found her,
> Her, and her young son, and all her gear,
> He should put, and push her from the land,
> And command her that she never again come there."]

Having provoked yet another jealous mother-in-law, Custance is set adrift again. When Alla discovers the fraud, he puts his mother to death because "she traitour was to hire ligeance" (895). Here the Man of Law alludes to the essential element defining the crime of treason, the violation of the bond of fealty between subject and king. Donegild's betrayal of Custance naturally violates that political bond. Moreover, her forged letter to the constable is evidence of two of the acts proscribed by the Statute of Treasons of 1352: imagining the death of the queen and counterfeiting the king's seal (Hornsby 142). The letter, forged under the king's imprint, masquerades as being authenticated by the king; in the process it authorizes the setting adrift, a virtual death sentence, of his queen. Treason was a hybrid of felony, the first significant crime defined by the common law. This creation of a class of crimes that violate the king's peace also marks the beginning of the king's law. The key element of a felony, as with treason, was violation of the faith one owed to one's feudal lord. Notably, the knight's false accusation of Custance is referred to as "tresoun" (619). He commits an act of moral treason against the king's law and Custance when he falsely swears to her guilt.

The forms of law invoked in this part of the "Man of Law's Tale" confirm the inviolable link between good law and God's law. The tale asserts that law is the mechanism by which truth is preserved and fraud punished, and God is an active participant in helping the law police the truth. Notably, the law of the "Man of Law's Tale" is the common law. Its divinity is insisted on not just in the way God works through it, but also in the law's central role in ensuring that Britain was Christianized. While Custance brings the faith with her, it is the power of that faith through law—the miracle of the knight's punishment as a result of his false oath—that is the catalyst for Alla's conversion (see Kolve 297–371). Even while in the safekeeping of heathen rulers, the law remained God's instrument. In this way, the "Man of Law's Tale" dramatically attests to the divine origins of the common law, and perhaps as well to that of his profession.

Chaucer's portrait of the Man of Law in the "General Prologue" is a snapshot of a profession in the making. It catches the English common lawyer at the point when he is beginning to define himself as one whose sole practice was in the common law of the king, whether at the king's courts as pleader or presiding over the king's judicial commissions. The common lawyer is just beginning to set himself apart from others claiming legal ability, a distinction implied in the pairing of the Franklin and the Man of Law in the "General Prologue." When the "Man of Law's Tale" is combined with the details of his portrait, we catch a glimpse of the common lawyer's mindset. Part of that mindset is a confidence in the crucial role law and lawyers play in society, a confidence that over the centuries grew into an arrogance that would provoke a character in another famous poet's work to suggest that the world would be a better place if all lawyers were dead.

REFERENCES

Baker, J. H. *An Introduction to English Legal History*. 3rd ed. London: Butterworths, 1990.

———. *Readings and Moots at the Inns of Court in the Fifteenth Century,* Vol. II. London: Selden Society, 1990.

———. "Learning Exercises in the Medieval Inns of Court and Chancery." *The Legal Profession and the Common Law*. London: Hambledon Press, 1986. Pp. 7–23.

———. "The Legal Profession, 1450–1550." *The Legal Profession and the Common Law*. London: Hambledon Press, 1986. Pp. 75–98.

————. *The Order of Serjeants at Law.* Selden Soc. Supplemental Series, Vol. 5. London: Selden Society, 1984.

Brand, Paul. *The Origins of the English Legal Profession.* Oxford: Blackwell, 1992.

Chaucer Life-Records. Eds. M. M. Crow and C. C. Olson. Oxford: Clarendon Press, 1966.

Clanchy, M. T. *From Memory to Written Record, England, 1066–1307.* Cambridge, Mass.: Harvard University Press, 1979.

Dawson, J. P. *The Oracles of the Law.* 1968. Rpt. Westport, Conn.: Greenwood Press, 1978.

Delasanta, Rodney. "Chaucer and Strode." *Chaucer Review* 26 (1991): 205–218.

Dyer, Christopher. *Standards of Living in the Later Middle Ages.* Cambridge: Cambridge University Press, 1989.

Eberle, Patricia J. "Crime and Justice in the Middle Ages: Cases from the *Canterbury Tales* of Geoffrey Chaucer." *Rough Justice: Essays on Crime in Literature.* Ed. J. L. Friedland. Toronto: University of Toronto Press, 1991. Pp. 19–51.

Fortescue, Sir John. *De laudibus legum anglie.* Ed. and Trans. S. B. Chrimes. Cambridge: Cambridge University Press, 1942.

Goodrich, Peter. *The Languages of Law.* London: Weidenfeld and Nicolson, 1990.

Hornsby, Joseph. *Chaucer and the Law.* Norman, Okla.: Pilgrim Books, 1988.

Ives, E. W. *The Common Lawyers of Pre-Reformation England.* Cambridge: Cambridge University Press, 1983.

Kolve, V. A. *Chaucer and the Imagery of Narrative.* Stanford, Calif.: Stanford University Press, 1984.

Lyon, Bryce. *A Constitutional and Legal History of Medieval England.* 2nd ed. New York: W. W. Norton, 1980.

Manly, J. M. *Some New Light on Chaucer.* Rpt. Gloucester, Mass.: Peter Smith, 1959.

Mann, J. *Chaucer and Medieval Estates Satire.* Cambridge: Cambridge University Press, 1973.

The Pastons. Ed. Richard Barber. New York: Viking Penguin, 1984.

Patterson, Lee. *Chaucer and the Subject of History.* Madison: University of Wisconsin Press, 1991.

Pocock, J. G. A. *The Ancient Constitution and the Feudal Law.* Reissued. Cambridge: Cambridge University Press, 1987.

Postan, M. M. *The Medieval Economy and Society.* Berkeley: University of California Press, 1972.

Ramsay, Nigel. "What Was the Legal Profession." *Profit, Piety and the Professions in Later Medieval England.* Ed. Michael Hicks. Gloucester: Alan Sutton Publishing, 1990. Pp. 62–71.

Readings and Moots at the Inns of Court in the Fifteenth Century. Vol. II. Eds. S. E. Thorne and J. H. Baker. Selden Society, Vol. 105. London: Selden Society, 1989.

The Riverside Chaucer. 3rd ed. Gen. Ed. Larry D. Benson. Boston: Houghton Mifflin Co., 1987.

Robinson, F. N., ed. *The Works of Geoffrey Chaucer.* Boston: Houghton Mifflin Co., 1990.

Select Cases in the Court of the King's Bench under Richard II, Henry IV and Henry V. Vol. VII. Ed. G. O. Sayles. Selden Society, Vol. 88. London: Bernard Quaritch, 1971.

Simpson, A.W.B. "The Early Constitution of the Inns of Court." *Legal Theory and Legal History*. London: Hambledon Press, 1987. Pp. 17–32.

Vale, Brigette. "The Profits of the Law and the 'Rise' of the Scropes: Henry Scrope (d. 1335) and Geoffrey Scrope (d. 1340) Chief Justices to Edward II and Edward III." *Profit, Piety and the Professions in Later Medieval England*. Ed. Michael Hicks. Gloucester: Alan Sutton Publishing, 1990. Pp. 91–102.

Wentersdorf, K. P. "The *Termes* of Chaucer's Sergeant of Law." *Studia Neophilologica* 53 (1981): 269–274.

Year Books of Edward IV. 10 Edward IV and 49 Henry VI. A.D. 1470. Ed. N. Neilson. Selden Society, Vol. 47. London: Quaritch, 1931.

Year Books of Richard II, 2 Richard II, 1378–79. Ed. M. S. Arnold. London: Ames Foundation, 1975.

Chapter 12

A Frankeleyn Was In His Compaignye

ELIZABETH MAUER SEMBLER

Little can be said with surety about the franklins of fourteenth-century England. Historical, social, and literary scholars have disputed with each other for at least the last century about the role and place of franklins in late medieval English society. But this much is certain: the franklins, by definition, were freeholders; that is, they held their lands free of military and labor obligations to their respective lords. The term *franklin,* then, refers not to a professional classification but to a legal one, applicable during feudal times but obsolete now.

The questions arise when scholars attempt to determine the social position, the rank in the hierarchy, of medieval franklins. Were franklins considered in their time to be part of the landed gentry? Or were they ranked just below that class and thus not numbered among the ''gentils''? If we turn to two standard dictionaries for an answer, we are disappointed, for even here there is no agreement. The applicable entry in *The Oxford English Dictionary* for ''franklin'' reads: ''A freeholder; in 14–15th c. the designation of a class of landowners, of free but not noble birth, and ranking next below the gentry'' (6: 148). But the entry in the *Middle English Dictionary* reads: ''A landowner and member of the gentry ranking immediately below the nobility; a freeman, a gentleman'' (3: 860).

This lack of consensus on the social status of franklins troubles literary critics in particular, who wish to better understand Chaucer's Franklin and the tale he tells on the pilgrimage. Because the Franklin seems to place an emphasis on ''gentillesse,'' a quality supposedly exclusive to the ''gentle'' classes, many Chaucer critics argue that the Franklin is preoccupied in this way because he is insecure about his own social rank and ''gentillesse.'' These critics thus interpret the portrait of the Franklin and his tale satirically. Other critics argue that the

Franklin is completely secure in his social position. As Mary J. Carruthers writes in "The Gentilesse of Chaucer's Franklin,"

> Clearly the Franklin is an important man, but whether his function in the tale is satiric or idealized, whether he is to be regarded as a moral blockhead or a wise counsellor especially of the verbal extravagant young Squire, is a matter of irreconcilable critical disagreement. (283)

This critical disagreement is based in part on the lack of definitive historical information on the exact status and role of the franklins in late fourteenth-century England. In fact, some of the historical scholars who raise questions about the status of franklins, while they refer extensively to historical documents to present their case, also rely on Chaucer's portrait of a franklin to draw their conclusions.

In his book *English Villagers of the Thirteenth Century,* George Caspar Homans writes that the franklins of that century were of the highest of three classes of villagers, ranked above cotters and husbonds. The franklin paid rent for his land but was free of military obligations and labor services to his lord. The franklin might be called upon by his manorial lord, however, to represent his manor's interests at various legal sessions, including the courts of the hundred and shire. And the franklin might also be asked by the lord to supervise at the harvest of the crops (242–250). Writes Homans, "In short, there is good evidence that in rural England in the thirteenth century a small class of freeholders existed, less wealthy than the gentry, more wealthy than the husbonds and cotters, and that these men were called franklins" (250). Yet Homans, when discussing the franklins of the fourteenth century, refers only to Chaucer's Franklin to make his point: "In the century to come, if we can judge from Chaucer's franklin, members of this class throve and gained much wealth and power" (250).

N. Denholm-Young, in *The Country Gentry in the Fourteenth Century,* places franklins below the gentry in rank. And yet he mitigates his position with a reference to Chaucer's Franklin:

> [W]e are told [Denholm-Young does not specify by whom or where] that the franklins are the class immediately below the gentry and in the poll-tax for the West Riding of Yorkshire of 1379 the franklins are assessed at 3s. 4d. and the knights at 20s. So the franklin is "one sixth of a knight." Yet Chaucer's Franklin had sat in Parliament and had been sheriff. By blood to gentility or chivalry they might (at any rate when on pilgrimage) be socially acceptable. (24)

R. H. Hilton, in his book *The English Peasantry in the Later Middle Ages,* also refers to Chaucer's Franklin in his discussion of the rank. But while he echoes the apparent contradiction noted by Denholm-Young between the historical evidence and Chaucer's portrait, he does not use it to weaken his own position;

instead, he declares Chaucer's literary portrait "rather misleading." Hilton places the Franklin squarely in the peasant upper stratum, along with the yeoman and demesne farmer, but he notes that, contradictorily, Chaucer's description of his Franklin's political and social role, as well as his way of life, puts him firmly among the country gentry (25–27).

The "General Prologue" of the *Canterbury Tales* tells us much about the social and political role and way of life of one particular, fictitious franklin. Whether that information should then be used to draw conclusions about the whole class of fourteenth-century franklins is open to debate. Nonetheless, Chaucer does sketch this one franklin vividly. We are given first in the "General Prologue" a physical description of the man, with his white beard and sanguine temperament. Next, Chaucer devotes twenty-one lines to describing the Franklin's love of food and his gracious hospitality. Chaucer then ends the portrait (along with the details of the Franklin's dagger and purse) with a list of the administrative positions that the Franklin has held. These concluding lines of the portrait are troublesome to both historical and literary scholars and relate directly to the question of the Franklin's social status. Would a man of the Franklin's rank be chosen for these jobs?

> At sessiouns ther was he lord and sire;
> Ful ofte tyme he was knyght of the shire;
>
> . . . .
> A shirreve hadde he been, and a contour.

(I (A) 355–359)

> [At sessions there was he lord and sire;
> Very often times he was knight of the shire;
>
> . . . .
> A sheriff he had been, and an auditor.]

To be "lord and sire" at sessions is to be justice of the peace. In 1368, the powers of the justices of the peace were secured by statute. Justices of the peace were to maintain the peace and determine and inquire into felonies and trespasses (a quorum of lawyers being necessary for the determination of felonies). And they were to inquire into labor laws, weights and measures, and forestalling and regrating. (Forestallers intercepted sellers on the way to market and tried to raise prices artificially; regrators bought goods with the intention to resell them at a higher price in the same market.) By the late fourteenth century, there were eight justices in every county, who were "established as an integral part of the machinery of English justice" (McKisack 202).

The knights of the shire were among the commoners summoned to Parliament. Writs addressed to the sheriffs of all English counties (except Chester and Durham) directed them to organize the election of two knights of every shire, two citizens of every city, and two burgesses from every borough, from among the most able, to come to Parliament (McKisack 187). "Knights of the shire" were not necessarily knights; as May McKisack writes, "From an early date it seems to have been accepted that men of substance in the shire, whether knights or not, were competent to represent it" (188). The elections for Parliament were conducted in the county courts by the sheriff and other substantial county officials. They were not the kind of popular elections that we have today (Robertson 276).

The sheriffs themselves were also responsible for appointing bailiffs to help make arrests and collect revenues. The sheriffs presided over the county courts and the hundred courts, where they could review petty offenses; they summoned jurors for the preliminary sessions of the justices of the peace; they summoned jurors for trial juries; they executed writs; they collected royal revenues, including fines; they made accountings of these revenues to the Exchequer (Robertson 276).

The Franklin's fourth office was "contour." Scholars disagree about what the contour did: some define the word as "accountant" or "auditor" (Benson 29; Robertson 275); Nigel Saul defines it as a pleader in court, or lawyer ("Social Status" 19). The Franklin's immersion in the legal world perhaps led him to the Man of Law, his pilgrimage companion.

At the end of his description of the Franklin in the "General Prologue," Chaucer observes: "Was nowher swich a worthy vavasour" [I (A) 360]. The word "vavasour," like "contour," is obscure. It does not define a legal officer or professional; it indicates that the Franklin was a landowner (Robertson 277). Some scholars have devoted detailed essays to explaining the term. Both Peter Coss and Roy J. Pearcy locate the vavasour in the romance literary tradition. Pearcy describes the Arthurian-romance vavasour, with whom he believes Chaucer's Franklin shares many characteristics:

They are provincials in comparison with knights, who have much closer contact with the royal court. Since vavassors are frequently family men with grown sons and daughters, they are usually old, on occasions explicitly grey-haired patriarchs, and their life style is characterized by settled domesticity, in comparison with knights who are conventionally young and unattached. They are also hospitable, since by providing lodging for knights they are brought into contact with the world of knight-errantry. Finally, they acquire through these standard traits something of a pastoral pundit quality, simplicity and clear-sightedness combining with long years of varied experience to make them trustworthy and wise. (36)

Caroline D. Eckhart, in another of the essays devoted to defining the "vavasour," links the term to the Vavasours, an old family from the West Riding of Yorkshire, and suggests that Chaucer may have in part been drawing on his knowledge of members of this family when he used the word. But, she notes, "at this distance it is difficult to know exactly what the reference implies" (245).

The list of offices that Chaucer's Franklin held—justice of the peace, knight of the shire, sheriff, contour—is used as evidence by some scholars to argue for the Franklin's well-respected place in the social hierarchy of the day. For those who believe that franklins were considered part of the landed gentry, the Franklin's appointment or election to these powerful positions of status and rank is proof for their argument. But historian Nigel Saul read the Franklin's resume differently. He argued that the great majority of sheriffs and justices of the peace in the late fourteenth century were not franklins but knights or very rich esquires. The franklins may have held lesser positions in the county, Saul wrote, perhaps in the commissions appointed to collect parliamentary subsidies.

The [*Canterbury Tales'*] Franklin's record of officeholding is thus a reflection more of his group's aspirations than of the reality of their achievement. A generation or two later the position would be different. Men of the Franklin's condition would indeed be appointed to the peace commissions and picked for shrievalty, for by then they were being gathered within the fold of gentle society. But in the late fourteenth century this time was still some way off. ("Chaucer and Gentility" 46)

For Saul, the Franklin is the one pilgrim in the *Canterbury Tales* whose "position in the pecking order is open to question" (46).

As noted above, it is with this question that Chaucerian scholars have particularly struggled. For many, assessing the Franklin's exact status has been a key element of their interpretation of his tale. By focusing on the emphasis the Franklin puts on gentillesse in his comments to the Squire and in his tale, these scholars argue one of two positions: we are either to take the Franklin seriously as a gentleman expounding on gentillesse and the ideal marriage, as exemplified by Dorigen and Arveragus, or we are to read him as Chaucer's satire of a middle-class social climber who yearns to be considered gentle and tells a tale of gentillesse that is acquired, as in the case of the clerk, not bred, as in the case of Arveragus and Aurelius.

In 1906 Robert Kilburn Root wrote that the Franklin was a "self-made man . . . uncomfortably conscious of a certain lack of 'gentility,' one who is "conscious that, with all that he has acquired and attained, he can never be quite the complete gentleman" (271–272). In 1926, Gordon Hall Gerould argued for the other side, describing the Franklin as rather learned and eminently dignified, a member of a landholding class of very good social position. He examined charters (from the reigns of Henry II and John, the twelfth and early thirteenth centuries), poetry, social documents from the fifteenth century, and Chaucer's portrait of the Franklin. One of the sources he used to illustrate his point was Sir John Fortescue's *De Laudibus Legum Angliae,* a document written between 1463 and 1471. Gerould quoted both the original Latin and a 1775 English translation, which reads in part, "There is scarce a small village in which you may not find a knight, an esquire, or some substantial householder, commonly called a Frankleyne; all men of considerable estates: there are others who are called Freeholders, and many Yeomen of estates sufficient to make a substantial Jury" (270). That Fortescue classified franklins with knights and esquires rather than with freeholders and yeomen led Gerould to conclude, "Franklins were gentlefolk" (270). By including this document, Gerould, it appears, was not disturbed by the fact that it appeared sixty or seventy years after Chaucer died, a time when, as Nigel Saul pointed out (as mentioned above), the franklins were just being "gathered into the fold of gentle society" ("Chaucer and Gentility" 46). As for the Franklin's tale, wrote Gerould, if the Franklin spoke of "gentillesse," it was not because he wanted to prove his immersion in it but rather because "he was at the moment so much impressed by the contrast between the Knight's son and his own" (279).

In his 1955 work *Of Sondry Folk: The Dramatic Principal in the Canterbury Tales,* R. M. Lumiansky argued Root's position. He noted the Franklin's strong desire for social advancement (182) and wrote that these social aspirations "lead him to conduct himself as he thinks befits the nobility" (186).

In 1981, Henrik Specht, perhaps hoping to put the issue to rest, devoted a two-hundred-page book to the subject of the status of franklins in general and Chaucer's in particular, concluding as Gerould did that Chaucer's Franklin was a secure member of the gentry.

In *Chaucer's Franklin in the "Canterbury Tales": The Social and Literary Background of a Chaucerian Character,* Specht drew on legal treatises, manorial records (custumals, surveys, and court rolls), public records (tax returns, the *Rolls of Parliament, Statutes of the Realm*), and chronicles and other literary works. He tried to prove definitively that some, if not many, franklins, including Chaucer's franklin, were considered gentlemen.

Based on his study of legal records, Specht concluded that franklins were substantial freeholders "(which) set them apart both in legal theory and in manorial practice from their unfree neighbors holding in villeinage. Thus they emerged as a fairly independent group with holdings of comfortable size, owing sometimes rent, sometimes services of a relatively light nature" (65). Specht argued for the financial clout of franklins as well and used the 1379 poll tax returns to show that they were on equal terms with almost nine out of every ten esquires (88).

When assessing the franklins' social status, Specht grouped many franklins among the "gentles," as opposed to the "churls." The distinction between these two groups, Specht argued, was the most significant social distinction in the fourteenth-century society, even more significant than the division between the three estates (clergy, military, and labor force) (94). "Gentle" was a term applied to both the nobility (i.e., the parliamentary peerage) and the gentry.

The means to support a way of life and a scale of living which excluded manual labour, but included the show and display, the genteel behavior, and the administrative duties which were to a great extent the preserve—and the obligation—of the gentry thus appear to have been perhaps the most important requirement for the validity of a claim to gentle status. . . . [M]any franklins in the fourteenth century would by these criteria of gentility be members of the gentry. (107–108)

Chaucer's Franklin, based on his description in the "General Prologue," is a gentleman, Specht concluded: "His luxurious proclivities and generous hospitality—described with a conspicuous absence of satire—make him a worthy representative of the extrovert country squire of his own time, and of the England of a later period" (119).

Furthermore, Specht wrote, the Franklin's role as a justice of the peace, knight of the shire, and sheriff was in keeping with the fourteenth-century practice of sometimes drawing on the country gentry to fill these roles. As for social climbing, Specht claimed: "The franklins could hardly aspire to a social group of which they were already—especially with a record like Chaucer's Franklin—esteemed honourable members" (146).

Among those literary critics convinced by Specht's study was Helen Cooper. In her 1989 guide to the *Canterbury Tales,* Cooper noted that Specht's study was the most detailed on the status of franklins and the implications of Chaucer's portrait (46). On the Franklin himself, Cooper wrote: "One matter can be resolved: the Franklin is not inherently a social climber, or a *nouveau riche.* The evidence is strongly that franklins were landed members of the minor gentry, with a long-standing stake in land ownership" (45).

But not everyone was convinced. In 1987, David Williams, in *"The Canterbury Tales": A Literary Pilgrimage,* still wrote of the Franklin as a *nouveau riche,* a man who had risen from a lower class solely because of financial success, a man "who attempts to deny and camouflage his roots and convince himself and others of his inherent nobility by acquiring and displaying the accoutrements and accomplishments of his new class" (43). When discussing how the clerk in the Franklin's Tale absolved Aurelius of his debt, Williams noted, "Now that's class! Or so, at least, the author of the tale would like his audience to believe" (47). Thus Williams related the teller of this tale to the tale he told:

The Franklin has constructed his tale with great care so that his conclusion, that the least socially distinguished is the most noble, is inescapable. He desires that from his fiction will emerge a view of reality in which natural aristocracy achieved through virtue is superior to legal aristocracy achieved through accident of birth. And this view of reality will, he believes, fulfill his personal ambition to be noble. (47)

Williams made no specific reference to Specht's work, but in 1989, Paul Strohm, in *Social Chaucer,* did, and he refuted it. Referring to Specht's assertion that the Franklin was considered "gentil," Strohm wrote that this conclusion was "finally not tenable; whatever franklins were to become, such late fourteenth-century documents as the 1379 poll tax show that they had not yet attained gentility when the *Canterbury Tales* were composed" (107). Strohm, like Williams before, connected the Franklin to his tale by stressing the issue of social status:

Thus the Franklin reveals himself as an exponent of a view entirely appropriate to his station—in this case, the view that trouthe may be severed from outdated feudal practices and may inform the practices of all strata of society, gentle and non-gentle alike, as they go about the business of their lives. (108)

Strohm, in refuting Specht, referred to the work of Nigel Saul, a historian mentioned above. Saul, too, was not convinced by Specht. In the essays quoted above, "The Social Status of Chaucer's Franklin: A Reconsideration," written in 1983, and "Chaucer and Gentility," written in 1992, Saul challenged Specht's conclusions. "He [Chaucer's Franklin] is after all only a franklin, inferior in quality to those of noble and gentle birth. For that reason his remarks in the tale are concerned to emphasize that gentillesse is dependent not on a man's birth or ancestry but on his manners and behavior" (21–22), wrote Saul in 1983. Saul drew on the 1379 poll tax: "If a franklin paying 3s.4d. according to the poll tax schedule of 1379 was a substantial figure in his own vill, where he overshadowed the peasants, the great majority of whom paid only 12d., nevertheless he was unlikely to cut much of a figure outside it. He was after all not usually the lord of a manor, and the evidence of the poll tax returns suggests that his holdings were unlikely to extend outside his own vill" ("Social Status" 15). It is this argument that convinced Strohm.

Saul also took issue with the fact that Specht named an actual person as a living model for Chaucer's Franklin. The speculation on the role model for the Franklin actually began in 1926, when John Matthews Manly had guessed that Chaucer based his portrait of the Franklin on Sir John Bussy of Lincolnshire. Manly pointed to Bussy's record of service—several times a justice of the peace, a knight of the shire, and a sheriff—and to his home's proximity to that of Thomas Pynchbeck, whom Manly believed was Chaucer's model for the Man of Law, the Franklin's companion on the pilgrimage. Bussy was a landowner; his widow possessed eleven manors and land in eight other places. His family was of great importance in the region. And while the terms *franklin* and *vavasour* were rare in the fourteenth century, both were especially connected with the district of Lincolnshire (162–165).

But Bussy was a "Sir," a title of rank that Manly acknowledged might throw doubt on Bussy's being linked to the Franklin. Manly, however, pointed out that some knighthoods were inherited or purchased without military obligation. Thus, even though Bussy may technically have been a knight, perhaps he was of a different sort than the Knight on the Canterbury pilgrimage. To differentiate between them, Chaucer made the Bussy character a franklin (164–167).

Specht rejected Bussy and chose William de Spaygne, a prominent administrative official in the service of John of Gaunt, as a possible model for Chaucer when he created his Franklin. Specht based his choice on de Spaygne's association with those with whom Chaucer was associated and his record of service; he too had been a justice of the peace, sheriff, and knight of the shire, among other positions. Yet Specht acknowledged that it was not possible for him to find evidence of de Spaygne owning substantial lands. He concluded:

To claim, however, that de Spaygne was actually the model for Chaucer's Franklin forms no major part of my purpose in this chapter. . . . [I]t may be argued, I think, that Chaucer created the Franklin from real life, drawing on his personal observation of the social scene of his own day. . . . But he portrayed the Franklin in a way so as to make him a worthy representative of a particular social group, rather than an easily recognizable portrait of an individual. (141)

Saul nonetheless objected to the identification of de Spaygne at all. Saul noted, "Since he created in his Franklin a figure so unrepresentative, Chaucer is unlikely to be thinking of someone known to him. If he existed, a franklin who was a sheriff and frequently sat in Parliament would be easy to track down. In fact, no such man existed" ("Social Status" 20).

Saul did offer the Hydes of Denchworth in Berkshire as an example of the kind of people Chaucer was satirizing in his portrait of the Franklin. Denchworth was a vill divided into several manors held by absentee lords; in one of these manors, Circourt, the Hyde family held the hide of land from which they took their name. And while no poll tax returns are available to confirm the Hydes' identity as franklins, they were of free blood in the fourteenth century, noted Saul. Saul presented this family history:

It was in the time of the elder John Hyde that the fortunes of the family began noticeably to advance. In 1382 Hyde acquired the Lovedays manor, and by 1399 he had assembled lands in the north of the vill which he conveyed to feoffes under the name of the "manor of Hyde". His son John was known as a gentleman in 1418, and his grandson, another John, as an esquire [armiger] in 1448. The case of the Hydes is probably exceptional only for the opportunity afforded them by weak lordship to acquire one after another of the manors into which Denchworth was fragmented. It may well be the enhanced pretensions of such men that Chaucer was satirizing. (23)

Perhaps. Perhaps not, as Specht and Gerould and others would argue. And perhaps we will never resolve the issue of the social status of franklins in Chaucer's day. Were these men, and Chaucer's representative, considered gentlemen? Were they secure in their gentility? The debate rages on.

REFERENCES

Benson, Larry, ed. *The Riverside Chaucer*. 3rd ed. Boston: Houghton, 1987.

Bowman, Mary R. " 'Half as She Were Mad': Dorigen in the Male World of the 'Franklin's Tale.' " *Chaucer Review* 27 (1993): 239–251.

Carruthers, Mary J. "The Gentilesse of Chaucer's Franklin." *Criticism* 23 (1981): 283–300.

Cooper, Helen. *Oxford Guides to Chaucer: "The Canterbury Tales."* Oxford: Oxford University Press, 1989.

Coss, P. R. "Literature and Social Terminology: The Vavasour in England." *Social Relations and Ideas: Essays in Honour of R. H. Hilton*. Eds. T. H. Aston, P. R.

Coss, Christopher Dyer, and Joan Thirsk. Cambridge: Cambridge University Press, 1983. 109–150.

Denholm-Young, N. *The Country Gentry in the Fourteenth Century.* Oxford: Oxford University Press, 1969.

Eckhart, Caroline D. "Chaucer's Franklin and Others of the Vavasour Family." *Modern Philology* 87 (1990): 239–248.

"Frank(e)lein,-in,en." *Middle English Dictionary.* 1952 ed.

"Franklin." *Oxford English Dictionary.* 1989 ed.

Gerould, Gordon Hall. "The Social Status of Chaucer's Franklin." *PMLA* 41 (1926): 262–279.

Hilton, R. H. *The English Peasantry in the Later Middle Ages: The Ford Lectures for 1973 and Related Studies.* Oxford: Oxford University Press, 1975.

Homans, George Caspar. *English Villagers of the Thirteenth Century.* 1941. New York: W.W. Norton, 1975.

Lumiansky, R. M. *Of Sundry Folk: The Dramatic Principal in the Canterbury Tales.* Austin: University of Texas Press, 1955.

McKisack, May. *The Fourteenth Century: 1307–1399.* Oxford: Oxford University Press, 1959.

Manly, John Matthews. *Some New Light on Chaucer.* 1926. Gloucester, Mass.: Peter Smith, 1959.

Pearcy, Roy J. "Chaucer's Franklin and the Literary Vavasour." *The Chaucer Review* 8 (1973): 33–59.

Robertson, D. W., Jr. "Chaucer's Franklin and His Tale." Essays in Medieval Culture. Princeton, N.J.: Princeton University Press, 1980. 273–290.

Root, Robert Kilburn. *The Poetry of Chaucer: A Guide to Its Study and Appreciation.* 1906. Rev. ed. 1922. Gloucester, Mass.: Peter Smith, 1957.

Saul, Nigel. "Chaucer and Gentility." *Chaucer's England: Literature in Historical Context.* Ed. Barbara A. Hanawalt. Minneapolis: University of Minnesota Press, 1992.

———. "The Social Status of Chaucer's Franklin: A Reconsideration." *Medium Aevum* 52 (1983): 10–26.

Specht, Henrik. *Chaucer's Franklin in the "Canterbury Tales": The Social and Literary Background of a Chaucerian Character.* Copenhagen, Denmark: Publications of the Department of English, University of Copenhagen, 1981.

Strohm, Paul. *Social Chaucer.* Cambridge, Mass.: Harvard University Press, 1989.

Williams, David. *"The Canterbury Tales": A Literary Pilgrimage.* Boston: G. K. Hall, 1987.

LIST OF RELATED CRITICAL WORKS

Brewer, D. S. "Class Distinction in Chaucer." *Speculum* 43 (1968): 290–305.

Crane, Susan. "The Franklin as Dorigen." *Chaucer Review* 24 (1990): 236–252.

Fyler, John M. "Love and Degree in the Franklin's Tale." *Chaucer Review* 21 (1987): 321–337.

Olson, Paul A. *The "Canterbury Tales" and the Good Society.* Princeton, N.J.: Princeton University Press, 1986.

Chapter 13

An Haberdasher . . .

LAURA C. AND ROBERT T. LAMBDIN

Geoffrey Chaucer's selection of the haberdasher as one of the guildsmen in the "General Prologue" of the *Canterbury Tales* might seem a curious choice, for the haberdashers, also known as hurrers, were not incorporated into a formally recognized brotherhood until 1447, when they were confirmed by Henry VI and named the Merchant Haberdashers. This group was the result of the joining of the Hurrers, or Cappers, and the Milliners, a group that gained its name because the bulk of the merchandise they chiefly dealt in came from Milan, Italy (Herbert 531). The haberdashers of Chaucer's time were mostly in the business of selling men's clothing and accessories, including hats, shirts, ties, gloves, and kerchiefs. In addition, they were milliners, or creators of women's hats. In keeping with Chaucer's apparently tactful and careful approach to the selection of guildsmen named in the "General Prologue," the haberdasher guild appears to have been as neutral as possible in the political struggles of late fourteenth-century England.

Ernest Kuhl discusses the conflict between the victuallers, or the food-preparing guilds, and the nonvictuallers which reached its height in October 1386, when ten nonvictualling companies openly denounced the mayor of London in Parliament (654). Clearly, the guilds had been "formed so recently that Chaucer could not help but see in them a striking and novel symbol of the rising middle class" (Lindahl 21), so rather than omit this group altogether because of the political upheaval, Chaucer probably included a few representatives of less powerful guilds to further the eclectic mix of pilgrims. John Gardner defines the guildsmen of the "General Prologue" as men who have all done well financially, have risen in their guilds, and because of their professions (373), not because of any inner qualities, are fit to be guild aldermen (237). While the scarce information concerning the guildsmen who appear in the "General Prologue'' hardly allows for any probing analysis of their characters, Chaucer most likely chose to include this group so that he would have representatives from every walk of life. Perhaps, as Thomas Kirby notes, this is simply one of the many passages that we are unable to fully understand and appreciate because we are so far removed from it (504).

Literary criticism concerning the guildsmen has been primarily devoted to establishing a rationale for their inclusion in the *Canterbury Tales.* Since none of the guildsmen are mentioned again after their seventeen-line introduction in the ''General Prologue'' [I (A) 361–376], this group seems rather an odd assortment, for ''a cursory glance at once reveals the fact that Chaucer did not choose representatives from the prominent companies of his day'' (Kuhl 652). Furthermore, none of the five companies mentioned in the ''General Prologue'' was among the thirteen chief mysteries summoned in 1351 to elect the common council (Harwood 414). Indeed, it was not until 1450 when the Haberdashers were finally incorporated to rank as number eight among the twelve livery companies of London. This confirmed the earlier incorporation of 1447, when the haberdashers combined with the cappers or hurrers into one brotherhood (Garbáty 703), even though haberdashers had been elected to the ministry as early as 1328. Apparently, Chaucer may have ''refused to make them members of the larger trade guilds, and so they are all heaped together in a single guild that had to legislate for several trades and bring everybody together for social and religious activities'' (Hussey 95). While it has been suggested that Chaucer forced these guildsmen into one group with mischievous intent (Hussey 95), their lack of development in the ''General Prologue'' makes this notion purely speculative.

However, this does not answer the question regarding the guilds Chaucer selected for inclusion nor why he chose to name guildsmen of mid- to low stature. For lack of a better reason, one might believe the guildsmen to represent a satiric attack on this new class (Lisca 321). D. W. Robertson feels that the tradesmen ''with their somewhat gaudy holiday attire, wisdom based on property and income, and ambitious wives, were intended as amusing examples of persons seeking to rise above their station'' (81). Similarly, it seems that the

> main emphasis in the sketch of the guildsmen is upon their *nouveau riche* characteristics.
> . . . [Their] equipment and clothing are ostentatiously new, and their wives, who have no reason to complain about lack of money, are extremely appreciative of their place in society. (Lumiansky 58–59)

What becomes clear here is that Chaucer's guildsmen do represent a change in the makeup of the people of England, a prominent middle class. Whether their attendance provided an indication of a new class or is a humorous jab at a newly mobile, wealthy group, the inclusion of the guildsmen in the ''General Prologue'' encourages intriguing speculation concerning their roles in late fourteenth-century England.

When we specifically examine the historical position and occupation of haberdashers, it seems that little has changed concerning their trade. This group has always been involved with men's and women's fashions and accessories, primarily in the making of hats and headwear; however, in Chaucer's time and before it seems that this group dealt with more than just apparel. "Parchment makers sometimes sold their wares through haberdashers" (Hollander 142), perhaps as stationery designed for men of stature. Furthermore, haberdashers may have been associated with the powerful Drapers guild, which dealt largely in cloth and dry goods (McCutchan 315). It seems likely, however, that the haberdashers were even more closely associated with the mercers (Garbáty 693), who dealt in textiles or woven fabrics. In fact, by this time the mercers felt themselves so closely related to the haberdashers that during the reign of Richard II (1367–1400), the mayor of London fined the mercers for entering themselves as freemen of the Haberdasher Company (Garbáty 704). Also by 1332, the haberdashers' shops had absorbed all the best grades of ornamental trifles that were on the market such as fine clasps and elaborately designed pins (Thrupp 7).

In Richard II's reign, haberdashers were divided into two fraternities separately dedicated to St. Catherine and St. Nicholas, respectively. This was the direct result of there being two distinct types of haberdashers: those who dealt mainly in headware (the hurrers), and those milliners who dealt in small wares such as brooches, spurs, capes, and glasses. Also associated with the haberdashers were pins; before the introduction of these small but invaluable tools, it is believed that English ladies depended on skewers made from thorns to secure their garments (Herbert 533). In addition, Mary Andere notes that perhaps monasteries made pins, since there are various allusions to this in literature (44), including the *Canterbury Tales,* where we are told that the friar brought knives "And pyns for to give faire wyves" [I (A) 234] ["And pins for to give to the fair wives"]. This sufficed until around 1376 when the Company of Pinmakers returned two men to the Common Council, so pins were extremely expensive and usually available only to the wealthy. Because of their scarceness, pins were acceptable as New Year's gifts to ladies, and special monetary gifts were earmarked specifically for the purchase of pins, which were regarded as essential for any gentleman. The term *pin money* derives from the customary bonus presented a merchant at the conclusion of a financial transaction "for her pyns" (Andere 44–45).

By 1372 the haberdashers' guild had seemingly gained more respect and stature: in this year they "promulgated their first set of ordinances and returned two members to the Common Council," and a bit later they established a Haberdasher's Court (Garbáty 703–704). That haberdashers had the prominence to be elected to such high positions demonstrates their growing monetary stockpiles and their political influence. This new social import further encouraged the burgeoning numbers of apprentices in this field of men's fashions, allowing for the establishment of a section of town devoted only to such establishments.

If the haberdashers had remained solely linked to the mercers, their inclusion in the "General Prologue" would make a lot more sense, for the mercers believed St. Thomas of Canterbury to be their patron saint (Fullerton 519). However, it seems that St. Katherine was the patron to whom haberdashers primarily directed their prayers, more often than to St. Thomas of Canterbury. By the year 1381, St. Katherine appears for the first time connected with the guild of haberdashers in the bishop of London's Registry of that year (Garbáty 703). The main import of pinpointing the date of the haberdashers' selection of a patron saint is to make it clear that by the time Chaucer penned the "General Prologue" this guild had already established its own separate identity. However, during Chaucer's time there were few haberdasheries to be found in London; William Herbert notes that even by the reign of Edward VI (1547–1553) there were not more than a dozen in all of London; but, by 1580, they were on every street in Westminster (534).

Haberdashers may have been recognized as a particular group by the time of the *Canterbury Tales,* but, in terms of import, in comparison with the other guilds included in the text, the haberdasher was only of moderate rank: "They are not the smallest companies nor the largest. But they are the largest not involved in the political squabble of the day" (Kuhl 665). Even if Chaucer did not carefully select the guilds represented, it is evident that—unless Chaucer meant this omission as a satirical attack—the guildsmen did not impress him enough to elicit details, dress or character, as did most of the other pilgrims (Herndon 44). Chaucer did not elaborate on these characters, even though the political crisis concerning the guildsmen had passed.

Later around the sixteenth century, haberdashery split from one into two distinct groups: those who dealt in small wares, such as needles, tapes, or buttons, and those who dealt with hats (Kuhl n. 60). But, according to the *OED,* the division into two kinds of haberdasher occurred during the sixteenth century (Andrew 329). Thus the role of the haberdasher in fourteenth-century England was still a mixture, and so the role will be defined here by a cursory examination of the styles of headwear and drygoods popular during this era.

In England, the idea of wearing fashionable clothing or making an individual statement through attire, particularly among common men, was relatively unimportant until around the reign of Edward III (1327–1377). Unlike most countries, England has never had a typical peasant costume. All people of the same gender have usually worn similar attire, varying mostly in the cost of fabrics used, so "dress in England has acted less as a barrier between one class and another than in any other country" (Settle 8). In fact, male and female fashions were also very similar, making it difficult to determine the sex of effigies represented on tombstones from this early English period. Clothing gained importance, especially by the reign of Richard II (1377–1399), and "it is important to remember, in this connection, that in the Middle Ages, Man took his clothes even more seriously than Woman and, as in the animal kingdom, was usually the more finely clad of the two sexes'' (Houston v). This information helps explain the sudden prominence of haberdashers in Chaucer's time and after.

Medieval English style incorporated a few racy features from France and Italy, but the dress code was usually moderate and in good taste (Von Boehn 214). As Chaucer seems to satirize in his description of the guildsmen and their wives, the rising middle class sometimes overstepped the bounds of propriety in an ostentatious attempt to outshine the gentry. Indeed, a prosperous townsman had more reason and opportunity to display wealth through dress than did his noble countrymen who were not at court: "The burghers who could see each other daily at church and in the marketplace and street, and take mutual stock of each other's appearance, felt a far greater incentive to vary their costume than did the knights in the seclusion of their country fastnesses'' (Von Boehn 216). Chaucer notes such aspects as the livery dress of the various companies with their long sleeves purfiled, or bordered, with fur, their shoes piked (or peaked), their girdles and purses and their hair cut and curled (Settle 16). By doing such, he was demonstrating that the guildsmen's dress had evolved and, much to the horror of the gentry, had become similar to that of the powerful rich. Dress had gradually become more and more a symbol of status until sumptuary legislation was attempted in 1363 because fashion had obscured any type of class distinction. This attempt to control attire proved impractical to enforce, and by 1379, it seems to have fallen by the wayside (Thrupp 147–148). Indeed, the description of a sheriff of the fourteenth century could be that of an aristocrat:

His hair rounded by his ears and curled: a little beard forked: a gown, girt to him down to his feet, of branched damask, wrought with the likeness of flowers: a large purse on his right side, hanging from a belt from his left shoulder: a plain hood about his neck covering his shoulders and hanging back behind him. (Pendrill 15)

Clearly, attempts to legislate fashion had failed.

The fashions of the latter part of the fourteenth century may be attributed to the arrival of Anne of Bohemia, queen of Richard II. Many extravagant styles became the norm, including long-toed boots which grew to such lengths that they had to be tied at the knees. Also new was the custom of cutting cloth into small pieces and having it sewn back together—at a cost of about twenty times its original price (Pendrill 14). By the late fourteenth century, typical male attire consisted of a shirt worn as an undergarment and rarely seen outside the domestic domain, and a flared tunic reaching to the knees (among the more daring, this tunic was worn skin tight and very short—just barely covering the buttocks). Also, gipons or doublets were adopted for civilian use by the 1370s. Changes in this style from its traditional military use included the addition of extra padding in front and a skirt that grew steadily shorter, barely covering the hips. This portion of clothing was usually joined by a seam, and there were sometimes side vents that could be buttoned. The sleeves of these outer garments extended to the knuckles, expanding into a funnel shape.

A variation of these sleeves was the "grande assiette" which was "cut so that the sleeve was inserted with a circular seam overlapping the front and back of the bodice (Cunnington and Cunnington 78). Also, a hooded surcoat or cote-hardie with loosely hanging, very long sleeves became fashionable. The sleeves were fairly close fitting to the elbow; the hanging flap became longer and narrower, and was known as a *tippet*. These sleeves could cover cold hands and were sometimes elaborated with notched or scalloped patterns cut out. During the last quarter of the fourteenth century, the cote-hardie, closely buttoned down the front, developed a collar (Cunnington and Cunnington 80).

The brightly hued tights, sometimes of two different colors, were tied at the waist with strings and were much like contemporary pantyhose in texture (Brooke 20). Men of greater means wore parti-colored hose from the ankle to the waist, the violent contrast in the tint of each leg produced a curious and bizarre effect. Among the most popular color schemes were black/white, blue/white, and red/black (Pendrill 13). Over the hose and the gipon was worn the girdle, usually very ornate and long. The knightly girdle, prominent from 1350 to 1410, was worn by nobles over their outerwear and consisted of decorative metal plaques joined and fastened in front by an ornamental buckle. These were always worn at the hip and probably required the wearer to be sewn or hooked in by someone else (Cunnington and Cunnington 80–81).

With this burst of fashion awareness came the need to accessorize and embellish costumes. There were also many new types of hats and headwear that came into style for both men and women. At the center of this flurry of activity and interest was the haberdasher. Around 1315 the hood was more like a bunch of loosely draped cloth around the neck; later this cloth was pulled up around the head and often tied like a turban, a look that remained popular throughout the fifteenth century as well. By the end of the thirteenth century, the fashions of hoodwear included the addition of the liripipe, or a tail. During the fourteenth century it became chic for men to wear draped turbans, prominent heretofore on the Continent, with very long liripipes that could either be wrapped around the neck or left hanging down the back. The style then shifted so that by the end of the fourteenth century, the liripipe became part of the folds of the turban. This produced a style resembling a cock's comb, accounting for the term *coxcomb*, which designated a dandy. The liripipe eventually dwindled, becoming merely an ornament that may be seen today in the cockade, a knot or ribbon worn as a badge on a British coachman's hat (Wilcox 57). Hoods with long points of varying lengths hanging down in back matched well when they were worn with the popular, elongated, extremely pointed shoes called cracowes (Houston 110).

It seems that individual tastes in fashion were primarily reflected in the type and angle of the hood, the fit and length of the tunic, and the sleeve style of a man's costume. By Chaucer's time, the cap became a favorite type of headwear. Nobility favored beaver caps lined with scarlet cloth or green velvet. Plain, colored caps were for the ordinary folk, while simple black caps known as "hures" were worn by even more common people (Pendrill 14).

Whereas earlier in the century the elaborate brooches and pins sold by haberdashers were the primary form of ornamentation, buttons—also apparently sold by haberdashers—became popular by the mid-fourteenth century for decorative uses beyond their practical application. In addition, around this time plumes began to be affixed to hats, usually pinned to the front brim with some sort of jewelled clasp (Cunnington and Cunnington 87). Also popular was fur trim on hats, coats, and shoes (Pendrill 13).

By the 1360s, men's hats had evolved into a style known as the *chaperon,* which consisted of three pieces—the gorget, hood, and liripipe. A French variation of this was called the *rondlet,* or padded roll; this style was fitted around the head and then stuffed with some type of material, usually silk or linen. The gorget was cut into scalloped shapes called dagging which protruded from the top of the hat and fell over the shoulder. The liripipe was suspended from the rondlet over the right shoulder, a technique that added balance to this style. A variation of this form of hat was popular in the court of Richard II. The men of his favor embellished their hats with lush, imported materials that were embroidered with silk or gold (Amphlett 34–38).

In addition, the hats of this period became more decorative as trimming and accessories were added to further accentuate the hats. Plumes, usually dyed ostrich or peacock feathers, were frequently added, either fixed upright in front or behind, attached with a brooch or a jewelled pin. Conveniently, all of these accouterments would have been available at the local haberdashery. Finally, hat bands with decorative designs became quite the rage, and hats were often slung behind with attached strings. The materials of choice were either felt, beaver, or showy textile (Cunnington and Cunnington 87–89).

By the 1380s two other headcoverings, both worn with a hood or cloak, emerged. Both were probably made small and round so that hoods could be pulled over them in inclement weather. The "bycocket" hat had a crown and an upturned brim that came to a point in the front. This style was often decorated and worn by both men and women. The crown was decorated with either a real or an embroidered peacock feather; the facing of the upturned brim was adorned with *menu-vair,* or squirrel's belly hair. Knotted streamers tied and held the hat on during inclement days. Larger forms of this hat were made of beaver fur and ostrich feathers (Amphlett 39–40).

While veils and wimples continued to dominate women's headwear, this time was one of evolving ornamentation. After Richard II's marriage to Anne of Bohemia, England was witness to some of the most showy headwear meant to accentuate, not hide, hair. Up to this point hair had not been on display; this fashion was so rigorously followed that even the hairs on the neck were removed; however, by the late thirteenth century, hair became so emphasized that many fantastic decorations and adornments were added, such as horns, pads, or boxes. It seems that "new" or "chic" meant more absurd—and fashionable

(Brooke 28–29). Such can be seen on the Wife of Bath who, as described in the "General Prologue," seems to be wearing an example of an outlandish, huge hat.

Particularly popular in headgear was the goffered veil, or Nebula headdress made of a half-circle of linen, possibly layered, which formed an arch around the face of the wearer, ending at the temples or extending to the chin. Also an ornamental fillet, which consisted of attached side pieces resembling pillars and hugging the cheeks, gave the face a squared look. Through each of these hollow pillars would be drawn a tress of hair. If a tiara or coronet was worn, it was measured to fit over these adornments (Cunnington and Cunnington 95). Elaborate headdresses seem to have been most popular in England and Germany. They were generally made of taffeta, silk, or wool, and, as were some men's hats, were adorned with lush embroidery. These decorative head ornaments remained fashionable past Chaucer's time and frequently included jewels, either real or artificial, sewn into gold net foundations (Amphlett 33).

Still important during this time, though not particularly chíc, was the wimple. Like the other dominant styles, these simple adornments sometimes were transformed to create eccentric forms. These coverings, which wrapped in folds around the neck and over the head, were originally used as protection from harsh weather. By the late 1300s, the wimple had evolved to variations that were pinned to the hair and left a space exposed between the fabric and the neck. To further this style, women would part their hair in the middle and form it in ripples down to the ears. The ends would be plaited and turned up to the top of the head (Amphlett 32).

During Chaucer's time the haberdasher took on an increasingly important function in society. As the guildsmen became a part of a growing middle-upper class—one that was no longer bound to the manor and one that could base its wages on supply and demand—their fashion choices exhibited all of the entrapments and displays of a proud and upwardly mobile class. Thus we are presented with the gaudily attired guildsmen of the "General Prologue." While many questions arise over Chaucer's selection of the five particular guilds represented, an examination of any particular type brings insight into the changes occurring in England at the end of the fourteenth century. The haberdashers had not reached their height, yet their inclusion in the work shows that this guild was beginning to be recognized. Perhaps Chaucer wished simply to make a comment on the strange popular styles of his day. Certainly an individual as observant as Chaucer would have noted and taken great pleasure in reflecting, even in this short passage, the folly of an evolving class that had not quite arrived in terms of stature.

REFERENCES

Amphlett, Hilda. *Hats: A History of Fashion in Headwear*. Buckinghamshire: Sadler Ltd., 1974.

Andere, Mary. *Old Needlework Boxes and Tools.* Plymouth, UK: David and Charles Newton Abbot Devon, 1971.

Andrew, Malcolm. "Portrait of the Guildsmen." In *A Variorum Edition of the Works of Geoffrey Chaucer: Volume II: The Canterbury Tales, "The General Prologue"; Part One B: Explanatory Notes.* Norman: University of Oklahoma Press, 1993. Pp. 326–337.

Brooke, Iris. *A History of English Costume.* New York: Theatre Arts Books, 1972.

Cunnington, C. Willard, and Phillis Cunnington. *Handbook of English Mediaevel Costume.* Boston: Plays, 1969.

Fullerton, Ann B. "The Five Craftsmen." *MLN* 61 (1946): 515–523.

Garbáty, Thomas J. "Chaucer's Guildsmen and Their Fraternitee." *JEGP* 59 (1960): 691–704.

Gardner, John. *The Poetry of Chaucer.* Carbondale, Ill.: University of Southern Illinois Press, 1977.

Harwood, Britton J. "The Fraternitee of Chaucer's Guildsmen." *RES* 39 (1988): 413–417.

Herbert, William. *The History of the Twelve Great Livery Companies of London.* 1834. Vol. 2. New York: Kelley Publishers, 1968.

Herndon, Sarah. "Chaucer's Five Guildsmen." *Florida State University Studies* 5 (1952): 33–44.

Hollander, A.E.J., and William Kellaway. *Studies in London History.* London: Hodder and Stoughton, 1969.

Houston, Mary G. *Medieval Costume in England and France.* 1939. London: Adam and Charles Black, 1965.

Hussey, Maurice. *Chaucer's World: A Pictorial Companion.* London: Cambridge University Press, 1968.

Kirby, Thomas. "The Haberdasher and His Companions." *MLN* 53 (1938): 504–505.

Kuhl, Ernest. "Chaucer's Burgesses." *Transactions of the Wisconsin Academy of Sciences, Arts, and Letters* 18, 2 (1916): 652–675.

Lindahl, Carl. *Earnest Games: Folkloric Patterns in the "Canterbury Tales."* Bloomington: Indiana University Press, 1987.

Lisca, Peter. "Chaucer's Guildsmen and Their Cook." *MLN* 70 (1955): 321–324.

Lumiansky, R. M. *Of Sundry Folk: The Dramatic Principle in the "Canterbury Tales."* Austin: University of Texas Press, 1955.

McCutchan, J. Wilson. " 'A Solempne and a Greet Fraternitee.' " *PMLA* 74 (1959): 313–317.

Pendrill, Charles. *London Life in the Fourteenth Century.* 1925. Port Washington, N.Y.: Kennikat Press, 1971.

Robertson, D. W. *Chaucer's London.* New York: John Wiley and Sons, 1968.

Settle, Alison. *English Fashion.* London: Colling, 1946.

Thrupp, Sylvia L. *The Merchant Class of Medieval London: 1300–1500.* 1948. Ann Arbor, Mich.: Ann Arbor Paperbacks, 1962.

Von Boehn, Max. *Mode and Manners.* 2 vols. 1932. New York: Benjamin Blom, 1971.

Wilcox, R. Turner. *The Mode in Costume.* New York: Scribner's, 1958.

Chapter 14

. . . And a Carpenter . . .

JULIAN N. WASSERMAN AND MARC GUIDRY

The two things that strike us most in regard to the Carpenter of the "General Prologue" are both negative attributions, at least in the context of the *Canterbury Tales*. In contrast to the other sondry folk wending their way to Canterbury—such as the churlish Miller, the worthy Knight, or the bawdy Wife of Bath—the Carpenter-Guildsman has no individual identity. When we meet him, he is lumped in with his fellow guildsmen (the Haberdasher, Weaver, Dyer, and Tapestry-maker). Even more damning, he never tells a tale, so we are apt to forget all about him almost as soon as Chaucer mentions him. However, carpentry is hardly the least memorable craft in the *Canterbury Tales*. Indeed, the carpenter's craft is the defining context of both the "Miller's Tale" and the Reeve's angry response, two of the most memorable of all the tales of Canterbury. We are told that the Reeve in his "youthe . . . hadde lerned a good myster: / He was a wel good wrighte, a carpenter" (I.613–614) ["youth . . . he learned a good mystery: / He was a very good wright, a carpenter"]. The Reeve's association with carpentry is all the more notable because the Miller, in order to "quyte" or ridicule the Reeve (who is the Miller's professional rival), tells a tale about the cuckolding of a carpenter. Carpentry, it would seem, has a more significant place in the world of Chaucer's pilgrims than the deceptive anonymity of the Carpenter-Guildsman would suggest.

Why might Chaucer be so interested in the "good myster" or craft of carpentry? The general importance of carpentry in the Middle Ages is indicated by St. Bonaventure (1221–1274), who considered the building trades (*fabricatio*) to be one of seven major types of work (5: 519–522). But carpentry had special relevance to Chaucer. When he was writing the *Canterbury Tales,* Chaucer was employed for a short time as Clerk of the King's Works, from July 12, 1389 to June 17, 1391 (see Benson xxiv–xxv for biographical information on Chaucer's appointment as Clerk of the King's Works). While in this office, he was responsible for Crown projects that required skilled carpenters—such as repairing the royal residences, constructing scaffolds for the knightly combats at Smithfield, and rebuilding and enlarging the London wharf where wool was brought and stored for customs. Thus, Chaucer the poet was also Chaucer the civil servant who recruited, supervised, and paid carpenters and other artisans of the building trades. He probably even had to pursue runaway carpenters and imprison them, as carpenters and masons (stone workers) often ran away from Crown building sites where they were usually impressed into labor against their will, often at wages lower than those they could command on the private market. Chaucer would have had at least one additional reason for representing carpenters in the *Canterbury Tales*. As the fortunes of the Herland family attest, the status of carpenters was on the rise in the late fourteenth century. They were building expensive public works as well as more and more private residences around England. Chaucer as Clerk of the King's Works might well have worked directly with Hugh Herland who as the King's Carpenter from 1375 to 1405 was responsible for what has been termed the single "greatest feat of medieval English Carpentry," the timber roof of the great hall of Westminster (Brown et al. 203). This rise in status, certainly on a par with that of the pilgrim Franklin, made the figure of the Carpenter the perfect type for the aspiring middle-class professionals who come under such scrutiny in Chaucer's greatest poem.

The Carpenter in the portrait of the Five Guildsmen is one of the more successful masters of his craft, since he conspicuously wears an expensive silver-mounted knife (I.367) and has enough "catel" (property) and "rente" (income) to fancy himself an "alderman" (a representative on the London City Council; I.372–373). Like John, the carpenter of the "Miller's Tale," the Carpenter-Guildsman apparently owns a spacious house and has servants working for him. As such, he is the medieval equivalent of the modern small businessman, probably not only a skilled laborer but also a small-time contractor. Chaucer thus envisions the Carpenter, along with his fellow guildsmen and their class conscious wives, to be a bustling member of the upstart middle class who at the close of the fourteenth century challenged the lower ranks of the nobility for political and economic influence in London. However, there is perhaps a hint of sarcasm in the Carpenter's portrait. As far as is known, no carpenter ever served as a London alderman in the fourteenth century (see Hope, Birch, and Torry 30; Salzman 37; and especially Thrupp 39, 78, who points out that of 260 aldermen elected in the fourteenth century, only nine came from the lesser craft companies). Moreover, most carpenters would have been stuck at the lower level of the urban social structure because they did not produce a good that could be sold retail or even wholesale, excluding them from the more powerful groups of London merchants. In other words, Chaucer, himself the son of a wine merchant and an esquire in service to Edward III and Richard II, seems to be poking fun at the self-importance of the nouveau riche in the portrait of the Five Guildsmen (see especially Andrew, Moorman, and Ransom 813).

The Carpenter—along with the Haberdasher, Weaver, Dyer, and Tapestry-maker—is a member of "a solempne and a greet fraternitee" (I.364). Ann Fullerton presents evidence that a guild of carpenters was formally incorporated "by the letters-patent of Edward III on the seventh of July 1344, as 'The Masters, Wardens, Assistants, and Commonality of the Mystery of the Freemen of the Carpentry of the City of London' " (517). However, Hope, Birch, and Torry note that on special occasions it was possible for groups of people otherwise unaffiliated to wear the same livery (37). This organization was probably a parish guild, a kind of social aid and pleasure club based not on trade affiliation but on neighborhood residency. Under this system, the residents of a given neighborhood in London would band together under the auspices of the local parish church and pay dues that would be used to finance social functions and help out distressed members of the group (Leeson 25–26). It is likely that the Carpenter also belonged to a guild affiliated strictly with his craft. Indeed, the term *myster* applied to the carpenter-reeve's training or skill might likewise be applied to the guild organization that represented those who practiced that craft.

In 1333 the "Brotherhood of Carpenters of London" had become organized enough to draw up their own "Boke of Ordinances." The first document to make a reference to the Guild or Fraternity of Carpenters is dated 1271 (Hope, Birch, and Torry 118). All but one of the sixteen ordinances dealt with social and religious, rather than trade, matters. The most important ordinance arranged for burial services for deceased carpenters and their family members. In an age marked both by religious devotion and sudden death (the Black Death raged in the fourteenth century), the value of this benefit cannot be overestimated. Medieval people were intensely concerned about the repose of the souls of the dead, and craftsmen saw their obligation to their deceased brethren as familial in nature. The carpenters were expected to attend the funerals of their deceased fellows and even memorialize them by paying for chantry masses (masses at which a priest was paid to chant or sing prayers on behalf of the deceased). Other guild ordinances provided for aid for any members who became sick (like John who breaks his arm—*Canterbury Tales,* I.3829), poor, or aged. For example, the rules of the Brotherhood of Carpenters, compiled in 1313, stipulate that the brotherhood pay 14d per week to any brother or sister who had lain ill for at least a fortnight. Levies could be collected should the common fund be insufficient to cover such costs (see Myers 157). The carpenters' fraternity also regulated the administration of small loans to members when the guild treasury was flush and mediated the settlement of disputes among members, thereby enabling them to escape court costs and, in certain cases, imprisonment. The fraternity would have also arranged for the celebration of religious feasts and social gatherings. Carpenters were reputed to be heavy drinkers, and, in fact, carpenters' contracts usually stipulated the provision of an after-dinner drink at the expense of their employers.

The sole ordinance of 1333 that dealt with the operation of the carpenters' trade called on each master carpenter "to work his own brother before any other'' (Leeson 25). The strong sense of solidarity among the London carpenters of the fourteenth century was in part motivated by the pressure of cheap labor from the provinces. Outsiders called ''forrens/foreigns'' came to London in search of work and offered their services for wages lower than the rate the carpenters set for themselves. Yet, as the carpenters' ''Boke'' indicates, economic matters were only one aspect of their fraternal order. In the Middle Ages few, if any, would have thought to separate the professional sphere of activity from the social and spiritual spheres. The world of work of the medieval carpenter was infused with his spiritual and social concerns. He saw his craft as a way to extend his communal ties and store up merits in heaven. As for the sense of community afforded by the association of the craft guilds, D. W. Robertson, Jr., notes that an unfavorable reflection on one carpenter would be an insult offered to all his brethren. Robertson thus sees Osewald's angry response to the Miller's tale as offense taken from an attack on his professional community rather than a personal attack regarding his personal circumstances (123).

We witness the sacred nature the carpenters accorded their work in the mystery plays they performed at Whitsuntide (the week following the seventh Sunday after Easter) or Corpus Christi (one week after Whitsuntide). The mystery plays appeared in cycles that would dramatize for the illiterate laymen (most medieval people couldn't read) the greatest events of the Bible, from the Creation in the Old Testament to the Last Judgment in the New Testament. The term *mystery play* refers to both the Christian mystery of Christ's redemption of humankind and to the ''mysteries'' or crafts of the artisan-performers. Throughout England in the streets of towns such as Chester and York, guilds put on plays that were dramatically appropriate to their craft. For instance, the goldsmiths performed the visitation of the Magi, the bakers performed the Last Supper, and cooks, who were used to snatching things out of the fire, performed the Harrowing of Hell. For their part, carpenters often reenacted Noah's building of the ark.

The version of the Noah play in the York Cycle implicitly compares God as divine artificer, who created the world in six working days, to the figure of Noah as a wright or carpenter, who made the ark out of wood. The York Noah play contains actual instructions on how to cut timber, make boards, and construct the ark, suggesting that the wright's craft is divinely inspired. The Noah play was mounted variously by carpenters, shipwrights (carpenters who specialized in shipbuilding), mariners, and watermen. Elsewhere, carpenters performed other plays appropriate to their craft. For instance, in Dublin, at the Christmas ceremonies of 1528, carpenters performed a play about Mary and Joseph, the patron saint of carpenters, for the earl of Kildare.

The religious and charitable concerns of medieval carpenters should not, however, blind us to the daily economic realities they faced. In the fourteenth century English carpenters fought hard to consolidate any economic gains they had made. Along with their fellow builders the masons, English carpenters had a long history of fighting for increased wages, a trend seen in the following daily wage averages for the royal palace at Woodstock:

Year	1346	1351	1354	1359	1365	1380
Wages	3d	3½d	4d	4d	5d,4d	5d,4d

(Salzman 74)

On the whole wages for carpenters were, relatively speaking, high, but the work on large projects was seasonal, stopping altogether in winter (Salzman 58). Other work was irregular. As for the local carpenter, most often his pay was negotiated piecemeal by contract which stipulated among other things the nature of the building and details such as the number of windows, monies to be paid, materials to be used, dates of completion and penalties for failure to meet contractual obligations (Salzman 47; on contracts see also Atkinson 7). One way carpenters might raise their wages was to arrange to be paid for provision of materials.

Without a yearly allowance, or stipend, a master carpenter's income was based on needed repairs and odd jobs. In this regard, one might well consider the odd jobs of Lawrence Wright, master carpenter of Ripon (Harvey and Oswald 305). Surviving fabric rolls show that in 1354 this master carpenter worked on raising the feretory of St. Wilfrid with "estriche" boards; spent a week repairing the belfry for 3s; and was paid 3s for another week's work cutting "thakbordes" for covering the house of the plumbery. January of 1355 found him cutting more "thakbordes" at the reduced winter rate of 2s/6d per week, and in April he mended bell-clappers along with "other minor works." In June, he erected a scaffold in the choir with other carpenters. Surviving records show that 8d was paid to provide Wright and his fellow carpenters with drink. While we may remark the wondrous variety of his jobs repairing clappers and cutting "thakbordes," we might also ask what was he doing, and more importantly what was he earning, between these tasks?

Even work on major projects could be irregular, if not unreliable, as is seen in the weekly count of workers at Windsor Castle beginning in February of 1344:

Cutting masons	15	58	106	137	127
Laying masons	—	18	64	73	41
Carpenters	4	8	15	14	14
Smiths	—	3	3	5	5
Quarriers	—	72	121	71	63
Laborers	17	211	401	180	180
Total	36	370	710	480	430

(Salzman 36)

Although the number of carpenters remained relatively stable in this brief census, the fluctuations of masons could have drastic effects for carpenters, who were paid in part to provide equipment and other support for the masons.

Though theoretically more mobile than many craftsmen, carpenters were not nearly as mobile as masons who, unless formally attached to a castle or cathedral that would necessitate ongoing maintenance, found little permanent work in the towns (Salzman 32). Also, it is noted that most carpentry work could be done in the carpenter's yard in the town, thus contrasting the stationary carpenters with the more mobile masons (Atkinson 14). Consequently, the lives of the more mobile masons, who often had to be brought in for major undertakings, centered around the temporary lodge erected at a construction site such as Windsor, while the carpenters remained more commonly associated with the town guild. The construction of the mason's lodge, as well as the housing for all the craftsmen on a major project, however, might provide more work for the carpenters. For example, housing had to be procured for some 710 skilled workers at Windsor in the harsh month of February of 1344.

In many ways the trade guilds were set in motion by the ambitious building programs of English monarchs. From Edward I to Henry VIII, English monarchs recruited large numbers of carpenters and other skilled craftsmen for royal works (Leeson 32). During that period, some 1,500 castles and even more churches were built. Windsor Castle, as we have already seen, in the fourteenth century provides an excellent example of the magnitude of such projects and their impact on the professional guilds. In 1359, Edward III had some 1,600 masons from thirty countries working on the castle (Leeson 36). But because these were buildings of stone, far more masons were employed than carpenters, as is demonstrated by the February 1344 figures for Windsor. Moreover, it is likely that most of these laborers were originally impressed into service since contracts gave the king's builders the right to impress workers who, because of the plague, were as important a resource to the King's Works as timber (Leeson 36–37). From the thirteenth century on, patent rolls contain orders stipulating the number of workmen to be impressed into service on a given project. Pressed into service and brought to projects such as Windsor, these workers then became vulnerable to the precarious fortunes of the building projects themselves. At Windsor the weekly expenses of the castle fell from £100 to £9 as events in the war in France diverted both the royal attention and resources, leaving carpenters as well as masons without work or income and in many cases far from home, creating another destabilizing element in regard to the workforce (Salzman 36).

Such fluctuations of supply and demand in regard to the labor force, as well as the shifting nature of the labor force itself, inevitably led to a drawn out tug-of-war over control of wages in the building trades. As early as 1212 there was an attempt to regulate craft wages, carpenters' fees being set at 3d a day plus food or 4d without provisions. By 1327, wages had risen to 5d a day in York, arguably the second most important city in fourteenth-century England (Salzman 68). The London rate, traditionally higher, was 6d a day plus an after-dinner drink (Robertson 93). Throughout the period, a number of forces began to push wages up. Foremost, to be sure, was the regularly recurring Black Death, especially the outbreak of 1348–1351, which decreased the labor pool to the advantage of most mobile professions such as masonry and carpentry where craftsmen could take to the road, often breaking contracts and leaving the periods of apprenticeship unfulfilled in order to move on to higher paying jobs (Leeson 38). Ironically, such movement to greener pastures literally threatened the pastures themselves, the farmlands losing needed workers to the cities. One result of such migrations was that in 1306 and 1339 carpenters who came to London on royal contracts were met with pickets, and in 1339, five London carpenters were actually charged with using physical violence to prevent "forrens" from entering London and working for less than the standard 6d plus drink (Leeson 24; Salzman 72). In Oxford, the town's two carpenters banded together declaring themselves a guild, albeit a rather exclusive one, in order to keep out "forrens" who had taken to the road and were willing to work at cut rates that were still higher than those they had left behind (Salzman 29). Nonguildsmen in many trades might work illegally at night, but if caught by the watchful guildsmen, their goods were seized and publicly burned (Leeson 28). At the Corpus Christi procession in York in 1419, the members of the carpenters' and cobblers' guilds set on the members of the skinners' guild with clubs and Carlisle axes. Medieval shoes were made of leather and wood, and the skinners, who were handlers of and dealers in leather skins, were probably taking business away from the carpenters and cobblers by paying "forrens" cheaper wages to make shoes, or were making shoes themselves at cut-rate prices (Mills 155). As this incident illustrates, trade rivalries were a constant fact of medieval urban life. The carpenters of each town not only vied with "forrens" but also competed with artisans from other woodworking crafts, such as the tilers and plasterers who roofed and covered the wooden frames of houses. Even without the plague or the policing and elimination of low-wage goods, wages often were driven higher during harvest time when master carpenters had to compete with the harvest overseer for the limited labor pool of unskilled or minimally skilled labor (Salzman 74).

In 1349 Parliament attempted to check the trend toward higher wages by instituting the Statute of Labourers in which wages were theoretically frozen at former, lower rates. In 1350, the lord mayor decreed that maximum wages for craft work, including those of carpenters, should be kept at 6d a day without the customary after-dinner drink (Leeson 38; Robertson 93). In 1351 the Statute, particularly directed at holding down the wages of agricultural laborers and "those employed in the building trades," was reissued, setting the prescribed rates at 3d a day for a master carpenter and 2d for nonmasters outside the city (see Brentano 78). London rates were set at 6d without food or drink in summer (Easter to Michaelmas) and 5d during the shorter winter days (Salzman 72). In 1360 Parliament announced the banning of all "alliances and covens of masons and carpenters," apparently in reaction to wage fixing at the Crown's Windsor Castle construction site (Leeson 35). That same year also witnessed an attempt to further strengthen the Statute of Labourers by increasing the penalties for accepting wages higher than those mandated. But the realities were that the labor market made violation of the Statutes commonplace, and those violating the statutes might still turn a profit after paying the imposed fines (Leeson 38). In 1389 Parliament, alarmed by the increasing agitation of the London craft guilds, passed a petition against the wearing of any livery (the uniform of a guild; Chaucer's Five Guildsmen have their own "lyveree," I.363) given under color of guild fraternity (Unwin 124–125). This was about the time Chaucer was writing the "General Prologue," a charged moment in the life of London when skilled laborers were discontented and organizing daily into increasingly factional special interests.

The corollary of the struggle to regulate wages was the effort to define the working day for which those wages were paid. To a great extent, the patterns of day labor remained the same despite the ongoing struggles over the rise and control of wages. As we have already noted in regard to the daily wages paid London carpenters, members of the craft were paid for a day's work according to the season, with the longer summer days from Easter to Michaelmas paying more than the shorter winter ones (Salzman 56–57). During those days, the average carpenter could expect to begin work at sunrise and complete his labor as the sun set. A break would be taken at the nones, actually the ninth hour, which came to be known as the "noon" break (Salzman 61). On Saturday a carpenter might expect to work three-fourths of a day at half wages. Rainy days did not necessarily halt work, much of which might be continued in relative comfort under the protection of the lodge at a major construction site. The York ordinances of 1352 and 1370 define the workday as daybreak to sunset, and as with most local ordinances, they likewise stipulate feast days such as those of patron saints of the guild and town. Christmas and Easter would also afford four to seven days' rest (Salzman 56–57).

Overseeing and enforcing the day's hours and wages was the master carpenter. For the crafts of both masonry and carpentry, the term *master*—with increasing frequency—no longer referred to a "master" of a craft or its lore but to the master, or supervisor, of underworkers. A master mason/carpenter was more akin to the modern architect than his fellow craftsman. Even more frequently, major work was done under the supervision of the clerk of the King's Works, who was responsible for the payment of wages, provision of materials, and impressment of workers (on the clerk of the King's Works, see Salzman 16–24; Harvey and Oswald 6; Brown, Colvin, and Taylor 189–201). In part, the creation of this new administrative position was due to the increased demands for literacy among those who headed projects, for medieval building was rooted in the subtleties of contracts. Arguably, Chaucer's knowledge of the intricacies of the written word rather than his knowledge of building per se made him qualified and successful as clerk of the King's Works (Salzman 8). Indeed, in the litigious Middle Ages, there were not a few contractual disputes and lawsuits over faulty workmanship and deceptive practices (Salzman 24, 29), such as the use of cheaper, unseasoned timber. If clerk of the Works was something akin to the producer of a modern movie, the architect or master mason/carpenter was analogous to the director responsible for the design of the project at hand. As such he had to provide plans and details and even scale models from which others might work. Sometimes this would be in the form of ground plans called "plattes" (Salzman 16; also see Atkinson 5–7 for a discussion of the role of the "architect" as well as the procedure for drawing up plans). Although some master masons and carpenters took part in the more skilled operations, since the thirteenth century there had been an increasing tendency for those elevated to the position of king's carpenter or mason to restrict their duties to design and oversight (Gimpel 114–115). The architect-mason might, however, lend a hand at carving, which was considered a more prestigious activity.

Because such large projects were primarily stone, master masons seem clearly to have had the ascendancy, serving as architects far more frequently than master carpenters (Salzman 24; on the role as well as the history of the master carpenter, see Brown, Colvin, and Taylor 203, 216–222). That dominance is reflected in the London Council where masons seem far more powerful than the carpenters, who along with other "lesser" fraternities failed to send a representative alderman to the London Council. During the fourteenth century, however, Hugh Herland, who was appointed as the king's carpenter, was clearly an important figure, with a hand seemingly in all royal works. In a rare tribute to a carpenter, Herland's portrait appears along with those of William Wyrford, mason, and Thomas, glass painter, in the great East window of Winchester College, although it should be noted that Herland's name is not given in the portrait, which is simply labeled "The Carpenter." Still, Herland is listed in household account rolls for 1393 as regularly dining with the clerk of the Works and William Wyrford, the king's mason, during the completion of the project, and the portrait is almost universally held to be his (Harvey and Oswald 7–8).

The carpenter of the "General Prologue" could only aspire to the sort of position held by Herland. Still, as we have seen, carpenters' fortunes were on the rise. For instance, two carpenters, along with two masons, were by patent inspectors for the city of London, their duties being to report nuisances, encroachments, and divide property (Salzman 37). In 1323, the master carpenter of Ely was provided furs worth 4s4d as part of his salary, a sign of respect and an indication of his rising status (Salzman 47). Either the city inspectors or the master carpenter at Ely could be considered the equivalent of Chaucer's carpenter.

In stark distinction to the master carpenters was the yeomanry (literally "the young men"), a group composed of daily wage laborers called journeymen (from the French *journée,* meaning day), and the servants apprenticed for several years to the masters of the craft (see Atkinson 14; Leeson 41). Although they have been compared to modern trade unions, medieval guilds were essentially associations of employers. In most carpenters' guilds in medieval England, only masters could join, and in all cases, only masters could hold office in the guild. Most master carpenters were themselves laborers, putting a hand in any work they did for a patron, but they also employed journeymen for a lesser

wage than they themselves drew and relied on the cheap child labor of apprentices. At a young age (usually at eight to ten years of age), the apprentice was
contracted to a master for a period of about seven years (Leeson 29–30; Robertson 79–80). The master carpenter promised to teach his apprentice the skills
of the craft and, usually, to feed, clothe, and house him in exchange for the
apprentice's labor, which often included domestic duties. Apprenticeship was
the medieval version of modern vocational education, the major difference being
that the apprentice was bound not to run away. The master thus assumed parental
responsibilities over the apprentice, instructing his charge not only in the secrets
of the craft but in moral matters as well. Often apprentices found themselves in
debt to their masters upon completing the term of their apprenticeship. Consequently, once the apprentice became a journeyman, he found it difficult to raise
the money necessary to open his own carpentry shop and, in his turn, become
a master. In addition, in late fourteenth-century England the masters of all crafts
began limiting guild membership to their own sons and relatives. Journeyman
status became "the great dividing line of labor—only a minority of men ever
joined the ranks of independent masters" (Epstein 115). When we read Chaucer's portrait of the Five Guildsmen, we should keep always in mind the hierarchical yet unstable social and economic structure of late medieval England.
The merchant guilds dominated the craft guilds; the masters dominated the yeomanry; and increasingly in the fifteenth century the richer craft masters would
become leading capitalists and dominate their poorer counterparts. We can better
understand, then, the pompous air of Chaucer's Carpenter when we relate his
apparent status as a consummate master of his craft to this ongoing division
among the ranks of working carpenters.

Whatever his rank within his craft, the working carpenter, in the course of
practicing his "myster," had an unusually varied repertoire of tasks, ranging
from the parlor tricks of his trade to miracles of seemingly biblical proportions,
from the minuscule, carving wooden pins to hold tiles in place, to the mundane,
fashioning the handles for his own tools, to the magnificent, connecting the 67-
foot span of the hammerbeam roof of Westminster Hall. (Examples of hammerbeam ceilings can be seen in Atkinson, figures 62–69; other examples of
this art form are found in plates 11B, 26, and 27 of Brown, Colvin, and Taylor.
Also, Gimpel 39 gives an illustration of a master carpenter supervising construction.) In fact, the carpenter of the fourteenth century might perform a wide
variety of work, as we have already seen in the case of Lawrence Wright, the
master carpenter of Ripon. Regardless of his position, the work of a general
carpenter required many skills applied to a wide range of different tasks, from
clappers to scaffolding.

Clearly, the great works of castle and cathedral were primarily the domain of
the mason. Still, carpenters were needed as much for the construction of the
lodgehouse and tools, including the barrows, as for direct contributions such as
gates, doors, windows, or even roofs for the edifice (Gimpel 140). Even more
crucial to such major projects was the carpenters' responsibility for designing

and constructing the elaborate hoists that were essential for raising men and materiel to the dazzling heights of both castle and cathedral (Gimpel 96). Of particular importance was the carpenters' job of providing scaffolding (Gimpel 137; see also Coldstream 51. Gimpel 125 provides a striking manuscript illustration of an on-site accident in which a scaffold collapses). New ironwork made carpenters able to meet the increasingly complex demands of scaffolding for the innovative and dramatic changes in vaulting. Such scaffolding could be extremely expensive, consuming vast amounts of lumber. In 1324, Westminster Abbey required 25 pieces of alder at 20 feet, 400 of alder at 38 feet, and 61 of ash at 42 feet (Salzman 318). Essential to the construction of vaults and arches were the "centeryngs," or the massive beams, that supported and held together the members of an arch or vault until the final keystones were laid and the mortar set (Salzman 320).

Although large projects such as work on castles and cathedrals might require increasing specialization (such as carvers and joiners, sawyers, and even the various "wrights," both cart or ship), a practicing master carpenter such as Lawrence Wright, who was neither so elevated as to be an architect-carpenter nor so humble as to be a general laborer, was something of a jack-of-all-carpentry-trades. In York, where the craft had developed a number of specializations, the "junours (joiners), cartwrights, caruours (carvers), and sawers," (Smith xxxvi) though recognized as specialists, were all members of the same carpenters' guild, and a good general carpenter could be said to have and need all these skills, especially in a small village. As J.A.W. Bennett has pointed out, Chaucer's Reeve's "myster," or craft, probably was a valued asset in his job as reeve where he would be called upon to perform numerous "other minor works" from maintaining existing structures to overseeing the creation of new ones (92). Even during times of recreation, carpenters were never far from their craft. For instance, they might be responsible not only for their own part in a pageant but also for the scaffolding and the rolling stages on which all their fellow guildsmen performed their plays (Smith xxxv). For carpenters, there was always a steady stream of work from carts to doorjambs. Whether stone or wood, all buildings required doors and shutters, glass windows being the exception rather than the rule (Harris 20) and, in more elaborate and costly projects, paneling and dividing screens (Salzman 318). Carpenters were responsible not only for buildings but for their furnishings as well, including cupboards, bedsteads, tables, and chairs. Thus the local carpenter could usually find enough work, though on average such work was seasonal and was paid by day or week.

Reflective of the wide variety of tasks undertaken by the working carpenter was the equally wide variety of tools at his disposal. As D. W. Robertson notes, the common carpenters who worked for daily wages "ordinarily possessed only their skills and a few tools" (80). Nevertheless, those tools might represent a considerable accumulated investment for men of small means—including assorted axes, adzes, chisels, gouges, planes, saws, drills with shell bits, hammers, and mallets (Harris 19; Salzman 340–346). For the carpenter's apprentice, the seven-year period of apprenticeship in large part consisted of learning the uses of and acquiring the specialized tools of his trade. Tools were so reflective of the craftsman that in the fifteenth-century poem, "The Debate of the Carpenter's Tools," the carpenter's tools come alive, much like the enchanted broom of the sorcerer's apprentice, and discuss the character and prospects of their owner (Salzman 340). In some cases carpenters had to protect the tools on which their livelihood depended. The account rolls of the work on Restormel Castle include the provision of planes for carpenters who refused to use their own tools for fear of damage done by nails embedded in reused lumber on the project (Salzman 340). Of all of these tools, the most efficient was probably the "wright's axe" which could be used to fell the timber and square the lumber at the beginning of the task; it also was handy in finishing work at the job's end. "Merkyngaxes" were used for marking or notching. Saws, though equally specialized, were generally two-handled. In addition to the tools required for cutting and shaping wood, the carpenter would also need a variety of files and whetstones for keeping those tools sharp. For smoothing rough surfaces, the rough skin of the dogfish (hundysfishskyn) was used much like modern sandpaper. Records of Westminster list its price in 1355 as 9d. Glue was made from fish-sounds (Salzman 346). For the average construction, oak pegs, also made by the carpenter, were the norm. On the larger building sites of cathedrals and the King's Works, the presence of ironmongers might mean the use of nails—a relative luxury in medieval construction—of which there were a surprising variety ranging from transom nails to roof nails to tile nails, and everything inbetween (Salzman 304–317). Ironmongers at the larger sites meant not only nails but increasingly better tools and scaffolding, which in turn enabled the creation of ever more complex vaulting. At the cathedral at Autun, a full 10 percent of expenditures went to maintaining the ironmonger's forge (Gimpel 137). The symbiotic relationship between the ironmongers and the carpenters, no doubt, had its ups and downs. We need only note that in the "Miller's Tale" the local blacksmith provides jolly Absolon with the red hot tool for the requiting of Nicholas's cuckolding of the Carpenter. On the other hand, late fourteenth-century rolls record a legal controversy between the ironmongers of Chester and their brother carpenters over "whether Fletchers, Bowers, Srugers, Coopers, and Turners should help one or the other [guild] or have their own play in [the town's mystery] cycle" (Lumiansky 204).

Whatever the final product of the carpenter's craft—whether tool handle, house, or vaulted ceiling—it began with the base material of wood. Indeed, it was the act of working with wood that defined the work, at least in the mind of the guildsman, as an act of carpentry, even if the end product was a shoe as in the controversy with the skinners' guild at York. Part of the carpenter's task was not only the making of the desired object, whether tile pins or shutters, but also the gathering of materials. Contracts frequently specify the required task of providing lumber along with specifications as to the size, quality, and type of wood to be used. Carpenters not only had to harvest and cut trees but also convert the wood into seasoned lumber, unseasoned wood being a serious fire hazard. Thus Richard Ploughwright, a carpenter from Trumpington, the site of the carpenter-reeve's tale, entered into a contract with one John Pilate in which it is specified that "the 'sparre' used was to be of value not less than 2d" (Harvey and Oswald 208–209). In 1390 William de Newhall, master carpenter in Chester and Flint, was ordered "to deliver one oak out of the wood of Ewloe" for the repair of coal mines (Harvey and Oswald 193–194). In 1353 the carpenter John Potte contracted to rebuild the great bridge to the outer gate of Farnham Castle. His client, the bishop of Winchester, was by stipulation of contract to supply the lumber. Since the Crown had first claim on resources such as timber, carpenters with influential patrons frequently sought protection of materials from the King's Works. For instance, Chaucer's patron John of Gaunt, on October 11, 1374, was able to "order that all the timber within the rape of Hastings, Sussex . . . be delivered to William Wintrigham," his own master carpenter, for the sake of several large building projects. Further orders were issued in 1380 for the cutting of oaks on July 1, 1380 and in the following February for the provision of more oaks for rafters, along with the cutting of twelve oaks for "the furtherance of the works" (Harvey and Oswald 297). Yet carpenters such as Wintringham also provided and were paid for lumber of their own provision, with or without the aid of a royal exemption. Thus in 1388, one finds Wintringham supplying timber for the works of London Bridge. Many powerful carpenters became timber merchants, and it was not unusual to see families, such as that of William Wright of Ripon, making considerable parts of their income merely supplying timber (Harvey and Oswald 305–306).

Timber, of course, had to be converted into usable beams. The most common method was to produce one rough beam (boxed heart) using axes or adzes. (On the conversion of timber into usable lumber, see Harris 17–18; Coldstream 23, 45, presents several manuscript illustrations.) Such beams might be split or sawed in half for rectangular rather than square beams. Planks, such as Lawrence Wright's "thakbordes" might be sawed as well. Such beams might often be 10 to 20 feet long. Lengths over 30 feet were not uncommon. Occasionally, beams could be found that were up to 50 feet in length. Sawing of beams was occasionally done on trestles but was most often done in pits with two man saws (Harris 17). Because the production of lumber was a major part of the contracted job, timbers were often simply reused. It was just such reuse of beams that caused the carpenters of Restormel Castle to be wary of damaging their own planes on hidden nails.

By far, houses and common buildings were the most frequent building projects (on the timber-framed house, see Harris 13–60; Salzman 320). Stone houses were very rare in most towns; the majority of buildings were timber framed. Such houses were often framed or prefabricated with the joining holes drilled and joints fashioned at the carpenter's yard or "framing ground." Next, the frames were transported to be assembled at the desired location (Harris 15). Because of the preciseness of the joints and the complications of assembling parts at the site, beams were marked with chiseled carpenters' marks, many of which are still visible today in exposed beams (Leeson 37; Salzman 342). Framing would begin with a floor frame to which side and middle frames were attached and then raised by pulleys and ropes. As Richard Harris notes, buildings were essentially a series of frames held together not by gravity as are edifices of stone, but by carefully constructed joints (Harris 8), joints being to medieval timber-framed buildings what nails are to modern houses. Motrice and tenon joints, "the basis of all traditional framing," usually consisted of a round oak peg (tenon) in a round hole (mortice), although in their more monumental form mortise and tenon joints could be found in the construction of Stonehenge. To construct long beams, usually near the main posts of a building, the medieval carpenter might also employ several types of scarf joints, a joint made by grooving, halving, or notching two pieces of wood and then aligning them (Harris 13). Lap joints—formed by layering and sometimes intricately intersecting two wood pieces—were employed more selectively in later buildings and "were generally found only between rafters and collars and in cruck construction." A "cruck" consists of "long curved timbers, framed together in pairs and joined by a tie beam or collar, which rise from the ground level to support the roof purlins of the building" (Harris 8). The complicated but beautifully detailed lap-dovetail assembly—a joint the intricacy of which approaches sculpture—was "in almost universal use in all buildings" from the thirteenth century and "is fundamental to the British tradition of timber framing" (Harris 13). The French, suffering decimation of their forests earlier and at a greater rate than the English, developed advanced methods of joining smaller pieces of timber to achieve the longer lengths demanded by increasingly grandiose projects (Gimpel 139).

Once the building was framed, the beams were left exposed, and the panels, or spaces between the framing beams, might be filled with a number of materials, the most common being "wattle and daub," a basket-like interweaving of oak or hazel or sometimes ash "wattles" or strips covered with a mixture of clay, dung, and straw (Harris 19). Bricks, because of their tendency to absorb and retain dampness, were seldom used. Increasing specialization meant that plasterers might be designated to fill in spaces between beams while tilers roofed the finished house, although the rural working carpenter might still perform all of these duties. While the plasterers and tilers were at work, the carpenter might then construct the screens, shutters, and interior furnishings. The average carpenter would certainly be capable of the common repairs, and the modest master carpenter with the aid of an apprentice or a journeyman might well oversee and complete the construction of a timber-framed building.

That feat, in and of itself, was a transformation worthy of great reverence both by Chaucer and his audience. In fact, nowhere is the sense of the "myster(ie)" of the craft of carpentry so well captured as by Richard Harris who observes that "Creating a building from trees is a bit like alchemy. Instead of turning base metal to gold, the alchemist-carpenter had to turn trees into beams, into frames, into buildings" (Harris 3). That observation might, in turn, remind us that, although the carpenter pilgrim might himself stand in the shadows, the pilgrimage—with its conversions, verbal constructions, and even its own tale of an alchemist—began at the Tabard, most likely a timber-framed building, and had as its own goal an apt emblem of the exalted heights of the worldly wright's art, the great cathedral at Canterbury, itself a microcosm of the Heavenly Jerusalem built by a Lord who also practiced the "good myster" of the carpenter's craft.

REFERENCES

Alford, B.W.E. and T. C. Barker, *A History of the Carpenters' Company.* London: George Allen and Unwin Ltd., 1968.

Atkinson, Thomas Dinham. *Local Style in English Architecture, An Enquiry into Its Origin and Development.* London: B. T. Batsford, Ltd., 1947.

Bennett, J.A.W. *Chaucer at Oxford and Cambridge.* Oxford: Clarendon Press, 1974.

Benson, Larry D., ed. *The Riverside Chaucer.* Boston: Houghton Mifflin, 1987.

Bonaventure. *De Decem Praeceptis, Collatio IV,* in *Opera Omnia.* Florence, 1891.

Brentano, Lujo. *On the History and Development of Guilds, and the Origin of Trade Unions.* London: Trubner and Co., 1870.

Brown, R. Allen, H. M. Colvin, and A. J. Taylor. *The History of the King's Works, Volume I: The Middle Ages.* London: Her Majesty's Stationery Office, 1963.

Chaucer, Geoffrey. *A Variorum Edition of the Works of Geoffrey Chaucer, Volume II, The Canterbury Tales, The General Prologue, Part One A,* ed. Malcolm Andrew, Charles Moorman, and Daniel J. Ransom. Norman: University of Oklahoma Press, 1993.

Coldstream, Nichola. *Masons and Sculptors,* Medieval Craftsman Series. Toronto: University of Toronto Press, 1991.

Ditchfield, P. H. *The Story of the City Companies.* London: G. T. Foulis and Co. 192?.

Epstein, Stephen A. *Wage and Labor Guilds in Medieval Europe.* Chapel Hill: University of North Carolina Press, 1991.

Fullerton, Ann B. "The Five Craftsmen." *MLN* 61 (1946): 515–523.

Gimpel, Jean. *The Cathedral Builders,* trans. Teresa Waugh. New York: HarperCollins, 1992.

Harris, Richard. *Discovering Timber-Framed Buildings.* Aylesbury, UK: Shire Publications, Ltd., 1978.

Harvey, John, and Arthur Oswald. *English Medieval Architects, A Biographical Dictionary Down to 1550.* London: B. T. Batsford, Ltd., 1954.

Hope, Valerie, Clive Birch, and Gilbert Torry. *The Freedom: The Past and Present of the Livery, Guilds and City of London.* Buckingham, England: Barracuda Books Ltd., 1982.

Leeson, R. A. *Traveling Brothers.* London: George Allen and Unwin Ltd., 1979.

Lumiansky, R. M., and David Mills. *The Chester Mystery Cycle.* Chapel Hill: University of North Carolina Press, 1983.

Mills, David. "Religious Drama and Civic Ceremonial." In *The Revels History of Drama in English. Vol. I: Medieval Drama.* Eds. A. C. Cawley, Marion Jones, Peter F. McDonald, and David Mills. London: Methuen, 1983.

Myers, A. R. *London in the Age of Chaucer.* Norman: University of Oklahoma Press, 1972.

Robertson, D. W., Jr. *Chaucer's London.* New York: John Wiley and Sons, 1968.

Salzman, L. F. *Building in England Down to 1540.* Oxford: Clarendon Press, 1952.

Smith, Lucy Toulmin, ed. *The York Plays: Plays Performed by the Crafts or Mysteries of York on the Day of Corpus Christi in the 14th, 15th, and 16th Centuries.* New York: Russell and Russell, 1963.

Thrupp, Sylvia. *The Merchant Class of Medieval London (1300–1500).* Ann Arbor: University of Michigan Press, 1962.

Unwin, George. *The Guilds and Companies of London.* London: Methuen and Co., 1908.

Chapter 15

... A Webbe ...

GWENDOLYN MORGAN

If one accepts the commonplace notion that Chaucer presents a cross-section of medieval society in his *Canterbury Tales,* it must be with the concession that the Weaver's virtual absence creates a glaring gap in his parade of characters. The Weaver tells no tale of his own, figures in no one else's, and receives only a brief description in common with four other guildsmen in the "General Prologue." He does not, apparently, merit even association with the Merchant, a member of the most wealthy and powerful guild made so primarily through the clothmaking profession. Nonetheless, he represents that trade which wrought the greatest social and economic changes of medieval England.

This in itself makes it unfortunate that the Weaver is lost in the unfinished portion of the *Tales.* (According to Chaucer's original plan, of course, he would have been assigned four tales—two on the way to Canterbury and two on the return trip—along with all the other pilgrims.) The loss is made the greater by the fact that Chaucer was a product of "the solempne and greet fraternitee" of citizens classified, organized, and governed by the various trade guilds in the midst of whose representatives the Weaver finds himself.

Understanding the peculiar significance of the weaver in medieval English society requires a review of the English wool commerce and of the clothmaking trade in Europe. This, combined with an understanding of the monumental changes occurring in the social and industrial spheres at the very time that the weaving profession becomes a major element of the English economy, goes far to explain his paradoxical position.

A HISTORY OF ENGLISH WOOL

Cloth had always been a major staple of commerce, both between the various areas of Europe and between Europe and the East. Indeed, during the high

Middle Ages, before coinage became common, cloth was a popular means of payment. Moreover, English wool, finer and stronger than that produced elsewhere, held a central position early in this important trade. As John Tovey (10) observes, "even before the Roman Conquest very fine woolen cloth was being woven at Winchester, and by A.D. 300 was being exported as far as Eastern Europe," Although the disruption of trade with the continent following the departure of the Romans caused production virtually to cease, by the mid-seventh century, trade in raw English wool was again thriving.

Throughout the Middle Ages, wool remained the most important English export. By the twelfth century, Flanders had established itself as the major cloth-producing and finishing center in Europe, and so English wool, along with smaller amounts of silk, cotton, and alum (necessary to finish cloth) from the East, was channeled into the hands of the skilled Flemish weavers, a portion of the finished cloth being exported back into England at a considerable profit to the craftsmen and merchants of the Low Countries. It was not long, however, before the English monarchy recognized the power that might be exerted through control and taxation of this necessary commodity.

In the thirteenth century, England established wool staples—compulsory markets—for its wool on the Continent, along with high export taxes which reached 33 percent in the fourteenth century. For 150 years, the monarchy manipulated trade and exerted political influence by relocating these staples, finally settling the market in Calais in 1363, where it remained for almost two hundred years. The wool taxes supplied the English exchequer with its major source of income, and merchants receiving charters to deal in exportation of the commodity ("Staplers") formed the most prestigious and wealthiest segment of the middle class. Indeed, control of the wool trade eventually became one of the primary causes of the Hundred Years' War with France.

Even so, exportation of the raw wool had begun to decline by the early fourteenth century owing to the level of taxation. Seeking to maintain their primary source of profit, English merchants assisted in persuading numbers of the talented Flemish weavers to settle in England and train native craftsmen in their techniques. English fabric soon sold for less in continental markets than that locally produced from the highly taxed, imported, raw wool. By the end of the century, English cloth dominated the market, as it continued to do for hundreds of years afterward. Today, English woolens still enjoy a reputation as among the finest available.

THE WEAVING TRADE

Wool and woolen cloth, then, shaped the English economy and influenced international policy throughout the Middle Ages, but how was the weaver involved in events of such magnitude? The answer is, in a variety of ways. First, members of his profession supported a large number of related trades, representatives from several of which travel together with the Weaver of Chaucer's "General Prologue." Second, the application of his craft—the process and the organization of weaving in England—offered a basis for the medieval and later the eighteenth-century industrial revolutions. Third, the weavers' guild and its position among the other guilds led, finally, to social and political changes so dramatic that the tripartite society of medieval England crumbled under their pressure.

Woolen cloth production has changed little since Chaucer's day, the various processes remaining the same, although many have been partially or fully mechanized and the division of labor into the distinct provinces of separate artisan groups has disappeared. Wool collected from the sheep and cleaned must be carded and spun into yarn, which is then woven into cloth. The raw cloth is softened and tempered by "fulling," a process early on accomplished by trampling the cloth and in the later Middle Ages by water-driven fulling mills. The fulled fabric must then be finished, that is, provided with a durable and uniform surface. Only properly finished fabric may be dyed, and from there fashioned into clothes and other goods.

The actual process of weaving, "making cloth by interlacing two sets of threads at right angles to each other, the longitudinal threads being the warp and the threads across being the weft" (Tovey 12), requires a loom, a frame that holds the warp in place while the weaver uses a shuttle to run the weft through the threads in a particular pattern called the "weave." Chaucer's weaver and his associates would have used the English four-post loom, a large, free-standing design that has a solid seat for the weaver built in the middle of the loom (between the posts) for ease in working the cloth. The English loom remains in common use by hand-weavers today.

As were most craftsmen during the Middle Ages, those performing the various steps in cloth production organized themselves into individual guilds, which in turn protected their particular provinces from encroachment by related crafts and policed themselves for observation of proper training and acceptable product quality. Eileen Power offers a succinct description of the cloth-producing guilds and their influence on the first capitalist guild in her biography of Thomas Paycocke, a fifteenth-century clothier:

The preliminary processes of spinning and carding were always by-industries, performed by women and children in their cottages; but the weavers, who bought the spun yarn, had their gild [sic]; and so had the fullers, who fulled it; and the shearmen, who finished it; and the dyers, who dyed it. All could not sell the finished piece of cloth, and in the group of interdependent crafts, each with its gild, we sometimes find the weavers employing the fullers and sometimes the fullers the weavers. Moreover, since weaving is a much quicker process than spinning, the weaver often . . . found it hard to collect enough yarn to keep his loom busy; and, as the market for cloth grew wider . . . the need was felt for some middlemen to specialize in the selling of the finished cloth. So by degrees there grew up a class of men who bought wool in large quantities and sold it to the weavers, and then by a natural transition began, not to sell the wool outright, but to deliver it to the weavers to weave, to the fullers to full, and to the shearmen to finish at a wage, receiving it back again when the work was done. (153)

By the mid-fourteenth century, the clothier also took under his control the preliminary processes of carding and spinning and the responsibility of selling the finished cloth to the draper, the mercantile middleman who would have the cloth dyed (if it had not already been so under the direction of the clothier) and sell it either in his own establishment or to the wool merchant for mass distribution and sale. On occasion, the draper and the wool merchant were one and the same.

It might also be observed that the process by which one became a fully accredited weaver followed the usual apprentice-journeyman-master division seen in other of the craft guilds. A master weaver apprenticed a young man interested in the trade for a term, usually seven years, providing him with room and board, training in his craft (and sometimes in other basic skills such as arithmetic, reading, and writing), and on occasion clothes and/or a small salary. After completing his apprenticeship, the weaver then became a journeyman who might work for himself, "journeying" around the countryside, or for a master weaver in return for wages. When a journeyman had served a period considered sufficient by his guild and demonstrated significant skill at his craft, he could be declared a master weaver and a full and influential member of his fraternity.

THE WEAVER AS PROLETARIAT

Despite his position at the center of cloth production, the weaver was often the lowest paid (next to the spinners) and least politically and socially powerful of the guilds. In continental and English cities alike—which were, by and large, autonomous and self-regulated units—the trade guilds usually formed the backbone of local government. Universally, the most powerful and prosperous guild was that of the merchants, of whom Chaucer offers a fairly standard portrait. Despite the fact that all the guildsmen were free-born and of common birth, it was not long before class distinctions appeared between the merchant and lesser elite and the laborers. Corruption among ruling groups and their prolonged economic and other abuse of the lower tradesmen led, by the end of the thirteenth century, to widespread unrest and not infrequent rioting. Such uprisings, sometimes led by the weavers themselves, continued into the fourteenth and fifteenth centuries, at one point leaving the rebels in control of the city of Flanders. Between the distrust and resentment bred on both sides of these conflicts, the ever decreasing availability of raw English wool on the continent (a result of the English monarchy's policies of taxation and monopoly), and the refusal of certain continental weaver guilds to compromise the quality of their product with inferior wool, the woolen cloth-producing industries of the mainland found themselves in irreversible decay by Chaucer's day.

In England, of course, the cloth trade thrived accordingly. However, the weavers themselves were no better off and, although they certainly participated in various demonstrations of social unrest, they lacked the effectiveness of their continental counterparts. By the time the cloth industry grew to significance in England, the weavers had lost whatever concentration of numbers and social and moral support of other exploited urban tradesmen they might have once enjoyed; for, as the industry grew, the powerful clothier, rather than deal with the strict monopolies, regulations, and higher wage scales enforced by city guilds, took his weaving business to the rural districts. Such a move was made more attractive as fulling mills came into use; dependent on water power, these machines and those who operated them were located increasingly in districts where such was readily available (Ferguson 126–127). Under such circumstances, the old weaving guilds gave way to independent piece workers by the early fourteenth century.

Nonetheless, the weaver, often unwillingly, continued as a political and economic force. As Ferguson puts it, the "transformation of England from a wool-producing to a wool-weaving country was an event of epoch-making proportions," for it "marked the beginning of that process of industrialization which in the course of time made England the workshop of the modern world" (126). Not only did expansion in the influence and function of the clothier and the wool merchant betoken a nascent capitalism, but the clothier actually organized the production of woolen cloth on an assembly line or factory basis. First in his own house, then in separate buildings, the clothier set up multiple looms and hired journeymen to work them, while similarly maintaining control over the other steps in the clothmaking process. A detailed description of such a "mini-factory" is offered in Thomas Deloney's 1597 *Pleasant History of Jack of Newbury.*

Needless to say, the weavers were not pleased with the clothier's production arrangements. Power observes that "either they were forced from the position of free masters into that of hired servants, obliged to go and work in the clothier's loom shop, or else they found their payment forced down by the competition of the journeymen" ("Thomas Betson" 162). This reduction in status resulted, as it had earlier on the continent, in considerable strife between the entrepreneurs and their laborers, and the disgruntled weavers again drifted toward the marginalized movements of social and political unrest. However, not all weavers viewed themselves as the exploited proletariat in the new capitalism. Some clung to the old perceptions of social order, substituting the clothier for earlier, more feudal connections, and maintained amiable relations with their paternal employers. Fifteenth-century clothier Thomas Paycocke, for example, bequeathed upon his death substantial sums of money and forgave debts to "my wevers, fullers and shermen . . . Kembers, Carders and Spynners" (Power, "Thomas Paycocke" 160–161) ["my weavers, fullers, and shearmen . . . Combers, Carders, and Spinners"].

So early organized and, to a certain extent, mechanized through the fulling mills and large, commercial looms, the weaving profession and cloth-producing industry as a whole nonetheless remained virtually unchanged until the eighteenth century. Then, in 1733, John Kay's invention of the flying shuttle, a device that significantly reduced effort and production time on the English loom and that produced a more regular weave, spawned a series of innovations in the

weaving process. Thereafter, "the traditions of the craft died out almost everywhere during the Industrial Revolution, but sufficient remained in rural areas
and in the records and writings of master weavers for a very complete picture
to be drawn" of the craft during the previous centuries (Tovey 11). It is perhaps
worth noting that the vain early attempts of weavers and other cloth-workers to
establish fair wages and working conditions, and control over their industry, did
finally come to fruition following the Industrial Revolution: factory cloth-
workers were among the leaders of the labor rights movements. In the twentieth
century, like so many other crafts, the art of hand weaving has reestablished
itself on a small but tenacious scale, and in England today one will still find
guilds of weavers and master weavers.

The weaver, then, by virtue of the process of his trade and of his position
within the early capitalist movement, stands at the center of many of the social,
political, and economic upheavals of England during the Middle Ages. He is
both mainstay, providing the most reliable and enduring source of national income and creating employment for great numbers of workers at the peripheries
of his craft, and revolutionary, becoming the first true urban proletariat as factory
and piece worker. However, in England his presence in these areas, though
essential, is obscure, just as is his presence in Chaucer's *Canterbury Tales*. In
history as in Chaucer, he is overshadowed by the more powerful merchant and
clothier who, without him, could not have attained their positions of power.

THE PUBLIC IMAGE OF THE WEAVER

The development of the clothmaking industry in England took place in an
extremely volatile social and economic environment. Despite the importance of
the wool trade to the English economy, a more general economic slump, primarily affecting the rural lower classes, stretched from the last quarter of the
twelfth century to the beginning of the sixteenth. The weaver's position in this
situation was peculiar indeed. A laborer in the capitalist system responsible for
the new power and wealth of the urban middle class, the weaver nonetheless
resided in the countryside where the effects of the reversal were most felt. He
thus seems to have been, rightly or wrongly, at once associated with the Peasants' Revolt of 1381 and the uprisings of the 1440s, as well as with the successful urban middle-class entrepreneurs feared and resented by the older
aristocracy. Without the cloth trade of the high Middle Ages, the English economy would have crumbled and England's influence on the continent drastically
reduced, yet the industry was continually held up as a metaphor for declining
morals, criminal activity, unscrupulous opportunism, and the general decay of
society. Consider, for example, the mid-thirteenth-century sermon of Berthold
of Regensburg: "The first [tricksters] are ye that work in clothing, silks, or wool
or fur . . . to steal half the cloth, or to use other guile; mixing hair with your
wool or stretching it out longer, whereby a man thinketh to have gotten good
cloth, yet thou hast stretched it to be longer than it should be, and makest a

good cloth into useless stuff'' (Coulton 90). Two hundred years later, William Langland's depiction of clothmakers in *Piers Plowman* seems to differ virtually not at all:

> Thanne drowe I me amonges draperes my donet to lerne,
> To drawe þe lyser alonge þe lenger it seemed;
> Among þe riche rayes I rendred a lessoun,
> To broche hem with a pak-nedle and plaited hem togyderes,
> And put hem in a presse and pynned hem perinne,
> Tyl ten yerdes or twelue hadde tolled out threttene.

> (11.211–216)

> [Then I drew among drapers my duty to learn,
> To draw the edge out until longer it seemed;
> Among the striped cloth lengths I was taught a lesson,
> I pricked them with a packing needle and plaited them together,
> And put them in a press and pinned them therein
> Until ten or twelve yards had stretched out to thirteen.]

It is worth noting that the character speaking these lines is Covetousness and that he goes on to describe his wife, a weaver of woolen cloth who cheated her spinners out of a fifth of their just wages by manipulating the scales used to weigh the yarn (11.217–220).

The weaver, then, did not enjoy a favorable reputation in Chaucer's day. His was not even the ambiguous position of the plowman, who at least was extolled as the ''salt of the earth'' in Langland's vision and other fifteenth-century lyrics even if he was equally condemned as a rabble-rouser and sluggard in Gower's sermons and other reactions to the rural unrest. How much the clothmaker was responsible for his poor image is unclear. Even so, the suggestion that he profited greatly from whatever dubious practices might have imbued his profession, or that he exercised any significant amount of control over the industry or the social classes involved in it, is certainly unfair. Instead, the weaver appears as the true proletariat of the Middle Ages, an exploited laborer on whose shoulders stood the capitalist clothiers and merchants, men whose social position, political power, and personal wealth grew steadily while the status and influence of the weaver accordingly declined.

CHAUCER'S WEAVER

Returning to Chaucer's Weaver, it should by now be obvious that, even in his brief appearance in the ''General Prologue,'' his depiction is inaccurate. Here, he is grouped with other guildsmen as a wealthy, pretentious social upstart:

An Haberdasshere and a Carpenter,
A Webbe, a Dyere, and a Tapycer—
And they were clothed alle in o lyveree
Of a solempne and a greet fraternitee.
Ful fressh and newe hir geere apiked was;
Hir knyves were chaped nought with bras
But al with silver, wrought ful clene and weel,
Hire girdles and hir pouches everydeel.
Wel semed ech of hem a fair burgeys
To sitten in a yeldehalle on a deys.
Everich, for the wisdom that he kan,
Was shaply for to been an alderman.
For catel hadde they ynogh and rente,
And eek hir wyves wolde it wel assente;
And elles certeyn were they to blame.
It is ful fair to been ycleped "madame,"
And to goon to vigilies al bifore,
And have a mantel roialliche ybore.

(361–378)

[An Haberdasher and a Carpenter,
A Weaver, a Dyer, and a Tapicer—
And they were all clad in one livery
Of a dignified and a great fraternity.
Very fresh and new their gear trimmed was;
Their knives were mounted not with brass
But all with silver, wrought very clean and well,
Their belts and their purses every bit.
Well seemed each of them a fair burgess
To sit in the guildhall on a dais.
Everyone, for the wisdom that he knows,
Was suitable to be an alderman.
For property they had enough and income,
And also their wives would it well assent;
And otherwise certain were they to blame.
It is very fair to be called "madam,"
And to go to vigils in front of everyone,
And have a mantle royally carried.]

While it was true that the wealthy burgers, merchants, and members of the more powerful trade guilds had begun to threaten the traditional English caste system and to cross class boundaries (the burgesses sat in the House of Commons in the first step taken by the British political system toward true democracy), it was not so for the weaver, who remained an exploited, usually propertyless laborer. When the other guilds were at the height of their power, his was at its nadir. The average weaver certainly could not afford knives chased with silver or to hire his own cook. Thus, his presence among these other, prosperous guildsmen is an anomaly.

Nonetheless, the elements of this description do apply to guilds in general, who often had their own distinctive livery and who formed an influential middle urban class. The description of the Weaver's compatriots, along with that of the Merchant, reflect the general aspirations of the class and their infringement on the traditional rights of the aristocracy. As Cooper notes, "the silver chasing on their knives is illegal, such ornament being the prerogative of the gentry" (47). Similarly, the indications of political and economic power, as has already been observed, are in concert with historical fact, as is the deliberate separation of the Merchant from the other guilds. Ultimately, this new citizen class did bring about the demise of the tripartite society.

Chaucer's treatment of the weaving profession, too, reflects practice in that he places the Weaver alongside a haberdasher, a tapester, and a dyer, professions dependent on the cloth he produced. The more powerful draper and clothier, however, are conspicuously absent. Even the reference to the Wife of Bath as a weaver of cloth recalls the cottage industries of spinning and carding, and the very real competition the weaver faced among such rural households. Finally, it again emphasizes the association of the weaving craft with the countryside, rather than with the city, as was the case with most artisans.

By serendipity or design, then, the Weaver's shadowy presence in the "General Prologue" is most appropriate. True to the perceptions of the aristocracy for whom Chaucer wrote and to which he aspired, the Weaver is guilty by association with both rural and urban unrest, with the breakdown of the old social order and the rise of capitalism. Positioned in some no man's land between the Wife and the guildsmen, he is in Chaucer, as in history, without real power or presence, neglected, abused, an unintentional hero and victim to early English capitalism.

REFERENCES

Bennett, H. S. *Chaucer and the Fifteenth Century.* Oxford: Oxford University Press, 1947.

Berlow, Rosalind Kent. "The Development of Business Techniques Used at the Fairs of Champagne from the End of the Twelfth Century to the Middle of the Thirteenth Century." *Studies in Medieval and Renaissance History.* Vol 3. Ed. Howard L. Adelson. Lincoln: University of Nebraska Press, 1971. Pp. 3–32.

Bloch, Marc. *Land and Work in Medieval Europe.* Trans J. E. Anderson. Berkeley: University of California Press, 1967.

Cantor, Norman. *The Civilization of the Middle Ages.* New York: HarperCollins, 1993.

Cooper, Helen. *The Canterbury Tales.* Oxford: Oxford University Press, 1989.

Coulton, G. G. *The Medieval Scene.* London: Cambridge University Press, 1930.

Ferguson, Wallace K. *Europe in Transition: 1300–1520.* Boston: Houghton Mifflin, 1962.

Hay, Denys. *Europe in the Fourteenth and Fifteenth Centuries.* New York: Holt, Rinehart and Winston, 1966.

Herlihy, David, ed. *Medieval Culture and Society.* New York: HarperCollins, 1968.

Keen, Maurice. *A History of Medieval Europe.* New York: Frederick A. Praeger, 1968.

Langland, William. *The Vision of William Concerning Piers the Plowman.* c. 1376–1387. *Medieval English Literature.* Ed. Thomas J. Garbáty. Lexington, Mass.: D. C. Heath, 1984.

Le Goff, Jacques. *Time, Work, and Culture in the Middle Ages.* Trans. Arthur Goldhammer. Chicago: University of Chicago Press, 1980.

Mann, Jill. *Geoffrey Chaucer.* Atlantic Highlands, N.J.: Humanities Press International, 1991.

Mills, Dorothy. *The Middle Ages.* New York: G. P. Putnam's Sons, 1935.

Power, Eileen. "Thomas Betson: A Merchant of the Staple in the Fifteenth Century." *Medieval People.* 10th ed. New York: Barnes and Noble, 1963. Pp. 120–151.

———. "Thomas Paycocke of Coggeshall: An Essex Clothier in the Days of Henry VII." *Medieval People.* 10th ed. New York: Barnes and Noble, 1963. Pp. 152–173.

Rowland, Beryl. "Chaucer's Working Wyf: The Unraveling of a Yarn-Spinner." *Chaucer in the Eighties.* Eds. Julian N. Wasserman and Robert J. Blanch. Syracuse, N.Y.: Syracuse University Press, 1986. Pp. 137–150.

Thompson, James Westfall. *Economic and Social History of Europe in the Later Middle Ages (1300–1530).* New York: Frederick Ungar, 1958.

Tovey, John. *The Technique of Weaving.* 2nd ed. New York: Charles Scribner's Sons, 1975.

Chapter 16

. . . A Dyere . . .

DIANA R. UHLMAN

Composing the frame for his *Canterbury Tales,* evidently intent on representing those of various "estaat" (I.714) and "degree" (I.40), Chaucer includes among the pilgrims "An Haberdasshere and a Carpenter, / A Webbe, a Dyere, and a Tapycer" (I.361–362; all references will be to *The Riverside Chaucer*). These pilgrims, first identified individually by occupation, are then immediately lumped together, dressed in the colorful uniform of one guild organization. How much should we make of Chaucer's specification of the guildsmen's occupations? Does it matter that one of the guildsmen is said to be a dyer?

Chaucer uses concrete detail to give his rapidly sketched portraits the bite of reality, and designating the occupations of the guildsmen plays off the way in which a man's identity and status in urban London was established. It was through acceptance into an official trade organization—like the Dyers' Guild—that a Londoner received "the freedom of the city," meaning he was considered a citizen of London and could claim the rights, privileges, and obligations that attached thereto. Trade affiliation held real significance, so that when John Doe signed his name, he didn't just write John Doe; he wrote John Doe, Fishmonger, or John Doe, Dyer (and perhaps he even wrote John Dyer, identifying with the craft so completely that it became his surname). In actuality, a successful man's designated craft affiliation might be a bit misleading in that success usually came from developing a business that extended well beyond the boundaries of any particular craft-trade. Since none of the guildsmen reappears outside the "General Prologue" to tell a tale or react to one, there is no development to give the craft designations additional meaning. Perhaps what is most important about the individual craftsmen is their collective guild membership.

Nevertheless, Chaucer had a welter of crafts and trades from which to choose—brewer, butcher, vintner, skinner, tailor, painter, mercer, grocer, draper, fuller, chandler, glover, ironmonger, goldsmith—and these are just a few: in the late 1300s, more than a hundred crafts are believed to have had organized groups in London. Why then might Chaucer choose to place among his guildsmen a dyer? Most critics agree that the guildsmen are portrayed as shallow aspirants to a more exalted social status based solely on their success in acquiring and displaying material wealth. Taking this into consideration, we can explore the historical context of the dyer's craft along with its literary associations and illuminate possibilities, however ultimately impossible it is to know what might have been done with the Dyer-guildsman had Chaucer further developed *The Canterbury Tales.*

DYES AND DYEING: THE CRAFT

The production and sale of cloth was one of the major domestic and international businesses in the Middle Ages, and the display of one's wealth through the wearing of beautifully dyed and finished "drapery" was more than anything a sign of status. Those at the bottom of the economic and social scale had to be content with rough woolen cloth, left its natural color or crudely dyed. Drab, washed-out color, along with coarse texture, indicated poverty and insignificance. Fabrics that used premium raw materials and that required long finishing processes and expensive dyes testified to one's wealth and ascent up the social scale. Take, for example, the guildsmen's livery—their dress uniform: with its soft, smooth texture, its deeply dyed, true colors, and its rich sheen, the expensive cloth projected the prosperity and importance of the men.

England in the Middle Ages produced beautifully finished and dyed woolen cloth, but the process, we must remember, was still a craft process. Almost everything had to be done by hand and depended for quality on the skill and knowledge of the individual doing the work. Wool had to be sorted, cleaned, carded, or combed and spun into yarn. Weaving, first of the highly skilled processes involved in clothmaking, followed. After that, several finishing processes were necessary to bring the cloth raw from the loom to its refined state. Fulling, the first of these, used "fuller's earth" (a highly absorbent, claylike substance) and water to scour, clean, and thicken fabric. Soaked cloth had to be stretched on frames and dried to keep it from shrinking too much and unevenly. While still damp, a fine nap was raised by rubbing the cloth with instruments using fuller's teasles, the dried heads of prickly thistles. In the fulling and finishing processes, other organic compounds—butter among them—were used to make the fabric pliable and soft. Shearmen were involved in these later stages, taking their name from the instruments they used to skim over the surface of the cloth, removing stray threads, and giving the cloth a completely uniform appearance. The best fabrics depended on repetition of these processes; the desired end product had a beautiful drape, a velvety surface, and a soft "hand."

Dyeing could take place before weaving: combed or carded fleece or spun wool could be put in the dyebath (thus, "dyed in the wool"). Or cloth could be dyed after fulling as part of the finishing. Whenever it was undertaken, dyeing was a complex craft—a science and an art handed down from experienced dyers to those who worked with them. The aniline, benzene-based dyes we employ today weren't synthesized by chemical engineers until the nineteenth century. In the Middle Ages, dyes were extracted from naturally occurring sources, from insects, shellfish, and plants. The three dyes most used in Europe—madder, weld, and woad—came from plants: madder, producing red tints; weld, yellow; and woad, blue. Other plant sources for red were brazilwood and orchil, a lichen. The deepest, richest reds—crimson and purple, colors of status since ancient times—were extracted from shellfish (purpura and murex) and from insects (kermes and cochineal). Kermes and cochineal were collectively called *grain* in Middle English, perhaps because the source of the exotic dye was misunderstood and thought to be seeds or because the dye came packaged in small pellets. Grain was very expensive and highly desirable; its saturated color never faded or ran. Thus, in the Middle Ages, people often used the expression that something was "dyed in the grain," or "ingrained," meaning something was so thoroughly imbued that it was virtually natural. Using limited dyestuffs, the most sophisticated medieval dyers boasted that they could produce as many as ten different shades of red, six different blues, three greens, and several kinds of black, grey, and brown.

Woad offers an excellent illustration of the knowledge, skill, and judgment required of a master dyer. Properly handled, alone or in combination with other dyes, woad could produce shades from a pale blue-green, through bright blue, to black. But woad was especially important because, in addition to color, its particular chemistry fixed other more "fugitive" dyes (like orchil and brazilwood) and made them permanent. Thus, most dyeing processes began by "woading" the cloth, whatever the final color to be achieved. The dye, when dyers bought it from woadmongers, had already been through an extensive preparation process that could take up to a full year: woad leaves had to be crushed, dried, fermented, and aged. An additional fermentation of the clay-like substance was required when the dyer prepared a vat just prior to dyeing, and depending on its earlier preparation, the strength of the woad could vary a great deal. As the dyer mixed the vat, he had to evaluate, adding organic matter like bran to increase the fermentation, and potash, from wood ashes, to fix the active ingredient chemically. Achieving the color desired depended on many variables: on having a properly prepared dyevat; on the type and quality of the wool to be dyed; on the amount of time the cloth spent in the dyevat; and on successive dippings in the same and/or different dyebaths. Woaded green, for example, was produced by first woading the cloth, then boiling it in alum and tartar (obtained from winelees), and finally immersing it in a vat of prepared weld.

Dyeing involved complex chemistry, skilled artistry—and also hot, smelly, hard labor. Dyevats were cauldrons over direct flame; woad, for example, had to be heated for a good three hours before dyeing. We know that woad fermentation had a distinctly foul odor because Elizabeth I forbade it in any area through which she passed, the smell sickened her so much. While in the vat, heavy woolen material had to be constantly stirred. Dyers wore the evidence of their labor on their hands: in Italy, dyers were ridiculed as "blue nails." Discolored hands were a sign that dyeing, however skilled, was still manual labor. On that basis, Italian dyers were excluded from membership in prestigious guilds intended for merchants who kept their hands clean, letting others do the work for them, while they managed, supervised, and handled accounts and money.

DYES AND DYEING: THE BUSINESS

As early as the 1100s, there were English towns known for cloth production, and town records refer to groups representing craftsmen's interests. Dyers are mentioned, but less frequently than weavers or fullers. A writ from the town of Lincoln, executed 1154–1160, contains the earliest mention of dyers: it declares that no one be allowed to enter Lincoln for the purpose of dyeing cloth or engaging in retail trade unless that individual has been admitted into the town's guild of merchants. This record suggests a very close connection between dyeing and retail trade. Probably the merchants of Lincoln bought the cloth undyed and then did the work in their own dyehouses or contracted the work out to dyers whom they controlled. The record thus illustrates a struggle that would go on throughout the Middle Ages: those who specialized in some aspect of production (like dyeing) sought to control competition in that area, to guarantee work and good wages, while those whose interests lay in buying and selling sought to control production of the commodity, to ensure low prices and better profits from sale.

Perhaps the merchants of Lincoln were particularly concerned with controlling the dyeing of cloth because their city was becoming famous for a particular hue of bright green, known as Lincoln green. Certainly, dyeing was an essential step in giving cloth its identity and value. Cloth was often generically known by its color, names deriving from the official French vernacular of the day. The Magna Carta (1216) regulated the size of "dyed cloths" like "russets" (madder-dyed red) and Henry III's household accounts (1233–1235) show that he bought, in addition to russets from Leicester and "blues" from Beverly, brown "burnets," gray-blue "plunkets," and undyed "blanket," to be colored scarlet at his orders.

In the twelfth and thirteenth centuries, however, English cloth was considered generally inferior on the world market. It was the city-states of Italy (especially Venice and Florence) and the Low Countries (especially Flanders) where the arts, crafts, materials, and trade involved in fine clothmaking, known to the Greeks and Romans, were rediscovered through contact with the East, Byzantium, and the Arabs. In fact, English cloth production was hindered during the early centuries of the Middle Ages because huge profits could be made by exporting the raw material—excellent quality English wool.

In the 1300s, with the Royal Treasury exhausted by the ongoing war with France, Edward II and Edward III realized that more money could be made on export of a finished product that kept craftsmen and laborers busy at home, used domestic raw materials and infrastructure for production, and limited the need for import and reliance on another country. They made rules and regulations that encouraged English clothmaking, restricting the export of wool and the import of finished cloth, prohibiting export of fulling and dyeing materials like woad, madder, and wood ashes, and granting franchises to weavers, fullers, and dyers. In 1364, for example, Walter Lister of Leeds paid 4 shillings to be named official dyer for the village of Bradforddale. Edward I and Edward II also encouraged master craftsmen from Flanders and Italy to emigrate. Some masters brought to England whole workshops; along with one foreign clothmaker, Nicholas Appelman, came several dyers and fullers who settled to work in Winchester. This policy was not always popular, however. We know about Nicholas Appelman and his workshop because a writ for their protection had to be issued in 1337—presumably local clothmakers were not happy with the competition for jobs that the foreigners represented.

The promotion of cloth production worked very well. By Chaucer's adulthood in the 1370s, weaving, fulling, dyeing, and finishing of cloth took place in the country all over England while merchandising clothmaking materials and trading in finished cloth was centralized in London. The guilds—or companies—that had grown prominent in England's capital were primarily organizations for merchants—with wealthy wholesalers, exporters, and distributors at the top, a main body of well-to-do shopkeepers, and a substratum of working craftsmen who aspired to trade. Many of the companies engaged in the cloth trade in some way to some extent. Members of the Company of Mercers (the word *mercers* comes from the same root as merchant and merchandise) certainly imported exotic cloth like silk and dealt in domestic cloth on a retail level. Those of the Company of Grocers (from *grossier*—one who deals in gross, or wholesale) were importers and distributors of woad, grain, and the other dyes and dye chemicals. John Churchman, Grocer, sued Geoffrey Chaucer for unpaid bills in the 1390s, and at the same time, he sued several dyers for money due for dyestuffs bought on credit. And certainly the Tailors, whose main activity was garment-making, bought and distributed large quantities of cloth. One company, however, specialized in the wholesale cloth trade and controlled a great deal of cloth production, besides: the Drapers' Company.

Because they had the capital to finance the lengthy, multifaceted production process, Drapers established themselves as middlemen between the various crafts involved in cloth production. Drapers bought wool, gave it out for spinning, and took it to weavers; they arranged to have cloth fulled, dyed and finished; they bought and distributed, or lent money for buying, fuller's earth, teasels, dyes, and other necessary materials. Affluent Drapers, like John of Northhampton, a controversial mayor of London in the 1380s, owned their own fulling mills and dyehouses, employing weavers, fullers, and dyers on a piecework basis. The Drapers sought regulations that strengthened and legitimized their monopoly; in 1364 they petitioned and obtained a charter from the king that gave their company sole right to manage the making and sales of cloth, explicitly denying that right to craftsmen associated with weaving, fulling, or dyeing guilds. The opening to the charter complains about dyers, weavers, and fullers who have been "making cloth" instead of "following their own craft" and who have been "refusing to work on the cloth of others except at excessive prices." It accuses them of committing fraud and "forestalling," buying up a commodity (cloth, in this case), and then raising the price before reselling. In other words, the Drapers were angry that dyers, weavers, and fullers were interfering in cloth trade and not simply acting as paid labor, working under the Drapers' orders and supervision.

Dyers thus had to struggle to keep from being reduced in status to mere sweated labor. They had to fight to maintain independence and enough power to ensure that business went to qualified dyers who were members of their guild, thereby keeping up wages and opening opportunities to rise in the cloth business. The Ordinances of the Bristol Dyers from 1407—just after the death of Chaucer and from the English city second only to London—vividly records this struggle. The members of the Dyers' Guild are definitely on the defensive; the Ordinances claim that new regulations are needed because cloths have been "greatly impaired of their colours and other defects to the great loss and damage of the owners of the said cloths" and "to the great shame of the dyers and the drapery of the town." But the merchant drapers who have brought the complaints are willing to concede that those at fault are not true dyers, not members of the Dyers' Guild. Rather, they are people of "divers crafts . . . who were never apprentices nor masters of the [dyeing] craft." The Dyers' Guild obviously opposes these outlaw craftsmen: because of them, legitimate guild members "go vagrant for lack of work." The Ordinances outline the agreement reached to remedy the situation: the Dyers' Guild will name two Master Dyers who will, under pain of a fine, guarantee that those admitted into the guild "are able and well learned in the said craft of dyeing, to save and keep the goods of the good folk who are wont to be served for their money." As further guarantee of quality work, these same Masters will inspect the work of all members, investigating complaints of abuse or defect and negotiating with merchant representatives for damages. Guild dyers agree to work for any Bristol merchant who asks, "taking for their labour reasonably as has been accustomed and used before these times"—in other words, without raising prices. In return, the labor market for authorized members of the Dyers' Guild will be protected, not only against unknown outlaw dyers, but also against those of "divers crafts"—perhaps fullers or weavers—who have been taking on dyeing work.

The domination of the dyers by those who capitalized and merchandised cloth production is obvious when we realize that the prominent merchant companies involved in cloth—the Mercers, the Grocers, the Drapers, the Tailors—all obtained official charters from the Crown in the fourteenth century, while none of the groups representing cloth-craftsmen were chartered until the Dyers were given one in 1471 by Edward IV. Besides struggling with the domination of merchant interests, dyers found themselves in tense and quarrelsome competition with closely related crafts like fullers and shearmen for control over what business there was in cloth finishing. However, perhaps because they were so close to the final product and by their skill could either add value or ruin it, dyers did manage to hold onto a certain sufficient independence and retain some leverage among the various forces. The London Dyer's Guild had established itself with a set of ordinances as early as 1188, and its fourteenth-century incarnation was making sure dyers were paid higher than average wages. It may have lacked the ultimate sanction of a king's charter, but the Dyers' Guild in Chaucer's time was nevertheless very active, ranking just below the most prestigious companies in the first tier of minor guilds. This is illustrated by the Dyers' role on ceremonial occasions: when companies are listed in parades with the king or for watches and vigils, the Dyers are consistently named twelfth or thirteenth, vying with the highest of the minor guilds like the Ironmongers, Salters, Shearmen, Brewers, and Scriveners.

DYERS OF THE FOURTEENTH CENTURY

With all this in mind, how might success and advancement be achieved as a dyer? A young dyer could get his start formally, as an apprentice (paying to live and work with a master dyer), or informally, as a relative or servant in a dyer's household. After seven years learning the trade, an apprenticed dyer was granted the freedom of the city; someone who had learned the trade informally could obtain the freedom through a sponsor by paying a redemption fee. He could now set himself up as an independent craftsman: the will of a certain John Hicheman, Dyer, shows that he possessed tools and stock connected with his trade that were valued at about 10 marks—a relatively modest sum. If the young dyer did not inherit from a father like John Hicheman and had no source of capital to help him set up with his own tools, he was obliged to become a journeyman dyer, working from day to day at someone else's dyeworks. One of the best opportunities came if a young dyer could marry the inheriting widow or daughter of a master dyer—thereby obtaining tools, perhaps a dyeworks, and an established dye business; to finance himself further, he could take on apprentices and obtain loans from their families, or he might save enough to join in a partnership. A successful master dyer probably focused on trade, shifting responsibility for production and labor onto the journeymen, apprentices, and servants he employed. Often the cloth was owned by drapers and the dyestuffs were given out by grocers, but the entrepreneurial craftsman managed to scrape together the capital to amass some stocks of his own. A dyehouse was already a substantial investment of capital, and ownership of one meant that the dyer was probably in a position not only to dye cloth on contract but also to finance cloth deals on his own. A dyer might also be in the service of the king or the household of a particular aristocrat.

One can assume that success as a dyer depended on the individual's business acumen, hard work, and good opportunities, as well as on his knowledge, experience, taste, and skill with dye. It was possible in the fourteenth century for an individual dyer to get a start in business and rise above the common level of the journeymen dyer who lived by piecework. But wealthy London tradesmen were not self-made; they were the result of families who over three or four generations built up a collective fortune, allying capital, property, and influence through good marriages, careful conduct of trade, and successful business ventures. Using records of business transactions, admittance to guilds, wills, and the like, historians can track many examples of families who began their climb upward as traders in the provincial counties of England, moved into London at some point to capitalize on its larger and more profitable prospects, became known in London business and social organizations like the guilds and fraternities, and married into already established London merchant and trade families. The ultimate goal for the scions of such families was the step into the aristocracy itself.

Two dyers who lived in the fourteenth century can give us a sense of the extremes a craftsman might inhabit, as well as the tensions, mentioned earlier, between working craftsmen and merchants. William de Pappesworth is an example of a young man who was sent to London by a prosperous family in the provinces, perhaps as an apprentice to a dyer. In 1311, William was admitted to the freedom of the city as a dyer. Thirteen years later, he was elected to a three-year term as one of twenty-four aldermen for the city (1324–1327). His will indicates that the Pappesworth family held a large estate in Cambridgeshire and drew significant sums from rents in London. Chaucer himself was from a family not unlike the Pappesworths. By the time the *Canterbury Tales* was written, Chaucer's family, originally located at Ipswich, had been importing wine and serving the monarchy as customs officials for three generations. They had attained (and, even more importantly, managed to retain) social and economic standing that was unequivocally upper middle class, just on the verge of entering the aristocracy (Chaucer's granddaughter would marry an aristocrat). As controller of Customs (1374–1386), and deeply knowledgeable about the trade in wool and cloth, Chaucer was part of the ambitious urban middle class.

But it should be noted that Pappesworth's achievement was a rare instance early in the century; a dyer might have been "shaply for to been an alderman" (I. 372) and may well have had the ambition to become one, but only in Pappesworth's case is it actually known to have happened. The mayors and aldermen of London were almost exclusively from the eight most prestigious, mercantile guilds: Mercers, Grocers, Drapers, Goldsmiths, Fishmongers, Vintners, Skinners, and Tailors. Attempts were made throughout the century, most notably in the 1370s, to lessen the power of the big guilds by sharing more electoral control with the smaller, minor crafts groups. But in fact the guilds associated with cloth working were steadily reduced through the fourteenth century to an insignificant, secondary position.

A dyer at the other end of the social and economic spectrum exemplifies the unrest among crafts-workers who felt thwarted in their expectations for higher wages and expanded opportunities. Geoffrey Litester (*litester* being a Middle English synonym for dyer) was a principal leader during the burst of civil unrest called the Peasants' Revolt, or the Rising of 1381. While Wat Tyler and his group of peasants and workers marched on London, raised havoc, and made demands that their position in relation to their masters and employers be improved, Litester rallied the disgruntled to revolt around Norfolk (a principal textile-producing area). During the anarchy of the several days of the rising, Litester was crowned "King of the Commons," and his supporters rioted in the major Norfolk towns, murdering several foreign—Flemish—textile workers. A similar phenomenon went on in London: unprotected foreign workers were clearly the easiest targets for the frustrated crafts-workers. Geoffrey's reign was short-lived; he was hung, drawn, and quartered for his leadership.

A dyer was associated through his occupation with one of the minor, unimportant guilds. Could he nevertheless hope to move up? Membership in the right organizations, then, as now, aided upward mobility by providing contact with the more powerful. Certainly a father could look to the future and pull together whatever funds might be spared to apprentice his son with a member of one of the more prestigious guilds—say, with a draper. And why shouldn't a highly successful dyer, who wanted to become more of a force in the buying and selling of cloth, drop his affiliation with the Dyers and join the Drapers' Company? Such a move was known to have happened, but very rarely; evidently, guild affiliation, once declared, was considered part of the individual's identity, and loyalty was highly valued. There was a back door to membership in a prominent guild, however. To enhance their prestige, most prominent and wealthy London companies extended honorary membership to royalty and aristocrats, and certain companies even made honorary membership available to up-and-coming individuals of other crafts. The substantial membership dues they paid for the privilege helped bolster the company's coffers. This may be the best explanation for why, although the pilgrim guildsmen would not have belonged to the same guild on the the basis of their occupations, as ambitious members of the London entrepreneurial class, they nevertheless could have become members of the same "solempne and . . . greet fraternitee" (I.364). Not all of the major guild-companies extended such possibilities. Indeed, some groups—like the Drapers—evidently felt exclusivity was better and refused admittance to upstarts from the lower guilds. But the powerful Company of Tailors (which counted among its honorary members King Richard II, Queen Anne, and assorted dukes), recorded in 1399 that William Calandrer, Dyer, paid a hefty fee to join the guild-fraternity.

THE DYER-GUILDSMAN IN THE *CANTERBURY TALES*

When Chaucer made one of the guildsmen a dyer and another a weaver, he drew attention to the cloth-producing industry that was so central to British commerce and politics. But despite his realism, Chaucer positively avoided direct comment on historical and political situations of his day. He favored, rather, the indirect approach, commenting on the values at work in his society. The activities involved in the production of cloth are among the primal activities of human culture—and of literary culture. Clothmaking and trading were not only central facts of everyday medieval life; they also resonated poetically. We all know that tales are "woven," but what metaphoric associations did dyeing carry for Chaucer and his audience?

Chaucer was much influenced by Boethius's *Consolation of Philosophy,* a piece of classical philosophy he translated from Latin into Middle English. Written by the imprisoned Boethius in the time of the Roman Empire's collapse, the *Consolation* asks the question, "What is the ultimate good?" and in the process discusses values that appealed to thinkers in the Middle Ages. To vivify his abstract discussion, Boethius several times uses as a metaphor the dye taken from the purpura shellfish, the dye whose scarcity made its purple color the symbol of imperial power. This painstakingly extracted dye represents all the luxury commodities that act as status symbols, in pursuit of which humans sacrifice their sense of what's truly important. The dye represents one of the "false goodes" that Boethius says cause us to forget the "verray goodes"— the true Good (see Chaucer's translation, Book III, Metrum 8, p. 415). Metaphorically, Boethius calls purpura the "venym [venom] of Tyrie," referring to the Phoenician city of Tyre which was the center of the dyer's trade, and playing on the similarity between the shellfish extract and the more sinister reptilian secretion. The dye, innocent in itself, nevertheless has the poisonous effect of a scarce commodity associated with status and power; it corrupts the values of those who covet it, and it instigates conflict among men for its possession.

One of Chaucer's short poems, "The Former Age," was inspired by this section of Boethius's *Consolation* and also uses dyes and the Middle English dyer—or litester—metaphorically. As the title suggests, the poem uses the classical idea of a Golden Age or First State of Man, a time when humans were simple, unaffected, and at peace, and through comparison, condemns a contemporary society that is precisely the opposite—violently decadent, materialistic, and immoral. To illustrate that those in the Age of Innocence fulfilled their needs simply, in harmony with nature and without desire for more, Chaucer uses negation and the dye/dyer metaphor:

> No mader, welde, or wood no litestere
> Ne knew; the flees was of his former hewe. . . .
>
> (651, 11.17–18)
>
> [Not madder, weld, nor woad nor dyer
> Not knew; the fleece was of his natural hue. . . .]

In other words, in the ideal society, naturally colored wool straight from the sheep was fine; neither madder, weld, nor woad—nor the specialized knowledge of the dyer—was needed to add an artificial red, yellow, or blue appearance to the already perfectly good material. The image reverses to suggest that in the corrupt times that have followed, wool is not valued simply because it protects and keeps us warm. No, it must have false color forced on it because what we hypocritically value is the appearance to be made with it. Dyes and dyeing imply all that is done to turn plain wool into the elaborate and expensive drapery that acts as a status symbol to meet medieval—or modern—need: the need to achieve wealth, status, and power. Dyes and dyeing are apt metonomies for the giant industry and commerce of cloth, a "bysinesse" that, fueled by the desire for "profit" and "richesse," leads to "darknesse" and "cursednesse." The curse is the curse of "coveytyse"—covetousness, avarice—the materialistic lust for more and more. And the darkness is moral benightedness, for as Boethius warns, in pursuit of more we are distracted from seeking the simple good.

Like "The Former Age," but in a more comic spirit, the *Canterbury Tales* also deals with avarice and its corrupting effects on society. The idealized characters like the Knight and the Parson are humble in appearance and action; the Knight fights and the Parson preaches, fulfilling their function in society for the good of the whole, rather than capitalizing on their roles by pursuing individual advancement. The most contemptible character, the Pardoner, is their exact reverse: rather than using his occupation to work for the good, he exploits his position to enrich himself and behaves in a way that will ultimately undermine people's faith, the church, and society. Ironically, he chooses *radix malorum est cupiditas*—avarice is the root of all evil—as the theme for his sermon, and his tale illustrates that cupidity brings death not only to the body, but also to the soul.

The guildsmen are literally and figuratively somewhere in the middle, between ideal and contemptible, noble and base. In other medieval literature that satirizes the different classes of society, tradesmen are stereotyped as practitioners of deceitful fraud, motivated by greed. But Chaucer shifts the focus of this common characterization to the men's social context. Having himself sprung from this class and having long worked with it as the controller of Customs, Chaucer reflects on the particular problem that the entrepreneurial spirit breeds in the "rising" class. They can become caught up in possessing the symbols of status and displaying the signs of materialist success—wearing the uniform of the right club, sporting new gear like silver-tipped knives, owning land in the country and real estate in the city, taking precedence in processions on ceremonial occasions, having their wives called "madame." They can become so caught up that they equate having "catle . . . ynogh and rente" ["property enough . . . and income"] with what gives a man the "wisdom" to lead. Scrambling their way to success in an acquisitive society, they have disconnected from the underlying values that give such positioning purpose and meaning. In pursuit of their individual good, they have lost sight of the social good.

The way Chaucer specifies the occupations of the guildsmen adds depth to this issue in the following way: the Dyer preens himself on holiday with his guild-brothers, wearing a uniform that erases his occupational difference, rather than staying at home, working and being content to serve society with the specialized knowledge and skills of his craft. He has grown wrongly ambitious for more, in the name of some upwardly mobile materialist success, deserting his lawful employment to hang around in a company of likeminded craftsmen and petty tradesmen. Does the Dyer carry the metaphorical trace of his occupation (as seen in "The Former Age"), a superfluous occupation at best, at worst, an occupation in the service of false appearance and covetousness? Does the Dyer suggest the way humans allow themselves to be misled, equating appearance with moral worth and seduced by show at the expense of more important values?

The guildsmen tell no tales. As modern readers we accept the idea that the *Canterbury Tales* is an incomplete work, with the understanding that the meaning of all literary texts is to some degree irresolvable. But that doesn't keep us from reading—and interpreting—based on what we know about the historic context that clings to all texts.

REFERENCES

Bolton, J. L. *The Medieval English Economy 1150–1500.* London: Dent, 1980.

Epstein, Steven A. *Wage Labor and Guilds in Medieval Europe.* Chapel Hill: University of North Carolina Press, 1991.

Fisher, H.E.S., and A.R.J. Jurica. *Documents in English Economic History: England from 1000 to 1760.* London: G. Bell, 1977.

Goodall, Peter. "Chaucer's 'Burgesses' and the Aldermen of London." *Medium Aevum* 50 (1981): 284–291.

Harwood, Britton. "The 'Fraternitee' of Chaucer's Guildsmen." *Review of English Studies* 39 (1988): 413–417.

Hurry, Jamieson B. *The Woad Plant and Its Dye.* Oxford: Oxford University Press, 1930.

Leggett, William. *Ancient and Medieval Dyes.* Brooklyn, N.Y.: Chemical Publishing Co., 1944.

Purdon, L. O. "Chaucer's Use of Woad in *The Former Age.*" *Papers on Language and Literature* 25 (1989): 216–219.

Robinson, Stuart. *A History of Dyed Textiles.* Cambridge, Mass.: MIT Press, 1969.

Salzman, L. F. *English Industries in the Middle Ages.* Oxford: Clarendon Press, 1923.

Swanson, Heather. "The Illusion of Economic Structure: Craft Guilds in Late Medieval English Towns." *Past and Present* 121 (1988): 29–48.

Unwin, George. *The Gilds and Companies of London.* London: Methuen, 1908.

Walton, Penelope. "Textiles." *English Medieval Industries: Craftsmen, Techniques, Products.* Eds. John Blair and Nigel Ramsay. London: Hambledon Press, 1991. Pp. 319–354.

Chapter 17

... And a Tapycer

REBECCA STEPHENS

By including a tapicer, or tapestry-maker, in the group of guildsmen described in the "General Prologue" to the *Canterbury Tales,* Chaucer offers a clue about an art form that is otherwise scantily documented in existing histories of the time. The appearance of this well-dressed artisan suggests that England shared the continental appreciation of tapestries, or woven paintings, which adorned the walls of castles, grand country residences, and churches during the Middle Ages. If Chaucer did in fact read his tales in the court of Richard II, he may have done so in halls lined with tapestries for warmth and decorative appeal. But like so many aspects of Chaucer's life and times, and like the few remaining samples of medieval tapestries themselves, the actual status of the art and the extent of its popularity in England must be pieced together from incomplete evidence and a larger picture of European history.

THE ART OF TAPESTRY-MAKING

Tapestry-making is a form of weaving, executed on a large wooden loom. Its end product, however, is more complex than the weaver's cloth, which serves as material for clothing and other sewn articles. A tapestry features a design actually woven into the cloth. This design can be an illustrative scene, as complex and realistic as a painting. Or it can be a repetitive arrangement of shapes and borders, or possibly a combination of the two. Tapestry differs from the related art of embroidery in that embroidery superimposes a design onto a pre-existing background fabric.

Among Chaucer's guildsmen, the tapicer claimed the highest status as artisan. "A tapissier was an artist with whom a loom took place of an easel, and whose brush was a shuttle, and whose colour-medium was thread instead of paints.

This places him on a higher plane than that of mere weaver'' (Candee 5). For the construction of his high-warp loom, the tapicer called on his fellow pilgrim, the carpenter. And the dyer, also a fellow guildsman, showed tremendous expertise in blending and creating colors for the wool. Even today, many fourteenth-century tapestries retain a subtlety of shading and tone that is considered true to their original state.

During the European peak of the art in the fourteenth and fifteenth centuries, a team of artists and craftsmen often worked together to create a tapestry. A designing artist supplied the "cartoon," a simple sketch of the intended design of the piece. A directing artist supervised translation of the design from paper to thread, selecting wools and silks for their proper color and texture. A team of tapicers then performed the actual weaving, assisted by apprentices in training for the craft (Candee 5). Chaucer's tapicer may have worked alone or in a group such as this. His prosperous appearance, however, suggests an involvement with the more artful design functions rather than the less creative and less lucrative hands-on weaving.

Some translations of the *Canterbury Tales* describe the tapicer as a rug or carpet maker. In *Rugs and Carpets of the Western World,* Weeks and Treganowan write that carpets and tapestries are woven in the same manner. These historians distinguish between the two in terms of weight or durability. Rugs and carpets can withstand considerable wear and are intended for use on the floor. Tapestries, which are often made of more delicate thread, generally cannot endure foot traffic and are therefore meant for use as wall hangings or table rugs. Except for these differences in durability and function, tapestries and carpets share a common history and will be treated together.

A SOCIAL HISTORY OF TAPESTRY

Tapestry-making is an ancient art, dating back at least to the third century and contributing to the cultural artifacts of the Far East, the Middle East, Egypt, India, and Peru. The designs, or subject matter, of a culture's tapestries tell an informative story of its values as they chronicle significant historical events.

In Northern Europe the art took hold during the Gothic period, as the Holy War of the Crusades came to an end and increased political stability encouraged creative activity and construction. Louis IX of France, having driven the Spanish invaders from the southern regions of his country, returned to Paris in the middle of the thirteenth century with a number of luxurious carpets as spoils of war. In the following years, he sought to make France a center of cultural distinction. He fostered an atmosphere of comfort and leisure at court, with plays, musical entertainment, and poetry readings. The royalty and the wealthy bourgeois also began to build country houses and hunting lodges, and their leisurely lives soon included a sort of transitory existence, as they moved from one home to another for a change of scenery and pastime (Weeks 36). The Spanish carpets that Louis brought home inspired him to develop the art of tapestry-making in France. He pressed into service a number of artisans for this purpose.

The quickly trained French tapestry-makers met an insatiable market among the lords and ladies of the country chateaux. Cold and drafty, and often constructed of massive, windowless walls, these houses needed the warmth and beauty that large panels of tapestry could offer. In contrast to the bold, heavily outlined designs of Spanish tapestries, the early French creations featured airy and "capricious" spreads of flowers and greenery (Weeks and Treganowan 35). These designs reflect the individual taste of those who commissioned them, as they suggest that the tremendous demand allowed the tapesters little time to consult and translate the subject matter of other arts and literature.

Tapestries soon became more than useful and attractive household furnishings. Mercedes Viale writes that "To own a tapestry was a sign of wealth, grandeur and power; and on public occasions, they were displayed ostentatiously as evidence of their owner's social importance" (24). Arras, another term for tapestry derived from the northern French city that refined the art under the patronage of Philip the Bold and Philip the Good, also came to be synonymous with dowry. This suggests that tapestries alone could place a woman among the ranks of desirable brides.

In spite of their great economic and social value, tapestries endured tremendous wear and tear in the hands of their owners. The pieces were often carried on horseback from one residence to another, and some even accompanied kings and princes to the battlefield. Although a tapestry could be made originally to fit a particular wall space, removal to another location might require that its edges be trimmed. The cut sections would then be reconnected and fitted to a new set of doorways and windows. Between this cutting and exposure to the elements during transport, medieval tapestries suffered a great deal of damage. Of the thousands of hangings that the period is thought to have produced, only a few hundred examples remain today.

The medieval tapestries that do exist today, in fact, offer a somewhat distorted view of the typical subject matter of the art form. This distortion results from the fact that the best preserved tapestries come from churches and cathedrals, where they enjoyed a relatively stationary existence. Unlike the tapestries of the royal and wealthy landowners, those belonging to churches were kept in place in the naves and between the pillars and arches. Naturally, these pieces had religious themes, drawn from the Old and New Testaments. Subjects included scenes from the lives of the saints, the administering of sacraments, and the Apocalypse as told in the Book of Revelation. Some art historians speculate that these themes enjoyed less popularity among secular owners, who preferred mythological and chivalric figures, heraldic emblems, hunting scenes, and the floral patterns mentioned earlier. Religious themes, when used, mingled with fictional and historical figures in a sort of textile panache. Charles V of France, for instance, owned a tapestry entitled *Nine Heroes,* which featured the Old

Testament figures Joshua and David, the classical statesmen Caesar and Alexander, and the Christian King Arthur (Verlet et al. 20).

By the last quarter of the fourteenth century, the art of tapestry-making flourished in the French cities of Paris and Arras, and in the country then known as Flanders (a territory now divided between France and Belgium). Germany, Switzerland, Italy, and Spain boasted their own tapestry industries as well. Viale writes that travel helped to spread both patronage and expertise in the craft: "Emperors and popes, princes and knights, priests, pilgrims, merchants, strolling players and stone carvers were always on the move: and so no doubt were the tapestry weavers with their looms" (23). Still, the extent of England's involvement with the art remains a matter of speculation. The fall of Flanders as a weaving and textile center sent a number of weavers to England, where quality wool was available and its market value protected with trade and price restrictions. Possibly, some tapestry-makers joined this exodus, in which "Flemish skills laid the foundation for England's textile greatness" (Bennett 28).

In spite of a renewed interest by historians and museums in early tapestries, the documented evidence of their production and use in England remains sparse. Among the first carpets to appear are the two handwoven " 'fote cloths' " commissioned by Egebric, abbott of Coyden, some time prior to the year 992 (Weeks 90). In 1252, when Eleanor of Castile, bride of Edward I, arrived in London with a dowry of Oriental carpets, the "austere" British reportedly reacted negatively to her ostentatious taste (Weeks 90). For hygienic reasons, the English chose not to cover their floors with carpets, at least until the end of the sixteenth century. Instead, they put down layers of hay, straw, or fragrant foliage, changing them daily.

Candee documents one occasion on which fourteenth-century dukes encountered and received as gifts continental tapestries. A meeting "to arrange peace" between France and England took place in Lelingien in 1393, in a rustic church made hospitable with a rich lining of tapestries. An inventory also notes that Philip's tent was furnished with the finest Flemish pieces and that, "As a means of pleasing the English dukes and the principal envoys, Philip gave to them superb gifts of tapestries, the beautiful tapestries of Flanders such as were made only in the territory of the duke" (33). The flow of tapestries from the Continent to England continued, particularly on occasions such as royal marriages. Marguerite of Anjou is believed to have brought "The Chatsworth Hunt" series from France when she married Henry VI in 1444 (Verlet 51).

This evidence indicates an English interest in the tapestries, but it offers little information about how the art was practiced in England. In the sixteenth century, Henry VIII's Cardinal Woolsey chose to import tapestries in order to furnish his rooms in the continental fashion. "As his tastes were advanced beyond those of his neighbors and beyond the creative capacities of craftsmen in his own country, he was forced to turn to other countries for many household luxuries" (Weeks 91). If a domestic industry did develop in England, art historians have yet to document it.

So it is difficult to determine the national heritage and the level of expertise of Chaucer's tapicer. Nor can we know if he encountered samples of his craft in the Cathedral at Canterbury, because post-Restoration Puritans destroyed the church's collection of medieval art. These religious fanatics considered the art superstitious and therefore sinful (Waddams 20). Had the tapicer lived one hundred years later, he would have witnessed the beginning of decline in his art. The influence of the Italian Renaissance made its way to Flanders, and tapestries became more pictorial, "peopled with nude figures and subjects taken from fables" (Verlet 63). In approximately 1515, Pope Leo X commissioned a Flemish tapestry based on a cartoon by the painter Raphael. Suddenly, the art of tapestry shifted from an original and creative invention of the designers and weavers to an imitative craft that copied images produced in another medium. Under the patronage of Leo X and European statesmen, tapestry-making turned into a high-volume industry. Multiple copies were often woven from one design, a practice that would have alarmed the early Flemish tapesters.

In the eighteenth century, tapestry virtually lost its status as art, as original pieces hung alongside decorative fabrics, bedspreads, and tablecloths. "From the heroic richness of Gothic days, from its status as a unique and precious work of art, tapestry had now sunk to a position ranking no higher than curtains, sets of chairs, china, or other items of household decoration" (Verlet 116). A number of twentieth-century artists, most notably the French tapestry-maker Jean Lurcat, have revived the art by blending the memory of its medieval inspiration and integrity with contemporary contexts and materials. In recent decades, several major museums in the United States and Europe have collected and preserved early samples of the great medieval tapestries.

THE TAPICER AS GUILDSMAN

Ultimately, Chaucer's silent tapicer may be important to the "General Prologue" not for his particular art, but rather for his association with the other guildsmen. Ample evidence exists to document the structure and function of the English guild system before and during Chaucer's lifetime. Against this historical support, Chaucer's choice of detail and the grouping of these particular guildsmen stand out for its ironic tone.

As numerous editors and translators have pointed out, the livery, or uniform, worn by the guildsmen suggests their association with the parish guilds of the fourteenth century. Secular rather than religious, these guilds included every free man or citizen of a town. Early forms of parish guilds date back at least to the eighth century. An example is the "Frith-gild," known to exist in London and York, which performed a peacekeeping function. Religious dimensions begin to appear in guild documents in the tenth century. These include prayers, charitable missions, and in one case financial support of a local monastery (Westlake 3). The Black Death of the mid-fourteenth century took its toll on the membership and the resources of guilds, as the members covered burial expenses and helped to support the victims' survivors. The system endured, however, and in Chaucer's time had begun an evolution that would manifest itself in the trade and craft guilds associated with the fifteenth century.

From their earliest history, English guild members gathered for feasts and celebrations. Fourteenth-century guilds established feast days in their charters and statutes, most coinciding with the high holy days of the Church: Corpus Christi Day, Assumption Day, and days of tribute to various saints. Strict codes of behavior governed such rituals as the drinking of ale, attendance of nonmembers, and the participation of unskilled tradesmen at the feasts. Chaucer supposed that his finely attired guildsmen led the procession on their chosen feast day, with their wives enjoying positions of status and privilege. Donald R. Howard suggests that the wives "are great social climbers" (76), while John H. Fisher simply confirms the accuracy of their portrayal as aldermen's wives (16). In its speculative and playful tone, this passage of the "General Prologue" mocks the solemnity of the feast and perhaps casts this annual ritual as a show of pomp rather than a pious tribute to a holy figure or event.

By focusing on the guildsmen's finery, Chaucer foregrounds the material aspects of their guild. Some fourteenth-century parish guilds regulated trade and set standards of quality for the various crafts, functions assumed later by the specialized trade and craft guilds. Early trade unions, emerging in the sixteenth century, narrowed their focus even more in the economic and professional interest of their members. In Chaucer's time, however, master craftsmen generally operated under provisions established by the parish guilds or by subgroups of these organizations. The craft guilds that existed met with resistance from the general citizenry, who feared the possibility of unfair privilege from the Crown (Smith 64). Chaucer's hyperbolic account of his guildsmen's appearance may be a comment on this tension, or a hint that greed can foster regulatory abuse. This particular combination of guildsmen—all potential dealers in finery and ornament—resonates with irony as it pits the spiritual against the material and hints at the victory of the latter, even among the pious pilgrims to Canterbury.

REFERENCES

Bennett, Anna C. *Five Centuries of Tapestry.* Rutland, Vt.: Fine Arts Museums of San Francisco and Charles E. Tuttle Co., 1976.

Candee, Helen Churchill. *The Tapestry Book.* New York: Tudor Publishing Co., 1935.

Coulton, G. G. *Chaucer and His England.* 5th ed. London: Methuen and Co., Ltd., 1930.

Fisher, John H., ed. *The Complete Poetry and Prose of Geoffrey Chaucer.* New York: Holt, Rinehart and Winston, 1989.

Howard, Donald R., ed. *Geoffrey Chaucer: The Canterbury Tales: A Selection.* New York: New American Library, 1969.

Smith, Toulmin. *English Guilds.* London: Early English Text Society by N. Trubner and Co., 1870.

Verlet, Pierre, Michel Florisoone, Adolf Hoffmeister, and Francois Tabard, eds. *The Book of Tapestry: History and Technique.* New York: Vendome Press, 1965.

Viale, Mercedes. *Tapestries.* London: Paul Hamlyn, 1966.

Waddams, Canon Herbert. *Canterbury: The Ancient Seat of Kentish Kings.* London: Pitkin Pictorials Ltd., 1972.

Weeks, Jeanne G., and Donald Treganowan. *Rugs and Carpets of Europe and the Western World.* New York: Weathervane Books, 1969.

Westlake, H. F. *The Parish Guilds of Mediaeval England.* London: Society for Promoting Christian Knowledge (New York: Macmillan Co.), 1919.

Chapter 18

A Cook They Had With Hem
For the Nones

CONSTANCE B. HIEATT

The occupation of Chaucer's Cook, Hogge of Ware, is easier for us to understand than that of any of the other Canterbury pilgrims: most of us know something about cooking, and all of us know something about food. Even his personal
foibles may strike us as familiar. Many of my colleagues fondly remember the
excellent cook under whose regime the culinary standards of our faculty club
reached unheard-of heights. Alas, he turned up drunk once too often, and so the
president of the university had to fire him. But, of course, to place Hogge in
his fourteenth-century context means that we must know something more specific about the conditions under which he worked and the food that he cooked.

The Cook makes three appearances in the course of the *Canterbury Tales:* in
the "General Prologue," the "Cook's Prologue and Tale," and the "Manciple's
Prologue." The first of these passages is the shortest. It follows the description
of five prosperous London guildsmen, traveling as a group:

> A COOK they hadde with hem for the nones
> To boille the chiknes with the marybones,
> And poudre-marchant tart and galyngale.
> Wel koude he knowe a draughte of Londoun ale.
> He koude rooste, and sethe, and broille, and frye,
> Maken mortreux, and wel bake a pye.
> But greet harm was it, as it thoughte me,
> That on his shin a mormal hadde he.
> For blankmanger, that made he with the beste.

[I (A) 379–387]

> [A cook they had with them for the occasion
> To boil the chickens with the marrow bones,

And powder-marchant tart and galyngale.
Well could he know a draught of London ale.
He could roast, and simmer, and broil, and fry,
Make stew, and well bake a pie.
But great harm it was, as I thought,
That on his shin an ulcer had he.
For blankmanger, that he made excellently.]

This tells us almost as much about the guildsmen as about the Cook himself: hiring a private cook to ensure the gourmet quality of their meals on such a trip would have cost them a pretty penny. And this is a cook who is a master of his trade. Not only was he expert at all the basic techniques of cooking (roasting, boiling, broiling, and frying); his repertoire also included the expensive, elaborate dishes characteristic of medieval *haute cuisine*. The spices with which he seasoned his special chicken dish, which gets two whole lines here, and the rice and almonds which were the base of his notable "blankmanger" were imported from the east and were quite beyond the means of humbler households.

But we have also been informed that he was very familiar with London ale and that he had an unattractive skin eruption on his leg. There has been much discussion of that "mormel." It may or may not indicate that he has led a life of extreme dissipation, but it surely suggests a lack of personal hygiene which, as Jill Mann has suggested, is unpleasantly juxtaposed with the Cook's skill in making a delicate dish. We would all prefer to think that our favorite foods were prepared in immaculate kitchens by well-washed hands; today, as then, this may not always be the case.

When we meet the Cook for the second time in the Prologue to his tale, we find out first that he greatly enjoys a truly dirty joke. His immediate reaction to the "Reeve's Tale" is loud laughter and approbation of this second indecent story in a row. But Hogge (as he here identifies himself) thinks one or two hot ones isn't enough, and he offers to continue the series. The Host agrees, telling him to make it good, but adds a few stinging professional insults:

For many a pastee hastow laten blood,
And many a Jakke of Dovere hastow soold
That hath been twies hoot and twies coold.
Of many a pilgrym hastow Cristes curs,
For of thy percely yet they fare the wors,
That they han eten with thy stubbel goos,
For in thy shoppe is many a flye loos.

(4346–4352)

[For many a meat pie have you let blood,
And many a Jack of Dover have you sold
That has been twice hot and twice cold.
By many a pilgrim have you been cursed,
For of your parsley yet they fare the worse,

That they have eaten your stubble fed goose,
For in your shop is many a fly loose.]

This casts a new light on the Cook's professional activities. We now know that he is the proprietor of a cookshop, the medieval equivalent of a caterer and fast-food and take-out restaurant. The Host has suggested that the premises are unsanitary, with flies buzzing around—and probably falling into—the food, and that the Cook has engaged in at least one dangerous and fraudulent practice: reheating cooked food, so that yesterday's stale (or possibly spoiled) food could be passed off as freshly cooked. In a world without refrigeration, this was clearly dangerous, and a fifteenth-century city ordinance insisted that cooks must not "bake rost nor seeth Flessh nor Fisshe two times to sell."

It is also possible that the Host is accusing the Cook of making unsavory or illegal "pastees." In 1379 the city ruled,

Because the pastelers [pasty makers] of the city of London have heretofore baked in pasties rabbits, geese, and garbage [giblets and other odds and ends of poultry], not befitting and sometimes stinking, in deceit of the people, and have also baked beef in pasties and sold the same for venison, in deceit of the people; therefore, by assent of the four master pastelers and at their prayer, it is ordered and assented to:

In the first place—that no one of the said trade shall bake rabbits in pasties for sale, on pain of paying, the first time, if found guilty thereof, 6s. 8d. to the use of the Chamber and of going bodily to prison, at the will of the mayor; the second time, 13s. 4d. to the use of the Chamber and of going etc.

Also, that no one of the same trade shall buy of any cook of Bread Street or at the hostels of the great lords, of the cooks of such lords, any garbage from capons, hens or geese to bake in a pasty and sell, under the same penalty.

The regulation specifies the same penalties for baking beef pasties and selling them for venison, and for baking and selling a whole goose or part of a goose in a pasty. It is clear that passing off beef as venison was a fraud, and that chicken livers and giblets might have been sitting around too long, but it is difficult to know today exactly why rabbits and geese were especially liable to go bad. Other pasties were not forbidden; another regulation of 1378 lists the prices to be charged for capons and hens baked in pasties, and the price for baking in a pasty a capon or a goose provided by the customer—which must have been safer than trusting the "pasteler" (or cook) to provide a fresh bird.

But Roger (for which Hogge is a nickname) was not a "pasteler" or pie-man: since he ran a cook shop, he would have belonged to a separate guild, and he may have been one of those cooks of Bread Street referred to in the regulation, although cook shops also clustered in other locations—notably, Eastcheap and Thames Street. A cook shop sold a great variety of roast poultry (among other things), and it must have been a temptation to make use in pasties of the "garbages" removed from these roasted birds, or to sell them to the members of the guild that specialized in such pasties.

Some may wonder why a cook would "let blood" in order to make pasties. Medieval cooks were expected to kill, pluck, and eviscerate their own poultry. A typical recipe for a roast bird tells us, "Cut a swan in the rofe of the mouth touward the brayn of the hed, & let hym blede to deth; & kepe the blod to colour the chaudon [a sort of giblet gravy] with, or cut the necke and let hym dye. Then skale [pluck] hym, draw [eviscerate] hym, rost hym, & serve hym forth." Another fifteenth-century ordinance spoke of cooks "with their hands dirtied and fouled" who, in attempting to sell their wares, offended passers-by by plucking at their clothing, and a group of cooks in Coventry were fined for throwing poultry entrails into the street.

Thus almost everything in the Host's words cited above contains unpleasant insinuations or is potentially libelous. However, the Host is not, as some readers have thought, accusing the Cook's geese of being old and tough: a "stubble goose" is a mature goose fattened up at harvest time. While younger ("green") geese have sometimes been said to be preferable, the English have traditionally enjoyed a well-fattened stubble goose as a treat for Martinmas (November 11). And note that the Host goes on to urge the Cook not to be angry at words he has spoken in "game": although it doesn't amount to much of an apology when he ends, "A man may seye ful sooth in game and pleye," which suggests he meant every insulting word of it.

And so Roger evidently understands the Host when he threatens to retaliate with a story about an innkeeper. Here, as elsewhere in the *Canterbury Tales'* links, we are viewing a hostile confrontation between members of rival professions. Tavern-keepers were the third group (along with cooks and pie-men) of the guilds known as victuallers, and there was considerable overlap in the wares they offered to the public. Nor is this the only fellow pilgrim with whom a cook may have reason for conflict, as we see in the Manciple's Prologue, the third and last passage in which Hogge of Ware is a central character.

This begins with the Host remarking that the Cook seems to be napping on horseback and is likely to fall off his horse. He asks the Cook why he is so sleepy at this time of the morning, suggesting he may have been troubled with fleas all night, or had too much to drink, or spent an active night with a prostitute. But while this may sound insulting, the Cook doesn't take offense, and simply replies that he would rather sleep than have the best gallon of ale in Cheapside. The real insults come from the Manciple, who says, among other things,

> Thyne eyen daswen eek, as that me thynketh,
> And, wel I woot, thy breeth ful soure stynketh:
> That sheweth wel thou art not wel disposed.
> Of me, certeyn, thou shal nat been yglosed [flattered].
> See how he ganeth [yawns], lo, this dronken wight,
> As though he wolde swolwe us anonright.
> Hoold cloos thy mouth, man, by thy fader kyn!

The devel of helle sette his foot therin!
Thy cursed breeth infect wole us alle.
Fy, stynkyng swyn! Fy, foule moote thee falle!

[IX (H) 31–40]

[Your eyes are dazed also, as that I thought,
And well I know, your breath very sour stinks:
That shows well you are not feeling well.
From me, surely, you shall not be flattered.
See how he yawns, lo, this drunken man,
As though he would swallow us right now.
Hold closed your mouth, man, by your father kin!
The devil of hell set his foot therein!
Your cursed breath will infect us all.
Fi, stinking swine! Fi, foul must you fall!]

Fighting words indeed, but the Cook evidently deserves them because his anger at the Manciple causes him to fall off his horse. The Host, however, reminds the Manciple that it may not be in his best interests to make an enemy of the Cook; the Manciple agrees and makes his peace by offering the Cook some wine. (Strangely, the Cook is able to thank him for this obviously super-fluous drink.) The Manciple's job was to buy the provisions for one of the Inns of Court; naturally, his professional success depended on his getting the most for his money. He would no doubt have had to buy food from a cook shop, at least from time to time, and thus his financial interests and those of the Cook would have been in direct opposition. And since, clearly, this particular manciple is likely to cook his books for his own profit, it would be unwise of him to provoke the Cook into exposing him by pointing out what he had *really* paid, as against what he asked his employers to reimburse him for.

A basic point here for readers of the "Cook's Tale" is that the Cook's ex-treme drunkenness confirms the hint in the "General Prologue" that he was entirely too familiar with London ale. Note also that it has been proposed that the Cook is modeled on an actual Roger of Ware, a cook of London who was found guilty of being a "common nightwalker," which means someone who was habitually in the streets after curfew and was suspected of keeping company with thieves and prostitutes. It is interesting that Harry Bailly, the only Canter-bury pilgrim (aside from Geoffrey Chaucer) whose full name is given, also has the name of an actual fourteenth-century counterpart, an innkeeper in South-wark. It is also interesting that we learn both names in the same passage—the Prologue to the Cook's Tale—and that Harry Bailly's remarks assume a prior acquaintance between the two.

But whether or not the Cook is modeled on a real, not-so-model citizen, we can easily see that the tale he is assigned—what we have of it—is exactly what we would expect of him. The central character, Perkyn Revelour, is, at the beginning of the tale, an apprentice working in a cook shop. As the proprietor of such a shop, our Cook would have known that Perkyn's behavior was intolerable for an apprentice. The master cook's business would certainly be impeded by an apprentice who took every excuse to rush out of the shop in pursuit of fun and games. Thus Hogge's attitude toward his central character is not one of approval, and presumably if we had a complete tale to examine, we would find that Perkyn got his comeuppance, one way or another.

Readers may suspect that a fragment that breaks off just after introducing a "wyf that heeld for contenance/ A shoppe and swyved for hir sustenance" [that is, a woman who kept a shop for the sake of appearances, but actually earned her living as a prostitute] would have been even more indecent than the two tales that precede it, and this is quite in keeping with the Cook's ribald admiration of the "Reeve's Tale"; but that does not necessarily mean that the Cook himself was given to gambling, the company of prostitutes, and other low forms of "revelry." He was, after all, very successful in his profession, and, indeed, he was a cut above most of the cooks associated with cook shops of the period.

The average London cook shop was a very small place of business, occupying a frontage on the street of from 6 to 12 feet. To judge by the price regulations laid down in 1378, such a shop's normal offerings were fairly limited. This ordinance set prices for various roast meats and poultry, ranging from 1d for ten roast finches to 20d for roast bittern, and including roast pig and roast lamb for 8d and 7d, respectively; the ordinance includes pasties (8d for "the best capon baked in a pasty") and eggs (boiled?), which were to be sold at ten for 1d.

All of these were "basic" foods for medieval Londoners and just the kind of thing people were likely to patronize a cook shop for, although some—like the bittern and finches—may sound pretty exotic to us today. Most Londoners did not have kitchens properly equipped to do roasting and baking, and even those who did evidently found such items useful additions to a basic meal when unexpected guests had to be fed. But there is little evidence that cook shops usually sold other prepared foods. No doubt they sold sauces to go with the roasts; medieval diners expected a sauce with their meat, and the cook shop's goose evidently came with a sauce or stuffing containing parsley.

It is highly doubtful, however, that cook shops ever sold the elaborate "pottages" characteristic of court and upper class cooking, or indeed much of anything beyond the sort of items listed in that 1378 ordinance. To be sure, the unfortunate country bumpkin of the fifteenth-century poem "London Lickpenny" says

> Cokes to me they toke good intent
> called me nere for to dyne
> and proferyd me good brede ale and wyne
> a fayre clothe they began to sprede
> rybbes of beef bothe fat and fyne
> but for lack of money I might not spede.

[Cooks to me they offer good intent
called me near to dine
and offered me good bread, ale, and wine
a fair cloth they began to spread
ribs of beef both fat and fine
but for lack of money I may not speed.]

Later he is offered hot peasecods (fresh green peas cooked in the pod, to be eaten more-or-less as we eat artichoke leaves) and hot sheep's feet (I have no idea how these were cooked), among other things. But the cooks who offer the ribs of beef are likely to have been tavern-keepers: pie-men and cook shops were not allowed to sell ale or wine. And the peasecods and sheep's feet may have been offered by hucksters specializing in these goodies—perhaps vendors with carts, but in any case probably vendors who had no connection with a cook shop.

Yet we are told that Hogge of Ware, a cook of London, is well known for two of the sophisticated dishes found on aristocratic menus and in the cookery books that claim to come from the highest social circles: "mortreux" and "blankmanger." Both dishes appear in many versions, made with chicken or other poultry—or, in the case of mortreux, pork—on "flesh-days," and with fish on days when "flesh" was not permitted. They can be found in the menus for notable feasts printed in Austin's *Two Fifteenth-Century Cookery-Books:* "blamanger" is in the menu for the funeral feast of Nicolas Bubwith, bishop of Bath and Wells, and "mortrewys" is in the menu of the induction feast of his successor, John Stafford.

By today's standards, the "fish-day" versions of these dishes are more appealing. To give some examples:

Blaunch mortruys of fisch. Take haddok, codlyng, or thornebak, sodyn; pyke out the bonys, do awey the skuyn. Grynd the fisch. Make a mylke of almondes yblaunchyd, & temper up the fisch therwith; take payndemayn [bread] grated & sigure [sugar] therwithe. Set hit on the fyre. When hit boyleth, loke hit be stondyng. Messe hit forth & strew on blaunch poudyr. (MS Beinecke 163)

[Blanch mortar of fish. Take haddock, cod, or thornback; pick out the bones, do away with the skin. Grind the fish. Make a milk of blanched almonds, and temper up the fish therewith; take bread grated and sugar therewith. Set it on the fire. When it boils, set it to standing. Mess it forth and strew on blanched powder.]

The dish is named for the mortar in which the fish (or meat, in a "flesh-day" version) was ground. Almond milk was made by steeping finely ground almonds in water or broth and then either wringing the mixture through a cloth or forcing it through a fine strainer. The "blaunch poudyr" added as a finishing touch seems to have been based on sugar and ginger, but it may also have contained other mild spices. If made very thick, as many parallel recipes say it should be, the end result of this recipe will resemble a modern Scandinavian "fish pud-ding": but of course the almond milk gives it a subtly different flavor.

Blamanger of Fysshe. Take rys, an sethe hem tylle they brekyn, & late hem kele; þan caste þerto mylke of almaundys; nym [take] perche or lopstere & do þerto, & melle [mix] it; þan nym sugre with pouder gyngere, & caste þerto, & make it chargeaunt [thick], and þan serve it forth. (MS Harleian 279)

[Blamanger of Fish. Take rice, and simmer them till they break, and let them cool; then cast thereto the milk of almonds; take perch or lobster and do thereto, and mix it; then mix sugar with powdered ginger, and cast it thereto, and make it thick, and then serve it forth.]

Again, the cook must draw up an almond milk as a key ingredient; but the fish (or poultry on a "flesh-day") does not need to be ground in a mortar and can simply be chopped or pulled into small pieces. However, one recipe, which calls for pike or haddock instead of perch or lobster, advises the cook to rub the cooked fish through a strainer, which would give results much like grinding. Note that the rice was supposed to be cooked until it was very soft and mushy; this dish can be, and probably was, packed into a mold and unmolded onto a platter.

The Cook's other major specialty is probably also represented in Austin's feast menus: "Brewys" and "Chykonys y-boylid" appear on the supper menu of a Trinity Sunday feast for Henry IV, and "Browes" and "Chekenos boiled" on the menu for the installation of John Stafford as archbishop of Canterbury. Neither menu mentions marrow bones; nor does the title of a contemporary recipe. Instead, the writers emphasize the accompanying "brewis" (i.e., toast used as a "sop"). What King Henry and the archbishop were served was this:

Schyconys with þe Bruesse. Take half a dosyn chykonys, & putte hem into a potte; þen putte þerto a gode gobet of fressh beef, & lat hem boyle wel; putte þerto percely, sawge levys, saverey, noȝt to smal hakkyd; putte þerto safroun ynow; þen kytte þin brewes & skalde hem with þe same broþe; salt it wyl. (MS Harleian 279)

[Chicken with the brews. Take half a dozen chickens, and put them into a pot; then put in a good gob of fresh beef, and let them boil well; then add parsley, sage leaves, savory, not too small hacked; put thereto saffron now; then cut your brews and scald them with the same broth; salt it well.]

Comparing this recipe with a contemporary French one for "Trumel de Beuf au Jaunet" makes it evident that the beef to be used is the leg and that this is, thus, chicken cooked with marrowbones. The French recipe emphasizes the beef, but it is otherwise the same. The dish is clearly the ancestor of a modern French Pot au feu, or Potée Normande.

Unfortunately, it is impossible to say exactly what went into the "poudre-marchant tart" with which the cook seasoned his chickens. The name means that this is a ready-made spice mixture, available at the spice merchants' shops, but there is no record at all of what the basic ingredients were. (Bowden's comments on this question, p. 32, are simply wrong; the phrase "pouder Marchant" appears in the recipe *before* the one she confidently assumed has a recipe for that "powder.")

It is equally impossible to say what sort of "pye" the Cook was likely to have baked, although that re-warmed "Jakke of Dovere" may have been a pie. Pies of all sorts turn up in medieval recipes and on medieval menus. Some are actually pasties, that is, meat, poultry, or fish, with or without various seasonings, wrapped in a sheet of pastry and baked. Others are open tarts of various sorts, including "crustards," which contained egg-based fillings (plus meat or fish) and closely resembled a modern quiche; this type turns up most frequently in the records of aristocratic feasts. But there were also closed pies, usually with a filling of more than one type of meat, which could be quite a production: one recipe calls for a filling of beef, pork, veal, or venison, plus capons or pheasants, dried fruits, a vast assortment of spices, and boiled egg yolks.

But there were also less ambitious pies. One of the more appealing is as follows:

Pies of Parys. Take and smyte faire buttes of porke and buttes of vele togidre [i.e., chop them], and put hit in a faire potte. And putte thereto faire broth and a quantite of wyne, and lete all boile todgidre til hit be ynogh; and þen take hit fro the fire and lete kele a litel, and cast therto raw yolkes of eyren and poudre of gyngevere, sugre and salt, and mynced dates, reysyns of corence [currants]. Make then coffyns [pie shells] of feyre past, and do it therynne, and kevere it & lete bake ynogh. (MS Harleian 4016)

[Pies of Paris. Take and chop fair butts of pork and butts of veal together, and put it in a fair pot. And put thereto a fair broth and a quantity of wine, and let it all boil together till it is enough; and then take it from the fire and let it cool a little, and put thereto raw yolkes of eggs and ginger powder, sugar and salt, and minced dates, and currants. Make then coffins of fair pastry, and put it therein, and cover it and let it bake enough.]

Miniature versions of this pie, which can be made without the top crust, have proved popular among modern diners.

A final culinary problem here is: what, exactly, was the parsley the Cook's customers ate with their roast goose? Virtually all the sauces recommended as an accompaniment for goose in England and France called for garlic; the sauce supplied by Roger's cook shop may, then, have been a simple "green sauce" of the kind that was a usual accompaniment to fish. The *Forme of Cury*'s version of this sauce is typical:

Verde Sawse. Take persel, mynt, garlek, a litul serpell [thyme] and sawge; a litul canel [cinnamon], gynger, piper, wyne, brede, vyneger & salt; grynde it smal with safroun, & messe it forth.

[Green Sauce. Take parsley, mint, garlic, a little thyme and sage; a little cinnamon, ginger, pepper, wine, bread, vinegar and salt; ground it small with saffron, and mess it forth.]

But a versatile cook like the highly reputed Hogge of Ware may have been capable of producing a far more sophisticated treatment, which starts out as a stuffing:

Sawse Madame. Take sawge, persel, ysope and saveray, quinces and peeres, garlek and grapes, and fylle the gees þerwith; and sowe the hole þat no grece come out, and roost hem wel, and kepe the grece þat fallith þerof. Take galyntyne and grece and do in a possynet [pot]. Whan the gees buth roasted ynowh, take hem of & smyte hem on pecys, and take þat þat is withinne and do it in a possynet and put þerinne wyne, if it be to thyk; do þerto powdour of galyngale, powdour douce, and salt and boyle the sawse, and dress þe gees in disshes & lay þe sewe [sauce] onoward. *Forme of Cury*

[Sauce Madame. Take sage, parsley, sopped and savory, quinces and pears, garlic and grapes, and fill the geese therewith; and sew the hole that no grease comes out, and roast it well, and keep the grease that falls thereof. Take gelatine and grease and put them in a pot. When the geese are roasted enough, take them and cut them in pieces, and take that that is within and do it in a possynet and put therein wine, if it be too thick; add thereto powder of galyngale, powder douce, and salt and boil the sauce, and dress the geese in dishes and lay the sauce onward.]

This may not have been suitable for the clientele of a London cook shop. But we know that our Cook also cooked for private parties: that is how he happens to be among the Canterbury pilgrims, in the company of, among others, Geoffrey Chaucer.

REFERENCES

Austin, Thomas, ed. *Two Fifteenth-Century Cookery Books: Harleian MS. 279 (ab. 1430, & Harl MS 4016 (ab. 1450) with Extracts from Ashmole MS. 1439, Laud MS. 553, & Douce MS. 55*. EETS 91; London: Oxford University Press, 1888; repr. 1964.

Benson, Larry D., general ed. *The Riverside Chaucer,* 3rd ed. Boston: Houghton Mifflin, 1987.

Bowden, Muriel. *A Commentary on the General Prologue to the Canterbury Tales.* New York: Macmillan, 1949.

Brodie, Alexander H. "Hodge of Ware and Geber's Cook: Wordplay in the 'Manciple's Prologue.' " *NM* 72 (1971): 62–68.

Hammond, P. W. *Food and Feast in Medieval England.* Stroud, Gloucestershire: Alan Sutton, 1993.

Hieatt, Constance B. " 'To boille the chiknes with the marybones': Hodge's Kitchen Revisited." In *Chaucerian Problems and Perspectives: Essays Presented to Paul E. Beichner.* Eds. Edward Vasta and Zacharias P. Thundy. Notre Dame: Ind.: Notre Dame University Press, 1979. Pp. 149–163.

————, ed. *An Ordinance of Pottage: An Edition of the Fifteenth Century Culinary Recipes in Yale University's MS Beinecke 163.* London: Prospect Books, 1988.

————, and Sharon Butler, eds. *Curye on Inglysch: English Culinary Manuscripts of the Fourteenth Century (Including the* Forme of Cury*).* EETS ss. 8; London: Oxford University Press, 1985.

————. *Plein Delit: Medieval Cookery for Modern Cooks.* Toronto: University of Toronto Press, 1976, rev. ed. 1979. [A 2nd ed., forthcoming in 1995, with Brenda Hosington as co-author, contains adaptations of all the recipes printed above.]

Howard, Donald R. *The Idea of the Canterbury Tales.* Berkeley: University of California Press, 1976.

Kolve, V. A. *Chaucer and the Imagery of Narrative: The First Five Canterbury Tales.* Stanford, Calif.: Stanford University Press, 1984.

————. "London Lickpenny." In Eleanor Prescott Hammond, ed. *English Verse Between Chaucer and Surrey.* Durham, N.C.: Duke University Press, 1927.

Mann, Jill. *Chaucer and the Medieval Estates Satire: The Literature of the Social Classes and the General Prologue to the Canterbury Tales.* Cambridge: Cambridge University Press, 1973.

Myers, A. R. *London in the Age of Chaucer.* Norman: University of Oklahoma Press, 1972.

Riley, Henry Thomas, ed. and trans. *Memorials of London and London Life in the 13th, 14th, and 15th Centuries.* London: Longmans, Green, 1868.

Robertson, D. W., Jr. *Chaucer's London.* New York: John Wiley and Sons, 1968.

Scattergood, V. J. "Perkyn Revelour and the *Cook's Tale.*" *Chaucer Review* 19 (1984): 14–23.

Stanley, E. G. "Of This Cokes Tale Maked Chaucer Na Moore." *Poetica* 5 (1976): 36–59.

Tupper, Frederick. "The Quarrels of the Canterbury Pilgrims." *JEGP* 14 (1915): 256–270.

Chapter 19

A Shipman Ther Was, Wonynge Fer By Weste

SIGRID KING

Chaucer's unnamed Shipman is an interesting character of a sort who would have been very familiar to the author during his maritime experiences as customs official and envoy for Edward III. As an envoy, Chaucer sailed to France and Italy several times, between 1366 and 1373. In June of 1374, Chaucer was appointed controller of the custom on wool in the Port of London, a post he held for twelve years. The world of the port custom official was inextricably bound to the maritime world. Donald Howard notes that for Chaucer, "the world of imports and exports, of international shipping; the smell of salt air and the creak of ships' rigging was a preponderant part of his life during what turned out to be his most formative and productive years as an artist" (203). During his first months as customs official, in August of 1374, Chaucer was sent to Dartmouth to obtain the release of the *Seinte Marie et Seinte George,* a Genoese ship being detained there. Howard believes that while in Dartmouth, Chaucer learned about the pirate John Hawley and later based the pilgrim Shipman on him (203). Yet interestingly enough, except for a passing reference to a shipman at the close of "The House of Fame," Chaucer's portrait of the Shipman in the *Canterbury Tales* is the only reference possibly reflecting this part of his life in his writing. This chapter provides a historical context for the fourteenth-century English shipman and the shipping industry, and explores what we can learn about the Shipman from his description in the "General Prologue" and from his tale.

THE MEDIEVAL SHIPMAN AND THE "GENERAL PROLOGUE"

Jill Mann claims that the material of the Shipman's description in the "General Prologue" is "given its first literary expression in Chaucer" and asserts that the Shipman is his "original creation" (168). Chaucer's description is rich with details that develop the historical picture of the Shipman, and we will use it as a starting point for our examination of his role in history. The Shipman was considered part of the working man's estate, the middle strata, into which the majority of Chaucer's pilgrims fit (Saul 45). The Shipman's clothing demonstrates his active life at sea: his all-weather, knee-length woolen "gowne" allows him quick movement, and his dagger, hanging "under his arm adoun," leaves his hands free for tying rope and hoisting sails (I.391, 393). The description that he is tanned by the sun indicates the amount of time he spends on the deck of his ship, and his discomfort riding the "rouncy," or large carthouse, is a humorous reference to the fact that he is most accustomed to traveling by water (I.390). Mann points out that the most important qualities for a shipman were "loyalty, prudence, and courage" because of the dangers of a life at sea (170). The Prologue mentions that "with many a tempest hadde his berd been shake" (406) ["With many a tempest had his beard been shaken"]. It is interesting to note that honesty is not among the essential traits listed for the shipman in estates literature, and that omission indicates the complex nature of this historical figure.

While the Shipman initially appears to have the narrator's approval in his description in the "General Prologue," as with most of Chaucer's pilgrims, we find evidence that he may not be quite deserving of the narrator's naive admiration. In fact, several comments actually identify him with the many pirates who flourished during Chaucer's lifetime. The description begins with a reference to the Shipman dwelling "fer by weste," possibly in "Dertemouthe," a location synonymous with the haunt of pirates in the fourteenth century (I.388–389). Dartmouth was a small but well-known port town, which records show had only 506 inhabitants over the age of fourteen in 1377 (Manly 181). Many of those inhabitants were involved in the marine trade, either as merchants, sailors, or ship owners. The term *shipman* usually refers to the master, or captain, of a ship, although, as we will discuss later, it has been used to refer to the ship owner as well. During this period, merchants, sailors, and ship owners engaged in piratical practices out of Dover.

Many readers are not aware of pirates in England until the sixteenth century, when Queen Elizabeth's "deare Pyrat" Sir Francis Drake brought back plunder for his monarch. After Drake's success, English-based piracy reached its heyday from the sixteenth through the eighteenth centuries, with the likes of Henry Morgan, Edward Teach (or Bluebeard), John Avery, and Bartholomew Roberts. Chaucer's Shipman is not explicitly described in the terms we are accustomed to associating with these later pirates, but a careful examination of his practices within the historical context of piracy reveals that he engaged in privateering just the same.

Records of pirates go back as far as classical Rome and continue through the thirteenth century when Marco Polo encountered the fierce Malay pirates in his travels in Asia. Throughout its history, piracy has always been a constant source of fear and economic loss for merchants. Early English privateering has a complex history. Although Edward I and Edward II had practiced rigorous naval campaigns against piracy, by the death of Edward II in 1327, the navy had fallen into neglect (Gosse 96). During Edward III's reign, the government focused less on building new ships than on "conscripting sailing ships and their crews when needed" (Unger 172). The Crown actually issued commissions for privateering during the fourteenth century so that English ships could arm and revenge themselves against attacks. In times of naval warfare, these same English trading ships would be pressed into service along with the king's navy. To help protect maritime trade along the southeast coast, the league of the Cinque Ports was formed. The cities were granted privateering privileges by the Crown in return for their protection. Philip Gosse notes that "conditions in the Channel and even the North Sea very quickly became worse with these authorised pirates about than they had been before" (96). Many coastal landowners were involved in the privateers' activities and benefited financially from them. As a result, many of the pirates were never prosecuted.

When the narrator calls the Shipman a "good felawe," a term Larry Benson defines as having the double meaning of "good companion" or "rascal," his diction captures the double nature of these privateers (815). At times, they practiced a legitimate shipping trade, bringing wool to the Continent and returning with wine and other goods. However, even on these legitimate voyages, the Shipman might engage in illegal practices. The narrator of the "General Prologue" reveals that the Shipman steals wine from merchants while they return from Bordeaux (a popular source of imported wine), and he takes no heed of "nyce conscience" (I.398). Muriel Bowden provides an explanation of how shipmen would "tap" the casks of wine they were carrying as cargo, when the merchants left them unguarded on the long voyage to England (194). The resulting shortage would be blamed on the merchant once the wine arrived at its English destination. The fourteenth-century *Viri fratres serri Dei* complained that "sailors and peasants, who used to be so honest, are so corrupted by fraud that hardly one of them is upright" (quoted in Mann 171).

The Shipman's morality is clearly one of expedience, as lines 399 and 400 reveal: "If that he faught and hadde the hyer hond, / By water he sente hem hoom to every lond." ["If that he fought and had the higher hand / By water he sent them home to every land."] By reading between the euphemistic lines, we understand that the Shipman drowns his enemies. The fourteenth-century *Memoriale Presbiterorum* warned confessors that pirates "not only kill clerks and laymen while they are on land, but also when they are at sea, they practice wicked piracy, seizing the goods of other people and especially of merchants as they are crossing the sea, and killing them mercilessly" (quoted in Mann 171). Edward III is said to have done the same in a naval victory over the Spanish in 1350.

In addition to the Shipman's piratical deeds, the narrator also admiringly mentions his nautical skills and provides some basic information about the Shipman's routes. He praises the Shipman's ability to recognize the tides, currents, harbors, and positions of the moon, and claims that he is hardy and prudent, having weathered many storms (I.401–403, 405–406). Improvements in several important navigational tools took place during the fourteenth century. The compass developed from a "primitive pointer" to a "needle swinging freely on a dry pivot" (Unger 174). Shipmen also made increased use of coastal charts with port locations and tide tables, and coastal communities placed an increased number of lights along dangerous coasts to warn shipmen (Unger 175). Because of these advances, the sailing season could be extended to include winter.

The Shipman's primary routes are alluded to in lines 404 to 409 of the "General Prologue," as including Hull (on the Yorkshire coast), Carthage (probably Tunisia, or Cartagena, Spain), Gotland (an island off the Swedish coast), the Cape of Finistere (off Galicia Spain), and Brittany, indicating the wide-ranging nature of the Shipman's voyages. England's trade routes were focused on the southeastern coast in the Cinque Ports—Dover, Sandwich, Hastings, Winchelsea, and Rye (Villiers 68). England's chief export was wool, which was sent to Calais, and woolen cloth, which was sent to various ports on the Continent. Ian Serraillier argues that Chaucer's merchant was probably a wool merchant, "for one of his main concerns was to keep free from pirates the stretch of sea between Ipswich and Middleburg, both ports appointed to handle the export of wool" (30).

In the last line of the "Prologue's" description, the Shipman's vessel is referred to as the "barge" named *Maudelayne* (I.410). If Chaucer means "barge" literally, he is describing a ship that is "single-masted, but with oars, undecked but with fore- and after-castles and perhaps a top-castle, about eighty feet long on the keel with raked bows and stern, and about twenty feet wide" (quoted in Benson 815). The two castle-like structures originally served as vantage points for marine warfare, but over time became the quarters for the ship's officers, from which they could view the length of the ship. The barge weighed from 100 to 150 tons and could have up to eighty oars. With one man on each oar, that would make the number of oarsmen larger than the average size of the barge's sailing crew. Richard Unger describes the barges as a "common part of war fleets in the fourteenth century" that were also "found effective doing convoy duty, privateering or carrying important individuals" (171, 172).

If the term *barge* is not to be taken literally, we may assume that Chaucer could mean other fourteenth-century vessels, such as cogs or galleys, with three masts and castles at the bow and stern, which frequently carried cargo for trade, despite being "plagued by pirates" (Villiers 68). Shipbuilders added the second and third sails as ships became larger and more difficult to manage. These larger galleys required more oarsmen, so shipmen who had various duties on smaller ships became confined to the oar bench on the galleys.

For a more detailed description of medieval ships, we can refer to Serraillier's description of Edward III's twenty-ship navy, which defeated the French at Sluys in 1340 and was used primarily for transporting soldiers and supplies: "The typical fourteenth-century ship was tub-like in shape, with stem and stern raised and fitted out like castle turrets. There were cabins inside the castles, with ladders leading to the decks, a single mast surmounted with a crow's nest or fighting-top, a square sail, and a large hawse-hole for the anchor-cable. Rudders were beginning to take the place of steering-oars'' (43). In addition to the increasing use of a rudder, mariners also created a legal code for shipmen. The Consulate of the Sea and the Laws of Oréron were adopted as standard maritime law. These regulations included the stricture that if a pilot lost a ship through carelessness, he must give financial satisfaction or be put to death; ships were ordered to mark their anchors with buoys; and shipmasters were required to ask their crew, "Gentlemen, what think ye of this wind?" when it shifted, inviting an opportunity to leave port (Villiers 72).

HISTORICAL COUNTERPARTS TO THE SHIPMAN

The Shipman may be a reference to a specific fourteenth-century English pirate, or he may be a composite of several men, mixed with some fiction. The man most frequently cited as the probable historical counterpart for the Shipman is John Hawley of Dartmouth. In 1378 he was part of a royal commission licensed to seek out and destroy the king's naval enemies. The *Magdaleyne* or *Maudeleyne* was the name of one of his vessels (Manly 174). While he was originally enlisted in 1374 to help defend Dartmouth from the sea (the same year that Chaucer went to Dartmouth as a customs official), Hawley was "especially notorious in the years immediately preceding the composition of the *Canterbury Tales* for his naval actions in his own interests" (Manly 174). In 1385 a complaint was brought against Hawley claiming that he had used his men and four of his ships to attack three vessels carrying wine and other goods. From the raid, Hawley made off with "fifteen tonnels" of wine (Manly 173). The case against Hawley was well-known and continued until 1394. Hawley was also implicated in a raid of a Genoese ship in January of 1386, an attack on the wine-carrying barge *La Trinite* in March of 1386, and in the theft of twenty-one "tuns" of wine from a Dutch ship in October of 1387. By 1389 Hawley had complaints filed against him by merchants from Rochelle, France, and Flanders. His attacks on merchant ships are recorded through 1404.

Hawley was not just a brigand, however. Manly points out that he was also a respected citizen of Dartmouth, held various offices, and, at times, even filed charges against other ship owners for seizing goods from his own ships. Hawley served as justice of the peace, mayor of Dartmouth, customs collector in Devonshire and Cornwall, and eventually admiral's deputy. Hawley was not the only official who engaged in piratical actions; at one time, the mayor of Winchelsea was also accused of privateering acts.

Although Manly cites many similarities between Hawley and the Shipman, he feels, as other critics do, that Hawley cannot have been the only source for the Shipman. The Shipman could also have been patterned after the master (or captain) of the ship rather than the owner. The Dartmouth *Maudeleyne* had at least two recorded masters during the latter half of the fourteenth century:

George Cowntree (1379) and Peter Risshenden (1391) (Karkeek 410). Others believe the Shipman may be a reference to Piers Risselden (possibly the same person as Peter Risshenden), who with John Hawley, captured the three wine-carrying ships in 1386 (Manly 171). Margaret Galway identifies the Shipman as the Basque, John Piers, who lived in the west of England from 1385 to 1388, captured a ship named the *Magdaleyne* in 1383, killed its crew, and threw them overboard (501, 502). Piers was known as an excellent navigator and was described as wearing a costume similar to that of the Shipman.

Today, we think of the privateer as a legendary character of the past, but shipmen still exist in legitimate roles as merchant marines, ship's captains, and sailors in the national navy. These modern shipmen are more carefully monitored by maritime law than were their medieval counterparts. The less legitimate legacy of the Shipman lives on in the Indonesian pirates who still maintain a presence in the Pacific. The "good felawe" of the "General Prologue" also remains to some extent in the twentieth-century "good fellow," or Mafia member, whose claim that merchandise "fell off the back of a truck" is a modern permutation of the shipman's siphoning of the merchant's wine.

THE "SHIPMAN'S TALE"

The "Shipman's Tale" is the first in fragment VII and may be considered Chaucer's earliest fabliau, although the *Tales* include other fabliaux, such as the "Miller's Tale," the "Reeve's Tale," and the "Cook's Tale." Although the speaker is not identified at the beginning of the story, his identity becomes clear when the Host addresses him at the end as "Sire gentil maister, gentil maryneer" (Payne 129). The adjective "gentil" is surely ironic, for the Shipman cannot be considered a member of the "gentil" estate, and his fabliau is certainly not "gentil." The story is based on a popular motif, the lover's gift regained, in which "a man pays a woman for her sexual favors with money borrowed from her husband and then tells the husband he has given the repayment to the wife" (Benson 16). In the "Shipman's Tale," the young beautiful wife is married to a Seint-Denys merchant, whose cousin, the thirty-three-year-old monk, Daun John, is also her lover. The interesting twist in the "Shipman's Tale" is that the wife proves herself as quick-witted as her lover. Because the wife outwits her husband and escapes censure, most critics believe the tale was originally intended for a female narrator, possibly the Wife of Bath. At one point the speaker refers to wives as "we," which would certainly support the attribution of this tale to the Wife.

While the tale may have originally been intended for the Wife of Bath, it is appropriate for the Shipman because he would have been "well acquainted with merchants and their attitude toward money" (Benson 17). The Shipman is established as an antagonist to the merchant in the "General Prologue," which describes how he had stolen wine from merchants while they slept on their voyage from Bordeaux. The pilgrim merchant also mentions pirates in the "Pro-

logue,'' when he expresses his wish that ''the sea were kept for any thyng /
Betwixe Middelburgh and Orewelle'' (276–277) [''the sea were kept for any
thing / Between Middleburgh and Orwell'']. Howard argues that shipmen and
merchants were ''natural adversaries, like millers and reeves, or friars and summoners,'' and that Chaucer ''must have meant to have the Shipman and Merchant tell tales against each other'' (436). Historically, we can see that the
Shipman may not only have stolen wine from the Merchant whose goods he
transported, but he may also have boarded merchants' ships and raided their
merchandise to fill his own coffers or the coffers of the port town he represented.
One of the central ironies of the story is that while the Merchant takes the risky
voyages to Bruges and Paris, his household, which he considers safely under
control, is undermined.

The ''Shipman's Tale'' clearly critiques the commodification of human relations and demonstrates how the exchange of capital can undermine moral
relations. Paul Strohm analyzes the tale as one that suggests ''an inextricable
melding of human and monetary values, of the commodification of exchange
relations in both the human and material spheres, of the extension of a mercantile
ethos to all spheres of activity'' (100). The narrator criticizes the wife for her
desire for material goods, and the deception in the tale centers around the borrowing of money and repayment in flesh. While the tale critiques these exchange
systems, it does not strongly condemn its main characters and it maintains a
detached tone. Paul Ruggiers describes the tale as ''worldly, cynical, and disillusioned,'' a description that seems perfectly suited to the Shipman, a man
whose living frequently consists of stealing from others (80).

Just as the tone is appropriate for the Shipman, the focus of the satire is also
linked to his world view. While the Wife and the Monk are the characters who
commit the immoral act, the Merchant is the butt of gentle satire. Like the
pilgrim Monk, Daun Piers, the Shipman's Monk, Daun John, is an ''outrider,''
who is as comfortable in the secular world as in his cloister, but the narrator
does not condemn him. Instead, as Ruggiers notes, ''we like him because we
see him in situations, like prayer, which elicit our respect; or in actions, like
blushing, which we associate with modest bearing'' (82). At the same time, we
also like the wife because of her cleverness and wit. The beginning of the tale
seems to condemn her at first, but then the narration switches with the pronoun
''we'' into her voice, and we hear her refer to her ''sely housbonde'' (VII.11).

The Merchant, as the focus of the satire, displays an inordinate concern with
the world of finance and shuts himself up in his ''countour-hous'' ''that no man
sholde hym lette / Of his acountes'' (VII.77, 86–87) [''country house'' ''that
no man should him disturb / Of his accounts'']. His attention to the maintenance
of his financial affairs is at the expense of the maintenance of his domestic
affairs. When his wife comes to fetch him for dinner, she exclaims

> What, sire, how longe wol ye faste?
> How longe tyme wol ye rekene and caste

Youre sommes, and youre bookes, and youre thynges?
The devel have part on alle swiche rekenynges!
Ye have ynough, pardee, of Goddes sonde.

(215–219)

["What, sir, how long will you fast?
How long a time will you reckon and calculate
Your sums, and your books, and your things?
The devil has part in all such reckonings!
You have enough, by golly, of what God has sent.]

She chides him for his focus on money and his lapse in the role of host to Daun John.

The Merchant's response to his wife demonstrates another aspect of the merchant mentality that the Shipman would mock: his desire for a dependable, regulated world. The merchant says that among his profession, "Scarsly amonges twelve tweye shul thryve / Continuelly, lastynge unto oure age" (228–229) ["Scarcely among twelve two shall thrive / Continually, lasting unto our age"]. He continues,

And therfore have I greet necessitee
Upon this queynte world t'avyse me,
For everemoore we moote stonde in drede
Of hap and fortune in oure chapmanhede.

(235–238)

[And therefore I have great necessity
Upon this tricky world to take heed,
For evermore we must stand in dread
Of risk and fortune in our business ventures.]

Ruggiers describes the Merchant's ethos as "a careful concern for a care-ridden world that assures no man security, a world ruled by chance and fortune, a world in which a man must wear the face and appearance of success while brooding over the failures of the day and presenting a prosperous air to the world" (84). Certainly, one of the Merchant's primary concerns is the unpredictable loss of goods to pirates. The Shipman would take particular delight in his ability to upset the controlled world of the Merchant through his privateering and through his narrative of the Merchant's cuckolding.

When Daun John asks the Merchant for the loan of 100 francs, the Merchant's reply indicates how much his world centers around the control of exchange:

But o thyng is, ye knowe it wel ynogh
Of chapmen, that hir moneie is hir plogh.
We may creaunce whil we have a name,

But goldlees for to be, it is no game.

(287–290)

[But one thing is, you know it well enough
Of chapmen, that her money is her plow.
We may borrow money while we have a name,
But to be goldless is no laughing matter.]

Little does the Merchant realize how his own money will be exchanged, as "frankes" for "flankes" (101–102) when the Monk uses it to receive sexual favors, and then the wife, in the end, uses her sexual favors as "credit" to pay off the loan to her husband.

The portrait of the Shipman that emerges from an analysis of his tale and description in the "General Prologue" is in keeping with the cynical nature of the profession of Shipman during Chaucer's lifetime. We will probably never know whether the Shipman was meant to represent someone specific, such as John Hawley, or just to depict another aspect of the working man's estate. What we do learn, however, is that the Shipman had a canny knowledge of the emerging commercial world and knew not only how to work within that world legitimately, but also how to exploit it. Chaucer's Shipman can be admired for his nautical skills and bravery in the face of danger. He also serves as a reminder to readers that the medieval world Chaucer depicts is full of complex and seemingly contradictory characters who can continue to surprise and fascinate us when we read the *Canterbury Tales.*

REFERENCES

Benson, Larry D., ed. "Notes to the 'General Prologue' and the 'Shipman's Tale.' " *The Riverside Chaucer.* 3rd ed. Boston: Houghton Mifflin, 1987.

Bowden, Muriel A. *A Commentary on the General Prologue to The Canterbury Tales.* 2nd ed. New York: Macmillan, 1967.

Galway, Margaret. "Chaucer's Shipman in Real Life." *Modern Language Review* 34 (1939): 497–514.

Gosse, Philip. *The History of Piracy.* New York: Burt Franklin, 1968.

Howard, Donald R. *Chaucer: His Life, His Works, His World.* New York: E. P. Dutton, 1987.

Karkeek, P. Q. "Chaucer's Shipman and His Barge 'The Maudelayne,' With Notes on Chaucer's Horses." *Essays on Chaucer* 5. London: Chaucer Society, 1894.

Manly, John M. *Some New Light on Chaucer: Lectures Delivered at the Lowell Institute.* New York: H. Holt, 1926.

Mann, Jill. *Chaucer and Medieval Estates Satire: The Literature of Social Classes and the General Prologue to The Canterbury Tales.* Cambridge: Cambridge University Press, 1973.

Payne, Robert O. *Geoffrey Chaucer.* 2nd ed. Boston: Twayne, 1986.

Ruggiers, Paul G. *The Art of the Canterbury Tales.* Madison: University of Wisconsin Press, 1965.

Saul, Nigel. "Chaucer and Gentility." *Chaucer's England: Literature in Historical Context.* Ed. Barbara Hanawalt. Minneapolis: University of Minnesota Press, 1992. Pp. 41–58.

Serraillier, Ian. *Chaucer and His World.* New York: Henry Z. Walck, 1968.

Strohm, Paul. *Social Chaucer.* Cambridge, Mass.: Harvard University Press, 1989.

Unger, Richard W. *The Ship in the Medieval Economy 600–1600.* London: Croom Helm, 1980.

Villiers, Capt. Alan. *Men, Ships and the Sea.* Washington, D.C.: National Geographic Society, 1973.

Chapter 20

With Us Ther Was a Doctour of Phisik

EDWIN ELEAZAR

INTRODUCTION

The seventeenth different pilgrim introduced in the "General Prologue" of *The Canterbury Tales,* the Doctour of Phisik, is described no less ambiguously than are any of the other major figures, such as the Prioresse, the Pardoner, or the Physician's nemesis in the professional world, the Man of Lawe. The Pilgrim Chaucer's treatment of this fourteenth-century medical practitioner is so equivocal that modern critics have had difficulty concluding whether he should be viewed in either a positive or a negative light. Those who approach the "General Prologue" description as at least mildly satiric generally address the Physician not as an individual embodying both human virtues and human foibles, but rather as a type of the entire medical profession, a group that was severely lampooned in fourteenth-century literature as being fraudulent and materialistic. Assuming this attitude, modern scholars have often dismissed Chaucer's Doctour as either a braggart, an atheist, an embodiment of the deadly sin of avarice, or an out-and-out medical fraud. Other critics, however, approach the Physician from the much more sympathetic angle of our modern understanding of medieval medical history, taking into account the practitioners' place in medieval society, the extent of their education and medical knowledge, and their moral training. Those who adopt this latter approach invariably conclude that given the medical knowledge of the fourteenth century and the social constraints placed on European physicians during that era, that Chaucer the Pilgrim is perfectly justified in claiming this medical man was a "verray, parfit praktisour" (422).

These two apparently antithetical views of the Physician arise quite naturally from the details of his outward appearance and behavior as recorded in the "General Prologue" (A, 411–444)—a set of details that renders him, both morally and professionally, as neither fish nor fowl. In the "Prologue" description, Chaucer begins positively, claiming of the Doctour that "In al this world ne was ther noon hym lik, / To speke of phisik and surgerye," implying (albeit not too clearly) that the Doctour is both a master physician and a surgeon, a somewhat unusual combination in fourteenth-century England (A, 412–413). This Doctour of Phisik is firmly grounded in astronomy and is a master diagnostician, who once having discovered a patient's illness may be relied on to administer the best of then-current medical practice—particularly, astrological talismans and herbal remedies (A, 414–424). To obtain pharmaceuticals for his clients, he has formed close alliances with local apothecaries, and both they and he profit from this arrangement (A, 420–428). Furthermore, the Physician has shared with Chaucer the Pilgrim some of the details of his medical training, especially his study in the writings of all the major Greek, Arab, and English physicians—"Deyscorides, and eek Rufus, / Olde Ypocras, Haly, and Galyen, / Serapion, Razis, and Avycen, / Averrois, Damascien, and Constantyn, / Bernard, and Gatesden, and Gilbertyn," and even the works of the mythical Æsculapius, to whom many medieval medical compilations were ascribed (A, 429–434; Benson, "Notes" 816; Curry 3). As any good physician of the age was expected to have been, he is of temperate diet (A, 435–437) and doesn't spend money lavishly (A, 441).

A number of details in the "Prologue" description also imply that the Physician may not be of exemplary moral character, and that both he and the profession he represents are being made the butts of some mild satire. First, Chaucer claims, somewhat enigmatically, that the Physician's study is "but litel on the Bible" (A, 438), a novel sort of behavior, certainly, for a man who was probably trained as a cleric and at the very least should be attempting to emulate the Great Physician, Jesus Christ. Second, this medical man wears expensive clothing of red and blue lined with silks and has saved scrupulously the money he has earned during the plague years. Obviously, neither action would qualify him for the title of Mr. Charity, 1489, and neither would the last detail we are given of him in the "General Prologue." There, we are told that since he believes potable gold is a "cordial," a good heart medicine, that he loves gold especially (A, 443–445), and for those who wish to view the Physician as one element of Chaucer's larger social satire, these details have been sufficient to cast doubt on the good doctor's motives for being on this pilgrimage. When added to other questionable details such as his use of "magyk natureel," his use of astrology and talismans, and his collusion with pharmacists, this is reason enough for some critics to label him a quack (Robertson, *Chaucer's London* 208; Root 219). Such charges were often leveled at physicians during the fourteenth century—that they were materialistic atheists who practiced medicine only for profit, and not for charity's sake. The inclusion of details such as these may indicate that Chaucer is taking his place in an already long line of famous poets who disdained the Doctour's profession, a line headed by Francis Petrarch, who in 1365 wrote a lengthy, scathing commentary to his friend Boccaccio on the lack of learning, the intemperance of diet, and the greed he felt characterized the physicians of his era (Moriarty 305–310).

We must remember, however, that even those very details that seem to indicate our Physician is not of the highest moral character are equivocal. His use of "magyk natureel," astrology and magic talismans, which seems to us moderns so obviously suspect (Bowden 204; Mann 93; Robertson 207–208) has been found proof positive of the Physician's knowledge of standard medical practice by at least one major scholar (Benson, "Astrological" 64–65). Even his collusion with apothecaries, which appears somewhat lacking in circumspection and has been cited as evidence of the Physician's deviance from basic ethical standards, has been described as standard fourteenth-century medical practice recognized by no less an influential body than the medieval medical faculty of the University of Paris (Renn 5).

Obviously, these conflicting details from the "Prologue" concerning the Physician's character can be understood in all their equivocal splendor only through an analysis of the medical profession in fourteenth-century England. In order to gain a clear insight into the motives of Chaucer's Physician, we must look at the social background from which he most likely rose, the sort of education he might have had, the extent of his medical knowledge, and the modes of practice he most likely employed. Only by attempting to develop a complete picture of the milieu in which the Physician operated will we be able to assess the man and the tale he tells.

SOCIAL BACKGROUNDS/EXPECTATIONS

Prior to the thirteenth century in Europe, the ranks of physicians and surgeons had been made up largely by members of the clergy or by religious women. These folk had studied medicine either in cathedral schools or privately and had given their lives to waiting upon the sick and infirm. It was they who created the earliest hospitals in the Western world, a legacy that dates from at least the fourth century to the present day (Inglis 57–58). But it was not until the thirteenth and fourteenth centuries that medicine became a standard course of study in most European universities and that medical faculties began to train a wide range of students from various social backgrounds. Even in the late Middle Ages, medical students were of a decidedly religious stamp. Their ranks were composed predominantly of men drawn from the beneficed clergy, the major orders, the secular clergy, and occasionally, laymen (Siraisi 25; Ussery 30–31). The lay group was formed almost exclusively of men from wealthy urban families, although there is some evidence that members of the lower classes became medical students under special circumstances (Siraisi 26; Talbot 52). The attraction of medical studies to these constituents was not overly dissimilar from the attractions such studies hold out today. For the layman, achieving a medical degree was the attainment of a sort of social distinction. As one historian has put it, the layman who became a doctor of medicine, if he were at all energetic and ambitious, had at least the hope of achieving "a good living, a dignified position, and a rich wife" (Schachner 373). In actuality, however, very few physicians ever amassed great wealth or garnered eminent social status, and most were forced to live rather modestly at a lower social status than that generally achieved by lawyers (Siraisi 23, 26).

Prior to the thirteenth century, the attainment of a medical degree was one method of achieving high office within the Church, especially for secular clerics (nonmonastic clergy). Secular clerics had been prominent in hospital work from the tenth century onward, particularly in hospitals near cathedrals where these men held ecclesiastic positions. In the thirteenth century, as the Church began to discourage and at times even forbid men in major orders to study medicine, the position of secular clerics with medical training became even more important within the ecclesiastical hierarchy, since these men had to "pick up the slack" as monks, deacons, subdeacons, priests, canons, and friars left the medical field. For the secular clergy, a medical career held out hope for preferment within the Church, possibly attachment to royal service, or at the least a reduction in the number of his religious duties around the cathedral.

As late as the latter half of the fourteenth century, the vast majority of men studying medicine in medieval universities were clerics, especially in England at Oxford and Cambridge where, apparently, the entire faculty of medicine was composed of religious men (Talbot 51; Ussery 28–31). This predominance of clerics within the discipline in England is all the more amazing given the existence of further evidence that indicates the study of medicine was actively discouraged at Oxford and Cambridge, since officials feared such study led to the development of materialistic/atheistic thinking (Arnold 179). For these and other related reasons, the study of medicine came in a distant third in popularity to the studies of civil and canon law generally throughout all medieval universities. The practice of civil law offered greater monetary remuneration and temporal power, while the study of canon law offered more rapid preferment within the Church (Schachner 372–373). Much of this information obviously militates against any reading of the Physician of *The Canterbury Tales* as the embodiment of avarice, since quite clearly Chaucer's medical man would have had to brave some stringent official opposition to his studies and could have made much more money and gained a higher degree of social prominence had he gone into the study of law.

Other critical questions about our Physician's financial health and his social status are further complicated by the "General Prologue's" ambiguity over whether or not the Doctour of Phisik is both a physician and a surgeon, this difficulty arising obviously from lines 411–414, where Chaucer claims, "With us ther was a Doctour of Phisik; / In al this world ne was ther non hym lik,/ To speke of phisik and of surgerye, / For he was grounded in astronomye." ["With us there was a Doctor of Medicine; / In all this world there was not another like him, / To speak of medicine and of surgery, / For he was well instructed in the science of astrology"]. Walter Clyde Curry treats these lines as an indicator that the Physician has been boasting about his professional expertise to the naive pilgrim Chaucer, but that the wary reader can see this man is capable only of speaking about the nature of surgery. He is incapable of practicing the surgeon's craft (3). Similarly, Huling Ussery argues that our Physician is not a practicing surgeon. Following J. M. Matthews's translation of "to speke of" in line 413 as "with respect to," Ussery reads these lines as "In all the world there none his equal with respect to [practitioners of] phisik and surgerye, because he was a good astronomer," meaning that the Doctour's skills surpass those of other physicians and certainly those of surgeons, who also used astrology in their practice (110–111). This reading fits snugly with Ussery's general thesis that Chaucer's Doctour is a cleric and therefore, unlikely to be both a physician and a surgeon (6–21). As C. David Benson points out, however, this is not necessarily the case, since Guy de Chauliac, author of one of the most famous surgical manuals of the period, describes himself as both surgeon and doctor of physic, and by Ussery's own admission, the combination of both practices in one person was not unheard of in England (Benson, "Notes" 816; Ussery 11, 59–60). Subsequent discussion will assume that the Doctour may have been a practitioner in both fields.

Becoming a surgeon, as our pilgrim physician may have done, did not require university training, although at many medieval universities the discipline was taught. In general, however, surgery was considered a craft and, therefore, separate from the profession of medicine (phisik). The reason for this separation in the fourteenth century is twofold. First, the two groups of health care workers were considered separate in some of the earliest medical texts with which the medievals were conversant, most notably in the works of Galen (A.D. 131–201), the Roman physician whose writings served as the basis of received medical wisdom throughout the Middle Ages. This separation was perpetuated, clearly, in the works of the Arabian authors who developed Galen's teachings further in the ninth and tenth centuries. They generally elevated the physician over the surgeon in the medical scheme of things, ascribing to the physician the superior realm of book knowledge as his sphere of influence, while relegating the surgeon to the realm of physical manipulation of the traumatized body. Subsequent medical texts produced in the Western universities during the eleventh, twelfth, and thirteenth centuries fed upon and institutionalized these positions. Thus to a major extent, the division between surgeons and physicians during the fourteenth century was the result of material in scholarly texts that "exalted the 'noble physician' to heights where any kind of manual operation was unthinkable" (Talbot 54).

Ecclesiastical legislation, in the form of a decree from the Fourth Lateran Council of 1215, also played a hand in widening the division between these two forms of medical practice, especially in Northern Europe and in England. This decree forbade both regular and secular clergy either to make surgical incisions or to cauterize wounds (Siraisi 26; Ussery 31). As a result, from the early thirteenth century onward, we find the ranks of surgeons filled increasingly by laymen—by Muslims and Jews as well as by lay Christians. Clergymen were not totally excluded from study in the field of surgery, however, since they could obtain papal dispensation to practice both surgery and cautery (Siraisi 26). However, the English surgeon was ordinarily a layman who had studied the craft in a guild under the direction of a master surgeon and had obtained a license to practice from the local authorities.

Consistent with their conservative clerical backgrounds, neither Oxford nor Cambridge taught surgery during the fourteenth century, so if our Physician is indeed a Doctour and a university-trained surgeon, he must have derived his training from a university in Southern France or Italy—for example, the universities of Salerno, Montpellier, or Bologna. In any event, this additional skill would indicate possibilities for a second source of income to supplement his primary calling as a *medicus*.

EDUCATION

The Physician's title as "Doctour of Phisik" indicates that he has achieved the highest rank possible for a medical practitioner and must have received it from a university (Ussery 21). However, Chaucer's description of the Physician in the "General Prologue," and the details relating to his background that the man gives within his tale tell us little about the trials he had to endure to achieve his position in English society. We do know that he has studied an impressive list of medical authorities, and his tale indicates that he has at least a passing familiarity with Livy's works (or perhaps with the *Roman de la Rose*), but beyond that we know nothing about his educational background. He gives us not one clue as to which of the several English or continental schools he might have attended, nor how long he was there. It would seem logical to assume that he graduated from an English university, but by the end of the fourteenth century, only two schools, Oxford and Cambridge, offered programs leading to the degree of Master or Doctour of Phisik, and neither university's program was what we might call a "world beater."

The Faculty of Medicine at Oxford, for example, which had been formed at the end of the thirteenth century, had only one teaching doctor in 1414, and he was not British. Furthermore, the study of medicine appears to have been actively discouraged in many Oxford colleges, particularly at Merton, where there was even a statute forbidding it (Talbot 68–69). Over the course of the entire fourteenth century, the Oxford medical faculty seems to have consisted of not much more than forty teachers and students, all of whom were either men in orders or beneficed and secular clergy. No records of laymen studying medicine at Oxford exist until the fifteenth century (Siraisi 56). If Chaucer intended his audience to envision the Doctour as a surgeon and therefore a layman, then he may not have wished his audience to recognize this man as an Oxford graduate, since the faculty there had such a decidedly clerical air about it during the fourteenth century.

The situation at Cambridge was quite similar to that at Oxford. The Faculty of Medicine, which was probably formed after the Oxford group, was just as small. Since the university's records were destroyed by fire in 1381, no testimony survives which describes exactly how large the program was nor who was involved in it. We do know that between 1488 and 1511, of 3,827 degree candidates university-wide, only 28 obtained degrees in medicine. Apparently, the faculty was rather less distinguished than Oxford's, if that is possible, since fifteenth-century statutes had to provide for the hiring of off-campus proctors for degree candidates in case no Doctour of Medicine was available on the faculty (Talbot 68–69).

Nothing in the text of the *Canterbury Tales,* however, indicates that the Physician was necessarily educated at either of the English universities, and if he had the means to attend university on the Continent, he might have attached himself to any one of a number of major institutions, several at which Englishmen apparently distinguished themselves highly.

The first major university of the Middle Ages to have a strong Faculty of Medicine was located at Salerno, on the southwestern coast of Italy. This school was happily located within the confluence of Greco-Roman, Arabian, and Jewish cultures, and thus it was at Salerno that the first fusion of the Western monastic medical tradition with the Arabic/Jewish tradition occurred (Cartwright 14; Schachner 51–52). By the middle of the twelfth century, this university had become the most important center of medical instruction in the West, thanks primarily to the works of one member of the abbey at Monte Cassino, Constantine the African. Constantine was apparently from Carthage and had traveled widely throughout Arabia as a young man, collecting a wide variety of texts in his travels. In his later years, he translated many of the major Arabian and Greek medical texts into Latin. Among these were the *Viaticus* and *Liber de stomacho* of Abu Djezzar, the *Liber oculis* of Hunain, the *Liber diætarum universalium et particularium* of Isaac Judæus, *Al-Maliki* of Haly Abbas, and the *Megatechne* of Galen (the last two authors being ones the Physician claims to have read). This opening of the Arabian and Jewish traditions to the West created a ferment of ideas and expanded the boundaries of medical practice and education, which first bore fruit at the University of Salerno. The first major development involved the creations of a series of commentaries on medical texts—the *Liber Gradum* of Mesuë, the *De elementis* of Isaac ibn Amaram, the *Isagoge* of Johannitius, the *Tegni* of Galen, and the *Aphorisms* and *Prognostics* of Hippocrates, among many others, each written by faculty members for instructural purposes. These various commentaries would eventually be grouped together in one volume entitled the *Articella,* which would become the standard medical instructional text throughout the Middle Ages (Talbot 39–41).

Not only did the Salernitan faculty spearhead the training of medical students, but they also trained many students in the craft of surgery. A most interesting sidelight in this area are the "ladies of Salerno," Abella, Rebecca, Costanza, and Trotula, women who were trained at the university to perform surgery and who may or may not have been restricted to gynecological practice (Cartwright 42). Of this group, the most important is Trotula, whose actual existence has long been doubted but was recently verified (Benton 44; Dronke 180–182; Green 442; Siraisi 27). Trotula not only practiced as a surgeon, but also became an author in her own right, creating several gynecological texts that were widely circulated throughout medieval Europe and gave rise to three fourteenth-century Middle English texts, *The Knowing of Woman's Kind in Childing,* the *Liber Trotuli,* and the *Book of Rota* (Barratt 27–28). After the thirteenth century, however, women were excluded from study in most medieval universities, Salerno included (Siraisi 27).

A second major continental school, and a more likely candidate for the *alma mater* of Chaucer's Physician, was the medical school at Montpellier in southern France. By 1137, this institution had a fully developed faculty, many of whom had been educated in the school at Salerno. As was the case with its mother school at Salerno, Montpellier was located within the confluence of several medical cultures, and here the early Salernitan tradition, which was largely Greco-Roman, received a heavy overlay of Eastern Arabic and the Spanish Moslem/Jewish influence. As at Salerno, intellectual ferment was set off by the translation of texts previously unavailable to Christian physicians, particularly works from Barcelona, Segovia, Leon, and Pamplona on astronomy and mathematics. By the middle of the twelfth century, the Latin translations of two monks at Montpellier, Gerard of Cremona and Mark of Toledo, were already having an effect on the quality of instruction and the prestige of the Montpellier medical faculty. Thanks to these two men, medieval physicians gained access not only to even more of the works of Galen and Hippocrates than were previously available, but also to works such as Albucasis's *Chirurgia,* Isaac Judæus's *De elementis* and *De definitionibus,* Al-Kindi's *De gradibus,* Rhazes's *Almansor,* Avicenna's *Canon,* and Serapion's *Breviarium,* the last three of which are by authors Chaucer's Physician prides himself on knowing. The cumulative effect of all this intellectual ferment was that Montpellier began to outstrip Salerno as a teaching institution during the thirteenth century and began to attract more students, becoming a major center for English scholars, in particular (Talbot 57–60).

That Montpellier was a major center of study for English scholars is readily attested to by the "roll call" of the famous medical men who studied or taught there. One of the earliest examples is "Ricardus Anglicus" (Richard the Englishman), author of the *Micrologus,* a treatise on prognosis, anatomy, pharmacy, and therapy, which circulated widely throughout Europe. Other medieval English physicians and authors connected with Montpellier include Adelard of Bath, Robert of Chester, Daniel Morley, Henry of Winchester, and perhaps, but not certainly, both Gilbertus Anglicus and John Gaddesden, the two English authorities from the Physician's reading list in the "General Prologue" (Talbot passim, 56–110).

A third major continental university that might have provided the Physician

with his medical education was the University of Paris, which was more prox-
imate to London than either Salerno or Montpellier, and by the thirteenth century
had the reputation of being one of the three best institutions in the West, the
other two being Montpellier and Bologna (Siraisi 59–60). The Parisian faculty
had its origins in about the same time frame (mid-twelfth century) as did its
sister school to the south, Montpellier. Since the city of Paris was a major
political and cultural hub during this period, the school naturally garnered most
of the major medical thinkers of the time, either to study or to teach there, and
as a result, the medical faculty perceived its own course of study to be vastly
superior to those of the more provincial universities. An Oxford scholar transferring to the University of Paris, for example, could expect to be granted less
than half his time spent at England's primary medical college in lieu of time
spent at the Parisian institution (Talbot 68). The major differentiation between
Paris and the schools of Montpellier and Salerno, at least for our purposes here,
is that throughout the fourteenth century, the Parisian faculty did not instruct
students in surgery, which both Montpellier and Salerno did (Siraisi 179; Ussery
11). Paris was, however, the sort of institution at which Chaucer's Physician
might well have obtained all the knowledge he claims to have been exposed to.
But then, he could just as likely have received it at any one of a number of
other institutions that we cannot possibly discuss here—specifically, the schools
at Bologna, Padua, and Ferrara, each of which was in some way important in
the development of medical training during the Middle Ages.

Courses of medical study at the major universities discussed above differed
slightly in the number of years required for completion, but the instructional
methods they employed were quite similar, as were the stages through which
the degree candidate rose. Instruction was quite dissimilar from what most medical students might expect to receive today, being primarily the rote learning of
theory with only a bare minimum of practical application or hands-on experience. Generally, the students' primary duty was to attend lectures on medical
texts. At Paris, these usually consisted, during the first year, of instruction in
the *Isagoge* of Johannitius (a systematic survey of the major areas of medical
knowledge), followed by gradually more specific texts (usually Hippocrates'
Aphorisms and *Prognostics*), and then finally the works of Rhases, Avicenna,
and Galen. Students learned these texts catechistically and were not expected,
generally, to question or argue with the authoritative pronouncements they found
therein. During the months from October through Easter, students held debates
on the texts they were studying and presented oral theses before their peers.

As far as practical, hands-on studies were concerned, medieval universities
did allow opportunities for students to be involved in dissections upon occasion,
but with nowhere near the frequency that medical students perform them today.
The reasons for this were multiple. To a certain extent, the situation devolved
from a number of ecclesiastical laws designed to prevent clergy from performing
surgery or to keep Crusaders from boiling Christian corpses overseas and returning with the bones for burial in their homeland. However, this does not

account entirely for the medieval reticence for dissections, since papal dispensations were frequently granted for that purpose. More important was the fact that the medievals had no way of preserving a cadaver for more than a couple of days. Thus, they were constrained to perform autopsies during the dead of winter only. However, the most likely reason for the dearth of dissections in the universities during the Middle Ages was the fact that most of the teaching faculties assumed that students would gain little knowledge beyond that available in the anatomical texts of Galen and later Arabic writers (Siraisi 89).

The course of these studies was also somewhat more lengthy than that required of medical students today. Generally speaking, to reach the level of Doctour of Phisik as our Canterbury-bound physician has, a student had to rise through four levels, or degrees, within the university: Scholar, Bachelor, Licentiate, and Doctour/Master. In what follows, we will discuss the curriculum as it existed at Oxford in the fourteenth century, although other schools would have had slightly different requirements for the length of time one had to spend at each stage. At the Scholar level, the Oxford student was expected to have spent nine years studying and lecturing in the *trivium* (logic, grammar, and rhetoric) and the *quadrivium* (geometry, astronomy, arithmetic, and music). Mastery of these areas of study was considered absolutely essential as prerequisites to study in medicine, since students used all of them in writing theses, debating, and lecturing (Curry 4–5). Even subjects like music, which seem at a wide remove from the concerns of medical men, had actual relevance, since a doctor was expected to base part of his diagnosis for certain illnesses on the rhythm and music of the patient's pulse. The nine years spent at this level consisted of four years for the attainment of the B.A., three years for the M.A., and a two-year regency in which the candidate lectured and attended to other duties around the Faculty.

The next three levels, Bachelor, Licentiate, and Master, were devoted to the study of medicine. After the regency period at the Scholar level, students were expected to spend four years in study at the Bachelor level before requesting permission to enter medical practice. Upon successful completion of the course of study, students obtained the B.M. or Bachelor's of Medicine. After this, they spent two more years of medical study at the Licentiate level, after which they received a license to practice from the university chancelor and were incepted by the medical faculty. After two more years of lecturing, the student was then granted the highest degree available to a medical practitioner, the D.M. or Master of Medicine, which brought with it the title of ''Doctour.'' Thus the average medical student was required to spend at least seventeen years attached to the university before he could even think about setting himself up in private practice (Talbot 68–70; Ussery 7–10).

For surgeons, education could be quite a bit simpler. In England, surgeons generally were educated within the guild system, which meant that one apprenticed himself to a ''Master'' surgeon for six or seven years before being allowed to enter practice. However, not all surgeons were educated this way. As has been mentioned earlier, the southern European schools did not share the northern schools' distaste for surgical studies. Indeed, much of the development of surgical innovation during the Middle Ages may be attributed to scholars lecturing in the universities, not from practitioners working in guilds. One of the earliest and most influential textbooks on the subject of surgery was the *Surgery* of Roger Frugardi of Salerno, as revised by his student Guido of Arezzo in 1170. This compilation of surgical material from Haly Abbas, Hippocrates, and Oribasius became the standard textbook not only at Salerno, but also at Montpellier and Bologna (Talbot 53). In the thirteenth century at Montpellier, Guillaume de Congenis practiced and taught surgery and produced his own text based largely on Frugardi's *Surgery* and the Arabic texts of Rhazes (Talbot 93). At Bologna, the standard text in the fourteenth and fifteenth centuries was the Surgery of Bruno Longoburgo (c. 1252), which was the first text to include extensive amounts of material from the Arabian author Albucasis (Siraisi 164; Talbot 68–70).

This openness to the teaching of surgery in the southern European schools should not be viewed as open rebellion against any ecclesiastical decrees, especially those proceeding from the Fourth Lateran Council (1215), since there is a good bit of evidence to indicate that practicing surgeons within the universities were laymen, especially Roger Frugardi. Furthermore, it is clear that even secular clergy often received papal dispensations to perform both dissections and surgery during this period (Siraisi 178). Thus, if Chaucer's Doctour is both a physician and a surgeon, he had ample opportunity to study both medicine and surgery in many of the major continental universities, even if he could not obtain such in either of the English schools or at the University of Paris.

MEDICAL THEORY

The medical theory that our physician would have learned at any university during the fourteenth century was a mixed bag of materials taken from the Greek, Roman, and Arabian/Jewish traditions of medical inquiry. Thus any discussion of medieval medical theory and practice which the Physician followed must begin with a discussion of their development from the early Greeks to the fourteenth century to clarify the origins of its several elements.

The first major medical thinker to affect the development of medicine in the West was the Greek philosopher, Empedocles of Sicily (400 B.C.). Convinced that the human body was but a microcosm of the universe, Empedocles postulated that it must be made up of the same four elements that Thales of Miletus (639–544 B.C.) had assumed to constitute all matter in the universe—earth, air, fire, and water. To these elements he assigned pairs of four different qualities: dry, moist, hot, and cold. Thus earth was recognized as a cold, dry element, air as hot and moist, fire as hot and dry, and water as cold and moist. This is the source of the "humoral theory," the idea that the human body is composed of four humors: black bile (which correlates with earth, since it is cold and dry), blood (with air, hot and moist), yellow or red bile (with fire, hot and dry), and phlegm (with water, cold and moist). In this system, disease arose in the body when these humors became in any way imbalanced (Jones 543–545). Thus a medical man could help a patient to right this imbalance by introducing natural substances into the body which would counterbalance the negative effect of the humors. The Greek medical texts that formed the basis of received medical knowledge during the Middle Ages devoted much space to pharmacopeias, lists of recipes of herbal and other natural substances that supposedly provided certain qualities of heat, dryness, coldness, and moisture to offset any possible humoral imbalance a physician might recognize in his patient (Cartwright 3).

Extensive lists of pharmaceutical recipes served as a hallmark of the writings of the first major medical practitioner in history, Hippocrates (c. A.D. 460), a Greek physician who was not only the supposed source of the Hippocratic oath, but also the source of the aphorism, "Ars longa, vita brevis," to which Chaucer alludes in the opening line of *The Parliament of the Fowl*. Hippocrates's importance in the history of medicine resides primarily in the fact that he removed the study of medicine from the realm of philosophy and made it a more practical concern. Evidently, he gathered together a great deal of medical knowledge from a wide range of sources and collected them in two major works studied in every major medieval university, the *Aphorisms* and *Prognostics*. His works are the source for the common medieval practices of prescribing herbal teas and bloodletting, as well as prescribing more mundane remedies such as taking fresh air, exercise, and diet to correct or avoid any imbalance in the body's four humors (Cartwright 4). So closely was Hippocrates's name related to pharmaceutical recipes that the Host can refer mockingly to the Physician's prescribing herbal teas or *ypocras* (elsewhere know as *Hippocras*) in the introduction to the "Pardoner's Tale" (C, 306). Here, of course, his half-joking thrust depends on the common belief that physicians could provide aphrodisiacs in the form of love philters (Baird 1).

The next major medical figure in the Greco-Roman tradition, Galen (A.D. 131–201), was the most important medical authority of antiquity, at least by medieval lights. Galen was even more practical minded than was Hippocrates, and he had written more widely, and on a more diverse range of subjects, than had any of his predecessors. He had dissected animals and applied what he had learned from those dissections to his understanding of the workings of the human body (Cartwright 9). He may have even dissected human cadavers himself, and certainly his writings advocated such, particularly in his treatise "On Anatomical Procedures" (Siraisi 191). From Galen's work, medieval physicians derived their concept of the physiologic system. Galen described the workings of the human body as being simply *Nature,* which he saw consisting of three spirits: animal spirits, vital spirits, and natural spirits. Animal spirits emanated from the brain and were transmitted throughout the body via the nerves, while the vital spirits, engendered in the heart, were transmitted by the arteries. The natural spirits rising from the liver moved out into the body through the veins. All of these spirits, as well as the four humors, were distributed throughout a person's body by the beating heart, which accepted blood charged with natural spirits from the liver, then charged it with vital spirits, and finally shot it up to the brain to pick up a dose of animal spirits. In Galen's view, all spirits and humors were distributed and redistributed throughout the body in a sort of ebb and flow motion arising from the heart. It would not be until the seventeenth century that physicians would begin to understand the concept of blood circulation, which is so central to modern medical practice (Jones 538–539).

Most of the Arabian authorities whose works influenced the development of post-twelfth century medieval medicine were themselves heavily influenced by Galen and Hippocrates, so the effect of increased knowledge about Arabic medicine in the West was not revolutionary but supplementary. The major figures of Arabian medicine, Rhazes (Abu Bec Mohammed Ibn Zacariya Ar-Razi, A.D. 900), Avicenna (Abu Ali al Hussein ibn Abdallah ibn Sina, A.D. 980–1037), and Averrois (A.D. 1126–1198) moved the course of medical knowledge forward by contributing ideas related to astronomy, pharmacy, surgery, and alchemy. Astronomy, or what we now call astrology, for the educated physician was doubtless one of the most important fields of his study, since his knowledge in this realm was the major distinction between himself and a simple *empirical* practitioner, like an eye doctor (Siraisi 68). Furthermore, since the physiology of the human body was so intimately tied to the forces of nature, as Galen and Hippocrates argued, it only made sense that the human body with its ebb and flow of spirits and humors should be, like the sea, affected by the influences of the sun, moon, and stars. Arab thinkers were not the source of any new theory in this regard, since Hippocrates had written in his *Astronomia:* "A medical man . . . cannot be considered a perfect physician if he is ignorant of astronomy; no man ought to commit himself into his hands" (quoted in Curry 7). They merely supplied more detail about the supposed effects of the sun, moon, and planets than had been provided before, so that in the Middle Ages, physicians and surgeons felt themselves much more aware of the effects of stars and planets on internal organs, and thus they were more concerned than their counterparts prior to the twelfth century with tables and charts of astrological data and the use of amulets and talismans (Benson, "Astrological" 64–65; Curry 23–24; Nicholas 176–177, 164–175). Thanks in part to these Arabian authorities, whose works he had studied at university, Chaucer's Doctour of Phisik is able to keep "his pacient a ful greet deel / in houres" (A, 415–416) and can "fortunen the ascendent / of his ymages for his pacient" (A, 417–418) ["He kept that he gained in pestilence. / For gold in medicine is medicine for the heart, / Therefore he loved gold in particular"].

In the fields of pharmacy and surgery, the effect of Arabic knowledge on the monastic tradition of the West was again largely supplemental. Most influential in the realm of pharmacy was the *Grabadin* of Mesuë (Yuhanna ibn Masawayn, d. A.D. 857), a pharmacopoeia that contained over 1,400 separate herbal and chemical recipes. In surgery, the *Chururgie* of Albucasis had a profound effect on the development of surgical texts in the West, as has been noted above.

But it was in the area of alchemy that Arabic thought had its most profound effect on the development of Western medicine. Alchemy was a philosophical science *cum* mystical art that had its origins in Northern Africa during the first four centuries *Anno Domini.* It had become popular in the Byzantine Empire and was picked up by the Muslims who invaded during the eighth and ninth centuries. The early alchemists drew their basic principles from the same Hellenistic sources that Galen had received his physiological concepts related to spirits and humors—the concept that all matter is constituted of the four elements earth, air, fire, and water—and sought for ways to create gold and silver from baser substances by a process called transmutation. Arabian alchemists added elements of Chinese philosophy to the art, including the concept of the existence of a universal "medicine"—a magical elixir that would turn any base metal into gold and that when consumed would confer immortality on the recipient (Cartwright 14; Hallam 19–20; Reidy lii-lxiv). Thus medieval Western authorities, such as John of Gaddesden, whom our Physician claims to have read, taught that powdered gold in a solvent, or potable gold, when drunk was an effective cure for heart attacks (Jones 580). Chaucer alludes to this concept for comic effect in his description of the Physician in the "General Prologue": "He kepte that he wan in pestilence. / For gold in phisik is a cordial, / Therefore he lovede gold in special" (A, 442–444).

It was from this diverse set of backgrounds that the medieval medical system was developed and, as we shall see, from which much modern medical practice proceeded. Indeed, medieval physicians lacked only two key bits of knowledge that separate them from their modern counterparts: understanding of the blood circulatory system and knowledge of the existence of microorganisms. Lacking a scientific understanding of these two concepts, they turned to two ancient authorities, Galen in his *Tegni* and Avicenna in his *Canon,* for an understanding of the causes of disease. In general, medievals viewed disease as having three causes: birth defects, humoral (or complexional) imbalance, and trauma. Birth defects were usually left untreated, and the second, complexional imbalance, was particularly the realm in which the physician was supposed to operate, while the third, trauma, was the surgeon's sphere of activity (Siraisi 120).

Overarching this disease theory was the idea that God and Nature were in control of all order and health in the universe, and that when the body was operating in an orderly fashion, such was an expression of divine justice (Alford 386). When that body was not in order, such was an expression of disorder, or chaos in Nature. The physician's place in medieval society may be encapsulated as being that person in the community who was best able to effect a "remedy by his knowledge the physical consequences of the Fall. He [was] an instrument of God's justice" (Alford 390). The ultimate sources of his power were God and Nature; therefore, he was not expected to be God-like, or infallible as most doctors are today. Instead, he was but a mere servant of Greater Powers, and if his medicine failed to heal, it was not particularly his fault, though infrequently, physicians were charged with incompetence (Siraisi 42). The Church Fathers had taught that disease was the visible expression of spiritual sickness, that there was only one True Physician who could heal the soul and the body—Christ, and that the medieval medical man was similarly his instrument. Therefore, a physician was expected to be moral, since his own spiritual purity affected the efficacy of his cure (Alford 390; Skerpan 42–44).

PRACTICE

The medieval medical man had learned in his studies of Galen and the *Isagoge* of Johannitius that disease was anything that contravened the just laws of nature, a so-called *contra-natural*. These contra-naturals militated against the human body's *natural* elements (its humors, bodily members, virtues, operations, or spirits), and the medical man had to help his patients use the *nonnaturals* (fresh air, exercise, rest, sleep, food, emotion, repletion, and excretion) to counterbalance the afflicting contra-naturals and thereby to effect a cure (Siraisi 100–101).

To diagnose an illness, the physician employed a variety of techniques, many of which survive in present-day medical practice. One of the major techniques was diagnosis by touch. First, the physician could not only gauge the patient's feverishness by touch, but he could also palpate, or press on any area of the body, and could check for certain characteristic sounds made by thumping on the bodily members. His readings in the works of Rhazes and Hippocrates would have prepared him to diagnose a wide range of illnesses based on these thumpings. He could also check for hardness or softness (blockage) in one of the organs thought to produce the various bodily humors, such as the liver (blood, red, yellow, and black bile) and the gall bladder (receptacle of red/yellow bile). He could not, however, palpate the brain, which was supposed to be the source of phlegm. Thus to determine the source or nature of a suspected phlegmatic imbalance, he had to resort to other diagnostic techniques. Second, with the sense of touch, he could take a patient's pulse and gather a great deal of information about what he perceived to be the ebb and flow of the patient's vital forces, or spirits. From his reading of the *Canon* of Avicenna, he would have known that a healthy patient's pulse was proportionate and created ''human music.'' Thus he could tell a great deal about the patient's health by the deviance from proportionality in pulse (Siraisi 125–127).

A more effective method of diagnosis, albeit a less hygienic one for the medical man, was the examination of excreted bodily fluids and wastes—particularly feces, urine, blood, and vomit. The principle here was, of course, that the body threw off excessive humors via the excreta and that study of them could help the physician decide on a cure. As distasteful as it seems to us moderns, the medieval physician did not hesitate to employ as many of his five senses as possible in the analysis of these waste substances, and he generally had at his command numerous charts describing what to look for in each specimen. For example, if he drew blood from a patient, he might check it for its greasiness (supposed to be a sign of leprosy), its taste, its temperature, and its coagulative strength. He might also let a sample stand for a period of time and check the degree of its separation into constituent fluids, a means by which he would then be able to determine humoral imbalances (Siraisi 124).

Uroscopy was evidently the medieval physician's most basic diagnostic tool, since the urinal flask was a popular symbol of the physician in the fourteenth century. Indeed, Harry Bailly mockingly blesses the Physician's "urynals" in the introduction to the "Pardoner's Tale" (C, 305), and the Physician's portrait in the Ellesmere manuscript even depicts him in the awkward and dangerous position of analyzing a flask of urine while riding horseback toward Canterbury. The medieval physician analyzed a patient's urine for color (clarity or cloudiness, sediment, viscosity), smell, and taste. The color gave him an indication of the complexion (humoral balance) of the patient's internal organs, whether their temperature was just right (in which case the urine would be either gold or redgold), too cold (milky yellow), or too hot (brown). The viscosity gave an indication of possible humoral imbalance, and the existence of sediment might be viewed as a symptom of leprosy. Before taking any sample, however, the doctor familiarized himself with the patient and took into account her or his age, sex, and eating habits, all of which, he was well aware, could affect the color and smell of the specimen (Baird 4).

Once the physician had used these means to determine the problems occurring within the naturals, he would rely on his training in astrology to aid in completing his diagnosis and administering his cure. Since Walter Clyde Curry has given a detailed description of the procedure (13–20), no lengthy discussion need detain us here. Suffice it to say that from casting a patient's horoscope, a physician had learned that he could tell how the stars and planets were currently acting on the afflicted parts of the body, and how the patient's humors were being affected. Thus he could tell not only when to administer the separate parts of his cure, but also when the cure should take full effect, if his diagnosis was correct. Once having cast the hours, the physician had a choice of cures that he could use either separately or in tandem. As physicians do today, he might give the patient directions for what sort of air he or she might take, how much exercise might be needed, how much rest, and what emotions or sorts of food to avoid. The other nonnaturals of repletion and excretion were elements that he could directly help the patient control, primarily through the principle of purgation.

One widely used purgative technique was blood-letting (phlebotomy)—that is, opening a vein and releasing a certain amount of blood into a cup to release excess humors. Blood-letting was also a cure for overeating, a concept that arose from the fact that both Galen and Avicenna described the digestive system as being directly related to the blood system. The medievals envisioned a digestive system in which food ingested into the stomach was turned there into a milky substance, called *chyle,* which was then sent to the liver where it was cooked into blood and melded with the various bodily humors. Blood was then dispersed to the various extremities where it was consumed, creating heat and motion

(Siraisi 106). Thus a fever indicated a surfeit of blood, some of which had to be let out for the patient's own good. Phlebotomy might be used in cases where the doctor suspected that the patient's disease was the result of gluttony or sloth, but even more importantly, it was apparently a weekly regimen for many adults, since letting a little blood upon occasion was thought to have some prophylactic effect. For this reason, there existed an entire subculture of medical practitioners whose primary job it was to phlebotomize the masses. These practitioners went by a variety of titles—blood-letters, leeches, barbers, and barber-surgeons, to name a few—and we may assume that they did not hesitate to extend their medical services beyond the simple act of phlebotomy. Obviously, they created quite a cadre of competitors for the regular, licensed physician. But in one regard, these simple empirics were deficient; they were not trained in "astronomye." Only the licensed physician, with his book knowledge of the best and least dangerous hours in which to cut, was considered worthy of a patient's complete trust (Jones 564–566).

The use of pharmaceuticals was the other principal method by which doctors generally tried either to balance the humors or to purge a surfeit. In the former instance, they could seek to balance the humors by providing medicinal compounds that contained qualities directly opposite to the complexional imbalance within the patient's body. For example, an excess of phlegm (the cold and moist humor) might be counterbalanced by a hot and dry medicine like a mixture of sugar and/or cardamom dissolved in wine or oil (Cartwright 3). They had learned this concept from the Greeks, especially from the works of Dioscorides, Hippocrates, and Galen, and the average physician had access to long descriptions of the pharmacological properties of most herbs and spices. But it was from the Arabs that most of the physician's knowledge of plant cures was taken. Often, a doctor would make a medicinal compound himself, taken from plants he had collected locally and had recited incantations over to increase their "magical" properties (Coulton, *Garner* 143), or he could have an apothecary perform the same function. Yet another method of creating humoral balance was for the doctor to prescribe an emetic or a laxative, or perhaps both in tandem, to purge the patient "bynethe and eke above" as Pertelote advises Chaunticleer to be purged of his "colere and malencolye" in the "Nun's Priest's Tale" (B2, 2953, 2946).

Surgeons, on the other hand, did not need to have command of this sort of elaborate pharmacological knowledge. Their sphere of disease control, handling trauma, required no elaborate diagnosis, and as far as being conversant with all the finer points of astronomy, all a surgeon really had to deal with was knowing when or when not to let blood. He had to have some limited knowledge of pharmacology, since he treated surgical wounds, but generally, these were very simple medicines—herbs and spices mulled in wine or oil, upon occasion sulfur or mercury, which he spread between the wound and a dressing that was changed occasionally. In actual practice off the battlefield, surgeons took on whatever traumas they thought they could handle without killing their patients, which meant that they did a great deal of treatment for simple problems such as setting broken bones, removing hemorrhoids, stitching cuts, removing ulcers and blemishes, repairing fistulas, and opening urinary tract obstructions. But they did not hesitate to perform more delicate surgery such as the removal of cataracts or even brain surgery (Siraisi 154–155; Talbot 93). Contrary to popular belief, medieval surgeons did have access to anesthetics, although these were certainly not as effective as those discovered in the nineteenth century. Recipes survive from the fourteenth century giving directions for making anesthetics from opium or mandragora dissolved in wine, as well as for a substance Chaucer calls dwale (A, 4161), which may have been simply a sleeping potion, or perhaps deadly nightshade, *atropa belladonna* (Jones 572–573).

The expertise and book learning that physicians and surgeons had to offer did not come cheap in the fourteenth century, and for the most part, only the wealthy upper classes could afford their services. The lower classes' medical needs were generally met by barbers and barber surgeons, by unlicensed physicians, apothecaries, leeches, bone setters, midwives, folk doctors, and quacks (Ussery 6). When all these failed, one cure for physical maladies was available to all—pilgrimage to a saint's shrine. Perhaps because of this competition from other sources, the physician's only hope for an adequate income was to cast his lot among the upper classes and to become attached to as many prosperous households as he possibly could. Physicians and surgeons who did attach themselves to noble or royal households did quite well, but the average physician's earnings were modest, at best, and many lived below the poverty line. To boot, wealthy families and sometimes the municipalities that hired physicians and surgeons were notoriously lax in paying for services rendered. For example, when the famous Paduan physician Pietro d'Albano died in 1316, the city apparently owed him three years' salary (Siraisi 22).

To overcome problems such as these, fourteenth-century physicians often took the precaution of requiring prepayments for services rendered, a practice for which they were often lampooned in satirical literature, since it was regarded as an evident lack of charity. But as physicians themselves often pointed out, behavior that made them appear avaricious actually may have grown from charitable impulses, since doctors often overcharged their wealthy clients in order to provide free care for the poor (Alford 392). In times of plague, physicians certainly had their hands full and could charge more than the going rate from those who could afford it. This might be a satiric point to which Chaucer alludes in his "General Prologue" description when he says of the Doctour that "He kepte that he wan in pestilence," implying that the Physician had gouged the poor in their time of need and was now living off such ill-gotten gains. On the other hand, we must remember that physicians took great risks in attending to the sick from all classes of society during these outbreaks, and certainly in the years of the Black Death, their ranks were decimated.

It is little wonder, then, that Chaucer's Physician has entered into a "friendship" with the local apothecaries, one that causes both to "wynne." Such a practice, despite its satirization in the literature of the period, was clearly considered a good one. It is also no surprise that he is "esy of dispence." He is probably not attached to any major household, nor is he making vast amounts of money healing the sick. The only outward sign that bespeaks any affluence is his flashy, silken attire, but even these robes might have been a gift or a payment from some wealthy patient. The "General Prologue" gives no precise indication of whether our physician is indeed the "verray parfit praktisour" that the gullible Pilgrim Chaucer claims, or whether he's a fraud. As is typical in Chaucer's work, we are given only ambiguous external clues, and our judgment of this man's spiritual health is dependent solely on the degree of charity we are willing to grant what we see.

CHAUCER'S PHYSICIAN AND HIS TALE

Critics have generally not behaved charitably toward either the Physician or his tale, often viewing neither in a very favorable light. Both Kinney (76–79) and Corsa (13–20) have discussed the wide range of criticism related to the tale and its teller, but a brief overview may not be inappropriate here.

Criticism from earlier in this century has characteristically found the tale an inappropriate choice for the Physician, so much so that at least two readers, R. K. Root and A. C. Baugh, have argued that it was originally written for another, earlier work, perhaps *The Legend of Good Women* (Baugh 485; Root 219). E. T. Donaldson concurred with this view and even left the story out of his 1958 edition of the *Tales*. In recent years, this position has been restated by Brian S. Lee (1987), who has argued that the tale "seems to bear no relation at all to [the Physician's] character."

To support this assertion, Lee points out that for a man who supposedly loves gold so much and reads the Bible so little, the Doctour of Phisik's story is remarkably absent of the former and fully informed by the latter (144).

It is also possible to view the tale as wholly appropriate to the Physician as does Huling Ussery, who argues: "The *Tale* as a whole may be considered appropriate to its teller because, as a moral, virtuous, learned account of chastity and goodness opposed to evil, it is appropriate to a cleric" (120). Similarly, Muriel Bowden points out that the "Physician's Tale" "is in itself a 'gode tale,' if not the merry one with which a physician is advised to divert a patient" (208–209), while Lee C. Ramsey claims that the "Physician's Tale" improves upon its sources (Livy and the *Roman de la Rose*) by creating a more subtle indication of the nature of the world where "despite pieties and even despite . . . good intent, innocence does not survive . . . where personal knowledge of sin is the best qualification for a parent, guardian, or judge" (197). More recently, Marta Powell Harley has analyzed those sections of the tale that have caused critics the most trouble: the description of Virginia's physical and spiritual beauty (C, 9–71, 105–117), the "digression" on governesses (C, 72–104), the beheading of Virginia (C, 213–253), and the moralized ending (C, 277–

286). Harley has found these digressions consistent not only with the tale's moral force, but also with the religious training physicians received in the medieval universities (16).

Most critics do not accept this position, however, and instead approach the tale as a badly botched moral exemplum—one that grants much more insight into the Physician's moral character than it does into Chaucer's poetic or narrative art. For some critics, Chaucer's sabotaging of this tale is clearly conscious and satiric. For example, Robert Longsworth argues that the tale is deliberately an "imaginative and moral failure," that indicates the Worm of Conscience "is plainly at work beneath those sanguine and silken robes" (233). Other scholars cite a host of reasons for the Physician's story-telling failure, including the following: (1) that Chaucer is fleshing out our understanding of the Physician's limited biblical knowledge, (2) that the physician bungles the tale because he doesn't allow his saint (Virginia) to face her accusers as do those female saints faced with the dilemma of rape or death in the saint's legends (Crowther 135), (3) that the Physician's definition of "virginity" is physical rather than spiritual (Hallissy 34), (4) that his narrative exposes his fraudulence (Robertson, "The Physician's" 137), his materialism/atheism (Arnold 179), his inability to diagnose the causes of human suffering (Brown 137), or his inability to "look beyond the body into the soul" (Skerpan 49), and (5) that he is "glad of sorwe" and "unhele" because "therein lies his profit" (Kempton 25).

In a related argument, two other critics argue that the tale is an obvious failure, but that the failure is largely of Chaucer's own making and is not a clear indicator of the Physician's moral character. Thomas L. Kinney argues that Chaucer has "lost control of the total effect of the tale" and "opened up the conscious level of the tale to an unconscious pattern recognizable by a popular audience." This happy accident, he argues, depicts a young girl's refusal to accept the call to adult sexuality (83–84). Similarly, Sheila Delany discusses the "depoliticization of a political anecdote," evident in the tale's reduction of the civic rebellion found in Livy's version. This, she argues, indicates that Chaucer had set himself the literary task to "transform a political anecdote into a moral tale: to rework a tract for the times into a tract for all time. But in this case at least, the material is simply not that tractable" (57).

The consensus, then, is that the "Physician's Tale" is not one of Chaucer's stunning successes, perhaps because, as Richard Arnold has pointed out, neither the teller nor his narrative is ever fully apprehensible by the audience (172). However, we can detect a broad series of correlations between the Physician and his story which indicate that Chaucer has chosen the best character possible to deliver this narrative to the pilgrim assemblage. Clearly, as Ussery and Harley indicate, this tale's highly moral theme makes it fully appropriate to the clerical background of the Physician's university training. Moreover, the story's conflict is resolved in a surgical manner (Preston 228–229), since Virginius removes the source of the affliction, Virginia's head, in the same sort of cold, dispassionate manner surgical texts taught that a practitioner should affect when cutting or burning human flesh. In his role as surgeon and executioner, Virginius becomes the dispassionate "secretary of Nature," dispensing heavenly justice and returning the balance of nature so horribly imbalanced by Appius's sin. Ironically, this man whom the Prologue implies loves potable gold, since it is such a good medicine for the heart, tells a tale that has no cordial effect, but instead almost causes Harry Bailly to have a "cardynacle," a heart attack. Our Physician, then, is an impotent man, a harmless drudge whose tale is as ineffectual as the material medicine he regularly dispenses. The gold of his tale is not potable, and his medicine effects no cure.

REFERENCES

Alford, John A. "Medicine in the Middle Ages: The Theory of a Profession." *Centennial Review* 23 (1979): 377–396.

Amoils, E. R. "Fruitfulness and Sterility in the *Physician's'* and *'Pardoner's Tales.'* " *English Studies in Africa* 17 (1974): 17–37.

Arnold, Richard A. "Chaucer's Physician: The Teller and the Tale." *Revue de L'Université D'Ottawa* 51 (1981): 172–179.

Baird, Lorrayne Y. "The Physician's 'urynals and jurdones': Urine and Uroscopy in Medieval Medicine and Literature." *Fifteenth Century Studies* 2 (1979): 1–8.

Barratt, Alexandra. *Women's Writing in Middle English.* London: Longman, 1992.

Baugh, Albert C., ed. *Chaucer's Major Poetry.* New York: Appleton, Century, Crofts, 1963.

Benson, C. David. "The Astrological Medicine of Chaucer's Physician and Nicholas of Lynn's *Kalendarium.*" *American Notes and Queries* 22 (1984): 62–66.

———. Explanatory Notes. *The Riverside Chaucer.* 3rd ed. Ed. Larry D. Benson. Boston: Houghton, 1987. Pp. 815–817, 901–904.

Benton, John. "Trotula, Women's Problems, and the Professionalization of Medicine in the Middle Ages." *Bulletin of the History of Medicine* 59 (1985): 30–53.

Bowden, Muriel. *A Commentary on the General Prologue of the Canterbury Tales.* New York: Macmillan, 1948.

Brown, Emerson, Jr. "What Is Chaucer Doing with the Physician and His Tale?" *Philological Quarterly* 50 (1981): 129–149.

Bullough, Vern L. "The Medieval University at Paris." *Bulletin of the History of Medicine* 31 (1957): 197–211.

———. "Medical Study at Medieval Oxford." *Speculum* 36 (1961): 600–612.

Campbell, Anna Montgomery. *The Black Death and Men of Learning.* 1931. New York: AMS Press, 1966.

Cartwright, Frederick F. *A Social History of Medicine.* New York: Longman, 1977.

Chaucer, Geoffrey. *The Riverside Chaucer.* 3rd ed. Ed. Larry D. Benson. Boston: Houghton Mifflin, 1987.

Corsa, Helen Storm. Introduction. *The Physician's Tale.* By Geoffrey Chaucer. *A Variorum Edition of the Works of Geoffrey Chaucer* 2. 17. Norman: University of Oklahoma Press, 1987.

Coulton, G. G. *A Medieval Garner.* London: Constable, 1910.

———. *Life in the Middle Ages.* 2 vols. 1910. Cambridge: Cambridge University Press, 1967.

Crowther, J. D. W. "Chaucer's Physician's Tale and Its 'Saint.' " *English Studies in Canada* 8 (1982): 125–137.

Curry, Walter Clyde. *Chaucer and the Medieval Sciences.* 1926. New York: Barnes and Noble, 1960.

Delany, Sheila. "Politics and the Paralysis of Poetic Imagination in *The Physician's Tale.*" *Studies in the Age of Chaucer* 3 (1981): 47–60.

Dronke, Peter. *Women Writers of the Middle Ages.* Cambridge: Cambridge University Press, 1984.

Goddu, André. "The Effect of Canonical Prohibitions on the Faculty of Medicine at the University of Paris in the Middle Ages." *Medizinhistorisches Journal* 20 (1985): 342–362.

Green, Monica H. "Women's Medical Practice and Health Care in Medieval Europe." *Signs* 14 (1989): 434–473.

Hallam, Elizabeth M. "Alchemy." *The Middle Ages: A Concise Encyclopedia.* Ed. H. R. Loyn. London: Thames and Hudson, 1989. Pp. 19–20.

Hallissy, Margaret. *Clean Maids, True Wives, Steadfast Widows: Chaucer's Women and Medieval Codes of Conduct.* Westport, Conn.: Greenwood Press, 1993.

Harley, Marta Powell. "Last Things First in Chaucer's *Physician's Tale:* Final Judgement and the Worm of Conscience." *Journal of English and Germanic Philology* 91 (1992): 1–16.

Hirsch, John C. "Modern Times: The Discourse of the 'Physician's Tale.' " *Chaucer Review* 27 (1993): 387–395.

Inglis, Brian. *A History of Medicine.* Cleveland: World, 1965.

Joseph, Gerhard. "The Gifts of Nature, Fortune, and Grace in the *Physician's, Pardoner's* and *Parson's Tales.*" *Chaucer Review* 9 (1975): 237–245.

Jones, Ida B. "Popular Medical Knowledge in Fourteenth Century English Literature, Part II." *Bulletin of the Institute of the History of Medicine* 5 (1937): 538–588.

Kempton, Daniel. "*The Physician's Tale:* The Doctor of Physic's Diplomatic 'Cure.' " *Chaucer Review* 19 (1984): 24–38.

Kinney, Thomas L. "The Popular Meaning of Chaucer's 'Physician's Tale.' *Literature and Psychology* 28 (1978): 76–84.

Lee, Brian S. "The Position and Purpose of the *Physician's Tale.*" *Chaucer Review* 22 (1987): 141–160.

Longsworth, Robert. "The Doctor's Dilemma: A Comic View of the *Physician's Tale.*" *Criticism* 13 (1971): 223–233.

Mann, Jill. *Chaucer and Medieval Estates Satire: The Literature of Social Classes and the General Prologue to the Canterbury Tales.* Cambridge: Cambridge University Press, 1973.

Middleton, Anne. "The *Physician's Tale* and Love's Martyrs: 'Ensamples Mo Than Ten' as a Method in the *Canterbury Tales.*" *Chaucer Review* 8 (1973): 9–32.

Moriarty, Catherine. *The Voice of the Middle Ages.* New York: Bedrich, 1989.

Nicholas of Lynn. *The Kalendarium.* Ed. Sigmund Eisner. Athens: University of Georgia Press, 1980.

Preston, Raymond. *Chaucer.* New York: Sheed and Ward, 1969.

Ramsey, Lee C. " 'The Sentence of It Sooth Is': Chaucer's *Physician's Tale.*" *Chaucer Review* 6 (1972): 185–197.

Reidy, John. Introduction. *Thomas Norton's Ordinal of Alchemy.* Early English Text Society. 272: ix–lxxv.

Renn, George A. "Chaucer's Doctour of Phisik." *Explicator* 45, no. 2 (1987): 4–5.

Robertson, D. W. *Chaucer's London*. New York: John Wiley, 1968.

———. "The Physician's Comic Tale." *Chaucer Review* 23 (1988): 129–139.

Root, Robert Kilburn. *The Poetry of Chaucer*. Gloucester, Mass.: Peter Smith, 1957.

Rubin, Stanley. *Medieval English Medicine*. New York: Barnes and Noble, 1974.

Schachner, Nathan. *The Medieval Universities*. New York: A. S. Barnes, 1938.

Siraisi, Nancy G. *Medieval and Early Renaissance Medicine: An Introduction to Knowledge and Practice*. Chicago: University of Chicago Press, 1990.

Skerpan, Elizabeth Penley. "Chaucer's Physicians: Their Texts, Contexts, and the *Canterbury Tales*." *Journal of the Rocky Mountain Medieval and Renaissance Association* 5 (1984): 41–56.

Talbot, C. H. *Medicine in Medieval England*. London: Oldbourne, 1967.

Ussery, Huling E. *Chaucer's Physician: Medicine and Literature in Fourteenth Century England*. Tulane Studies in English 19. New Orleans: Tulane University Press, 1971.

Chapter 21

A Good Wive Was Ther of Biside Bath

JUDITH SLOVER

In the "General Prologue" of the *Canterbury Tales,* Chaucer introduces Alison of Bath as the type of woman whom the patriarchy feared, hated, and preached against. Yet Chaucer, perhaps ironically, also describes her as a "worthy wife" [I (A) 459]. Today we profess to know the role of "wife." Yet within the last half-century, this role has undergone many emendations, "glosyngs," and re-interpretations. Modern readers trying to reconcile the contradictions inherent in Chaucer's Wife of Bath, who appears to be representational of both the ideal fourteenth-century wife and the feared autonomous woman, need only recall the confusion in our society today, when roles are rapidly changing within the social context. In many ways, Alison of Bath throws the conception of women's roles "up-so-doun," and yet in many other ways exemplifies the life of merchant-class women. In the "General Prologue," Chaucer has given us a double-edged portrait of Alison, Wife of Bath. Despite her imperfections, she may still be deserving of the appellation "worthy" (459), which will be further acknowledged in her prologue and tale.

MEDIEVAL WOMEN

In the Middle Ages, women were identified by their roles in life as wives, widows, mothers, or maidens, and were "portrayed in relation to a man or group of man [*sic*]" (Klapisch-Zuber 285). Thus they were effectively reduced to the status of chattel, allowing them little autonomy. However, substantial historical evidence exists showing that within the sphere of wifely duties, considerable autonomy existed. While peasant women worked in the fields, "artisan-class women worked in their husbands' shops, which on occasion they took over at his death" (Klapisch-Zuber 308). Women of nobility often managed great estates when the men went to war. Yet because of women's supposedly weak natures, men "imposed a closely circumscribed domain in which women exercised a degree of autonomy . . . primarily the house, a space both protected and enclosed, and, within the house, certain even more private places such as the bed chamber, the work areas, and the kitchen" (Klapisch-Zuber 305). The major tasks assigned to women were the conservation and prudent use of the resources the husband brought into the home (Klapisch-Zuber 306). Despite the different spheres of work, women's work was not denigrated or considered less than men's work, just different (Hanawalt 219). Marriage was considered a partnership, both economic and emotional (Hanawalt 219), but "a married couple was not simply an economic unit in the eyes of society, but also a social and convivial one. . . . Wills indicate a high degree of trust and even affection" (Hanawalt 218). In fact, in looking for wives, men were advised to look for women who were courteous, wise, and meek, and were admonished not to make their wives angry (Hanawalt 206). Women were instructed to honor their husbands and to be meek; not to get drunk too often or go to masculine entertainments (wrestling and cockbaiting); to do their work well, governing their households prudently; to be generous but not envy another's riches; to marry their daughters as soon as possible; and not to beat their children ("How the Good Wife Taught Her Daughter" 106–108).

One area in which Alison is an exemplary wife is in her trade of "clooth making" (447). By the fifteenth century, some women were "apprenticed in the clothing trades" (Bishop 228) rather than marrying. Not only were women being apprenticed in the clothing trade, but many also earned additional income for the family by selling woven goods, ale, or bread, thus being frugal and maximizing the resources the husband brought into the home.

The Wife of Bath is also an example, albeit a poor one, of her social class. Her elaborate clothing, her heavy headdress, her red close-fitting stockings, her soft shoes, noted so prominently in the "General Prologue" (lines 453–457) flaunt her wealth and status, thus picturing "the folly of the bourgeoisie—its appetite for goods, both social and economic—as the ancestral license of women. . . . If she [the Wife of Bath] is an arch-woman (all women ever), she is also a player in the fourteenth-century cloth trade and marriage market who in her own way shares the most censured vices of the merchant class—pushiness, greed, guile, vanity, love of precedence" (Justman 345). Capitalizing on Alison's technique of appropriating the text to her own ends and using synonymous terminology, she liked to shop, she obtains what she goes after, she is concerned about money, she is smart, she accepts herself as she is, she is self-assured, and she makes sure people notice her. Most of these character traits, while portrayed negatively, can also be seen as survival skills for a woman alone in a world controlled and dominated by men. When she jockeys for position in church, boasts about her five husbands, overdresses, and flirts with men, she is showing not only her social status, but also her lack of breeding. Well-bred women were supposed to be modest in dress and actions, thrifty, resourceful, and so busy with their wifely duties that they rarely had time to think about anything other than their work and responsibilities.

Although Alison herself seems to have no children, throughout much of history, women have been relegated to domestic service because of the biological function of childbearing. This role was increasingly important in the Middle Ages when populations and whole families were decimated by various plagues, estimated at killing from one-third (Cipolla 146) to one-half (Bishop 309) of the population of Europe. In the noble and wealthy merchant classes, fully one-half of a woman's life, from the age of eighteen to forty (if she lived that long), was occupied by pregnancy (Klapisch-Zuber 299). Death of both mother and child was common during childbirth, and considering that nearly half of all children who survived childbirth died before their twentieth birthday, the biblical admonition to "be fruitful and multiply" nearly guaranteed that a woman be pregnant during most of her childbearing years so that an heir of the lineage of the father—and less importantly, the mother—would survive to inherit.

Because of the emphasis on progeny, the marriageable age for women was surprisingly low, especially among the noble class, although most artisan women did not marry until their mid-twenties (Anderson and Zinsser 371). Alison's first marriage at twelve years of age was not uncommon. Although today we have laws to prevent marriages at such an early age, "children having children," some as young as ten years of age, is not that uncommon. While "virginity before marriage was a concern of moralists, it apparently did not worry prospective husbands" (Hanawalt 196), at least among the lower classes, but was a common concern with the nobility. Alison mentions escapades in her youth, and her nonvirgin status did not seem to discourage any of her five husbands. Before marrying, men frequently waited until they had established themselves in their businesses or inheritances, and the average husband was usually ten years or more older than his wife (Klapisch-Zuber 296–297). Young girls of the nobility were often forced into marriage by their families. Because of this, the Church demanded that consent from the two parties involved, the man and the woman, not their families, be obtained at appropriate ages, making the spouses, not the lineages, important in the marriage ceremony. The change from lineage to individuals, "prompted a considerable revolution, at least in theory, by according to the woman a place equal to that of the man in the administration of the sacrament of marriage" (Klapisch-Zuber 292). In fact, some evidence demonstrates that "while most young women had marriages arranged for them, one-third may have had free choice in selecting husbands" (Hanawalt 201).

While seeming to give women a certain autonomy of choice in the matter of marriage, women were still forced by their families to consent to unpalatable marriages owing to the threats of disinheritance, seclusion in a nunnery, or ostracization. The best a woman could hope for in regard to an unhappy marriage was that she could outlive her husband, which, if she survived childbearing, was almost certain. Then, as now, women lived longer than men, and given that women were much younger than men at marriage, they could hope to have some relatively happy years after their spouses' demise. Despite the risks of childbirth, however, "most women appeared to survive it, for the wills indicate that the overwhelming majority of men were survived by wives, usually their first" (Hanawalt 217). The wills also show that many men thought of their wives with affection, so perhaps many marriages were convivial.

Because the inheritance issue was so important, women's sexual fidelity was imperative. Thus "women's bodies required unflagging surveillance to guard against fraudulent changelings who might discredit the great body of the lineage" (Klapisch-Zuber 292). The "whore madonna" dichotomy is a product of the Middle Ages, so it is not surprising that the "proper 'use' of wives meant that the man must constantly be on guard against their [women's sexual] demands" (Klapisch-Zuber 305). This echoed religious teachings, for during much of the Middle Ages, the Church only approved sexual activity for the sake of procreation. By the fourteenth century, however, some theologians "no longer forbade copulation between barren partners" (Klapisch-Zuber 300), leaving Alison's search for future husbands unfettered by Church dictum in considering her barrenness due to age. Even today, however, procreation is the only truly acceptable reason for sexual activity within the dictates of the Roman Catholic Church, although it remains a private matter. But other female behavior was more radically stigmatized by society in the fourteenth century. Women who did not heed advice and were insubordinate to their husbands were not only censured by their husbands, but also "were subject to collective disapproval as well" (Klapisch-Zuber 307). From the twelfth to the seventeenth century, a woman's insubordination or rebellion "necessitated control just as it always had. Proper female behavior—acting in a way that men deemed appropriate—meant acquiescing to the male-defined ideal, yet another way of bowing to male authority" (Anderson and Zinsser 432). Infidelity to the wife was a private matter between the spouses, yet enough evidence exists to show that it was a community concern as well. The *fabliaux*—comparable to our traveling salesmen or milkman jokes—while evidencing women's intelligence, virtually assume that females will cuckold their husbands, occasionally forcing societal disapproval in the form of the husband's public embarrassment by parading him through town wearing the cuckold's horns, or like John the Carpenter in the "Miller's Tale," married to and outwitted by another Alison, laughed at and considered "wood" [I (A) 3848]—crazy and/or foolish—by the townsfolk. From the Kinsey reports in the 1940s to University of Chicago statistics from October 1994, estimates of marital infidelity this last half-century vary from 15 to 75 percent—women actually represent the lower end of the spectrum, while males tend to dominate the upper half. However, the opprobrious social stigma of the fourteenth century does not exist today, or is minimal against adultery, but the old public laws condemning adulterous acts are still on the books. At least one case has been tried in the courts in the last decade. The "live-and-let-live" attitude may be changing, however, thanks to the advent of the new plague, AIDS, resulting in statistics that show increased fidelity in monogamous relationships. Another factor in the lack of societal control may be the consideration that 50 percent of all marriages end in divorce. Thus, if infidelity is an issue, it is between the husband and the wife and is not a concern of the community as it was in the fourteenth century.

A concern for many young women marrying older men was widowhood. Most widows did not remarry and were often left to fend for themselves. Widows who had brought dowries into the marriage were substantially better off than women who did not, unless they had sons who would care for them. While it is verifiable that most widows did not remarry, during adverse economic times, until the plagues exterminated much of the population, it was not uncommon for younger men, usually unestablished younger sons, to marry older, wealthy widows. This served a two-fold purpose: the younger man not only established himself, independent of his family fortunes, but was given resource management and financial training. When his first wife died, he was financially able to support a wife and children, and usually married a young woman and started his family. In Alison's case, however, it appears that she outlived her twenty-year-old husband, Janekyn, husband number five, for she states that she is looking for a sixth. These marriages of older women and younger men are occurring today. While women traditionally marry men two to ten years older, there is increasing uneasiness among women who have put off marriage and childbearing to further their careers, for the available pool of men in this age range is much smaller than the number of women looking for mates. Some women have begun dating and marrying men from two to twenty years younger, just as older men have traditionally married younger women. Social stigma still exists, of course, but such alliances appear to be better accepted now than in the past, especially the fourteenth century when "the earliest mentions of boisterous popular rites attest to public curbs on matrimonial choices. Widows who remarried and remarriages in general brought down the fury of youth on couples they judged inappropriate or intemperate" (Klapisch-Zuber 307). Perhaps this attitude accounts for Alison's jockeying for position in church: by not allowing Alison her "proper" place, the women of the community may have been exerting social pressure to show her the "error of her ways."

Social pressure was also applied to some women who were not docile. Like Alison, some ran in search of idle pleasure, "powdering and painting themselves—surely not for the sake of winning their husbands' affections"—and followed "all the vagaries of fashion, not so much for the men's sake as because they want to be like other women" (Walsh 186). Again, are women today so different? In 1994, John Mellancamp redid Van Morrison's "Wild Nights," where he recites "the girls passed by, dressed up for each other." Men often tell women that they wear too much makeup, shadowing the advice of the fourteenth century. Most men today also do not really care how women dress and are ignorant of "fashion," as long as they are neat and clean—women often dress to impress other women with their style-consciousness, à la *Cosmopolitan,* again reflecting fourteenth-century attitudes.

Misogyny was another attitude that the women of Chaucer's time had to fight. The Church preached that women were like Eve, still causing a fall from grace for men through their sensuality and disobedience. Following a long Western tradition dating back to the early Greek and Hebrew cultures, the Church was particularly virulent against women in the second half of the Middle Ages. Before the year 1000, women who had substantial income often left it to the Church to establish monasteries. Some women chose to retire to these convents to pursue knowledge, some even taking their dowries with them. In some instances, a woman abbess was the superior over both men and women, responsible for the education and dedication to God of the religious community. From the advent of Christianity, women's status had been slowly deteriorating. Some women were bishops in the early Church and held other esteemed positions as well, but church ruling after church ruling slowly eroded the rights of both lay and secular women. By the year 1000, women were again relegated to the home and children, under the dominion of their husbands. Yet in the twelfth and thirteenth centuries, "women openly and enthusiastically embraced doctrines and roles that contradicted all the institutional Church had come to represent. . . . —a call for the 'equality of all believers.' This more than any other assertion gave women a nature like man's and promised them roles outside the family, outside the convent, roles of authority within the faith independent of their relationship to fathers, husbands, and sons" (Anderson and Zinsser 226). But laws were passed, particularly on the Continent, that forbade women from willing money away from the family, or they were not given money to will—it was in trust for their lifetimes. Convents and monasteries became separate establishments, with the Mother Superior of a convent answerable to a male clergy.

The teachings of the Church were based on the misogynous preaching of the Pauline texts and of such writers as Jovanian, whose *Adversus Jovinianum,* along with Theophrastes's *Aureolus* were some of the "auctoritees" the Wife of Bath twisted to her own ends. Other contemporary writings stressed the subordination of women to men, such as Deschamps's *Miroir de Mariage* and Jean de la Meun's *Roman de la Rose.* In many ways, the Wife of Bath exemplifies La Vielle in the *Roman de la Rose.* They appear to be similar characters, except that La Vielle is educating a young woman in how to subvert and control men, whereas Alison is not merely subverting the patristic textual injunctions but is trying to educate misogynists. Ironically, she is turning their own arguments against them and is using them as a defense of her actions. Anderson and Zinsser assert that European women who were "unable to see beyond their culture's attitudes . . . have mastered the strategies of those in subordinate positions: manipulating, pleasing, enduring, surviving" (vii), just as Alison does in her life.

Today, many misogynist attitudes are disappearing but still survive (some implied and some not so unexpressed). The Clarence Thomas/Anita Hill dispute before the United States Congress in 1992 showed that sexual harassment (which implies a male "right") still survives. Date rape is another exposed phenomenon that also indicates a lack of respect for women which is born from misogynistic attitudes, comparable to the "Wife of Bath's Tale." Physical abuse of women is also a link from the past; at some times the Church admonished men to beat their wives, and at other times not to beat their wives. There are now laws that offer some protection to wives of abusive husbands. Indeed, legislation is becoming stronger with harsher penalties against men who beat women, despite the reluctance of authorities to interfere in the affairs between a man and a woman. Alison herself dealt with her abuse and consequent deafness from Janekyn in a very direct way: she hit him back. But Alison defends herself not only physically, but intellectually as well.

The intellectual life of women in the Middle Ages is a disputed topic. Traditional wisdom holds that women were not allowed to be educated, with most women only learning enough arithmetic and reading skills to help their husbands keep accounts and keep track of the household belongings. There is some evidence however, that women, particularly those connected with the nobility or the Church—whether noble or serf—were given a modicum of education. For instance, in Italy, "from the end of the fourteenth and during the first half of the fifteenth centuries, . . . women were being afforded opportunities for education equal to those of men, and they were availing themselves of these opportunities very successfully" (Walsh 168). Convents, particularly those belonging to the Benedictine Order, were "occupied rather intently with the task of developing the minds not only of the members of the [religious] community. But of the children of the nobility and even of the tenantry of the monastery who were confided to them" (Walsh 160). Alison appears to have had at least some education. While it is possible that her knowledge was gained aurally—she does say that Janekyn read her the stories—the depth of her knowledge and her ability to argue using logic and rhetoric are usually products of education. Wilson and Makowski have "defined the methodology of general misogamic satire as a dissuasion by inversion employing everyday specificity, exemplary documentation, and current misogynous topoi rendered by an experienced persona who is ironically unreliable and whose attacks on women and wives frequently backfire on him. All of these observations hold true for the Wife of Bath's *Prologue*" (151). Alison uses her intelligence in diverting the misogynistic attacks against women back to the directors of the attack, the clergy and men generally, and husbands specifically.

As can be deduced from attempting to define the role of "wife" in the fourteenth century, the indigenous contradictions of the role are often the same as those found in the definition today, or indeed, in any time. Women as wives had certain well-defined tasks: childbearing, housekeeping, cooking, nursing, organizing, and often income-producing occupations. The contradictions arise when these tasks are juxtaposed one against another and against a repressive atmosphere endemic with domination by a masculine hierarchy. The qualities a young woman needed to possess and to bring to a marriage were those bounded by ethics and morality instituted by church and social paradigms—virtue, obedience, loyalty, meekness, fortitude, and endurance. Wives were supposed to be "helpmates," implying an equality, but while the social and religious structures imposed on them often thwarted their attempts to be equal, at least in individual cases, such as with Alison and with both Prudence in the "Tale of Melibee" and, to a lesser degree, Dorigen in the "Franklin's Tale," some women did obtain a degree of autonomy and equality, using their intelligence in their own and their families' best interests. While a sense of equality may have been achieved in the private sphere of home, in the public sphere conformity with the social ideals of masculine superiority frustrated efforts to gain equity. Wives were, and sometimes still are, subject to their husbands' authority. Was Alison a "worthy" wife? Financially, she was commendable. Morally, she was virtuous—at least with Janekyn, her charitable church donations, and her pilgrimages to holy sites—despite her earlier lewd behavior. She was steadfast in her opinions, and while neither obedient nor meek, she was true to herself. Just like any woman, and the role of wife itself, Alison is a mass of incongruities and contradictions, so the reader must decide whether Alison truly deserves Chaucer's appellation of "worthy."

THE WIFE AND HER TALE

Alison's tale encompasses a wide range of ideas, as does her Prologue, and is not easily categorized; it has variously been described as an Arthurian romance, a fairy tale, and an *exemplum*. Since it corroborates her Prologue, it may be perceived as an *exemplum* redefining feminine mastery as equality in marriage. The question of the "Wife of Bath's Tale" is the same one that persons of both genders ask today: "What does a woman want?" Yet the tale appears to be another example of Alison's ideal marriage.

Alison herself is the exemplum of the feared autonomous woman, turning patristic and popular misogynistic arguments against the perpetrators of those same arguments and making no apologies for doing so. While incriminating herself as one of "those women," she ridicules the misogamists, arguing against the "philosophical and ascetical branches of misogamy in a masterfully ironic way" (Wilson and Makowski 151). She rationalizes every argument, feeding it through her own experience, using her highly skilled command of language and rhetoric, as well as her thorough understanding of the writings of the Church Fathers to temper or modify the traditional patristic Church views regarding women and marriage. Alison's "*exemplum* about the condemned knight admirably proves her case for learning from women and experience, and coherently exemplifies her objections to the clerical antifeminist tradition" (Knapp 49). Her "auctoritee," which has come to her through her own experience, is unconventional and perhaps anti-Church, but is not as iconoclastic as we envisage. The traditional view, of course, was that humans could understand God not through earthly experience, but only through divine revelation, reserved almost exclusively for the Church hierarchy. The Wife of Bath twists this idea "up-so-doun," as she does many other Church teachings, and she relies on her own experiences to dispute old ideas and teach a different way of thinking. In effect, she recreates the text in light of her own experiences by using what she reads and ignoring the patristic glossing which tells her what she should understand from the text. Thus she dyes the words in her own tones, in her own tints, and becomes the master of someone else's words; as Knapp explains, she appropriates the text to her own ends. She does not, as many critics maintain, "misinterpret" the text. She fully comprehends what she "ought" to discern (according to the misogynists), but by weaving her own experience through the framework of the texts, she reveals the falsity of doctrine.

Traditionally, the physical life has been equated with Eve and the spiritual life with Adam. Eve presumably—according to patristic teachings—precipitated the *felix culpa* of humankind through her sensuality, by seducing Adam into carnal sin. Thus anything connected with the bodily senses, including bodily, worldly experience, was rejected because of its connection with the fall from grace. Because Alison filters what she reads and hears through the threads of her "liberal education," the knowledge she has to offer to a patriarchal hierarchy is scorned. The Prologue to the "Wife of Bath's Tale" thus becomes, "for the age in which it was written, a revolutionary document. It embodies the protest of human nature against the doctrine that made the single life purer and nobler than the wedded. The audacity of the performance will not be fully recognized unless we bear in mind that the doctrine attacked was the doctrine universally accepted" (Lounsberry 523–524). Alison's philosophy of marriage involves recognition for her intelligence, acknowledgment as a person, and validation of her "claims to prestige and a certain kind of status" (Gottfried 205), a mutuality of attitude that inverts and subverts the patriarchal teachings.

Subtly arguing in a logical fashion to correspond with her ideas expressed in the Prologue, the Wife has transferred Eve's sin of carnality to the male figure, the Knight. Again, she has shifted the focus of not merely the words, but the idea of original sin, placing the onus squarely on the male figure and absolving the female figure from sin when the Knight rapes the girl, just as modern laws are viewing rape as an act of violence perpetrated against a woman and exonerating her from "asking for it." Alison transforms the patristic view of Eve as the seducer into the view of man as aggressor and violator, usurper of body and mind. The rape itself signifies not only physical assault, but mental abuse as well: the abrogation of physical and mental powers subsumed in violated Eve.

After Alison begins her tale—and incidentally attacks the Church, paralleling perhaps the rape of the maiden—the Knight appears at Arthur's court, strengthening the "biblical ideal of male sovereignty" as "the erring knight is brought before King Arthur for punishment. Then, however, a quick inversion takes place as the Queen . . . steps into the place of authority, and Arthur concedes control to Guinevere" (Williams 147). This is another analogy to the Wife's interest; Arthur bestows jurisdiction on his wife. Another comparison to the Prologue is that just as the women of the court forgave his sin after his penance because he was a "lust bachelor," so did Alison make amends with Janekyn after his capitulation.

The Knight's penance was hard; he had to discover what it was that "women moost desiren" (905). After questioning and searching, and receiving different answers, dispiritedly he turned toward the court. He was distracted by maidens dancing, luring him to try once more to find the answer. The maidens disappeared, leaving an old hag (analogous to Alison) in their place. She promises to tell him the answer if he will promise her what she asks. He rashly promises, and they go to court to give his answer: "Women desiren to have sovereynetee / As wel over hir housbond as hir love, / And for to been in maistrie hym above. / This is youre mooste desir, thogh ye me kille" (1038–1041) ["Women desire to have sovereignty / As well over their husbands as their love, / And for to be in mastery above him. / This is your most desire, though you kill me"].

"Sovereynetee" to Alison, and perhaps to others, does not necessarily mean only "rulership"; it may also imply the best among equals. For instance, why does Chaucer choose to place the Tale in Arthur's court, when French courts were more famous as courts of love? Is it possible that he placed it in Arthur's court to recall the signification of the Round Table—where all were treated as equals, none above the others? If so, another link is created between theme and plot, between Prologue and Tale, and sovereignty, like mastery, can be redefined by the Wife within and without the gender-biased hierarchy as equality.

The Wife, having redefined words, appropriating the meaning to her own uses, now teases patriarchal perceptions. After the women of the Court have taught the Knight to respect females, and he acknowledges that he could only have received an answer from a woman—the Hag—then the old woman holds him to his promise: he must marry her. He does not go gently, that good knight! He fights against his vow, kicking and screaming all the way: "Allas and weylawey! / I woot right wel that swich was my biheste. / For Goddes love, as chees a newe requeste! / Taak al my good and lat my body go" (1058–1061) ["Alas and alas! / I know very well that such was my promise. / For God's love, as choose a new request! / Take all my goods and let my body go"]. " 'My love?' quod he, 'nay, my dampnaciaoun! / Allas, that any of my nacioun / Sholde evere so foule disparaged be!' " (1067–1069) [" 'My love,' said he, 'nay, my damnation! / Alas, that any of my family / Should ever so foul degraded be!' "]. He still has not learned his lessons properly.

The Wife, through the Hag, makes the Knight, representing the universal male (and coincidentally Alison's husbands), pay his debts in full. Since he was a lusty knight, condemned for a sexual infraction, the forced rape of a woman, why did he "fare ye thus with me this firste nyght? / Ye faren lyk a man had lost his wit" (1094–1095) ["fare you thus with me this first night? / You fare like a man who has lost his mind"]. He could not accept sexual intimacy with the old Hag, perhaps an echo of Alison's and Janekyn's relationship. He continues to be cruel to her, though, saying: " 'Though art so loothly, and so oold also, / And therto comen of so lough a kynde, / That litel wonder is thogh I walwe and wynde. / So wolde God myn herte wolde breste!' '' (1100–1104) [" 'You are so ugly, and so old too, / And thereto descended from such base-born lineage, / That little wonder is though I wallow and twist about. / So would God my heart would burst!'"]. His rudeness engenders another lesson, not one in humility, as one might expect from the Prologue, but in "gentilesse." The Hag, like the Wife, fragments the text of the "auctoritees" she summons to her aid, again sermonlike, "glozing" the texts to her own purposes. She lectures the Knight on his pride of ancestry, on living virtuously, poverty, patience, and wisdom. Near the end of the lesson, she echoes the opening lines of the Prologue: "thogh noon auctoritee / Were in no book" (1208–1209). Her logic appears indisputable; he becomes as silent as women were supposed to be. She has used the weapons of the patriarchs against the hierarchial authorities, and she has won.

When the Hag gives the Knight the last riddle, he knows the answer: give all authority to her, just as Janekyn did Alison. He has finally accepted feminine teachings of learning through personal experience. Like Christian teachings, through losing, he wins. Actually, both win: The Knight, "by his full recognition of her 'otherness' is rewarded by her free acceptance of him. Thus, in the mutual recognition of the other, in each giving only to find that the giving is the taking, in this lies the ideal love-marriage relationship" (Whittock 127). Again, corresponding to the end of the Prologue, once the female has gained "maisterie" or "sovereynetee", she allows him equality, obeying "hym in every thyng / That myght doon him pleasance or likyng" (1255–1256) ["him in every thing / That might do him pleasure or please him"].

Alison and the Hag's relinquishing of control meant that they had authority to give, and their respective husbands would know that their wives could regain control at any time they were mistreated or not consulted. As long as the women were treated with respect and attention to their individualities as persons, the husbands had nothing to fear; both men learned to respect the feminine ideal of education through experience, not books. In fact, Alison's "*exemplum* about the condemned knight admirably proves her case for learning from women and experience, and coherently exemplifies her objections to the clerical antifeminist tradition (Knapp 49). Both Alison and the loathly lady have contrived to have husbands with whom each "can share both authority and experience" (Knapp 49).

In examining the evidence, particularly the parallels within the Prologue and Tale, despite Alison's assertions that a woman wants "maisterie," it is not female domination she seeks. She does not want her husband to tell her what to do, certainly, but more than this, she desires respect for her opinions, intelligence, and experience, resulting in an "equalitarian relationship at the end of the *Tale* (1230–56) which elaborates on the vital equilibrium established in Alice's last marriage to Jankyn" (Long 274). If we redefine mastery as a type of equality, then the conjunction of the Tale to her Prologue make sense. Both women demanded mastery, and once given it, were "trewe" and "loving" wives. In the historical period in which the *Canterbury Tales* was written, equality in a marriage could be perceived as mastery by other members of the community, but certainly not by many thinking people, perhaps not by Chaucer himself. Thus, when Alison discusses mastery, she is really talking about equality, being consulted, treated like a thinking being, and, above all, respected and recognized as an intelligent person who has learned her lessons in life through experience.

FINAL THOUGHTS

The Wife of Bath is a larger-than-life figure, the epitome of the misogynous lessons against women's independence. She represents a certain type of wife, but not the "ideal" wife of a masculine-dominated society. The ideal wife was meek, hardworking, thrifty, unambitious intellectually, sexually repressed, and fertile. From this perspective, Alison was not a "paragon" or model for others. Viewing her through modern eyes, readers can observe her, if not dispassionately, at least through lenses that are sometimes undistorted by misogyny. Today she can be examined as a female, a woman who existed—albeit on the pages of literature (which is all too easy to forget, for she seems like a real person)—and fought for her rights and happiness as a human being. If she emerges as a loud, offensive, greedy, formidably aggressive woman, at least she does ascend from the ordinary, and she is not submerged by the vicissitudes of life or her repressive society. She manipulates, subverts, endures, and survives with "jolite" and joy in the living, undaunted by life. Like the fiery phoenix or like Botticelli's "Birth of Venus," she arises and is (re)born anew after each hardship in life, lusty, cheerful, and determined.

REFERENCES

Anderson, Bonnie S., and Judith P. Zinsser. *A History of Their Own: Women in Europe from Prehistory to the Present.* Vol. 1. 1988. New York: Harper and Row, 1989.

Bishop, Morris. *The Middle Ages.* Boston: Houghton Mifflin, 1985.

Cipolla, Carlo M. *Before the Industrial Revolution: European Society and Economy, 1000–1700.* New York: W. W. Norton, 1976.

Gottfried, Barbara. "Conflict and Relationship, Sovereignty and Survival: Parables of Power in the *Wife of Bath's Prologue.*" *Chaucer Review* 19, no. 3 (1985): 202–224.

Hanawalt, Barbara A. *The Ties That Bound: Peasant Families in Medieval England.* New York: Oxford University Press, 1986.

Hodges, Laura F. "The Wife of Bath's Costumes: Reading the Subtexts." *Chaucer Review* 27 (1993): 359–376.

"How the Good Wife Taught Her Daughter." *The Past Speaks to 1688: Sources and Problems in English History.* Eds. Lacey Baldwin Smith and Jean Reeder Smith. Toronto: Heath, 1981.

Justman, Stewart. "Trade as Pudendum: Chaucer's Wife of Bath." *Chaucer Review* 28, no. 4 (1994): 344–352.

Klapisch-Zuber, Christiane. "Women and the Family." *Medieval Callings.* Trans. Lydia G. Cochran. Ed. Jacques LeGoff. Chicago: University of Chicago Press, 1990. Pp. 285–311.

Knapp, Peggy. "Alisoun of Bathe and the Reappropriation of Tradition." *Chaucer Review* 24, no.1 (1989): 45–52.

Long, Walter C. "The Wife as Moral Revolutionary." *Chaucer Review* 20, no. 4 (1986): 273–284.

Lounsberry, Thomas R. *Studies in Chaucer: His Life and Writings.* Vol. 2. New York: Russell, 1962. 3 vols.

Root, Jerry. " 'Space to Speke': The Wife of Bath and the Discourse of Confession." *Chaucer Review* 28 (1994): 252–274.

Walsh, James J. *High Points of Medieval Culture.* 1937. Freeport, N.Y.: Books for Libraries Press, 1969.

Whittock, Trevor. *A Reading of the Canterbury Tales.* London: Cambridge University Press, 1968.

Williams, Michael E. "Three Metaphors of Criticism and the *Wife of Bath's Tale.*" *Chaucer Review* 20, no. 2 (1985): 144–157.

Wilson, Katharina M., and Elizabeth Makowski. *Wykked Wyves and the Woes of Marriage: Misogynous Literature from Juvenal to Chaucer.* Albany: State University of New York Press, 1990.

Yamamoto, Dorothy. " 'Noon Oother Incubus But He': Lines 878–81 in the 'Wife of Bath's Tale.' " *Chaucer Review* 28 (1994): 275–278.

Chapter 22

And Was a Povre Persoun of a Toun

ESTHER M. G. SMITH

Chaucer's pilgrims portray a spectrum of representative Englishmen of the fourteenth century. They also portray universal and timeless human characteristics. Although the group are on a religious pilgrimage, the tone of their traveling companionship is that of a group of strangers who have met on vacation—until the last tale, told by the Parson. Their manners range from the gentility of the Knight and the Prioress to the churlish quarreling and cynicism of such characters as the Miller, the Reeve, the Cook, and the Summoner, and their tales range from romance and classic fabliaux to bawdy comedy. But Chaucer recalls them all to the true purpose of their journey—a pilgrimage not only to a great cathedral and the site of a saint's martyrdom but also to Celestial Jerusalem—by the final tale, a sermon on damnation and salvation, preached by an ideal "religious."

After the withdrawal of Roman control of much of Europe, the Roman Catholic Church gradually assumed responsibility for many civilizing functions. It established and maintained not only religious organizations and instruction, but also law and order, education and economic stability, travel and communication. As secular communities redeveloped into townships, dukedoms, and kingdoms, the religious and secular institutions fought over the jurisdiction of these civilizing functions, and unfortunately, the Church sometimes outdid the secular groups in corrupt motives and methods. Nevertheless, there were always individuals who sought to live by high spiritual standards, and most people maintained a simple faith in the doctrines religion taught.

Sometimes those strongly committed to spiritual values became leaders in reform movements that developed into organizations that served throughout Europe. One such organization was the mendicant order of friars and nuns known as the Dominicans, an order founded in 1215 by the scholarly St. Dominic of

Caloruega, Spain (1170–1221). He and his followers were dedicated to improving the education of the clergy. Thus they increased the number and quality of schools beyond those already established by the Church. Another of the dedicated individuals was St. Francis of Assisi, Italy (1182–1226). Francis and Dominic knew each other and were friends, although sometimes their followers were rivals. Francis sought to counteract the ostentatious wealth of many church dignitaries by emphasizing voluntary poverty and labor. However, his teachings succumbed to the inevitable requirements of institutional development, especially the necessity of raising adequate funds to build and maintain permanent residences, schools, and other places of service. Eventually, men talented in raising charitable contributions but without sincere religious principles—men such as Chaucer's Friar—corrupted the group's work.

Still another originally well-intentioned but ultimately abused practice was the assignment of offices and the bestowal of benefices (land held by a feudal lord or the Church and the church and parish which this land included, for the sake of the income it provided from tithes and offerings). Such a source of income was assigned, supposedly by the Church and/or the feudal lord, to persons who needed such support while they studied at a university or carried out other religious or secular duties that were not directly related to the parish. The actual duties of the parish were then fulfilled by clerics who were less fortunate and were often poorly paid and poorly trained. While only a few recipients of such absentee benefice-incomes were thereby made wealthy, some received several such gifts, a practice called pluralism. Despite the abuses this practice led to, the bestowing of benefices on relatives or friends continues to this day in the English Church.

Two events of great significance to European history took place during Chaucer's lifetime, although neither is directly referred to in his writing. One, known first as the Babylonian Captivity, was the period during which the papal seat was in Avignon, France, rather than Rome; then it was called the Great Schism, when there were papal seats in both Rome and Avignon. Following a bitter struggle between Pope Boniface VIII and Philip IV, Clement V was elected pope and chose to stay in his native France rather than riot-prone Rome. While several of the French popes were sincere, learned, pious, and efficient, their administration of the world's largest business organization was materialistic and permeated with corruption. Their greatest revenues and therefore greatest disputes came from ecclesiastical appointments, by lay rulers or the church, to bishoprics and abbacies. Finally, in 1377, Pope Gregory XI returned the papal seat to Rome. However, the French were unwilling to concede defeat, and for a time there were two, even three, popes. Not until 1417, with the election of Martin V as pope, did this century of disgraceful conduct come to an end.

The second event was the life of John Wycliffe (1320–1384), an eminent theologian at Oxford University. His death from natural causes, in 1384, saved him from being burned at the stake as a heretic. Although Wycliffe founded no religious order, many of the lower clergy rallied to his beliefs and went about the countryside preaching and teaching from portions of the Bible which he translated from the Latin Vulgate into the vernacular. This group then became known as the Lollards. A summary of the movement's radical beliefs was presented to Parliament in 1395 under the title "Conclusions." The central doctrine was the responsibility of the individual believer in his relationship to God, without the intercession or authority of the clergy, a concept sometimes called "the priesthood of the believer." This point of view argues that the Bible is the only true source of authority. Therefore, the scriptures should be available to all. This belief resulted in numerous translations—and martyrdom for some of the translators—a struggle with ecclesiastical authority that ended in England with the Authorized or King James Version, commissioned by James I, in 1611.

Other examples of Wycliffe's significant departures from Catholic doctrine were the denial of "transubstantiation" (a belief that the bread and wine served at Communion became the very body and blood of Christ), the rejection of the use of other sacraments and images, of prayers for the dead, of auricular confession, of celibacy for the clergy and chastity for nuns, and the insistence on the submission of the clergy to secular law. Many of these principles were the goals of the Reformation, a century before Martin Luther, and are still central to modern evangelical churches and democratic governments.

The fact that the Parson's conduct and tale reflect several of these convictions has led many scholars to label him a Lollard, although he was not an itinerant preacher but a true pastor of his parish. Chaucer says he would "nat his benefice to hyre / And leet his sheep encombred in the myre / and ran to London unto Seinte Poules / to seken him" ["not his benefice to hire / And left his sheep stuck in the mire / And ran to London into St. Paul's / to find himself"] a better position. Instead, he "dwelte at hoom, and kepte well his folde" [I (A) 507–510] ["dwelt at home, and kept well his fold"]. The effectiveness of his example is testified to by the presence of the Plowman, his brother. Both men exhibit the spiritual qualities that all the reformers sought to teach and that Chaucer affirms in his exposé of several of the other characters. Although the two were "pouvre" in money, they were "riche" in "hooly thought and werk" [I (A) 478] ["holy thought and work"]. The Plowman was a "trewe swynkere (worker)" who lived "in pees and parfit charitee" ["in peace and perfect charity"], for "God loved he best with all his hoole herte. . . . /And thanne his neighebor right as hymselve" [I (A) 531–535] ["God loved him best with his entire heart . . . / and then his neighbor exactly as himself"], fulfilling the Great Commandment named by Jesus in Luke 10:27.

The Parson fulfilled another ideal of the reformers: he was a "learned man, a clerk" [I (A) 480]). Chaucer does not explain how this poor man was able to afford a good education; perhaps he was the recipient of charity. His education is substantiated in his tale by his knowledge of both the Bible and many theological sources. His devout teaching was supported by his conduct. He had compassion for his parishioners; he was unwilling to "cursen for his tithes" [I (A) 486] ["excommunicate those who did not tithe"], preferring if there was any doubt of their ability to pay to take the money out of his own meager resources. He never permitted bad weather to keep him from walking everywhere in his parish to serve all his people. Thus "first he wroghte, and afterward taughte," [I (A) 497] the gospel. For "to drawen folk to heven by fairnesse, / By good ensample, this was his bisyness" [I (A) 519–520] ["to draw folk to heaven by fairness, / By good example, that was his business"]. However, if any person persisted in sin, whether he was of high or low degree, "Hym wolde he snybben sharply" ["he would rebuke him sharply"]. Chaucer concludes that "A better preest I trowe that nowhere noon ys" [I (A) 523–524] ["A better priest I believe that nowhere none is"].

The Parson's tale, the longest of the Tales, is really a treatise, in the manner of a sermon, on Penitence and the Seven Deadly Sins. The thirteenth and fourteenth centuries produced a wealth of such works, many by clergymen but some by laymen. Initially, they were chiefly written to assist the parish priests in the conduct of their duties, but they became popular with the increasingly literate public and often were studied and revised by the universities.

According to W. A. Pantin, in his excellent history of the period, *The English Church in the Fourteenth Century,* the best known of these treatises is the "*Oculus Sacerdotis,*" written by William of Pagula, a scholarly churchman of the Salisbury Diocese, in the early fourteenth century. This work, which was to be widely used and often incorporated in later works, contained three parts. Part I was a manual for priests hearing confession. "Special injunctions and interrogations are given as suitable for particular sorts and conditions of men and women, such as drunkards or wrathful men" (Pantin 197). There is even advice for the health of expectant mothers. It also gives detailed instruction in canon law, identifying prescribed penances, sins whose absolution is reserved to the bishop or pope, and sins that incur excommunication.

Part II is a program of instruction for the parish priest's teaching and preaching. Among the practical instructions he was to give his people are such warnings as the danger of letting infants be smothered or overlaid in bed. (The Parson explains, near the conclusion of his tale, that such sins of carelessness, as well as efforts at birth control or abortion, are homicides and therefore deadly sins. The Catholic Church still so labels abortion.) Other instructions range from commanding parents to have their children confirmed within five years of birth, if the bishop is available, to warning foresters and beadles not to force unwarranted collections. Detailed instructions are given for annual confession, Easter communion, devotions at Mass and tithe-paying, and against usury, magic arts, and incantations to cure sick men or animals. Four times a year the priest was to explain to his parishioners, in their vernacular, the fourteen articles of faith, the seven sacraments, the seven works of mercy, the seven virtues, the ten commandments of the law and the two of the gospel, and the seven deadly sins. This part ends with remedies for each sin.

Part III of the *Oculus* deals with the seven sacraments, partly from a theological point of view and partly from a canonical and practical point of view, discussing such special problems as the baptism of a person unable to speak, and a long list of the advantages and disadvantages of matrimony. Among the many derivative or similarly inspired works Pantin presents, he mentions Chaucer's "Parson's Tale," describing it as "a good, straightforward, rather conventional example of a treatise on confession and on the seven sins and their remedies" (Pantin 226–227).

Since the subject matter of most of these treatises was such complex concepts as the ten commandments, the seven deadly sins, the seven sacraments, and the articles of the creed, a variety of literary techniques was used to make the concepts memorable. The most common method was dividing each major point into minor points, the method of philosophical scholasticism. Any modern reader of the "Parson's Tale" is a bit nonplussed by his constant use of this technique. For example, he has sixteen subdivisions for the sin of pride: Inobedience, Avautynge, Ypocrisie, Despit, Arrogance, Inpudence, Swellynge of Herte, Insolence, Elacioun, Inpacience, Strif, Contumacie, Presumpcioun, Irreverance, Pertinacie, and Veyne Glorie; and then frequently adds three or more divisions of each subdivision. However, numbering major points is still part of most sermons and lectures, essays and dissertations.

Sometimes ideas were emphasized by pairing, as the seven vices and the seven virtues, or the seven gifts of the Holy Ghost and the seven petitions of the Lord's Prayer, or, well beyond the "sacred sevens," were twelve abuses in religion and twelve abuses in the world, or the fourteen pains of Hell and the fourteen blessednesses of Heaven.

While the Parson disclaimed ability to use alliteration or rhyme, both common devices even today, he did use illustrations from experience and observation, and the timeless appeal to authority. He naturally quotes from the Bible, not only its words of wisdom but also to cite the example of Jesus and such good characters or prophets as David, Ezekiel, Isaiah, Jacob, James the Apostle, Jeremiah, Job, John the Evangelist, Mary Magdalene, Matthew, Micah, Moses, Noah, Peter, Paul, Solomon and Zechariah, and even such bad examples as Judas and Simon the Pharisee. His authorities outside the Bible include Saints Ambrose, Anselm, Antony, Augustine, Basil, Bernard, Damasie (Pope Damasus), George, Gregorie, Isadore, Jerome and John Crisostom, and the wise pagans Galen and Seneca.

The period was a classic one for preaching, with an abundance of influential sermons and great preachers from every walk of ecclesiastical life: bishops, friars, monks, and secular chaplains. And since both preachers and laymen were aware of the abuses in the religious structure, their criticism was bold and frequent—until the reaction of the privileged class set in, a reaction that condemned Wycliffe and John Huss and precipitated the Reformation. Chaucer masks his criticism behind his narrator pose as an unsophisticated Canterbury pilgrim, until he gets to the "Parson's Tale." Here are not only almost every sin common to humankind named and judged against a strong belief in right and wrong, Heaven and Hell, but also many of the faults previously ascribed to the other pilgrims.

The "Parson's Tale" is usually labeled a discourse on the seven deadly sins. Actually, it begins with a long and earnest plea for Penitence, in which terms are carefully defined and the appropriate penance is described. His emphasis on each individual's responsibility for his own sin and the sincerity with which he should seek reformation reflect the Lollard position: "For, certes, if he be baptized withouten penitence of his olde gilt, he receyveth the mark of baptisme, but nat the grace ne the remission of his synnes" [X (I) 97] ["For, surely, if he was baptised without penitence of his old guilt, he received the mark of baptism, but not the grace nor the remission of his sins"].

The dictionary lists the seven deadly sins as pride, covetousness, lust, anger, gluttony, envy, and sloth. The Parson treats the sins in a slightly different order: de Superbia (pride), de Invidia (envy), de Ira (anger), de Accidia (sloth), de Avarica (greed), de Gula (gluttony), and de Luxuria (lechery). When he says that there are two kinds of pride, one within a man and the other without the man, he gives considerable detail, as for expensive, exotic, or elaborate clothing, mentioning embroidering, notching of borders, stripes, fur trim, folding, punched or slit designs, and immodestly short coats. When he asks the rhetorical question as to the source of pride, he answers that it may come from a person's health, physical strength, or good looks, or from his wit and knowledge, or from his sense of righteousness—for none of which should he take credit, since they are the gifts of God. With such many-faceted analyses he deals with each sin.

He deals with this multitude of human weaknesses with vivid images and common sense reasoning, often showing how the sins are intertwined. Of the sin of anger he says that pride blows on the flames of the fire of anger and that envy "holdeth the hoot iren upon the herte of man with a peire of longe toonges of long rancour" [X (I) 555] ["holds the hot iron upon the heart of man with a pair of long tongs of long rancor"]. However, he recognizes that there are different levels of sinning. He labels habitual drunkenness a deadly sin, for it destroys a man's reason, but the drunkenness that is the result of someone not knowing the strong effect of a drink would be only a venial sin.

He reserves some of his strongest condemnation for those who seek spiritual office out of avarice:

For as seith Seint Damasie, "Alle the synnes of the world, at regard of this synne, arn as thyng of noght." For it is the grettestse synne that may be, after the synne of Lucifer and Anticrist. . . . For they putten in theves that stelen the soules of Jhesus Crist and destroyen his partimoyne. [X (I) 787, 789]

[For as said Pope Damasus, "All the sins of the world, in regard of this sin, are like possessions of nothing." For it is the greatest sin that may be, after the sin of Lucifer and the Antichrist. . . . For they put in thieves that steal the souls of Jesus Christ and destroy his inheritance.]

So much for Chaucer's view of absentee benefices and pluralism, and several of his "religious" pilgrims.

Following each explanation of a transgression, the Parson offers the remedy, assuring the sinner of God's mercy and the blessedness of reform. His thorough knowledge of human nature makes him more than a spokesman for religious doctrines. There is little emphasis on liturgical rituals and great emphasis on the psychology of sinning. His recognition that many sinners find it hard to trust divine understanding and mercy or to believe that they will be given the spiritual strength to resist bad habits and temptation makes his preaching compassionate, his character convincing. Chaucer's "Retraction" also attests to the sincerity with which he speaks through the Parson. Chaucer asks Jesus to give him the grace to bewail his guilt and study for the salvation of his soul, following the steps of penitence, confession, and penance that his ideal parish priest has so convincingly preached.

REFERENCES

Besserman, Lawrence. "Glossyng Is a Glorious Thyng: Chaucer's Biblical Exegesis." In *Chaucer and Scriptural Tradition.* Ed. David L. Jeffrey. Ottawa: University of Ottawa Press, 1984. Pp. 65–73.

Bishop, Morris. *The Middle Ages.* Boston: Houghton Mifflin, 1968.

Bloomfield, Morton W. "Fourteenth Century England: Realism and Rationalism in Wycliffe and Chaucer." *English Studies in Africa* 16 (1973): 59–70.

Catholic England: Faith, Religion and Observance Before the Reformation. Translated and annotated by Robert Norman Swanson. Manchester and New York: Manchester University Press, 1933.

Finke, Laura A. " 'To Knytte Up Al this Feeste': The Parson's Rhetoric and the Ending of the *Canterbury Tales.*" *Leeds Studies in English* 15 (1984): 95–107.

Glowka, Arthur Wayne. "Chaucer's Parson and the Devil's Other Hand." *Interpretations* 14, no. 2 (Spring 1983): 15–19.

Grennan, Eamon. "Dual Characterization: A Note on Chaucer's Use of 'But' in the Portrait of the Parson." *Chaucer Review* 16 (1982): 195–200.

Lawrence, C. H. *The English Church and the Papacy in the Middle Ages.* New York: Fordham University Press, 1965.

McKisack, May. *The Fourteenth Century, 1307–1399.* Vol. 5 in *The Oxford History of England.* Oxford: Clarendon Press, 1959.

Moorman, John R. H. *Church Life in England in the Thirteenth Century.* Cambridge: Cambridge University Press, 1955.

Oberman, Heiko A. "Fourteenth-Century Religious Thought: A Premature Profile." *Speculum: A Journal of Medieval Studies* 53 (1978): 80–93.

Pantin, William A. *The English Church in the Fourteenth Century.* Cambridge: Cambridge University Press, 1955.

Trevelyan, George M. *England in the Age of Wycliffe.* 4th ed. London: Longmans, Green, 1909.

Chapter 23

With Hym Ther Was a Plowman, Was His Brother

DANIEL F. PIGG

Certainly, one of the most memorable aspects of Chaucer's writings for a general audience or for a scholarly one is the descriptions of the pilgrims in the "General Prologue" to the *Canterbury Tales*. From the ideally presented Knight to the dishonest Miller to the morally and physically bankrupt Pardoner, we admire the curious and subjective eye of the Chaucer pilgrim. Among the pilgrims he describes, the Plowman stands out to readers perhaps most markedly by his silence; he does not tell a tale, has no verbal interaction with other pilgrims, and has no reference made to his presence by other pilgrims. Such a lack of prominence has led Jill Mann to contend that "Chaucer's interest in the ploughman seems perfunctory; the portrait in the *Prologue* mentions enough traditional characteristics to ensure our recognition of an ideal stereotype, but shows little feeling for his position" (73). Donald R. Howard even labels this Plowman's portrait "an anachronism" as a result of Chaucer's idealization of his estate (102).

Yet in the Middle Ages, the plowman was both valuable and most certainly vital to the economic well-being of society, especially amidst the crises of the fourteenth century. That Chaucer represents him is no mistake; in fact, that he is the only representative apart from the yeoman of the *laboratores* (the laboring class) is probably significant in the poet's overall enterprise of selectively depicting late medieval society. Rodney Hilton has shown the great disparity of land held by this class; peasants were by no means on equal footing. Considerable diversity existed among the group, with the ownership of a plow and plow team as an indication of higher status (*Class Conflict* 140–145). Overall, Chaucer's Plowman is a sign of stability and material and economic innovation—perhaps even success. As we will see here, silence can sometimes speak volumes.

The description of the Plowman quoted below is the briefest portrait given of a single pilgrim and requires concentration to understand the subtlety of play the poet uses in juxtaposing the Plowman's portrait against the shifting social realities and changing mentalities:

> With hym ther was a Plowman, was his brother,
> That hadde ylad of dong ful many a fother;
> A trewe swynkere and a good was he,
> Lyvynge in pees and parfit charitee.
> God loved he best with al his hoole herte
> At alle tymes, thogh him gamed or smerte,
> And thanne his neighebor right as hymselve.
> He wolde thresshe, and therto dyke and delve,
> For Cristes sake, for every povre wight,
> Withouten hire, if it lay in his myght.
> His tithes payde he ful faire and wel,
> Bothe of his propre swynk and his catel.
> In a tabard he rood upon a mere.

(Prologue, 529–541)

> [With him there was a Plowman, was his brother,
> Who had hauled full many a cartload of dung;
> A true worker and a good man was he,
> Living in peace and perfect charity.
> God loved he best with all his whole heart
> At all times, when it pained him or pleased him,
> And then his neighbor exactly as himself,
> He would thresh, and moreover make ditches and dig,
> For Christ's sake, for every poor man,
> Without payment, if it lay in his power.
> His tithes paid he very full and well,
> Both of his own labor and his possessions.
> In workman's clothes, he rode upon a mare.]

Paul A. Olson (36–39), Jill Mann (67–74), and Muriel Bowden (238–245), among others, have noted the interconnected relationship with other members of the social order that the Plowman exhibits. He creates by his actions a web of social interaction establishing community and dependence leading to charity. In fact, Olson contends that the description "centers in love rather than in the labor" (36). The change in emphasis is typical of estates literature of the period (Olson 36). Yet we should not be lulled into the view that Chaucer's Plowman is a completely unproblematic figure living in the midst of quiet. Actually, the converse is true. Writing in a period after the Peasants' Revolt when the plowman was adopted by William Langland as well as the anonymous author of *Pierce the Plowman's Crede* and of the *Plowman's Tale,* Chaucer fashions this "General Prologue" figure so that he bears obverse signs of ideological friction and potential volatility. In fact, the period following the Black Death saw the departure of many plowmen to urban centers where economic success seemed greater (Britnell 166). Thus Chaucer's Plowman is at the heart of socioeconomic change in the late fourteenth century.

Attitudes toward labor in the Middle Ages provide an important lens for understanding Chaucer's Plowman. Jacques Le Goff has isolated a number of ambiguities in labor philosophy. He characterizes this ''ambivalence'' to the presence of several binary views contributed by Greco-Roman, Judeo-Christian, and Germanic societies (71–86). Of these sources, Judeo-Christian thought read through the filters of the commentary tradition presented labor not only as a punishment stemming from the disobedience in the Garden of Eden but also as a requirement, according to St. Paul, if one is to be given anything to eat (2 Thess. 3:10). And yet labor could be ennobling—perhaps even nostalgically so in a period of agricultural decline and movement away from villages to urban centers. The literature of the period, especially *Piers Plowman,* which critics have noted may have inspired Chaucer's description of the Plowman (Mann 67–74), depicts labor as contributing to the physical, emotional, and spiritual success of the individual, the family, and the larger community. As several social historians have observed, the further opening of the markets in the late Middle Ages contributed to the growing equation of labor and capital (Hilton, *Class Conflict* 139–151; Rösener 140–143, 271–275). Thus, if labor were not in itself ennobling, the insertion of market value made it at least valuable.

These conflicting views of labor occupied an uneasy coexistence in medieval culture. Medieval society, according to Le Goff (73), was able to reconcile these seeming contradictions with the development of the tripartite model of social organization (those who pray, fight, and work). It is perhaps worth observing, however, that the laborers are the most subservient group in this social model, so rather than a reconciliation of ideas surrounding labor, it may be more accurate to say that work was pushed to the extremities of the model. A mid-fifteenth-century proverb, ''Wele better it were the plough lye stylle / Than efter honger for to tyll'' (Whiting 464), shows the marginalization of agricultural labor, even if in a paradoxical manner. Thus this ecclesiastically developed and employed model was useful in justifying ''divisions of labor'' and in accounting for the use of power and force to maintain the ideology that the triangular model embodies. *Laboratores* thus work to support the efforts of those who fight and those who pray. Another model of social organization, noted in one of Thomas Brinton's sermons in the 1370s, uses the human body as a metaphor. Here peasants are predictably the feet necessary to support and move the entire body (Owst 587). With any of these ideological models the emphasis remains the same: stability is predicated on an acceptance of the assigned roles.

All of these views have at least the sanction of the Church and of the king's court. Yet these official views often found expression in culturally based forms which, at times, threatened to undermine the voices of the dominant powers. Medieval writers, and dramatists in particular, had to deal with the implications of the archetypal Cain, the first plowman. While playwrights generally depicted him as the first person to deal seriously with a hostile and unproductive world, the Wakefield Master saw much potential in Cain as a symbol for social critique. At the beginning of the *Mactacio Abel*, Cain drives his oxen and plow onto the stage. The harshness of the elements, the unruliness of the animals, and the witticisms of his servant Garcio contribute a somewhat sympathetic image of the medieval plowman. Before the pageant begins, Garcio says to the audience, "Some of you are his men" (73). Thus the archetypal plowman Cain comes to represent the destructive potential within a viewing audience, some of whom have been plowmen outside the village of Wakefield. Given that homicide among peasants was a particular problem in the planting and harvesting seasons (Hanawalt 23), the murder in the pageant assumes an even greater poignancy. Whether the author of the pageant had in mind the need to establish distance between Cain and his laboring "offspring," whether he was simply domesticating the biblical story to fit the needs of a late medieval audience, or whether he was attempting to further problematize labor through a representative plowman can only remain a matter of conjecture. What most certainly arises is Le Goff's notion of "ambivalence" in the hands of a likely ecclesiastical writer.

What medieval readers or hearers of the Plowman's portraits would have done, however, is to compare the description with the material manifestation of this person in their world. They would have been the first audience to ask and to answer the question about how historically accurate Chaucer's pilgrim portraits are. In the case of the Plowman, they would have found a mixture of the real and the ideal. In contrast to many of the pilgrims, the Plowman seems quite realistically drawn, even if he seems devoid of the distinctive features of personality that we can identify in the Wife of Bath, the Miller, or the Pardoner. We need to concentrate on the description of his activities, his attitude, and finally on his connection with the Parson to understand Chaucer's construction of this character.

Chaucer's Plowman seems to be a prosperous individual, given his activities in labor and the items he owns. That the poet calls him a "plowman" rather than a "cottager," for example, is an important indication of his economic status within the wider class we call peasants (Hilton, *English Peasantry* 20–22). It is likely he lived with his family in a modestly substantial house by peasant standards; he must certainly have owned a plow and a team of oxen, although horses were in many areas assuming the place of oxen. Whether he would have owned a hook plow or a wheeled plow (heavy plow) is difficult to determine. If we use artistic media from *The Luttrell Psalter* as any indication of which plow was common in England approximately contemporary with the writing of the Plowman's description, then he would be using a wheeled plow. By the fourteenth century, the wheeled plow had grown in usage, especially given its ability to move more deeply into the soil while the hook plow only scratched the surface and required cross-plowing of a field (Rösener 107–113). Lynn White, Jr., has also shown that the use of the wheeled plow altered the status of tenants, because it produced an equipment-to-land ratio that assigned land on the basis of whether or not a tenant owned a plow rather than on "the needs of a family" (56). The question that often arises from the patently obvious economizing of labor and machinery is, How extensive was ownership of a plow and plow team? Barbara Tuchman notes that 75 to 80 percent of the peasants did not own a plow or plow team (173). Werner Rösener proposes a much less ominous 40 percent without a plow and plow team (138). Although these figures are clearly diverse, they do show how valuable a plowman would have been in his village community. Poorer tenants might borrow his plow for their own fields that were most likely smaller than his typical holding of a virgate of approximately 30 acres (Hanawalt 22; Townsend 74).

In the twentieth century, unencumbered by feudal obligations, the plowman would be a stellar figure of agribusiness. From a medieval perspective, a plowman could also be relatively prosperous, as wills often bear record. Barbara Hanawalt, a medieval historian who focuses on the material history of English peasantry, notes in the will of John atte Wall, a prosperous plowman, the following articles limited solely to agriculture: "two iron-bound wagons, one for dung, a cord, a plow, a horse harrow, a dung fork, a sheep fork, a mattox, a flail, an ax, a sieve, a sack, and a seed lip" (46). All of these items are tools of the trade that suggest he was at least adequately prepared to undertake agricultural labor. His material culture shows him to be a person who understood his economy, and the success that the plowman could achieve could elevate him along with other "upwardly mobile" peasants into the judicial roles in the village in a period following the Black Death as the labor market became even more fluid (Hilton, *Class Conflict* 148).

The "General Prologue" portrait also includes his labor in threshing grain and in making ditches. These activities were common for a medieval peasant and thus require little explanation. The first was a step in the movement after harvesting in order to prepare the grain for its use in the production of bread. That he was engaged so directly in every aspect of agricultural production may not be unusual, but as he was working with a shrinking workforce throughout the second half of the fourteenth century, the suggestion of the "division of labor" may be disappearing. Studies have shown almost an 80 percent drop in the number of peasant workers in the fourteenth century (Campbell 95–97). As with threshing grain, making ditches could serve several useful purposes. They could be used to separate a field from a grazing area so that animals would not disturb the crops. They could be used for draining fields or other inundated areas. Evidence suggests that these ditches were typically deep enough for a drowning to occur (Hanawalt 27). As a "trewe swynkere" (531), he was obviously concerned with the success of his crops, and these ancillary activities to plowing show that his focus was wide enough to include the entire cycle of production.

Yet this Plowman was not merely concerned with the agricultural success of his virgate. Chaucer suggests that he follows the ten commandments and that his religion is one with social consequences. Of all the areas of medieval life, the spiritual state of individuals is the most difficult to assess. Traditionally, literary and historical scholars have turned to literary texts and legal documents—especially wills—as the religious barometers for the period. And while there are pitfalls in investing too much credibility in either area, we can say that a general level of religious devotion existed among the peasant group. They, too, may have felt some of the aspects of lay piety developing throughout the fourteenth and fifteenth centuries, but it is unlikely that they would have owned Books of Hours, devotional or religious texts, or endowed their parish churches as did the growing, powerful merchant class. What evidence of religious devotion we do find might be called "relics." Hanawalt again finds in a peasant will "a painted cloth of the crucifix" (49). In literary representations of the period, apart from the drama, the plowman always appears as a religious figure or as one who is critiquing the abuses of the religious community—a tone in keeping with literary production of the late Middle Ages.

Another part of the Chaucer pilgrim's fascination with description is his concern with dress. Here again, the poet displays keen insight: "In a tabard he rood upon a mere" (541). Chaucer often uses the clothing the pilgrims are wearing to indicate their disfavor or discontentedness with their social status. The wives of the guildsmen are particularly notable on this point as they are attempting to imitate their social superiors. Clothing for the peasant class was valued for its functionality. Durability was certainly an important factor. Sumptuary laws, for the most part, mandated dress, and as Hanawalt observes, "Men wore loose tunics and cote-hardie, hoods and wide-brimmed straw hats" (62). Records of theft from peasant homes, however, show some tendencies away from humble dress (Hanawalt 62). If there were a clothing revolution underway—and the necessity of sumptuary laws suggests there was—Chaucer's Plowman and Langland's plowman would likely scorn anything that would outwardly misrepresent the mental and spiritual qualities they attempt to figure forth.

Perhaps the most important clue to understanding Chaucer's Plowman is his connection with the Parson, yet for many readers the identification of "brother" (529) has been an enigma. Jill Mann contends that the connection is inspired by Chaucer's knowledge of Langland's Piers, who brings together both aspects of preaching and plowing (68). But the ideas of preaching and plowing had wider currency in medieval thought as Stephen A. Barney and Donald R. Howard (101–102) have demonstrated. Stemming from imagery in scripture supported by commentary, "The plowshare is the preacher's tongue; the plow is the symbol of the penitential act; a farmer or ox is a symbol of a preacher" (Barney 276). Seen in this way, the Plowman becomes a mirror image of the Parson in a symbolic way. He activates on a literal level what the Parson through his own words and works initiates in the hearts of hearers. Thus not only does Chaucer see no disharmony between the two figures, but he also shows how one supports the other by solidifying the letter as well as the spirit of work. After a period of social unrest in 1381 in which the peasants called for an end

to feudal obligations and in the wake of labor disputes culminating in the propagation of the Statutes of Labourers of 1351 to return the wages of peasant
workers on manors to levels of pre-plague England, finding a point of equilibrium was essential. A representative of the group that originated and taught the
vital importance of social order and responsibility is united with a representative
of the group that was most threatening to undermine the continuance of that
order. And while it is certainly true that the reformation/restoration strains found
in *Piers Plowman* do not echo in these Chaucerian lines, we can find here a
model in the Parson and Plowman for peace and unity amidst change albeit
Chaucer's vision lacks Langland's apocalyptic urgency.

Chaucer's Plowman will likely remain a figure often noted while never heard
in the "General Prologue." Bearing evidence of both social reality and idealism
in the late Middle Ages, Chaucer's Plowman stands as a testimony of one who
has fought with the elements of nature, of self, and of society and has been
successful in establishing "pees and parfit charitee" (532).

REFERENCES

Barney, Stephen A. "The Plowshare of the Tongue: The Progress of a Symbol from the
    Bible to *Piers Plowman.*" *MS* 35 (1973): 261–293.
Benson, Larry D. *The Riverside Chaucer.* 3rd ed. Boston: Houghton Mifflin, 1987.
Bowden, Muriel. *A Commentary on the General Prologue to the Canterbury Tales.* Lon-
    don: Macmillan, 1967.
Britnell, R. H. *The Commercialisation of English Society 1000–1500.* Cambridge: Cam-
    bridge University Press, 1993.
Campbell, Bruce M. C. "Population Pressure, Inheritance and the Land Market in a
    Fourteenth-Century Peasant Community." *Land, Kinship and Life-Cycle.* Cam-
    bridge: Cambridge University Press, 1984. Pp. 87–134.
Hanawalt, Barbara. *The Ties That Bind: Peasant Families in Medieval England.* New
    York: Oxford University Press, 1986.
Hilton, Rodney. *Class Conflict and the Crisis of Feudalism: Essays in Medieval Social
    History.* New York: Hambledon Press, 1985.
———. *The English Peasantry in the Later Middle Ages: The Ford Lectures for 1973
    and Related Studies.* Oxford: Clarendon Press, 1975.
Howard, Donald R. *The Idea of the Canterbury Tales.* Berkeley: University of California
    Press, 1976.
Le Goff, Jacques. *Time, Work, and Culture in the Middle Ages.* Trans. Arthur Goldham-
    mer. Chicago: University of Chicago Press, 1980.
Mann, Jill. *Chaucer and Medieval Estates Satire: The Literature of Social Classes and
    the General Prologue to the Canterbury Tales.* Cambridge: Cambridge University
    Press, 1973.
Olson, Paul A. *The Canterbury Tales and the Good Society.* Princeton, N.J.: Princeton
    University Press, 1986.
Owst, Gerald R. *Literature and the Pulpit in Medieval England.* Cambridge: Cambridge
    University Press, 1933.
Rose, Martial, ed. *The Wakefield Mystery Plays.* New York: W.W. Norton, 1961.

Rösener, Werner. *Peasants in the Middle Ages.* Trans. Alexander Stützer. Urbana: University of Illinois Press, 1992.

Townsend, Robert M. *The Medieval Village Economy.* Princeton, N.J.: Princeton University Press, 1993.

Tuchman, Barbara W. *A Distant Mirror: The Calamitous 14th Century.* New York: Alfred A. Knopf, 1978.

White, Lynn, Jr. *Medieval Technology and Social Change.* New York: Oxford University Press, 1962.

Whiting, Bartlett Jere. *Proverbs, Sentences, and Proverbial Phrases: From English Writings Mainly Before 1500.* Cambridge, Mass.: Harvard University Press, 1968.

Chapter 24

The Millere Was a Stout Carl for the Nones

LAURA C. AND ROBERT T. LAMBDIN

INTRODUCTION

Arguably one of the most popular of Chaucer's pilgrims in the *Canterbury Tales* is Robyn the Miller. His bawdy tale, which accentuates his coarse life as a hard-working and equally hard-playing individual, is forever charming. Through the clear depiction of this miller in the "General Prologue" and the incidents that befall him during the journey, whether by design or not, Chaucer individualized Robyn, a stout, big-boned fellow with a passion for wrestling, to a greater extent than most of the other pilgrims. He was

> . . . short-sholdred, brood, a thikke knarre;
> Ther was no dore that he nolde heve of harre,
> Or breke it at a rennyng with his heed.
> His berd as any sowe or fox was reed,
> And therto brood, as though it were a spade.
> Upon the cop of his nose he hade
> A warty, and theron stood a toft of herys,
> Reed as the brustles of a sowes erys;
> His nosethirles blake were and wyde.
>
> [I (A) 549–557]

> [. . . short shouldered, broad, a stout fellow;
> There was no door that he would not heave off its hinges,
> Or break it at a running with his head.
> His beard as any sow or fox was red,
> And therto broad, as though it was a spade.
> Upon the top of his nose he had
> A wart, and on it stood a tuft of hairs,

Red as the brustles of a sow's ears;
His nostrils black were and wide.]

Yet of import beyond Robyn's interesting physical characteristics are the possible reasons why Chaucer included him in the pilgrimage. He probably would have had to leave his mill in the country to join the pilgrims at the Tabard, so one assumes that members of this particular vocation rarely went on pilgrimages.

Hindering vacations or "religious" journeys was not the only limitation of the trade. Simple logistics created many peculiar problems; for example, mills were located in isolated areas some distance apart, making it impossible for millers to unite as a guild. This profession, as well as a miller's place in the hierarchy of medieval British society, presents some insight into the changes that were occurring in England during this period. If any of the pilgrims illustrates a link between the gentry and the peasants, it would be the miller, a member of a group that had no identifiable stature, being neither upper nor lower class.

During the Middle Ages, a miller would have been, obviously, someone who ran or operated a mill. In Chaucer's time, larger, stream-powered mills had replaced the old hand mills that had been used for hundreds of years in England. There had been a vast improvement in plowing techniques; since horses had been better harnessed for greater ease of domestic use, many serfs no longer had to plow by hand. These occurrences led to huge changes and vastly improved working conditions for an agrarian society. Grain productivity reached new heights, so there developed demand for more sophisticated grinding implements; among the most important devices created and perfected were the water mills. The Romans had originally created small mills that were used domestically and also the larger mills that were used by the general populace. Because the Romans had failed to harness water as a means of turning the mill wheels, these great mills depended on slave labor. From these prototypes evolved the water mills that spread slowly over Europe; by the seventh century, versions of the water mill had made their way to England (Van Bath 70–71).

Perhaps the mill of Chaucer's Miller would have been the overshot type used for shallow water, with wooden wheels about 9 inches wide. Such mills were usually housed in one-storey structures with a projecting loft, or a "lewcome" (Bennett 112). Next to the grinding facility would have been a modest home with a kitchen, parlor, and one-bed chamber where the entire family slept. Behind the mill would have been a grain barn and a "levesel," or a canopy with a sedge roof which covered the back door or steps of the mill (113–114).

Mills were often found in remote areas by streams, usually near sharp changes in the ground level where water would run faster. Sometimes water for mills was artificially dammed, and some mills were hung under bridges or placed on barges to take advantage of the water's power and of the force of gravity. One bid was made to erect a mill on the rocky coast of Brittany. The builders hoped to take advantage of the high and low tides to power the mill, but the task proved unworkable, owing to the ebb and flow of the tides. Mills continued to be popular constructions, and the *Domesday Book* contains references to some 1,306 mills in the counties of Lincolnshire, Norfolk, Suffolk, Essex, Cambridgeshire, and Huntingdonshire (Van Bath 70–72).

In the Middle Ages, mills were usually constructed so that they could be versatile in their grinding. These flexible mills, besides grinding grain, were also used for creating mustard, beating oak bark for the tanneries, rolling metal, sawing timber, pulverizing goods for dyes, and, after the thirteenth century, making paper—which would later usurp parchment as writing material. Each of these different operations required different sets of millstones. The miller had one set of stones for grinding wheat, and others for malt or barley. Different stones were mandated because of the different textures and sizes of the varying grains. Additional income was generated by the mill pool which provided fish and eels—with the fishing rights all being retained by the mill. This meant that all who wished to harvest from the pond would be required to compensate the millers for using "their" water. In addition to owning the fish and the other living creatures of the pond, the mill also claimed the riparian rights, or all access to everything that grew on the banks of the mills, including brush and grass which would have been used in mortar or as thatch for roofs (Bennett 111–112).

As milling became a more socialized industry, the English followed the example set by the Romans hundreds of years earlier and relegated mill work to serfs which, as George Fenwick Jones indicates, made the vocation of milling fall into social disrepute (6). Installing a water mill was a costly prospect, one that most of the populace could never hope to undertake because constructing the mill race, and then transporting, fashioning, and setting the millstones required a substantial investment. Regular maintenance only added to this prohibitive cost, for the grinding tools were often in need of repairs or replacement (Duby 16). These overhead costs meant that only the extremely well-to-do, such as manor owners or religious orders, could afford to construct and operate these needed facilities. To establish total monopolies, those in charge often had all privately owned grinding devices located and destroyed. Furthermore, by the time of Chaucer's writings in the late fourteenth century the situation had shifted because the position was so lucrative: "times are changing: the miller or his predecessor could well have bought the freedom of the mill" (Bennett 91).

As one means of recouping some of the operation costs, lords or abbots who built mills required that all those who rented and toiled on their lands must use only their mill. For example, at Ramsey Abbey, it was decreed that all tenants were obligated to use the abbey's mill and, therefore, all of the abbey's corn was sent there. If tenants were unable themselves to grind enough wholemeal for a day's supplies, they had to have the mill grind it. Only if the mill was too busy or if it was broken down could tenants take their crops elsewhere. Those caught using another mill without authorization were convicted of failing to render suit to their lord's mill and fined sixpence (Coulton 55). In essence, the mill became a means through which the rich and the powerful controlled and later constrained the other members of society. It was a monopoly because only the elite could own mills that all of their social lessers in the immediate area were forced to use (Fossier 100).

When it eventually became possible for prosperous millers to own their own mills, much of the hatred that the peasantry had felt previously toward the gentry for creating monopolies was shifted to millers. Millers were unpopular members of society because the people would bring their goods to these mills and unload them only to have thieving millers use their "golden thumbs" to measure the bushels. On average, a typical sack of the peasantry held around four bushels, medieval measure, about a fifth less than modern bushels. Once the sack was turned over to the miller, only he would know for certain how much flour or goods the load would make, so he was able to pinch and grab or take his extra cut without any threat of reprisal. This is illustrated in a popular proverb of the fifteenth century: "If any sack would not dance to his [bag]pipe, it had to let itself be tolled twice in punishment" (quoted in Jones 12).

Since there was literally no competition for the worker's goods, millers had no real reason to provide even adequate service to their customers; the peasants were at their mercy. This brings to mind the nursery rhyme which may sound amusing but preserves the harsh reality of the millers' power:

> As the wheel wen round he made his pelf:
> One hand in the hopper, the other in the bag,
> As the wheel went round he made his grab . . .
>
> (Quoted in Bennett 114)

> [As the wheel went round he made his fortune:
> One hand in the hopper, the other in the bag,
> As the wheel went round, he made his grab . . .]

The general populace was forced to depend on these churls to process their crops. Oddly, in a way almost everyone was more fortunate than the clerks. Since clerks had no right to use the mills and colleges did not own mills, they were put in the most untenable of positions. Clerks had to speak kindly to the miller and never antagonize him, for the miller had no real obligation to grind for them.

Jones explains that people had additional reason to dislike and suspect millers of unfair practices. As the rhyme indicates, millers made their best profits by literally skimming off the top of the grain. Because they could steal during two different parts of the process, when the bushels were brought in and when the grain was bagged, at least two onlookers were needed to catch the thief. This theme seems to have been continental in nature for, in Germany, a book called *Wendunmuth* mocks a miller whose business fails, forcing him to ask alms of a baker. When the miller admits to the baker that he once had seven peasants obliged to him, the baker expresses his surprise that the miller would have to beg (8–9). Undoubtedly, by Chaucer's time the characterization of millers was clear; one could anticipate and understand that Robyn would tell a bawdy tale.

But there was yet a third way for the miller to gouge the populous. Serfs who were forced to use the area mill were also obliged to pay the miller a "multure," or toll. This toll was theoretically fixed by law, but since the miller controlled the only mill available to the majority of the masses, he could easily "tollen thries" [I (A) 562] or charge literally any toll he so pleased (Bowden 124). As one might expect, millers quickly accumulated much wealth, which created an atypical social position for them. Many millers considered themselves to be of the upper class, which may explain why Robyn wore a "blew hood" (564). Headwear of certain colors were theoretically illegal for the lower classes, and it seems that many medieval writers clad their characters in certain ways as a means of satire. In this case, Robyn *believes* that he is of an upper class, and he is arrogant enough to wear the hood (Jones 6).

That Robyn was seemingly able to get away with this type of dress illustrates a unique dialectic: while the millers were essentially a part of the laboring class, they also, because of wealth, could be considered part of the gentry. Naturally, millers were subject to ridicule and distrust from both the landed gentry and the laborers. Millers had lots of money to spend and were able to step above the boundaries that had evolved between the classes, but nobody wanted them. Because they were still seen as serfs in the eyes of the gentry, millers were barred from carrying weapons, a privilege granted only to freemen. So, like the Jews and the peasants, millers were forced to depend on the protection of their lords or rulers. Thus, even after they lost their unfree status, millers were often prohibited from bearing weapons at certain times; in Germany a law was passed which banned millers from being armed when entering a tavern (Jones 6–7).

What is forgotten in all this is that the tolls the millers extracted were nominal compared to what the feudal lords took, the bulk of the money made from the millers' tolls. In spite of this, the peasants' resentment of these payments was largely diverted to millers (and, later, to reeves), who were easily capable of robbing both their masters and the tenants. Thus the millers evolved into a class of people who are commonly depicted in the literature of the time as untrustworthy, boorish, and churlish. Millers were so geographically separated that they could not form guilds, so they could not protect their reputations as could those better organized. This lack of respect caused problems such as in Germany, where millers were denied many benefits of the law. In addition, millers' bloodlines were considered corrupt, so that their "tainted" children frequently had to take up milling or some other equally despicable vocation (Jones 9). What becomes clear here is that the image of the miller was commonly that of thief or rogue, much like Robyn, the Miller.

CHAUCER'S MILLER

Just after the Knight has finished his long, courtly narrative, Harry Bailley calls on the Monk to come forward and present a tale. The Miller breaks up the

Host's plan of observing social order in the telling of the tales by drunkenly asserting that *he* will "quyt" the Knight's tale. Thus begins the "poetic self-consciousness" of Chaucer's work: "The allocation of such a tale to the Miller is a dramatic device so plausible, so flattering to the expectations of rank, that it seems natural" (Pearsall 171). This, along with Robyn the Miller's quarrel with Oswald the Reeve establishes a "certain baseness of intellect and ethos" (Ruggiers 53). The Miller, an earthy, tactless, vigorous, ribald cheat, tells a tale that is appropriate for him; indeed he does, as many critics note, tell a tale which effectively, in a way, requites the Knight (Owen 76). A sign of Chaucer's artistry is how well his audience is prepared for the Miller's antics.

In the medieval period, the appearance of the Miller in the *Canterbury Tales* would have probably been instantly noted as cliché. A plethora of rhymes and anecdotes relating to the nature of Millers as "churls" and "cheats" were known by most (Jones 8). Yet Chaucer has included explicit information in the "General Prologue" as if to emphasize the physical person of the Miller. His portrait, while only some thirty lines long, "concentrates, as no [description of pilgrims] previous only on appearance, and matches with a vigor of language the crude vitality of the man" (Owen 76). Chaucer stresses Robyn's physical features. He begins by noting the Miller's strength and athletic prowess, especially the notion that Robyn wins a ram at every wrestling match. Then, perhaps to highlight Robyn's animal-like nature, we are told that he also likes to beat down doors with his head, thus becoming a literal ram. The animal references continue as we are shown that his beard is as red as a fox's fur. Too, the tuft of hair that protrudes from the wart on his nose is as red as the brustles of a sow's ears. His black nostrils emphasize the furnace of his mouth and perhaps highlight the foulness of his speech.

Ironically, the most prominent cliché concerning millers—that of the "golden thumb"—takes up only one line of his description (Owen 76–77). Thus the impression given to us by Chaucer is one of Robyn's strength and roughness, not of his role as a thief and a cheat. Therefore, we are not surprised when we learn that Robyn's behavior echoes his appearance. His speech is as crude as his looks. He likes to gossip, tell bawdy jokes, and batter down doors with his head, when he is not ripping off his clients by stealing their grain or overcharging for his work (Lumianski 50). So, it appears that Chaucer manages the scene with the Miller and the Host so that they emerge more fully realized than before. This artistic method is a remarkable change from the common "flat" medieval fashion that was prominent in works such as *Confessio Amantis* or *Handlyng Synne* (Bennett 71). In every way, Robyn is just as we have been led to believe millers were, except that this miller also played the bagpipes.

Perhaps Robyn's playing of the bagpipes is a means by which Chaucer uses ordinary materials of life to achieve artistic purpose in his works (Block 239). The bagpipes in medieval England played a wide role in all types of social life. They functioned as military instruments and were used in church services and ceremonies. Predominantly, however, bagpipes became known as a folk instrument to be played at weddings, dances, and even funerals. Thus the bagpipes became associated with the lower class. Since Robyn was rude, crude, and therefore definitely rustic, his use of the bagpipes draws attention not only to his proclivity for making music, but it also reinforces his social and rural background (Block 239–240). Despite his wealth and wearing of the blue hood, our miller is still rooted in the peasantry.

THE MILLER'S TALE

The rural idea is reinforced when we acknowledge that the Miller in his tale replaces knightlore with folklore, which Donald Howard sees as "leaving the world of legends and noble deeds, the long ago and far away, for the native countryside and the ordinary people, the world of 'funny things that happened'" (238). The Miller's tale ends with the pilgrims laughing, swearing, and talking to each other. In essence, they gossip and titter over the duping of the base folks of the "Miller's Tale," a far cry from their response to the "Knight's Tale," which they saw as proper and noble.

Robert Dudley French finds that during the Middle Ages, stories like those told by the Miller and the Reeve probably circulated in great numbers (215–217). There is just something about raunchy humor which seems to appeal to humankind. In Chaucer's case, this makes it unlikely that he had a written source for his "Miller's Tale," and even more doubtful that any of the events of the story are original. While no one source for the tale has been found, there are other fabliaux that contain elements of the "Miller's Tale" (French 215–217). Perhaps Chaucer was "consciously creating people with whose characters the action of a borrowed plot would not be inconsistent—in other words, through a character he was motivating as much as possible a fabliau whose action originally had little or nothing to do with character" (Beichner 118).

It is in the Prologue that the Miller creates the frame for his tale, which is a clear indication of Chaucer's artistry (171). The "Miller's Tale" is the first of the low comic tales, and it appears that Chaucer felt some concern about including it or he would not have provided the disclaimer about "turning the page." It may be that the allocation of such a tale to the Miller is a dramatic device so plausible that it seems natural; indeed, the Miller even apologizes in advance for his fabliau. The Miller's attempts to pragmatize this ideal thus turns the "Miller's Tale" into a complex piece of narrative engineering, as a link to both the "Knight's Tale" and the "Reeve's Tale." In essence, Robyn's requiting of the Knight is actually a repayment of an old debt to Oswald (Pearsall 172–173).

The Miller uses low humor to parallel the themes of the "Knight's Tale:" two young men fall in love with the same girl, long for her, and make commentary upon lofty manners. Thus Pearsall sees that the Miller's claim that he will "quit" the Knight does not mean that he is trying to put down the Knight; rather, he is trying to repay the Knight for entertaining him (173–174). However, in his presentation of the tale, Robyn has treated the characters by blending realism with fantasy. The details of the town, the vocations, and the domestic life are quite real, so much so that it has been noted that "we could find our way blindfold [*sic*] about old John's with its cat-flap in Nicholas's bedroom door (3440), or the gable-end over the stable from which the three tubs will come triumphantly floating (3571)" (Pearsall 182–183). But the story itself is all a figment of Robyn's imagination, a comic fantasy rich in characterization, setting, witty allusiveness, and a versatile style. The word play is especially delightful, and the interweaving of plots make this one of the masterpieces of all literature.

It is on account of its many merits that Bernard Huppé sees the "Miller's Tale" as a superb work on its own, but he finds it in no way a serious requiting of the Knight. He adds that it is clear that the Miller has no real clue or ability to understand the "sentence" of the "Knight's Tale"; therefore, the Miller's work serves to reveal the "ignorance of his own soul [better] than it does to requit the Knight" (85). These two tales contrast two views of reality, two very different lifestyles. The Knight presents a learned, literarily toned work expounding the chivalry of a "matter of Greece and Rome" piece. The Miller would probably see this as a pretentious, overwrought story and tell his tale in hopes of revealing the foolishness of the genteel (Huppé 86). However, this may all be contentious hearsay that serves as fodder for scholarly debate. It is quite the opposite in terms of Robyn's role in influencing Oswald the Reeve's choice of a tale, for Robyn is the direct cause of the Reeve's bitter retort.

The Miller's requiting of the Knight has opened up another quarrel, that between the Miller and the Reeve. That the Reeve would be a natural adversary for the Miller is clear. Few, if any, of the pilgrims would be more likely to argue or have a conflict than these two. Their dispute is typical of their respective positions and vocations. A reeve's main duties were to protect his lord's businesses and to give assurance to the bailiff, much the same way as his modern successor. Additionally and most important here, reeves were responsible for seeing that the grain was properly garnered (Tupper 265–268). Muriel Bowden adds that a reeve was to inspect the estate regularly, buy needed supplies, and impose fines on the workers who merited them (125). Since both money and goods were usually in short supply among those overseen by the reeve and dependent on the miller, there would be a good bit of competition for funds. Thus, Robyn and Oswald would have good cause to be at odds with each other.

It is also possible to see these two characters as the outstanding misfits of an agrarian social order, since both held liminal positions between the higher and the lower classes (Lindahl 111–112). Among the greater duties of reeves was ensuring that all of the workers were productive. Chaucer has made it clear that Oswald accomplishes this by frightening the workers; thus he would be neither loved nor respected by those over whom he held dominion. Millers, as we have noted, also abused peasants. Disputes between these two types could go even deeper because both reeves and millers held privileged positions. They were among the few who were freeholders on an estate. For example, in fourteenth-century Spelsbury, there were six freeholders; one was the miller, another, noted as the richest, was the reeve (Lindahl 111). But this was not always true, and another possible reason that the Reeve and Miller would be apt to quarrel was that even though reeves held power over millers in terms of overseeing and regulating them, they were not always better off financially than their correlatives. Millers often made more money than reeves and were therefore more powerful financially, if not socially. This made reeves, who were poorer, seem lesser in terms of titular balance. Thus, Chaucer's stark description of Oswald's appearance may give another clue about the character's animosity, for the Reeve even appears less financially successful than the Miller.

Since members of both of these vocations were in a separate class, they were forced into direct competition; the rest of society was largely unsympathetic toward them, which normally would have forced them to accept each other if for no other reason than for the company. However, the nature of their jobs made millers and reeves despise each other. Since the reeve was charged with overseeing the mill and he earned a portion of his wages based on the returns on the grain which was ground at the mill, the more a miller took, the less a reeve could filch. Thus one gained at the expense of the other (Lindahl 113).

In terms of the pilgrims' word play in their separate tales, the Reeve is no competition for the Miller. Oswald is described as choleric, or angry, so he is unlikely to rhetorically "quit" wily Robyn. Too, the Reeve is no physical match for the Miller; Robyn is a stout man who likes to wrestle. The Reeve is slender and appears beaten down by life. In his prologue he even admits that the tap to his life is running dry. Thus he is very much unlike the Miller, who "almost thrusts his face into ours. As his appearance suggests, he is a lout and a great talker, quarrelsome, too" (Hussey 108). In terms of one-upsmanship, it seems that Oswald's nature dictates that he will be no match for Robyn.

And so consideration must arise concerning the question of prudence of Chaucer's selection of the Miller and his tale. Such an intrusion must have artistic significance; when Chaucer apologizes and invites the audience to turn to another tale, it seems only to whet the collective appetite. His inclusion of the "Miller's Tale" signifies perhaps only Chaucer's ability to make merry (Ruggiers 64). Still, this explanation does not answer all of the questions posed by the Miller and Reeve's quarrel: why doesn't the carpenter of the five guildsmen respond similarly to the criticism of his trade? Why does Oswald object so strenuously? Lumianski believes that this is because Oswald probably knows which story Robyn is going to tell and is therefore already starting to prepare his story about the cuckolding of a miller (51). This would give Harry Bailley good reason to separate these two rascals, and so they left the Tabard with Robyn leading the way, Oswald at the rear.

Regardless of the quarrel or the prevalent questions, Chaucer uses the stereotype of a vocation so despised to make a point: England is changing and will never be the same again. In this new society, one blotted by the remnants of the plague and the growing capitalistic tendencies, it is everyone for himself. While they may travel securely in a group, all the pilgrims are still individuals. And none of them is presented in more particular depth than Robyn, the Miller.

REFERENCES

Beichner, Paul E. "Characterization in *The Miller's Tale*." 1960. In Richard Schoek and Jerome Taylor, eds. *Chaucer Criticism: The Canterbury Tales*. Notre Dame, Ind.: University of Notre Dame Press, 1978. Pp. 117–129.

Bennett, J.A.W. *Chaucer at Oxford and Cambridge*. Toronto: University of Toronto Press, 1974.

Block, Edward A. "Chaucer's Millers and Their Bagpipes." *Speculum* 29 (1954): 239–243.

Bowden, Muriel. *A Reader's Guide to Geoffrey Chaucer*. New York: Noonday, 1964.

Coulton, G. G. *Medieval Village, Manor, and Monastery*. 1925. New York: Harper, 1960.

Duby, Georges. *Rural Economy and Country Life in the Medieval West*. London: Edward Arnold, 1968.

Fossier, Robert. *Peasant Life in the Medieval West*. Trans. Juliet Vale. Oxford: Basil Blackwell, 1988.

French, Robert Dudley. *A Chaucer Handbook*. 1927. New York: Appleton, 1947.

Howard, Donald. *The Idea of the "Canterbury Tales."* Berkeley: University of California Press, 1976.

Huppé, Bernard F. *A Reading of the "Canterbury Tales."* New York: State University of New York Press, 1964.

Hussey, S. S. *Chaucer: An Introduction*. London: Methuen, 1971.

Jones, George Fenwick. "Chaucer and the Medieval Miller." *MLO* 16 (1955): 3–15.

Lindahl, Carl. *Earnest Games: Folkloric Patterns in the "Canterbury Tales."* Bloomington: Indiana University Press, 1987.

Lumiansky, R. M. *Of Sundry Folk*. Austin: University of Texas Press, 1955.

Owen, Charles A. *Pilgrimage and Storytelling in the "Canterbury Tales."* Norman: University of Oklahoma Press, 1977.

Pearsall, Derek. *The Canterbury Tales*. London: George Allen, 1985.

Ruggiers, Paul G. *The Art of the "Canterbury Tales."* Madison: University of Wisconsin Press, 1967.

Tupper, Frederick. "The Quarrels of the Canterbury Pilgrims." *JEGP* 14 (1915): 256–270.

Van Bath, B.H. Slicher. *The Agrarian History of Western Europe A.D. 500–1850*. London: Edward Arnold, 1963.

Chapter 25

A Gentil Maunciple Was Ther of a Temple

JOHN H. FISHER

The Manciple is perhaps the least likely character to have been included among Chaucer's Canterbury pilgrims. There cannot have been more than a dozen manciples in England at the time and only two who could have been described as "of a temple" ("General Prologue" 567). A manciple was the purchasing agent for a college or an inn of court. The inns of court were in effect the lawyers' colleges, architecturally closely resembling the Oxford and Cambridge colleges. In early English, "inn" meant simply residence or habitation. The inns of court were the lawyers' residences—court in this sense referring to the law courts rather than the royal court. *OED* derives "manciple" from Latin *mancipium* meaning an acquisition by purchase, hence a bondsman, a slave, which makes Chaucer's epithet "gentil maunciple" (567) particularly ironic. In Medieval Latin *mancipium* developed into *manceps,* a buyer of provisions, sometimes the manager of a public bakery. *OED* says the term is not found in Old French, but it is found in Godefroy under *mancipe,* with a citation reading *manciple.* The only meaning in Godefroy, however, is "esclave, serviteur," so it would appear that the Medieval Latin transfer from "purchased" to "purchaser," and especially to a college official, was adopted only in English.

The use of the word "manciple" in English is severely limited. The earliest citation is from the *Ancrene Riwle* (ca. 1200) in the collocation *thes feondes manciple,* which *OED* takes as the original Latin meaning, the devil's bondsman. The other two *OED* citations before 1410 are from Chaucer and from a political poem, *Topias* (1401), "Ones I was a manciple of Merton halle." *MED* contains the *AR* citation and another from Trevisa's translation of Higdon (1378) likewise meaning bondsman, four citations of manciple as a surname, and four citations from Chaucer.

The Tatlock and Kennedy *Concordance* lists thirteen usages by Chaucer, three in the "General Prologue," two in the "Reeve's Tale," seven in the "Manciple's Prologue," and one in the first line of the "Parson's Prologue." The two in the "Reeve's Tale" refer to the manciple of Soler Hall, Cambridge; all of the others refer to the Pilgrim Manciple. *OED* and *MED* have a few other citations after 1410, but the evidence seems to indicate that Chaucer was the only person before 1400 to record the term as the purchasing agent for a college. Now it is clear that Chaucer did not invent this usage. The other instances, few as they are, indicate that it was an accepted title for a college servitor, like bursar or proctor. But I find it very interesting that the office/title was sufficiently prominent in Chaucer's consciousness that he—unlike Gower or Langland—chose to include it among his estates. Jill Mann does not record the term in her lists of estates (203–206), although her designations are, of course, all translations.

Chaucer identifies his manciple very precisely as "of a temple." There could have been only two such manciples in England. Two of the inns of court occupied buildings that had belonged to the Knights Templars until the order was suppressed in 1314. After 1324 they were rented to the lawyers. The two Temple inns were called Middle Temple and Inner Temple. One may still visit the round Templars' church on the Temple grounds just off Fleet Street. The other two inns of court, off Chancery Lane, were Lincoln's Inn, built on the ruins of the Blackfriars' monastery, which had become part of the estate of Henry Lacy, earl of Lincoln, and Gray's Inn, the former residence of the lords Gray of Wilton. The manciples of these establishments were the only nonuniversity manciples in England, and only two of them were "of a temple."

Along with Manly (12), Rickert, Robinson (665), and others, I take the precise identification of the Manciple as support for the tradition of Chaucer's education in the inns of court. Manly and Rickert offer what seems to me telling evidence in support of the tradition, Rickert substantiating the statement in Speght's Life of Chaucer that "Master Buckley did see a record in the same house [i.e., the Inner Temple] where Geffrye Chaucer was fined two shillings for beatinge a Franciscane fryer in fletestreate." No records of the inns from Chaucer's time survive today. William Buckley was the keeper of the records of the Inner Temple in Speght's time (1598), and Rickert hypothesized that there may have been early records from the Inner Temple still extant in his time.

The tradition of Chaucer's education in the inns has not been popular with recent commentators. I have had my say about the matter in *The Importance of Chaucer* (Chapter 2) and will not bolt it to the bran here. Chaucer could not have held the important administrative posts he did throughout his career without the equivalent of an MBA, which he got from studying for six years in the inns of chancery and the inns of court. His first appointment as controller of Customs in 1374 specifies that he must keep the records in "manu sua"—in his own hand (*Life Records* 148)—that is, in the official "chancery hand" taught by the writing masters to aspiring clerks in the inns of chancery. The critics' failure to accept this aspect of Chaucer's education is the result of their failure to understand how the inns operated. They think that the inns had to be like modern law schools, with formal faculty and curricula, which of course they weren't. They were merely the law students' and lawyers' residence halls, where the students lived while they "read" law as apprentices to practicing attorneys, as all would-be lawyers did until this century. After being called to the bar, many of them continued to live or have offices in the inns, as they still do today.

Not to understand this aspect of Chaucer's education is to miss so much of his delicious satire on law craft and law commonplace. The inns of court had many feasts with entertainment (for which, of course, the manciples had important responsibilities). Many of the Elizabethan plays, like *Comedy of Errors* and *Twelfth Night,* were first presented at inns of court celebrations, and the inns would have provided the most appropriate audiences for Chaucer's sophisticated humor. The humor of *Parliament of Fowls* lies in the proclivities revealed by the language of the different kinds of birds, which is just the sort of thing that lawyers are most trained to observe. One interest of the "Knight's Tale" is the way it is structured around the definitions of law at the beginning of the *Corpus juris civilis,* the summary of Roman law that formed the basis for all legal education. The *Corpus* begins by distinguishing three kinds of law: natural law *(lex naturalis),* the law of peoples *(lex gentium),* and civil law *(lex civilis).* The desire of Palamon and Arcite for Emelye exemplifies natural law—sex, the propagation of the species, which we share with animals. The tournament Theseus arranges exemplifies the law of peoples—might makes right, to the victor belong the spoils. The parliamentary settlement through which Palamon and Emilye finally marry exemplifies civil law—negotiation and equity. We can follow legal tropes like these throughout Chaucer's writings. Clearly, they were always at the surface of his mind, and it is not at all surprising that along with the Man of Law as the Don Quixote of the legal estate, he would include a Sancho Panza to gloss its shortcomings.

One puzzle is the placement of the Manciple in the series. If they are both examples of the legal estate, why isn't he associated more closely with the Man of Law? The pilgrims in the "General Prologue" are carefully arranged: the gentry (Knight, Squire, their servant, the Yeoman), the clergy (Prioress, Monk, Friar), the haute bourgeoisie (Merchant, Clerk, Lawyer, Franklin), the artisans (Guildsmen, Shipman, Physician, Wife of Bath), the peasants (Plowman and his brother the Parson), and the rascals (Miller, Manciple, Reeve, Summoner, Pardoner). It is not my privilege to relish here all the fun Chaucer has with the categories and characters. Malcolm Andrew, in his volume of explanatory notes for the "General Prologue" in the Variorum edition of Chaucer's writings, has brought together all of the observations by the commentators on the structure of the "General Prologue" and the natures of the pilgrims, including the Manciple. His notes (pp. 478–485) are essential to any consideration of the Manciple. But my question remains: Why is the Manciple placed among the rascals, and why is his description so bare? Unlike the Miller and the Reeve on each side of him, there is no description of his physical appearance, his clothes, his manner. There is no interest in the Manciple as a "person." The only interest is in his function, his ability to cheat his more than thirty learned masters (i.e., the attorneys in his Temple inn). This fraudulence evidently seemed to Chaucer akin to the fraudulence of the Miller, the Reeve, the Summoner, and the Pardoner. But even here the Manciple is different because he displays none of the personal vice we observe in the other rascals.

Perhaps the very colorlessness of the Manciple is an aspect of Chaucer's ingrained caution—he never directly criticized anyone of power or importance. The Manciple was the only figure among the rascals whom it might be possible to identify; after all, there were only two of them. The colorlessness kept specific identification to a minimum. In the structure of the "General Prologue," it is not unusual for the representatives of the estates to be separated: the religious estate should in a broad sense include the Parson, the Summoner, and the Pardoner. The artisan estate could include the Miller and the Reeve (himself a carpenter, just as the Wife of Bath is a weaver). Merely placing the Manciple between the Miller and Reeve was comment enough. Chaucer never overstates, but part of the delight in the pilgrim assembly is contemplating reasons for the apparent disorder in such a calculated order.

The Reeve and the Manciple are indeed two of a kind. Their responsibilities and their misdeeds were similar. Themselves "lewed," uneducated men ("General Prologue" 574), they were able to swindle their more educated masters so cunningly that no auditor could incriminate either one. Like the Manciple, the Man of Law was a "purchasour" (318), but of estates, not of meat and beans. The Man of Law was a distinguished officer of the courts; everything he did appeared to be by the letter of the law. But an aspersion is cast. "Al was fee symple to hym *in effect*" (319). "In effect"—then it must not really have been so. He was evidently adept at breaking entails and buying, or helping others to buy, property that ought legally to have been passed on through inheritance. Chaucer is as circumspect in his criticism of the Lawyer as of the Manciple. But the underbelly of the profession is revealed in the way the cunning Manciple gets away with charging his shrewd masters more than he spends for their provisions. The lawyer may be merely illegitimate; the Manciple is downright dishonest as he "sette her aller cappe" (586). Finagling with money, licitly or illicitly, is the name of the legal game.

Another reason why the Manciple is interesting is for a reason that Chaucer could not have imagined but in which he played an important part. I have argued in the last chapter of *The Importance of Chaucer* and in articles such as "A Language Policy for Lancastrian England" and "Chancery and the Emergence of Standard Written English" that Chancery and Chaucer played crucial roles in the reestablishment of English as the official language of England. From 1066 until 1400 French and Latin were the official languages in the sense that all legal and governmental business was recorded in these languages. The Lancastrian administration, inaugurated in 1399 by Henry IV's usurpation of the throne, began to use English for official activities in order to secure parliamentary support for the usurpation. To enhance the prestige of English, which until then had been regarded as a colloquial patois, the Lancastrians began to commission the production of handsome manuscripts and the composition of original poems and other belles lettres in English. Gower and Chaucer were featured as the principal exhibits from earlier times, and Lydgate and Hoccleve were the first writers whose poems were commissioned by the Lancastrians. Chaucer especially became the cynosure for both language and literature throughout the fifteenth century, as brilliantly surveyed by Seth Lerer in *Chaucer and His Readers.*

Chaucer could hardly have imagined the change in the status of English that would begin in the year of his death. He wrote his poetry in the Franglais of the London business community, the language people spoke, not the language in which they read and wrote. All of his own bureaucratic business was carried on in Latin and French. He did not have enough confidence in English to commission a single presentation manuscript of a single one of his poems. But such was his native genius that his compositions were at once recognized, and have been recognized ever since as prototypes of consummate expression in English.

The political elevation of English began with the decision of Henry V in 1416 to use English for his official promulgations and correspondence. His Signet scribes employed his own lexicon and accidence (Fisher, *Anthology*; Richardson; Henry V was the first English king by whom there are holograph letters preserved). The Chancery scribes then employed the language of the Signet missives. (We have edited and discussed these early documents in *An Anthology of Chancery English.*) The guild scribes in London then employed the Chancery forms, developing a relatively uniform language that has been designated Chancery Standard (Samuels). Eventually, Caxton and the early printers—themselves members of the London business community—began to print in Chancery Standard (Fisher, "Caxton"). Throughout the fifteenth and sixteenth centuries, Chaucer was constantly cited as the cynosure for polished English (Lerer), regularly associated with the king and the court—even though the Chancery connection was not perceived, as it has not been until very recently.

Now none of this casts much direct light on the character of the Manciple in the "General Prologue," but it certainly makes him a significant figure. He and the Man of Law stand as testimonials to the milieu in which Chaucer moved and from which modern English language and literature emerged.

The relationship of the Manciple to his tale remains as moot as most of the relations between tellers and tales in the Canterbury collection. Recent criticism, as represented, for example, by David Benson and Derek Pearsall, is turning away from George Lyman Kittredge's argument that "Chaucer always knew what he was about" (151) and that the *Canterbury Tales* should be read as a drama: "the Pilgrims do not exist for the sake of the stories but vice versa. Structurally regarded, the stories are merely long speeches expressing, directly or indirectly, the characters of the several persons" (155). Recent manuscript study (as represented by Norman Blake, *The Textual Tradition of the Canterbury Tales,* and Fisher, "Animadversions") indicates pretty strongly that all the manuscripts of the *Tales* were compiled by editors and scribes rather than by Chaucer himself, and that the orders of the tales in the manuscripts and the ascriptions of at least some of the tales are editorial rather than authorial.

The "idea" of a composition in which participants tell stories that reveal their characters is Chaucer's own contribution, and I have tried to point out the way the idea grew on him as he began to assemble fragments VI, VII, and VIII of the compilation ("Chaucer's Last Revision of the *Canterbury Tales*"). It seems to me that the source of the idea was the formularies, which served as textbooks for the writing masters who taught composition in the inns of chancery (*Importance of Chaucer* 63). These formularies were collections of letters in different styles, appropriate to different recipients and occasions—a letter to a bishop, to a king, to a parent, to a friend. The students were supposed to imitate these models in mastering the *ars dictaminis,* the art of letter writing. It was but a short step from learning to compose letters in different styles to creating a collection of stories told in different voices.

None of this, again, has a direct bearing on the character or function of the Manciple. His tale is not one of those, like the Reeve's or Miller's, in which the headnote is knitted into the fabric of the characterization and narration. As Andrew's notes make clear, cooks and manciples traditionally worked closely together, and the ribald incident of the Manciple's berating the drunken Cook and then reviving him with wine are appropriate to this domestic affinity. But this episode does not seem to be related either to the character of the Manciple in the "General Prologue" or to the story that follows. Some association between the headnote and the tale might be elicited from the fact that the Manciple's gratuitous comments to the Cook ("Manciple's Prologue") nearly get him in trouble and the crow's comments to Phebus ("Manciple's Tale" 271ff) do get him in trouble. A similar link can be noted between the cautions against loose talk and the lawyer's need for verbal discretion.

Salamon's advice at 319 in the "Manciple's Tale," "My sone, keep wel thy tonge," is curiously similar to Genius's admonition to the Lover in Gower's *Confessio Amantis* III.768, "Mi Sone . . . hold thi tunge." Composition of the *Confessio* dates between 1385 and 1390. This is the same period as for the composition of *Legend of Good Women*. R. W. Frank has argued that in *LGW*, Chaucer was developing his technique of brief verse narratives by reworking stories from Ovid. The "Manciple's Tale" is the most directly Ovidian of any of the *Canterbury Tales;* hence it may date from the same period. The tale of how the crow turned black may have been composed for independent performance (at an inns of court feast?) and then been incorporated like Palamon and Arcite and Melibeus when Chaucer began to assemble his compilation. This would suggest that its assignment to the Manciple is arbitrary.

The Manciple remains interesting chiefly for his association with, and Chaucer's own possible association with, the inns of court, and for the enigmas of why Chaucer elected to include such an inconspicuous figure and to place him where he did among the pilgrims.

REFERENCES

Andrew, Malcolm. Explanatory Notes to the General Prologue to the *Canterbury Tales*. In *A Variorum Edition of the Works of Geoffrey Chaucer*, Vol. 2, *The Canterbury Tales, The General Prologue*. 2 vols. Part One A, Commentary, Text, Collations, Bibliography, by Malcolm Andrew, Daniel J. Ransom, et al. Part One B, Explanatory Notes, by Malcolm Andrew. Norman: University of Oklahoma Press, 1993.

Benson, David. *Chaucer's Drama of Style*. Chapel Hill: University of North Carolina Press, 1986.

Blake, N. F. *The Textual Tradition of the Canterbury Tales*. London: Arnold, 1985.

Chaucer Life Records. Eds. M. M. Crow and C. C. Olson. Oxford: Clarendon Press, 1966.

A Concordance to the Complete Works of Geoffrey Chaucer. J.S.P. Tatlock and A. G. Kennedy. Washington, D.C.: Carnegie Institution, 1927.

Fisher, John H. "Chaucer's Last Revision of the *Canterbury Tales*." *MLR* 67 (1972): 241–251.

———. "Chancery and the Emergence of Standard Written English in the Fifteenth Century." *Speculum* 52 (1977): 870–899.

———. "Caxton and Chancery English." In *Fifteenth-Century Studies*. Ed. Robert F. Yeager. New Haven, Conn.: Archon, 1984. Pp. 161–185.

———. "Animadversions on the Text of Chaucer." *Speculum* 63 (1988): 779–793.

———. "A Language Policy for Lancastrian England." *PMLA* 107 (1992): 168–180.

———. *The Importance of Chaucer*. Carbondale: Southern Illinois University Press, 1992.

———, Malcolm Richardson, and Jane L. Fisher. *An Anthology of Chancery English*. Knoxville: University of Tennessee Press, 1984.

Godefroy, Frederic. *Dictionnaire de L'Ancienne Langue Française*. Paris: Librarie des Sciences, 1938.

Kittredge, George L. *Chaucer and His Poetry* (1915). Cambridge, Mass.: Harvard University Press, 1970.

Lerer, Seth. *Chaucer and His Readers*. Princeton, N.J.: Princeton University Press, 1993.

Manly, John L., ed. *The Canterbury Tales*. New York: Holt, 1928.

Mann, Jill. *Chaucer and Medieval Estates Satire*. Cambridge: Cambridge University Press, 1973.

Middle English Dictionary. Ann Arbor: University of Michigan Press.

Oxford English Dictionary. Oxford: Oxford University Press.

Pearsall, Derek. *The Canterbury Tales*. London: Allen and Unwin, 1985.

Richardson, Malcolm. "Henry V, The English Chancery, and Chancery English." *Speculum* 55 (1980): 726–750.

Rickert, Edith. "Was Chaucer a Student in the Inner Temple?" In *Manly Anniversary Studies*. Chicago: University of Chicago Press, 1923.

Robinson, F. N., ed. *The Works of Geoffrey Chaucer*. 2nd ed. Boston: Houghton, 1957.

Samuels, M. L. "Some Applications of English Dialectology." *English Studies* 44 (1963): 81–94.

Chapter 26

The Reve Was a Sclendre Colerik Man

RICHARD B. MCDONALD

INTRODUCTION

Relatively few documents exist which detail the professional responsibilities of workers in the Middle Ages, but in order to understand certain characters within a medieval work, like Chaucer's *Canterbury Tales,* it is necessary to recreate what medieval workers of specific professions did from those historical and literary sources that do exist. Literary sources often provide today's readers with most of their information concerning how individuals in the Middle Ages conducted their daily lives, but all too often the characters on which literary works specifically focus are of the noble class, and as a result, relatively little is known about the daily lives of peasants. In some instances, we can easily imagine what the responsibilities of a peasant worker might be. Certainly, a medieval cook would have difficulties in performing his duties which from our technologically advanced perspective we cannot imagine, but we assume that a cook's responsibilities on the most basic level have remained unchanged: a cook prepared food for others to eat. But the professional duties of some of Chaucer's other characters are much harder for us to envision. There are no modern-day reeves, and there are not any jobs today which more than remotely approximate what a reeve would have done. A foreman supervising sharecroppers for a large landowner seems the closest relative to this now extinct position, but a foreman was never as involved in the professional or private lives of his tenants as a reeve would have been. Even though a reeve held a position of authority, his legal rights differed little from those of the peasants he supervised.

A reeve was a serf just like the individuals he oversaw. In addition, as the conditions of serfdom, or villeinage, changed, so did the responsibilities and the importance of being a reeve. During the time that Chaucer is writing, at the end of the fourteenth century, reeves were a well-respected, if not well-liked, part of every medieval village. Each medieval village had a reeve, although a number of small villages technically could be under the jurisdiction of the same person. Being a reeve placed a peasant in a position of authority over the other peasants of his village. Although occasionally female peasants might be listed as land-holders on a medieval manor's court roll, the use of the word "he" in discussing reeves is all but absolutely appropriate; there is little evidence to support the notion that women were ever entrusted with the position. The reeve was an elected post that gave one peasant authority over and relative responsibility for the actions of the other peasants within the village. The reeve was accountable to the lord of the manor for the conduct and productivity of the village's serfs.

THE LIFE OF A PEASANT

Because our understanding of peasants' lives and their responsibilities to their lords is limited, an understanding of what it meant to be a reeve first requires us to comprehend what it meant to be a peasant. As already noted, medieval documents outlining the peasant lifestyle are very few, but by analyzing certain written codes restricting the freedoms of villeins (the serfs who lived in medieval villages), we can get a basic idea of what life might have been like. A villein (serf) was a member of the village's unfree class who received whatever land he had from the lord of the manor and technically had no personal possessions—everything owned by a villein was legally his lord's. Although some members of a medieval village's population would have been considered freemen, most villages were comprised of a large proportion of villeins. Historians today have difficulty determining exactly what real differences there would have been be-tween the lives of freemen and villeins. Both freemen and villeins often had similar contractual relationships with their manorial lord. Freemen had more freedom of movement, and villeins were technically owned by their lord, but the differences in their lifestyles and the hardships of their lives are often hard to differentiate clearly (Harvey 331).

The reeve of most manors would be better off financially than the freemen of his village, but the reeve was always technically a villein. John Hatcher, in his "English Serfdom and Villeinage," points out that, although villeins them-selves could theoretically purchase the status of freemen, "the purchase of free-dom, manumission, appears to have lain well down the list of priorities of even the wealthiest villeins and to have been overshadowed by the attractions of acquisitions of more land" (269). The unfree were more interested in securing the rights to farm more land than securing their rights to personal freedom. This may have been the case only because the amount of personal freedom even freemen had was directly related to their economic situation. Land meant eco-nomic freedom; apparently, the title of freeman meant nowhere near as much. Often freemen would buy or sublease land from villeins submitting to the same type of labor agreement as a villein (Hatcher 270).

The conditions under which both freemen and villeins accepted land from the noble of a manor differed from age to age and from region to region, but it is possible to make some general statements about what medieval farmers, both free and unfree, had to do in order to receive land from which they made their living. Strictly free individuals might rent land from a noble at a fixed rate, and this amount would remain relatively stable throughout the tenant's lifetime. Villeins received land that they could farm as their own in return for providing services to the lord's manorial farm. Villeins owed the lord work and produce in proportion to the amount of land that they held from the manor. The more land one had from the lord the greater one's obligations were (Gies and Gies 133). One example of the villagers' responsibilities is provided by surviving copies of the work schedule at Elton. A virgater, someone who held a reasonable quantity of land from the lord, varying between 18 and 32 acres (Gies and Gies 246), could be expected to devote up to 117 days of work to the lord each year. Half and quarter virgaters owed an amount of time proportional to their land-holdings. On many manors quantities of grain, poultry, and even livestock were also expected from virgaters, with proportionally less being owed by individuals with smaller farms. The work requirements varied with the seasons, as would be expected in a farming community. At Elton, a region with work requirements slightly higher than average, from September 29 (Michaelmas) to August 1, virgaters owed two days of work per week. From August to September 8, they owed three days a week and from September 8 to 29, virgaters owed five days of work a week (Gies and Gies 134). During periods of intense work, like the Autumn harvest, villeins would be expected to put in long hours of work to complete the harvest and would often be treated to a harvest dinner provided by the lord (Gies and Gies 140).

The reeve would be held responsible for ensuring that all tenants of the lord's land provided their services in an appropriate and timely fashion. "His main duty was seeing that the villagers who owed labor service rose promptly and reported for work. He supervised the formation of the plow teams and saw to the penning and folding of the lord's livestock, ordered the mending of the lord's fences and made sure sufficient forage was saved for winter" (Gies and Gies 54). The reeve was in charge of keeping detailed records of services provided by villeins and was the chief recordkeeper for all facets of the lord's farm. The reeve's yearly report (or reeve roll) included all cash, produce, and service payments for land let out by the lord, and noted when these payments were due as well as when they were received. Rents that went unpaid or underpaid were also explained within the report. The reeve's responsibilities included keeping track of all the expenses of the farm as well as maintaining reports on grain storage and livestock (Gies and Gies 55). Each year at Michaelmas, the reeve presented his roll to the lord or his appointed auditors. At this same time, in conjunction with the manor court, reeves were elected by a contingent of other peasants who had significant landholdings. The reeve retained his office for at least one year, although there was no limit on how often one could be reelected. (Chaucer's

Reeve seems to have served in his capacity for a long period of time.) A manor court was held each year to resolve grievances of villeins and to assess fines for tenants failing to observe community standards.

THE REEVE'S DUTIES

The structure of the medieval village farm required a high degree of cooperation between all villagers. Usually, individual farms were not separated from other farms by fences, and often plowing would require the pooling of numerous farmers' oxen or horses. Because an individual's landholdings would frequently not be located all in the same field, it was necessary for farmers to team up with different individuals in order to plow both their own fields and those they were required to farm for the lord. The medieval village and manor farms often comprised part of what is called an open field system, with the farmland of all being located together, near or surrounding the village. Fences were used only to separate certain groups of fields from others in order to ensure that livestock was kept out of fields that were being used to grow produce. There were strict regulations about where and when livestock could be grazed, and fines are common in manor court records for individuals who let their livestock stray (Keen 53).

Although the villagers held differing amounts of land from the lord and owed various degrees of responsibility to the manor farm, the open field system required them to perceive their land in terms of its relation to the rest of the community. Medieval plots of land were often assigned in long, continuous plowing strips, or furrows. It was possible that a villein could plow the equivalent of an entire acre of land before reaching the end of one furrow; this system made plowing both efficient and more communal. By plowing for great distances in straight lines, the amount of time spent turning the plow was greatly reduced. With one's entire holdings in a given field sometimes limited to only one furrow, a farmer would often work side by side with his neighbors, even when the teamwork required for plowing was complete (Keen 51).

Working effectively in such close proximity to one's neighbors was a constant reminder of the communal nature of the work done on the farm. To minimize the altercations between neighbors with differing expectations for their farms, each village developed its own set of community bylaws. These bylaws often worked to protect not only the concerns of the manor farm, but individual villein farms as well. Individuals who failed to plow their fields in a timely manner, be it their own field or their obligation to the lord, could be fined at the manor court, and it would be the reeve's job to represent the interests of both the community and the lord in such matters (Keen 55).

Some of the most intricate laws of the community revolved around the harvest and when certain activities could be allowed to occur. It was beneficial for all to allow livestock to graze in the newly harvested fields, but this process could not take place if certain individuals did not keep pace with the rest of the harvesters. The grazing of animals on harvested fields alleviated some of the need for the manuring of land (another contractual obligation that villeins had to their lord), and provided livestock with a healthy food source and a new grazing area so that the fields in which they were previously grazing could replenish their grasses or be cultivated for other crops. Often fields used as pastures would be rotated for other uses so that crops could benefit from the manuring the land received as a result of the grazing livestock.

Community regulations also helped to protect the poorest members of the community and the elderly. The right to the gleaning of the fields—collecting loose beans and other produce dropped during the harvest—was reserved for the most fragile of the poor and elderly. The community was willing to help out its own poor through the privilege of gleaning, but there were strict regulations about who could do so and when. Able-bodied individuals found gleaning, when they could be working for wages during harvest, would be fined, and the poor of other villages were prohibited from gleaning. The gleaning privilege was a means of supporting the community, not a means of supporting the poor in general (Keen 54).

MAINTAINING COMMUNITY MORAL STANDARDS

Reeves were the officials in charge of both controlling the communal activities of the farm as well as ensuring consistency in the requirements of services between all villeins. Reeves were not only in charge of enforcing regulations as they applied to farm labor, but they were the community's principal agent in charge of enforcing its moral standards, standards set primarily by the same relatively well-off group of peasants who elected the reeve each year. Anyone who did not conform to the standards set by the community could be fined and brought before the manor court. Misbehavior in the form of poor work habits, drunkenness, or promiscuity could result in a fine, and recurrent fines could eventually result in a tenant's eviction from the community (McIntosh 3). Drunkenness was not an uncommon occurrence, and the brewing and selling of ale was a common way for wives to improve the economic situation of the household. Even in the fields it seems that drinking was acceptable, as many of the tenant agreements for special harvest work periods stipulate that each worker should receive a given amount of ale each day, often one gallon per worker (Gies and Gies 140). The reeve planned for all the provisions for events such as harvest workdays in accordance with the lord's orders and the community's expectations.

However complicated the management of a farm became, it always fell on the reeve to balance the accounts of the lord's farm, and often this balancing of accounts required the reeve to give money from his own pocket to the lord (Gies and Gies 55). For all his work the reeve received no salary, but he was released from his villeinage obligations to the lord. In addition to not having to farm the manor land, he received concessions in terms of the right to pasture his own animals with the lord's herd, and he took at least some of his meals at the manor house. It may be that the job of reeve was made profitable by what was not recorded in the reeve rolls, but, obviously, there is no official record of what is not recorded in the account books. Chaucer maintains that the Canterbury Reeve had an outstanding ability to balance his books to his lord's approval and his personal benefit. Chaucer tells us that:

> Wel koude he kepe a gerner and a bynne;
> Ther was noon auditor koude on him wynne.
>
> ("General Prologue" 594–595)

> [Well could he keep a granary and a bin;
> There was no auditor who could win against him.]

The reeve would have understood the accounts of the farm better than anyone else, putting him in an excellent position from which to exploit his knowledge. Chaucer implies that his Reeve has used his superior knowledge of the manor farm to steal from the lord; not only has the Reeve stolen from him, but he has done it so craftily that when the lord is in need of something that the Reeve has unethically acquired, the Reeve lends it back to the lord and receives thanks for his generosity:

> His lord wel koude he plesen subtilly
> To yeve and lene him of his owene good,
> And have a thank, and yet a coat and hood.
>
> ("General Prologue" 610–612)

> [His lord he could please subtly
> To giving and loaning him some of his own goods,
> And get his thanks, and yet a coat and hood.]

Even though many reeves were expected to profit from their position on the manorial farm, the position of reeve was not always one coveted by the peasantry. Numerous communities had to enforce laws that made the peasant elected as reeve accept his responsibilities; these communities often rotated the responsibilities so that no one had to accept the duty too often (Williamson 53). In some villages one could pay a fee to be absolved of having to serve as reeve for a year.

As land grew more scarce in the fourteenth century, the composition of the community became more confusing. More and more villeins began to split their holdings up among numerous tenants, making the job of the reeve even more difficult (Mertes 92). There was not enough land for all villeins to have large tracts so many made their living as laborers on others' lands as well as obtaining what little land they could for themselves. It was not uncommon for large tracts of land, which in earlier years were assigned to one tenant, to be controlled by numerous farmers, sometimes more than ten. Reeves now had to keep track of the movements of many more people and the individual responsibilities owed to the lord by each person were proportionally lower. To resolve the unwieldy number of individuals responsible for the duties once owed by one man, the reeves often held tracts of land accountable for the same responsibilities and let the individuals determine who would provide what to the lord. In situations where the land had been divided among family members, this was more feasible than in instances where small tracts of land were sold off to entire strangers. Eventually, new means of collecting the services due to the lord were necessary to simplify the reeve's accounts and to ensure that the lord continued to profit from his farm. Converting the tenants' responsibilities to pure rent payments, divisible equally among all of the landholders, was the most common solution.

Although land scarcity in the fourteenth century made the reeve's job more complicated in terms of discerning individual responsibilities, the reeve had always needed a quick wit and a resourceful knowledge of farm husbandry. "The medieval manor was a well supervised business operation and the reeve who played so central a role in it was not the dull-witted clod traditionally evoked by the words 'peasant' and 'villein' " (Gies and Gies 55). Reeves were chosen from among the wealthiest peasants, and at a time when one's livelihood was directly determined by one's ability to run a profitable farm each and every year, the fact that reeves were successful villeins testifies to their resourcefulness. But the resourcefulness of reeves was a double-edged sword, both to the village and the lord. The village needed a resourceful individual to ensure that they as a community prospered, but the reeve was at least as interested in furthering his own conditions as he was in helping the community. The lord also benefited from a capable farmer/businessman in the position of reeve, but the more competent the reeve, the more likely he would be able, if so inclined, to abuse the benefits of his office, while presenting the lord with reasonably believable books. Most nobles thought it wise to check the reports of their reeves closely (Gies and Gies 56). Many lords found that setting quotas in the areas of livestock, produce, and rent collections made it possible for them to be assured that the reeve produced an acceptable profit for them each year, but these quotas made it even more likely that a reeve would increase production so that he could line his pockets with whatever surplus there was over and above the quotas.

THE REEVE'S RELATIONS TO OTHER MEDIEVAL PROFESSIONS

As peasants, reeves had no formal education; thus they needed the services of clerks in order to formally prepare the accounts of the farm for the year. This relationship between the reeve and clerk may be one reason why Chaucer's Reeve is partial to clerks. Certainly, the reeve's superior knowledge of farming combined with the formal education of the clerks created a combination most ably equipped to balance the manor's books to the lord's expectations. It is quite possible that clerks may have benefited from an accounting of the lord's resources which would be acceptable to the lord and profitable to the reeve. Although historians are not quite in agreement about the relationship between reeves and clerks—most find the reeve went to the clerks only to write out the formal reeve roll—Chadwick in his discussion of medieval life as depicted in Langland's *Piers Plowman* (ca. 1362) asserts that at least some reeves actually had clerks working for them. Chadwick finds that Langland's poem suggests reeves and clerks were two reasons why lords should look closely at their accounts (56).

Osewold's (Chaucer's Reeve) selection of clerks to serve as main characters in his tale is often attributed to the fact that, in his attempt to requite the Miller he is borrowing the Miller's use of a clerk to cuckold a carpenter (Osewold's second profession) and going it one better by employing two clerks to embarrass a miller. Julia Holloway explains the antipathy between the Miller and the Reeve in terms of their being established as opposites, both in the "General Prologue" and in their respective prologues and tales. While the Miller leads the pilgrimage riding at the head of the group, the Reeve "rides ever the hynderesste." The Miller is a stout, relatively young man, and the Reeve is a lean old man. Holloway asserts that, while the Reeve is a northerner from Norfolk, it appears at least from the Miller's oaths to St. Thomas of Kent that the Miller is a southerner (100). One striking reason for the antipathy between the two is the result of the Reeve's position within medieval society. Certainly, Chaucer's Reeve is presented as being unethical and willing to abuse the powers of his office for his own gain, but as a reeve he may have taken very seriously his roles of protecting both the other peasants of the community and the profits of his lord's farm. Chaucer's Miller was a cheat, using his thumb of gold to increase the weight of the products he milled in order to increase the customer's fee. Osewold would be familiar with this type of individual, and much of his professional life would have been devoted to not being cheated by such a miller and to protecting his community as best he could from any unscrupulous tradesmen. Reeves and millers would be almost natural enemies, each trying to maximize his profits by getting what he deserves from a transaction, plus whatever else he could acquire by cleverly outwitting his opponent.

The clean-shaven, closely cropped reeve does not seem the type to begin a public argument (in his personal life, as in his personal appearance, he attempts to keep his accounts as neat as possible), but it is the Miller's tale of a cuckolded carpenter which activates the Reeve's professional aptitude for squaring accounts and outwitting opponents. Chaucer tells us that Osewold is a carpenter, and some critics have suggested that this is merely a device intended to facilitate the rivalry between the Miller and the Reeve (Cooper 114). Although reeves were selected for their farming abilities, managing skills, and social status, carpentry was also a necessary profession in all medieval villages (Gies and Gies 149). Each villein household was responsible for the building and upkeep of their homes and could be fined (by the reeve) for noncompliance. Although all peasants did some of their own carpentry, most villages had professional craftsmen as well. In a smaller village, this craftsman may not have had enough demand for his services to support his family. Often tradesmen in such a village farmed first and practiced their trades second in order to supplement the family income. The reeve's status as a carpenter implies that he may have fallen into this category; he certainly takes enough pride in his skills as a carpenter to be passionately offended by the Miller's story.

SETTLING ACCOUNTS

The Reeve both begins and ends his tale by referring to his desire to "quite" (requite) the Miller. It is generally agreed that Osewold's fabliau about a miller, whose wife is cuckolded and daughter is deflowered by two clerks, is a direct attack against the Miller and is meant as a form of retribution for the insult the Reeve felt because of the Miller's tale. Osewold's attempt to even the score seems appropriate for one whose job it was to collect what was due to the lord and balance the accounts. His tale is an attempt at balancing the accounts, but it seems that the Reeve is not merely interested in collecting what is due (evening the score); he also wants to exact a degree of interest over and above what would settle the account.

The Reeve, it seems, intends his tale as a direct assault on the Miller, and his claims to the truth of the tale are arguably made in order to create the appearance that Robyn (the Canterbury Miller) and Simkin (the Reeve's miller) are one and the same. Osewold is attempting within his truthful tale (he makes a claim for his story's "verray Sooth") to portray a miller very similar, if not identical, to Robyn (Kiser 128). Because Osewold sees himself portrayed in the gullible carpenter of the Miller's tale, he wants to ensure that his audience identifies Robyn with the miller in his story.

The source of the Reeve's "true story" of a miller is found in at least two French tales and quite possibly in one Flemish tale. All three stories concern a miller and his family who try to outwit two clerks and who in turn receive some degree of sexual degradation at the hands of the clerks. Although Chaucer is more likely to have known the two French versions of the story, *De Grombert et des deux clers* and *Le Meunier et les .II. clers,* Peter Beidler advances a convincing argument that the Flemish tale *Een bispel van .ii. clerken* contains occurrences similar to Chaucer's tale which neither of the French tales possesses (291). Whichever of the sources Chaucer chose to borrow from, what is interesting in his version of the tale are the ways that the story is altered to make the miller look more contemptible and more like Robyn. Helen Cooper explains:

The opening descriptions of the dishonest, violent and bald miller and his proud wife have no parallels in the analogues, and their daughter is rather less attractive than she is elsewhere. Chaucer's version is clearly not a simple translation of any source; and the immediate stimulus to many of the changes he makes is the *Miller's Tale* itself. It is the potential for parallelism in the two plots that makes him put this story here, so that the Reeve can "quite" the Miller with his tale. That the location is Cambridge and that the Miller's name for the cuckolded carpenter, John, now belongs to the man who cuckolds the miller are both inspired by the Miller's Tale. The description of Simpkin with his dishonesty, his wrestling skills, his weapons kept handy (he has four, from a sword to a knife), his broad nose and his ability to play the pipes are all reminiscent of the pilgrim Miller as described in the General Prologue. (111)

Just as the Reeve's tale seems suitable to his purpose of getting even with the Miller, the description of the Reeve (in the "General Prologue") and the tone of the Reeve's Prologue seem fitting to the type of man Chaucer seems intent on portraying. Cooper finds that "The Reeve . . . is the most clearly visualized" of all the pilgrims to Canterbury. His stature, his hair, and even his horse are described with more care than most of the other pilgrims (55). The clear presentation of the Reeve may very well reflect Osewold's resemblance to his occupation. He is presented carefully by Chaucer with no "outright accusations of dishonesty" (Cooper 55); his careful depiction parallels the way in which the manor's accounts would need to be carefully prepared for approval by the lord. Both Chaucer's presentation of Osewold and the Reeve's presentation of himself could easily be characterized as cunning. Certainly, a reeve would need to be cunning in order to be successful, and an ineffective reeve would be unlikely to have the leisure to go on a pilgrimage; most peasants lived barely above the starvation level.

Numerous details about the Reeve reflect his superior ability at settling accounts favorably. Not only does he have the leisure to attend pilgrimages and Chaucer's approval as one who "noon auditor koude on him wynne," but his depiction as a "Norfolk" reeve again emphasizes his parsimoniousness with money. Alan Fletcher explains that during Chaucer's day there was a societal stereotype that associated the people of Norfolk with fraudulence and deceitfulness. Some medieval documents indicate that the inhabitants of Norfolk were considered both "crafty and treacherous" (Fletcher 100). Fletcher points out that Langland also portrays Norfolk men as avaricious (102); to make the peasant from Norfolk a reeve as well would only multiply the audience's expectation that the Reeve would be greedy and deceitful.

Assertions like those made by Fletcher reveal some of the expectations that a medieval audience might have had for a character like Chaucer's Reeve, but other critics have noted even more abhorrent stereotypes evoked by the Reeve. Edward Vasta outlines numerous ways that Chaucer's Reeve fulfilled the stereotype associated in the Middle Ages with the devil. According to medieval beliefs, the devil, much like the Reeve, came from the North; entrapped and punished men (the Reeve seeks to punish the Miller); was stern and pitiless; was known for boasting, lying, anger, and covetousness (four traits extolled by the Reeve in his prologue); possessed a sharp wit; and was a shrewd thinker (Vasta 126–127). Chaucer's Reeve indeed seems to fulfill stereotypical expectations of reeves, Norfolkers, and the devil, but his vengeful tale is most clearly understandable in terms of his professional responsibilities alone. Osewold's status as demonic and a Norfolker only increases the audience's expectation that they are dealing with a corrupt and covetous reeve—a stereotype they may not have had to look far to find fulfilled. The Reeve's desire to settle accounts with the Miller, as well as exacting revenge above and beyond the Miller's insult, would have portrayed an individual that the medieval mind could have readily identified.

We can never recapture the thoughts of medieval readers of the *Canterbury Tales,* but by attempting to understand what certain archaic elements within the *Tales* may have meant to Chaucer's contemporary readers, we can gain a greater appreciation of the artistry that Chaucer employs in the creation of his characters and the stories those characters tell. Chaucer's depiction of the Reeve would not have been difficult for medieval readers to understand. Poetry of the Middle Ages may be notorious for its allegorical (extended symbolic) meaning, but as twentieth-century readers, we must keep in mind that, although poets sometimes obscured meaning for the sake of creating reader interest, some meanings that we find difficult are only made so by the temporal and cultural divide that separates us from medieval readers.

Although Osewold certainly would not have been identical to reeves Chaucer's readers knew, the type of reeve he was would have been familiar to them. They may have literally experienced the influence of unethical reeves in their own lives, either as nobles or as peasants. Attaining a glimpse of what medieval readers would have thought was common knowledge about reeves allows us a greater understanding and appreciation of the masterpiece Chaucer has created.

REFERENCES

Beidler, Peter G. "Chaucer's 'Reeve's Tale,' Boccaccio's *Decameron,* IX, 6, and Two 'Soft' German Analogues." *Chaucer Review* 28 (1994): 237–251.

———. "The Reeve's Tale and Its Flemish Analogue." *Chaucer Review* 26 (1992): 283–292.

Chadwick, D. *Social Life in the Days of Piers Plowman.* 1922. New York: Russell and Russell, 1969.

Chaucer, Geoffrey. *The Riverside Chaucer.* Ed. Larry D. Benson. 3rd ed. Boston: Houghton, 1987.

Cooper, Helen. *The Oxford Guides to Chaucer: The Canterbury Tales.* Oxford: Oxford University Press, 1989.

Fletcher, Alan J. "Chaucer's Norfolk Reeve." *Medium Aevum* 52 (1983): 100–103.

Gies, Frances, and Joseph Gies. *Life in a Medieval Village.* New York: Harper, 1990.

Harvey, P.D.A. *The Peasant Land Market in Medieval England.* Oxford: Clarendon Press, 1984.

Hatcher, John. "English Serfdom and Villeinage: Towards a Reassessment." *Landlords, Peasants and Politics in Medieval England.* Ed. T. H. Ashton. Cambridge: Cambridge University Press, 1987.

Holloway, Julia Bolton. *The Pilgrim and the Book: A Study of Dante, Langland and Chaucer.* New York: Peter Lang, 1987.

Keen, Maurice. *English Society in the Later Middle Ages 1348–1500.* New York: Penguin, 1990.

Kiser, Lisa J. *Truth and Textuality in Chaucer's Poetry.* Hanover: University Press of New England, 1991.

McIntosh, Marjorie Keniston. *Autonomy and Community: The Royal Manor of Havering, 1200–1500.* Cambridge: Cambridge University Press, 1986.

Mertes, Kate. *The English Noble Household 1250–1600: Good Governance and Politic Rule.* Oxford: Blackwell, 1988.

"Reeve." *Dictionary of Medieval Knighthood and Chivalry: Concepts and Terms.* New York: Greenwood, 1986.

Vasta, Edward. "The Devil in Chaucer's Reeve." *American Notes & Queries* 22 (1984): 126–128.

Williamson, Janet. "Norfolk: Thirteenth Century." *The Peasant Land Market in Medieval England.* Ed. P.D.A. Harvey. Oxford: Clarendon Press, 1984.

Chapter 27

A Sumonour Was Ther With Us In That Place

Chaucer's Summoner is the one pilgrim whom the poet treats with unmitigated scorn. Whereas the other characters of the *Canterbury Tales* have some redeeming qualities that endear them to the reader, the Summoner has none (Owen 79). His physical repulsiveness is paralleled only by his moral and spiritual corruption. The open hostility that the portrayal reveals has led scholars to wonder whether the character is based on a historical individual with whom Chaucer had contact. The poet clearly possessed detailed knowledge of the Summoner's ecclesiastical office as well as an understanding of its attendant abuses, and much of the hostility that Chaucer displays is related to the Summoner's role in executing his professional duties. Thus it is expedient to begin with an examination of the structure of the ecclesiastical court system and a study of the Summoner's occupation.

Much of the information about summoners has been drawn from the records of the ecclesiastical courts of thirteenth- and fourteenth-century England. The church apparatus of medieval England included a judicial branch that was responsible for punishing sin. This court system was hierarchical, and the summoner was one of the lowest officials in this vast superstructure. At the top of the institution were two men, the archbishop of Canterbury and the archbishop of York. The entire court system was under the jurisdiction of these individuals. However, the land was further divided into numerous smaller segments called dioceses, and each of these dioceses was managed by a bishop, who was the "primary judicial authority." But even the diocese was too broad an area to be administered by a single man, so the ecclesiastical courts had yet smaller branches (Thompson 41). The immediate delegate of the bishop's authority was the vicar general, who was allowed to hear cases in the bishop's place and who even had the authority to pass sentence (Thompson 46, 51). A further subdivision of the realm was the provincial chapter presided over by an archdeacon, whose authority was often exercised by rural deans (Scammel 7). It was at this lowest level that the majority of the litigation took place, and much of it was informal.

The ecclesiastical court had jurisdiction over a variety of offenses, including slander and libel, breach of contract, disturbing the peace, and perjury (Rodes 128–129). However, its predominant concern was with sexual misconduct (Hahn and Kaeuper 74), and these violations included prostitution and adultery (Rodes 130). Such offenses were handled at the lowest level of the court system, the rural chapter. However, some offenses were reserved for the bishop's judgment: "perjury in matrimonial cases, willful murder, usury, sins against maidens and nuns, assaults on clerks in holy . . . orders, . . . conspiracies . . . (Thompson 55–56).

The judicial branch of the Church was also engaged in the supervision of many social programs, such as the regulation of "physicians, surgeons and midwifes." In addition, the courts were responsible for licensing marriages, for administering the property of the dead, and for distributing poor relief (Rodes 130).

Proceedings in the judicial branch could be initiated in several ways. Charges could be brought by an interested party who witnessed a crime or who was victimized (Rodes 140). A charge of libel, for instance, had to be initiated by the victim, and often sexual offenses were reported by neighbors who had observed the flagrant illicit activities (Rodes 128). Proceedings could also be instigated when the king demanded legal action (Rodes 140). However, in the most common cases, charges were brought by the bishop or one of the bishop's deputies, licensed to ferret out transgressors and bring them to justice (Rodes 140). Among these deputies were the parish priests who were obliged to "denounce fornicators and other malefactors" (Scammel 11).

The punishments exacted by the ecclesiastical courts were various. Generally, the accused was compelled to submit to the court's authority through threats of excommunication, or on occasion, the court would seize the individual's assets (Rodes 142). When the accused did come under the court's auspices, punishment was dealt out summarily, with little opportunity for a lengthy defense (Rodes 141). The mildest punishment administered by the Church authority was the promissory oath, in which the guilty swore they would never again commit the offense (Rodes 135). Other punishments included fines and public beatings (Hahn and Kaeuper 77). Sometimes these penalties were interrelated. For instance, threats of monetary penalties could be used to secure the promissory oaths (Rodes 135), and the fines might be exacted with beatings (Scammel 18). However, the punishment that inspired the greatest fear was excommunication. Those who were thrown out of the Church suffered public humiliation as well as permanent alienation from society.

The administration of justice in the diocese needed to be monitored by those officials with the most power. This need was addressed by the obligatory visitation of the bishop and the archdeacon to the diocese at regular intervals. By law, the bishop was required to attend each section of the diocese once every three years, while the archdeacon was to visit annually (Rodes 137). However, usually the bishop did not live up to this obligation. His first act after his installment was to visit the diocese. At that time, the clergy and significant laypeople would gather at a convenient central location (Thompson 45); people accused of crimes would be summoned to account for their actions and to face punishment or acquittal (Rodes 135–136). After the bishop's initial visitation, further obligations were fulfilled by a deputy whose idea of justice might be to extort money with threats of prosecution (Thompson 62).

Because the court jurisdiction was quite large and the administrative visitations were infrequent, it became necessary to appoint officials who were responsible for guaranteeing the attendance of malefactors at court proceedings (Haselmayer 44). The common title for these individuals was "apparitor"; however, Chaucer popularized the name "summoner" with his portrayal in *The Canterbury Tales*. The apparitor was a vital part of the court apparatus because it was necessary to have an effective and methodical means of serving summonses. In official British records, the first mention of this occupation, dated 1237, reveals that former practices for bringing offenders to justice were irregular and inefficient. By the end of the same century, the position was widespread, existing in Worcester, Hereford, Exeter, Bath, Wells, London, Canterbury, and Winchester (Haselmayer 44–45).

Two basic classes of apparitors emerged that were defined by their affiliation with the upper administration of the diocese. The more powerful of these individuals was the apparitor general, who was employed by the bishop. This class of apparitor enjoyed jurisdiction over the entire diocese. The other category was the archdeacon's apparitor, whose scope was localized. That is, he was in charge of a very limited section of the district (Haselmayer 45–46). When the distinction between the two categories began to disappear, measures were taken to reestablish it. The distinguishing feature severing the dignity of the upper office from that of the lower was the designated means of travel. Only the bishop's official was permitted to ride on horseback; the archdeacon's apparitor was consigned to travel by foot. A record from 1338 reveals the distinction: " 'Whereas it was ordained that our archdeacon of Wells shall have one apparitor in each deanery of the said archdeaconry, on foot, and that no apparitor on horse henceforth shall be admitted by any subject of our said archdeaconry, except our general apparitor' " (quoted in Haselmayer 49).

There do not seem to have been any qualifications necessary to merit an appointment to the office of summoner, except perhaps literacy. There is some indication that the summoner, following the completion of an assignment, was required to write a report certifying that he had executed his task properly. A document delineating this practice is extant: "By the authority of which I peremptorily cited the aforesaid Mr. John Paxton on June 23rd, being found personally in the Cathedral Church of Chichester, etc., to appear of Monday, etc., in the said Chapter-house before you the Rev. Father or your Commissaries to do and receive etc." (quoted in Haselmayer 47–48). The literacy of many apparitors is confirmed by occasional references to these officers as "clerks." Moreover, there are records of former clerks being appointed to the position of apparitor. Johannis Sayer de Claketon and Robert de Baac, both former clerks, were made summoners in the dioceses of London and Bath, respectively. The necessary literacy of apparitors clearly elevates the appointment above the mass of occupations filled by the uneducated. There is even some indication that the office could be a stepping stone to a place of greater eminence. William de Grafton became a member of the clergy and was able to retain his position as apparitor, executing his duties through a deputy (Churchill 457).

The duration of the individual apparitor's office does not seem to have been stipulated by the ecclesiastical courts. Thus the tenure of each position varied from situation to situation. In some instances the position was conferred for life. The above-mentioned William de Grafton was the recipient of such an appointment. Others include Robert de Brassyngton and Thomas Elyngton, who were appointed for the period of life, with the privilege of naming a deputy to act in their absence (Churchill 457). One appointment was made for the duration of the bishop's rather than the apparitor's life (Haselmayer 46).

The apparitor's principal duty was not only to distribute summonses to individuals required to appear in the ecclesiastical courts, but also to guarantee that these individuals actually attended the hearing (Haselmayer 46). Commissions delineating the duties of the apparitor were quite complex:

Under the powers conveyed the man so appointed was to cite any ecclesiastical persons whatsoever, religious or secular, as well clerks as laymen of whatsoever preeminence, condition or state they might be, of the city diocese or province of Canterbury, to appear before the Archbishop, or his deputy, Auditors or commissaries in whatever causes, business or suits . . . or moved at instance of the parties and concerning all excesses or crimes committed, whose cognition and punishment belonged to the ecclesiastical court, or to the Archbishop's jurisdiction by custom or right. (Churchill 480–481)

As this quotation implies, the apparitor's opportunities to deliver citations were not restricted to those issued by the court. In certain dioceses, the summoner acted as an investigator, licensed to issue subpoenas at will: "The courts they served evidently turned them into policemen either by allowing them to cite verbally or by arming them with blank citations to be filled out at need; either way they could then circulate in the community and cite anyone they thought needed citing" (Rodes 138). This opportunity to cite broadly did not appear until the last quarter of the fourteenth century. In 1387, the bishop of Hereford appointed an apparitor and assigned him duties similar to those of a policeman, encouraging him to expose criminal offenses (Haselmayer 48).

Not all the summoner's tasks were related to the citation of criminal offenders. One function involved the search for the beneficiaries of decedent estates (Churchill 417) and the execution of other tasks connected with the "probation of wills'' (Haselmayer 46). The appointment of Master John Lynton reveals the emphasis on this aspect of the vocation:

[T]o sequestrate and keep safe the goods of all those dying in the province of Canterbury who possess goods in different dioceses and to cite the executors and administrators of their goods to appear before the Archbishop and his commissaries in that behalf, on a day and at a place to be fixed by him, to produce the testaments and to receive in form of law the administration of goods and to do whatever else is required. (Churchill 417)

In 1443 Archbishop Stafford selected Christopher Furneys for a position with similar duties. The apparitor was to call beneficiaries before the bench, sequester the goods of the deceased, and guard those valuables from ''inferior officials, correctors and ministers'' (Churchill 417).

Often the apparitor acted as a functioning member of the proceedings within the court session. For instance, in some cases, he performed the duties of a bailiff with the charge of shuffling the court participants about the chamber (Haselmayer 48) and calling for the presentation of depositions (Churchill 335). The anonymous medieval poem, *Satire on the Consistory Courts,* depicts a summoner directing people within the courtroom (Haselmayer 49). Other responsibilities were more dignified. There is evidence that some apparitors were required to take the depositions of witnesses who lived at a substantial distance from the court, a practice that can be observed in the commission of John Dawbourne, apparitor to Master John Perche (Churchill 401). Finally, the summoner could be a witness in some legal actions (Churchill 335).

Financial compensation for the position of apparitor was not substantial, and this led to many of the notorious abuses of the office. The apparitor's salary was a percentage of the court fines generated by the summonses he served (Haselmayer 50). If the summoner wanted to increase his income, he had to ferret out more sin; he had to bring as many people as possible before the judicial bench, and this meant pursuing sin with great zeal, both where it existed and where he could make it appear to exist. Thus much of his income was derived from ''petty graft'' (Haselmayer 50), and he became infamous for blackmail, bribery, and luxurious living (Rodes 138).

Perhaps the most contemptible practice of the apparitor involved the accusation of crimes against the innocent in order to extract money from them. An ample number of documents from the era detail this corruption among court officials. In 1350, a man impersonating an apparitor accused several Church officials of fornication with numerous women in the parish. However, the charges were not taken seriously, and the impostor fled retribution. In another case, John de Alleford, summoner in the County of Surrey, attempted to use his office to extort money from the prioress of Saint Mary in the village of Clerkenwell. He told her that the archbishop was too old to make visitation and that he had been deputized in that office. After being seized by officials, he confessed that his intentions were to wring money from the prioress (Haselmayer 53).

A specific method of extortion involved compelling the innocent to pay a fine "in order to avoid the inconvenience, danger, and embarrassment of prosecution" (Hahn and Kaeuper 81). Particular examples of this practice can be drawn from the ecclesiastical records of the late thirteenth century:

The inquest jurors say that John de Berstrete, the subdean, maliciously charged Gilbert Fitzwarin with adultery though he was innocent and had him summoned from chapter to chapter until he made fine with him in 12d. which he took from him unjustly.

Sibil le Walesch of Norwich was caused by John le Rodeprest to be cited before John the subdean of Norwich because there was a quarrel between them over the boundary between their properties. So he was amerced 12 d. unjustly before the dean. (quoted in Hahn and Kaeuper 83)

The British Parliament made an official complaint about the practices of summoners:

The said summoners make their summons to diverse people maliciously as they are going along in their carts through the fields, and elsewhere, and accuse them of various wrongful crimes, and they force people to pay a fine . . . or alternately the said summoner summons them 20 or 21 leagues away to two places on one day, to the great hurt, impoverishment, and oppression of the said poor Commons. (quoted in Hahn and Kaeuper 82–83)

Yet another abuse of the apparitor's office pertains to his leniency toward the guilty. The official would sometimes allow the malefactors to escape justice if they could make sufficient payment (Lumiansky 139). Some citizens complained that this practice encouraged further violations of the public morality, such as venality and fornication (Hahn and Kaeuper 87). However, this practice had an additional objective. The summoner would be indulgent toward sinners who offered to reveal the sins of others.

The various injuries perpetrated by the apparitors made them subject to the people's anger and sometimes even led to physical violence against them. In Hertfordshire a group of citizens attacked an apparitor and forced him to swallow the citation that he was commissioned to serve on a villager (Thompson 55). In 1304 the dean of Ospring in Kent, Richard Christien, assigned to deliver summonses for the archbishop, was hindered in the pursuit of his duties by a mob that injured his horse, stole his money, and tossed him in a ditch (Hahn and Kaeuper 85). In both Winchester and Hereford between the years of 1378 and 1383, an apparitor in pursuit of his duties was killed by criminals (Haselmayer 52).

Actions against the practices of summoners were not confined to vigilantes and criminals. Church leaders attempted to check the abuses of the local officials by imposing regulations. Archbishop Boniface tried to dictate guidelines for the office in his Provincial Constitution:

an apparitor or beadle whether of an archdeacon or other prelate in carrying out his work was to demand nothing by way of procuration or other servitude or service but to take the hospitality offered. They were not to use others for executing their orders nor might they pronounce sentences of excommunication, suspension or interdict save by special orders of their lords. (Churchill 456–457n)

In 1295 the diocese of Winchester dictated standards for determining the evidence necessary to summon people to the court (Haselmayer 44–45). The Council of London in 1342 condemned the practices of apparitors with great vigor, citing "the use of horses by apparitors other than the Apparitor General, the use of deputies, the use of boys as assistants, long and expensive visits with country clergy, and illicit collections of gifts at the consistory with threats to those who refused to contribute" (Haselmayer 54). Finally, Edward III in 1372 demanded that efforts be made to end extortion among Church and court officials (Hahn and Kaeuper 83). The lengthy period of time between these examples demonstrates that either the official regulations had no effect or their effects simply did not endure.

Geoffrey Chaucer possessed a detailed understanding of the corruptions of ecclesiastical officials. *The Canterbury Tales* contains portraits of two separate apparitors. The first of these is the subject of "The Friar's Tale," and the second is one of the pilgrims. It is in "The Friar's Tale" that we find a prolonged condemnation of the ecclesiastical courts and particularly of the summoners.

The Friar tells of the damnable practices of the Summoner and begins by revealing the official's efforts to blackmail parishioners. He observes the court's self-serving preoccupation with the sin of lechery, an obsession he attributes to the vice's profit potential. No "Lecchours" could escape "pecunyal peyne" (court-imposed fines). The summoner's ability to recognize fornicators and solicitors was the source of his income: "And for that was the fruyt of all his rente, / Therefore on it he sette al his entente" (1373–1374) ["And for that was the fruit of all his income, / Therefore on it he put all his purpose"]. The Friar reveals his summoner's professional secrets. The summoner hires spies who report offenses, and he offers some violators immunity from prosecution if they will agree to expose others:

> For subtilly he hadde his espiaille,
> That taughte hym wel wher that hym myghte availle.
> He koude spare of lecchours oon or two,
> To techen hym to foure and twenty mo.
>
> (1323–1326)

> [For subtly he had his network of spies,
> That taught him well where that he might avail.
> He could spare of lechers one or two,
> To lead him to four and twenty more.]

The summoner of "The Friar's Tale" hires pimps who "tolde hym al the secree that they knewe" (1341). These informants expose their own customers, and as payment, the summoner allows them to continue to operate. Yet another abuse involves the employment of prostitutes who lure men into sin, and when the liaison is exposed and the couple brought before the bench, the summoner releases the woman and fines the man (1359–1362). From this racket, the apparitor generates much money, but he does not report his profits to the archdeacon who would want a percentage; he runs a private swindle for his own enrichment.

The Friar also denounces the summoner's practice of accusing the innocent. In the long inventory of allegations preceding the Friar's narrative, the clergyman accuses the apparitor of bringing charges without a warrant and threatening his victims with excommunication if they refuse to comply with his demands:

> Withouten mandement a lewed man
> He koude somne, on peyne of Cristes curs,
> And they were glade for to fille his purs
> And make hym grete feestes atte nale.
>
> (1346–1349)

> [Without summons a lewd man
> He could summon, on threat of excommunication,
> And they were glad for to fill his purse
> And make him great feasts at the ale house.]

The final line suggests that the offenders could sometimes appease the summoner with food and ale. The victims are happy to obey in order to avoid having to appear in court and risk a conviction. In his tale, the Friar tells a story of a widow exploited by a summoner. The summoner confesses that the widow is entirely blameless, but he is confident he can make her pay by threatening her with litigation. He tells her that she must appear "Tomorn bifore the erchedeknes knee / T'answere to the court of certeyn thynges" (1588–1589) ["In the morning before the archdeacon's knee / To answer to the court of certain things"]. The summoner knows that the woman is too decrepit to make the journey and that she will have to pay in order to avoid excommunication for failing to respond to the warrant. She protests that she cannot survive the trip, that she cannot meet the fine of "Twelf pens," and that she never committed adultery or was summoned before the court in her life. The summoner even threatens to seize her property (her new frying pan) in order to compel her to comply. The woman curses the shameless apparitor and is abruptly rescued by the devil who, in response to her condemnation, carries the summoner off to hell.

The Summoner pilgrim, the second of Chaucer's portraits, is an archdeacon's apparitor, and it is clear from the depiction that Chaucer was quite familiar with the duties and requirements of the office. The Summoner pilgrim has been given license to cite the public at will, whenever he finds sin; he is not restricted to serving citations issued by the court. It is his duty to uncover corruption and to bring the guilty before the archdeacon's bench. He can even threaten offenders with excommunication if they resist his notice. Moreover, there is also some indication that the Summoner serves as a bailiff or a witness, since his pretenses to learning are represented by the few phrases of Latin that he gleaned in his long hours in the courtroom. If he only served summonses, there would be no reason for him to spend so much time at court. The shallowness of the Summoner's learning is also consistent with historical detail. There were no educational requirements for the office of apparitor, and it is fairly clear the Chaucer's Summoner has no intellectual depth. However, he may be able to read. After all, he does cite ancient authorities in the digression on anger in his tale.

In the "General Prologue," the narrator reveals that the Summoner pilgrim is guilty of many of the notorious abuses of the ecclesiastical office. He concentrates on the Summoner's greed and hypocrisy. The Summoner is described as hot and lecherous, yet he punishes lust in others. However, the Summoner is willing to be generous and overlook sexual transgression if he receives financial or material reward: "He wolde suffre for a quart of wyn / A good felawe to have his concubyn" (649–650) ["He would allow for a quart of wine / A good fellow to have his concubine"]. He controls all of the young people of the diocese because he knows their secret lusts and can bring them before the archdeacon at will. He uses this knowledge to wring money from them: " 'Purs is the ercedekenes helle' " (658).

The fact that the Summoner and the Pardoner ride together on the pilgrimage may be significant both in the racket that the Summoner runs and in his animosity toward the Friar. The Summoner and the Pardoner are close friends. They even sing a lewd song together in the "General Prologue." Perhaps their union extends to their professional activities. The Summoner profits from exposing sinners, and the Pardoner benefits from absolving them. This partnership may account for the Summoner's contempt for the Friar's vocational avarice. The holy man is stealing the Pardoner's business by shriving the sinful in exchange for money, and the Summoner has an interest in maintaining his profitable association with the Pardoner.

The Summoner's appearance, as described in the "General Prologue," is appropriate to his occupation. The Middle Ages regarded physical repulsiveness as a sign of spiritual and moral corruption (Andreas 142; Mann 137), and certainly the Summoner is the most revolting of the pilgrims. The narrator complains that the Summoner's appearance frightens the innocent: "Of his visage children were a aferd" (628). His body "bears the marks of vicious living" (Curry 37). He is afflicted with a disease called apolicia, a form of leprosy that results from "evil diet, and a hot liver, and the disordering of a man's complexion in his youth, of late drinking and great surfeiting" (Curry 40). The signs of illness can be seen in his "fyr-reed face," his "scalled browes," and "the knobbes sittynge on his chekes" (Curry 41). Chaucer also includes in his portrait the causes of the disease: "As hoot he was and lecherous as a sparwe" (626), and "Wel loved he garleek, onyons and eek lekes, / And for drynken strong wyn, reed as blood'' (634–635 [Curry 45]) [''As hot he was and lecherous as a sparrow''] and [''Well loved he garlic, onions, and also leeks, / And to drink strong wine, red as blood'']. The Summoner's physical condition is one of the hazards of his occupation. His work provides him too much opportunity to satiate his lust and to live riotously off of the populace.

The Summoner's countenance is not the only part of his person that is unpleasant. He has a disposition that is appropriate to one who makes his living cheating, threatening, and manipulating others. The Summoner's vulgar and vituperative tale is the product of a ''diseased and embittered scoundrel'' (Lumiansky 140), and his deep insights into the subtle extortion techniques of Friars is suspect. In the *Canterbury Tales,* the animosity between the Friar and the Summoner accounts for much of the conflict between the pilgrims. They exchange insults on three occasions, the most prominent examples being the tales that they tell about members of each other's profession. This resentment is traditional, resulting from competition between the two vocations to fleece money from the same victims (Lumiansky 131). Both individuals are extortion artists. The medieval Friar survived by begging and the Summoner by taking bribes (Lindahl 118–119). The rivalry for money was probably fierce since much of the English populace was quite poor, and the level of this resentment is illustrated in the animosity between the two pilgrims. As these two individuals attack each other in order to discredit the other's profession, they only succeed in exposing their own faults and weaknesses (Corsa 184). When the Summoner satirizes the Friar, he reveals much about himself and his occupation.

The Summoner is so infuriated by the Friar's narrative that he shakes like an ''aspen leef.'' A portion of this rage may result from a sense of frustration that the Friar is beyond his control. The clergyman is of lower social rank than the Summoner, yet the Summoner has no jurisdiction over friars, as the holy man is quick to point out:

> To telle his harlotrye I wol nat spare;
> For we been out of his correccioun.
> They han of us no jurisdiccioun,
> Ne nevere shullen, terme of alle hir lyves.

(1328–1331)

> [To tell his wickedness I will not spare;
> For we are exempt from his authority.
> They have of us no jurisdiction,
> Nor never shall, during all their lives.]

The Friar suggests that he will satirize the Summoner with impunity. The anger that the Summoner must feel, being forced to listen to the criticism of a man who is beneath him in social position, is aggravated by jealousy resulting from the friar's infamous wealth and political power (Lindahl 119). In his vocation, the Summoner must have ample opportunity to punish those who anger him, so listening to the Friar's admonishment and knowing that there is little he can do to penalize him must be particularly galling. This frustration accounts for the hysterical tone and the erratic construction of the Summoner's narrative (Birney 109).

In his tale, the Summoner details a friar's efforts to wring money from an unfortunate couple who have recently lost a child. The central emphasis of the tale is to reveal the holy man's hypocrisy and dishonesty: he lies about his concern for the couple's loss, turning the situation into yet another opportunity to get money. The Friar tells how he saw the child ascending to heaven in a vision, when in reality, he was not even aware that the child had died until the grieving parents told him. He uses the false account of his revelation to assert his favor with heaven, and from there, he argues that the couple should give him more money so that he can pray for them and help them to avert any other disasters (Allen 1). He even suggests that God's beneficence toward friars results from their lives of abstinence, and he condemns gluttony:

> "Blessed be they that povere in spirit been."
> And so forth al the gospel may ye seen,
> Wher it be likker oure professioun,
> Or hirs that swymmen in possessioun.
> Fie on hire pompe and on hire glotonye!
>
> (1923–1927)

> ["Blessed are they that poor in spirit be."
> And so forth all the gospel may you see,
> Where it more closely resembles our profession,
> Or they that are surrounded by possessions.
> Fie on their pomp and on their gluttony!]

This is particularly hypocritical since friars were notorious for eating and drinking heavily. However, the irony of the Summoner's accusations lies in the fact that he shares this flaw. He denounces friars for shamelessly manipulating and exploiting the poor, a practice that accounts for his own livelihood. Thus, in his diatribe against friars, he exposes the ruthless practices of his own vocation. The accusations against the friars are subtle indicators of the Summoner's own professional swindles. Both summoners and friars convince their respective victims that they must pay in order to stave off potential disaster. Thomas and his wife must give money to avoid any other misfortunes similar to their child's death, and the old lady of "The Friar's Tale" must pay to avoid excommunication and peremptory property loss.

Both the Summoner and the Friar, quite contrary to the obligations of their respective offices, cynically use a Church institution to gain wealth. The Summoner denounces friars for promising to pray for parishioners in exchange for money. At the same time, the holy man does not even bother to keep up with the couple's misfortunes, and when he finally hears of their loss, he does not offer comfort but tries to make them feel guilty in order to compel them to give more money. Clearly, the Summoner's Friar has no interest in the couple's salvation, but only in his own enrichment. This may be a legitimate claim regarding the behavior of friars, but the Summoner is equally uncommitted to the legitimate execution of his office. He breaks many of the laws that he is charged to uphold. The narrator suggests that the Summoner keeps prostitutes for his own enjoyment at the same time that he fines others for fornication. The Summoner exploits the legal system by forging writs with which he summons the innocent to court, and he blackmails the young who are unmarried and sexually active. In all of these enterprises, the Summoner places self-interest and desire for wealth above his obligations to the court.

The Summoner accuses friars of incurring the wrath and scorn of those who are the victims of extortion plots. Thomas, the bedridden man in the "Summoner's Tale," becomes infuriated by the Friar's insensitivity and greed, and to insult him, he deceives the Friar into a degrading position, breaking wind in the holy man's hand and obtaining the Friar's promise to divide the fart equally among his fellow clergymen. Here, the Summoner exposes his own professional hazards in his efforts to reveal the Friar's. The Summoner's activities make him the object of public scorn and even violence. In the prologue to his tale, the Friar indicates that summoners are "ybet at every townes ende" (1285), and the subject of the "Friar's Tale" is dragged off to hell on the condemnation of one of his victims. The Host of the pilgrimage reveals a subtle contempt for the Summoner, treating the official harshly while regarding the Friar with reverence (Mann 143).

Perhaps the part of the Summoner's narrative that most clearly reveals his character and occupation is the Friar's digression on anger. It is clear from the beginning of his tale that the Summoner is a man of wrath, and because of his profession, he has become accustomed to forcing people to oblige him. Moreover, he has ample opportunity to get revenge on those who offend him; he need only threaten them with a false summons. In the "Summoner's Tale," the Friar moralizes with Thomas when he perceives that the sick man has become angry. However, his digression on anger is more a warning against provoking angry people than a sermon against the damnable consequences of wrath (Birney 116). The holy man tells three moral anecdotes against anger. These include the stories of an angry potentate, of Cambyses, and of Cyrus the Persian. In each of these stories, he reveals the dire consequences of angering a vindictive man, and he concludes with a quotation from Solomon:

> Ne be no felawe to an irous man,
> Ne with no wood man walke by the weye,
> Lest thee repente.

> (2086–2088)

> [Nor be any fellow to an angry man,
> Nor with no mad man walk by the way,
> Lest you repent.]

The emphasis of the scripture is on avoiding the company of wrathful people. Perhaps this speech by the Summoner's Friar is intended as a threat to the Friar pilgrim. The Summoner has already been revealed to be unscrupulous, vindictive, and furious. In the fictitious friar's speech, he has included a warning against provoking him further and against keeping his company. After all, the ill-humored Summoner first initiated the tension between himself and the Friar in the Prologue to the "Wife of Bath's Tale," and thus revealed his readiness to argue and his tendency toward unrestrained anger (Lumiansky 131).

Chaucer's Friar and Summoner are portraits of two damned souls. In their rivalry for the money of the afflicted English peasants, they reveal each other's darkest professional secrets and open themselves up for condemnation. Chaucer was very familiar with the duties and corruptions of the apparitor. In exposing the Summoner's hypocrisy and depravity, the poet aims his satiric barbs at the corruptions of the entire ecclesiastical court system (Lumiansky 139). Perhaps the poet's portrayal of the Summoner is intended to be socially productive, inspiring a reformation of the apparitor's office and an end of abuse. In any case, it certainly reveals the hostility that the English populace felt toward corruption among governmental and religious officials.

REFERENCES

Adams, John F. "The Structure of Irony in *The Summoner's Tale*." *EC* 12 (1962): 126–132.

Allen, David G. "Death and Staleness in the 'Son-less' World of *The Summoner's Tale*." *SSF* 24 (Winter 1987): 1–8.

Andreas, James. " 'Newe Science' from 'Olde Bokes': A Bakhtinian Approach to *The Summoner's Tale*." *Chaucer Review* 25 (1990): 138–151.

Beichner, Paul E. "Baiting the Summoner." *MLQ* 22 (1961): 367–376.

Birney, Earle. *Essays on Chaucerian Irony*. Toronto: University of Toronto Press, 1985.

Churchill, Irene Josephine. *Canterbury Administration*. 2 vols. New York: Macmillan, 1933.

Clark, Roy Peter. "Doubting Thomas in Chaucer's *Summoner's Tale*." *Chaucer Review* 10–11 (1975–1976): 164–176.

Corsa, Helen Storm. *Chaucer: Poet of Mirth and Morality*. Notre Dame, Ind.: University of Notre Dame Press, 1964.

Curry, Walter Clyde. *Chaucer and the Medieval Sciences*. New York: Barnes and Noble, 1926.

Fleming, John V. "The Antifraternalism of *The Summoner's Tale*." *JEPG* 65 (1966): 688–700.

Gallacher, Patrick J. "*The Summoner's Tale* and Medieval Attitudes Towards Sickness." *Chaucer Review* 21 (1986): 200–212.

Hahn, Thomas, and Richard Kaeuper. "Text and Context: Chaucer's *Friar's Tale*." *Studies in the Age of Chaucer*. Ed. Thomas Heffernan. Vol. 5. Knoxville: University of Tennessee Press, 1983.

Harwood, Britton J. "Chaucer on 'Speche': *House of Fame, The Friar's Tale*, and *The Summoner's Tale*." *Chaucer Review* 26 (1992): 343–349.

Haselmayer, Louis A. "The Apparitor and Chaucer's Summoner." *Speculum* 12 (1937): 43–57.

Haskell, Ann S. "St. Simon in *The Summoner's Tale*." *Chaucer Review* (1970–1971): 218–224.

Hennedy, Hugh L. "The Friar's Summoner's Dilemma." *Chaucer Review* 5 (1970–1971): 211–217.

Levitan, Alan. "The Parody of Pentecost in Chaucer's *Summoner's Tale*." *University of Toronto Quarterly* 40 (1970–1971): 236–246.

Lindahl, Carl. *Earnest Games: Folkloric Patterns in The Canterbury Tales*. Bloomington: Indiana University Press, 1987.

Lumiansky, R. M. *Of Sundry Folk: The Dramatic Principle in The Canterbury Tales*. Austin: University of Texas Press, 1955.

Mann, Jill. *Chaucer and Medieval Estates Satire*. London: Cambridge University Press, 1973.

Merrill, Thomas F. "Wrath and Rhetoric in *The Summoner's Tale*." *TSLL* 4 (1962–1963): 341–350.

Owen, Charles A. *Pilgrimage and Storytelling in The Canterbury Tales*. Norman: University of Oklahoma Press, 1977.

Pearsall, Derek. *The Canterbury Tales*. London: Unwin Hyman Press, 1985.

Richardson, Janette. "Friar and Summoner, The Art of Balance." *Chaucer Review* 9 (1975): 227–236.

Rodes, Robert E. *Ecclesiastical Administration in Medieval England*. Notre Dame, Ind.: University of Notre Dame Press, 1977.

Scammel, Jean. "The Rural Chapter in England from the Eleventh to the Fourteenth Century." *English Historical Review* 86 (1971): 1–21.

Thompson, A. Hamilton. *The English Clergy*. Oxford: Clarendon Press, 1947.

Wentersdorf, Karl P. "The Motif of Exorcism in *The Summoner's Tale*." *SSF* 17 (1980): 249–254.

Zeitlow, Paul N. "In Defense of the Summoner." *Chaucer Review* 1 (1966–1967): 4–19.

Chapter 28

With Hym Ther Rood a Gentil Pardoner

ELTON E. SMITH

The Summoner and the Pardoner were oddly united in a pilgrimage to the Shrine of St. Thomas à Becket, martyred archbishop of Canterbury Cathedral. The Pardoner is one of the most ambiguous and therefore intriguing of the Canterbury pilgrims, and so many estimates have been made of his personality. In the development of Christian ritual and dogma, the earliest form of pardon was related to the baptism of adults by immersion, until the seventh century. A youth or adult claimed allegiance to Jesus and was baptized as testimony to that loyalty. This meant that all previous sin was thereby forgiven. However, infant baptism made that forgiveness meaningless, so that pardon increasingly referred to sins after infant baptism and before and after confirmation. The development of a subdivided design for life after death—Inferno, Purgatorio, Paradiso (Dante, *Divina Commedia* 1265–1321) was an elaborate formulation of the dogma that had been centuries in articulation).

In the Gospel according to St. Matthew, when Jesus, outside Caesarea Philippi, asked his disciples who he was, Peter replied "Thou art the Christ, the Son of the Living God." In appreciation, Jesus praised his perceptiveness: "Blessed art thou, Simon Bar-Jonah: for flesh and blood hath not revealed it unto thee, but my Father which is in heaven [Paradiso]."

Then, most significantly for the matter of pardon, he proceeded: "Thou art Peter and upon this rock I will build my church, and the gates of Hell [Inferno] shall not prevail against it. I will give unto thee the keys of the kingdom of heaven: and whatsoever thou shalt bind on earth shall be bound in heaven; and whatsoever thou shalt loose on earth shall be loosed in heaven."

This remarkable passage divides Catholics who consider it a gift to Peter and his successors, and Protestants who consider the rock (petra) which is the root of the martyred saint's Greek name, to represent Jesus who specifically claimed to be the Rock at the conclusion of the Sermon on the Mount (Matthew 8:24), or at least that the rock consists of "these words of mine."

The Catholic interpretation led directly to the primacy of the bishop of Rome, the crossed keys on the papal coat of arms, absolution, and excommunication. How will the power to absolve sin be exercised? According to the plenary theory of the Atonement, the Church was heir to a Treasury of Merit—all the forgiveness that flowed from the cross of Christ plus the merit from the calendar of martyred saints (Harris).

Remission of sin and the resulting satisfaction of the debt was performed by confession plus punishment. However, by "withdrawals" from the Treasury of Merit in the form of indulgences, the duration or harshness of the punishment could be materially reduced. This become especially important in relieving the deceased in the torments of the Purgatorio and ushering the cleansed sinner into Paradiso, and in the Last Rites whereby the sinner may die in a state of Grace.

The system quickly outgrew Purgatorio or the Last Rites. Around A.D. 258, when Bishop Cyprian (later to be martyred) knew the people of Carthage would soon face persecution, he granted a *libellus pacis,* or certificate of peace, en masse, absolving all the penitents of Carthage. At the Council of Clermont in 1095, Pope Urban II included in his encyclical: "Whosoever, out of pure devotion and not for the purpose of gaining honour or money, shall go to Jerusalem to liberate the Church of God, may count that journey in lieu of all penance"(Hastings). Thus a Crusader received an automatic indulgence; later, those who sent a representative to fight or who supported a Crusade by their alms could claim an indulgence.

As the veneration of holy relics developed, this also granted pardon by indulgence. By 1300, Boniface VIII granted indulgences of one-year duration for pilgrims to Christ's Tomb in Jerusalem and the basilicas of the Holy Apostles in Rome. In this welter of pilgrimage, relics, and Crusades, *The Penitential Books* developed to match precise indulgences of duration and vigor with psalms, fasts, mortifications, flagellations, Stations of the Cross, Hail Marys, social service, and so on. By 695 at Tribur and 923 at Rheims, these precise tables of indulgence were made official. Indulgences attached to holy objects (The Crucifix, Rosary, medals, beads, relics) were called "real." The "chief indulgences" were linked to a Crusade, a pilgrimage to Rome, Jerusalem, Compostella, Portiuncula (Assisi), or objects blessed by the pope.

Abuses were early recognized, the most historical being the activities of Johann Tetzel (ca. 1465–1519), Dominican preacher and inquisitor general of Poland. In 1503, 1506, and 1517 he preached indulgence missions for the Teutonic Knights along the Rhine and for the reconstruction of St. Peter's Cathedral in Rome. An Augustinian friar, Martin Luther, was so outraged that he engaged Tetzel in a famous theological debate. This is the basis for the canard that the reconstruction and enlargement of St. Peter's cost the Catholic Church the Protestant Reformation. The Lateran Council of 1215 countenanced the system of indulgences by regulating that a bishop might grant an indulgence for 50 days, an archbishop for 100, and a cardinal for 200. Even Thomas Aquinas accepted indulgences for the dead, and the whole system was further authorized under Sixtus IV in 1476. This official recognition provided the essential background for the activities of Chaucer's Pardoner.

But by 1667, the abuses of the penitential system had become so scandalous that Clement IX, as part of the Catholic Counter-Reformation, charged a commission of cardinals "to correct and suppress abuses, to do away with false, apocryphal, and indiscreet indulgences" (Hastings).

Perhaps the most compelling traits concerning Chaucer's Pardoner with his partner the Summoner are in terms of contrast. The Pardoner's traveling comrade is described as the "bourdon" [I (A) 673], or bass voice of the early organs, whereas the Pardoner is the treble "trompe" [I (A) 674], loud and shrill. The Pardoner claims to have come straight from the Papal Court in Rome, but admits that his personal origin is Rouncivale, the hospital of the Blessed Mary of Rouncivale, near Charing Cross, itself a cell of the Convent of Nuestra Señora de Roncesvalles in Navarre. Founded in 1229 by William Marshall, earl of Pembroke, John of Gaunt (Chaucer's patron) was one of its patrons. So notably corrupt was the sale of pardons by unauthorized persons that in 1382 and again in 1387 it was investigated and thus was satirized as a fraudulent charity in both popular song and writing.

The Pardoner's appearance—blond, lank hair and a Veronica handkerchief in his cap—was eccentric [I (A) 708], yet he was considered a "noble ecclesiaste," probably for his talent as preacher (well-supported by his tale). His voice was as high and bleating as a goat's, yet, when in village squares or on the church steps he sang out the popular invitation "Com hider, love, to me!" they came! So smooth was his chin that Chaucer swears he was a gelding or a mare [I (A) 691], yet later the enraged Host threatens to take his gonads in his hand and squeeze [VI (C) 952] them. Both these statements might be true; a "castratti," gelded for the continuance of his soprano voice, might be reduced to silence by the coarse threat to grasp what he obviously did not have!

He carries his Papal Bull of Indulgence, a pillow-case he claimed to be the Virgin's veil, a fragment from the sail of St. Peter's fishing boat, a cross of mixed metals, and a glass case full of pigs' bones, which he represents as the fingers or toes of wonder-working saints. He knows his relics are meretricious, yet he claims a Holy Jew's sheep-bone to be efficacious in ridding cattle or sheep of worms, stone, or scabs, and to stop the physical abuse of women by their husbands. He also carries a mitten which, worn for the sowing of seed, will guarantee a bumper harvest. Knowing the invalidity of his tokens, he yet claims such effectiveness that "Ne was their swich another pardoner" [I (A) 603] ["Nor was there such another pardoner"]. Indeed, his admissions of falsehood are in no sense confessional. He is boasting that believing nothing himself he can make others believe. The nineteenth-century Robert Browning, in describing the Renaissance "superbia" of the duke in "My Last Duchess," is studying just such blatant pride. Satan's "non serviam" in John Milton's *Par-*

adise Lost is of similar character: "Because I am the Duke of Ferrara, I am above the judgment of men; Because I am an archangel, I refuse to serve anyone, even the Highest."

The Pardoner chooses for his text *Radix malorum est Cupiditas* (I Timothy 6:10), yet preaching fervently and effectively against avarice in others, exclaims that he has no intention of imitating the holy poverty of the Apostles: "Nay, nay, I thoughte it nevere, trewely!" [VI (C) 442] ["No, no, I thought it never, truly!"]. He is not there to correct sin but to collect money. And nothing can stop him. The poor parson of the country church must stand aside and watch him collect more money from his parishioners in a single sermon than they have given to the support of the Church in a whole year because of the authority of his papal patent. And when he leaves, the elderly and children will be left in poverty, starvation, and disease.

When the poor parson is asked to tell a story, he obliges with a scholastic meditation on the Seven Deadly Sins. Called "beel amy" by the Host, the Pardoner is asked to tell a mirthful tale full of jokes. Swearing to do so by St. Ronyon, he insists on stopping for ale and food. The gentle folk on the pilgrimage disagree with the Host and require a "moral thyng" instead. So the Pardoner, a truly vicious man, will think up a moral tale while he drinks! He is the perfect instance of the sacerdotal theory that the office elevates the man. Personally repugnant, professionally he is superb at his job.

In his prologue to his own tale, the Pardoner uses the composite definition current in his age. Avarice is not only for money, but it includes gluttony, drunkenness, gambling, and lechery. The seven deadly sins were divided into two categories: spiritual—pride, envy, anger, sloth or despair; and carnal—avarice, gluttony, and lechery. Thus the Pardoner's interest is focused not on the spiritual qualities modern men might most deplore, but on carnal sins of the flesh with the longing for strong drink included in the longing for rare and vast quantities of food.

With professional pride he describes his customary church oration. Expressed in lofty language, with a voice sonorous as a bell, he delivers his memorized homily—always on the subject of avarice (perhaps better "greed" since it includes money, food, drink, and sexual desire "a joly wenche in every toun" [VI (C) 462]. First, he announces that he has come from Rome, via Rouncivale. Then he displays his Papal Bull to sell pardons, with the seal of the local lord on the document. In addition, he has bulls from cardinals, patriarchs, and bishops, so no cleric dare attempt to silence him. Using his few Latin words, he produces a devotional atmosphere before showing off his relics, which are efficacious except in cases of cardinal sins, including adultery (lines 378–388), which he will deal with in a private audience following the Mass. With these pardons he has managed to gain 100 marks (two-thirds of a pound or 13 shillings, 4 pence) per year.

His pulpit manner is almost ludicrous, a caricature, as he perches high in the raised pulpit, looking down on the people right and left below. Telling a hundred jokes, he stretches forth his neck while his hands gesture and his tongue clatters busily. Caring nothing about whether his congregation dies in sin, he reckons that many sermons are of evil intention, some to please and flatter the people, some hypocritical, vainglorious, and exalting hate, whereas he preaches not to free them from sin but to win their money. If some in the congregation are too important to debate openly, he will sting them by descriptions everyone will recognize. Though avaricious himself, he preaches against avarice and causes others to repent, but money, not repentance, is his aim. Using many illustrations, he preaches old stories venerated by and familiar to the peasantry.

Finally, although describing himself as a "vicious man" [VI (C) 459], he begins his moral tale—gripping, brief, powerful—one of the best short stories in existence. The tale is drawn out of the scourge of the Black Death, when half of Europe succumbed to the plague. Because of the Flemish reputation for drunkenness and gluttony, he follows three dissolute young gentry of Flanders, ostensibly seeking Death to kill the villain who has robbed them of their fellows. Profanely swearing by parts of Jesus' body (as if the Jews had not rent it enough), they delay, to let dancers, fruit-sellers, and singers arouse that lechery which is related to gluttony (Proverbs 20:1; Ephesians 5:18). Was it not drunkenness that caused Lot to commit incest unwittingly with his own daughters (Genesis 19:30–36) and Herod, full of wine, to order the beheading of John the Baptist (Matthew 14:3–12; Mark 6:17–29)? Seneca (3 B.C.–A.D. 65), the Latin moralist, pointed out that the only difference between the drunkard and the insane is that the insane state lasts longer.

Returning to biblical reference, the Pardoner reminds his hearers that Gluttony was the cause of the Fall of man (entirely superficial! Disobedience or rebellion are the proper themes of Genesis 3). So dear was the cost of this appetite for the forbidden fruit that the immediate consequence was the expulsion of Adam and Eve from the Garden of Eden, and the long-range consequence the necessity of Christ's sacrifice on the cross. Becoming very flamboyant, he first quotes the moderately coarse dictum of I Corinthians 6:13: "Meats for the belly and the belly for meat, and God shall destroy them both" (also Philippians 3:18). Then moving to barnyard medievalism, he graphically portrays the throat as the drunkard's toilet and cries out: "Oh belly! Oh stinking anus—full of dung and corruption, making a foul sound at either end" [VI (C) 533].

Developing the theme of gluttony, he expatiates on the trouble a cook takes to strain, pound, and grind a perfectly edible substance into a gourmet delight that will tickle even the drunken palate, knocking the marrow out of hard bones, treasuring everything soft and sweet, spicing with sauces and roots to renew the appetite of the satiated diner.

Wine first leads to lechery, violence, and wretchedness, and then makes the drinker disgusting, with disfigured countenance, sour breath, a body foul to embrace, and a voice so nasal it cannot even pronounce the name of the great champion of the Book of Judges, Sampson who, a Nazirite, drank no wine!

Making one thick of tongue, dead to self-respect, drunkenness is the sepulchre of man's wit and discretion.

Perhaps from personal experience, the Pardoner warns especially against potent Spanish white wine from Lepe, sold in the Fishmarket and Cheapside, London. In a stirring peroration to what is really a continuation of his prologue, rather than his tale, he cries: "Hearken, Lords! I dare say that all the sovereign victories of the Old Testament, granted by the Omnipotent God, were achieved by human abstinence and prayer" (573–577). Even Attila the Hun bled to death on his wedding night as the result of drunken revels!

Having finished with gluttony for food, drink, and sex, he now moves to gambling (gluttony for wealth). Gambling stands self-indicted as mother of lying, swearing, and murder, the wasting of time and property, usually accompanied by blaspheming the name of Christ (Matthew 5:34; Jeremiah 4:2; the Second Commandment, Exodus 20). Quoting from late Greek chronicles, the Pardoner depicts the scorn of Spartans for gambling Corinthians and of the king of Parthia who held the Greek Demetrius as a gambler, of no honor or reputation. He even mentions the numbers 7 and 3, prime in the game of Hazard, and the Holy Blood at Hayles (Gloucestershire), which was often invoked in British oaths.

Although an overlong preface to a superbly succinct tale, a stunning survey of social and religious evils of late fourteenth-century England has been provided. The tale itself is rooted in the medieval experience with plagues, the funeral bell tolling for a young man whose boon companions are on an all-night drinking spree. Speared to the heart by a man called Death, he was one of a thousand thus brought low. The three comrades with alcoholic bravado swear by God's Arm and Worthy Bones to find and slay the slayer of their friend (Leviticus 19:12). Within one-half mile, Chaucer injects the aesthetic chill by the majestic, enigmatic presence of an Old Man who cannot die. Skillfully, he directs the roisterers up a lane to eight bushels of gold coins. Drunkenness and avarice take over; the youngest poisons the drink he brings from the inn; his friends kill him in a mock duel; then the dead comrade kills them by the poisoned wine. The slayers of Death are slain by their own inhumanity and sin, although, in medieval fashion, the Enemy Fiend [VI (C) 340] is held responsible. There follows an outburst of denunciation by the preacher of traitorous homicide, wickedness, gluttony, licentiousness, gambling, and blasphemy, so unnatural in view of Christ's purchase of our salvation by his heart's blood.

Having shouted in denunciation and wept in pity, the Pardoner is now ready for his sales pitch. Congratulating them on their good fortune to have him in their midst and admitting that the pardon of Jesus Christ is best, he brazenly touts his bulls, pardons, and relics, making only one serious error. Looking about, he decides to start with the Host, "the most ensnared in sin" [VI (C) 479]; he offers to him the first kiss upon his relics for only a groat (Dutch coin).

In a profane rage at having been singled out as a notorious sinner (perhaps because he was a bartender and publican), the Host replies: "No, no! That would only convey Christ's curse. You would make me kiss your old breeches, swearing them to be saints' relics, even though smeared by your own excrement! [The anal and excremental humor of Chaucer]. But by the true Cross which St. Helen [mother of Constantine the Great, founder of the church of the Holy Sepulchre in Jerusalem] found, I would rather have your testicles in my hand than your holy relics. Let's cut them off and I'll help you enshrine them in a hog's turd'' [VI (C) 946]. With the Pardoner too speechless to reply to the coarse attack, the Host refuses to jest further with an angry man. The Knight, as appropriate to his station and personality, makes peace, so they kiss and the assemblage moves on its way.

The tale itself, one of the most vivid in British literature, has many forbears in Chinese and oriental literature, but its most striking resemblance is to the Gilgamesh epic of ancient Babylon, an epic of some three thousand lines which after a millennium of oral transmission was finally (Ca. 2000 B.C.) transcribed on twelve tablets for the great library of Ashurbanipal at Nineveh. When the hero Gilgamesh's best friend En-kidu drowns, the survivor vows to kill Death. His ancestor Ut-na-pishtim (the biblical Noah), who had survived the Great Flood, told him about a plant that conveyed eternal life. But when Gilgamesh carelessly left the plant unguarded, a serpent stole it away. When Gilgamesh turned to the shade of En-kidu for consolation, he received only the communication that a gloomy future awaits all the dead, king and commoner alike. In this earliest of forms, just as Chaucer later spelled it out, friendship leads to death, and death is triumphant—a tale well-suited to the character and vocation of the Pardoner: ''—And lo, sires, thus I preche, / and Jhesu Crist that is oure soules leche, / So graunte yow his pardoun to receyve, / For that is best; I wol yow nat deceyve'' [VI (C) 915–918] [''—And lo, sirs, thus I preach, and Jesus Christ who is our soul's physician, / So grant you his pardon to receive, / For that is best; I will not deceive you''].

Before he displays relics and pardons, the Pardoner, as double-dealing a pilgrim as any on the road to Canterbury, candidly shares the fact that Christ's pardon is superior to any he has to sell, perhaps indicating that some small measure of divine grace has rubbed off on him from his profitable dealings with holy things.

The history of the tortured relationship between crime and punishment runs the gamut from the horrendous blood feud arising from the rape of Dinah (Genesis 34) to the nineteenth-century buffoonery of the Lord High Executioner (Gilbert and Sullivan's *Mikado*) and his seriocomic refrain:

> My object all sublime
> I shall achieve in time,
> To make the punishment fit the crime,
> The punishment fit the crime.

After so savage an example of the unlimited "blood feud," the *lex talionis* "Eye for an eye and tooth for a tooth" (Exodus 21:24; Leviticus 24:20; Deuteronomy 19:21; Matthew 5:38) seems remarkably restrained. However, toward the climax of the Sermon on the Mount, Jesus said that this landmark ethical advance was insufficient for citizenship in the Kingdom of God: "Love your enemies, bless them that curse you, do good to them that hate you" because that is the way God forgives (Matthew 5:45–48).

Hence, the first definition of grace is that great good gift that came to people because they did not deserve it, and the prime exemplum would be the Pardoner's frequent references to the death on the cross of the guiltless Savior for a guilty and unregenerate world.

However, the Pardoner would have no interest in free gifts; instead, he is permanently arrested at the stage of the *lex talionis*. To him, the forgiveness of sin requires penance: contrition of heart, confession of mouth, and satisfaction [X (I) 108]. Paying little heed to the first two, spiritual and oral, he is deeply interested in the third. The first two (*culpa*) are easy, but punishment (*poena*), on earth or in purgatory, may be very hard. This is the point at which he peddles his indulgences to shorten the duration or lessen the rigor of proper punishment.

If he prefers a penitential system to the free operation of grace, he is even more troubled by Paul's doctrine than by Jesus' largesse: "For by grace are ye saved through faith; and that not of yourselves; it is the gift of God" (Ephesians 2:8). Thus the Pardoner becomes the victim of a church that preferred Deuteronomy to Matthew; in turn, he victimizes for penance over free forgiveness.

REFERENCES

Blamires, Alcuin. *The Canterbury Tales.* "Medieval Intellectual Contexts," p. 21; "Social and Political Historicism," p. 26. Atlantic Highlands, N.J.: Humanistics Press International, 1989.

Bowden, Muriel A. *A Commnetary on the General Prologue to the "Canterbury Tales."* University of North Carolina Studies in Romance Languages and Literature, 1965. Pp. 177–207, 274–290.

Brown, Carlton, ed. Intro., Chaucer, *The Pardoner's Tale.* Oxford: Clarendon Press, 1963.

Brown, Peter, and Andrew Butcher. *The Age of Saturn: Literature and History in the "Canterbury Tales."* Oxford: Basil Blackwell, 1991.

Bryan, W. F., and Germaine Dempster. *Sources and Analogues of Chaucer's "Canterbury Tales."* Chicago: University of Chicago Press, 1941.

Chance, Vane. " 'Disfigured Is Thy Face': Chaucer's Pardoner and the Protean Shape-Shifter Fals-Semblant." *Philological Quarterly* 67 (1988): 423–435.

Chapman, Coolidge O. "The 'Pardoner's Tale': A Medieval Sermon." *Modern Language Notes* 41 (1926): 506–509.

Clouston, W. A. "Originals and Analogues of Some of Chaucer's "Canterbury Tales." *Chaucer Society,* 2nd Series: 417–436.

Coulton, G. G. *Chaucer and His England.* 4th ed. London: Methuen, 1921.

Curry, Walter Clyde. *Chaucer and the Medieval Sciences.* Oxford: Oxford University Press, 1926.

Delasanto, Rodney. "Sacrament and Sacrifice in the 'Pardoner's Tale.' " *Annuale Mediaevale* 14 (1973): 43–52.

MS Digby 86. Text printed in *English Lyrics of the Thirteenth Century*. Oxford: Oxford University Press, 1932.

Dinshaw, Carolyn. "Eunuch Hermeneutics." *Etude de la Langue Française* 55 (1988): 1: 27–51.

Faulkner, Dewey R., ed. *The "Pardoner's Tale": A Collection of Critical Essays*. Englewood Cliffs, N.J.: Prentice-Hall, Twentieth Century Interpretations, 1973. (Essays by Ralph W.V. Elliott and Robert P. Miller.)

Gibaldi, Joseph, ed. *Approaches to Teaching Chaucer's "Canterbury Tales."* D. W. Robertson, Jr., "The Intellectual, Artistic, and Historical Context," p. 129. Modern Language Association of America, 1980.

Gittes, Katherine S. *Framing the "Canterbury Tales": Chaucer and the Medieval Frame Narrative Tradition*. Westport, Conn.: Greenwood Press, 1991.

Haines, R. Michael."Fortune, Nature, and Grace in Fragment C." *Chaucer Review* 10 (1972): 220–235.

Harris, William H., and Judith S. Levey. *The New Columbia Encyclopedia*. New York and London: Columbia University Press, 1975.

Hastings, James, ed. *Encyclopaedia of Religion and Ethics*. New York: Chas. Scribner's Sons, 1915. (Articles on Johann Tetzel, Indulgences.)

Jusserand, J. J. "Chaucer's Pardoner and the Pope's Pardoners." *Chaucer Society Essays* 5:13, 421–436, 2nd Series No. 19. London: 1884.

———. *English Wayfaring Life in the Middle Ages*. Trans. L. Toulmin Smith. London, 1899; revised, 1921.

Lea, Henry Charles. *A History of Auricular Confession and Indulgences in the Latin Church,* 3 vols. Philadelphia: Lea Bros. and Co., 1896.

Luongo, A. "Audience and 'Exempla' in the Pardoner's 'Prologue and Tale.' " *Chaucer Review* 11 (1979): 1–10.

Malcolm, Andrew, ed. *Critical Essays on Chaucer's "Canterbury Tales."* Toronto: University Press, 1991.

Manly, John M. *Some New Light on Chaucer*. Lowell Institute Lectures. New York: H. Holt and Co., 1926.

Merrix, Robert P. "Sermon Structure in the 'Pardoner's Tale.' " *Chaucer Review* 17 (1983): 235–239.

Miller, Clarence H., and Roberta Bux Bosse. "Chaucer's Pardoner and the Mass." *Chaucer Review* 6 (1972): 171–184.

Mirus, John. "Instructions for Parish Priests." *Early English Text Society* 31 (1968).

Moore, Arthur K. "The Pardoner's Interruption of the 'Wife of Bath's Prologue.' " *Modern Language Quarterly* 10 (1949): 49–57.

Nichols, Robert E., Jr. "The Pardoner's Ale and Cake." *Publications of the Modern Language Association* 82 (1967): 498–504.

Owen, Nancy H. "The Pardoner's Introduction, Prologue, and Tale: Sermon and Fabliau." *Journal of English and Germanic Philology* 66 (1967): 541–549.

Owen, W.J.B. "The Old Man in the 'Pardoner's Tale.' " *Review of English Studies,* New Series II (1915): 49–55.

Owst, Gerard Robert. *Preaching in Medieval England*. Cambridge: Cambridge University Press, 1926.

Roache, Joel. "Treasure Trove in the 'Pardoner's Tale.' " *Journal of English and Germanic Philology* 64 (1965): 1–6.

Rowland, Beryl. "Chaucer's Idea of the Pardoner." *Chaucer Review* 14 (1979): 140–154.

Sherwood, Miriam. "Magic and Mechanics in Medieval Fiction." *Studies in Philology* 44 (1947): 567–592.

Small, J., ed. "English Metrical Homilies from Mss. of the 14th C." *Northern Homily Collection.* Edinburgh, 1862. Pp. 79–82.

Spearing, A. C., ed. Intro., *The Pardoner's Prologue and Tale.* Cambridge: Cambridge University Press, 1965.

Steadman, John. "Chaucer's Pardoner and the *Thesaurus Meritorium.*" *English Language Notes* 41 (1965): 4–7.

Tupper, F. "The Pardoner's Tavern." *Journal of English and Germanic Philology 13* (1914): 553–563.

Williams, David. *The "Canterbury Tales": The Historical Context.* Boston: G. K. Hall and Co., 1987.

Wright, Thomas, ed. *Political Poems and Songs.* 2 vols. Rerum Britannicatum Medii Aevi Scriptores, Rolls Ser. *ii,* 78, 1859–1861.

Chapter 29

Harry Bailly: Chaucer's Innkeeper

Thomas C. Richardson

The Innkeeper of Chaucer's *Canterbury Tales,* or "Oure Hooste" as the narrator identifies him, has received relatively little critical attention. Since he does not tell a story, he is most frequently discussed secondarily in the context of his encounters with other pilgrims in the links between tales, where with his blustery personality he engages in biting, frivolous, or comic dialogue with them, punctuated throughout by a great variety of oaths. Few studies are devoted solely to him. However, even though the reader does not have the advantage of a tale from the Innkeeper, his significance should not be underestimated, either in terms of the full development of his character or the function of his character in the *Canterbury Tales* as a whole.

The Innkeeper occupies a unique position in Chaucer's story. He is the only traveler on the pilgrimage for whom no tale is intended; he is also the only traveler who does not make the journey under the pretense of undertaking a pilgrimage. As a character, he serves as a narrative device for establishing unity among the tales; as "governor," "juge and repertour" of the pilgrims and their stories, he usually controls the transitions from one tale to the next. Most importantly, however, he changes the character of the journey itself. Once the Host has won the agreement from the pilgrims for his "voirdit," the destination is no longer the shrine of Thomas à Becket in Canterbury; it is the Tabard Inn in Southwark. The purpose is no longer the "hooly blisful martir for to seke"; it is a "soper at oure aller cost."

"Oure Hooste" is the Innkeeper for the Tabard Inn in Southwark, where the pilgrims gather to begin their journey, and he is identified in the Prologue to the "Cook's Tale" as Harry Bailly. Although one can only speculate on the extent to which Chaucer may have modeled his characters on real people, it is important to note that there were in Southwark in Chaucer's day both a Tabard Inn and an innkeeper named Harry Bailly.

J. M. Manly in *Some New Light on Chaucer* provides details about Bailly. A "Henri Bailly" was one of two burgesses representing Southwark in the parliaments of 1376–1377 and 1378–1379. The Subsidy Roll for Southwark for 1380–1381 includes "Henricus Bailiff, Ostyler, Christian Uxor eius—ijs." Henry Bailly was also "one of the four controllers of the subsidy for Southwark" (79). Other records list a Henry Bailly as a witness to a deed (dated 1387) and a specially appointed coroner (dated 1392 and 1393). Manly notes that the statute pertaining to coroners requires that they be "chosen of the most lawful and wisest knights, who can, may, and will best attend upon that office" (82). It is also noted that Bailly was appointed because other coroners had "neglected their duties." Manly makes it clear that one cannot be certain that Henry Bailly was Innkeeper for the Tabard Inn or that all references to Henry Bailly are to the same person. However, he argues that it is highly unlikely that there was more than one Henry Bailly, so that one may "safely conclude that the host of the Tabard in Chaucer's day actually was named Harry Bailly and consequently that the Host of the *Canterbury Tales* was modeled upon him" (83).

Manly further argues that the Host's wife is also named in the *Canterbury Tales*, although his attempts to connect the Host's wife in the *Tales* to the extant records are far from convincing. In the Prologue to the "Monk's Tale," following the narrator's "Tale of Melibee," the Host mentions his wife, who has not accompanied him on the pilgrimage:

> I hadde lever than a barel ale
> That Goodelief, my wife, hadde herd this tale!
>
> (VII.1893–1894)

> [I would rather than a barrel of ale
> That if Goodlief, my wife, had heard this tale!]

Manly asserts that "Goodelief" is correctly written as one word, not as "goode lief" as earlier editors had done, and that Goodelief is the name of Harry Bailly's wife. To support his case, he relies on Professor Rickert's research into fourteenth-century records that indicate frequent references to "Godlef" as a woman's name. Manly also honestly admits that he cannot convincingly connect this name with the "Christian" of the Subsidy Roll, other than speculation that Goodelief might have been a second wife or that Chaucer simply used a different name (81). Regardless of the factual basis for the Innkeeper's spouse, it is to be expected that the Innkeeper's wife assisted him in the business and played a substantial role in both the business and social life related to the innkeeping trade. In the context of Chaucer's story, no doubt the Host's wife ran the inn while the Host was away.

The narrator of the *Canterbury Tales* describes the Tabard Inn as a spacious, comfortable inn for travelers and their horses, and the Host provided food, drink, and service appropriate to a high-class lodging establishment:

> The chambres and the stables weren wyde,
> And wel we weren esed atte beste.
>
> . . . .
>
> (I.28–29)
>
>   Greet chiere made oure Hoost us everichon,
> And to the soper sette he us anon.
> He served us with vitaille at the beste;
> Strong was the wyn, and wel to drynke us leste.
>
> (I.747–750)
>
> [The chambers and the stables were wide,
> And well we were accommodated at best.
>
> . . . .
>
>   Great cheer had our Host for every one of us,
> And to the dinner he set us immediately.
> He served us with victuals of the best sort;
> Strong was the wine, and we were pleased to drink.]

The extant documents regarding the Tabard and similar inns would lend credence to the narrator's superlative descriptions. The function of the fourteenth-century inns, by law, was to lodge travelers and their horses. The inns tended to cater to middle- and upper-class travelers who desired—and could afford—luxury accommodations. Martha Carlin, in her significant study of medieval Southwark, points out that innkeepers often rejected pedestrians because the innkeepers' major profits came from the sale of food and alcoholic beverages rather than the lodging itself (559). Muriel Bowden also notes that there are records of numerous complaints about the high cost of inns outside of London in the fourteenth century (292). Even into the sixteenth century William Harrison continues to praise the quality of the inns: "we have plentie of ale, beere, and sondrie kinds of wine, and such is the capacitie of some of them that they are able to lodge two hundred or three hundred persons, and their horsses at ease, and thereto with a verie short warning make . . . provision for their diet." Innkeepers competed for "goodnesse of interteinement of their ghests, as about finesse and change of linnen, furniture of bedding, beautie of roomes, service at the table, costlinesse of plate, strengthe of drinke, varietie of wines, or well using of horsses." They also competed for the "gorgeousness" of their signs (quoted in Carlin 556).

Even with the substantial incomes from their lawful business of receiving and feeding lodgers, most of the innkeepers of Southwark "had a second major source of income in the illegal markets that they allowed or maintained in their inns and inn-yards" (Carlin 559), primarily from the illegal sale of dairy products and poultry but some also from the sale of drink to nonlodgers and in some cases even in prostitution. Victuallers were supposed to have rights to the sale of food on and off premises, and taverns existed for the sale and consumption of alcoholic beverages. Separate houses of prostitution existed as well. Although there were distinctive regulations for innkeepers, victuallers, tavern-keepers, and prostitutes, certainly the innkeepers had the advantage of being able to provide for all their travelers' ''needs'' in a place where regulations were rarely enforced.

Most of the property in the Southwark of Chaucer's day was owned by the Church; the site of the Tabard is no exception. The abbot of Hyde acquired the site of the Tabard and adjoining tenements in 1304–1306, and the abbey retained the property until 1538. The property consisted of two tenements. The northern tenement is described ''as measuring in width 20-3/4 ells plus one inch [77.9 feet] on the streetside, twenty-two ells [82.5 feet] 'in the middle, in the garden,' and 33-1/4 ells plus one inch [124.78 feet] at the east end, along the common ditch of Southwark. The southern tenement was described in a grant of 1298 as containing a hall and a chamber with a stone wall, a kitchen with a brewhouse, adjacent solars, and a gate with a shop on its north side. There also were two shops on the south side of the gate that were not included in the grant'' (Carlin 225).

The lease of the Tabard in 1538 provides some mention of the inn's features, ''notably the stables, yard and privies, and a newly-built house or 'lodgynge' with glazed and latticed windows, adjoining the kitchen on the south side of the well'' (Carlin 554–555). An inventory of the Tabard included ''two parlors . . . ; a hall with a trestle table and benches; a kitchen with a well in it; two cellars; seven chambers . . . ; a 'drynkynge bower' containing a table nailed to two posts, two benches, six boards and three wicker lattices; two adjacent tenements; and a courtyard with a well and a watering trough'' (Carlin 555).

The Tabard Inn, like other inns and taverns, was identified by the sign in front of the establishment. The sign displayed a *tabard,* a sleeveless or sleeved jacket bearing an embroidered heraldic coat of arms. As John Stow notes:

Amongst the [inns], the most auncient is the Tabard, so called of the signe, which as we now tearme it, is of a Iacquit, or sleevelesse coat, whole before, open on both sides, with a square coller, winged at the shoulders: a stately garment of old time, commonly worne of Noble men and others, both at home and abroad in the warres, but then (to wit in the warres) their Armes embrodered, or otherwise depict upon them, that every man by his coate of Armes might be knowne from others. (2: 62)

The fact that the Tabard Inn is in Southwark, and not London, is also significant, both in terms of the realism of the pilgrimage story and in the thematic function of the character of the Innkeeper—and for better reason than the fact that in the first half of the fourteenth century, the poet's step-grandfather, Richard Chaucer, a vintner, was a property owner in Southwark. Martha Carlin summarizes the character of Southwark in Chaucer's time:

Medieval Southwark was a chimera. It was a suburb of London but outside the City's jurisdiction; a Parliamentary borough without a charter of incorporation; a collection of autonomous manors; a haven of criminals and forbidden practices in the shadow of the City of London and the royal court and law courts at Westminster. . . . To the Londoners of its own day, medieval Southwark was simultaneously a dumping-ground of unwanted industries and residents, a commercial rival, an administrative anachronism and a perpetual jurisdictional affront. (7)

Although there may have been some disadvantages in being a "dumping ground," being outside the jurisdictional control of London was obviously advantageous to the growth of the innkeeping trade. From the second half of the fourteenth century through the sixteenth century, Southwark "developed something of a specialized industry in innkeeping, and also became a center for victualling, brewing and alehouse-keeping" (Carlin 540). Although the evidence concerning the development and character of innkeeping in Southwark is not extensive, it is clear that there was a flourishing and growing innkeeping industry in fourteenth-century Southwark.

There are several reasons why this trade might have developed so successfully at the time. Located across the Thames and to the south and east of the city, Southwark was the major gateway to and from London from southern England and the Continent. The expansion of the innkeeping trade naturally corresponded with the increasing political, commercial, and legal importance of London. Also, Southwark was outside the gates to the city of London, so that travelers to and from the city could arrive at their lodgings late or leave early, when the city gates were shut. More importantly, however, Southwark was not subject to London's extensive and strict hosting laws in the late fourteenth century. As Carlin notes, London's laws stipulated "that hostelers be freemen (or else able to produce good character references and sureties), that they sell provisions for men and horses at officially-set rates, . . . that they be responsible for their guests and disarm them, that they lodge no evildoers and report all suspicious persons who arrived at their hostelries, that they keep strict hours" (547). Innkeepers of Southwark were subject to few restrictions, which were at most loosely enforced, and the potential profitability of innkeeping was much greater in Southwark than in London.

Finally, the prevalence of the Stews, or houses of prostitution, should not be overlooked as an attraction for travelers to and from London—or for travelers whose sole purpose was to patronize the Stews. Developing concurrently with innkeeping in the Southwark of the fourteenth century—and no doubt contributing to the innkeeping trade—was a thriving business for licensed houses of prostitution. The Stews were administered by the officers of the bishops, "the bailiff, steward and constables of their manor" (Carlin 478).

The Stews were always a source of controversy and concern among government and Church officials who debated the morality of prostitution and the criminal activity associated with the dissolute lifestyles of those who frequented the Stews and the taverns. In 1387, for example, the bishop of Winchester enjoined the staff of St. Thomas's Hospital against going to "taverns or other dishonest or suspect places." Ironically, however, the Stews were primarily on the property owned by the bishop of Winchester. Flemish women in particular were noted for prostitution, or at least were often singled out for criticism and attacks as part of a general persecution of the Flemish in London and its suburbs. Southwark brothels were raided during the Peasants' Revolt of 1381, and in a proclamation of 1393 Flemish women were forbidden from roaming about the city of London, day or night (Carlin 481–482). Attitudes toward the Flemish people are important in the *Canterbury Tales,* especially in the "Cook's Tale" and the "Pardoner's Tale."

The Southwark brothels were regulated, as were inns and taverns. Brothels were not permitted to lodge guests or to sell food and drink. Stewholders must be men, and payments to prostitutes were regulated. However, it was London more than Southwark that was concerned with the regulation of prostitution in Southwark. Since London had no legal authority over Southwark, the city was not able to impose legal sanctions directly against the Stews, although they tried several means of indirect control. London officials limited the prostitutes' accessibility to the city and the Londoners' accessibility to the Stews. For example, an order in 1391 from the mayor and aldermen of London would not permit boatmen "to bring any man or woman to the Stews between sunset and sunrise, nor tie up his boat within twenty fathoms of the shore during that time, 'lest evildoers be assisted in their coming and going' " (Carlin 483). Considerable efforts by London officials to keep prostitutes outside the city of London only contributed to the development of the Southwark trade. Furthermore, prostitution expanded from the licensed Stews to the taverns and inns. A complaint filed in Parliament in 1433 addressed the problem of "stewholders who had set up hostelries and taverns in the high street of Southwark, where they received thieves, prostitutes and other misdoers, just as they had done at the Stews" (Carlin 556).

The Southwark Poll Tax roll for 1381 includes several men and their households whose occupations were listed as "stuynmönger." Among those listed were "Richard Bailif and his wife Margery, with servants Constance and John" (Carlin 481). Records from the bishopric of Winchester indicate that a woman named Cristina la Frowe was fined for prostitution in the bishop's Southwark court (Carlin 479). Perhaps Chaucer's model for the Innkeeper of the *Canterbury Tales* is really a composite of "Baillys" in fourteenth-century Southwark and "Christian" was more than an innkeeper's wife!

Although the Innkeeper is not assigned a tale as a vehicle for insight into his character, his character is developed carefully and consistently throughout the *Canterbury Tales.* Through the narrator's descriptions and the Host's interactions with other characters, between what is said and what is not said in the tales, the reader comes to understand much about the Host and to speculate about even more—especially when Harry Bailly is set in the context of his role as Innkeeper at the Tabard Inn in late fourteenth-century Southwark.

The pilgrim narrator describes the Innkeeper as he does other pilgrims: that is, he presents his impressions—"so as it semed me"—drawn from the pilgrims in the short time they are all assembled in the Tabard prior to beginning the pilgrimage. Like his descriptions of most of the pilgrims in the "General Prologue," the narrator's preliminary description of the Host is full of complimentary terms:

> A semely man Oure Hooste was withalle
> For to been a marchal in an halle.
> A large man he was with eyen stepe—
> A fairer burgeys was ther noon in Chepe—
> Boold of his speche, and wys, and wel ytaught,
> And of manhood hym lakkede right naught.
>
> (I.751–756)

> [A seemly man our host was indeed
> To be a master of ceremonies in a hall.
> A large man he was with large eyes—
> A fairer burgess was there not in Cheapside—
> Bold of his speech, and wise, and well taught,
> And of his manliness he lacked nothing at all.]

The Host seems to be educated and wise, outgoing, an effective burgess, attractive, and not lacking in "manhood." According to the narrator, he has all the qualities necessary to be a marshal in a lord's hall. The marshal had supervision of the household as a whole and was in charge of the house in the lord's absence: "at all tymes of the day the marshall shall have his commondmentes fulfillid in every office of the house" (Bowden 293). He is also described as "a myrie man"—so much so that the narrator uses "myrie" or "myrthe" seven times in his twenty-six-line introduction to the Host in the "General Prologue." In spite of the fact that he sets up a competition for tale-telling based on the criteria of best "sentence and solaas," throughout the *Tales* the Host calls on the pilgrims to tell a "myrie tale" or a "jape," often disdaining, in fact, any serious attempts at tales of "sentence" or moral instruction, admonishing the Clerk, for example, to tell a "myrie tale" in plain language and keep his "heigh style" to himself. It is for the purpose of entertaining one another to and from Canterbury, after all, that the Host proposes the story-telling scheme (as well as to ensure their return to the Tabard Inn, where they will require food and accommodations for themselves and their horses once again).

At the conclusion of the "General Prologue," the Host seems to be well suited to the role of "governour" of the pilgrimage. However, as is the case with most of the pilgrims, the superlative descriptions begin to fade as the tales progress and as the narrator—thus the reader—learns more and more about the pilgrims through their stories and their interactions with one another. Apparently, even the Host's plan for the pilgrimage is altered. Bailly originally proposes that each pilgrim tell two stories on the road to Canterbury and two on the return to the Tabard, and the story teller judged by the Host to tell tales "of best sentence and moost solaas" will win a supper at the Tabard at the expense of all the other pilgrims. The Innkeeper proposes this plan after everyone had paid for supper—and, no doubt, he is certain that the pilgrims can pay for their suppers on their return. The Host's comments later suggest an adjustment of the plan, as he says to the Franklin that "ech of yow moot tellen atte leste / A tale or two, or breken his biheste" (V.697–698) ["each of you must tell at least / A tale or two, or break his promise"].

The Host speaks as if he is very familiar with pilgrims and pilgrimages, as if he had profited from this kind of arrangement before. Yet, it seems that for a governor of a pilgrimage the Host is much given to swearing, as if he is more accustomed to an association with a secular clientele than with religious pilgrims. At the conclusion of the Knight's story, the Host "lough and swoor," and consistently his responses to the tales include many and various oaths. At the end of the "Man of Law's Tale," the Host stands up in his stirrups and calls on the Parson to fulfill his obligation to tell a tale: "Sir Parisshe Priest . . . for Goddes bones, / Telle us a tale . . . by Goddes dignite! (II.1166–1169) ["Sir Parish Priest . . . for God's bones, / Tell us a tale . . . by God's dignity!"]. The Parson asks, "What eyleth the man, so synfully to swere?" (II.1171) ["What ails the man, so sinfully to swear?"]. The Host responds by swearing again, and the Shipman interrupts, protesting that he will not hear any preaching.

The Host begins the story-telling process by fixing the drawing of straws so that the Knight wins and tells the first tale, preserving a social order that is obviously important to the Host. The Host calls on the Monk to follow the Knight and tell the second tale, but he is quickly interrupted by the drunken Miller, who insists that he will "quite" the Knight's tale. The Reeve follows the Miller to attempt revenge for the Miller's story of a cuckolded carpenter, and the Cook responds to the Reeve even before the Host has a chance to comment. Thus the extent of the Host's actual ability to govern is very early called into question, and at several points in the journey (such as in the "Monk's Tale," the "Squire's Tale," and following the "Pardoner's Tale") the Host loses control of an orderly process.

By the time the Cook begins his tale—only three stories into the pilgrimage—the Host has become more than a "juge and repertour"; he has entered into the competitiveness among the personalities of the pilgrimage—a role that increases as the story-telling progresses. The incomplete "Cook's Tale" raises questions about the Host that only become fully realized in the "Pardoner's Tale."

The Host agrees to the Cook's request to follow the Reeve with "a litel jape," but not without first launching a brief but pointed attack on the Cook, accusing him of serving bad food in unsanitary conditions and hinting at the rivalry of the victualling and innkeeping trades:

For many a pastee hastow laten blood,
And many a Jakke of Dovere hastow soold
That hath been twies hoot and twies coold.
Of many a pilgrym hastow Cristes curs,
For of thy percely yet they fare the wors,
That they han eten with thy stubbel goos;
For in thy shoppe is many a flye loos.

(I.4346–4352)

[For many a meat pie have you let blood,
And many a Jack of Dover have you sold
That has been twice hot and twice cold.
By many a pilgrim have you been cursed,
For of your parsley yet they fare the worse,
That they have eaten your stubble fed goose;
For in your shop is many a fly loose.]

The Cook and the Host address each other by name, implying a familiarity that extends beyond one night together in the Tabard Inn. Roger the Cook responds to the Host by promising to tell a story about an innkeeper before the pilgrimage is over:

And therfore, Herry Bailly, by thy feith,
Be thou nat wrooth, er we departen heer,
Though that my tale be of an hostileer.

(I.4358–4360)

[And therefore, Herry Bailly, by your faith,
Be not angry, before we depart hear,
Though that my tale is of an innkeeper.]

The Cook is already prepared to continue the story pattern set by the Miller and the Reeve, so he delays his tale of a "hostileer." Although he does not tell the tale then, he promises the Host that he will tell it before the journey is over to "quit" the Innkeeper for his insults of the Cook. Nonetheless, the Cook's story cannot be completely divorced from associations with the Host. The "Cook's Tale" is about Perkyn, an apprentice in a "craft of vitailliers" who preferred the tavern, playing dice, and riotous living to his work. Perkyn had a friend whose wife "heeld for contenance / A shoppe, and swyved for hir sustenance" (I.4421–4422) ["held for the sake of appearance / A shop, and copulated for a living"].

Although the incomplete "Cook's Tale" is not supposed to be about the Innkeeper, there are several images that connect this tale to other clear associations with the Host. The setting of the tale in "Chepe" echoes the narrator's description of the Host in the "General Prologue"; the wife/prostitute whose shop is a cover for her brothel and the Cook's reference to the Flemish saying associate the story with Southwark and the Stews; and the story of the young man who loves the tavern and playing dice connect the story with the "Pardoner's Tale," in which the Stews, gambling, a tavern, and the Flemish figure prominently and which elicits such a violent response from the Host. The Cook, then, introduces a number of issues about the Innkeeper that are developed as the story-telling journey continues.

Besides his desire to be entertained with merry stories, the Innkeeper was obsessed with male sexuality. Of course, the narrator prepares the audience for the Host's special interests in his reference to the Host's own apparent manliness. Still, the Host is not merely interested in sexual stories; he comments on the story tellers as well. When the Host calls on the Monk to tell a story, he does so with extensive commentary on the Monk's manhood:

> I pray to God, yeve hym confusion
> That first thee broghte unto religioun!
> Thou woldest han been a tredefowel aright.
> Haddestow as greet a leeve as thou hast myght
> To parfourne al thy lust in engendrure,
> Thou haddest bigeten ful many a creature. . . .
> Religioun hath take up al the corn
> Of tredyng, and we borel men been shrympes.
>
> (VII.1943–1948; 1954–1955)

> [I pray to God, give him destruction
> Who first brought you into religion!
> You would have been an excellent copulator of fowls.
> Had you as great a leave as you might have
> To perform all your lust in the act of procreation,
> You would have begotten many a creature. . . .
> Religion has taken up all the corn
> Of treading, and we laymen have been shrimps.]

At the conclusion of the "Nun's Priest's Tale," which follows the "Monk's Tale," the Host uses similar language to refer to the Nun's Priest, again regretting that the Church has enlisted all the best men for celibacy rather than for sexual activity. The Host blesses the priest's breeches and testicles, and then continues:

> But by my trouthe, if thou were seculer,
> Thou woldest ben a trede-foul aright.
> For if thou have corage as thou hast myght,
> Thee were nede of hennes, as I wene,
> Ya, moo than seven tymes seventene.
> See, which braunes hath this gentil preest,
> So gret a nekke, and swich a large breest!

He loketh as a sperhauk with his eyen.

(VII.3450–57)

[But by my truth, if you had been a secular,
You would have been a rooster alright.
For if you have as much heart as you might,
You would need many hens, I suppose,
Yes, more than seven times seventeen.
See, what brawn has this gentle priest,
So great a neck, and such a large breast!
He looks like a sparrowhawk with his eyes.]

The natural questions, of course, are why would the Host be so concerned with the sexuality of these churchmen? And how would he know about their sexual prowess? Is Harry Bailly making judgments based on appearance only, or does he have inside information from their stay at the Tabard Inn? Why does he need to make these points to the pilgrims? Obviously, the sexuality of the Host himself is the real issue, as well as perhaps the full nature of Harry Bailly's innkeeping trade.

It is the Host himself who seems to challenge the narrator's assessment of the Host's manhood. Prior to his comments on the Monk's sexuality, the Host confesses to Goodelief's opinion of his manhood, clearly setting his character in contrast to that of the Monk:

"Allas!" she seith, "that evere I was shape
To wedden a milksop, or a coward ape,
That wol been overlad with every wight!
Thou darst nat stonden by thy wives right!"
    This is my lif, but if that I wol fighte;
And out at dore anon I moot me dighte,
Or elles I am but lost, but if that I
Be lik a wilde leoun, fool-hardy.
I woot wel she wol do me slee som day
Som neighebore, and thanne go my way;
For I am perilous with knyf in honde,
Al be it that I dar nat hire withstonde,
For she is byg in armes, by my feith:
That shal he fynde that hire mysdooth or seith,—
But lat us passe awey fro this mateere.

(VII.1909–1923)

["Alas!" she said, "that ever I was shaped
To have married a milksop, or a cowardly ape,
Who has been overborn by every man!
You dare not stand by your wife's right!"
    This is my life, but unless I will fight;
And out of doors immediately I must hasten,

Or else I am but lost, but if that I
Am like a wild lion, fool hardy.
I know well that she would have me slay some day
Some neighbors, and then go my way;
For I am perilous with a knife in my hand,
Albeit I do not stand up to her,
For she is strong, by my faith:
That shall you find that she misdid or said,—
But let us pass away from this matter.]

The Host reiterates the shrewish behavior of his wife at the end of the "Merchant's Tale." He refers to her as "a labbyng shrewe" with "an heep of vices mo." He regrets that he is married to her and says that he could elaborate on her flaws, but someone from the pilgrimage would certainly tell her. There were laws to protect men from shrewish women, as Bailly must have known, especially directed at prostitutes (Bailly would not have wanted to pay the fines, however): "A prostitute who was a scold or caused an affray was to be imprisoned for three days and three nights and fined 6s. 8d., although other women of the manor were not to be 'brought in to prisoun for scoolding like as commun wommen ben,' but presented at the annual leet instead" (Carlin 486). There is not enough textual evidence to make many claims about the Host's wife in the *Tales,* but the Host makes clear his opinion. From the Host's perspective "Goodelief" must certainly be an irony; it must also be considered, however, that Goodelief's assessment of Harry is accurate.

The pieces in the puzzle that is the Host's character come together in his response to the Pardoner's story and personal invitation to the Host to repentance. It is the Host's inconsistency of response to the Pardoner that provides the most telling insight into his character and puts the other details in perspective. Throughout the tale-telling, the Host good-naturedly interacts with the other pilgrims in the exchange of insults or potentially embarrassing comments, such as with the Cook or Nun's Priest. After the Host has addressed the Monk's sexuality, the Host says to the Monk:

But be nat wrooth, my lord, though that I pleye.
Ful ofte in game a sooth I have heard seye!

(VII.1963–1964)

[Be not angry, my lord, though that I play.
Very often in a game of truth I have heard say!]

However, the personal banter between the Host and Pardoner leads to such anger that the Knight must intervene. The Host's response to the Pardoner stands in stark contrast to the responses to the Nun's Priest and the Monk, even though the Pardoner is also at least loosely connected to the Church. Rather than praising the Pardoner's manhood, the Host wants to emasculate the Pardoner and enshrine his testicles in a "hogges toord." At the end of the "Pardoner's Tale," the Host's personal attacks have reduced the smooth-talking Pardoner to silence. The Host himself, who normally speaks incessantly about mirth and play, is driven to mean-spirited seriousness.

Donald Howard argues that the "Host's response is far more of a surprise than the Pardoner's 'afterthought,' and is harder to understand because we haven't the insight into the Host that we have into the Pardoner" (365). Actually, however, the reader has had more insight into the Host than the Pardoner; the Host has been on the stage for many more lines than the Pardoner until the Pardoner tells his story. Furthermore, the Pardoner's story is finally as much about the Host as about the Pardoner.

When the Host calls on the Pardoner to tell a tale, it is with an exchange of oaths "by Seint Ronyan," an off-color play on two meanings of runion: the male sex organ and an insulting term applied to women. The Host addresses the pardoner as "beel amy" and encourages him to tell the group "some myrthe or japes right anon." The Pardoner readily agrees, but "the gentils gonne to crye" to the Host that the Pardoner not be permitted to tell a ribald story but that he be required instead to tell "us som moral thyng." The Pardoner agrees to this as well, but only after he has had time to think about "some honest thyng while that I drynke" (VI.328).

What the Pardoner comes up with is a story about greed *(radix malorum est cupiditas)* that leads to death; the story is set in a Flanders that could well have doubled for late fourteenth-century Southwark:

> In Flaundres whilom was a compaignye
> Of yonge folk that haunteden folye,
> As riot, hasard, stywes, and tavernes,
> Where as with harpes, lutes, and gyternes,
> They daunce and pleyen at dees bothe day and nyght,
> And eten also and drynken over hir myght,
> Thurgh which they doon the devel sacrifise
> Withinne that develes temple, in cursed wise,
> By superfluytee abhomynable.
> Hir othes been so grete and so dampnable
> That it is grisly for to heere hem swere.
> Oure blissed Lordes body they totere—
>
>   (VI.463–474)

> [In Flanders once was a company
> Of young folk that made a habit of folly,
> Of riot, dice playing, brothels, and taverns,
> Where with harps, lutes, and citerns,
> They dance and play at dice both day and night,
> And eat also and drink over their might,
> Through which they do the devil's sacrifice
> Within the devil's temple, in cursed ways,

By superfluity abominable.
Their oaths were so great and damnable
That it is grisly for to hear them swear.
Our blessed Lord's body they tore in pieces—]

The Pardoner preaches against not only greed, but also swearing, drunkenness, gluttony (which he names the "cause first of oure confusion"), and lechery, which he says is closely related to gluttony. In other words, the Pardoner condemns much of the behavior associated with the innkeeping trade that has developed in Southwark and so condemns the Innkeeper in the process. The Host—who loves to swear, offers a dinner (not at his expense) as a pilgrimage prize, is possibly involved in prostitution, and loves money—is made the subject of the "Pardoner's Tale." At the end of the tale, when the Pardoner calls on the pilgrims to step forward and buy his pardons, he specifically calls on the Host to lead the way, "For he is moost envoluped in synne." Perhaps, too, the Pardoner understood better than anyone the sexual inadequacies (or preference) of the Host. There is no reason for the Host to be so angry if the truth of his character has not been exposed.

Although the *Canterbury Tales* does not end with the return to the Tabard Inn and the completion of the Host's original plan, a discussion of the Host should not end without some speculation on the leading contender for the supper based on the available stories. Most of the pilgrims can be eliminated quickly: the Pardoner, obviously, and the Cook, as well as other pilgrims, such as the women and the Franklin, whom the Host does not like; the Monk, Squire, and Chaucer the pilgrim, whose dull tales are interrupted; the Miller and the Reeve, the Friar and the Summoner, whose tales in part are personal weapons. There are really only two serious candidates, the Knight and the Nun's Priest, both of whom tell tales of "sentence and solaas." The Host probably prefers the story the Nun's Priest tells and seems to admire the man himself; however, the social status of the Knight may finally give him the edge.

Chaucer's Canterbury pilgrims gathered at the Tabard Inn in Southwark to begin their pilgrimage to Canterbury because the lodging was comfortable, the food and drink were good, they could begin their journey early, and all of them—from the Pardoner to the Parson—would be well-accommodated in Southwark. The Host himself was a very capable innkeeper, a merry man who was eager to provide for the comfort of his well-paying lodgers.

It is unlikely that the reader of the *Canterbury Tales* will ever know much more about the life of "Henricus Bailiff, Oystler," or ever know for certain whether Chaucer's "Harry Bailly" is anything more than a coincidence of fiction. It is enough to know that Chaucer has given the reader a very real Harry Bailly, who is real because his character is consistent with what is known about the details of the innkeeping trade in late fourteenth-century Southwark and, more importantly, because out of the art of Chaucer's fiction Harry Bailly emerges as a fully credible human being.

REFERENCES

Benson, C. David. *Chaucer's Drama of Style: Poetic Variety and Contrast in the Canterbury Tales*. Chapel Hill: University of North Carolina Press, 1986.

Besant, Walter. *London South of the Thames*. London: Black, 1912.

Bowden, Muriel. *A Commentary on the General Prologue to the Canterbury Tales*. 2nd ed. New York: Macmillan, 1967.

Burford, Ephraim John. *Bawds and Lodgings. A History of the Bankside Brothels*. London: Peter Owen, 1976.

Carlin, Martha. "The Urban Development of Southwark." Dissertation, University of Toronto, 1983.

Cooper, Helen. *The Structure of the Canterbury Tales*. Athens: University of Georgia Press, 1984.

Coulton, G. G. *The Medieval Village*. Cambridge: Cambridge University Press, 1926.

Gaylord, Alan T. "Sentence and Solaas in Fragment VII of the *Canterbury Tales:* Harry Bailly as Horseback Editor." *PMLA* 82 (1967): 226–235.

Hanawalt, Barbara, ed. *Chaucer's England: Literature in Historical Context*. Medieval Studies at Minnesota, Volume 4. Minneapolis: University of Minnesota Press, 1992.

Hill, John M. *Chaucerian Belief: The Poetics of Reverence and Delight*. New Haven, Conn.: Yale University Press, 1991.

Howard, Donald R. *The Idea of the Canterbury Tales*. Berkeley: University of California Press, 1976.

Huppé, Bernard F. *A Reading of the Canterbury Tales*. Albany: State University of New York, 1967.

———, and D. W. Robertson, Jr. *Fruyt and Chaf: Studies in Chaucer's Allegories*. Princeton, N. J.: Princeton University Press, 1963.

Jensen, Emily. "Male Competition as a Unifying Motif in Fragment A of the *Canterbury Tales*." *Chaucer Review* 24 (1990): 321–327.

Keen, William. "To Doon Yow Ese: A Study of the Host in the *General Prologue of The Canterbury Tales*." *Topic* 17 (1969): 11.

Knight, Stephen. *Geoffrey Chaucer*. Oxford: Blackwell, 1986.

Lumiansky, R. M. *Of Sundry Folk: The Dramatic Principle in The Canterbury Tales*. Austin: University of Texas Press, 1955.

Malone, Kemp. *Chapters on Chaucer*. Baltimore: Johns Hopkins University Press, 1951.

Manly, John Matthews. *Some New Light on Chaucer*. New York: Holt, 1926.

Mann, Jill. *Chaucer and the Medieval Estates Satire*. Cambridge: Cambridge University Press, 1973.

Memorials of London and London Life in the XIIIth, XIVth, and XVth Centuries. Trans, and ed. by Henry Thomas Riley. London: City of London, 1868.

Munimenta Gildhallae Londoniensis, Liber Albus. Ed. Henry Thomas Riley. Rolls Series, 12 (1859).

Page, Barbara. "Concerning the Host." *Chaucer Review* 4 (1970): 1–13.

Pichaske, David R., and Laura Sweetland. "Chaucer on the Medieval Monarchy: Harry Bailly in the *Canterbury Tales*." *Chaucer Review* 11 (1976–1977): 179–200.

Portnoy, Phyllis. "Beyond the Gothic Cathedral: Post-Modern Reflections in the *Canterbury Tales*." *Chaucer Review* 28 (1994): 279–292.

Rendel, William, and Phillip Norman. *The Inns of Old Southwark*. London, 1888.

Richardson, Cynthia C. "The Function of the Host in *The Canterbury Tales*." *TSLL* 12 (1970): 326.

Scheps, Walter. "'Up Roos Oure Hoost, And Was Oure Aller Cok': Harry Bailly's Tale-Telling Competition." *Chaucer Review* 17 (1982–1983): 5–20.

Stow, John. *A Survey of London*. Ed. Charles Lethbridge Kingsford. 2 vols. Oxford, 1906.

Strom, Paul. *Social Chaucer*. Cambridge, Mass.: Harvard University Press, 1989.

Taitt, P.S. "Harry Bailly and the Pardoner's Relics." *Studia Neophilologica* 41 (1969): 112–114.

Wallace, David. "Chaucer and the Absent City." In *Chaucer's England: Literature in Historical Context*. Ed. Barbara Hanawalt. Minneapolis: University of Minnesota Press, 1992. Pp. 59–90.

Williams, Celia Ann. "The Host—England's First Tour Director." *English Journal* 57 (1968): 1149–1150.

Chapter 30

I Demed Hym Som Chanoun For To Be

CHRISTINE N. CHISM

The Canon, like most of Chaucer's pilgrims, has two strings to his bow where his livelihood is concerned; he is both a canon and an alchemist. This practical duplicity pervades his character from the moment he first appears, gasping behind the pilgrims as though seeking their protection from pursuing fiends. It shows in his raiment: white and black; in his entourage: silent, apprehensive master and resentfully garrulous servant; even in his horse: a dapple grey, like the one Chaucer the pilgrim rides (a detail to which we will return later). To understand the Canon's role in the *Tales*, it is helpful to examine both of his occupations, canon and alchemist—their histories, self-definitions, and common practices—so that we may then consider the way he responds to his social responsibilities. Finally, we may ask why Chaucer found the amalgam of canon and alchemist appropriate to a pilgrim who is at best a credulous dupe and at worst, according to his own servant, a devil in human form.

CANONS

We will begin with the overt occupation, that of Canon. The word comes from the Greek word meaning "rule" and in ancient times designated the clergy of any large church. From the very beginning, therefore, canons had an institutional affiliation with a particular church or cathedral. After the eighth century, the practice of the canonical lifestyle became more formalized and began to connote adherence to canonical rules or guidelines for living, laid down by Church authorities. In 816, Chrodegand, bishop of Metz, devised his *Rule for Canons* which summoned the clergy of his own cathedral to embrace the common or apostolic life—living as much like the New Testament apostles as possible (Gasquet 222–225). This involved living communally, eating at a common refectory, sleeping in a common dormitory, sharing goods in common with other canons, and devoting oneself to a life of prayer and the chanting of the Divine Office, much as early monks did. In fact, these early canons were almost impossible to distinguish from the Benedictine monks—with one essential difference. Although property was to be shared if possible, they were not forbidden to own it. In the fervor of eighth-century Church reform, other foundations soon followed the example of Chrodegand's, promoting this more apostolic but not entirely monastic life. Those who undertook it became known later as Regular Canons—canons of the rule. (For the definitive early history of the Augustinian Canons, see Rev. J. C. Dickinson's *The Austin Canons and Their Introduction into England.*)

This regulated lifestyle, however, was not for all tastes. Throughout the ninth, tenth, and eleventh centuries, many canons vigorously refused the strictness of Chrodegand's rule. In some wealthy churches they had organized into administrative groups called canonries where, like regular canons, they staffed the churches, held services, and undertook parish duties. They held considerable power in their canonries and in many cases lived a liberal life, eating meat, keeping their own houses and personal income, and wearing fine clothes made of linen, a cloth forbidden to monks (Lynch 209–210). They were called secular canons, and throughout the eleventh century, it was the dearest endeavor of Church reformers to persuade them to adopt stricter rules and become regular canons.

The Fourth Lateran Council of 1059 took steps in this direction, emphasizing the relative gentleness of canonical rule in relation to monastic rule. Secular canons could lead a modified common life that would allow them to continue to draw and keep income from personal estates or supplementary benefices, while sharing in common all funds derived from the Church establishment.

Despite such accommodating gestures, at first would-be reformers met with indifferent success. The secular canons could be quite territorial about their administrative power in cathedral matters and were not necessarily eager to relinquish their dominant status for a life of apostolic poverty. In fact, they could be downright murderous. During a dispute over cathedral authority with his canons at Bordeaux, Archbishop Geoffrey de Lovoux was forced to flee for his life (see Daniel-Rops 233). The privileges of Church authority could be very rewarding to the unscrupulous. H. Daniel-Rops describes the abuses that had overtaken the secular canons' religious practice:

Many canons were preoccupied with tapping the revenues of the chapter rather than with singing matins; many of them too, were no better than gyrovagues [monks who would wander irresponsibly from cloister to cloister], continually absent from their stalls. Some were guilty of even more deplorable vices—violence and sexual immorality. (Daniel-Rops 130)

So widespread were such abuses that they proved resistant to direct prosecution. However, where legislation failed, compromise made some headway. In the twelfth century, Chrodegand's *Rule for Canons* was replaced by the newly discovered *Rule of St. Augustine*—a flexible rule that attempts to accommodate the needs of both regular and secular canons, while discouraging abuses (see C. H. Lawrence 273–279). This rule, like the monastic rule of St. Benedict, establishes a community of devotion along apostolic lines. However, rather than stressing extremes of poverty, devotional performance, and submission, it legislated moderation and reasonable compromise. As with monks, a regular canon's day was structured around the singing of the divine office six times a day—the canonical hours. However, the rituals tended to be shorter than in monasteries. Canons also had fewer dietary restrictions than monks, could replace monastic manual labor with study and recreation, and, crucially, could retain personal property. Because the apostolic life involved the cure of souls—attention to parish duties as well as monastic ones—some foundations gave their canons pastoral duties that would take them out of the cathedral close. They maintained parish churches attached to their houses, fulfilled the duties of a parish priest, and assisted the bishop in the administration of his diocese.

In England, by the end of the twelfth century, there were three chief orders of regular canons. The first were the Augustinian, or Black Canons, so called for the black habit and overcloak they wore. They established their first English house at St. Boltoph's at Colchester by 1107. They were soon joined by the second great canonical order, first founded in 1119 by St. Norbert (1085–1134) at Premontre in France. St. Norbert was a German nobleman who was galvanized to take up the religious life at the age of thirty when his horse was struck by lightning. He seems to have retained a certain fervor of illumination throughout his religious life, preaching vigorously against Church abuses, denouncing the laxity that had infected canonical practice, and calling for a stricter return to apostolic principles—a uniting of both monastic and parochial endeavors (Daniel-Rops 131–132). His order was called Premonstratensians, or White Canons, because they adopted a habit of bleached wool. Over the next two centuries they established thirty great establishments throughout England. (For the fullest history of the Premonstratensian Order, see H. M. Colvin's *The White Canons in England.*)

The third group, the Gilbertines, was also founded in the twelfth century, by St. Gilbert, rector of Sempringham, who took elements from the Augustinian rule and joined them with elements from the rule of St. Benedict—again, betokening a return to a more strictly monastic life. The Gilbertines admitted both men and women, the men following a modified Augustinian rule and the women following the Cistercian version of the Benedictine rule. The men wore a black habit with a white cloak, and the women a black habit with a white cap (Gasquet 222–230). It is difficult to pinpoint to which order Chaucer's Canon belongs, with his white surplice and his black overcloak. It is more likely in terms of demographics and location that he belongs to the more numerous Augustinian order; he turns up in the shadow of Boughton under Blee, five miles from Canterbury, which featured a chapter of Augustinian canons. However, it is possible, too, that Chaucer gives him a piebald habit to introduce elements of all three orders—making him a kind of ur-canon, or one who plays fast and loose with his dress to show his evasion of canonical habit, or to sharpen the sense of duplicity that defines his character.

From its first establishment, the canonical life negotiates a compromise between monastic and pastoral service retaining possible extensions into both practices. There was enormous variety between canonries. Some foundations exempted their canons from all pastoral duties and allowed them to live in a fashion indistinguishable from that of the monastery. Others, especially those serving rural districts without large ecclesiastical centers, would stress the pastoral rather than the communal life. By Chaucer's time, the flexibility of the Augustinian rule was stretched even further; canons were allowed to live out of the cathedral chapter, preach publicly, devote themselves entirely to study, administrate hospitals, run schools, become missionaries in Eastern Europe, hear the confessions of the laypeople, and even seek supplemental sources of income by attaching themselves to the retinues of secular princes (Lawrence 137–141).

Such flexibility of practice immeasurably increased the outreach and appeal of the canonical orders. Throughout the twelfth and thirteenth centuries, they spread all over Europe and were establishing missions as far east as the Baltic Sea. By Chaucer's time, in England alone there were more than two hundred churches and cells of the Augustinian order and thirty Premonstratensian houses.

In addition, the *Rule*'s stress on compromise makes the canonical rule a bridge between the monastery and the laity; both the Black and White Canons of England were founded to bring together the active and contemplative pursuit of holiness. Ideally, a canon, like a monk, would devote time to the prayerful works of the spirit: the singing of the canonical hours, the chanting of masses as intercession on behalf of the dead in purgatory, devotional study, fasting, and administrative service within the cathedral chapter. However, like a parish priest, he would also play a more active role serving his congregation, hearing confessions, staffing hospitals and schools, visiting the sick, recuperating the sinful, and living a material life in the world in a way that exemplifies not only spiritual but social rectitude. A canon, in theory, brings together the active life and the contemplative life, the social body and the holy spirit, in one divine servitude.

This theoretically enabling flexibility also generates tensions that can confound the success of canonical order. Canonical history is long oscillation between the reformatory urgency of a return to the monastic apostolic life and the need to acknowledge the social and parochial engagements that monastic seclusion ignores. More than most medieval religious orders, canons teeter along the nebulous boundary between the sacred and the worldly. By definition, they continually negotiate between the monastery and the laity, struggling to maintain their regular flexibility without falling into abuses.

And they manage this with varying success. As early as 1204, Pope Innocent III inveighed against the canons of Languedoc:

The heretics are finding their strongest arguments in the lives of the prelates ... the archbishop of Narbonne ... exercises neither responsibility nor almsgiving, and often though sound in body, passes a week or two without entering his church. ... The members [clergy of the diocese] take such contagion from the sickness of their head, that many monks and canons regular have cast off the religious habit, keep public concubines, some of whom have been torn from the embraces of their husbands, practice usury ... or assume the parts of minstrels or buffoons. (Quoted in Coulton 2:302)

By the late fourteenth century in England, canons, like monks and friars, far from being famed for their apostolic piety, were noted for their greedy unscrupulousness. The effects of the Babylonian Captivity and the Great Schism had intensified the distrust of ecclesiastical figures generally. Simony was rampant (Flick 329–331). Like other Church officials, canons could evade the letter of their canonical law in any number of ways, and did so with a regularity that appalled Chaucer's contemporaries, even those within the Church.

The bishops aped the secular rulers in their dress, carried weapons, waged war, surrounded themselves with luxurious courts, and sold ecclesiastical privileges to worldly tyrants to the disgrace of the church and the oppression of the poor. ... The canons were as bad as the bishops and like them imitated the secular lords in dress, carried swords, and lived worldly lives. (Flick 329–331)

Bishop Redman had to caution the abbot general of the Premonstratensians not to believe the complaints of "certain runaway canons of our English province who apostatize and come fraudulently to you for the sake of getting something or of making some complaint under no matter what pretext" (quoted in Coulton 320). John Gower, Chaucer's fellow poet, waxes satirical on the subject:

Ensi comme Moigne, ensi Canoun / Ne tient la reule du canoun Mais l'un et l'autre nepourqant / La fourme de Religioun / Gardont, mais la matiere noun ... pour final governement / Danz Vice est Abbes au present, / Par quoi danz Gule et danze Peresce / Sont fait par le commun assent / Ses chapellains; et ensement / Danze Veine gloire se professe, / A qui nostre Abbes se confesse; / Danz Avarice ad la richesce, / Qui danz Almoisne ascunement / Ne soloit garder le covent. (Gower 11. 21157–21161, 21169–21180)

[Thus both Monks and Canons neglect the canon rule; however much they scrupulously follow the protocols of Religion, they neglect the substance. ... At the present, dan Vice is abbot, and by common assent dan Gluttony and dan Indolence are appointed his chaplains, while, following suit, dan Vain Glory is admitted to the order as a confessor to our Abbot. Dan Avarice claims the riches which dan Almsgiving is not allowed in any way to give to the poor. In this way, dan Conscience who used to guard the convent has been slain.]

Thus to many of Chaucer's contemporaries, the apostolic vigor that had given the regular canons and their successors, the Franciscan friars, such a powerful reformatory impact on both Church and society had spent its force. The flexible compromise between laity and monastery had fallen into a disrepute so profound that even clerical titles of respect can, in Gower's treatise, become stinging accusations. Gower accuses monks and canons of following the form of religious life but corrupting the matter; using a deceptive cloak of charity that allows them to keep alms from the poor while amassing riches for their own enjoyment. This general perception of canonical corruption is a touchstone for the character of Chaucer's canonical alchemist.

ALCHEMISTS

In one sense, it is not at all surprising that Chaucer's Canon moonlights as an alchemist. A great part of the alchemical writers through the Renaissance were churchmen of one sort or another, and many, perhaps owing to the flexibility of canonical observance in the fourteenth and fifteenth centuries, were canons. Fifty years after Chaucer's death, a canon of Bridlington, George Ripley, dedicated to King Edward IV one of the most elaborate English alchemical treatises, *The Compound of Alchymie, Containing Twelve Gates.* In it he offered for the king's perusal "Great Secretts which I in farre Countryes did lere" on condition that "to your selfe ye shall keepe it full secretly, / And only it use as may be to Gods pleasure" (Ashmole 109–10) ["Great secrets which I in far countries did learn" on condition that "to yourself you should keep it very secret, / And only use it as may be to God's pleasure"]. Ripley took care from the very beginning to avoid any hint of dereliction of ecclesiastical duty. Declaring himself "exempt from Claustrall observance," he goes on to assert not only the innocence of his investigations but also their profound social, epistemological, and religious value:

> He [Canon Ripley] did labour you to advance.
> He turned darknes into light
> Intending to helpe you to happy chaunce,
> Gyving Counsell that ye live right,
> Doeing to God no displeasaunce.
>
> (Ashmole 108)

> [He did labor you to advance.
> He turned darkness into light
> Intending to help you to a happy chance,
> Giving Counsel that you live right,
> Doing to God nothing displeasing.]

Similar protestations of the effortless congruity between religious and alchemical labors introduce alchemical writings from the twelfth-century translators of Islamic manuscripts through the speculative alchemists of the Renaissance. Arnold of Villanova, whom Chaucer quotes, glorifies the beneficial effects of alchemy, extending them to medicine, as well as religion and society. He linked the philosophers' stone to the elixir of life, a combination that proved irresistible to later alchemists. His *Treasure of Treasures, Rosary of the Philosophers, and the Greatest Secret of All Secrets* sparked a series of "alchemical rosaries" whose titles alone show the insistent linkage of alchemy and religion. They range from the *Summa Perfectionis* ("Sum of Perfection") through the *Pretiosa Margarita Novella* ("The New Pearl of Great Price"). Together they become a glittering litany that weaves together the allurements of holiness, riches, and secrecy.

Added to these baits was the patina of age. Alchemy had over a thousand years of history by the time it reached Chaucer. This history has three phases: the Egyptian, the Islamic, and the medieval. Historians generally agree that the first roots of what later became medieval alchemy lie in Egypt in the city of Alexandria, founded by Alexander the Great in 311 B.C. (For a much more detailed account of the Chinese influence in this regard, see Holmyard 33–42.) In one of the most helpful studies on the subject, Arthur John Hopkins traces the genesis of alchemy from the conjugation of strange bedfellows: the exquisite metalcraft of Alexandrian artisans and Platonic and Aristotelian philosophy. Almost coterminous with the founding of Alexandria, a school of philosophy had been established to explore and promote tenets drawn from the philosophies of Plato and Aristotle. Several of these tenets are crucial to the subsequent development of alchemy:

1. Hylozoism (the animate nature of the universe and all the matter in it).

2. The corollary that any event may be precipitated and determined by guiding animistic spirits.

3. Correspondence between macrocosm and microcosm (a unity of structure between, say, a city and the world, a single body and a social body, the mind of man and the order of the universe, etc.).

4. The corollary that what happens on a macrocosmic level will be mirrored in the microcosm and sometimes vice versa; this leads to the practice of such disciplines as astrology, sympathetic magic, and, of course, alchemy itself. (Hopkins 28)

To these principles, alchemical writers harnessed Aristotle's theory of the four elements—earth, water, air, and fire—and the four properties of matter—dry, cold, moist, and hot. But the central thesis that provided the basis of alchemical theory comes from Plato: the idea that all matter is inchoate, uniform, without any attributes, and ultimately unknowable until it is impressed by certain properties. These properties, or "forms," can stamp the passive matter and give it individual, knowable, and differentiable qualities, in the same way that a maker of gold statues can hammer and cast his material into different shapes. (For a more detailed account, see Benjamin Jowett's translation of the *Timaeus*, 1177–1178.) It is easy to see how this theory of matter would prove appealing to future alchemists. If one could maneuver to alter the impressed properties of a given element, one would be changing the element itself.

The culture of Egypt lent itself to practical applications of these principles, with its long history of expertise in practical artistry, the expertise that gave rise to such stunning achievements in architecture, stonework, weaving, woodworking, painting, and, notably, metalwork. The land was particularly famous for its dyes and colors; its very name "kmt" or "kemet" means "black," and is speculated to be an etymological root of "chem" which with the Arabic article "al" gave rise to "alchemy." This etymology was presented by Suidas in the eleventh century; Holmyard and Thompson suggest the alternative etymology of the Arabic article "al" with the Greek work "chyma," which means the fusing or casting of metal (10). Arthur Hopkins theorizes persuasively that the origins of Egyptian alchemy lie in the workshops of the Alexandrian dyers, sparked by the discovery that it was possible to tint metals different colors by certain chemical applications similar to those used in dyeing cloth. The exact secrets of these processes would be jealously guarded to protect the monopolies of the different workshops. Given the passage of time and the vagaries of transmission, such secret recipes could be misinterpreted as processes for actual transmutation by later translators who were unfamiliar with the metallurgical crafts, and dizzy with the influx of new philosophies and religions that came to Alexandria over the next six centuries, including new forms of Neoplatonism, Judaism, Gnosticism, and Christianity with all their fierce disputes and mutually excommunicating factions.

Traces of these earlier metallurgical recipes can be found in Egyptian alchemical literature for six centuries. It is during this time that sulphur became important to alchemical processes; the treatment of metals by calcium sulphide could produce a wide range of colors (Hopkins 48–49). Later alchemists would make sulphur one of the two foundational principles crucial to both the generation and the treatment of metals; the other was mercury.

Egyptian alchemical writings furnished the basic paradigms for subsequent theories of alchemy. Essential was the idea that the alchemist practiced the rarification of metals, a process that involved gradually adjusting the proportion of elements in the metals from the most base to the most noble. Earth was considered the lowest, then water, then air, and finally the most rarified of all, fire. The metals also had their scale of nobility. First were the earthy metals, copper, iron, tin, and lead, dedicated to Venus, Mars, Jupiter, and Saturn, respectively. Then came the transitional metal, Mercury, which was associated with both water and air, depending on its use. Finally came the highest metals, silver and gold, associated with the moon and the sun. In Egyptian writings there is also a mysterious metal beyond gold, called coral of gold: its color was a beautiful, iridescent purple.

Each stage of the process of transmutation involved the conjunction of two substances: the metal to be treated—called the "body"—and the substances with which the metal was treated—called the "spirit," ferment, or elixir. At each stage the ferment would permeate the metal, work through it, and change it as a yeast leavens bread. Each stage had a different ferment. The ferment itself usually incorporated a small portion of a more noble metal. For instance, mercury would be transmuted to silver by a ferment containing silver; silver would be transmuted to gold by a ferment containing gold. The most potent ferment of all was drawn from coral of gold; a tiny portion was reputed to have the power to transmute vast proportions of all the baser metals to gold. It is from the concept of this super-ferment that the Islamic alchemists derived the idea of the philosophers' stone. (For a much fuller discussion of the theories of early alchemical ferments, see Hopkins 59–123 and Holmyard 14–104.)

Alchemists would mark the progress of their transmutations by noting the colors produced in the metals. The importance of a given color sequence becomes an overriding code in all subsequent alchemical writings. It was considered best to start out with as earthy and heterogeneous a metal as possible; most alchemists used an alloy of copper, tin, lead, and iron, which would be blackened by oxidation. This blackness invokes Plato's discussion of primal matter as neutral; its absence of color and differentiable qualities make it a better material for the endowing of more noble qualities. The Egyptian color sequence went black—white (producing silver)—yellow (producing gold)—purple (producing coral of gold). This last step distinguishes Egyptian transmutations from medieval ones, which end with the production of gold in a color sequence that usually goes from black to white to red.

Hopkins theorizes that the change is catalyzed by the use of the kerotakis of Mary the Jewess, which brought together the two most potent spirits in the production of metals—sulphur and mercury. The kerotakis apparatus for the first time enabled the sublimation of sulphur and the production of artificial sulphide of mercury—which is a bright red (115–118). By the fifteenth century, there was a lot of individual variation in this color scheme. George Ripley offers a particularly elaborate assertion:

> Pale, and Black, wyth falce Citryne, unparfyt Whyte and Red,
> Pekoks fethers in colors gay, the Raynbow whych shall overgoe
> The Spotted Panther with the Lyon greene, the Crows byll blue as lede;
> These shall appeare before the parfyt Whyt, Grey, and falce Citryne also:
> And after all thys shall appeare the blod Red invaryable,
> Then hast thou a Medcyn of the thyrd order of hys owne kynde Multyplycable.
>
> (Quoted in *Theatrum* 188)

> [Pale, and Black, with false Citron, unperfect White and Red,
> Peacock feathers in gay colors, the Rainbow which shall overgo
> The Spotted Panther with the Lyon green, the Crow's bill blue as lead;
> These shall appear before the perfect White, Grey, and false Citron also:
> And after all this shall appear the blood Red invariable,
> Then have you the Medicine of the third order of his own kind Multiplicable.]

We have very few surviving alchemical manuscripts from the early Egyptian period; the oldest are transcriptions dating from the tenth and eleventh centuries.

They include writings attributed to Democritis (first century), Synesius (third century), Zosimus (fourth century) who collected and organized many earlier writings, and Stephanus (seventh century) who taught at Constantinople. These writings cite the influence of even older semimythical figures like Hermes Trismegistos and Mary the Jewess who was reputed to be the sister of Moses and is credited with the invention of a special furnace that revolutionized alchemical processes: the kerotakis. Even through the Renaissance, these shadowy authorities kept their appeal for aspiring alchemists seeking antique origins for their procedures; in the "Canon's Yeoman's Tale," Chaucer mentions Hermes.

Egyptian alchemy seems to have declined from the fifth century on, and the surrender of Alexandria to the Islamic Ummayads in 649 marks its effective end. But the Ummayads and their successors the Abbasids quickly developed a lively interest in ancient and classical learning, establishing a capital at Baghdad in 750, which was to be a center of culture for five centuries. Islamic scholars at the academy in Baghdad continued the energetic translation of Greek and Roman manuscripts, preserving and commenting on countless works of classical literature that would otherwise have been lost. Among these works were those of the Egyptian alchemists. The Islamic scholar who seems to have taken them up is the controversial figure of Jabir ibn Hayyan or Geber. This scholar, originally the son of an apothecary, became so respected for his learning that by middle life he was accepted at the magnificent court of Harun al-Rashid. If we are to accept even a part of the manuscripts attributed to him, he apparently wrote over five hundred alchemical treatises. There is some controversy over whether Geber existed, let alone wrote every work attributed to him. To explain this amazing prolixity, some speculate that there were two Gebers, one eighth century and the other thirteenth century, whose works and identities are conflated. Whatever the case, the writings attributed to him exerted a considerable influence over subsequent alchemical literature, including that of his Islamic successors, Razi, Ibn Sina (or Avicenna as he was known to the West), and the Spanish Islamic scholar Maslama ibn Ahmad.

The Islamic contribution to the study of alchemy includes an intensified focus on the natural generation of metals from proportions of mercury and sulphur (often called the mercury-sulphur theory), an emphasis on pragmatic experimentation, and a certain caustic skepticism about the possibility of transmutation. (Halleux's discussion, 64–70, particularly stresses this experimental spirit.) In his treatise "The Book of the Remedy," Ibn Sina asserts that alchemy is an art of clever imitation; that the changes in metallic color do not reflect changes in substance; and that actual transmutation is impossible. These sentiments did not deter his twelfth-century Christian translators; medieval alchemists cheerfully canonized him as one of the great alchemical authorities.

It was largely through the Islamic occupation of Spain and the Christian conquest of Islamic Sicily that both alchemy and classical learning reentered the consciousness of the Christian West. When the abbot of Cluny, Peter the Venerable, hired the English scholar Robert of Chester to translate the Koran into

Latin in 1141, he did so in order to expose the dangerous heresies of a religion and culture whose palpable achievements had become very alluring to many of his religion. His strategy backfired. After the Koran, Robert of Chester began translating the Arabic "Book of the Composition of Alchemy," which only whetted the appetite for Islamic culture and learning. Throughout the twelfth century, Christian Europe took from the hands of its enemies works of Aristotle, Galen, Ptolemy, Euclid, and Hippocrates believed lost forever, and with them the sophisticated commentary, exegesis, and argument with which the Moslems had enriched and augmented their classical legacy. These twelfth-century translations stimulated a European renaissance of learning and university controversy which was to last two hundred years. Along with the classical and Arabic works came many alchemical treatises that incorporated Aristotelian philosophy so intimately that they proved irresistible.

The thirteenth-century encyclopaedists lent further credibility to alchemical practice, including it in their extensive works on minerals, theology, and natural philosophy. Of these scholars, two names are preeminent: Albertus Magnus, author of *De Mineralibus,* and Roger Bacon, author of the *Opus Majus,* who, like the Islamic alchemists, also stressed the importance of experiment over theory. Their works, while synthesizing and deploying Arabic alchemical theories, did not contribute much original material; this did not diminish their popularity. Throughout the fourteenth and fifteenth centuries, there was an explosion of alchemical writing: hermetic, allegorical, suggestive, and bristling with false attributions. Pseudo-Gebers, Ibn Sinas, Albertus Magnuses, and Roger Bacons sprang forth to reveal the ancient oriental secrets of alchemy to an enchanted audience.

By the late fourteenth century, alchemy had become the study of studies, as encompassing as—and often becoming—the search for the key to all mythologies. It was at once a hermeneuticist's dream and a pragmatician's nightmare, superbly ambiguous and supremely alluring. As Poisson comments dryly: "Scholasticism with its infinitely subtle argumentation, Theology with its ambiguous phraseology, Astrology so vast and complicated, are only child's play in comparison with Alchemy" (quoted in Read 29). Chaucer's tale rides the first waves of an obsession that was to crest over the next two centuries, spawning countless treatises, earnest acolytes, and cynical dissemblers in every city in Europe. England in particular became famous for the quality of its alchemists; by the late fifteenth century, continental scholars were journeying to England to translate English alchemical treatises into Latin. So widespread was the mania that soon after Chaucer's death, King Henry IV passed his edict of 1404 banning alchemical gold-making, for fear of the effect it would have on the national economy should even a fraction of its practitioners succeed. After that date, alchemists were forced to sue for royal licenses to pursue their craft (Ashmole xx–xxi).

These fourteenth- and fifteenth-century treatises are spectacular for their obscurity, treading the line between including the select few who could decipher their coded language and excluding the ignorant. The fourteenth-century pseudo-

Albertus Magnus begins his treatise the *Libellus de Alchimia* ("Little Book of Alchemy") with a bait that had already become conventional:

I, therefore, the least of the Philosophers, purpose to write for my associates and friends the true art, clear and free from error; however, in such a way that seeing they may not see, and hearing they may not understand. Therefore, I beg and I adjure you by the Creator of the world to hide this book from all the foolish. For to you I shall reveal the secret, but from the others I shall conceal the secret of secrets because of envy of this noble knowledge. . . .Beware, then of revealing to anyone our secrets in this work. A second time I warn you to be cautious; persevere in your labors and do not become discouraged, knowing that great utility will follow your work. (Magnus 3–4)

Such gestures appeal by establishing an intimate coterie from the center of which the envious ignorant can be derided, while the perceptive are flattered and teased by imponderables ("seeing they may not see")—even as they are warmly encouraged to persevere. It is this practice of encoding knowledge, speaking indirectly by means of figures and allegories, that distinguishes and enlivens the alchemical literature of Chaucer's day, tantalizing even as it defies comprehension.

This practice of verbal indirection suggests the power of the alchemist to manipulate both his elements and his language. It also makes an implicit analogy between alchemists and poets which can illuminate one facet of Chaucer's interest in the subject. To begin with, many alchemists were poets; countless late medieval alchemists wrote of their art in poetic allegories. The delightful fourteenth-century alchemical poem *Hermes Bird* makes the parallel even stronger. At the beginning of the alchemical allegory, the author writes: "Poyetys write wonderfull lyknes / And Covert kepe himselfe full clos," a description of poetic strategy that is uncannily Chaucerian (Ashmole 214). In fact, the seventeenth-century collector of alchemical poetry, Elias Ashmole, believed Chaucer to have been an alchemist, one of a long line of poet-alchemists who "fully knew the Mistery" (see Schuler 305–333). According to Ashmole, Chaucer was instructed in alchemy by the poet John Gower, and then passed his mantle to the fifteenth-century poet, John Lydgate (Ashmole 470). While such a genealogy may seem incredible, it reflects a perceived similarity between the disciplines that at times rings true. Both alchemical writers and the Chaucerian narrator of the *Canterbury Tales* seek a self-effacement that is epistemologically empowering. This strategy solicits the reader's involvement to share the secret while it teases with a plurality of interpretations. In both cases, the sheer difficulty of negotiating the textual indirection can become one of the most beguiling attractions of the process. But if you read for *results* it also becomes its greatest frustration.

CANONS AND ALCHEMISTS

It remains, then, to return to the question of why Chaucer wished to associate canons and alchemists. We know that he was not the only one to juxtapose religion and alchemy (see Pickering 140–149). Alchemical manuscripts typically begin by claiming spiritual cleanliness to be essential to the success of the process. The fourteenth-century alchemical poem, *Hermes Bird,* recalls the penitential function of the Canterbury pilgrimage when it interweaves penitential ritual with careful study and practical experience.

> Iyfe thow wilt thys warke begyn,
> Than schrevy the clene of alle thy Seyne:
> Contryte in hert wyth all thy thowght,
> And ever thenke on hym that the der bowght.
> Satisfaction thow make wyth ally thy myght . . .
> Yet nedeth the more to thy conclesyon,
> Take thow good hede now to thys lessen;
> Thow must have *Grace, Nature,* and *Resen,*
> *Spekelatif,* and *Coning,* wyth good Condition:
> Yet thow must have more now herto,
> *Experience,* wyth *Pracktik, Prudent* also;
> *Patient* that thow be, and *Holi in Lyfyngs.*

> [If you will this work begin,
> Then shrive yourself clean of all your Sin:
> Contrite in heart with all your thought,
> And ever thank him who with his sacrifice bought.
> Satisfaction you make with all your might . . .
> Yet need the more conclusion,
> Take you good heed now to this lesson;
> You must have *Grace, Nature,* and *Reason,*
> *Speculation* and *Cunning,* with good Condition:
> Yet you must have more now henceforth,
> *Experience,* with *Practicality, Prudence* also;
> *Patient* thjat you be, and *Holy in Livings.*

This beguiling association of spiritual and social value is evident in varying degrees throughout the entire history of alchemy. In addition, many of the most widespread medieval theories about alchemy and the canonical life revolve around a very similar set of metaphors. In the case of alchemy, the most crucial event in transmutation was the actual conversion of the metal by the elixir: the meeting of body and spirit. In alchemical manuals, this extended commerce of matter and spirit was as formalized and delicately sequenced as a pavane, and often figured in terms of sexual intercourse, marriage, and hybrid offspring. At every transmutation, the base and corrupted elements of the earth were to be penetrated by the most rarified spiritual exhalations, all to the ennoblement of the metal. In the case of canonical rule, a canon was to meld body and spirit in a different way, by merging the duties of the active and contemplative life. By fulfilling both monastic and pastoral imperatives, he situated himself at the crossroads of the spiritual and the worldly. The pinnacle of both the canon's and the alchemist's practice was to bring together unlike and often theoretically opposing practices and qualities. Both were to excel at potentially volatile compromises that bring about highly desirable ends.

And the end is paramount; it is the only justification for the undeniable (and even boasted) vagaries, frustrations, and repugnance of the process. In the *Romance of the Rose,* Jean de Meun puts into the mouth of Nature a testimonial to the possibility of alchemical transmutation but only if "one know how to carry the operation through to its conclusion, to take away the impurities from the impure metals and put them into pure forms according to their affinities, one resembling another" (11.16113–16115). And it is precisely here that Chaucer's Canon and his disgusted servant, the Yeoman, fail: "For alle oure sleightes we kan nat conclude" (VIII.773) ["For all our failures we cannot conclude"].

In Chaucer, the desired end of the multiplication of gold from the elixir becomes the endless multiplication of the process itself, a life spent in the never-ending repetition of failed experiments. Thus when we find Chaucer's Canon not living a life of monastic seclusion with his brethren within the cathedral chapter but instead racing about the countryside on a dapple grey, indulging himself in the luxury of a servant, and practicing alchemy in the seedier parts of a city, those facts alone are not necessarily damning evidence. It may be that, like the fifteenth-century canon-alchemist George Ripley, he has a dispensation or that his canonical order is one of the less strict ones allowing him to live outside the cathedral chapter, retain private property and personal servants, and even practice a second livelihood in addition to his ecclesiastical one, provided it was consonant with canonical ideals. What does become dubious about his lifestyle is not that it is double, or even that he practices alchemy, but rather that he cannot get results. He spends the time and substance he should be devoting to pastoral obligation in the pursuit of alchemical transmutation. And far from producing his spiritual and social ennoblement, it results in a debasement and corruption that seemingly have no end.

This endless degeneration is a fatal inversion of theories both of the canonical life and the alchemical process. Each discipline acknowledges corruption, but stresses its power to transform, enliven, and recuperate. Yet there is no doubt that, historically, the devilish "puffer" whose story the Yeoman tells was usually the rule rather than the exception in the profession. The history of alchemy is bedeviled by such stories of fraudulence; its own practitioners, somewhat ironically, continually caution the would-be acolyte against them. The author of the *Liber Patris Sapientiae* (Book of the Father of Wisdom) is particularly caustic; those who trust the famous books on alchemy are "foolys that glyde on the Ice; / They weene in grete Bokes schould be the Art / Of the Science of Alchemy, but they be not worth a fart" (Ashmole 195) ["fools that glide on the Ice; / They know in Great Books should be the Art / Of the Science of Alchemy, but they are not worth a fart"]. He then proceeds to contribute his secret nugget of alchemical wisdom. Generally speaking, however, his admonition was good. The alchemical manuals of the fourteenth century, despite their tone of disarming confidentiality, tend to lapse into impenetrable allegory at crucial moments. When Chaucer's canon-alchemist sells the priest a worthless recipe, he joins a cohort of alchemical fabricators, whose recipes would often work up to the crucial moment—the production of silver or gold—and only then, after the dupe had invested considerable effort and money in the process, baffle him.

A final question then presents itself. The Canon gets extremely unusual treatment in the *Canterbury Tales*. It would have required little effort to insert him in the "General Prologue"; his servant relates a very Prologue-like list of alchemical minutiae, which could easily have been excerpted. Instead, Chaucer draws attention to the Canon's abrupt arrival and his just as sudden departure; his yeoman ironically calls him a "passyng man" (VIII. 614), a suggestive pun that transforms "surpassing" into "ephemeral" and works as a microcosm of his livelihood. Alone of all the pilgrims, the Canon is not given an opportunity to define himself. Rather, he is betrayed by his servant while he anxiously seeks to hide himself, his face, his voice, his practice, his history, and his tale. To a large extent, the only gesture of self-definition he makes is a gesture of dissimulation; he reveals only his need to keep himself secret. (For discussions of the relationship of this tale to its companion pieces, the "Second Nun's Tale" and the "Manciple's Tale," see Weil 162–170 or Longsworth 87–96.) This should alert us to potential links to Chaucer, himself a master of such gestures.

We know that alchemy, the canonical life, and Chaucer's poetry are all concerned with interpretations of the written word. Canons were held to their canonical rule; in fact, they derive their very name, "canon," from the written canon laws of the Church. Alchemists informed, seduced, and deceived by the "derke parables" of their treatises, recipes, and poems (Ashmole 214). We have seen that the first two practices had, by the fourteenth century, become infamous for their inability to balance the opposing imperatives of their crafts—with an added sting of internal corruption. Is Chaucer passing a similar judgment on his own art? Did he place a tale about the impossibility of reaching a conclusion toward the end of his fragmentary collection of tales, because he knew he could never complete his original plan? Is he practicing deceptions similar to the alchemists' when he uses the strategic distances between author, narrator, teller, and tale, to revel in the space where the words are cousin to (and cozen) that which they describe? Does his language both delight and founder in its own "multiplicacioun" of "derke parables?" Is the poet like the alchemist of the Prologue, the helplessly addicted victim of an enchanting and frustrating art; or is he the diabolical cozener of the tale itself? The tale finally enacts the same dialectic as the alchemical tracts it mocks, withholding the secret answers even as it invites the reader's judgment.

REFERENCES

Primary Sources

Ashmole, Elias. *Theatrum Chemicum Britannicum*. New York: Johnson Reprint Corp., 1967.

Chaucer, Geoffrey. *The Canon's Yeoman's Tale*, 1. 773 in *The Canterbury Tales*. Ed. Larry D. Benson. Boston: Houghton Mifflin Co., 1987.

Gower, John. *Mirour de l'Omme*. In the *Complete Works of John Gower*. Ed. G. C. Macauley. Oxford: Clarendon Press, 1899.

Guillaume de Lorris and Jean de Meun. *Romance of the Rose*. Trans. Charles Dahlberg. Hanover: University Press of New England, 1983.

Plato. *Timaeus*. Trans. Benjamin Jowett in *The Collected Dialogues*. Eds. Edith Hamilton and Huntington Cairns. Princeton, N.J.: Princeton University Press, 1961.

Pseudo-Albertus Magnus. *Libellus de Alchimia*. Trans. Sister Virginia Heines. Berkeley: University of California Press, 1958.

Secondary Sources

Berthelot, M. *La Chimie au Moyen Age*. Vols. 1–3. Osnabrück: Otto Zeller; Amsterdam: Philo Press, 1967.

Colvin, H. M. *The White Canons in England*. Oxford: Clarendon Press, 1951.

Coulton, G. C. *Five Centuries of Religion*. Vol. 2. Cambridge: Cambridge University Press, 1927.

Daniel-Rops, H. *Cathedral and Crusade: Studies of the Medieval Church, 1050–1350*. Trans. John Warrington. London: J. M. Dent and Sons; New York: E. P. Dutton and Co., 1957.

Dickinson, J. C. *The Austin Canons and Their Introduction into England*. London: S.P.C.K., 1950.

Flick, Alexander Clarence. *The Decline of the Medieval Church*. Vol. 1. New York: Burt Franklin, 1930.

Gasquet, Abbot. *English Monastic Life*. Port Washington, N.Y.: Kennikat Press, 1904.

Halleux, Robert. *Les Textes Alchimiques*. Turnhout-Belgium: Brepols, 1979.

Holmyard, E. J. *Alchemy*. Baltimore: Penguin, 1957.

Hopkins, Arthur John. *Alchemy: Child of Greek Philosophy*. New York: AMS Press, 1967.

Lawrence, C. H. *Medieval Monasticism: Forms of Religious Life in Western Europe in the Middle Ages*. London: Longman, 1984.

Longsworth, Robert M. "Privileged Knowledge: St. Cecilia and the Alchemist in the Canterbury Tales." *Chaucer Review* 27, no./ 1 (1992): 87–96.

Lynch, Joseph H. *The Medieval Church: A Brief History*. London: Longman, 1992.

Patterson, Lee. "The Modernity of the Middle Ages." (forthcoming).

Pickering, James. "Chaucer's *Alchemy:* The Pilgrims Assayed." *Medieval Perspectives* 4–5 (1989–1990): 140–149.

Read, John. *Prelude to Chemistry*. New York: Macmillan, 1937.

Schuler, Robert M. "The Renaissance *Chaucer* as Alchemist." *Viator* 15 (1984): 305–333.

Thompson, Charles J. S. *The Lure and Romance of Alchemy.* London: George G. Harrup and Co., 1932; rprt. Detroit: Gale Research Co., 1974).

Weil, Eric. "An Alchemical Freedom Fight: Linking the Manciple's Tale to the Second Nun's and the Canon's Yeoman's Tale." *Medieval Perspectives* 6 (1991): 162–170.

Chapter 31

His Yeman Eek Was Ful of Curteisye

ROBERT T. AND LAURA C. LAMBDIN

One of the more curious events of the *Canterbury Tales* occurs in the final section of the Ellesmere Manuscript and provides us with the addition of a new story teller, the Canon's Yeoman. This peculiar circumstance occurs when the Canon and his Yeoman ride furiously in order to join the pilgrims, only to have the Canon leave after he is scrutinized by Harry Bailly. Prompted by the Host's questions, the Canon's Yeoman provides us with a fascinating glimpse at the science of alchemy, one of the oddest vocational trends of the time. There has been some speculation that the addition of the Canon and his Yeoman is spurious or was added late because Chaucer had been duped by an alchemist, notions that R. M. Lumiansky finds have no merit (227). Whatever the reason for this pilgrim's inclusion, it soon becomes clear that the vocation of the Canon's Yeoman must be perceived in a different light than that implied by his title because of his specific duties and knowledge. As Paul Ruggiers notes, the Yeoman, leaden-hued, disheveled, and impoverished, is knowledgeable about the ability of alchemy to separate the greedy from their money, yet he himself is unable to withstand the fever for gain and the fleeting promise of power (132).

The term *yeoman* suggests two things. First, at one point he must have owned a piece of land or property, or he must have had some kind of net worth, for this was implied by law; by the fifteenth century, a yeoman must have had an annual income of 40 shillings from his freehold property (Schmidt 3). The Canon's Yeoman confides that his addiction to alchemy has taken all his money: "Al that I hadde, I have lost therby" [VIII (G) 721]. Second, the term insinuates that he was some sort of assistant or servant. In its truest sense, then, the role of a Canon's Yeoman would have been to assist a literate and learned man of high office and esteem in the Church (Burland 66). Extensive book knowledge would have made the Canon a valuable commodity to the Church and, under normal circumstances, would have accelerated his promotion to that of serving in a cathedral or a collegiate church.

With this in mind, it would be easy to envision the Canon Yeoman's tasks as those appropriate for a servant to a man of high Church stature. Perhaps he would have overseen the Canon's affairs by setting dates, scheduling services, or keeping accounts. Yet the Canon is atypical and guilty of using his great knowledge for evil, worldly purposes; the Yeoman speaks of this when he says "For whan a man hath over-greet a wit, / Ful oft hym happeth to mysusen it" [VIII (G) 648–649]. Therefore this duo has forsaken the nice quarters and amenities they would have deserved because of the Canon's Church affiliation. Instead, they are forced to dwell

> "In the suburbes of a toun," quod he,
> "Lurkynge in hernes and in lanes blynde,
> Whereas thise robbours and thise theves by kynde
> Holden hir pryvee fereful residence
> As they that dar nat shewen hir presence"
>
> [VIII (G) 657–661]

> ["In the suburbs of a town," said he,
> "Lurking in hiding places and in lanes blind,
> Where these robbers and these thieves by kind
> Hold their secret fearful residence
> As they that dare not show their presence"]

Therefore, as Professor Conlee noted earlier in this book in his chapter on the Squire's Yeoman, it is understandable that the Canon's Yeoman would have been one of the lowest in status of all of those on the pilgrimage, for even if his master constantly promises huge future rewards, only a fool would knowingly participate in a lifestyle of poor health, deception, and poverty. He had to be callous and vain to go along with the Canon's antics as a cunning alchemist. Carl Lindahl takes the position that the Canon's Yeoman would have been only above the cook and the plowman in terms of status. Indeed, as the personal servant of a religious officer, he would have had less freedom than the cook, yet his position would have been elevated by that of his master. Therefore, the Yeoman would have been considered a better man, simply because of his relationship with a man of the Church (22–24).

Calling this newest pilgrim the Canon's "Yeoman" may be constructed as a bit of a misnomer, however. Indeed, as the events of the "Canon's Yeoman's Prologue" detail, the Canon and his Yeoman have strayed far from the notions of Canonical law and religion. This digression from the Holy Spirit to an unsuccessful venture into the dark chasm of the fires and harsh materials of alchemy has caused the servant to become deeply disturbed, particularly by their continued failures (Burland 66). Because of this pair's addiction to alchemy, it may be alleged that a more fit medieval title would be that of Canon's "puffer."

In alchemic terms, the name "puffer" referred to the hearths where alchemists worked which held a large pair of bellows installed permanently at one side. Additional equipment here included anvils, hammers, tongs, and pincers. The puffer was often depicted in medieval times, as with the Canon and his Yeoman, as the manipulator of the fires for an alchemist of the exoteric or uniformed type. In other words, these alchemists were not seeking spiritual awareness, only wealth, so they were considered base. The depiction of these alchemists typically showed them fanning the flames of a huge fire, which explains why they were often referred to as "laborers of the fire" (Read, *Through* 78–79).

Since an accurate thermometer was not invented until the late eighteenth century, precise regulation of the size and heat of fires was extremely difficult. But this did not keep those interested in extracting gold from base metals or discovering the legendary Philosopher's Stone, a ruby red stone that alchemists felt was the missing elixir or chief agent in the creation of gold (Taylor 66), from trying an amazing variety of means of creating the perfect fire. They relied on imprecise calculations to determine the required heat; this included using horse dung, water, and sand-butt for building a fire with gentle heat, while wood, charcoal, and coal were stoked to create a somewhat stronger heat. Thomas Norton later noted in *Theatrum Chemicum Brittanicum* (ca. 1652) that in alchemy the heat must be enough to "roast grosse meate," and he described a "wet fire" (*ignus humidus*). Norton also warned of a "fier of effusion," and for good reason. In the seventeenth century it was recorded that Johannes Oporinus, an alchemist's assistant much like Chaucer's Canon's Yeoman, was knocked out by an effusion fire during one experiment. He passed out after poisonous vapors "invaded his nose . . . and was revived only after being doused by a bucket of cold water" (Coudert 40).

Other accounts of chemical dangers express the consequences of puffing into fires involving certain chemicals without understanding the possible side effects or toxic reactions. It was documented that even as late as the seventeenth century these fires still were not understood and could be lethal. Alchemist Domenico Parodi was overcome by the gasses emitted during an experiment with antimony, an element now used with other metals to harden them and increase their resistance to chemical action, and died three days later (Coudert 40–41). As the Canon's Yeoman explains, these alchemists became what can only be perceived as addicted to the flames. It was because of these constant attempts to regulate fires in any way, with bellows, wind, or breath, that the base alchemists and their assistants were called "puffers."

The art of puffing to promote combustion and to attain a higher temperature dates back to antiquity. Egyptian drawings from around 1450 B.C. show the remote ancestors of the alchemic puffers working two pairs of bellows to stoke a furnace (Read, *Through* 79). Such early ideas were available to most civilizations, and the process evolved into a complicated array of hypothetical unknowns. By the fourth century B.C., these notions were pursued and expanded by the Greek Aristotle, who supposed that there were four elementary properties or qualities. These four formed two pairs of opposites: hot and cold, dry and wet, which, when combined pairwise, gave rise to the four fundamental elements: earth, air, fire, and water. Aristotle posited that these four elements were incorporated with a *prima materia,* an unknown that had no material existence until it became allied with some type of form. Only then could it enable one element to pass into another in a process he called transmutation. He further believed that somewhere behind these four elements was a shadowy and ill-defined fifth type that Aristotle called "ether" or the element of the stars. It is this missing element that medieval alchemists confused with the concept of the Philosopher's Stone (Read, *Through* 2–3).

The search for this missing fifth element led to the evolution of the craft of alchemy and its further emphasis on fire in medieval times. Allison Coudert notes that the fire was the most important and trickiest part of the alchemists' technique; the alchemists themselves felt this was the greatest mystery of the art (38). By using fire properly, alchemists believed that they could speed the course of nature by bringing base metals to the perfection of gold in a fraction of the time it took naturally. They often noted the difficulties in controlling their laboratory fires, and they grieved over the flames more than any other component of their craft. In a statement that may be applied to Chaucer's Canon's Yeoman, Coudert explains that alchemists constantly complained about slovenly or sleepy assistants who ruined months of work by failing to regulate their fires (38).

The difficulties concerning regulation were increased when it was theorized that the heat of the fire should be increased to its final, or red, stage. The speculation regarding this is exemplified by a quote attributed to the seventeenth-century alchemist Albertus Magnus in *Compositum de Compositis:* "Increase the fire until its force and power, the material is changed into a stone, very red, which the philosophers call Blood, or Purple, Red Coral, Red Sulphur" (Coudert 38). It was during this final stage that the puffers pumped the bellows and blew on the flames so hard that the materials being heated often spat or exploded in their faces, which accounts for the complexion of Chaucer's Canon's Yeoman as well as the group's nickname. Interestingly, the appellation "puffer" became a derogatory term associated with the less philosophical or religious alchemists—those interested in turning a fast buck—and was bestowed on these hooligans by the more spiritually minded alchemists who considered themselves disinterested in the material benefits to be had from producing gold (Coudert 38–39). Thus we can see that there was even a certain class distinction formed within this spurious art.

By the Middle Ages, the idea stoked by alchemy in terms of heat and transmutation, which was illustrated thousands of years earlier by the Egyptians, had evolved into an hierarchical structure. Read comments on this notion and concludes that the groups included those alchemists who "on the one hand were ranged the sheep, the elect fraternity of alchemic cognoscenti; on the other hand stood the goats, the worldly-minded seekers of gold, those alchemical 'outsiders' sometimes disdainfully known as . . . 'puffers' " (*Prelude* 23). So two groups of alchemists evolved; the Canon's Yeoman falls into the lesser second category and, perhaps, could have learned something had he been around the pilgrims when the Pardoner preached his sermon of *radix malorum est cupiditas.* (Perhaps ''the love of *gold* is the root of all evil'' would be more appropriate.)

The primary aim of the puffers, although they might often share the religious convictions of those alchemists known as ''adepts'' who searched for the Philosopher's Stone in the name of the Church, was to heat and mix elements that would combine and allow the alchemists to obtain the Philosopher's Stone as a key to material wealth and well being. Many adepts looked to the Philosopher's Stone as a spiritual grail, although it was probably true that most had a secondary interest in the Stone as a source of wealth, health, and long life (Read, *Through* 83). Thus it is clear that the puffers would have been jealous of their competitors in the quest for gold. To this extent, the true adept would have considered himself a guardian of the secrets of this ''divine art'' (Read, *Prelude* 92)—that is, if indeed he had really discovered and understood any such mysteries!

Dealing as they did with the unknown, these people became a suspicious, paranoid lot. Because alchemy had evolved into such a secret science, the participants often kept little or no records of their ''research,'' except in cryptic messages that meant nothing to anyone but themselves. Too, they often undid all that they had accomplished at the end of an experiment so that nobody could steal their findings and copy their work. Because of this destructive aspect of their job, the puffers were ''likened to Penelope who would undo at night what she would do by day'' (Read, *Prelude* 161). Furthermore, because there were so many variables in their experiments, most alchemists obsessed that they would be unable to duplicate any true science they may have stumbled on. It is ironic that such a previously inexact science evolved into one so exact: chemistry.

Because this science was so based on constant and inexact experiments, the unsophisticated puffers used other materials in their operations, regardless of any theoretical considerations. When Chaucer's Canon's Yeoman provides an intensive list of alchemic compounds, we must note its diversity (such as urine or egg whites). It would have been difficult to truly name any material known to these medieval chemists that was *not* at some time or another drawn into the course of their operations (Read, *Prelude* 134–135). Just about every substance, natural or unnatural, was subjected to the heat of the alchemists' fires in the hopes of producing the Philosopher's Stone. Selecting the correct ingredients was extremely frustrating, especially considering the many alchemists who professed their success at creating gold or finding the Philosopher's Stone and their silence about necessary materials. The author of *Gloria Mundi* (1678) claimed that the needed ingredients were right under every alchemist's nose:

[It] is found in the country, in the village and in the town, in all things created by God; yet it is despised by all. Rich and poor handle it every day. It is cast into the streets by servant maids. Children play with it. Yet no one prizes it, though next to the human soul it is the most beautiful and precious thing upon the earth and has the power to pull down kings and princes. Nevertheless it is esteemed the vilest and meanest of earthly things. It is cast away and rejected by all. (Quoted in Coudert 41)

The foolishness of the Yeoman's list in particular leads to an array of questions concerning the Yeoman which have split the critics.

Is he to be perceived as a loquacious fool as seen by Lumiansky and a host of other critics, or is he well versed in his craft and confessing his sins in realization of his losses and the effects of his cunning on others? Carl Lindahl sees the Yeoman's curse of the Canon to be potentially dangerous, for he is a servant insulting his master, but then he goes on to say that the Yeoman speaks only after the Canon, exposed as a fraud, is forced to abandon the company, so the Yeoman has avoided a face-to-face encounter (92). Too, this confession comes as a direct result of the prying questions of Harry Bailly; the Yeoman's renunciation of his evil pursuit may reveal, as John Gardner notes, that the Philosopher's Stone which these two so dearly cherish is "none other than Christ, by extension the Pearl of Price" (201); thus the Yeoman's confession might well bring him the riches he desires.

UNDERSTANDING THE "CANON'S YEOMAN'S TALE"

When the pilgrims arrive at Boughton-under-Blean, only about five miles outside of Canterbury, they are joined by two rushing, sweating new characters: the Canon and his Yeoman. This sudden and dramatic occurrence invites speculation; it seems likely that the pair join the pilgrimage intending to con as many members as possible (Kittredge, Manly, etc.), and it may also be the case that they are fleeing from other folks whom they had conned earlier (Lumiansky). It is possible that the Yeoman, suddenly struck by a desire to reform, has seized this opportunity to escape by encouraging his master to join the "joly compaignye" [VII (G) 583]. Clearly, this Yeoman is the only pilgrim who is a dynamic character, for his personality undergoes a major revision during the text. Indeed, although the narration does partially expose the fraud of alchemy, that it is all an illusion, this tale seems to exist for the teller (Kittredge 222).

The Canon's Yeoman may be introduced to remind the reader of how a true spiritual pilgrimage should conclude. With the help of the Host's inquiries (as an innkeeper he would be good at digging for information), the Yeoman slowly distances himself from both his master and his craft. The Yeoman finally drives the Canon away with open criticism and is able to look back over the seven disheartening and wasted years he has spent working for an alchemist. This review is followed by a narration about a universal alchemist figure, a text that— like many of the other pilgrims' tales—offers variations on the themes of deception and self-deception (Burlin 175).

The Canon is too old and set in his grifting ways, but the relatively young Yeoman seems mostly willing and able to reform. He confesses like the Wife of Bath and the Pardoner, but unlike them, he is not proud of his lifestyle or pleased with himself, and therefore he seems to want real change (Campbell 179). While the Yeoman's answers to Harry Bailly's first two questions can be seen as automatic "sales talk" that has been a part of his job for years, his answer about his boss's misused intelligence marks "a definite break, intellectual as well as emotional, with the Canon, and the beginnings of a struggle to separate himself from a long and fruitless habit" (Cook 33). The Host asks the perfect question just when the Yeoman seems about to fall silent: " 'Why artow so discoloured of thy face?' " [VIII (G) 664] [" 'Why are you so discolored in your face?' "]. This reference to his personal mark of shame, the once rosy, now leaden-hued visage, sets the Yeoman off:

There is an appealing irony in the notion of an alchemist's servant himself being changed from a healthy ruddiness of complexion to a leaden pallor (724–729)—the reverse of the hoped-for change from lead to gold—and in the ultimate effects of pursuing the science, which are to make men impoverished instead of wealthy (731–741). (Brown 486)

It is this grim reminder of his loss of a rosy skintone that makes the Yeoman "not mind using himself as a negative example to instruct others." He is himself a warning away from the practice of alchemy and away from those who need resources in order to practice alchemy (Cook 36).

Chaucer carefully developed the Yeoman's motivation to sin, making his confession seem designed to work with the "Parson's Tale" as an example of how the sacrament of confession should work (Ryan 299). The Yeoman starts slowly after his Prologue, with the *Prima Pars* showing mostly the quasiscientific, pragmatic aspects of the trade. The Yeoman recites a confused but fairly complete list of alchemical recipes, ingredients, and utensils, the point of which remains obscure. Is Chaucer satirizing the use of pointless technical terminology? If so, we have only to watch current television commercials to relate:

As members of a technological society, we recognize the fraudulent allure of scientific language to which we attach no concrete meaning—in advertisements for soap with hexachlorophene, lotion with benzoyle peroxide, detergent with enzymes, wheat germ oil with octacosanol, and vitamins with triacotanol, tetraconsanol, hexaconsanol and high content octaconsanol. We buy bikes with manganese molybdenum tubing, cameras with synchro-meterized flash integration and quartz-driven calcu-set modules, watches with polysulfone cases, and shoes with kinetic ribs, cantilevered outersoles, and butterfly-balancing systems. (Hilberry 442)

As has been often noted, the list of the *Prima Pars* seems too complete to have come from a common man of the era. Indeed, the material is so technical that it was once assumed that Chaucer himself was an alchemist. Eventually, however, sources for the information were discovered. Two nearly identical works by Vincent of Beauvais composed in the 1470s, *Speculum Naturale* and *Speculum Doctrinale,* contain the same written information as does the tale (although

Vincent's texts are more in-depth, such as minute descriptions of the nine grades of fires) (Aiken 385).

While the list was once considered rather silly, several pioneering studies (Lumiansky, Muscatine, Speirs) conclude that the list is part of Chaucer's literary art and is intended to help create a more "fleshed-out" or realistic character. It is also likely that the list is meant to show the Yeoman's lingering interest in alchemy, despite his protests. He can still impress himself, at the very least, with his scientific mumbo jumbo, and he can yet imagine the great joy he would feel if gold were actually created. Instead, despite his excitement, all that has ever happened as a result of these experiments are wasteful and inexplicable accidents that create only messes: "Some of the contents scatters on the floor and some into the ground in a fruitless, sterile orgasm—wasteful, nonproductive spilling of false seed—a worthless, failed 'multiplication,' an act of pseudo-creation" (Calabrese 287). The aspect of the Yeoman's psyche that requires further thought is that he remains fascinated by this fruitless occupation. Despite a lack of adequate compensation, the Yeoman is still desperately interested in his craft and therefore might be considered unlikely to change vocations.

Pars Secunda contains the actual tale, which does not begin until line 972, wherein a priest is conned by a canon/alchemist. The Yeoman insists that the canon in his tale is *not* the Canon he has served for the past seven years. This seems odd, and it is also strange that both characters of the tale, the canon and the priest, are men of the cloth. "The chantry priest is swindled by the alchemist in the second part just as the alchemist is swindled by the science in the first. That the victim is a priest and the alchemists are canons may be owing to current events for all we know" (Muscatine 216). The tale describes the ease of deception when one's audience is greedy, gullible, and wishes to believe in magic or a get-rich-quick scheme. The quicksilver remains the same; it is the priest who changes:

The alchemist is running a scam; and the metals themselves remain unaltered by the purportedly alchemical operations to which they are subjected. On the other hand, a transformation does indeed take place: by sleight of hand the protagonist substitutes one metal for another, and thereby deludes his victim into supposing that the substance of a single metal has been altered. (Longsworth 88)

The reader, like the priest, may become caught up in the process and wish to acquire more specific information about what takes place *after* the fire and elements have been set up in the way the alchemist suggests. Such knowledge is not to be gleaned from our Yeoman, who either does not know the required magic or will not share such privileged information:

Indeed, one of the most baffling features of the *CYT*—its two-part structure with its "two" canons—grows directly out of the poet's familiarity with the literature, for it duplicates the very structure of an alchemical treatise, a first part filled with an enormous melange of directions and ingredients, and a second part which dissolves into mystic mummery and allegory when it purports to describe the actual transmutation. (Grennen 547)

No specific information is given because the final steps are secrets guarded closely by alchemists.

The priest has no greater understanding than he did before, nor does the Yeoman seem to possess seven years' worth of magic/science. Has the Yeoman been conned like the priest? Is a reader to understand that there is only one canon and that the priest, who blows on the fire, is meant to signify the Yeoman? Lawrence Ryan finds that the Yeoman "doth protest too much" that there are two canons (303), but perhaps the two are separate sides of one man's character and are intended to reflect the dualism implied in the alchemical lifestyle: "There are two aspects of alchemy, after all—the spurious practice used for gulling people and the serious scientific search for the Philosopher's Stone—but the Yeoman's mind seldom makes a sharp and clear distinction between them" (Campbell 175). All the Yeoman knows is that he is much worse off than when he first met the Canon.

Although the confessional revealing makes the Yeoman's disillusionment and feelings of acute futility very clear, it is equally obvious that the servant still admires his old master and retains a fascination for alchemy. He feels a weary hopelessness that the craft will never produce the desired results, and he is tired of the required deception and dishonesty. However, the Yeoman never accepts moral responsibility for his own actions; he may feel some personal guilt, but all is mostly the fault of that "slidynge science" [VIII (G) 732] of alchemy. The reader is aware that the Yeoman leaves the Canon more to avoid the despair caused by his craft rather than to avoid the untruths necessary to finance alchemical undertakings.

Is the Yeoman's reformation truly underway, or will he revert to his former lifestyle? While his split from the Canon seems irreconcilable, the Yeoman may yet admire him in some ways. Another problem, more prohibitive to change, is that the Yeoman has trained for seven years as an alchemist's apprentice. Thus he might not only miss the Canon, but he may need his former master to employ him because he is trained for little else. However, since yeomen did simple daily tasks as defined by their masters, one assumes that this particular Yeoman could find a job performing uncomplicated tasks for a master in some other field. It is hard to decide whether the Yeoman sincerely wishes to distance himself from his craft. "He does have ambivalent feelings, after all, not only about his former lord but about what he is doing at this moment of major change in his life" (Campbell 174). He still seems excited about the possibilities of chemical experiments, so many critics (Chute, Cook, Reidy) believe that he will remain greedy and deluded; however, others (Gardner, Greenberg, Olmert) agree that he truly renounces his former lifestyle.

The Yeoman's mixture of spleen, yearning, and remorse is further confused by the suggestions that certainly the second Canon, and possibly the first, is a fiend that the Yeoman cannot escape without giving a full confession. The Yeoman stops short of total self-incrimination, so his confession seems far from true penitence. He may even be agonized by this half-repenting and evasion of blame. The Canon of the false religion of alchemy flees once his true nature is revealed, and the Yeoman is left to blame his former master entirely for their earlier misdeeds. He tells secrets to the audience not only for their protection and benefit, but also in an attempt to cleanse himself of any taint of wrongdoing. It has been suggested that the Yeoman fears the Canon as a truly satanic figure; therefore, he wants to get away from him but hesitates from fear to tell all (Ryan 229). The link has also been made between the Canon and an anti-Christ figure because the Yeoman uses diabolical terms to describe him (Rosenberg 567). Perhaps all the fire imagery is meant to symbolize the fires of hell, which have burned the Yeoman both physically and spiritually (Grennen 236).

Has alchemy become an addiction burned into the Yeoman's consciousness as a deep need that is impossible to drive away, even with a confession? He seems more disillusioned with alchemists than able to scorn alchemy, and he is frustrated by his own ignorance. It is as though "he believes in the efficacy of a knowledge that others do, though he does not possess" (Longsworth 89). Perhaps the Yeoman wants to become a reformed addict, rejecting the deceit that accompanies a lust for gold, but "the psychology is that of the confirmed gambler, one who knows better but cannot resist the seductions of yet another try" (Burlin 71). The Yeoman is a simple but hopeful man who has been introduced to an addictive lifestyle that has destroyed his self-respect, stolen his health, and used up all of his money. Although "meeting the Yeoman is a bit like listening to a man who has been to Alcoholic's Anonymous" (Cook 34), he still does not completely reject alchemy as science.

The science of alchemy was too caught up with various religious ideas (like the thought that God's creative breath was needed to produce the Philosopher's Stone) for it to be completely rejected by a man with any respect for the Church. "The poem's dualism of attitude is conventional. It corresponds to the division of the science between charlatans and puffers on one hand, and philosophers and mystics on the other" (Muscatine 215). The constant play between wisdom versus ignorance and science versus spirit is linked to the Yeoman's dichotomy of pleasing appendage of his master versus the rebellious informer he becomes. That the Yeoman's tone is dispassionate and educated at the end has made critics (Hartung 112; Herz 236) wonder whether this were not Chaucer speaking himself and forgetting his created character as persona. Indeed, the final section in which the Yeoman cites authorities like Arnold of Newton who wrote in Latin seems out of character.

Following his work on the Hengwrt manuscript of the *Canterbury Tales,* N. F. Blake suggested that the Prologue and the Tale may have been written by an unknown imitator. This inauthenticity seems unlikely if we find the piece to work with the "Second Nun's Tale" of St. Cecilia as part of a pair. "The principle of juxtaposing like with unlike in a mutually enriching way appears to be an example of the practice adopted by Chaucer with, say, the *Knight's Tale,* and *Miller's Tale"* (Brown 485). It has also been theorized that not only do the "Canon's Yeoman's Tale" and the "Second Nun's Tale" work together, but also that all of the stories from the "Second Nun's Tale" to the end of the *Canterbury Tales* are meant to be read as one extremely sober unit (Campbell 172). Certainly, the "Second Nun's Tale," with its lesson in how to regard the physical world from a spiritual point of view is the opposite of the graphic "Canon's Yeoman's Tale" with its many references to physical secretions:

Perhaps no figures in Chaucer are so tied to the body as the Canon and his Yeoman: the froth of sweat, the darkened skin, the thick bubble of piss and dung in the pot. . . . These images create them as body, as fluid, as appetite, and as process, . . . [completely opposite from the] sweatless spirituality fecund St. Cecilia. (Calabrese 278)

The comparison forces us to see the Yeoman as a real human being with a problem, one we can only hope will be purged at the shrine of St. Thomas à Becket.

REFERENCES

Aiken, Pauline. "Vincent of Beauvis and Chaucer's Knowledge of Alchemy." *Studies in Philology* 41, no. 3 (1944): 371–389.

Blake, N. F., ed. *"The Canterbury Tales" by Geoffrey Chaucer: Edited from the Hengwrt Manuscript.* London: York Medieval Texts, 1980.

Brown, Peter. "Is the 'Canon's Yeoman's Tale' Apocryphal?" *English Studies* 64 (1983): 481–490.

Burland, C. A. *The Arts of the Alchemists.* London: Weidenfield and Nicolson, 1967.

Burlin, Robert B. *Chaucerian Fiction.* Princeton, N.J.: Princeton University Press, 1977.

Calabrese, Michael A. "Meretricious Mixtures: Gold, Dung, and the Canon's Yeoman's Prologue and Tale." *Chaucer Review* 27, no. 3 (1993): 277–292.

Campbell, Jackson J. "The Canon's Yeoman as Imperfect Paradigm." *Chaucer Review* 17, no. 2 (1982): 171–181.

Chute, Marchette. *Geoffrey Chaucer of England.* New York: Dalton, 1946.

Cook, Robert. "The Canon's Yeoman and His Tale." *Chaucer Review* 22, no. 1 (1987): 28–40.

Coudert, Allison. *Alchemy: The Philosopher's Stone.* Boulder, Colo.: Shambhala, 1980.

Dickson, Donald R. "The 'Slidynge' Yeoman: The Real Drama in the *Canon's Yeoman's Tale."* *South Central Review* 2, no. 2 (1985): 10–22.

Duncan, Edgar Hill. "The Literature of Alchemy and Chaucer's *Canon's Yeoman's Tale:* Framework, Theme, and Characters." *Speculum* 43 (1968): 633–656.

Gardner, John. "Signs, Symbols, and Cancellations." In *Signs and Symbols in Chaucer's Poetry.* Eds. John P. Hermann and John J. Burke, Jr. Tuscaloosa: University of Alabama Press, 1981.

Greenberg, Bruce. *"The Canon's Yeoman's Tale:* Boethian Wisdom and the Alchemists." *Chaucer Review* 1 (1966): 37–54.

Grennen, Joseph E. "The Canon's Yeoman's Alchemical 'Mass.' " *Studies in Philology* 62 (1965): 546–560.

Hartung, Albert E. "Inappropriate Pointing in the *Canon's Yeoman's Tale,* G 1236–1239." *PMLA* 77 (1962): 508–509.

Herz, Judith Scherer. "*The Canon's Yeoman's Prologue* and *Tale.*" *MP* 58 (1961): 231–237.

Hilberry, Jane. " 'And In Oure Madnesse Evermore We Rave': Technical Language in the *Canon's Yeoman's Tale.*" *Chaucer Review* 21, no. 4 (1987): 435–443.

Kittredge, George L. "*The Canon's Yeoman's Prologue* and *Tale.*" *Transactions of the Royal Society for Literature* 30 (1910): 87–95.

Lindahl, Carl. *Earnest Games.* Bloomington: Indiana University Press, 1987.

Longsworth, Robert M. "Privileged Knowledge: St. Cecilia and the Alchemist in the *Canterbury Tales.*" *Chaucer Review* 27, no. 1 (1992): 87–96.

Lumiansky, R. M. *Of Sundry Folk.* Austin: University of Texas Press, 1955.

Manly, J. M. *Some New Light on Chaucer.* New York: Henry Holt, 1926.

Metlitzki, Dorothee. *The Matter of Araby in Medieval England.* New Haven, Conn.: Yale University Press, 1977.

Muscatine, Charles. *Chaucer and the French Tradition.* Berkeley: University of California Press, 1964.

Olmert, Michael. "*The Canon's Yeoman's Tale:* An Interpretation." *AnM* 8 (1987): 70–94.

Read, John. *Prelude to Chemistry.* Cambridge, Mass.: MIT Press, 1966.

———. *Through Alchemy to Chemistry.* London: Bell and Sons, 1961.

Reidy, John. "Chaucer's Canon and the Unity of the *Canon's Yeoman's Tale.*" *PMLA* 80 (1965): 31–37.

Rosenberg, Bruce A. "Swindling Alchemist, Antichrist." *CRAS* 6 (1962): 566–580.

Ruggiers, Paul G. *The Art of the "Canterbury Tales."* Madison: University of Wisconsin Press, 1965.

Ryan, Lawrence. "The Canon's Yeoman's Desperate Confession." *Chaucer Review* 8 (1974): 297–310.

Schmidt, Albert J. *The Yeoman in Tudor and Stuart England.* 1961. Charlottesville: University of Virginia Press, 1968.

Speirs, John. *Chaucer the Maker.* London: Faber, 1960.

Taylor, F. Sherwood. *The Alchemists: Founders of Modern Chemistry.* New York: Henry Schuman, 1949.

Chapter 32

"What Man Artow?": The Narrator as Writer and Pilgrim

KATHARINE WILSON

The little narrator in the *Canterbury Tales* is an enigma. He turns his searching gaze on everyone on the pilgrimage except himself, finishing up in a rush with "Ther was also a Reve, and a Millere, / A Somnour, and a Pardoner also, / A Maunciple, and myself—ther were namo" (542–544) ["There was also a Reeve, and a Miller, / A Summoner, and a Pardoner also, / A Manciple, and Myself— there were no more"]. Not a word about what he himself does for a living or where he stands socially. To find out who he is and what he does, we must look for clues in the text.

We know he's not just a talker who's telling a story once, but a writer who has produced a written copy of the story and knows it may survive to be read by others. His promise to produce a word-for-word transcript of the pilgrimage, to "reherce as ny as evere he kan / Everich a word" (732–733) ["repeat as close as ever he knows how / Every word"], would be a difficult promise to keep if he hadn't been taking notes the whole journey and writing up the stories to be read later. Perhaps the promise to produce a perfect copy is just hyperbole. What isn't hyperbole, however, is his caution before the "Miller's Tale." He acknowledges that his audience might "list it not yheere" (3176), not want to *hear* what he has to say, but then directs them in that case to "Turne over the leef and chese another tale" (3177) ["Turn the page and choose another tale"] and to choose responsibly: "Blameth not me if that ye chese amys" (3181) ["Blame me not if you choose poorly"]. His audience is not just composed of *hearers* but also of *readers* who are responsible for their own choices in a way that they could not have been if they had simply been listening while he talked.

Besides being a poet who both recites his work and writes it down, the narrator is also a pilgrim. He says it clearly: "in that seson on a day, / In Southwerk at the Tabard as I lay / Redy to wenden on my pilgrymage" (19–21) ["in that season on a day, / In Southwark at the Tabard as I lay/ Ready to go on my pilgrimage''']. But the fact that he is a pilgrim gives no clue to what he does in real life; beggars and kings alike could be pilgrims.

So we know the narrator not by his vocation, but by his avocations: writer and pilgrim. So what? Why not short-circuit this elaborate search for textual clues as to what the narrator does and just equate him with Chaucer? After all, the narrator and Chaucer are both literate, so they belong to a relatively small segment of medieval society and are likely to have had similar interests, jobs, and education. Also, to Chaucer's contemporary audience, Chaucer and the narrator could have been one; it's possible that Chaucer read his own poems aloud to the court. As Chaucer read the words of his narrator, ''I was of hir felaweship anon'' (32) [''I was of their fellowship straightaway''], his listeners easily could have merged the government employee with the narrator of the poem, and Chaucer the courtier could have ridden wrapped in pilgrim's robes.

But while Chaucer's hearers may have conflated him with the narrator, we can't know exactly how. It's impossible to question an audience that's been dead for six hundred years, and without knowing more about author or audience, it's dangerous to equate an author automatically with his or her characters; Shakespeare was not Hamlet, Herman Melville was not Ishmael, even though *Moby Dick* begins ''Call me Ishmael,'' and Mary Shelley, author of *Franken- stein,* was not a hodgepodge of resurrected body parts. Neither was Chaucer identical with the narrator in the *Canterbury Tales.* Chaucer was at various times a courtier, a civil servant, an ambassador, and a prisoner of war, but the text doesn't indicate that the plump little narrator tagging along with the jingling, colorful group speaks as any of those. The narrator remains a writer and a pilgrim, and it is as a writer and pilgrim that we must consider him.

THE WRITER

Calling the narrator a reciter and writer is a redundancy, because the first thing the narrator would have been prepared to do as a writer is to read out loud. Medieval writers were not only wordsmiths but also performance artists. William Woods considers the medieval connection between silent reading and vocalization so strong that reading silently to oneself in the Middle Ages would have seemed as insufficient as reading musical notation would be to a modern music lover (166). Modern authors are rarely adept at communicating their works vocally, but to the medieval author, writing a manuscript was only half the job; the other half was reciting it.

The narrator is like Chaucer in that Chaucer may have introduced the *Canterbury Tales* to the world by reading them out loud. While there's no absolute proof that Chaucer performed his works aloud, there are two pieces of circumstantial evidence. The first is simply that many other authors read their own works out loud, so there's no reason to suppose Chaucer didn't. The second is more individualized. A frontispiece of *Troilus and Criseyde,* painted shortly after

Chaucer's death, shows a man who resembles Chaucer, standing behind a lectern declaiming to an audience. Of course, although the narrator of the *Canterbury Tales* might have had an audience, he wouldn't necessarily have had the apparently noble one pictured in the frontispiece. Recitations appealed to the citizenry and peasants as well, and the entertainers known as jongleurs made their living off that fact.

A significant difference between modern and medieval writers is that medieval authors made no money with their pens. Only scriveners (copyists) made money from writing. For authors, there was no market and no reading public because the number of people able to read was relatively small. And even if a writer could have captured the imagination of every reader in England, other writers could have copied his work freely. There were no copyright laws, so every writer, including Chaucer, freely borrowed from other written works. Such borrowing benefited the public because borrowers, by retelling other's tales, made information available to a wider audience than the original authors could reach. Between the lack of readers and the lack of exclusive rights to any story, the narrator of the *Canterbury Tales* never could have paid his bills by selling copies of his work. Few would have bought it, and many would have copied it.

Even if literacy had been universal and copyright laws had existed, the narrator still could not have earned money by writing: there was no way to flood the market with books because there was no quick way to reproduce them. The first book printed in Europe with movable type emerged from Johann Gutenberg's press more than fifty years after Chaucer died. Until then, books had had to be written out individually by hand—a labor-intensive process that could take months per copy and put the price of books beyond the reach of any but the most dedicated reader.

Therefore, authors had to do something besides write if they were to earn a living. Once men had become educated, they had three choices of jobs: Church, government, or, if they were free-spirited or desperate and one doesn't define "literacy" too strictly, the itinerant entertainer's life of the jongleur.

For centuries, the source of literacy in England had been the Church, which not only taught its clergy to read and write, but also taught them to teach others to do so. ("Clergy" here refers to male clergy. Literacy doesn't seem to have extended as uniformly through the nunneries as it did through the monasteries, and nuns confined themselves to teaching their novitiates, while male clergy could instruct members of the secular world as well.) The literacy of the humbler village clerics was often barely above that of their flock, but still, until the end of the twelfth century, education was connected with monasteries or cathedrals so inextricably that to be a scholar was to be religious. G. G. Coulton tells of a religious official who entered religious life only to have a teaching career. "Samson, abbot of Bury St. Edmunds, told Jocelin frankly that, if he could have made bread and cheese by teaching outside, he would never have become a monk" (*Medieval* 580).

Great numbers of grade schools, universities, and colleges were founded throughout England during the fourteenth century. Children of both sexes could receive some schooling, but higher education was reserved for males. If females continued past the grade-school level, they generally did so at home. Many grade schools and "public" (privately funded) institutions were supported by individual philanthropists, churches, and workmen's guilds. The institutions of higher learning were for the most part at least nominally under religious control, but, even so, the Oxford students were such dedicated drinkers and brothel-visitors that in 1355 they clashed in open warfare with the citizens of the town. Still, even in Chaucer's time, secular teachers owed their abilities to the religious masters who had taught them or to the religious masters who had taught *those* masters before. One didn't have to intend to enter the Church to receive an education, but the education available was strongly flavored by that Church.

Writers in the Church not only taught in grammar schools, cathedral schools, and universities; they also preserved old manuscripts and produced new ones. For hundreds of years the high-ranking Church and monastic officials (who were generally the most educated of the churchmen) acted as the wardens of books, and kept Greek and Latin alive so that ancient documents could be read. The churchman had a double intellectual duty: to protect this storehouse of wisdom, and to add to it by writing new texts on history, theology, and philosophy.

But because of the technical demands of producing books, not every writer in the Church was a writer as we think of writers now. Rather than creating new books or even cataloguing old ones, many writers were copyists. With no copy machines, no typewriters, and no printing presses, the only way to multiply manuscripts was to copy each one out by hand. Many monks spent their lives doing just that. They glorified God and relieved what must have been unutterable tedium, by "illuminating," or illustrating, appropriate places in their manuscripts with ornate lettering, biblical figures, animals, angels, and demons.

If the narrator of the *Canterbury Tales* were a cleric at all, the life of a copyist/monk, or of a frugal parson like the "Poor Parson" on the pilgrimage, would be his most likely niche. He would be of fairly low rank because it's unlikely that a bishop, say, would have joined such a ragtag crew, or that he would have been treated as informally by the innkeeper if he had. He is certainly placed no higher than the Priest because the innkeeper addresses even the Priest casually, reserving nominal deference for the Knight, and teases the narrator unmercifully. The only way it's conceivable for the narrator to be a high-ranking churchman is if he has first deliberately disguised himself and then left that fact out of the *Canterbury Tales* altogether.

Even though the Church educated writers, it did not retain every one it taught. If the narrator wasn't a cleric, he could have been one of many Englishmen of letters who clustered in the courts to become either courtiers or government officials.

A courtier's duties in the royal household were wide-ranging. For instance, a Yeoman of the King's Chamber (as Chaucer once was) was a live-in, high-class servant/attendant who carried messages, went on errands, made beds, and did whatever else the chamberlain told him to. Squires (the rank Chaucer eventually achieved) might execute these same housekeeping duties, taste the king's food to test for poison, or entertain royalty, nobility, and visitors by singing, harping, and telling stories.

A government official's job sometimes overlapped with that of the courtier, and also depended on literacy—either an instant familiarity with Italian and French literature (to which he could refer in elaborate ambassadorial speeches) or an ability to write (which he would have needed in a job such as customs-official or comptroller, both of which Chaucer held).

But whether a writer became a civil servant or a courtier, he wasn't limited to legal writing. Courtiers, of course, might have needed to be expert creators of tales and poems for entertainment on long evenings. But civil servants, too, produced not only import/export documents and bills of lading, but also translations, romances, and poems for the amusement of their peers. And "for the amusement of their peers" is an important qualifier; poetry might have won a writer favor or prestige in the English court, but it's not certain that such poets were paid any money.

In fact, even Chaucer may not have earned anything for writing. Although some authorities believe that Chaucer received grants and pensions for his poems, others point out that there's no inevitable cause and effect between Chaucer's writing for the court and his receiving money from it. V. J. Scattergood deduces from the value of Chaucer's pensions (about what any competent government man would get) that Chaucer wasn't a paid writer but rather a paid public official, and that he wrote as a sideline (32). Again, D. W. Robertson, Jr., asserts that Chaucer "was always a member of the court first—whether as squire, customs official, or Clerk of the Works" (217).

The narrator could have been, like Chaucer, a non-nobly-born citizen who became a courtier or civil servant, with the pensions and grants attached to such a position. But no matter what court connections or pensions the narrator had, he probably was not a writer with a patron. Patrons were the rich and influential who paid money—sometimes irregularly, sometimes like any other wage—and even offered room and board in their households to writers. In return for financial support, a writer saturated his works with compliments to his patron. But although the custom of patronage was established in the French court by Chaucer's time, the English court didn't embrace the practice until well afterward, when John Lydgate was financed for his praises of Henry V. Chaucer's *The Book of the Duchess* did commemorate the death of John of Gaunt's wife, but even if John of Gaunt rewarded Chaucer for that particular poem, patronage probably would not have been a steady source of income for either Chaucer or the narrator.

Besides the writers in government and religion, another kind of writer/reciter existed. The jongleur, "half-minstrel, half-buffoon" (Coulton, *Medieval* 581), was a traveling entertainer for occasions such as funerals and weddings. Whether or not he could actually write, he had to be familiar with the classical, romantic, and popular sources that informed medieval literature, and able to rapidly adapt and recite stories from them at will. He had to be good at gauging his audience, too; he subsisted by passing the hat after his performances, and a performance that didn't please didn't pay. Jongleurs drifted from house to house and village to village, pursued by the imprecations of clergymen, who regarded them as ministers of Satan. It's unlikely that the narrator is this impoverished kind of entertainer. He has enough money to stay at inns during his pilgrimage (no easy task on the usual income of a jongleur). And although Bailly teases the narrator remarkably freely, he does not describe the narrator as a jongleur. Bailly does not say that the narrator is ragged or a crowd-pleaser, or that he pesters people for handouts. Rather, Bailly sketches the narrator as a small, silent, doll-like man who stares at the ground as if to search for rabbits, and who probably shrinks from the very kind of hearty cheer Bailly thrusts on him.

> And thanne at erst he looked upon me,
> And seyde thus: "What man artow?" quod he;
> "Thou lookest as thou woldest fynde an hare,
> For evere upon the ground I se thee stare.
>
> "Approche neer, and look up murily.
> Now war yow, sires, and lat this man have place!
> He in the waast is shape as wel as I;
> This were a popet in an arm t'embrace
> For any womman, smal and fair of face.
> He semeth elvyssh by his contenaunce,
> For unto no wight dooth he daliaunce."
>
> (694–704)

> [And then for the first time he looked upon me,
> And said thus "What man are you?" said he;
> You look as though you would find a hare,
> For ever upon the ground I see you stare.
>
> "Approach near and look up merrily.
> Now take care you, sires, and let this man have place!
> He in the waist is shaped as well as I;
> This was a puppet in an arm to embrace
> For any woman, small and fair of face.
> He seems abstracted by his countenance,
> For unto no man is he sociable."]

The narrator could indeed have been a courtier or a cleric (albeit not very high-ranking in either profession), but here on the road he is quiet, teasable, merely one of a crowd of pilgrims. And that's the second part of what the narrator does. Not only is the narrator a writer; he's also "Redy to wenden" (21). He's a pilgrim.

THE PILGRIM

Like saying prayers or giving alms, a pilgrimage was a devotion to God. It was a road trip to one of various holy places, planned for one or more reasons. The pilgrim

1. Might have been ordered by a religious leader to make a pilgrimage as a penance for sin.
2. Might have vowed, in the midst of sickness or trouble, to go on a pilgrimage as a kind of bargain with God to "buy" better times.
3. Might have survived sickness or trouble and wanted to thank God more tangibly than with prayers.
4. Might simply have wanted to go on a journey.

In theory, the purpose of a pilgrimage was religious. In practice, especially by Chaucer's time, pilgrimages could be excursions with a sense of religious duty scarcely more, and a noise level scarcely less, than a vanload of students setting out for spring break. Despite a handful of devout companions, the narrator has joined a rowdy bunch: the Summoner drapes himself in flowers and food, the Pardoner is a shyster, the Friar is a lecher, and at one point the Cook is so drunk that he falls off his horse, requiring "greet showvyng bothe to and fro / To lift hym up" (53–54) ["Great shoving both to and fro / To lift him up"]. Even the Miller's "baggepipe," with which "he broughte us out of towne" (565–566), is noisily inappropriate to play on a holy trip, or so one complaint (by a Lollard called Thorpe, discussed below) would have us believe. Bagpipes at the beginning of a journey are the medieval version of slapping a raucous cassette into a car's tape player, turning the volume up, and roaring onto the highway.

Despite extremely secular distractions, a pilgrimage was supposed to pay a debt to, or fulfill a contract with, God. Making a pilgrimage entailed much more than worshiping at the destination: traveling itself was usually so difficult that the journey itself was privation for the Lord's sake. The expense, danger, and time involved in a pilgrimage, of course, increased dramatically when the pilgrim traveled overseas to the most holy of holy places, Rome or Jerusalem, but even a local pilgrimage like the Canterbury trip had great potential for unpleasantness and danger.

The dangers of travel began with the daunting logistics of simply getting from point to point. Roads were not paved outside London; beyond the city gates, the flat, wide strip we think of as a road degenerated into the weedy ruts of cart-tracks, and those cart-tracks degenerated into mires. In 1499, bad road conditions actually killed one unfortunate glove-maker who had started out at night from Leighton Buzzard to Aylesbury on a horse laden with panniers of gloves. In the dark, neither rider nor horse saw a huge hole that had been dug in the middle of the road by a miller who had needed some clay to repair his mill. The pit that the miller left had filled with rain, and both rider and horse fell in and were drowned (Coulton, *Medieval* 323–324). Although the records don't indicate that this particular kind of disaster was common, or that clay pits dotted England's roads, travel was quite dangerous enough anyway. Besides being so dark at night that it was indeed possible for travelers to blunder into danger, even during daylight travel wasn't easy. Bridges and roads were muddy, rocky, desolate, and so subject to ruinous bad weather that maintaining them was a charity and a duty to God.

Bridge and road maintenance was charitable and holy because it mitigated the terrible problems travelers had to face, and therefore relieved human suffering. Since maintenance work was charitable and holy, who better to do it than monks? Their tasks were sometimes shared by merchants, who had a financial interest in reliable transportation. But although monks and merchants worked diligently to serve God and their purses, travel could not be made entirely easy. Rain turned dirt roads into soup; the mud caked walkers' shoes and spattered riders' clothes; if streams had no bridges, sometimes the shallow spots were not obvious, so people and horses blundered into deep water; when streams did have bridges, the bridges could collapse; wolves lurked in the forests, waiting for stragglers; and, generally, the outdoors often got closer to the traveler than the traveler wanted it to.

Even if travelers could keep Nature at a safe distance, they still had to deal with fellow humans, including convicted thieves and murderers sentenced to walk the main road to the closest seaport for passage out of England. Any offender so sentenced had to dress like "a felon condemned to death—a long, loose white tunic, bare feet, and a wooden cross in his hand to mark that he was under protection of Holy Church" (Coulton, *Medieval* 375). But although these criminals were thus easily identified, nobody accompanied them to be sure they kept wearing their felon's robes, behaved well on the journey, or reached the seaport at all. A criminal might set up an anonymous life in another town, become a mercenary soldier, or live in the wilds by scavenging, hunting, and preying on travelers.

Not every dangerous person on the road was a white-robed felon. Some were employed by the most powerful people in the area. Any man or woman who could afford the wages could hire retainers to defend his or her administration, land, or person, but protectors often became a kind of goon squad or mini-Mafia that robbed, vandalized, raped, and assaulted. A traveler set upon by these brigands had no legal recourse because the local authorities either supported the brigands or were intimidated into silence. This practice of employing quasi-hitmen was called "maintenance," and was so widespread in Chaucer's day that both Edward III and Richard II constantly issued edicts against it. The number and frequency of edicts shows how little attention anyone paid to them. Townspeople and travelers alike feared maintenance, but at least the townspeople knew when and where to be on the lookout. Travelers could be taken by surprise.

Yet despite bad weather, dangerous roads, marauders, and other perils, the pilgrims of the *Canterbury Tales* are so unconcerned that they tell stories. Why aren't they worried? Because these pilgrims are dangerous. Setting out from the Tabard Inn, fully half are bristling with blades, are experienced brawlers, or are accustomed to blood-letting. The group includes:

- The Knight, armored, armed, and fresh from battle.
- His son, who at an early age has already fought in several cavalry expeditions.
- The efficient, silent Woodsman who is a walking armory: arrows, bow, sword, and dagger.
- The Monk, who, even if not a fighter, is a huntsman.
- The Friar, whose neck "strong was as a champioun" (239) and who has a collection of knives to hand out to pretty matrons.
- The Frankeleyn, who carries an "anlaas" (357) [a broad, double-edged dagger that tapers to a sharp point].
- The Haberdasshere, Carpenter, Webbe, Dyere, and Tapycer, who own "knyves . . . chaped . . . al with silver" (366–367).
- The Shipman, who carries a dagger under his arm and dispatches losers quickly, sending them "hoom to every lond" (400).
- The Miller, who carries a sword, is a champion wrestler, and can rip a door off its hinges or smash through it with his head.
- The Reve, armed with "a rusty blade" (618).
- And the innkeeper Harry Bailly, who boasts, "I am perilous with knyf in honde" (1919) ["I am dangerous with knife in hand"].

Even the Wife of Bath reminisces about her free-for-alls:

> I with my fest so took him on the cheke
> That in our fyr he fil backward adoun.
> And he up stirte as dooth a wood leoun,
> And with his fest he smoot me on the heed
> That in the floor I lay as I were deed.
> . . . And neer he cam, and kneled faire adoun, . . .
> I hitte hym on the cheke.
>
> (III.792–808)

> [I with my fist so took him on the cheek
> That in our fireplace he fell backward down.
> And he started as does the mad lion,
> And with his fist he hit me on the head
> That on the floor I lay as if I were dead.
> . . . And near he came, and kneeled fairly down, . . .
> I hit him on the cheek.]

She's a strong, dirty fighter: she punches hard enough to knock a man into the fire, and when he returns the blow, she plays possum until she can get a good shot at him.

Nor are the other pilgrims pushovers. The Summoner "quook for ire" (III. 1667) ["trembled with ire"] at the Friar, the Friar insults the Summoner as "a rennere up and doun / With mandementz for fornicacioun" (III.1283–1284) ["a runner up and down / With summonses for fornication"], the Cook "wax wrooth and wraw" (IX.46) ["was angry and wrathful"] at the Manciple. This group is a fourteenth-century Magnificent Seven.

The narrator wasn't an original member of this group; he joins them after they arrive at the Tabard. He had started on his journey alone. But he doesn't fit the picture of the stereotypical solitary pilgrim, who traveled on foot, wearing a traditional gown or hair shirt and carrying a staff topped with a shepherd's hook or a cross. Such pilgrims were protected without weaponry; the robe and staff stated clearly that God's eye was on them. Human predators must have respected the robe and staff at least occasionally, because some professional pilgrims spent their lives on the road traveling alone from shrine to shrine, and couldn't have spent much time in solitary humility if doing so always meant being beaten, robbed, and left to die.

It would have been suicidally foolish to start out alone on a journey with neither a weapon nor an obvious sign of God's patronage, and the narrator doesn't seem to possess either. He doesn't say he carries a weapon himself, and we can be sure that he's not dressed in the attention-getting garb of the professional pilgrim because Harry Bailly teases him unmercifully about his appearance but doesn't mention the narrator's clothes. So with no spiritual or physical weaponry, the narrator wasn't intending to travel alone the whole way to Canterbury. He certainly ingratiates himself with the group quickly enough—between its arrival "at nyght" (23) and the time that "the sonne was to reste" (30), he is "of their felawshipe anon" (32). And since the group includes people as ill-assorted as a Prioress, a Miller, and a group of tradesmen rich enough to bring their own cook, this pilgrimage (despite warnings issued in medieval travel books against making friends with traveling strangers) seems to have made a practice of picking up stragglers.

So the fierce, armed pilgrims, fortified with weapons, noise, jokes, and religious purpose, start out from the Tabard. It's unclear how long they spend traveling, but a four-day trip would mean they could keep a reasonable pace and still have time to argue, jostle for position on the road, and retrieve the Cook when he falls off his horse. Four travel days from Southwark (just outside London) to Canterbury could have been apportioned like this (timetable from Coulton, *Chaucer* 154–168; distances are my approximations from Jennett's map of the *Pilgrim's Way,* facing 296):

1st day: Southwark to Dartford (15 miles)
2nd day: Dartford to Rochester (14 miles)

3rd day: Rochester to Ospringe (18 miles)

4th day: Ospringe to Canterbury (9 miles)

This well-used route was dotted with inns and places to hire horses. One could ride a horse from Southwark to Rochester for twelvepence and another horse from Rochester to Canterbury for the same price. But even if travelers owned their horses, travelers (and horses) needed food and places to sleep, and therein lay the next travail of travel: nighttime lodging.

Inns were usually set up with the sleeping quarters on the second floor, directly above the dining room, and smells and noise could filter up through the floorboards. A fifteenth-century manuscript (Coulton, *Chaucer* 139) illustrates the casual way strangers slept naked side by side on featherbeds or straw mattresses, or on straw pallets on the floor. The straw in the bed chamber and the food in the kitchen so often attracted bedbugs, fleas, lice, and rodents that travelers addressed the issue as matter-of-factly as modern road manuals warn of speed traps. J. J. Jusserand mentions a fourteenth-century manual of French conversation that includes a sample exchange between an innkeeper and a potential customer.

The servant sent forward to engage the room utters the fond hope "that there are no fleas, nor bugs, nor other vermin." "No, sir, please God," replies the host, "for I make bold that you shall be well and comfortably lodged here— save that there is a great peck of rats and mice" (62–63).

Lodging was not only uncomfortable but also expensive, especially when combined with meals. The 1331 expense account of six travelers from Oxford to Durham is instructive. One night's food, horse fodder, beds, fuel to heat the bedroom, and candles to light it cost *each* traveler "about four times a ploughman's daily wage" (Woods 67–68). However, every pilgrim in the *Canterbury Tales* seems to have brought money to spare. They agree to Harry Bailly's suggestion that they all chip in after their return to buy the best story teller a supper at the Tabard. This is a shrewd move on Bailly's part, for he isn't *giving* the supper away, just spreading the cost among himself and the thirty paying members of the party in such a way that they will be tempted to buy supper from him for themselves as well. After that, who knows? Some pilgrims may then eat and drink until it's too late to start back home, and must spend yet another night at the Tabard at still more profit to Bailly. No matter who gets the free meal, there are two winners in this bargain: the story-telling champion and Bailly himself.

Pilgrims could spend hefty sums for food and lodging on the way through town, but local residents weren't always happy to see the pilgrims coming. In 1410, a Lollard called Thorpe complained of how disruptive pilgrimages could be. His complaint should not be taken as the last word on the subject, because Lollards disagreed with the religion that sent pilgrims through town in the first place. Still, Thorpe's vivid description could have come straight out of the pages of Chaucer, from the Miller's pipes to the Monk's bells to the Pardoner and Summoner as they sing "Com hider, love, to me!" (672):

I know well that when divers men and women will goe thus after their own willes, and finding out one pilgrimage, they will ordaine with them before, to have with them both men and women that can well sing wanton songes, and some other pilgrimes will have with them bagge pipes; so that everie towne that they come through, what with the noise of their singing, and with the sound of their piping, and with the jangling of their Canterburie bels, and with the barking out of dogges after them, that they make more noise, then if the king came there away, with all his clarions, and many other minstrels. (Coulton, *Chaucer* 142–143)

Religious or irreligious, holy journey or pleasure trip, the pilgrimage eventually ended at the shrine: a church, a monastery, an abbey, or a convent that purportedly could heal body or soul. The shrine's curative powers derived either from its location—usually where a miracle had occurred—or from something it possessed. This possession could be a piece of religious artwork or, more importantly, a relic, which was a tangible scrap of anything connected with a holy person or event. The list of relics at various shrines reads like a combination junk shop and natural disaster: it's a jumble of the property, bodies, and severed limbs of the devout. Canterbury possessed:

- Thomas Becket's coffined body
- His severed head, which the privileged could kiss
- His haircloth underclothes
- A jewelled statue of the Virgin, which was said to have spoken to Becket when he prayed to it
- The whole arms (not weaponry, but body parts) of eleven saints, including St. George
- Fragments of the arms of two other saints
- Aaron's rod (Rome also claimed to own the original)
- Fragments of the Holy Sepulchre, the manger, and the rock on which the Cross stood
- The column to which Christ was tied to be whipped
- The stone on which Christ stood before the Ascension
- The bed of the Virgin
- Wool woven by the Virgin
- A piece of the clay from which Adam was made

Of all the English shrines, Canterbury was the most enduringly popular. Others went in and out of favor as they acquired different attractions, but Canterbury was a constant draw. Its resident saint, Thomas Becket, was murdered in Canterbury Cathedral on December 29, 1170, by four of Henry II's knights. In penance for this murder, Henry II journeyed to the shrine, thus initiating the tradition of other British kings doing the same. This royal luster and Becket's dramatic martyrdom attracted thousands of pilgrims annually.

Canterbury Cathedral lived up to the pilgrims' expectations with an extremely theatrical presentation of the blessed relics. The Cathedral itself was good theater, because upon entering it, the first thing the pilgrim saw was an awe-inspiring series of steps with Becket's coffin looming distantly and magnificently at the top. After recovering from this sight, the pilgrim would be shown various relics. Which relics were shown depended on the rank of the pilgrim, with rarer relics exhibited as the rank increased, but everyone saw the bejeweled statue of the Virgin. Then the pilgrim would ascend the steps to the altar, perhaps crawling on his or her knees. At the altar, the coffin supported on arches held the remains of Thomas Becket. Derek Brewer describes the dramatic ritual that attended the viewing of the shrine:

> . . . sick and lame pilgrims were allowed to place themselves between these [arches], rubbing their afflicted limbs against the marble which held the body. The shrine proper was at first invisible, concealed by a wooden canopy; at a sign this was raised, and the shrine appeared blazing with gold and innumerable jewels. While the pilgrims knelt, an officer of the monastery came forward and pointed out the various jewels with a white wand, naming them in English and, for the benefit of foreigners, in French, telling their values and the marvellous magical properties which were normally attributed to jewels in the Middle Ages. (215–217)

After the official finished the lecture, the wooden canopy was again lowered over the shrine. The pilgrims were then free to pray and exit past an offering-box strategically located at the foot of the stairs.

Religious demands on the pilgrim's purse continued long after the offering: outside the Cathedral, souvenirs were available for purchase. Each shrine sold a distinctive style of medallion or amulet, made of lead, silver, or pewter, and meant to be sewn onto clothing or worn as a necklace. To anyone familiar with the symbols of the various shrines, it would have been immediately obvious where any pilgrim had journeyed.

Canterbury	St. Thomas miniature jar
St. James's Compostella	shell
Amiens	head of St. John the Baptist
Rocamadour	Holy Virgin
Rome	A "vernicle:" a reproduction of the cloth with which St. Veronica wiped Christ's face when he was on his way to Calvary. The cloth miraculously received the imprint of Christ's features. (A vernicle was sewn to the cap of Chaucer's Pardoner.)

Canterbury sold two styles of amulet. The little lead or silver jar sometimes held holy water. The St. Thomas was a sketch in lead of a full-face view of the mitered head of Becket, in a circular frame or against a background of decorated arches that provided plenty of open spaces through which to pass needle to thread when sewing it to cloth.

If the pilgrim wanted something besides religious souvenirs, the town of Canterbury could provide it. If a pilgrim needed to eat but didn't want to stop at an inn, a long row of street stalls sold food and drink. And if the sight of the relics within the Cathedral hadn't been enough, the pilgrim could see more relics outside. Local residents, or itinerants like Chaucer's Pardoner, sometimes passed off common objects as relics, selling glimpses of the objects—or sometimes the objects themselves. Chaucer's Pardoner is an effective salesman with a good stock in trade:

> For in his male he hadde a pilwe-beer,
> Which that he seyde was Oure Lady veyl;
> He seyde he hadde a gobet of the seyl
> That Seint Peter hadde, whan that he wente
> Upon the see, til Jhesu Crist him hente.
> He hadde a croys of latoun ful of stones,
> And in a glas he hadde pigges bones.
> But with thise relikes, whan that he fond
> A povre person dwellynge upon lond,
> Upon a day he gat hym moore moneye
> Than that the person gat in monthes tweye;
> And thus, with feyned flaterye and japes,
> He made the person and the peple his apes.
>
> (I.694–706)

> [For in his bag he had a pillow case,
> Which was said to be Our Lady's veil;
> He said he had a piece of the sail
> That St. Peter had, when that he went
> Upon the sea, until Jesus Christ he took.
> He had a cross of latten full of stones,
> And in a glass he had pigs' bones.
> But with these relics, when that he found
> A poor person dwelling upon land,
> Upon a day he got him more money
> Than that person got in two months;
> And thus with feigned flattery and japes,
> He made the parson and the people his apes.]

Suitably purified, decorated, gorged, and entertained, the pilgrims would retrace the path homeward, still traveling together. Harry Bailley assumes that nobody will depart from the group until after they reach the Tabard.

> . . . ech of yow, . . .
> In this viage shal telle tales tweye
> To Caunterbury-ward, . . .
> And homward he shal tellen othere two . . .
> And which of yow that bereth him best of alle— . . .
> Shal have a soper at oure aller cost
> Heere in this place . . .
> Whan that we come agayn fro Caunterbury.
>
> (I.791–801)

> [. . . each of you, . . .
> On this journey shall tell tales two
> Towards Canterbury, . . .
> And homeward shall tell the other two . . .
> And which of you that does best of all— . . .
> Shall have supper at the cost of all of us
> Here in this place . . .
> When that we come again from Canterbury.]

Bailly's game depends on everyone's returning to the Tabard together. Company would lessen the dangers and increase the potential pleasures on the second half of the journey as well as on the first; it would have been common sense to travel both ways in a group.

So the little narrator is a writer and a pilgrim, but that still doesn't tell us what his actual job was. He's not indubitably Chaucer, or a civil servant, or a courtier, or a cleric, or in any obvious career path; he's not even labeled by his marital status as is the Wife of Bath. The only thing that the narrator indubitably is, is the man who went on an ordinary pilgrimage and then preserved the memory of it in an extraordinary way. But perhaps that, after all, is his job. The job of entertainer existed before the job of Reeve or of Summoner, and has outlived them as well.

As an entertainer, the narrator isn't necessarily a member of the ragtag class of jongleurs, just as he isn't necessarily a courtier passing the long winter evenings away, or a cleric stealing time from recopying the Book of Matthew to scribble his own words. He is son to the Old English *scop,* the honorable minstrel-poet who entertained the Anglo-Saxons; he's brother to Scheherazade, to Sherlock Holmes's Doctor Watson, even to Uncle Remus—any fictional retailer of others' stories.

Ultimately, this narrator's spare-time amusement is his full-time profession. All the other characters tell stories only if there's a supper to be won, but the narrator tells and tells even if there's nothing to tempt him. His entire narration of the *Canterbury Tales* is not an entry in the pilgrimage's story-telling contest, because he couches not only the stories but the pilgrimage itself in the past tense. Presumably the pilgrimage is over, along with the contest, by the time he starts telling about it. But even though both the journey and the free supper are a memory, he still revels in the stories. For him, and for us, that is enough.

REFERENCES

Benson, Larry D., ed. *The Riverside Chaucer.* 3rd ed. Boston: Houghton Mifflin Co., 1987.

Brewer, Derek. *Chaucer in His Time.* 1963. London: Longman Group Ltd., 1973.

Coulton, G. G. *Chaucer and His England.* New York: Russell and Russell, 1957.

————. *Medieval Panorama: The English Scene from Conquest to Reformation.* 1938. New York: W. W. Norton, 1974.

Jusserand, J. J. *English Wayfaring Life in the Middle Ages.* 4th ed. Trans. Lucy Toulmin Smith. London: Ernest Benn Ltd., 1950.

The Pilgrim's Way. Map. *The Pilgrim's Way from Winchester to Canterbury.* By Sean Jennett. London: Cassell and Co., Ltd., 1971. Facing 296.

Robertson, D. W., Jr. *Chaucer's London.* New Dimensions in History Series. New York: John Wiley and Sons, 1968.

Scattergood, V. J. "Literary Culture at the Court of Richard II." *English Court Culture in the Later Middle Ages.* Eds. V. J. Scattergood and J. W. Sherborne. New York: St. Martin's Press, 1983. pp. 29–43.

Woods, William. *England in the Age of Chaucer.* New York: Stein and Day, 1976.

Selected Bibliography

Aers, David. "Imagination, Order, and Ideology: The Knight's Tale." In *Chaucer, Langland, and the Creative Imagination*. London: Routledge, 1980.

Baugh, Albert C., ed. *Chaucer's Major Poetry*. New York: Appleton, 1963.

Bennett, H. S. *Chaucer and the Fifteenth Century*. Oxford: Oxford University Press, 1947.

Bennett, J.A.W. *Chaucer at Oxford and Cambridge*. Oxford: Clarendon Press, 1974.

Benson, C. David. *Chaucer's Drama of Style*. Chapel Hill: University of North Carolina Press, 1986.

Benson, Larry D., Ed. *The Riverside Chaucer*. 3rd ed. Boston: Houghton Mifflin, 1987.

Birney, Earle. *Essays on Chaucerian Irony*. Toronto: University of Toronto Press, 1985.

———. "The Squire's Yeoman." *Review of English Literature* 1 (1960): 9–18.

Bishop, Morris. *The Middle Ages*. Boston: Houghton Mifflin, 1985.

Blake, N. F. *The Textual Tradition of the Canterbury Tales*. London: Arnold, 1985.

Boitani, Piero, and Jill Mann, eds. *The Cambridge Chaucer Companion*. Cambridge: Cambridge University Press, 1993.

Bowden, Muriel. *A Commentary on the General Prologue to the Canterbury Tales*. New York: Macmillan, 1948.

Brewer, Derek. *Chaucer in His Time*. 1963. London: Longman Group Ltd. 1973.

Brooke, Iris. *A History of English Costume*. New York: Theatre Arts Books, 1972.

Brooks, Harold F. *Chaucer's Pilgrims: The Artistic Order of the Portraits in the Prologue*. New York: Barnes and Noble, 1962.

Butler, Lionel, and Chris Given-Wilson. *Medieval Monasteries of Great Britain*. London: Michael Joseph, 1979.

Calabrese, Michael A. "Meretricious Mixtures: Gold, Dung, and the Canon's Yeoman's Prologue and Tale." *Chaucer Review* 27 no. 3 (1993): 277–92.

Campbell, Mary B. *The Witness and the Other World: Exotic European Travel Writing, 400–1600*. Ithaca, N.Y.: Cornell University Press, 1988.

Chute, Marchette. *Geoffrey Chaucer of England*. New York: Dalton, 1946.

Cooper, Helen. *Oxford Guides to Chaucer: The Canterbury Tales.* Oxford: Oxford University Press, 1989.

Coudert, Allison. *Alchemy: The Philosopher's Stone.* Boulder, Colo.: Shambhala, 1980.

Coulton. G. G. *Chaucer and His England.* New York: Russell and Russell, 1957.

———. *Medieval Panorama: The English Scene from Conquest to Reformation.* 1938. New York: W. W. Norton, 1974.

———. *The Medieval Scene.* London: Cambridge University Press, 1989.

Crow, M. M., and C. C. Olson, eds. *Chaucer Life-Records.* Oxford: Clarendon Press, 1966.

Curry, Walter Clyde. *Chaucer and the Medieval Sciences.* New York: Barnes and Noble, 1926.

Daly, Lowrie J. *The Medieval University 1200–1400.* New York: Sheed and Ward, 1961.

Denholm-Young, N. *The Country Gentry in the Fourteenth Century.* Oxford: Oxford University Press, 1969.

Dillon, Janette. *Geoffrey Chaucer. Writers in Their Time.* New York: St. Martin's Press, 1993.

Dobson, E. J. *The Origins of Ancrene Wisse.* Oxford: Clarendon Press, 1976.

Durant, Will. *The Story of Civilization.* New York: Simon and Schuster, 1957. Vol. 6, *The Reformation: A History of European Civilization from Wycliffe to Calvin: 1300–1564.*

Dyer, Christopher. *Standards of Living in the Later Middle Ages.* Cambridge: Cambridge University Press, 1989.

Eisner, Sigmund. "Canterbury Day: A Fresh Aspect." *Chaucer Review* 27 (1992): 31–44.

Fisher, John. "Animadversions on the Text of Chaucer." *Speculum* 63 (1988): 779–793.

———. *The Importance of Chaucer.* Carbondale: Southern Illinois University Press, 1992.

———, Malcolm Richardson, and Jane L. Fisher. *An Anthology of Chaucer English.* Knoxville: University of Tennessee Press, 1984.

Fleming, John V. "The Antifraternalism of the Summoner's Tale." *Journal of English and Germanic Philology* 65 (1966): 688–700.

Fullerton, Ann B. "The Five Craftsmen." *MLN* (1946): 515–523.

Gardner, John. *The Poetry of Chaucer.* Carbondale: University of Southern Illinois Press, 1977.

Gies, Frances, and Joseph Gies. *Life in a Medieval Village.* New York: Harper, 1990.

Green, Richard Firth. *Poets and Princepleasers: Literature and the English Court in the Late Middle Ages.* Toronto: University of Toronto Press, 1980.

Herlihy, David, ed. *Medieval Culture and Society.* New York: Harper and Row, 1968.

Hermann, John P. "Dismemberment, Dissemination, Discourse: Sign and Symbol in the Shipman's Tale." *Chaucer Review* 19 (1985): 302–337.

———, and John J. Burke, Jr., eds. *Signs and Symbols in Chaucer's Poetry.* Tuscaloosa: University of Alabama Press, 1981.

Hieatt, Constance B. " 'To boille the chiknes with the marybones': Hodge's Kitchen revisited." In *Chaucerian Problems and Perspectives: Essays presented to Paul E. Beichner.* Eds. Edward Vasta and Zacharias P. Thundy. Notre Dame, Ind.: University of Notre Dame Press, 1965. Pp. 149–163.

Hill, John M. *Chaucerian Belief: The Poetics of Reverence and Delight.* New Haven, Conn.: Yale University Press, 1991.

Hollander, A.E.J., and William Kellaway. *Studies in London History*. London: Hodder and Stoughton, 1969.

Holloway, Julia Bolton. *The Pilgrim and the Book: A Study of Dante, Langland, and Chaucer*. New York: Peter Lang, 1987.

Hornsby, Joseph. *Chaucer and the Law*. Norman, Okla.: Pilgrim Books, 1988.

Howard, Donald R. *Chaucer: His Life, His Works, His World*. New York: E. P. Dutton, 1987.

———. *The Idea of the Canterbury Tales*. Berkeley: University of California Press, 1976.

Huppé, Bernard F. *A Reading of the Canterbury Tales*. Albany: State University of New York, 1967.

Hussey, Maurice. *Chaucer's World: A Pictorial Companion*. London: Cambridge University Press, 1968.

Jennett, Sean. *The Pilgrim's Way from Winchester to Canterbury*. London: Cassell and Co. Ltd., 1971.

Jones, Terry. *Chaucer's Knight: The Portrait of a Medieval Mercenary*. New York: Methuen, 1985.

Jusserand, J. J. *English Wayfaring Life in the Middle Ages*. 4th ed. Trans. Lucy Toulmin Smith. London: Ernest Benn Ltd., 1950.

Keen, Maurice. *English Society in the Later Middle Ages 1348–1500*. New York: Penguin, 1990.

———. *A History of Medieval Europe*. New York: Praeger, 1968.

Kendall, Alan. *Medieval Pilgrims*. New York: G. P. Putnam's Sons, 1970.

Kiser, Lisa J. *Truth and Textuality in Chaucer's Poetry*. Hanover, N.H.: University Press of New England, 1991.

Knapp, Peggy. *Chaucer and the Social Context*. New York: Routledge, 1990.

Knight, Stephen. *Geoffrey Chaucer*. Oxford: Blackwell, 1986.

Knowles, David. *The Evolution of Medieval Thought*. New York: Random House, 1964.

———. *The Religious Orders in England*. Cambridge: Cambridge University Press, 1950.

Kolve, V. A. *Chaucer and the Imagery of Narrative: The First Five Canterbury Tales*. Stanford, Calif.: Stanford University Press, 1984.

Lawrence, C. H. *The English Church and the Papacy in the Middle Ages*. New York: Fordham University Press, 1965.

Leggett, William. *Ancient and Medieval Dyes*. Brooklyn, N.Y.: Chemical Publishing Co., 1944.

Lerer, Seth. *Chaucer and His Readers*. Princeton, N.J.: Princeton University Press, 1993.

Lindahl, Carl. *Earnest Games: Folkloric Patterns in the Canterbury Tales*. Bloomington: Indiana University Press, 1987.

Lounsbury, Thomas R. *Studies in Chaucer: His Life and Writings*. 3 vols. New York: Russell, 1962.

Lumiansky, Robert M. *Of Sundry Folk: The Dramatic Principle in the Canterbury Tales*. Austin: University of Texas Press, 1955.

McAlpine, Monica E. *Chaucer's Knight's Tale: An Annotated Bibliography: 1900–1985*. Toronto: University of Toronto Press, 1991.

Malone, Kemp. *Chapters on Chaucer*. Baltimore: Johns Hopkins University Press, 1951.

Mandel, Jerome. *Geoffrey Chaucer: Building the Fragments of the Canterbury Tales*. Rutherford, N.J.: Fairleigh Dickinson University Press, 1992.

Manly, J. M. *Some New Light on Chaucer*. Rpt. Gloucester, Mass.: Peter Smith, 1959.

Mann, Jill. *Chaucer and Medieval Estates Satire*. Cambridge: Cambridge University Press, 1973.

———. *Geoffrey Chaucer*. Atlantic Highlands, N.J.: Humanities Press International, 1991.

Mertes, Kate. *The English Noble Household 1250–1600: Good Governance and Politic Rule*. Family, Sexuality and Social Relations in Past Times Series. New York: Basil Blackwell, 1988.

Miller, Robert P., ed. *Chaucer: Sources and Backgrounds*. Oxford: Oxford University Press, 1977.

Moorman, John R.H. *Church Life in England in the Thirteenth Century*. Cambridge: Cambridge University Press, 1955.

Moriarty, Catherine. *The Voice of the Middle Ages*. New York: Peter Bedrich, 1989.

Muscatine, Charles. *Chaucer and the French Tradition*. Berkeley: University of California Press, 1964.

Myers, A. R. *London in the Age of Chaucer*. Norman: University of Oklahoma Press, 1972.

Nolan, Barbara. *Chaucer and the Tradition of the Roman Antique*. Cambridge: Cambridge University Press, 1992.

Olson, Glending. "Chaucer's Idea of a Canterbury Game." *The Idea of Medieval Literature: New Essays on Chaucer and Medieval Culture in Honor of Donald R. Howard*. Eds. James M. Dean and Christian K. Zacher. Newark: University of Delaware Press, 1992. pp. 72–90.

Olson, Paul A. *The Canterbury Tales and the Good Society*. Princeton, N.J.: Princeton University Press, 1986.

Owen, Charles A. *Pilgrimage and Storytelling in the Canterbury Tales*. Norman: University of Oklahoma Press, 1977.

Owst, Gerald R. *Literature and the Pulpit in Medieval England*. Cambridge: Cambridge University Press, 1933.

———. *Preaching in Medieval England*. Cambridge: Cambridge University Press, 1926.

Pantin, W. A. *The English Church in the Fourteenth Century*. Notre Dame, Ind.: University of Notre Dame Press, 1962.

Patterson, Lee. *Chaucer and the Subject of History*. Madison: University of Wisconsin Press, 1991.

Pearsall, Derek. *The Canterbury Tales*. London: Allen and Unwin, 1985.

———. *The Life of Geoffrey Chaucer: A Critical Biography*. Oxford: Blackwell, 1992.

Pendrill, Charles. *London Life in the Fourteenth Century*. 1925. Port Washington, N.Y.: Kennikat Press, 1971.

Pickering, James. "Chaucer's *Alchemy*: The Pilgrims Assayed." *Medieval Perspectives* 4–5 (1989–90): 140–49.

Pollard, A. W. *Chaucer's Canterbury Tales: The Squire's Tale*. London: Macmillan, 1921.

Preston, Raymond. *Chaucer*. New York: Sheed and Ward, 1969.

Quiller-Couch, Sir Arthur T. *The Age of Chaucer*. London: Dent, 1926.

Read, John. *Prelude to Chaucer*. New York: Macmillan, 1973.

Rex, Richard. "Chaucer and the Jews." *MLQ* 45 (1984): 107–122.

Ridley, Florence H. *The Prioress and the Critics*. Berkeley: University of California Press, 1965.

Robertson, D. W., Jr. *Chaucer's London*. New York: John Wiley and Sons, 1968.

———. *Essays in Medieval Culture*. Princeton, N.J.: Princeton University Press, 1962.

———. *A Preface to Chaucer: Studies in Medieval Perspectives*. Princeton, N.J.: Princeton University Press, 1962.

Root, Robert K. *The Poetry of Chaucer*. Gloucester, Mass.: Peter Smith, 1957.

Ruggiers, Paul G. *The Art of the Canterbury Tales*. Madison: University of Wisconsin Press, 1965.

Scattergood, V. J. "Perkyn Revelour and the *Cook's Tale*." *Chaucer Review* 19 (1984): 14–23.

———, and J. W. Sherborne, eds. *English Court Culture in the Later Middle Ages*. New York: St. Martin's Press, 1983.

Schuler, Robert M. "The Renaissance Chaucer as Alchemist." *Viator* 15 (1984): 305–333.

Shoaf, R. A. *Dante, Chaucer, and the Currency of the Word*. Norman, Okla.: Pilgrim Books, 1983.

Skeat, Walter W., ed. *The Complete Works of Geoffrey Chaucer*. 7 vols. Oxford: Clarendon-Oxford University Press, 1894–1897.

Speirs, John. *Chaucer the Maker*. London: Faber, 1960.

Strohm, Paul. *Social Chaucer*. Cambridge, Mass.: Harvard University Press, 1989.

Szittya, Penn R. *The Antifraternal Tradition in Medieval Literature*. Princeton, N.J.: Princeton University Press, 1986.

Taylor, F. Sherwood. *The Alchemists: Founders of Modern Chemistry*. New York: Henry Schuman, 1949.

Thrupp, Sylvia. *The Merchant Class of Medieval London (1300–1500)*. Ann Arbor: University of Michigan Press, 1948.

Tuchman, Barbara W. *A Distant Mirror: The Calamitous 14th Century*. New York: Alfred A. Knopf, 1978.

Tupper, Frederick. "The Quarrels of the Canterbury Pilgrims." *JEGP* 14 (1915): 256–270.

Turner, Victor, and Edith Turner. *Image and Pilgrimage in Christian Culture: Anthropological Perspectives*. New York: Columbia University Press, 1978.

Unwin, George. *The Gilds and Companies of London*. London: Methuen, 1908.

Vasta, Edward. "The Devil in Chaucer's Reeve." *American Notes and Queries* 22 (1984): 126–128.

Von Boehn, Max. *Mode and Manners*. 2 vols. 1932. New York: Benjamin Blom, 1971.

Weil, Eric. "An Alchemical Freedom Fight: Linking the Manciple's Tale to the Second Nun's and the Canon's Yeoman's Tale." *Medieval Perspectives* 6 (1991): 162–170.

Weisberg, David. "Telling Stories about Constance: Framing and Narrative Strategy in the *Canterbury Tales*." *Chaucer Review* 27 (1992): 45–64.

White, Lynn, Jr. *Medieval Technology and Social Change*. New York: Oxford University Press, 1962.

Whittock, Trevor. *A Reading of the* Canterbury Tales. London: Cambridge University Press, 1968.

Williams, Arnold. "Chaucer and the Friars." *Speculum* 28 (1953): 499–513.

Williams, David. *"The Canterbury Tales": A Literary Pilgrimage*. Boston: G. K. Hall, 1987.

Woods, William. *England in the Age of Chaucer*. New York: Stein and Day, 1976.

Zeitlow, Paul N. "In Defense of the Summoner." *Chaucer Review* 1 (1966–1967): 4–19.

Index

About the Editors and Contributors

MICHAEL A. CALABRESE is an assistant professor of English at California State University, Los Angeles. He has published extensively in the fields of classical literature and Middle English literature.

CHRISTINE N. CHISM is an assistant professor of English at Allegheny College.

JOHN W. CONLEE is an associate professor of English at the College of William and Mary. Among his specialties are Old and Middle English literature.

CATHERINE COX is an assistant professor of English at the University of Pittsburgh, Johnstown. She is the author of several recent articles on Chaucer, the *Gawain*-poet, and William Langland, appearing in *Exemplaria, Christianity and Literature,* and elsewhere.

BERT DILLON is an associate professor of English at the University of South Carolina-Columbia. He teaches medieval literature, and he has written on Chaucer and Malory.

EDWIN ELEAZAR is an associate professor of English at Francis Marion University in South Carolina. He has spoken on such diverse works as *Beowulf* and the *Pearl* poet.

JOHN H. FISHER is professor emeritus of the University of Tennessee. His extensive list of publications includes an edition of Chaucer's *Works,* as well as several critical volumes on Chaucer's works.

MARC GUIDRY is completing his doctoral work at Louisiana State University. His interests include Old and Middle English, particularly Chaucer.

KARL T. HAGEN is a graduate student at the University of California, Los Angeles. He is writing his dissertation on the use and reception of medieval sermons and has published on Middle English metrics.

JOHN P. HERMANN is the author of *Allegories of War* and editor of *Signs and Symbols in Chaucer's Poetry.* He has taught at Illinois, UCLA, and Alabama, and is best known for his theoretical studies of medieval literary iconography.

CONSTANCE B. HIEATT is professor emeritus of English at the University of Western Ontario. She has published extensively in Old English, Middle English, Old Norse, and Old French language and literature, and has also published medieval recipes.

JOSEPH HORNSBY is an associate professor of English at the University of Alabama. He has published on law in the works of Geoffrey Chaucer and on Thomas Hoccleve. He is presently at work on a book-length study of the politics of representation in Hoccleve's poetry.

MAUREEN HOURIGAN is an assistant professor at Kent State University's Trumbell campus. In addition to her medieval work, she has researched and published extensively in the fields of composition and rhetoric as well as seventeenth-century British literature.

PEGGY HUEY is currently at the University of Alabama after graduating from the University of South Florida. Among her interests are Chaucer, the *Gawain-*poet, and Mandeville.

JAMES KELLER is an assistant professor of English at the Mississippi University for Women. He enjoys medieval English literature, but he has published extensively in Renaissance English literature as well, specializing in Christopher Marlowe.

SIGRID KING is an assistant professor at Francis Marion University in South Carolina. She has had work published in *Black American Literature Forum* and has work forthcoming in *[Re]presenting the Other Eighteenth Century, Feminist Literary Theory: A Dictionary,* and *Fraun in der Literaturwissenschaft.*

LAURA C. LAMBDIN is an assistant professor of English at Francis Marion University in South Carolina. She has published works on Malory, Chaucer, and various Victorian poets, in such journals as *Philological Quarterly* and *Arthurian Interpretations.*

ROBERT T. LAMBDIN is an assistant professor of English in the Provisional Year program at the University of South Carolina. He has several publications on Chaucer, and is currently working on the *Encyclopedia of Medieval Literature* with his wife, Laura.

RICHARD B. McDONALD is an English instructor at St. Petersburg Junior College and the University of South Florida, where he is currently completing his doctoral work.

GWENDOLYN MORGAN, professor of medieval and British Literature at Montana State University, is the author of *Medieval Balladry and the Courtly Tradition* and numerous articles on Anglo-Saxon and medieval literature.

DANIEL F. PIGG is an assistant professor of English at the University of Tennessee at Martin, where he teaches courses on medieval and Renaissance literature. He has published diversely on medieval texts from *Beowulf* to Chaucer's *Canterbury Tales* and Malory's "The Tale of Sir Gareth."

NANCY M. REALE is a master teacher and coordinator of Humanities in the General Studies Program at New York University. Her principal scholarly interest is the manner in which inherited texts are redefined and reinterpreted by successive authors. She has published articles on *The Owl and the Nightingale, riscrittura* in late medieval and Renaissance prose fiction, and Italian influences on Chaucer. She is presently at work on a book on epic poetry.

THOMAS C. RICHARDSON is vice president for Academic Affairs and professor of English at Mississippi University for Women.

ELIZABETH MAUER SEMBLER is a doctoral candidate and instructor of English at the University of South Florida at Tampa.

JUDITH SLOVER is a Ph.D. candidate and graduate assistant at the University of South Florida with interests in Old, Middle, and Renaissance English literature and a sprinkling of the fantastic genre. Her dissertation deals with links in all these areas. She has published in *SAR* and has presented conference papers on various topics such as *The Duchess of Malfi* and its links to women, witchcraft, and sovereignty, and women in Old English literature.

ELTON E. SMITH is a distinguished professor of English at the University of South Florida. On his massive publication list are many works about Victorian poets and authors. Of special note is his work *The Two Voices of Tennyson.*

ESTHER M. G. SMITH is a retired English professor and the author of many articles and books, including literary criticism, fiction, and poetry.

REBECCA STEPHENS is an assistant professor of English at Carlow College. Her interests include Modern British literature and eroticism in Chaucer. She has published extensively in these fields and presented numerous papers, most recently concerning Virginia Woolfe and Toni Morrison.

DIANA R. UHLMAN received her Ph.D. in 1991 and has been a visiting professor at Miami University and Bowling Green State University in Ohio. Her most recently published article, ''The Comfort of Voice, the Solace of Script: Orality and Literacy in *The Book of Margery Kempe*,'' appears in *Studies in Philology* (Winter 1994).

JULIAN N. WASSERMAN is a professor of English at Loyola University in New Orleans. He is a proficient scholar and the author of numerous works concerning Middle English literature.

KATHARINE WILSON teaches English at Rensselaer Polytechnic Institute, where she is pursuing her doctorate in Technical and Professional Writing. Her interests cannot be limited by space, and she will undoubtedly be on the cutting edge of modern technological theory.

ISBN 0-313-29334-1

9 780313 293344

HARDCOVER BAR CODE